WHAT IS AN *Aspen RoadMap?*

Aspen RoadMaps™ are comprehensive course outlines that lead you, step by step, through your law school courses—helping you prepare for class and study for exams. With a clean, modern design that is as easy to use as it is visually appealing, your RoadMap will guide you from the "big picture" to the careful details you need to know.

WHAT MAKES THE *ASPEN ROADMAP*™ FOR CRIMINAL PROCEDURE THE BEST?

The Aspen RoadMap™ for Criminal Procedure:

- ■ Is the newest, most up-to-date outline available, brought to you by the publishers of the successful Examples and Explanations Series.

- ■ Is written by Professor James Tomkovicz, one of America's best classroom teachers, and informed by his insights and teaching methods.

- ■ Gives you a comprehensive and accessible treatment of the controlling rules and doctrines in criminal procedure.

- ■ Provides the most complete set of study tools available to help you comprehend and reinforce your learning and prepare for exams.

- ■ Constructs a coherent analytical framework and captures and highlights the dispositive legal standards.

THE PRACTICAL COMPONENTS OF YOUR *ASPEN ROADMAP*™

- ■ ***The Casebook Correlation*** *Chart* helps you match sections of your casebook to this RoadMap™.

- ■ ***The RoadMap™ Capsule Summary***, cross-referenced to the outline text, provides a "big picture" view anytime you need it.

- ■ ***Chapter Overviews***, each no more than two pages long, highlight key concepts.

- ■ ***Hypotheticals*** are interwoven throughout to help further clarify important concepts.

- ■ ***Examples***—complete with accompanying analyses—are included in each chapter to provide lively and memorable illustrations of key points.

- ■ ***Chapter Review Questions***—complete with answers—reinforce your understanding.

- ■ ***Exam Tips*** help you target what you really need to know in order to maximize your study time and do well on exams.

- ■ ***Sample Exam Questions***, presented as short essays, are accompanied by model answers.

Dear Student,

I'd like to take this opportunity to welcome you to the *Aspen RoadMap*™ for Criminal Procedure. I am James Tomkovicz, Professor of Law at the University of Iowa College of Law, and I have taught Criminal Procedure for over 15 years.

During my years in the classroom and in the many hours I've spent talking to students outside of class, I have come to learn when and why you, as a student, might have difficulty in this course. From what other students have told me, I have developed specific approaches and effective techniques that can help you navigate your way around potential problems.

Your *RoadMap*™ covers the subject matter of two different law school courses. The Basic or Investigatory Criminal Procedure course may be a mandatory first-year course or an upperclass elective. It is concerned with constitutional regulation of the government's efforts to investigate crime, gather evidence, and apprehend criminals. The Advanced or Adjudicatory Criminal Procedure course focuses on constitutional safeguards that come into play during the more formal, courtroom phases of a criminal case. Particular emphasis is placed on the fundamental guarantees extended to defendants at trial.

The *Aspen RoadMap*™ for Criminal Procedure provides thorough yet concise explanations of the controlling rules and doctrines in Criminal Procedure and a coherent analytical framework to help you organize and clarify your study of law in both Criminal Procedure courses. Created to closely track the content and organization of the major casebooks in Criminal Procedure, your *Aspen RoadMap*™ provides a Casebook Correlation Chart that will make this *RoadMap*™ an invaluable companion to your casebook.

Good luck, and please remember that this book is not intended to replace the casebook, the relevant constitutional and statutory provisions and the opinions of the Supreme Court, or problems your professor has assigned. Use the outline in conjunction with these materials to review, reinforce, and clarify the learning that must begin with a study of the cases and other assigned materials. You'll find that you will be able to better understand—and maybe even enjoy—your course in Criminal Procedure.

Sincerely,

James J. Tomkovicz
Professor of Law

P.S. I'd welcome your suggestions for making the *RoadMap*™ even more useful. Please write to me at Aspen Law & Business, Law School Division, One Liberty Square, 10th floor, Boston, MA 02109 or e-mail me at james_tomkovicz@uiowa.edu

Aspen Publishers, Inc. A **Wolters Kluwer** Company

1185 Avenue of the Americas, New York, NY 10036

Criminal Procedure

James J. Tomkovicz

Professor of Law
University of Iowa College of Law

ASPEN LAW & BUSINESS
A Division of Aspen Publishers, Inc.

This publication is designed to provide accurate and authoritative information in regard to the subject matter covered. It is sold with the understanding that the publisher is not engaged in rendering legal, accounting, or other professional services. If legal advice or other professional assistance is required, the services of a competent professional person should be sought.

—From a *Declaration of Principles* jointly adopted by a Committee of the American Bar Association and a Committee of Publishers and Associations

Copyright © 1997 by Aspen Law & Business
A Division of Aspen Publishers, Inc.

All rights reserved. No part of this publication may be reproduced or transmitted in any form or by any means, electronic or mechanical, including photocopy, recording, or any information storage and retrieval system, without permission in writing from the publisher. Requests for permission to make copies of any part of this publication should be mailed to:

Permissions
Aspen Law & Business
A Division of Aspen Publishers, Inc.
1185 Avenue of the Americas
New York, NY 10036

Printed in the United States of America

Library of Congress Cataloguing-in-Publication Data

Tomkovicz, James J.
  Criminal procedure / James J. Tomkovicz.
    p.   cm.—(Aspen roadmap)
  Includes index.
  ISBN 1-56706-504-x
  1. Criminal procedure—United States. 2. Civil rights—United States. I. title. II. Series.
KF9619.3.T66   1997
345.73'05—dc21

97-21808
CIP

ACKNOWLEDGMENTS

Several people deserve thanks for their assistance and support during my efforts to complete this project. First, I appreciate Mark Russell's encouragement and organizational skills and Leslie Keros's excellent editorial input. Second, my colleague, co-author, and friend, Welsh White, and my colleague and friend, Barbara Schwartz, helped me understand and accurately capture the law of collateral remedies—no mean task. Third, my secretary, Jacki Williams, came through time and again when I needed her.

Three outstanding research assistants—Sarah Gayer, Brenda Claussen, and Will Anderson—provided absolutely invaluable aid of the highest caliber at every step of the way. Each of them worked tirelessly to ensure that this outline was as good as it could be. Much of the credit for the final product belongs to them. I hope they know how grateful I am for their dedication.

Finally, I would be remiss not to thank my wife, Nancy, and my children, Vivian, Michelle, and Henry. They generously allowed me to have the time needed to complete the project and restored my energy in innumerable, unmeasurable ways.

James J. Tomkovicz
Spring, 1997

SUMMARY OF CONTENTS

CONTENTS

12 THE EXCLUSIONARY RULES ... 209

18   THE RIGHT TO THE ASSISTANCE OF COUNSEL   335

19 THE RIGHT TO TRIAL BY JURY

21 APPEALS OF CRIMINAL CONVICTIONS   433

22 COLLATERAL CHALLENGES AND REMEDIES   449

CASEBOOK CORRELATION

Aspen RoadMap	Allen, Kuhns, Stuntz, **Constitutional Criminal Procedure,** (3rd Ed., 1995)	Kamisar, LaFave, Israel, **Modern Criminal Procedure,** (8th Ed., 1994)	Saltzburg, Capra, **American Criminal Process,** (5th Ed., 1996)	Weinreb, **Criminal Process** (5th Ed., 1993)
1. The Study of Criminal Procedure		1-2	1-31	
A. The Content of Criminal Procedure Courses	3-22			
B. Investigatory vs. Adjudicatory Criminal Procedure	32-49			
C. The Significance of the Study of Criminal Procedure	49-61			
D. Doctrinal Details and Larger Perspective				
2. The Processes of the Criminal Justice System		14-35		
A. Arrest	9-10		136-160	4-115
B. The Initial Charge and Initial Appearance	11		146-153	654-669
C. The Preliminary Hearing	12, 14		718-722	654-699
D. Formal Charges in the Trial Court	14-16		694-718	798-839
E. Pretrial Proceedings	17		728-739	280, 692-699, 902-907
F. The Trial Court	18		816-828	840-859
G. Post-Trial Motions and Sentencing			1130-1132	1277-1297
H. Appeals and Collateral Challenges			1352-1425	853-856, 1395-1400

N. Elevated Standards of Fourth Amendment Reasonableness	866-868, 876-885	181-186, 227-252	123, 176-187, 484, 490	73, 81, 385, 456, 463-464, 276
5. Government Involvement in the Commission of Crimes				
A. The Entrapment Defense	979-1003	399-415	447	
B. The Due Process Defense	980, 998, 1001	416-429		
6. Due Process Clause Regulation of Confessions			511-527	503-645
A. The Common Law Rule	1165, 1167, 1226-1229, 1381-1384, 1414-1419	440-504	512-513	
B. Due Process Doctrine	1278-1286	453-469, 572-575, 609-626	512-527	503-515
7. The Privilege Against Compulsory Self-Incrimination and Confessions		471-608	527-596	
A. Constitutional Foundations of *Miranda* Doctrine	1177-1221, 1226-1429	469-599	527-559	514, 523-536, 605
B. The Elements of *Miranda* Doctrine	1231-1329, 1386	508-598	555-564, 575-596	537-539, 545-550, 594-598
8. The Sixth Amendment Right to Counsel: A Foundation			559-622	
A. The Right to Counsel at Trial	141-175	67-88, 460	610-612, 659-675, 1059-1095	514-515, 681-682, 855
B. Pretrial Extensions of Right to Counsel	374-426	58, 81-82, 643-665, 671	611-614, 634-649, 664-678	508-523, 558-561
9. The Right to Counsel and Confessions		627-649, 666-671	559-623	
A. The Threshold Requirement: A Formal Initiation of Adversary Proceedings	1355-1380	572-585, 666-675	610	548-573
B. The Nature of the Critical Stage Defined by *Massiah*	1335-1368	627-649	602-616	508-517
C. Waiver of the Right to Counsel	320-321, 339-341, 1329-1381	628,1143-1156, 1349-1350	616-621	545-576, 523
D. Invocation of the Right to Counsel	1302-1329, 1358-1380	547, 552, 566-567	618-622	549-551

17. The Rigth to a Public Trial				
A. The Sixth Amendment Right to a Public Trial	1464, 1468	1460-1467	1024-1038	1224-1226
B. The First Amendment Public Right of Access to Criminal Procedures		1461-1467	1023-1029	1224-1226
C. Publicity and the Right to a Fair Trial		1434-1452, 1463-1465	999-1038	1028-1038
18. The Right to Assistance of Council				
A. The Nature of the Right to the Assistance of Counsel	155-180	1171-1200, 1157-1161	1097-1105, 1123-1124	681-699
B. The Scope of the Right to the Assistance of Counsel	174-183, 1360-1381	666-675, 1172-1190	654-678, 1045	1187-1224
C. The Substance of the Right to the Assistance of Counsel: The Right to Effective Assistance	86, 230-240, 244, 245, 289	1175-1216	1045-1114	1194-1214, 1232
D. Waiver of the Right to Counsel and the Right of Self-Representation	313-342, 320-321, 339-341	1143-1156	1114-1130	1194, 1214, 1221, 1223
19. The Right to Trial by Jury		1388-1432	915-999	
A. The Scope of the Right to Trial by Jury	64-79, 172	1389-1391	915, 918-920, 930	1038-1042
B. The Meaning of the Right to Trial by Jury	78, 117-137	1391-1394, 1400-1429	921-927, 933-940	1042-1043, 1048
C. Jury Selection	86, 107-118, 129, 133	1405-1431	933-978	1038-1076
D. The Substance of the Jury Guarantee During Trial	64-79, 117-137	1513-1514	979-988, 915-920, 942-945	1257-1258
E. Jury Deliberations and Verdicts	64, 81, 155	1392-1394, 1508-1516	927-933, 985-986 990-994	1253-1265
F. Waiver of the Right to Trial by Jury	67, 327	1388-1398	997-999	1043, 1045

Capsule Summary

This capsule summary contains a concise overview of the contents of the entire outline that follows and is intended to assist review by students who have studied the substance of the law covered in the text of the outline. The bracketed page numbers refer to the main outline.

PART I INTRODUCTION TO CRIMINAL PROCEDURE

Part I of this outline lays a foundation for the study of the law of criminal procedure.

 THE STUDY OF CRIMINAL PROCEDURE

The law explained in this outline is addressed by two criminal procedure courses—an "investigatory" course and an "adjudicatory" course.

A. CONTENT OF CRIMINAL PROCEDURE COURSES [p.4]

The law encountered in criminal procedure courses is primarily **constitutional law.** The focus is on constitutional rights that regulate criminal justice processes.

B. INVESTIGATORY VERSUS ADJUDICATORY CRIMINAL PROCEDURE [pp.4-5]

This outline discusses subjects that are typically covered in both a **basic "investigatory"** or **"police practices"** course (Part II) and an **advanced "adjudicatory"** or **"trial rights" course** (Part III).

1. **The "Police Practices" Course [p.4]**

    The police practices course treats **Fourth, Fifth,** and **Sixth Amendment guarantees** applicable to the **investigatory stages** of a criminal case. Topics include: **searches and seizures, government participation in crimes, confessions, identifications,** and **the exclusionary rules.**

2. **The "Trial Rights" Course [pp.4-5]**

    The trial rights course treats guarantees that apply to **adjudicatory phases** of criminal cases. Topics include **discovery, bail, pleas, speedy trials, public trials, counsel, juries, double jeopardy, appeals,** and **collateral remedies.**

C. **SIGNIFICANCE OF THE STUDY OF CRIMINAL PROCEDURE [p.5]**

    The primary concerns of both courses are fundamental constitutional liberties in the Bill of Rights—guarantees that play substantive and symbolic roles in defining our national character.

D. **DOCTRINAL DETAILS AND LARGER PERSPECTIVES [p.6]**

    The study of criminal procedure involves acquiring a working knowledge of numerous **doctrinal details.** It also should direct attention to **the bigger picture**— the role that each detail plays in defining the balance between individual freedom and societal security.

 THE PROCESSES OF THE CRIMINAL JUSTICE SYSTEM

The rights studied operate within state and federal criminal justice processes. A basic sketch of typical steps in those processes follows.

A. **ARREST [pp.7-8]**

    The first formal stage may be an **arrest**—the taking of a person into physical custody with or without a warrant.

B. **INITIAL CHARGE AND INITIAL APPEARANCE [p.8]**

    Before or after arrest, a **formal complaint** that alleges an offense may be filed. Soon after arrest, the suspect makes an **initial appearance** in court.

C.   PRELIMINARY HEARING [p.8]

The next stage may be a **preliminary hearing,** an *adversarial* stage in which a judge determines whether there is probable cause to require the defendant to stand trial.

D.   FORMAL CHARGES IN THE TRIAL COURT: INFORMATIONS AND GRAND JURY INDICTMENTS [p.9]

Serious charges must be formalized in either an **information**—a charging document prepared by a prosecutor—or an **indictment**—a charging document returned by a grand jury.

E.   PRETRIAL PROCEEDINGS [pp.9-10]

Prior to trial, defendants may bring **pretrial motions** and both sides may engage in **discovery.**

F.   THE TRIAL COURT: ARRAIGNMENT AND TRIAL [pp.10-11]

At an **arraignment,** which is the defendant's **first appearance in the** *trial* court, a plea is entered. **Trial** requires proof of guilt **beyond a reasonable doubt.** In a **jury trial,** the first stage is jury selection—the summoning of a panel, voir dire, and the exercise of challenges. After opening arguments, the prosecution presents its case-in-chief, the defense then has an opportunity to present evidence, and both sides may present rebuttal evidence. The judge then instructs the jurors, closing arguments are delivered, the jury deliberates and, if it can agree, returns a verdict. If the verdict is guilty, a **judgment of conviction** is entered.

G.   POST-TRIAL MOTIONS AND SENTENCING [p.11]

Both post-trial motions and **sentencing** follow the trial. Sentencing schemes vary greatly from jurisdiction to jurisdiction.

H.   APPEALS AND COLLATERAL CHALLENGES [p.11]

A defendant may then **appeal** the conviction. When opportunities for appeal are no longer available, a prisoner may bring a **collateral challenge,** claiming that his confinement is unlawful due to a flaw in the process leading to conviction.

 3   FOUNDATIONAL CONCEPTS AND PRINCIPLES

There are a few foundational concepts or principles that students of criminal procedure should understand.

A. APPLICABILITY OF THE BILL OF RIGHTS [p.14]

The guarantees of the **Bill of Rights apply only to the federal government,** not to the states.

B. THE DUE PROCESS CLAUSE AND STATE CRIMINAL JUSTICE PROCESSES [pp.14-15]

The **Fourteenth Amendment Due Process Clause,** through an interpretive process known as **"selective incorporation,"** requires the states to respect almost all of the rights contained in the Bill of Rights. Consequently, the constraints upon state investigatory and adjudicatory processes are almost identical to those upon federal processes.

C. INDEPENDENT STATE CONSTITUTIONS AND LAWS [pp.15-16]

While states cannot deprive individuals of rights guaranteed by the United States Constitution, they may provide **additional, independent** rights either by statute or state constitutional provision. In construing the provisions of a state guarantee, a state court may be guided by, but **is not bound by,** Supreme Court interpretations of the federal Constitution. And if a state court includes a **plain statement** that its decision rests on an **"independent and adequate"** state legal ground, that decision is insulated from reversal on federal grounds.

D. THE FEDERAL SUPERVISORY POWER [pp.17-18]

The **inherent supervisory power** authorizes federal courts to maintain fair processes of criminal justice and empowers them to impose **more demanding** standards on the *federal system* than those required by the Constitution or statutes. This power, however, is *rarely* invoked to limit the authority of federal actors.

E. BURDENS OF PROOF ON CRIMINAL PROCEDURE CLAIMS [pp.18-21]

Two **burden of proof** questions can arise: (1) **Who bears** the burden? and (2) **What is the magnitude** of that burden?

1. Who Bears the Burden of Proof? [p.19]

The defendant typically has the burden of establishing the elements of a claim that she has been deprived of a constitutional entitlement. The government, however, may well bear the burden of establishing a "justification" or a "rebuttal" of the defendant's claim.

2. What Is the Magnitude of the Burden? [pp.20-21]

Ordinarily, matters determinative of criminal procedure claims must be established by **"a preponderance of the evidence."** The party bearing this burden must satisfy the **"more likely than not"** standard. States may impose higher burdens such as **"clear and convincing evidence."**

PART II ## PROCESSES OF INVESTIGATION: RIGHTS AND REMEDIES

Part II of the outline discusses the topics covered in a basic or investigatory criminal procedure course. The topics include Fourth Amendment regulation of searches and seizures, the entrapment and due process defenses based on government participation in crimes, Fifth and Sixth Amendment restrictions on methods of securing confessions and on the admissibility of confessions, Fifth and Sixth Amendment restrictions on methods of securing eyewitness identifications and on the admissibility of eyewitness identifications, and the exclusionary rules that limit the government's ability to introduce unlawfully obtained evidence.

 ## 4 FOURTH AMENDMENT REGULATION OF SEARCHES AND SEIZURES

The Fourth Amendment contains two clauses. The **"reasonableness clause"** prohibits "unreasonable searches and seizures" by the government. The **"warrant clause"** specifies the showing needed to obtain a warrant to search and seize and the content required for a valid warrant.

A. THE THRESHOLD: DEFINITIONS OF SEARCHES AND SEIZURES [pp.27-35]

The Fourth Amendment regulates only **"searches"** and **"seizures"** by **"government agents."** A **"threshold"** question may be whether or not a "search" or a "seizure" has occurred. If government conduct constitutes a search or seizure, it must be reasonable. If conduct is not a search or a seizure, the Fourth Amendment does not regulate it at all.

1. Definition of a "Search": The "Privacy Violation" Approach of Katz v. United States [pp.27-32].

Whether an action constitutes a search depends upon whether it violates a constitutionally protected **privacy** interest.

a. "Reasonable expectation of privacy" doctrine [p.28]. A search occurs when the government's action invades or intrudes upon a **"reasonable expectation of privacy."** Two elements are necessary: (1) the individual alleged to have been searched must have exhibited **"an actual [subjective] expectation of privacy"**; and (2) that expectation must be one **"that society is prepared to recognize as reasonable."**

b. **"Actual (Subjective) expectations of privacy" [pp.28-29].**   To determine whether a person satisfies the actual expectation of privacy requirement, the relevant question is whether individuals in general who behave as this person has behaved have actual expectations of privacy. A person who actually expects privacy from the government may fail to meet this criterion based on the lack of an actual privacy expectation vis-à-vis a private entity.

c. **Expectations "that society is prepared to recognize as reasonable" [pp.29-32].** Ordinarily, the determinative inquiry in threshold "search" determinations is whether a privacy expectation is one **"that society is prepared to recognize as reasonable."** Several factors are relevant to this inquiry:

- **Voluntary disclosure to a third party.** It is not reasonable to expect that information that is **voluntarily disclosed to a third party** will remain private. Consequently, if a third party cooperates with the government by passing the information on to government agents either simultaneously or at a later time, there is no search.

- **Knowing exposure to the public.** It is not reasonable to expect privacy in information or activities **knowingly exposed to the public.** If a government agent occupies a lawful vantage point that is open to any member of the public, if that vantage point is routinely occupied by the public, and if the agent acquires information by the use of unaided senses, there is no search.

- **Lack of societal interest in protecting the privacy of matters.** If there is **"no societal interest in protecting the privacy"** of activities that take place in a certain area, an individual cannot have a reasonable expectation of privacy in those activities. A government intrusion upon such an area—a privately owned "open field," for example—will not constitute a search.

- **The fact that nothing, nothing of significance, or nothing "legitimate" will be learned.** A government act that can reveal **no information, no information of any significance,** or **no information that is "legitimate"** in nature cannot violate a "reasonable expectation of privacy." If it is **"virtually certain"** that an action will not enable the government to learn anything of legitimate significance—that is, if it does not have the *potential* to reveal legitimate, significant information—that action will not be deemed a Fourth Amendment search.

2. **Definition of a "Seizure" of Places and Effects [pp.33-34]**

   A **seizure of property** occurs when there is **"meaningful interference"** **with "possessory interests"** in the property. Thus, taking physical custody of an object, destroying or damaging an effect, or restricting access to a home all constitute seizures of property.

3. **Definition of a "Seizure" of a Person [p.34]**

   The determination of whether and when a **person has been "seized"** can be very significant. That topic is treated at length later in the outline. See Chapter 4, section G.2.

4. **Government Agent Requirement [pp.34-35]**

   The Fourth Amendment regulates only searches and seizures by **government agents.** It does not govern the conduct of **private parties.** An individual is a government agent whenever he or she acts for the state. If government agents "extend" a private party's search or seizure, the extension is subject to Fourth Amendment regulation.

B. **PROBABLE CAUSE TO SEARCH OR ARREST [pp.37-43]**

   1. **Probable Cause: A "Norm" of Reasonableness**

      As a general rule, both warranted and warrantless searches and seizures are unreasonable unless they are supported by showings of **probable cause.**

   2. **Probable Cause to Search [p.37]**

      Probable cause to search requires a showing that an item that is the legitimate object of government interest is presently in the place to be searched.

   3. **Probable Cause to Arrest [p.37]**

      Probable cause to arrest requires a showing that a crime was committed by the person to be arrested.

   4. **Staleness of Probable Cause to Search [pp.37-38]**

      The **staleness** of information may prevent a court from finding **probable cause to search.** Staleness occurs when information is initially sufficient to establish probable cause that an object is in a place, but the mere passage of time reduces the likelihood that the item is still present to a level below what is necessary for a finding of probable cause.

      Generally, **probable cause to arrest** cannot go **stale** because the mere passage of time does not reduce the likelihood that an individual committed an offense.

5. **Level of Probability Required [p.38]**

    The standard of probable cause is lower than the "preponderance of the evidence" or "more likely than not." Probable cause requires only a **"fair probability"** or **"substantial chance."** Thus, probable cause to search requires a "fair probability" that an item is presently in the place to be searched; probable cause to arrest requires a "fair probability" that a person committed an offense.

6. **The "Objective" Nature of Probable Cause [p.39]**

    Probable cause exists if the **objective** facts are sufficient to support a finding of the requisite level of probability. An officer's subjective intention or motivation is irrelevant to and will not defeat a finding of probable cause based on sufficient objective facts.

7. **Hearsay as a Basis for Probable Cause [p.40]**

    Showings of probable cause may properly be based on **hearsay**—information supplied by someone other than the individual applying for a warrant or seeking to justify a warrantless search.

8. **Evaluations of Hearsay-Based Probable Cause Showings: The *Aguilar-Spinelli* Two-Prong Test [pp.40-41]**

    At one time, whenever a probable cause showing depended on hearsay, the "proper weight" to be given to the hearsay first had to be determined by applying the *Aguilar-Spinelli* test. Two independent prongs had to be satisfied to support a probable cause finding.

    a. **"Basis of knowledge" prong [pp.40-41].** The **basis of knowledge prong** was designed to ascertain the facts and circumstances that led the supplier of the hearsay—often an informant—to his or her conclusions. Firsthand observations could provide an adequate basis to support a finding of probable cause.

    b. **"Veracity" prong [p.40].** The **veracity prong** was designed to ascertain the facts and circumstances indicative of the honesty or truthfulness of the person supplying the hearsay. Evidence of either an honest character in general or truthtelling on the particular occasion could provide sufficient evidence of veracity to support a probable cause finding.

    c. **Application of the two-prong test when hearsay is only part of the probable cause basis [p.41].** When a showing of probable cause depended in part on hearsay and in part on other information, the analysis involved two stages. In the **first stage,** the **hearsay alone** had to be evaluated according to the two-prong test. If probable cause was not established, a judge proceeded to the second stage. In the **second stage,** the hearsay had to be evaluated according to the two-prong test **in light of any corroborating information** provided to the judge.

9. **Abolition of the Federal Two-Prong Test; Continuing Adherence in Some States [pp.41-42]**

   In Illinois v. Gates, the Supreme Court **"abandoned" and "rejected" the two-prong test.** Showings of probable cause under the Fourth Amendment no longer have to satisfy that standard. Several states, however, continue to adhere to the two-prong test as the appropriate method of evaluating hearsay-based probable cause showings under their own constitutions.

10. **Evaluations of Hearsay-Based Probable Cause Showings: The *Gates* "Totality of the Circumstances" Test [pp.42-43]**

    The Supreme Court replaced the two-prong test with a **"totality of the circumstances"** standard for determining whether a showing that includes hearsay supports a finding of probable cause. A judge simply adds up all relevant information and determines whether a "fair probability" has been established.

    a. **Role of the two prongs [p.42].** The two prongs—basis of knowledge and veracity—remain **"highly relevant"** to assessments of the weight to be accorded hearsay. However, a deficiency in one prong can be compensated for by a strong showing on the other prong, and probable cause can apparently be found even though neither is satisfied.

    b. **Value of independent police corroboration [p.42].** Official investigative efforts that **corroborate** facts reported by an informant play a role in the totality approach. They can indicate a sound basis of knowledge, support veracity, or add independent weight to the totality and thereby increase the likelihood that probable cause will be found.

    c. **Anonymous tips [p.42].** Anonymous tips can properly count in the totality analysis. The weight to be accorded such tips will increase if corroborative facts support the tipster's basis of knowledge or veracity.

    d. **Significance and limits of the *Gates* totality approach [pp.42-43].** The totality standard frees judges from the restraints of the two-prong test, enabling them to find probable cause in more situations. There are, however, limits that preclude probable cause findings in certain situations. A magistrate must have a **"substantial basis"** for finding probable cause and **may not merely ratify "the bare conclusions of others."** Thus, an affidavit that contains nothing but an informant's or an officer's "conclusions," or both, may not be the basis of a probable cause finding. Once any additional information is provided, however, the totality approach does not prescribe rules that dictate whether probable cause may or should be found.

C. THE WARRANT REQUIREMENT [pp.45-47]

Warrants are documents issued by judges that authorize officers to conduct searches or seizures. A **search warrant** authorizes the search of a place and the seizure of objects. An **arrest warrant** authorizes the seizure of a person.

1. Warrants to Search [pp.45-46]

The text of the Fourth Amendment does not explicitly require officers to obtain search warrants before conducting searches. The question is whether a warrant requirement is implicit in the amendment.

   a. Search warrant requirement [p.45].   The prevailing view holds that there is a **search warrant requirement.** According to the doctrine, **"warrantless searches are per se unreasonable."** As a general rule, no amount of probable cause alone will validate a search; officers must present information to a judicial officer and obtain a search warrant **before** conducting a search.

   b. Rationales for the search warrant requirement [p.46].   The search warrant requirement **prevents unreasonable invasions of privacy and guards against hindsight justification of unjustified searches.** The warrant rule assures that probable cause showings are screened by neutral judicial officers *before* privacy is invaded, discourages officers from searching in the hope of justifying their acts by what is discovered during the search, and limits the scope of the searches and seizures conducted.

   c. Exceptions to the search warrant rule [p.46].   Although the search warrant requirement is a cardinal Fourth Amendment rule, it has **many exceptions.** There are many instances in which warrantless searches are constitutionally reasonable.

2. Warrants to Seize Persons [pp.46-47]

Except in one situation, arrests without arrest warrants are reasonable.

   a. Rule for felony arrests [pp.46-47].   While an arrest of a suspected felon in public requires probable cause, **no warrant is needed for a public felony arrest.** This conclusion is consistent with and based on the common law tradition and the prevailing view of federal and state lawmakers.

   b. Rule for misdemeanor arrests [p.47].   While there is no controlling holding, it is likely that a **public arrest for a misdemeanor not committed in the presence of the arresting officer requires a warrant.** On the other hand, **a public arrest for a misdemeanor committed in the officer's presence** probably **does not require a warrant.**

D. ISSUANCE OF WARRANTS [pp.48-52]

Explicit requirements for valid warrants are set forth in the second clause of the Fourth Amendment (the "warrant clause"). Implicit requirements for valid warrants have also been found in the amendment's text.

1. "Probable Cause" Requirement [p.48]

The Fourth Amendment prohibits the issuance of a warrant "but upon **probable cause.**" At the time a warrant is issued, the judge must be presented with facts sufficient to support a probable cause finding.

2. Misrepresentations in Probable Cause Showings [p.48]

Misrepresentations may invalidate facially adequate showings of probable cause and invalidate warrants issued on the basis of those showings. If it is shown by a "preponderance of the evidence" that **a false statement** that was made **knowingly and intentionally or with reckless disregard for the truth** was included in a showing of probable cause and that the **other information does not support a probable cause finding,** a warrant will be voided.

3. "Neutral and Detached Magistrate" Requirement [pp.49-50]

To be valid, a warrant must be issued by a **"neutral and detached magistrate."** To be neutral, the individual must be **impartial** with regard to whether the warrant should be issued. To be detached, the individual must not be affiliated with the **executive branch**—specifically, she must not have ties to law enforcement. A magistrate does **not need** to be a **lawyer** but must be **"capable of determining whether probable cause exists for the arrest or search."**

4. "Oath or Affirmation" Requirement [p.50]

The Fourth Amendment states that probable cause must be "supported by Oath or affirmation." The applicant for a warrant must swear or affirm that the information provided is true.

5. "Particularity" Requirements [pp.50-51]

The warrant clause requires that warrants **"particularly describ[e both] the place to be searched and the persons or things to be seized."**

a. **Particular description of the place to be searched [p.50].**   The terms of the warrant must particularly describe the place to be searched to guard against unjustified privacy invasions.

b. **Particular description of the persons or things to be seized [p.50].**   The terms of the warrant must particularly describe the persons or things to be seized to guard against unjustified liberty or property deprivations and to limit the scope of privacy invasions.

c. **Meaning of "particularity" [pp.50-51].** There is no bright-line standard of particularity. Descriptions in warrants must be as particular as is reasonable and practicable under the circumstances of each case. The degree of particularity demanded can vary based on the nature of the information available and the scope of the authority needed for an effective investigation.

d. **Mistaken descriptions and the particularity requirement [pp.51-52].** Warrants containing mistaken descriptions of places to be searched or persons or things to be seized, may be—but are not necessarily— unconstitutional. A warrant that includes a mistaken description of a place or a person or object is **sufficiently particular** if **at the time the warrant is issued** it is **reasonable to believe** that the probable cause to search or seize extends to the place, person, or object described. The warrant is **invalid** only if those applying for the warrant **knew or should have known of the mistaken description** in the warrant.

E. EXECUTION OF WARRANTS [pp.52-54]

Searches pursuant to warrants can be unreasonable because of the manner in which the warrants are executed.

1. **The Fourth Amendment "Knock and Announce" Principle [p.52]**

   The **knock and announce principle** that is part of the Fourth Amendment reasonableness inquiry creates a presumption in favor of announcement. A search may be unreasonably executed because officers failed to knock and announce their presence and identify themselves prior to entering a private place.

2. **Reasonable Unannounced Entries: "Specific" versus "Categorical" Justifications [p.53]**

   There is no rigid rule requiring a knock and announcement in every case. Adequate "countervailing law enforcement interests" can make an unannounced entry reasonable. It is not clear, however, what interests are sufficiently weighty to justify an unannounced entry. To determine whether an exemption from the "knock and announce" requirement is justified, the **specific** facts and circumstances of each case must be examined; **categorical** exemptions based on the type of crime involved are not valid. Moreover, officers need only demonstrate a **reasonable suspicion** that there are grounds for a "no knock" entry; probable cause is not required.

3. **Mistakes in Executing Warrants [p.54]**

   A search may be unreasonable because of a mistake by an officer in executing a warrant. If an officer **mistakenly interprets the warrant,** a search is unreasonable unless it is **reasonable at the time of execution to believe that the warrant authorizes the action.** If an officer executes a warrant that contains a mistake, the search is unreasonable unless it is **reasonable at the time of execution to not realize that the warrant description is mistaken.**

F. EXCEPTIONS TO THE SEARCH WARRANT RULE [pp.56-87]

The warrant requirement, a cardinal rule of Fourth Amendment law, is qualified by several exceptions. Each exception defines a situation in which a search is **reasonable without a search warrant.** Some exceptions also define situations in which searches are **reasonable without probable cause to search.**

1. Searches Incident to Arrest [pp.56-60]

Officers have limited authority to conduct **"searches incident to arrest."**

a. The showing needed to conduct a search incident to arrest [pp.56-57]. A search incident to arrest is justified when an officer performs a **lawful, custodial arrest.** The officer must have **probable cause to arrest,** must have **an arrest warrant** if the offense is a misdemeanor committed outside his presence, and must take the person **into custody.**

Probable cause *to search* is not required. Moreover, the fact that an officer has discretion to decide whether to arrest and discretion to decide whether to search an arrestee does not negate the authority to conduct a search incident to arrest.

b. Scope of search incident to arrest authority [pp.57-59]. Incident to an arrest, an officer may search the **person of the arrestee,** including any **containers** found in his possession. An officer may also search the **area within the immediate control of the arrestee**—the surrounding area into which he might reach to grab a weapon or destroy or conceal evidence. The permissible search is **temporally** and **spatially limited;** it may not be **remote in time or place** from the arrest.

After the arrest of an occupant of an automobile, an officer may search **the entire passenger compartment** and **containers** located inside. This authority exists even though the arrestee was not inside the automobile at the time of arrest, so long as she was a **recent occupant** of the vehicle—that is, she was in the vehicle **just prior to the arrest.**

Incident to an arrest in a dwelling, officers may also search **areas immediately adjoining the place of arrest** for the limited purpose of ascertaining whether **dangerous persons** are present.

2. The *Chrisman*–"at the Elbow of the Arrestee" Exception [pp.61-62]

In certain instances an officer may make a warrantless entry of a private place in order to monitor an arrestee.

    a. **The showing needed for the "at the elbow of the arrestee" exception [p.61].** The "at the elbow" exception applies if an officer makes a **lawful custodial arrest** and the **arrestee requests to enter a private place.** It is unclear whether it applies to cases in which an officer, for good reason, **requires an arrestee to enter a private place.**

    b. **Scope of the "search" [pp.61-62].** An officer may enter the private place, go wherever the arrestee goes, and observe objects in view. It is uncertain whether an officer has any authority to open closed spaces in the dwelling that fall within the area of control of the arrestee.

3. **Searches for Arrestees: The Doctrine of Payton v. New York [pp.62-64]**

Entries of private dwellings normally require search warrants. When an entry is made to arrest an individual who resides in the dwelling for a felony, a partial exception to the search warrant requirement applies.

    a. **The showing needed to justify entry [pp.62-63].** To enter a home to arrest a resident for a **felony,** an officer does not need a **search warrant,** but needs *only* **an arrest warrant** and **probable cause to believe that the person to be arrested is presently in the home.** These showings adequately protect the *privacy interests of the arrestee* in the dwelling.

    b. **Scope of the exception [pp.63-64].** Officers may enter the dwelling, may search places where the suspected felon could be found, and must end the search when the arrestee is found.

    The "*Payton* exception" does not justify an invasion of the privacy interests of an **innocent third party**—a person who is not the subject of the arrest warrant. To enter the home of an innocent third party to arrest a suspected felon, officers must have a **search warrant.**

    It is uncertain whether the "*Payton* exception" allows an invasion of the home privacy interest of an innocent third party when the individual sought to be arrested also has a privacy interest in the home. In that situation, a felony arrest warrant and probable cause to believe that the potential arrestee is in the home **may** be an adequate basis for invading the privacy interest of the innocent co-dweller. On the other hand, the innocent co-dweller **may** be entitled to the full protection of a search warrant.

4. **Exigent Circumstances Searches [pp.65-69]**

Exigent circumstances is a somewhat open-ended exception to the warrant requirement that permits warrantless searches when there is a sufficient showing of *need* to search without a warrant.

    a. **The showing needed to invoke the exigent circumstances exception [pp.65-69].** The exigent circumstances exception applies when officers have both **probable cause to search** and **an exigency.** At least some cases also require a showing of **an interest of sufficient importance.**

To qualify as an exigency, the circumstances must demonstrate not merely a need to *act* but a **need to** *search* **without a warrant.** Typically, this involves a showing that the purpose of searching will be defeated or that some serious harm will occur if officers have to apply for a warrant before searching. It is not clear **how likely** it must be that the particular need to search exists or **how specific** the exigency showing must be.

Hot pursuit is a recurrent type of exigency that exists when a pursued suspect flees into a private dwelling. A warrantless entry is justified when law enforcement officers or others have **immediately and continuously pursued** the suspect from the scene of a crime or some other place.

A warrantless entry of a **home** pursuant to the exigent circumstances exception (including the ''hot pursuit'' doctrine) is not permissible if the interest served by the entry is insufficiently weighty—that is, if there is probable cause to believe that **only a minor offense** has been committed.

b. **Scope of an exigent circumstances search [p.69].** A warrantless search under the exigent circumstances exception may extend **only** to those **areas where the object of the probable cause to search could be found** and may last **only so long as the need to search continues.**

5. **The ''Automobile'' or** *Carroll-Chambers* **Doctrine [pp.70-73]**

The **''automobile''** or *Carroll-Chambers* **doctrine** is a type of ''exigent circumstances'' exception that permits the warrantless search of vehicles because of their *mobility* and the *diminished privacy expectations* that individuals have in vehicles.

a. **The showing necessary to trigger the automobile doctrine [pp.70-72].** A warrantless automobile doctrine search requires at least a showing of **probable cause to search** a **vehicle** that is **readily mobile. All kinds of vehicles,** not only automobiles, are subject to warrantless search under the doctrine—for example, airplanes, boats, and motorcycles are included. The automobile doctrine allows warrantless searches of vehicles that have been **stopped in transit, found stationary in a public place,** or **found stationary on private property** belonging to another person. It is arguable, but seems *unlikely*, that a vehicle found stationary on private property (or curtilage) belonging to the vehicle owner does not fall within the exception and that a search requires a warrant.

It *may* also be necessary for the vehicle to be at least partially **in use for transportation purposes.** A vehicle that is exclusively or primarily **being used as a residence** *may* be outside the scope of the exception.

b. **Scope of an automobile doctrine search [pp.72-73].** Warrantless automobile doctrine searches may extend to **any part** of a vehicle **that there is probable cause to search. Locked compartments** and **separate containers** found inside the vehicle are included. While the search of a private container found outside a vehicle requires a warrant, a search of the same container located inside a vehicle may be conducted without a warrant so long as there is probable cause to search.

Warrantless searches of vehicles may be conducted **immediately at the place the vehicle is stopped or found** or **immediately after the vehicle is transported to the police station.** Moreover, delay in conducting the warrantless search will render the search unreasonable *only* if the delay is **indefinite** or, perhaps, if it **adversely affects privacy or possessory interests** in the vehicle.

6. **Inventory Searches of Vehicles and Arrestees [pp.74-78]**

The **"inventory search" exceptions** permit warrantless searches of vehicles or arrestees without showings of probable cause to search.

a. **Inventory searches of vehicles [pp.74-77].** A valid inventory search of a vehicle requires a **lawful impoundment** of the vehicle and a search pursuant to **standard police procedures.**

A lawful impoundment occurs when a vehicle is taken into custody for legitimate governmental purposes. There is adequate reason to impound a vehicle that is impeding traffic or threatening the public safety or convenience. The **decision to impound** may not be left to the **unfettered discretion** of the authorities; it must be based on **standard criteria** and on **something other than suspicion of criminal activity.**

The decision to inventory also cannot be left to the **unfettered discretion** of officers but must be made according to **standard police procedures.** "Standard" procedures need not command the search of all or no impounded vehicles, but they may allow officers to exercise judgment **"based on concerns related to the purposes of an inventory search."**

Officers do **not** have to **invite an owner to make other arrangements** for the safekeeping of belongings, but *may* have to grant an owner's request to make such arrangements.

The constitutionally permissible **scope** of a vehicle inventory includes **all generally accessible areas of the passenger compartment, trunks,** and **closed containers** inside the vehicle. However, an inventory may be no broader than what is authorized by the standard procedures governing the inventory.

b. **Inventory searches of arrestees [pp.77-78].** A valid inventory search of an arrestee requires a **lawful arrest.** Probable cause to search is unnecessary, but **probable cause to arrest** is required. For some misdemeanants, an arrest warrant is probably needed.

In addition, inventory searches (or "inventories") are reasonable only when the arrestee is **going to be incarcerated.** If the individual is going to be released from the station without being confined in jail, an inventory is unconstitutional.

Finally, the jurisdiction must have **standard police procedures** that govern inventory searches of arrestees. Officers may not be given **unfettered discretion** to decide which arrestees to inventory, but they may be allowed to decide as long as **standard criteria** guide their decisions.

An inventory of an arrestee may include a search of **the person of the arrestee** and **personal belongings and containers on the person or in the possession** of the arrestee. While inventories ordinarily are conducted **at the police station or jailhouse** before an individual is placed in a cell, it is permissible to perform an inventory prior to arrival at the station or jailhouse.

7. **Consent Searches [pp.79-83]**

When a person with authority gives the authorities **consent** to search, a warrantless search is permissible. Moreover, if the person giving consent lacks authority, a warrantless search based on that person's **apparent authority** is reasonable if the officer reasonably believes that the person has authority to consent.

a. **The showing needed for a consent search [pp.79-81].** A warrantless search based on consent requires **express or implicit consent** that is **voluntary,** not coerced. Voluntariness is determined based on the **totality of the circumstances.** While factors bearing on the **subjective strength of will** of the individual are relevant, some amount of **official coercion** is probably needed to render a consent "involuntary." **Knowledge of the right to refuse** is relevant but not necessary. A lawfully seized individual need not be advised that he is "free to go" before a consent can be found voluntary.

A valid consent requires **authority to consent.** The person giving consent must have **common authority** that rests on **mutual use of the property by persons generally having joint access or control for most purposes.** The scope of an individual's authority to consent may be limited if the individual uses or has access to or control over only limited spaces within a larger area.

b. **Scope of a valid consent search [pp.81-82].** The **scope of a consent search** is as broad as the consent given. An individual with authority may expressly limit the scope of the search permitted. When there is no express limitation, the standard for determining the permissible scope is one of **"objective reasonableness."** The dispositive inquiry is **what a reasonable person would have understood by the exchange** between the officer and the person giving consent.

c. **The "apparent authority" doctrine [pp.82-83].** A warrantless search based on consent by a person without actual common authority may still be reasonable if it falls within the **"apparent authority" doctrine.** If an officer has an **objectively reasonable belief that the person who has given consent has common authority,** the search is reasonable. If it is not reasonable to believe that the person has authority to consent, the search is unreasonable—*unless* the person does in fact have actual authority.

8. **The Plain View Doctrine [pp.84-87]**

    Although it is sometimes viewed as an exception to the search warrant rule, the **plain view doctrine** does not permit warrantless searches. It merely authorizes the warrantless **seizure** of an object under the following circumstances: (1) **lawful arrival at the place from which the object can be plainly viewed;** (2) **lawful access to the object seized;** and (3) **an object whose incriminating nature is "immediately apparent."**

    a. **Lawful arrival at the place from which the object can be plainly viewed [pp.84-85].** The **lawful arrival** criterion means that officers must not violate the Fourth Amendment in gaining access to the place that affords plain view of the object to be seized. If an unlawful search provides the view, it will taint the later seizure.

    b. **Lawful access to the object that is seized [p.85].** The **lawful access** criterion reflects the notion that officers must not violate the Fourth Amendment in reaching the place that allows seizure of the object. If a search is necessary to gain access to the object, **no amount of probable cause** will justify that search—a warrant or exception to the warrant requirement is required.

    c. **An object whose incriminating nature is "immediately apparent" [pp.85-86].** The **"immediately apparent"** criterion reflects the requirement of **probable cause to seize** the object. While it almost certainly does not mean that officers must instantly realize the grounds for a seizure, it does bar an independent search or seizure of the object itself in order to generate the probable cause required to seize it.

    d. **Rejection of the inadvertence requirement [p.87].** A justified plain view seizure does **not** require **inadvertent discovery** of the object. Even if officers are aware in advance that they will find an object that they have probable cause to seize, a seizure is reasonable if the criteria set out above are satisfied.

G. STOPS AND FRISKS: THE DOCTRINE OF TERRY v. OHIO [pp.90-103]

In the landmark case of Terry v. Ohio, the Supreme Court addressed a law enforcement practice known as a **"stop and frisk."** A "stop" is a limited detention of a person to determine whether a crime is occurring or has occurred. A "frisk" is a patdown of a person's outer clothing to determine whether he has a weapon.

1. The Holding of Terry v. Ohio [pp.90-91]

Because a stop is a *seizure* and a frisk is a *search*, both are subject to the Fourth Amendment reasonableness requirement. However, because a stop is not a "full" seizure and a frisk is not a "full" search, they do not require probable cause. They are reasonable if an officer is aware of facts that "lead him **reasonably to conclude** . . . that **criminal activity may be afoot** and that the [suspect] . . . may be **armed and presently dangerous.**"

2. The "Threshold" Question: When Is a Person "Seized"? [pp.91-93]

The Fourth Amendment regulates only encounters in which officers **"seize"** individuals. Because not every encounter between an officer and a suspect is a seizure, an important "threshold" question is when such a seizure occurs.

    a. **"Intent" requirement [p.91].** A seizure does not occur unless the officer has the **intent to acquire physical control or terminate the freedom of movement** of the individual. Seizures cannot be effected accidentally.

    b. **"Physical force" or "show of authority" requirement [pp.92-93].** A seizure of a person does not occur unless an officer uses **either physical force or a show of authority.** If an officer uses **any physical force,** even a slight touching of the person, **a seizure is complete.** The seizure may end, however, if the suspect flees.

    If the officer uses a **"show of authority,"** a seizure occurs *only* if **a reasonable person would not feel free to leave** *and* **the suspect submits** to the show of authority. If the suspect does not feel free to leave because of **self-imposed restraints,** a seizure occurs *only* if **a reasonable person would not feel free to decline the officer's requests or otherwise terminate the encounter** *and* **the suspect submits** to the show of authority. In a case involving a show of authority, no seizure can occur without **submission by the suspect.**

3. **Justification for Stops and Frisks: A "Reasonable Suspicion" [pp.94-96]**

   The showing needed to render a stop and a frisk reasonable is a **reasonable suspicion.**

   a. **The showing needed for a stop or temporary detention of a person [pp.94-95].** A seizure of a person—a stop or temporary detention—is constitutional if it is based on a **reasonable suspicion** that the person **is engaging in criminal activity** or that the person **was involved in or is wanted in connection with a completed felony.**

   b. **The showing needed for a frisk or weapons patdown of a person [p.95].** A limited search—a frisk or weapons patdown—is constitutional if it is based on a **reasonable suspicion** that the person being detained **is armed and presently dangerous.**

   c. **Definition of a "reasonable suspicion" [pp.95-96].** A reasonable suspicion is more than an inchoate, unparticularized, or inarticulate hunch. While a showing of reasonable suspicion must be supported by articulable, objective facts, the reasonable suspicion standard is **less demanding than probable cause.** Consequently, the level of likelihood required is something less than a "fair probability." The facts needed to establish a reasonable suspicion can be lesser in "quantity" and in "quality," and no single fact needs to describe "ongoing criminal activity." A judge must make independent, reasonable suspicion determinations and cannot simply defer to the judgments of officers.

4. **Scope of *Terry*-Stops: Limits on Temporary Detentions of Persons [pp.97-99]**

   The justification for allowing stops and frisks on less than probable cause is that they are less intrusive than "full" seizures and searches. An important question, therefore, is the permissible scope of the seizures and searches that are allowed on the basis of a reasonable suspicion.

   a. **Temporal factor: How long may a temporary detention last? [p.97].** While an investigative detention must be **brief** and cannot continue "indefinitely," there is no bright-line time limit. A "stop" may last only as long as officers are **diligently pursuing a means of investigation likely to confirm or dispel their suspicions quickly.** If the investigation is **dilatory** or **unnecessarily prolonged,** the detention is unreasonable in scope.

b. **Locational factor: May a suspect be moved during a *Terry* detention? [pp.97-98].** An officer may not **transport a suspect to the police station** on the basis of a reasonable suspicion. If the officer acts without judicial authorization, such a detention is considered a **de facto arrest** that requires probable cause. However, an officer with only a reasonable suspicion *may* be able to take a suspect to a police station as part of a temporary, investigatory detention if he obtains **judicial authorization for the seizure.**

While limited movements of a suspect to other locations are probably permissible based on a reasonable suspicion alone, the extent of the movements that are allowable during a stop is uncertain.

During a lawful vehicle stop it is always reasonable to order the driver and passengers to exit pending completion of the stop.

c. **Other relevant factors: How much may official conduct intrude on a suspect's liberty? [pp.98-99].** Other actions by officers that increase the intrusion on a suspect's freedom can exceed the scope of a permissible detention. Such actions could include intense questioning, the selection of an isolated or intimidating setting, the use of investigatory techniques such as sobriety tests or fingerprinting, and handcuffing the individual.

5. **Scope of *Terry*-Stops: Temporary Detentions of Effects [pp.99-102]**

The *Terry* doctrine permits **seizures of effects** independently of the detention of an individual.

a. **Permissibility of and grounds for seizing effects [p.99].** A limited detention of an effect is reasonable when officers have a **reasonable suspicion that it contains contraband narcotics.** It is uncertain whether any other reasonable suspicions justify seizures of effects, but it is clear that a mere reasonable suspicion that an object is stolen does **not justify** even the most limited seizure of that object for investigatory purposes.

b. **Allowable scope of seizures of effects [pp.99-102].** There is no bright-line standard prescribing the permissible scope of a seizure of an effect. When an object is seized from an individual both the **possessory interest** in the item and the **liberty interest** of the individual in her person are infringed upon, but when an object that is seized is not in the possession of an individual, only the **possessory interest** in the item is infringed upon. Consequently, the seizure of an object from the custody of an individual may last **no longer than a seizure of the person**—as long as the officer is diligently pursuing investigative means likely to confirm or dispel his suspicions quickly. The seizure of an object not in the possession of a person may not be subject to the same time limitations.

An object suspected of harboring contraband may be subjected to a **dog sniff.** However, an officer may not open or otherwise "search" the detained object on the basis of a reasonable suspicion. Moreover, the extent of an officer's authority to **transport a detained effect to another location** is uncertain.

6.   **Scope of _Terry_ Frisks [pp.102-103]**

A frisk based on reasonable suspicion must be limited to a **patdown of the outer clothing** of the suspect to detect large weapons—guns, clubs, and knives—but may involve a **thorough exploration of all areas of the person.** If the officer detects a weapon during the limited patdown, he may remove it. Otherwise, an officer may not reach beneath the outer clothing or conduct an additional search of the person (for example, by manually manipulating an object not believed to be a weapon).

A **limited weapons search of a vehicle** (a "vehicle frisk") is permitted if there is a reasonable suspicion that a **suspect is dangerous and may gain immediate control of weapons** from the vehicle. The search may extend only to **areas in the passenger compartment—including containers—that could contain a weapon and over which the suspect would generally have control.**

H. "PROTECTIVE SWEEPS" OF HOMES: THE DOCTRINE OF MARYLAND v. BUIE [pp.106-107]

In certain circumstances, officers may conduct **"protective sweeps"** of homes.

1.   **Showing Needed to Conduct a "Protective Sweep" of a Home [p.106]**

A protective sweep is justified if officers make a **lawful arrest in a home** and also possess **a reasonable suspicion that the house harbors a person posing a danger** to the officers.

2.   **Scope of a Sweep of a Home [pp.106-107]**

Protective sweeps may extend only to those areas of the home where it is reasonable to suspect there are dangerous persons. Moreover, the search of the home must be limited to a **cursory inspection of those spaces where a person may be found.** It can last **no longer than necessary to dispel the reasonable suspicion of danger** and **no longer than it takes to complete the arrest and depart the premises.**

I. DETENTIONS AND SEARCHES OF INDIVIDUALS PRESENT DURING SEARCHES OF PREMISES [pp.107-109]

In some circumstances, officers conducting searches of places may be authorized to detain or search persons who are present.

1. **Detentions of Individuals During Searches of Premises: The Doctrine of Michigan v. Summers [pp.107-108]**

   Officers have a limited authority to detain occupants of premises during a search of those premises pursuant to a valid warrant for contraband.

   a. **"Occupant" or "resident" limitation [pp.107-108].** Only **occupants** or **residents** of premises may be detained; visitors and short-term guests may not. Officers may detain those found **inside** the premises and may require those found **just outside** the premises to come inside and remain there. The authority to detain clearly applies to occupants of **private dwellings** and may extend to those who have equivalent relationships to other premises.

   b. **Potential "search warrant" limitation [p.108].** The authority to detain arises when officers are searching premises pursuant to a **valid search warrant** and may arise when officers are conducting a legitimate **warrantless search based on exigency.**

   c. **Potential "contraband" limitation [p.108].** A detention is reasonable if the officers are searching for **contraband** and may be reasonable when they are searching for **evidence** or other items.

   d. **Permissible scope of a *Summers* detention [p.108].** The detentions authorized may ordinarily last **while a proper search is being conducted,** but **in an unusual case** involving **special circumstances** or possibly **a prolonged detention,** it may be unreasonable to detain an individual during the entire time that a proper search is being conducted.

2. **Searches of Individuals During Searches of Premises [pp.108-109]**

   A search of a person who is on premises pursuant to a warrant that specifically authorizes the search of that person is valid, while the validity of a search pursuant to a warrant that authorizes the search of "all persons present" is debatable. The question here is the validity of a search of a person who is merely present in a place that is subject to a valid warranted or warrantless search.

   a. **Persons present in commercial establishments [p.109].** A person who is merely present in a commercial establishment—a customer, for example—**may not be searched** as part of the search of the premises even if there is a valid warrant to search the premises. Only particularized **probable cause to search the person** can justify such a search. The same conclusion would very likely govern analogous situations involving guests or visitors on private premises.

b. Occupants of private dwellings and individuals with analogous connections to commercial establishments [p.109]. It is uncertain whether occupants or residents of private premises or those with similar connections to commercial premises (such as business owners) are subject to **search** by virtue of their presence during valid searches of those premises.

J. SCHOOL SEARCHES [pp.111-114]

The **special relationship** between schoolchildren and school officials and the **special need** to maintain order in schools justifies limited searches without warrants or probable cause.

1. Conditions Necessary to Conduct a School Search [pp.111-112]

Warrantless searches of **schoolchildren** by **school officials** are reasonable if based on a **reasonable suspicion.**

a. Primary or secondary school setting requirement [p.111]. The authority to search applies only to **schoolchildren**—that is, students in **primary and secondary schools.**

b. School official requirement [p.111]. The authority may be exercised only by **school officials** when they are **acting in the interest of the school.** The school search doctrine does not authorize searches conducted **in conjunction with** or **at the behest of law enforcement.**

c. "Reasonable suspicion" requirement [pp.111-112]. The searching official must have **"reasonable grounds for suspecting"** that the search will produce evidence of **a violation of either the law or the rules of the school.**

2. Scope of an Authorized School Search [pp.112-114]

Reasonable school searches are limited in scope.

a. The school setting [p.155]. The search authorized must be performed **in the schol2 setting.**

b. The "person" of the student [pp.112-113]. Officials may search **the person of the student,** including **all personal belongings** on the student at the time of the search. The extent of the search of the student must be **reasonably related to the objectives of the search and not excessively intrusive in light of the age and sex of the student and the nature of the infraction.** Clearly, the search must not go further than is justified by the official's reasonable suspicion. Moreover, searches that are peculiarly intrusive on privacy may be unreasonable unless conducted by officials of the same gender and justified by a weighty interest.

    c. **Automobiles and other belongings not on the person of the student [pp.113-114].** A school search of a student's vehicle or other personal belongings not on her person *may* be justifiable on the same basis as a search of the student's person.

    d. **Lockers, desks, and other school property [p.114].** It is arguable that students have no legitimate expectations of privacy in lockers, desks, and other school property. If so, officials would not have to justify "searches" of those places.

  3. **Possibility of Random Searches of Schoolchildren [p.114]**

In some circumstances, school authorities **might** be able to justify **"random" searches of students**—that is, searches conducted **without any individualized suspicion.**

K. **PERMANENT AND TEMPORARY CHECKPOINTS OR ROADBLOCKS [pp.115-117]**

The temporary **seizure** of a motorist at a permanent or temporary traffic checkpoint can be reasonable **without individualized suspicion** that the detained motorist is involved in any sort of illegality.

  1. **Cases Upholding Permanent and Temporary Checkpoints [pp.115-116]**

In United States v. Martinez-Fuerte, the Supreme Court upheld a **permanent illegal alien detection checkpoint,** and in Michigan Department of State Police v. Sitz, the Court upheld a **temporary sobriety checkpoint.** Despite the fact that the motorists were briefly **seized** without individualized suspicion, the checkpoint detentions were deemed constitutional.

  2. **Criteria for Judging the Constitutionality of Checkpoints [pp.116-117]**

Instead of a bright-line standard for evaluating the constitutionality of a traffic checkpoint, the Supreme Court has provided three criteria.

    a. **Magnitude of the seizure [pp.116-117].** A suspicionless checkpoint stop can be sustained if the **magnitude of the seizure is limited or minimal.** The **objective magnitude** of the seizure depends on the **duration** and the **intensity of the investigation** conducted. "Brief" seizures that involve limited questioning and visual inspection constitute "limited" or "slight" objective intrusions.

    The **subjective magnitude** of the seizure hinges on its **potential to generate fear and surprise,** which can be diminished by visible signs of authority, the fact that other motorists are also being stopped, and limits on the officers' discretion to choose sites and methods of investigation.

    b. **Nature of the interest served by the checkpoint [p.117].** The **nature of the interest served by the checkpoint** is highly relevant. The decisions upholding checkpoints pointed to the **important law enforce-**

ment **interests** served and the **serious public dangers** combated by those checkpoints.

c. **"Need" for suspicionless stops and "effectiveness" of the checkpoint [p.117].** The **need for suspicionless stops,** the **effectiveness** of those stops, and the **extent to which they advance the public interest** are all relevant to the constitutionality of checkpoints. Nevertheless, checkpoints that result in relatively **small percentages of detection** are sufficiently **effective,** and judges should be reluctant to invalidate checkpoints based on their own assessments of need or effectiveness.

L. DRUG TESTING [pp.118-122]

Drug testing is a kind of search that can be reasonable despite the absence of a warrant, probable cause, or any kind of individualized suspicion. The constitutionality of "random" drug testing programs must be evaluated on a case-by-case basis.

1. Cases Upholding Random, Suspicionless Drug Testing [p.119]

In three cases, the Supreme Court has upheld blood, urine, and breath tests for drugs or alcohol. Skinner v. Railway Labor Executives' Association involved the testing of certain railroad employees. National Treasury Employees Union v. Von Raab involved the testing of certain customs service employees. Vernonia School District 47J v. Acton involved the testing of student athletes.

These cases make it clear that drug tests are Fourth Amendment **searches** and that they can be **reasonable** even though they are administered **randomly—that is, without any individualized basis for suspicion about the person tested.** The constitutionality of a particular drug testing scheme is determined by **balancing the nature and extent of the intrusion against the governmental interests that are promoted.**

2. Nature and Extent of the Privacy Intrusion [pp.119-120]

A random drug testing program can be constitutional if the **intrusion on privacy interests** is **limited.** An intrusion can be limited because the individual has a **diminished privacy interest** or because there are **restrictions on the government's conduct.**

a. **Factors that diminish an individual's expectation of privacy [pp.119-120].** An individual may have a **diminished expectation of privacy** because she is employed in a pervasively regulated industry; has a job that requires fitness, probity, judgment, or dexterity; is a schoolchild committed to the temporary custody of the state; or is a participant in school athletics.

b. **Factors that restrict the intrusiveness of the government's conduct [p.120].** The following can **restrict the intrusiveness of the govern-**

ment's conduct and thereby reduce the privacy intrusion effected by drug testing: the use of testing techniques that reveal only information about illicit drug or alcohol use; the use of commonplace testing methods administered by medical personnel; the lack of a need to disrobe; the absence of direct visual observation of the process of urination; the limited disclosure of test results; and the use of standardized testing processes that do not involve discretionary variation.

3. **Government Interests Promoted by the Tests [pp.120-122]**

The reasonableness of random drug testing depends on whether the intrusion is outweighed by the **government interests** that are promoted. The government interests hinge on the **nature of the interests** promoted, the **need for random testing,** and the **effectiveness of such testing.**

a. **Nature of the government interests promoted by the tests [pp.120-121].** While describing the interests in two drug testing cases as **compelling,** the Supreme Court has indicated that a government interest can support random drug testing if it is *"important* **enough to justify the particular search at hand."**

The cases approving drug testing have involved a **"special need beyond the normal need for law enforcement."** The testing programs were **not designed for criminal law enforcement,** and the results **could not be used in criminal prosecutions.** It is unclear whether a random program designed to enforce the criminal laws could be constitutional.

b. **Proof of a drug use problem in the particular case [p.121].** Proof of a drug use problem in the group subject to random testing is **relevant but not essential.** While such proof counts in favor of a finding of reasonableness, a program can be sustained without it.

c. **Extent to which government interests are promoted by the tests: Need and effectiveness [pp.121-122].** The **need for random, suspicionless drug testing** is **relevant** to the constitutionality of random drug testing. Such a need is established if a particularized suspicion requirement would impede efforts to further the interest at stake.

The **effectiveness** of random drug testing is also **relevant** to its constitutionality. The government, however, does not have to provide empirical proof of effectiveness.

4. **A Case Rejecting Random, Suspicionless Drug Testing**

In Chandler v. Miller, the Supreme Court found a Georgia drug testing scheme under which candidates for state office had to certify that they had submitted to a urinalysis test and had tested negative for illegal drugs to be unreasonable. Although the testing method involved was "relatively noninvasive," the Court concluded that the state's program was not supported by a "special need" because Georgia had not provided evidence of a drug abuse problem among state officials and its program was neither well designed to identify antidrug law violators nor a credible means of deterring drug users from seeking state office. Moreover, there was no good reason to conclude that suspicion-based searches would be insufficient. In sum, "public safety [was] not genuinely in jeopardy."

M. OTHER ADMINISTRATIVE SEARCHES [pp.123-127]

Administrative or **regulatory searches** are designed to enforce governmental regulatory schemes. Such searches serve **"special needs"** other than enforcement of the criminal laws. An administrative search can be reasonable in the absence of a search warrant or probable cause. The **reasonableness** of such a search is determined by balancing the governmental interests that are served against the invasion of privacy caused by the search. This balancing process has produced three general categories of constitutionally legitimate administrative searches.

1. **"Administrative" or "Regulatory" Searches That Are Reasonable If Supported by Search Warrants Based on Unparticularized, "Area-Wide" Showings of Cause [p.124]**

    Some administrative searches **require search warrants,** but the warrants need not be based on probable cause to search a particular place. Instead, they may be based on general considerations bearing on the objectives of the search to be conducted. More specifically, such a warrant may be issued if **"reasonable legislative or administrative standards for conducting an area inspection"** are satisfied.

    Warrants are required because the searches entail **significant privacy intrusions** and the requirement of **advance judicial approval will not frustrate the purposes** of the regulatory scheme. Particularized cause showings *are not* required because the regulatory programs have a **long history of acceptance,** the **public interests** could be frustrated by a particularized cause requirement, and the **privacy invasion is limited.**

2. **"Administrative" or "Regulatory" Searches That Require Neither a Warrant nor Any Showing of Cause [pp.125-126]**

    Some administrative searches are reasonable **without warrants or any particularized showings of cause.** The searches in this category have involved businesses that are subject to **close or pervasive governmental regulation;** regulatory schemes that promote **substantial governmental interests;** the **need for warrantless inspections** to carry out those schemes; and statutory inspection provisions that **provide notice that the searches are pursuant to law** and **limit the discretion** of the officials performing the searches. A **long history of close governmental regulation** has also played a role.

3. **"Administrative" or "Regulatory" Searches That Do Not Require Warrants but Do Require a Showing of Justification Less Than Probable Cause [pp.126-127]**

    Some administrative searches are reasonable **without warrants,** but must be supported by a **particularized showing less than probable cause.** The precise showing needed has not been defined.

    Searches have been classified in this category when **search warrant and probable cause requirements would frustrate** efforts to promote the **special needs** that underlie the regulatory scheme at issue.

N. ELEVATED STANDARDS OF FOURTH AMENDMENT REASONABLENESS [pp.127-133]

In many instances described in the preceding subsections, a "balancing" process has led to the conclusion that Fourth Amendment norms—probable cause and a warrant—must be lowered. In those situations, searches or seizures have been deemed reasonable without a warrant, without probable cause, or without either. The same balancing process can lead to **elevated standards of Fourth Amendment reasonableness** when governmental conduct causes particularly severe intrusions on privacy or liberty.

1. **Use of Deadly Force to Arrest [pp.128-130]**

    The use of deadly force to apprehend a suspect is a highly intrusive Fourth Amendment **seizure** that is not reasonable simply because an officer has probable cause to believe that the suspect has committed a felony.

    a. **Official conduct that is regulated: Any use of deadly force or only deadly force that kills? [p.128].**   The traditional definition of **deadly force** includes force used with the purpose of causing or with the knowledge of a substantial risk of causing death or serious bodily harm. A death or serious injury need not result. It is unclear whether the Fourth Amendment standards discussed in this subsection govern **all uses of deadly force** to apprehend suspects or **only uses of deadly force that kill or inflict serious injury** on a suspect. The latter seems to be the better view.

    b. **The showing needed to seize a suspect by means of deadly force [pp.128-130].**   Deadly force may be used only when it is **necessary** to apprehend a suspect who poses a **risk of serious physical harm.** Sometimes a **warning** is required before deadly force is used.

        More specifically, the use of deadly force is reasonable if a suspect **threatens an officer with a weapon** or if an officer has **probable cause** to believe that the suspect has committed **an offense involving the infliction or threatened infliction of serious physical harm.** While the offense need not be committed in the officer's presence and "probable cause" is sufficient, only offenses that involve the infliction or threat of **serious physical harm** qualify.

In addition, deadly force may be used only if it is **necessary to prevent an escape or serious physical harm.** Moreover, if it is feasible to issue a **warning** to the suspect, the officer must do so.

2. **Intrusions into the Human Body [pp.131-132]**

Searches inside the human body that are "more intrusive" than ordinary full searches must satisfy an elevated reasonableness standard.

a. **Magnitude of the intrusion: Threats to privacy, dignity, and health [p.131].**   A search of a human body may be more intrusive than an ordinary search in three respects. First, it may reveal **information of a more intimate or private nature.** Second, it may infringe upon **dignitary interests in personal privacy and bodily integrity.** Finally, it may threaten the **safety or health** and even **endanger the life** of the individual. To determine the reasonableness of such a search, the extent of the intrusion must first be assessed.

b. **The showing needed to justify a "more intrusive" search inside the body [p.132].**   If a search of a human body intrudes upon constitutional interests **more severely than an ordinary search,** a **more substantial justification**—perhaps **a compelling need**—is required. Government officials must obtain a **search warrant** and must demonstrate **more than probable cause** to believe that evidence will be found. If the search of a human body is no more intrusive than an ordinary full search of a person, home, or effect, Fourth Amendment probable cause and warrant norms will govern its reasonableness.

3. **Newsroom Searches and Nighttime Searches [p.133]**

The **search of a newsroom** is governed by the Fourth Amendment probable cause and warrant norms despite the potential intrusion on First Amendment interests. Whether the search of a private dwelling **at night** must meet more demanding standards has not been decided.

GOVERNMENT INVOLVEMENT IN THE COMMISSION OF CRIMES

The **entrapment defense** and the **due process defense** are assertions that an accused should not be held criminally liable because government agents were excessively involved in the commission of an offense. The **subjective version** of entrapment rests on the notion that legislators do not intend to punish those lured into crime by the government. It focuses primarily on whether the defendant was **predisposed** to commit an offense. The **objective version** of entrapment reflects antipathy toward unacceptable law enforcement conduct and focuses solely on the **conduct of the government agents.** The constitutionally based **due process defense** has not been clearly endorsed by the Supreme Court. Consequently, its legitimacy is uncertain. If such a defense does exist, it applies only to the rare case in which governmental misconduct in bringing about criminal conduct is so egregious that it is "**fundamentally unfair**" to prosecute an accused.

A. THE ENTRAPMENT DEFENSE [pp.138-141]

A claim of **entrapment** is an assertion that the defendant has a complete defense to a charge because government agents lured the defendant into committing the offense.

1. "Subjective" Version of the Entrapment Defense [pp.138-140]

The **subjective version** of the entrapment defense is concerned with identifying defendants who do not deserve or do not need to be punished for a crime. The subjective version discussed here is the one recognized in the federal system.

a. Doctrinal standards for the subjective version of entrapment [pp. 138-140]. Under the subjective version, entrapment is established when the offense was **the product of the creative activity of government officials.** This turns on whether **the government's conduct instigated** the offense and whether **the accused was predisposed.**

First, there must be sufficient "**instigation**" by a government agent who **lured the defendant** into committing the offense. The **criminal design must originate with government officials.** It is not enough that officials **merely afford opportunities or facilities** for committing an offense.

Second, the accused must not have been **predisposed.** A defendant who was predisposed to commit an offense cannot establish entrapment no matter what government agents have done. To defeat an entrapment claim on the basis of "predisposition," the prosecution **must prove beyond a reasonable doubt** that government agents did not implant the disposition to commit the crime in the mind of an **innocent person**—more specifically, that the defendant was **disposed to commit the crime prior to first being approached by government agents.**

b. Legal foundation of the subjective approach [p.140]. The federal "subjective" approach to entrapment rests on the premise that the legislature "could not have intended" to punish "innocent persons" who have been "tempted" into violating the law by government agents.

2. **"Objective" Version of the Entrapment Defense [pp.140-141]**

    The **objective version** of entrapment focuses exclusively on government conduct and is not concerned with predisposition. It is aimed at preventing government misconduct, safeguarding the judicial process, and preserving public confidence in the criminal justice system.

    a. **Doctrinal standards for the objective version of entrapment [p.140].**   Objective entrapment is established if the government uses **lawless means** or **means that violate rationally vindicated standards of justice.** If government conduct is **likely to induce those who would normally avoid crime and resist ordinary temptations**—that is, likely to instigate a crime by someone who is **not ready and willing to commit it**—an objective entrapment claim will succeed.

    b. **Legal foundation of the objective approach [pp.140-141].**   The foundation of the objective approach is uncertain, but it may be the judiciary's inherent **supervisory power** over the administration of criminal justice.

B. **THE DUE PROCESS DEFENSE [pp.142-143]**

    The Supreme Court has said that it "*may* someday be presented with a situation" that would support a **due process defense** to a criminal charge.

    1. **Nature of the Potential Due Process Defense [p.142]**

        A due process defense would be based on the **Fifth and Fourteenth Amendment Due Process Clauses** and would hinge entirely on whether the government's involvement in the defendant's commission of an offense was so extreme that it is **fundamentally unfair** to convict the defendant for that offense. Because the defense would be rooted in concern with unfair methods of law enforcement, predisposition would be irrelevant.

    2. **Doctrinal Standards of a Due Process Defense [pp.142-143]**

        To establish a due process defense, the conduct of law enforcement agents would have to be **so outrageous** that it would **violate fundamental fairness** or **shock the universal sense of justice** to use the judicial process to convict the accused. Any such defense would be quite narrow and available only in rare cases of extreme misconduct.

 6   DUE PROCESS CLAUSE REGULATION OF CONFESSIONS

The Fourteenth Amendment command that no state shall **"deprive any person of life, liberty, or property, without due process of law"** is the first constitutional basis invoked by the Supreme Court to restrict government **"interrogation" methods** and the **admissibility of confessions.** While other constitutional limitations have since been discovered, the **coerced confession doctrine** of the **Due Process Clause** continues to play an important role in regulating efforts to secure confessions and the use of those confessions to obtain convictions.

A.   THE COMMON LAW RULE [p.146]

Before the Due Process Clause was interpreted to restrain confession practices, a **common law rule** barred reliance on confessions "forced from the mind" of an individual by "the flattery of hope, or the torture of fear" because such confessions were thought to be **untrustworthy.**

B.   DUE PROCESS DOCTRINE [pp.146-151]

The Due Process Clause forbids the use of **coerced confessions.** Whether a confession is coerced is determined by evaluating the **totality** of relevant circumstances. Coerced confessions are barred because they are **unreliable** and because they offend principles of **accusatorial fair play.**

1.   Due Process Prohibition of "Involuntary" or "Coerced" Confessions [p.147]

The Due Process Clause is concerned only with confessions that are **involuntary** or **coerced** because an individual's **will was overborne.**

2.   "Totality of the Circumstances" Approach: External Pressures and Internal Attributes [p.147]

To determine whether a confession is involuntary or coerced, **the totality of the circumstances** must be assessed. Relevant circumstances include both **external pressures** brought to bear by law enforcement and **internal attributes** of the suspect.

3.   Official Coercion Requirement [p.147]

A confession is not "involuntary" or "coerced" unless it is the product of some amount of **coercive police activity.** If official coercion is present, the suspect's mental condition and susceptibility to that coercion are relevant, but the **confessant's state of mind alone** can never support a conclusion that a confession is barred by the due process doctrine. In other words, internal, subjective limitations on free will cannot by themselves render a confession coerced.

While the minimum amount of coercive activity necessary to support a due process claim is uncertain, it is clear that only coercion by a **state agent** can render evidence inadmissible under the Due Process Clause.

4.   "Inherently Coercive" Situations [p.149]

Some official actions generate so much pressure to confess that they are deemed **"inherently coercive"** and give rise to an "irrebuttable presumption" of coercion. In "inherently coercive" situations, there is no need to examine the subjective attributes of the individual because a statement made by any person is considered involuntary.

5. **Relevance of Promises and Trickery [pp.149-150]**

    Promises, deception, and trickery are **relevant** to the voluntariness inquiry insofar as they put pressure on a suspect to speak. However, a confession **will not necessarily be involuntary** because it was secured by means of a promise, deception, or trickery by a government official.

6. **Rationales for the Due Process Bar on Involuntary or Coerced Confessions [pp.150-151]**

    The use of a coerced confession to obtain a conviction violates the **substantive due process** guarantee of "fundamental fairness" because of the **risk that the confession is untrustworthy** and could lead to the **conviction of an innocent person.**

    The use of a coerced confession also violates the **procedural due process** guarantee of **fair methods and procedures.** It offends a fundamental principle of **fair play** in our **accusatorial system.**

    The Due Process Clause may also bar the use of coerced confessions in order **to deter future coercion** by law enforcement officers.

7. **Timing of the Due Process Violation [p.151]**

    An individual is deprived of due process when the government **uses a coerced confession** at trial. Some coercive methods may also deprive individuals of "liberty" without due process at the time they are used to obtain a confession.

THE PRIVILEGE AGAINST COMPULSORY SELF-INCRIMINATION AND CONFESSIONS: THE DOCTRINE OF MIRANDA V. ARIZONA

The Fifth Amendment **privilege against compulsory self-incrimination** provides that **"[n]o person . . . shall be compelled in any criminal case to be a witness against himself."** Miranda v. Arizona held that this Fifth Amendment privilege applies not only to the formal compulsion of court processes but also to the informal compulsion of police interrogation. The *Miranda* Court also announced a detailed scheme of Fifth Amendment safeguards governing the admissibility of confessions obtained during custodial interrogation. This chapter explains the foundations, elements, and scope of the *Miranda* doctrine.

A. CONSTITUTIONAL FOUNDATIONS OF THE *MIRANDA* DOCTRINE [pp.156-157]

The current constitutional foundations of the *Miranda* doctrine are somewhat different from its original premises.

1. The *Miranda* Court's Explanation [pp.156-157]

The *Miranda* Court reasoned that because **custodial interrogation** produces **inherent compulsion,** statements produced by custodial interrogation are compelled. Such statements are excluded from trials **because their use against an accused would violate his Fifth Amendment right not to be compelled to be a witness against himself.** The *Miranda* Court prescribed a set of "procedural safeguards" that are adequate to dispel the compulsion inherent in custodial interrogation. When those safeguards are employed, statements made are not compelled and their use is consistent with the Fifth Amendment.

2. Explanation in Opinions Subsequent to *Miranda* [p.157]

Later opinions have explained that statements made during custodial interrogation are **presumed to be compelled** but are **not actually compelled.** Consequently, the Fifth Amendment does not *require* that they be excluded. The *Miranda* safeguards, and the exclusion of statements made without complying with them, are **prophylactic** measures that provide "enlarged protection for the Fifth Amendment privilege." Exclusion ensures that the *Miranda* safeguards will be honored and **lessens the *risks* of compelled self-incrimination.**

B. ELEMENTS OF THE *MIRANDA* DOCTRINE [pp.158-171]

The *Miranda* doctrine has no application in the absence of either **custody** or **interrogation.** When both are present, any statement made by a suspect is inadmissible unless the procedural safeguards prescribed by the *Miranda* scheme are respected.

1. Applicability of *Miranda* to All Crimes [p.158]

Miranda doctrine applies to **all offenses, regardless of their nature or severity.**

2. Threshold Requirements for *Miranda* Protection: "Custody" and "Interrogation" [pp.158-160]

Miranda's requirements apply only to situations in which a person **in custody** is subjected to official **interrogation.**

    a. Definition of "custody" [pp.158-159]. **Custody** requires a **formal arrest or its functional equivalent.** A **formal arrest** occurs when a person is told that she is being arrested. The **functional equivalent of a formal arrest** occurs when a **reasonable person in the suspect's**

position would conclude that his **freedom of action has been curtailed to a degree associated with a formal arrest** or that he has been **subjected to restraints comparable to those associated with a formal arrest.** The **intentions or plans of an officer** that are not communicated to the suspect are irrelevant. The **suspect's subjective beliefs** are not determinative. And while a **police station setting** may be relevant, a suspect in a police station is not necessarily in custody and a suspect outside a police station may be in custody.

    b. **Definition of "interrogation" [p.160].** Interrogation requires **express questioning or its functional equivalent.** The functional equivalent is **words or actions on the part of the police that they *should know are reasonably likely to elicit an incriminating response from the suspect.*** An officer's **intent to elicit** is relevant but not determinative. A **suspect's unusual susceptibility** that is **known to the police** is also **relevant.**

    To trigger the application of the *Miranda* safeguards, the interrogation must be conducted by an individual who **the suspect knows to be a state agent.** However, a statement that is the product of **actual coercion** by an unknown state agent is barred by both the Due Process Clause and the Fifth Amendment privilege.

3. **The First *Miranda* Safeguard: Adequate Warnings [pp.161-162]**

Miranda requires that a suspect be warned of the **right to remain silent,** that anything said **can and will be used against him,** that he has a **right to consult with a lawyer and have a lawyer present during interrogation,** and that if he cannot afford one, **a lawyer will be appointed.** The warnings are **absolute prerequisites** and must be given **in all cases,** but they need not be given in the **exact form or language** prescribed in *Miranda*. Warnings that **reasonably convey** the information contained in the four original warnings are adequate.

4. **The Second *Miranda* Safeguard: A Knowing and Voluntary Waiver [pp.162-164]**

The government also must demonstrate that the suspect gave a **knowing and voluntary waiver** of the *Miranda* entitlements.

    a. **"Waiver" requirement [p.163].** The government must demonstrate **a waiver**—a choice to relinquish one's rights. An **express waiver is not required;** waiver can be **inferred** from a suspect's actions and words.

    b. **"Knowledge" requirement [pp.163-164].** A valid waiver of *Miranda* rights must be **knowing.** The government needs to show only that the suspect was aware of the matters contained in the *Miranda* warnings. No other knowledge is required.

    c. **"Voluntariness" requirement [p.164].** A valid waiver of *Miranda* rights must be **voluntary.** To render a waiver involuntary there must be **official coercion.** Once coercive police activity is shown, the voluntariness of a waiver is judged by examining the **totality of circumstances**—including the coercive conduct, the setting, and the subjective attributes of the suspect.

5. Additional *Miranda* Safeguards Based on Invocation of the Right to Remain Silent [pp.165-166]

Additional *Miranda* safeguards apply when a suspect **invokes the right to remain silent.**

    a. **The necessary predicate: An invocation of the right to remain silent [p.165].** An invocation of the right to remain silent is probably effective only when a suspect **clearly asserts or expresses a desire not to talk** to the authorities. An ambiguous or equivocal indication that a suspect *might not* want to talk probably does not invoke the right to remain silent.

    b. **Additional safeguards triggered by an invocation of the right to remain silent [pp.165-166].** When a suspect invokes the right to remain silent, **custodial interrogation must cease.** It may **resume if officers "scrupulously honor" the suspect's "right to cut off questioning."** Statements made in response to resumed interrogation will be admissible **only** if officers **scrupulously honor** the suspect's right **and** obtain a **waiver.** Whether the suspect's right has been "scrupulously honored" depends on several variables.

The amount of **time** between the invocation and the resumption is relevant. If interrogation is resumed after a **momentary respite or cessation,** the suspect's rights have *not* been "scrupulously honored," and a waiver cannot be valid. The minimum amount of time necessary is uncertain, but "more than two hours" is sufficient.

The fact that the resumed interrogation concerns a **crime different from** the subject of the initial interrogation provides support for a finding that the suspect's right has been honored, but under some circumstances a resumption regarding the same offense is probably allowable.

Additional factors that weigh in favor of a finding that the right to remain silent has been honored include resumption of the interrogation in a **different place,** resumption by **a different officer,** and the issuance of a **second set of *Miranda* warnings.**

6. Additional *Miranda* Safeguards Based on Invocation of the Right to Counsel [pp.167-169]

Invocations of the *Miranda* entitlement to counsel also give rise to "additional" procedural safeguards.

a. The necessary predicate: An invocation of the right to counsel [pp.167-168]. To invoke the right, a suspect's request for counsel must be **clear and unambiguous.** An invocation is clear enough *only* if **a reasonable police officer in the circumstances would understand the statement to be a request for an attorney.** An **ambiguous or equivocal** assertion is ineffective and raises no barriers to further interrogation.

Moreover, a suspect's **request to have the assistance or presence of someone other than a lawyer** has no effect on the *Miranda* inquiry and creates no additional impediments to interrogation.

b. Additional safeguards triggered by an invocation of the right to counsel [pp.168-169]. When a suspect invokes his right to counsel, interrogation must cease and may continue **only if an attorney is present or the suspect initiates further communications with the authorities.** Unless one of these conditions is satisfied, **no waiver can be valid** and statements that are the product of custodial interrogation are inadmissible.

The **presence of counsel** is a sufficient safeguard to allow the authorities to seek a waiver and conduct interrogation, but the fact that a suspect has **consulted with an attorney** is not a basis for continuing the interrogation.

If counsel is not present, a waiver is possible only if the suspect **initiates further communications, exchanges, or conversations with the police.** If the **authorities initiate** the communications, no waiver can be valid and no products of custodial interrogation are admissible.

Inquiries or statements that relate to the routine incidents of the custodial relationship are not **"initiation"** by either the suspect or the authorities. A suspect or an officer initiates by **evincing a willingness and a desire for a generalized discussion about the investigation.** It is unclear whether statements by officers that do not "relate to the routine incidents of the custodial relationship," yet do not demonstrate a desire to discuss the investigation, are "initiation" by the authorities.

The fact that a **different officer** conducted the interrogation that followed an invocation of counsel, the fact that the officer was **wholly unaware that the suspect requested counsel,** and the fact that the second interrogation concerned a **different offense** than the one that would have been the subject of the earlier session are all **irrelevant.**

7. **The New York v. Quarles "Public Safety" Exception to the** *Miranda* **Doctrine [pp. 170-171]**

The **public safety exception** to the *Miranda* doctrine allows officers to ask **questions reasonably prompted by a concern for the public safety** without reciting the warnings or obtaining a waiver. Statements obtained are admissible.

a. **Objective, "reasonable officer" standard [p.170].** An officer's **subjective motivation is irrelevant** to the public safety exception. The exception applies when officers ask questions *reasonably* **prompted** by a public safety concern.

b. **Nature and magnitude of the public safety interest [p.170].** While serious risks to life or health are sufficient public safety interests, it is uncertain whether other sorts of harm support the application of the public safety exception.

c. **Immediate and future threats to the public safety [pp.170-171].** Immediate threats of harm that can be prevented only by swift action qualify. It is uncertain whether a threatened harm that will not occur until some future time can support a valid "public safety" claim.

d. **Applicability of the "public safety" exception to other** *Miranda* **doctrine requirements [p.171].** The public safety exception currently permits officers to dispense with the **warnings** and **waiver** requirements. It is unclear whether the exception can justify a failure to abide by other *Miranda* doctrine requirements such as the demand that a waiver be voluntary or the additional procedural safeguards that are applicable when a suspect invokes the rights to silence or counsel.

e. **Actual compulsion and the public safety exception [p.171].** The public safety exception allows the admission of statements that otherwise would be *"presumed* compelled" by the *Miranda* doctrine. If a statement is *actually* **compelled,** the public safety exception cannot render it admissible because the Fifth Amendment privilege absolutely bars its use.

8 THE SIXTH AMENDMENT RIGHT TO COUNSEL: A FOUNDATION

he **Sixth Amendment** contains an explicit **right to counsel at trial.** The rights to counsel to protect against official efforts to secure confessions and eyewitness identifications are **pretrial extensions** of this explicit Sixth Amendment right to assistance at trial. This chapter explains that trial right and the reasons for its extension to pretrial contexts.

A. THE RIGHT TO COUNSEL AT TRIAL [pp.177-178]

1. Purpose of the Right to the Assistance of Counsel [pp.177-178]

Our **adversarial system** of criminal justice contemplates a contest between the prosecution and defendant. The assistance of counsel ensures fundamental fairness by making the defendant roughly equal to her opponent.

2. Nature and Substance of the Right to the Assistance of Counsel [p.178]

The Sixth Amendment grants the right to retain a lawyer and, for indigent defendants, the right to an appointed lawyer. The right to appointed counsel does not extend to those charged with misdemeanors unless a proceeding results in a sentence of **actual imprisonment.**

Whether counsel is retained or appointed, an accused has the right to **effective assistance.** "Ineffective assistance" of counsel deprives the defendant of her Sixth Amendment right.

B. PRETRIAL EXTENSIONS OF THE RIGHT TO COUNSEL [pp.178-179]

The Sixth Amendment right has been extended to a limited number of formal and informal pretrial stages of the criminal process.

1. Rationales for Extending Counsel to Pretrial Stages [pp.178-179]

The extension of counsel to pretrial stages rests on the fact that modern criminal justice systems have developed pretrial confrontations that are integral parts of the adversarial contest. If the accused were not entitled to assistance at these stages, the prosecution could gain advantages that would render the assistance of counsel at trial pointless. A pretrial right to counsel is essential to guarantee meaningful assistance and fundamental fairness at trial.

2. Scope of Pretrial Counsel [p.179]

The right to counsel extends only to **critical stages of the prosecution**—that is, only to pretrial events that pose serious threats to the fairness of the trial. Efforts to secure inculpatory statements and efforts to obtain eyewitness identifications both can qualify as "critical stages."

 THE RIGHT TO COUNSEL AND CONFESSIONS

In some circumstances, defendants have a **Sixth Amendment right to counsel** when the government seeks to secure inculpatory admissions. The *Massiah* doctrine defines the circumstances that constitute a "critical stage" of the prosecution and trigger the right to counsel. The elements of that *Sixth Amendment* doctrine are different from the elements of *Miranda's Fifth Amendment* protection against custodial interrogation.

A. THE THRESHOLD REQUIREMENT: A FORMAL INITIATION OF ADVERSARY PROCEEDINGS [pp.182-183]

The Sixth Amendment right to retained or appointed counsel **does not attach** until the **formal initiation of adversary judicial proceedings.** Arrest does not trigger the right. A **formal charge, preliminary hearing, indictment, information, or arraignment** is required. Moreover, attachment of the right to counsel is **offense specific**—a formal charge for one offense does not trigger a right to counsel for other offenses.

B. NATURE OF THE CRITICAL STAGE DEFINED BY *MASSIAH*: "DELIBERATE ELICITATION" BY A GOVERNMENT AGENT [pp.183-187]

Attachment of the right to counsel is merely a "threshold." After the right "attaches," an accused is entitled to counsel only at **"critical stages of the proceedings."** The critical stage identified by *Massiah* doctrine occurs when a government agent **deliberately elicits** incriminating information from a defendant.

1. Government Agent Requirement [pp.183-184]

The individual who elicits the incriminating information must do so on behalf of the government. Government employees and others who act at the instigation, behest, or request of the government qualify.

2. "Deliberate Elicitation" Requirement [pp.184-185]

An accused is entitled to counsel when the government **deliberately elicits statements.**

a. **An "intent" to elicit information is apparently required [p.184].** The deliberate elicitation requirement seems to require an actual *intent to elicit information* from the accused.

b. **Active elicitation is required [pp.184-185].** A government agent must **actively elicit** information. There must be **some action, beyond merely listening,** that is designed deliberately to elicit information from the accused. **Affirmative direct questioning** qualifies, but merely **engaging in or having conversations** with an accused also suffices.

c. **Both direct and surreptitious elicitation are included [p.185].** Both **direct elicitation by a known government agent** and **surreptitious elicitation by an undercover agent** are governed by *Massiah* doctrine and give rise to a right to counsel.

3. **Requirement of a "Basis for Attributing" the Elicitation to the Government [pp.185-187]**

When an undercover agent elicits information, an accused has a right to counsel only when there is a **basis for attributing** that agent's conduct to *the government*—that is, to the law enforcement agents who are regular government employees. Those "regular" agents must either **intentionally create** or **knowingly exploit** a situation that they **know or should know is likely to involve active elicitation by the undercover agent.** The following factors are relevant.

a. **Custody and undercover status [p.186].** **Custody** generates pressures that make an accused more likely to disclose information. Moreover, an accused is more likely to trust an **undercover agent** with information that he would not divulge to the authorities. Both factors support a finding of a basis for attributing the agent's conduct to the government.

b. **Compensation of the agent [p.186].** An agent who is **compensated only if he gains information** is more likely to elicit actively, whereas an agent who is clearly told that there will be no compensation if he actively elicits is less likely to do so. Compensation arrangements, therefore, can also play a role in the "attribution" inquiry.

c. **Instructions to the agent [p.187].** If the undercover agent is not given instructions about permissible conduct, or if the instructions forbid only certain kinds of elicitation, active elicitation is more likely. Clear instructions prohibiting all active elicitation make active elicitation less likely. Consequently, the instructions that "regular" agents give to the undercover operative can play a role in deciding whether there is a basis for attribution.

4. **Good Faith Investigations of Different, Uncharged Offenses [p.187]**

Inculpatory statements acquired in the course of a **good faith investigation** of an uncharged offense **may not be used to prove a charged offense** if they are deliberately elicited in violation of the accused's *Massiah* entitlement to counsel for the charged offense. Because the accused has no right to counsel for the uncharged offense, the statements *may* be used to prove that offense.

C. **WAIVER OF THE RIGHT TO COUNSEL [pp.187-189]**

The *Massiah* right to counsel **may be waived.** A **knowing and voluntary relinquishment** of the entitlement to assistance is required.

1. **An "Actual Relinquishment" That Need Not Be "Express" [p.188]**

An **express oral or written waiver** is not required; waiver can be inferred from an accused's conduct and the surrounding circumstances. The state, however, must demonstrate that the accused **did make a choice to relinquish** the right to assistance.

2. A "Knowing" Waiver [p.188]

A waiver must be **knowing.** In general, the *Miranda* warnings contain and convey adequate information for a valid waiver of the Sixth Amendment right. The accused *may* also have to be aware that she has been formally charged with an offense. If the accused has a lawyer who has attempted to contact her, a waiver is insufficiently knowing and is invalid unless the accused is aware of that fact.

3. A "Voluntary" Waiver [pp.188-189]

A waiver must be **voluntary**—that is, not coerced by official pressure. Once adequate coercive conduct by the government is shown, voluntariness is determined by examining the totality of relevant circumstances, including subjective characteristics of the accused.

D. INVOCATION OF THE RIGHT TO COUNSEL [pp.189-190]

When an accused **invokes** the right to counsel, **no waiver is valid unless the accused initiates further communications** with the authorities.

1. What Constitutes an Invocation? [p.189]

The standards for determining whether an accused has invoked the Sixth Amendment right are the same as those developed by *Miranda* doctrine. See Chapter 7, section B.6.a. However, an accused can effectively invoke the Sixth Amendment *Massiah* right by making a general request for appointed counsel at an appearance in court. The same request *does not* constitute an invocation of the *Miranda* entitlement.

2. What Constitutes "Initiation" of Communications by the Suspect or the Authorities? [p.190]

A waiver *may be found* after the accused has initiated communications, but *is invalid* if the authorities have initiated communications. The meaning of "initiation" is identical to the meaning for purposes of *Miranda* doctrine. See Chapter 7, section B.6.b.ii.

E. DIFFERENCES BETWEEN THE *MIRANDA* AND *MASSIAH* DOCTRINES [pp.190-191]

The distinct constitutional foundations of *Miranda* and *Massiah* have led to distinct doctrinal requirements.

1. Custody [p.190]

Miranda requires custody, but *Massiah* does not.

2. Formal Charges [p.190]

Massiah requires a formal charge, but *Miranda* does not.

3. **Interrogation and Deliberate Elicitation [p.190]**

Interrogation is necessary for *Miranda* to apply; it is sufficient but not necessary to satisfy *Massiah*'s deliberate elicitation demand.

4. **Undercover Agents [p.190]**

Massiah doctrine governs undercover agent activity; *Miranda* does not.

5. **Waivers [pp.190-191]**

Both entitlements may be waived knowingly and voluntarily. A waiver of the *Massiah* right *may* require more knowledge.

6. **Invocations of Counsel [p.191]**

Under both doctrines, an invocation of the right bars a waiver. A subsequent initiation of communications by the suspect permits a waiver; an initiation by the authorities renders any waiver invalid.

10 THE RIGHT TO COUNSEL AND IDENTIFICATION METHODS

In some circumstances, pretrial events designed to identify the perpetrator of an offense constitute "critical stages" of the prosecution at which an accused has the Sixth Amendment right to the assistance of counsel.

A. THE THRESHOLD REQUIREMENT: AN INITIATION OF ADVERSARY PROCEEDINGS [p.194]

The right to counsel **attaches only** at or after the **initiation of adversary judicial proceedings—by means of a formal charge, preliminary hearing, indictment, information, or arraignment.** Prior to that point, there is no Sixth Amendment right.

B. NATURE OF THE CRITICAL STAGE: A "TRIAL-LIKE CONFRONTATION" FOR PURPOSES OF IDENTIFICATION [pp.194-195]

Once the right "attaches," an accused has the right to counsel only at an identification procedure that qualifies as a *critical stage* **of the prosecution.**

1. **"Trial-Like Confrontation" Requirement [p.195]**

An identification session is a critical stage only if it involves the **actual, physical presence of the accused at a "trial-like" adversary confrontation with a witness.**

2. **"Accurate Reconstruction" Criterion [p.195]**

An identification session can **cease to be critical if accurate reconstruction at trial provides the opportunity to cure defects in the session.**

C. WAIVER OF THE RIGHT TO COUNSEL [p.196]

The Sixth Amendment right to counsel at an identification session **can be knowingly and voluntarily waived.** While the accused clearly must know of the entitlement to assistance, it is unclear whether any additional "knowledge" is required.

D. EXCLUSION OF EVIDENCE OBTAINED IN VIOLATION OF THE RIGHT TO COUNSEL [pp.196-198]

An identification obtained in violation of the Sixth Amendment right to counsel is **per se excluded** and may **never** be used against the accused at trial. A **subsequent identification** by the same witness is **presumptively barred,** but **may be used** if the government provides **clear and convincing evidence** that it came from an **independent origin**—that is, from observations of the accused other than those at the uncounseled identification session. Relevant factors include the following.

1. **Extent and Quality of the Witness's Opportunity to Observe the Crime [p.197]**

An independent origin is more likely if the witness had a good opportunity to observe the criminal at the time of the crime and less likely if the witness had a poor opportunity.

2. **Discrepancies Between Any Pre-identification Description by the Witness and the Defendant's Actual Appearance [p.197]**

Correspondence between a witness's postcrime **description** and the **actual appearance** of the accused supports an independent origin finding; discrepancies militate against such a finding.

3. **Prior Identifications or Failures to Identify the Accused [p.197]**

Prior, untainted identifications support an independent origin finding while earlier failures to identify the accused count against such a finding.

4. **Time Periods Between the Crime and the Two Identifications [p.197]**

The more time that has passed between a crime and an identification, the less supportable a finding that the identification is based on an independent origin.

5. **Facts About the Uncounseled Identification Session [pp.197-198]**

Unfairly suggestive aspects of an identification process render an independent origin less likely. A fair, nonsuggestive process enhances the case for an independent origin.

11 DUE PROCESS AND IDENTIFICATION METHODS

The **Due Process Clause** guarantee of **"fundamental fairness"** also imposes restrictions on government identification processes and can bar the use of identification evidence obtained in violation of those restrictions.

A. THE CONCERN OF THE DUE PROCESS CLAUSE: "UNNECESSARILY SUGGESTIVE" IDENTIFICATION METHODS [pp.202-203]

The Due Process Clause is concerned *solely* with identification methods that are **unnecessarily suggestive and conducive to misidentification.**

1. Government "Suggestion" Requirement [pp.202-203]

Due process is concerned only with unreliability that is the product of **suggestive** methods of identification. There must be something about the method that could improperly influence a witness and give rise to **a very substantial likelihood of misidentification.**

2. "Lack of Necessity" Requirement [p.203]

For due process to be offended, the suggestion in an identification process must be **unnecessary.** If there is a need for the suggestive process, there is no due process violation.

B. DUE PROCESS CLAUSE RESTRICTIONS ON THE ADMISSIBILITY OF IDENTIFICATION EVIDENCE [pp.203-206]

Unnecessary suggestion may, but does not automatically, result in the exclusion of an identification and subsequent identifications by the same witness. Only **unreliable** identification evidence is barred.

1. Due Process Clause Bars the Use of Tainted Identification Evidence [p.204]

Due process cannot be violated by an improper identification process. It can be violated only by the **use of an improperly suggested identification at trial.** Because of the risk of **irreparable misidentification, both the product of an unnecessarily suggestive session and any subsequent identification by the same witness are presumptively inadmissible.**

2. The Government May Use Any Identification Evidence if It Demonstrates "Reliability" [pp.204-206]

An identification at a suggestive session and a subsequent identification are **admissible** if the government demonstrates **reliability** by a preponderance of the evidence. An identification is "reliable" when it "stems from" the witness's observations at the time of the offense rather than from the improper official suggestion. Factors relevant to the reliability determination include the following.

a. **Witness's opportunity to view the offender at the crime scene [p.205].**   Strong opportunities to view support reliability findings; weak opportunities support unreliability findings.

b. **Witness's degree of attention [p.205].**   The greater the attention at the crime scene, the more likely an identification is reliable. Limited attention to the criminal undermines reliability.

c. **Accuracy of a witness's prior description [p.205].**   A witness's accurate description of a suspect prior to an identification supports reliability. Material inaccuracies in descriptions count against reliability.

d. **Witness's level of certainty [p.205].**   Greater certainty is thought to indicate reliability; uncertainty suggests unreliability.

e. **Time between the crime and the identification confrontation [p.205].**   The shorter the time between the crime and the disputed identification, the stronger the case for reliability. Long time periods point toward unreliability.

f. **Degree of suggestiveness in the identification process [pp.205-206].**   The greater the suggestion in an identification process, the less likely it is that an identification is reliable. The case for reliability is enhanced if the suggestion in a process is limited.

 12   THE EXCLUSIONARY RULES

The **exclusionary rules** bar from the courtroom evidence secured in violation of the constitutional provisions discussed in the preceding chapters. An exclusionary rule may be **deterrent** in nature—the object may be to discourage future violations. An exclusionary rule may be a **constitutional right of the defendant**—exclusion may be required because admission of the evidence would violate the Constitution. Or an exclusionary rule may rest on both of these bases.

A. THE EXCLUSIONARY RULES AND THEIR RATIONALES [pp.210-214]

The **exclusionary rules** rest on different constitutional guarantees. The rationale for each must be identified and analyzed.

1. **Fourth Amendment Exclusionary Rule [pp.210-211]**

    The Fourth Amendment exclusionary rule commands the exclusion of **evidence acquired by means of an unreasonable search or seizure.** At one time, Fourth Amendment exclusion was considered a constitutional right. Today, its **primary purpose is deterrence**—its object is to **remove incentives** for future unreasonable searches and seizures by putting the government in the **same evidentiary position** that it would have been in if it had not acted unconstitutionally. While **judicial integrity** is an additional reason for the rule, it is coextensive with the deterrent rationale.

2. **Due Process Clause Exclusion of "Coerced Confessions" [p.211]**

    The Due Process Clause excludes coerced confessions because their **use** is **fundamentally unfair.** Because a coerced confession may be **untrustworthy** and because its use offends notions of **accusatorial system fair play,** the introduction of such a confession violates a defendant's right to **due process.** The exclusion of a coerced confession also **deters** future coercion and may be intended for that purpose.

3. **The *Miranda* Exclusionary Rule [pp.211-212]**

    Exclusion under the *Miranda* doctrine is **not a constitutional right** because the admission of statements made in violation of the *Miranda* doctrine **does not violate the Fifth Amendment.** One clear goal of the *Miranda* exclusionary rule is to **deter** future failures to abide by *Miranda*'s dictates. Another rationale for exclusion is to *safeguard* **the right not to be compelled to be a witness against oneself** by eliminating the *risk* that a compelled statement will be used at trial.

4. **The *Massiah* Exclusionary Rule [pp.212-213]**

    The *Massiah* exclusionary rule is designed to **deter** future deprivations of the *Massiah* right to counsel. Because the **use** of statements acquired in violation of *Massiah* may violate the Sixth Amendment right to counsel, the *Massiah* exclusionary rule *may* also be a **constitutional right** of the accused.

5. **Exclusion of Identification Evidence Under the Fifth and Sixth Amendments [pp.213-214]**

    Identification evidence may be excluded by virtue of the Due Process Clause or the Sixth Amendment right to counsel.

    a. **Identifications obtained in violation of the Sixth Amendment *Wade-Gilbert* right to counsel [pp.213-214].** An identification acquired in violation of the accused's **Sixth Amendment right to counsel** and subsequent identifications by the same witness are excluded to **deter** future failures to respect the right to counsel. Such identifications *may* also be excluded because their use would violate the Sixth Amendment. If so, the *Wade-Gilbert* exclusionary rule is also a **constitutional right** of the accused.

b. **Identifications obtained in violation of the Due Process Clause safeguard against "unnecessarily suggestive" identification processes [p.214].** The **Due Process Clause** excludes the products of unnecessarily suggestive identification processes because the **use** of such identification evidence **violates the Constitution.** Consequently, a defendant has a **right to exclusion.**

B. OPERATION OF THE EXCLUSIONARY RULES: THE SCOPE OF EXCLUSION AND LIMITATIONS ON EXCLUSION [pp.214-239]

The exclusionary rules presumptively bar both the **immediate products** of illegalities and evidence **derived from** those products. However, a number of limitations on the scope of exclusion are imposed by doctrines that allow the use of illegally obtained evidence.

1. **General Scope of the Exclusionary Rules: Immediate and Derivative Evidence [pp.214-215]**

   The exclusionary rules presumptively prohibit the use of evidence acquired as the **immediate, direct result** of illegalities. In some cases, the bar on these **primary products** is absolute; in other cases, it is limited.

   By virtue of the **fruit of the poisonous tree doctrine,** the exclusionary rules also presumptively prohibit the use of **derivative evidence**—that is, evidence that is derived from immediate, primary evidence. This presumptive bar is not absolute; derivative evidence may qualify for admission under an exclusionary rule exception.

2. **Standing to Raise Exclusionary Rule Claims [pp.215-218]**

   Only individuals with **standing** may assert exclusionary rule claims.

   a. **Fourth Amendment standing limitation [pp.215-217].** An individual has standing to assert the Fourth Amendment exclusionary rule **only if his Fourth Amendment rights were violated** by the allegedly unreasonable search or seizure that led to the contested evidence.

      An individual has standing to object to **an unreasonable search** if he had **a legitimate expectation of privacy in the place searched.** Relevant factors include ownership of the place searched, legitimate presence in that place, guest status, ownership or possession of the item seized, prior use of or time spent in a place, one's relationship to the owner of the place searched, and a right to exclude others.

      Standing to object to **an unreasonable *seizure of the person*—an arrest or detention**—requires a showing that the individual was deprived of **physical freedom,** while standing to object to **an unreasonable *seizure*** *of property* requires a showing of an **ownership or possessory interest in the item seized.**

b. **Standing to raise other kinds of violations [pp.217-218].** The standing limitation on exclusionary rule claims has not been developed with regard to other kinds of violations. A limitation analogous to the Fourth Amendment standing doctrine undoubtedly applies to most, if not all, of them. Thus, an individual claiming *Miranda* exclusion, *Massiah* exclusion, or the exclusion of an eyewitness identification on right to counsel or due process grounds must demonstrate that the alleged official impropriety infringed on her own personal interests. The one possible exception may be the due process–coerced confession rule. It is *arguable* that an individual has standing to exclude a confession coerced from another person.

3. **Exceptions to the Exclusionary Rules [pp.218-222]**

The **exceptions to the exclusionary rules** permit the government to use evidence acquired as a result of illegal conduct. Some apply only to **derivative evidence;** others permit the introduction of **primary products.** Illegally acquired evidence that is admissible under an exception is **not** considered the **fruit of the poisonous tree.**

a. **"Independent source" doctrine [pp.219-220].** The **very same information** or the **very same item of evidence** may be discovered by both illegal and independent, legal means. The information or evidence discovered by the **legal means** is admissible under the **independent source doctrine.** This doctrine is not a true "exception" to the exclusionary rules because evidence admitted under it is **not the product of an illegality** and thus falls outside the presumptive bar of the exclusionary rules. To qualify for this doctrine, the source of the evidence must in fact be **independent** of the illegality.

b. **"Inevitable discovery" exception [pp.220-222].** Evidence that was **in fact discovered illegally** but **could have been acquired legally** may qualify for the **inevitable discovery exception.** The government must establish **by a preponderance of the evidence** that the evidence **ultimately or inevitably would have been discovered by lawful means.** The government's **good faith or bad faith** is irrelevant.

The inevitable discovery exception applies to evidence acquired in violation of the *Massiah* right to counsel doctrine and almost surely applies to evidence acquired by means of most, if not all, other types of illegality. It applies to **derivative evidence** and should also apply to **primary evidence.**

c. **Attenuation exception [pp.223-228].** Evidence that has been illegally acquired may also qualify for admission under the **attenuation**

exception. The government must show that the connection between the evidence and the illegality is "so attenuated as to dissipate the taint." More specifically, attenuation requires a showing that the evidence, although derived from an illegality, has been acquired by **means sufficiently distinguishable from the illegality to be purged of the primary taint.** Relevant factors include the time between the illegality and acquisition of the evidence, the presence of intervening circumstances—including a sufficient exercise of free will—and the nature and character of the official misconduct.

The attenuation exception applies **only to derivative evidence** and should be more readily applied to "live-witness testimony" than to other kinds of evidence. The attenuation exception is *arguably* inapplicable to exclusionary rules that are **constitutional rights.**

A presumptive attenuation exception was developed for *Miranda* exclusion by Oregon v. Elstad. The *Elstad* doctrine applies when officers fail to give *Miranda* warnings, acquire a statement by means of custodial interrogation, and then comply with *Miranda* and obtain a second statement from the same suspect. Because the connection between the first and second statement is considered **speculative and attenuated,** the second statement is **never excludable** by virtue of the initial *Miranda* violation. The *Elstad* doctrine does not apply if an initial statement is **actually coerced**—in that situation the government must demonstrate attenuation. Moreover, it is uncertain whether the exception applies to *Miranda* violations other than a failure to warn.

While the *Elstad* opinion also hints that the *Miranda* exclusionary rule does not presumptively bar **derivative evidence,** later reasoning has cast doubt on that hint.

d. **"Good faith" exception [pp.229-234].** The current **"good faith" exception** is a limited exception to the **Fourth Amendment exclusionary rule** applicable only to situations in which an illegal search or seizure is the fault of someone other than the officer. It allows **both primary and derivative products** to be admitted into evidence.

The *Leon-Sheppard* **good faith exception** applies only when an officer who has conducted an illegal search or seizure acted in **objectively reasonable reliance on a subsequently invalidated** *warrant*. The standard is wholly **objective**—an officer's **actual, subjective good faith or bad faith is irrelevant.** The objective standard requires officers to be **reasonably well trained** and to have **reasonable knowledge of what the law prohibits.**

The *Leon-Sheppard* **exception does not apply** if a warrant is invalid (1) because of a **knowing or reckless falsehood** by an officer, (2) because of a **magistrate's abandonment of her judicial role,** (3) because an underlying showing is so deficient that **official belief in the existence of probable cause is entirely unreasonable,** or (4) because a warrant itself is **so facially deficient that executing officers cannot reasonably presume it to be valid.**

There are two other variations of the "good faith" exception. The **Illinois v. Krull–"legislative authorization" variation** applies when officers illegally search or seize in **objectively reasonable reliance on a statute authorizing the search or seizure.** The **Arizona v. Evans–"court employee error" variation** applies when an unreasonable search or seizure is the result of **objectively reasonable reliance on a clerical error of a court employee.** It is unclear whether a good faith claim would succeed if the clerical error was made by police personnel.

The current "good faith" exceptions have no application to the vast majority of **warrantless searches and seizures.** Whether there should be exception for unreasonable warrantless searches or seizures based on **objectively reasonable beliefs that they are constitutionally valid** is an **open, debatable question.**

e. **Impeachment use of illegally obtained evidence [pp.235-237].** The **impeachment use exception** to the exclusionary rules permits illegally obtained evidence to be introduced to cast doubt on the truthfulness of trial testimony. The illegal evidence may be a prior inconsistent statement of a witness or it may simply contradict a witness's testimony.

The impeachment use exception may be used to avoid suppression under the Fourth Amendment exclusionary rule, the *Miranda* exclusionary rule, and the Michigan v. Jackson branch of the *Massiah* exclusionary rule. It may not be used to avoid the Due Process Clause's prohibition on *any* use of a coerced confession. It is uncertain whether evidence obtained in violation of other *Massiah* doctrine requirements is admissible for impeachment purposes.

Evidence obtained in violation of the Fourth Amendment may be used to impeach a **defendant's direct testimony and a defendant's answers to proper cross-examination** by the prosecutor, but it may **not** be used to impeach **a defense witness's testimony.** Evidence obtained in violation of *Miranda* or the *Jackson* branch of *Massiah* may be used to impeach a **defendant's direct testimony** and **probably** to impeach **a defendant's answers to proper cross-examination,** and **probably may not** be used to impeach **a defense witness's testimony.**

Both primary and derivative tangible and verbal evidence can fall within the impeachment use exception.

4. **Types of Proceedings in Which the Exclusionary Rules Apply [pp.237-239]**

All exclusionary rules apply at **trial.**

The Fourth Amendment rule does **not** apply to **grand jury proceedings.** Moreover, the Fourth Amendment rule may **not** be the basis of a **collateral, habeas corpus** challenge in federal court *if* a state has accorded the defendant a "full and fair" opportunity to contest the Fourth Amendment claim. The *Miranda* exclusionary rule, however, **may be** the basis for a **habeas corpus** petition even when a state has provided a full and fair opportunity to litigate the underlying claim.

The Fourth Amendment exclusionary rule applies in **forfeiture proceedings** in which the government seeks to forfeit property used in connection with a crime, but it may not apply to other kinds of forfeitures.

The Fourth Amendment rule does not bar from a **federal civil tax proceeding** evidence unlawfully seized in good faith by a **state police officer.** The rule is also inapplicable in a **civil deportation proceeding.** It is uncertain whether the Fourth Amendment exclusionary rule applies in *any* civil proceedings.

PART III # THE PROCESSES OF ADJUDICATION: RIGHTS AND REMEDIES

Part III of this outline discusses constitutional, and some statutory, rights and remedies pertinent to the **adjudicatory** stages of criminal cases. Most of these rights and remedies are **essential elements of a fair trial.** The topics of this part are typically addressed in an advanced criminal procedure course. They include discovery and disclosure, bail and preventive detention, plea bargaining and guilty pleas, speedy prosecution, public trials and pretrial publicity, the assistance of counsel, trial by jury, double jeopardy, appeals, and collateral remedies.

 ## 13 DISCOVERY AND DISCLOSURE

Discovery is the process by which the parties to litigation disclose to their opponents information about the case. Discovery in criminal cases was historically disfavored but has become increasingly available in modern times. While most of the law of

discovery is statutory, constitutional provisions require the government to provide certain information to defendants and protect defendants from being forced to divulge certain information to the government.

A. SOURCES AND CONTENT OF THE LAWS THAT GOVERN DISCOVERY IN CRIMINAL CASES [pp.252-255]

Because jurisdictions vary greatly in the amount and nature of the discovery allowed or required in criminal cases, this summary of the sources and content of discovery law is a general sketch of possibilities.

1. Sources of Discovery Law [p.252]

Discovery law in most jurisdictions is prescribed by statutes or rules of court. A few still have "common law" systems.

2. Content of Discovery Law [pp.252-255]

Instead of comprehensively describing the varying approaches to criminal case discovery, this section sketches possible variations and highlights aspects of the federal system.

a. Material subject to discovery [pp.253-254]. Most jurisdictions provide for both defense and prosecution discovery but require greater disclosure by the government. The prosecution might be required to disclose statements by witnesses, defendants, and codefendants; criminal records; test or examination results; documents; other tangible items; and witness lists. Federal Rule of Criminal Procedure 16 (FRCrP 16) mandates the disclosure of such items.

The defense might be required to disclose witness lists or statements; documents; tangible items; and test or examination results. Prosecution discovery might be conditioned on initial discovery requests by the defense or might be unconditional. FRCrP 16 gives the government an entitlement to various kinds of items and makes government discovery conditional on the defendant's request.

Specific provisions might require defendants to disclose certain information regarding a particular defense she intends to raise. Alibi and insanity defense provisions are typical. FRCrP 12.1(a) requires defendants to provide information regarding a prospective alibi defense to the prosecution and requires the prosecution to reciprocate.

b. Continuing duties to disclose [p.254]. Typically the parties have "continuing duties to disclose" that require them to disclose matters they learn after they have complied with a discovery request. FRCrP 16 contains such a duty.

    c. **Protection from discovery [pp.254-255].** If a party shows adequate grounds, a court may issue a "protective order" that prevents, limits, or delays the opponent's discovery of a discoverable item. FRCrP 16 allows courts to grant protective orders "upon a sufficient showing."

    d. **Sanctions for violations of discovery rules [p.255].** To enforce discovery provisions, courts may order immediate disclosure, continue trials, preclude parties from introducing undisclosed evidence, order mistrials, cite parties for contempt, or dismiss charges. FRCrP 16 grants judges ample authority to fashion appropriate sanctions.

B. THE GOVERNMENT'S CONSTITUTIONAL DUTY TO DISCLOSE [pp.255-257]

A defendant has **no general constitutional right to discover evidence** in the prosecution's possession, but the **Due Process Clause** imposes on the government a limited duty to disclose certain information to an accused.

    1. Duties Not to Use and to Correct False or Perjured Testimony by a Government Witness [pp.255-256]

    If the government **deliberately or knowingly introduces false or perjured testimony** or **knowingly allows false testimony to go uncorrected** and there is **any reasonable likelihood that the false testimony could have affected the judgment of the jury,** the **Due Process Clause** requires reversal of a conviction.

    2. Duty to Disclose "Exculpatory" Evidence: The Doctrine of Brady v. Maryland [pp.256-257]

    In addition, **due process** requires the prosecution to disclose some exculpatory evidence to the defense.

        a. **"Suppression" of evidence by the prosecution [p.256].** The government's constitutional duty can be violated by a **failure to disclose** evidence that is known either to prosecutors or to other agents acting on the government's behalf in the case. The government's good or bad faith is irrelevant.

        b. **The evidence must be "favorable to an accused" and "material" to guilt or punishment [pp.256-257].** The duty to disclose applies only to evidence that is **favorable to the accused** and **material to guilt or punishment.** Evidence is material **only if there is a reasonable probability that, had the evidence been disclosed to the defense, the result of the proceeding would have been different.** A failure to disclose evidence material to guilt requires a **new trial;** a failure to disclose evidence material to punishment requires a **new punishment proceeding.**

    c. **Significance of a "request" for the evidence [p.257].**   The standard of materiality and the duty to disclose are the same whether or not the defendant has requested the evidence. However, if the defense has made a **specific request** for an item, a failure to disclose may be more likely to affect the outcome of the trial.

    d. **Timing of the disclosure required by the *Brady* doctrine [p.257].**   Due process does **not** require **pretrial disclosure;** it is satisfied by disclosure at trial *unless* the delay significantly impairs the defense's ability to derive exculpatory value from the evidence.

    e. **Inapplicability of "harmless error" analysis [p.257].**   Violations of the due process duty to disclose **cannot be harmless.** An accused is entitled to have a conviction reversed or a sentence vacated.

C. CONSTITUTIONAL RESTRICTIONS ON REQUIRED DEFENSE DISCLOSURE [pp.258-262]

Due process and the **privilege against compulsory self-incrimination** restrict the government's power to require defense disclosure. The **entitlement to present evidence in one's defense** restricts the government's power to sanction defense noncompliance with discovery requirements.

    1. **Protection Against Discovery Afforded by the Due Process Clause [pp.258-259]**

    The **due process** promise of "fundamental fairness" does not entitle defendants to withhold what they know, but it does require discovery to be a **two-way street.** The state may not require a defendant to disclose information about a subject unless it grants that defendant a "reciprocal" right to disclosure from the government.

    2. **Protection Against Discovery Afforded by the Privilege Against Compulsory Self-Incrimination [pp.259-261]**

    The Fifth Amendment guarantee that **no person "shall be compelled to be a witness against himself"** is violated only if the government **compels** an individual to reveal information that is both **testimonial** and **incriminating.**

    a. **Requirement of a "testimonial" disclosure [pp.259-260].**   Under the Fifth Amendment, the government may not compel **testimonial** self-incrimination. A person may not be compelled to reveal thoughts or knowledge, but she may be forced to disclose nontestimonial evidence.

    b. **Requirement that the disclosure be "incriminating" [p.260].**   Because the Fifth Amendment only forbids compelling an individual "to be a witness **against himself,**" the government is only barred from forcing that individual to disclose **incriminating** evidence.

c. **Requirement that the defendant be "compelled" [pp.260-261].** The Fifth Amendment prohibits only **compelled,** testimonial self-incrimination—it protects the individual only when the state seeks to *force incriminating knowledge or thoughts from her mind.* If she has voluntarily committed incriminating thoughts to paper, she may be forced to furnish that paper to the government, and the thoughts may be used against her because the government has **compelled only the** *production* **of the testimony, not the** *testimony itself.* Any incriminating, testimonial content conveyed by the act of production itself, however, may not be used against the individual.

If an accused discloses testimonial, self-incriminating information at trial in response to the "force of historical fact" and "the strength of the State's case" against him, the Fifth Amendment is not violated because the "compulsion" to disclose is "legitimate." If the state does not *add* to that legitimate compulsion, but merely **compels an individual to accelerate the timing of a disclosure,** it does not violate the privilege. A "notice of alibi" rule that requires a defendant to disclose a planned alibi defense to the prosecution prior to trial does not violate the Fifth Amendment because it only compels an accelerated disclosure.

3. **Protection Against Discovery Sanctions Provided by the Sixth Amendment Right to Compulsory Process [pp.262-263]**

The **right to have compulsory process** for obtaining witnesses in the defendant's favor includes a qualified **right to offer the testimony** of those witnesses. The use of **evidence preclusion** as a sanction for defense discovery violations will violate that right unless the preclusion serves sufficient public interests. Preclusion can be constitutional when defense discovery violations are **designed to conceal a plan to present fabricated testimony** or when the failure to disclose is **willful and motivated by a desire to obtain a tactical advantage** that would minimize the effectiveness of the government's cross-examination.

 14 BAIL AND PREVENTIVE DETENTION

Prior to trial or following conviction, an accused may obtain **release on bail** or may be subjected to **preventive detention.** Release and detention decisions implicate important interests of the accused and of society. Constitutional provisions—the **Eighth Amendment Excessive Bail Clause** and the **Fifth and Fourteenth Amendment Due Process Clauses**—and state and federal "bail statutes" regulate bail and detention decisions. They are attempts to strike an appropriate balance between competing interests.

A. THE EIGHTH AMENDMENT RIGHT AGAINST "EXCESSIVE BAIL" [pp.266-270]

The **Eighth Amendment** mandate that **"[e]xcessive bail shall not be required"** limits state power to prescribe conditions under which a person may obtain release pending trial or appeal.

1. Nature of the Eighth Amendment Right [pp.266-267]

According to one view, the Eighth Amendment **does not grant a constitutional right to bail** and imposes **no restrictions on *legislative* authority** to grant or deny release on bail. It **merely precludes *courts* from requiring excessive bail** when the legislature has granted a right to bail. A contrary view holds that the Excessive Bail Clause **contains an implicit constitutional right to nonexcessive bail** and governs *both* **legislatures and courts**—that is, neither can require excessive bail.

2. Meaning of "Excessive" Bail [pp.267-269]

Bail is **excessive** if the conditions for release are **"higher" (more demanding or onerous) than what is reasonably calculated to serve a "compelling interest."** Bail conditions set at a level that is reasonably calculated to prevent flight, safeguard the judicial process, or protect the community from the accused are not excessive.

a. Necessity for individualized determinations of bail [p.268]. The Eighth Amendment requires an "individualized" determination of bail conditions for each accused based on the particular facts of her case. There must be "evidence" and a specific "showing" that the bail conditions prescribed are "reasonably calculated" to serve the state's interests in the accused's case.

b. Constitutionality of denying release on bail [pp.268-269]. A complete denial of release on bail is not "excessive" if that action is no more than what is "reasonably calculated" to serve a compelling state interest. If it is the only way to ensure that an accused will not flee, for example, a denial of release on bail will not violate the Eighth Amendment.

3. The Eighth Amendment and Bail on Appeal [pp.269-270]

It is unclear whether the Excessive Bail Clause regulates bail on appeal. The guarantee **may have the same force on appeal** that it has prior to conviction, requiring individualized assessments of the conditions reasonably calculated to serve compelling state interests. On the other hand, it **may have no application at all to bail on appeal.**

B. **CONSTITUTIONALITY OF MONEY BAIL FOR INDIGENTS [pp.270-271]**

Indigents who have not been able to obtain release on bail because of their inability to satisfy financial conditions have raised constitutional challenges based on the **Eighth Amendment Excessive Bail Clause,** the **Fourteenth Amendment Equal Protection Clause,** and the **Fourteenth Amendment Due Process Clause.** Most claims have been unsuccessful.

1. **The Eighth Amendment Challenge to Financial Bail Conditions [pp.270-271]**

Indigents have argued that financial conditions that result in detention are "excessive" if there are nonfinancial conditions that would serve the state's purposes and enable them to gain release.

2. **The Equal Protection Clause Claim [p.271]**

Indigents have claimed that the result of financial bail conditions is unconstitutional discrimination on account of financial status when they must remain in jail while those with resources gain release.

3. **The Due Process Clause Claim [p.271]**

Indigents have asserted that pretrial detention resulting from financial conditions is fundamentally unfair because it undermines the presumption of innocence and interferes with opportunities to prepare defenses.

C. **FEDERAL BAIL REFORM ACT OF 1984: RELEASE BEFORE TRIAL AND PENDING APPEAL [pp.271-273]**

In the federal system, the **Federal Bail Reform Act of 1984** governs release on bail pending trial and pending appeal.

1. **Bail Pending Trial [pp.271-272]**

A judge **must** order pretrial release *unless* the government establishes one of the limited bases for detention.

a. **Release on personal recognizance or an unsecured bond [p.271].** A judge must impose the **least restrictive** release conditions that will prevent flight and protect the community. More specifically, release **on personal recognizance** or **an unsecured appearance bond** is required unless it will not reasonably assure the defendant's appearance and the community's safety.

b. **Release on conditions [p.272].** If additional conditions are justified, the judge must order pretrial release on the **least restrictive condition(s)** that will reasonably assure the defendant's appearance and the community's safety. Several conditions are authorized.

c. **Factors to be considered [p.272].** Judges must make decisions based on the **nature and circumstances of the offense,** the **weight of the evidence,** the **history and characteristics of the accused,** and the **nature and seriousness of any danger** posed by release.

d. **Financial conditions that result in pretrial detention [p.272].** Under the Act, a judge **may not impose a financial condition that results in the pretrial detention of a person.** If a judge decides that a financial condition is the least restrictive condition needed to reasonably assure the defendant's presence and a defendant cannot meet the condition, the judge **must hold a detention hearing.**

2. **Bail Pending Appeal [pp.272-273]**

Pending appeal, detention is required unless the judge finds **by clear and convincing evidence** that the convicted defendant **is not likely to flee or endanger the community.** The judge must also find that **the appeal is not for purposes of delay,** that it **raises a substantial question of law or fact,** and that **if the appeal is decided in the defendant's favor** it is **likely to yield** a reversal, a new trial, a sentence that does not include imprisonment, or a reduced sentence that is less than the time served plus the expected duration of the appeal.

D. **CONSTITUTIONALITY OF PREVENTIVE DETENTION [pp.273-275]**

Preventive detention—denying pretrial release in order to prevent flight or danger—is subject to challenge on both **due process** and **excessive bail** grounds. Under certain conditions, however, preventive detention can be constitutional.

1. **Preventive Detention and ''Substantive'' Due Process [pp.273-274]**

Because **substantive due process** permits **punishment only for *past* offenses,** preventive detention is constitutional only if it is **regulatory.** It is regulatory if it is **not intended as punishment,** if it is **not excessive in relation to its purported regulatory purpose,** and if the **interest** it serves is **sufficiently important to outweigh the individual's liberty interest.**

a. **Whether detention is ''intended'' as punishment [p.273].** Whether detention is **intended as punishment** hinges on whether the legislative purpose is punitive or regulatory. If the purpose is to assure an accused's appearance or to protect the community, detention is **not intended as punishment.**

b. **Whether detention is excessive in relation to its ''regulatory'' purpose [pp.273-274].** Detention can be **excessive in relation to its regulatory purpose** if the imposition on a detainee's freedom is disproportionate to or greater than whatever is necessary to serve the regulatory purpose.

    c. Whether the regulatory interest is sufficiently important [p.274]. To justify the infringement on an accused's freedom, the regulatory interest served by detention must be **sufficiently important.** Sufficient interests include preventing future crimes, protecting individuals from identified threats, and preventing risks of flight or danger to witnesses.

2. Preventive Detention and "Procedural" Due Process [pp.274-275]

To satisfy **procedural due process,** a preventive detention scheme must contain safeguards against inaccurate deprivations of liberty. While the minimum constitutionally required process is uncertain, the safeguards contained in the Federal Bail Reform Act have been deemed adequate.

3. Preventive Detention and the Guarantee Against "Excessive" Bail [p.275]

Preventive detention is not **excessive** within the meaning of the Eighth Amendment if it is **"mandated on the basis of a compelling interest."** If the state establishes that detention is needed to serve a compelling interest such as flight prevention or community safety, the Eighth Amendment does not require release on bail.

E. FEDERAL BAIL REFORM ACT OF 1984: PREVENTIVE DETENTION [pp.275-276]

The Federal Bail Reform Act provides for preventive detention.

1. Limited Classes of Defendants Subject to Detention Hearings [p.275]

Under the Act, preventive detention requires a detention hearing. A detention hearing may be held only if (1) there is a serious risk the accused will flee, obstruct or attempt to obstruct justice, or threaten, injure, intimidate or attempt to threaten, injure, or intimidate a witness or juror; or (2) the case involves a crime of violence, an offense punishable by life imprisonment or death, certain narcotics offenses, or any felony if the person has at least two convictions of the preceding kinds of crimes.

2. Detention Hearing Requirement [p.275]

The Act requires a special detention hearing at which the accused has the right to counsel and opportunities to testify, present witnesses, cross-examine witnesses, and present information.

3. Finding Required for Detention [pp.276]

To order detention, a judge must find, based on facts supported by **clear and convincing evidence,** that **no condition(s) will reasonably assure the appearance of the person and the safety of any other person and the community.**

15 PLEA BARGAINING AND GUILTY PLEAS

Plea bargaining—negotiations between the prosecution and defense to resolve criminal charges—and **guilty pleas**—defendants' admissions of guilt in court—are important components of the criminal justice system. Both are subject to regulation by the Constitution and laws in each jurisdiction.

A. THE PLEA BARGAINING PROCESS [pp.280-285]

Various forms of plea bargaining have benefits for both the state and the defendant. However, a defendant has **no constitutional right to plea bargaining,** and some types of bargaining by the government are impermissible.

1. Permissible Kinds of Plea Bargaining by the Prosecution [p.281]

The government has broad discretion to select a bargaining method that will encourage a guilty plea. It may offer substantial benefits or a proper degree of leniency, may threaten to bring more serious charges if a defendant does not plead guilty, and may carry out that threat.

2. Limitations on the Prosecutor's Plea Bargaining Methods [pp.282-283]

Due process requires **fairness in securing agreement.** A prosecutor **may not punish an accused for exercising constitutional rights,** may not **retaliate** or **engage in vindictiveness** when an accused refuses to plead, may not **make threats or promises for improper reasons** (such as those based on race or religion), should not **bring additional or more serious charges without notice,** and should not **threaten unwarranted charges.** Moreover, bargaining must not deprive an accused of **freedom to accept or reject an offer.** Statutes may hold out substantial benefits but may not **needlessly encourage guilty pleas and waivers of constitutional rights.**

3. Remedies for Improper Plea Bargaining by the Prosecutor [p.283]

A **plea** resulting from improper bargaining **may be declared involuntary and invalid.** If so, a **conviction must be reversed.** If an accused resists improper bargaining and a prosecutor brings **improper charges,** a resulting **conviction must be reversed.**

4. Breaches of Bargains by the Prosecutor [p.284]

Due process requires that the **government fulfill a promise or agreement** when a guilty plea **rests in any significant degree on that promise or agreement.** When the government **breaches** an agreement, an accused is entitled to a **remedy**—either **withdrawal of a guilty plea** or **specific performance of the agreement.**

5. **Unexecuted Bargains and Withdrawn Offers [p.284]**

Because an unexecuted bargain has no constitutional significance, an accused's **acceptance** of a prosecutor's offer **does not give rise to a right to specific enforcement of the bargain.** Moreover, a negotiated plea entered by a defendant who is aware that the prosecutor has withdrawn a previous, more advantageous offer is valid.

6. **Federal Rule of Criminal Procedure 11 and Plea Bargaining [pp.284-285]**

Federal Rule of Criminal Procedure 11(e) governs plea bargaining in the federal system. It **authorizes plea discussions** for the purpose of reaching an agreement that the government will move for dismissal of charges, make a sentencing recommendation or not oppose a defense sentencing request, or agree that a specific sentence is appropriate if the defendant pleads guilty or nolo contendere. **Judges** may not participate in plea discussions and **are not bound to accept agreements.** Upon accepting or rejecting an agreement, judges are required to take prescribed steps.

B. **GUILTY PLEAS [pp.285-293]**

A guilty or nolo contendere plea—which may or may not be the product of plea bargaining—will result in a conviction. While a court may accept such a plea, the accused has **no absolute constitutional right to have a guilty plea accepted.**

1. **Requirements for a Valid Guilty Plea [pp.285-290]**

Because a guilty plea entails the **waiver of fundamental constitutional rights,** unless it is **voluntary, knowing, and intelligent** it **violates due process and is void.**

a. **A guilty plea must be "voluntary" [p.286].** A guilty plea must be a **voluntary** choice by the accused. An **improperly coerced** plea is invalid because it is both an unreliable admission of guilt *and* an invalid surrender of rights. Voluntariness is determined by considering all relevant surrounding circumstances—including official pressures and an accused's weaknesses. A plea is not involuntary simply because it is motivated by powerful inducements or threats or by fear of a more serious sanction after trial.

b. **A guilty plea must be "knowing and intelligent" [pp.287-288].** For a guilty plea to be **knowing and intelligent,** the accused must be **aware** of certain things and must be **mentally competent** to understand and choose. A defendant must have **full understanding of the true nature of the charges,** of the **direct consequences of a guilty plea,** and of the **nature of the protections being waived.**

c.   **An accused must be ''competent'' to enter a guilty plea [p.289].** An accused must be **competent to plead guilty**—that is, he must have **sufficient present ability to consult with his lawyer with a reasonable degree of rational understanding and a rational as well as a factual understanding of the proceedings against him.**

d.   **Validity of a guilty plea by a defendant who asserts innocence: The doctrine of North Carolina v. Alford [p.289].** A guilty plea can be constitutionally **valid even if** the defendant **refuses to admit guilt or asserts innocence** so long as the accused **voluntarily, knowingly, and understandingly consents to the imposition of punishment** and the record contains **a strong factual basis of guilt.**

e.   **Need for an adequate record to support a guilty plea [p.290].** Because waivers of constitutional rights cannot be presumed from silent records, a guilty plea is invalid unless the record contains an affirmative showing that it was voluntary, knowing, and intelligent.

2.   **Challenges to the Validity of Guilty Pleas [pp.290-292]**

Guilty pleas may be challenged on direct appeal or by means of a collateral challenge.

a.   **Claims that a plea was not voluntary, knowing, and intelligent [p.290].** On appeal or collateral review, an accused may contend that a plea was not voluntary, knowing, and intelligent.

b.   **Claims that a plea was based on ''ineffective assistance'' of counsel [pp.290-291].** On appeal or collateral review, an accused may attack a guilty plea on the basis that it was the product of **ineffective assistance of counsel** and thus violates the Sixth Amendment. To succeed, the accused must show both **deficient performance** by counsel and **prejudice** as a result.

c.   **Claims of ''antecedent'' constitutional violations [pp.291-292].** An ''antecedent'' constitutional violation occurs prior to the entry of a guilty plea and is independent of the validity of the plea. Ordinarily, a state defendant **may not bring a federal habeas corpus** challenge to a guilty plea **on the basis of an antecedent constitutional violation.**

The sole **exception** to this bar to habeas relief is for antecedent violations that **contest the power of the state to bring the defendant into court to answer a charge.** An antecedent claim that **the state may not constitutionally prosecute** the accused for a charge is **not barred** on collateral review.

3. **Federal Rule of Criminal Procedure 11 and Guilty Pleas [pp.292-293]**

    Federal Rule of Criminal Procedure 11 governs the guilty plea process in federal court. The rule requires a judge in open court to **inform the defendant** personally of a variety of matters. It prohibits acceptance of a plea unless the judge **determines that the plea is voluntary** by addressing the defendant personally in open court and **inquires** as to whether the plea is the result of plea discussions. Moreover, the rule requires an inquiry sufficient to satisfy the court of the **factual basis for the plea** and a **verbatim record** of the proceedings.

 THE RIGHT TO A SPEEDY PROSECUTION

To guard against the serious harms and unfairness that delay in investigating and prosecuting criminal offenses can cause to an accused, the **Due Process Clause** forbids some pre-accusation delays and the **Sixth Amendment Speedy Trial Clause** guarantees the **right to a speedy trial.** In addition, statutes such as the **Federal Speedy Trial Act** provide detailed schemes designed to promote expeditious resolutions of charges.

A. **THE DUE PROCESS CLAUSE AND PRE-ACCUSATION DELAY [pp.298-300]**

    A trial may violate the **due process** guarantee of **fundamental fairness** if **pre-accusation delay** by the government impairs the accused's **ability to present a defense.**

    1. **Elements Necessary to Establish a "Due Process–Pre-Accusation Delay" Claim [pp.298-300]**

        A successful **due process–pre-accusation delay** claim requires a showing of **delay** for **an insufficient reason** and **prejudice.**

        a. **Delay element [pp.85-86].**   The accused must show **undue delay.** The **relevant period** begins when an offense is completed and continues until a defendant is tried. Any **substantial delay** should suffice, but the **minimum time period** needed to raise a due process claim is uncertain.

        b. **Insufficient reason element [pp.298-299].**   Some reasons or justifications for official delay are clearly "insufficient," some are clearly sufficient, and still others are of unclear significance. **Intentional delay to gain a tactical advantage or to harass the defendant** will support a due process claim. A claim *might* also succeed if delay results from the government's **reckless disregard of circumstances known to the** prosecution, suggesting an **appreciable risk that delay would impair the ability to mount an effective defense.** On the other hand, **good faith investigative delay** or delay resulting from **any good faith effort to serve a legitimate government objective** cannot support a due process claim even if the decision to delay is *objectively unreasonable.* The significance of **negligent** or **nonnegligent, unjustified delay** is unclear, but it is unlikely that either would provide the basis for a successful due process claim.

    c. **Actual prejudice element [p.300].** In addition, **actual prejudice to the conduct of the defense** is **generally a necessary element** of a due process claim. Ordinarily, the defendant must show tangible harm to the opportunity to avoid conviction. In an egregious case, a **presumption of prejudice to the defense** *might* render proof of actual prejudice unnecessary.

2. Remedy for a Due Process Violation [p.300]

The only remedy for a valid due process pre-accusation delay claim is **dismissal of the charges and a permanent bar to conviction.**

B. THE SIXTH AMENDMENT RIGHT TO A SPEEDY TRIAL [pp.301-306]

The **Sixth Amendment** guarantee that **the accused shall enjoy the right to a speedy trial** ensures **orderly expedition, not mere speed.** Determinations of whether the Sixth Amendment has been violated require inquiry into **whether the right attached** and, if so, **whether the defendant was brought to trial with sufficient speed.**

1. Attachment of the Speedy Trial Right: The Time That Counts [pp.301-303]

Time begins to count toward a speedy trial claim only after the right has **attached** and continues to count only so long as the right has **not been suspended.**

    a. **Initial attachment of the right: When the speedy trial clock begins to run [pp.301-302].** The speedy trial right **attaches only upon an arrest or a formal charge** for an offense. Time prior to these events **does not count.** If a formal charge has been made public, the right **does attach** even though the accused is unaware of the accusation, has not been arrested, and has no other restraints on his liberty.

    b. **Suspension of the right: When the speedy trial clock stops running [p.302].** The clock stops running and time does not count if **formal charges are dismissed either by the prosecution or by a court** and the **accused is released from custody** and **is not subject to bail conditions.** However, if a prosecutor dismisses charges **in bad faith to evade the speedy trial guarantee,** the speedy trial clock *may* continue to run.

Moreover, if charges are **suspended** but not dismissed, the time continues to count.

   c. **Speedy trial right protection for prisoners [p.302-303].** Because prisoners have the right to a speedy trial, when an individual is incarcerated for one offense and formally charged with another offense, the right for the latter offense **attaches when the formal charge is filed.**

2. **Content of the Speedy Trial Right: The Barker v. Wingo Balancing Test [pp.303-306]**

   Speedy trial claims are resolved on a case-by-case basis by applying the **four-factor balancing test** of Barker v. Wingo. The four relevant factors are (1) the **length of delay,** (2) the **reason for the delay,** (3) the defendant's **assertion of the speedy trial right,** and (4) **prejudice** to the defendant.

   a. **Length of the delay [p.304].** The **length of delay** is "**a triggering mechanism.**" Without a minimum amount of time, a speedy trial claim cannot succeed. In general, **five months** has been considered **too short** a time, while periods **approaching one year** have been deemed **sufficient** to trigger balancing analysis. The length of delay also plays a part in the balancing process. It bears on the adequacy of a reason, the need for an assertion, and the appropriateness of presuming prejudice.

   b. **Reason for the delay [pp.304-305].** The **reason for each period of delay** must be determined and given proper weight. A **valid reason** for postponing a trial weighs on the state's side of the balance. Delay caused by official **negligence or overcrowded courts** weighs on the defendant's side, and **a deliberate delay to hamper the defense** weighs **heavily** on the defendant's side. In most cases, delay of a trial because of an **interlocutory appeal** from a trial court ruling will weigh on the government's side.

   c. **Defendant's assertion of the right to a speedy trial [pp.305-306].** While the failure to demand a speedy trial will not *necessarily* defeat an accused's claim, a **failure to assert provides substantial weight** to the government's side of the balance. On the other hand, **assertions provide substantial weight** in favor of a defendant's claim. Pro forma assertions do not help a defendant whose behavior indicates a lack of desire for a speedy trial, while failures to assert do not count against defendants who have good reasons for those failures. Both the frequency and the force of assertions are relevant.

   d. **Prejudice to the accused [p.306].** While **prejudice** will weigh on the defendant's side of the balance, a defendant **does not have to show prejudice** to prevail. Three types of prejudice are relevant: (1) **losses of liberty resulting from pretrial incarceration or bail constraints,**

(2) **anxiety and concern** caused by a pending accusation, and (3) **impairment of the ability to make a defense.** The third form of prejudice—the **most serious**—ordinarily requires **proof of actual, particularized harm.** In cases of excessive delay, however, **prejudice to the defense will be presumed.**

3. **Remedy for Violation of the Right to a Speedy Trial [p.306]**

   The **only possible remedy** for violation of the right to a speedy trial is **dismissal.**

C. THE FEDERAL SPEEDY TRIAL ACT [pp.308-310]

The **Federal Speedy Trial Act** was enacted by Congress to ensure expedition in the processing of criminal charges.

1. **Section 3161: Time Limits and Exclusions [pp.308-309]**

   The Act sets fixed **time limits** for certain steps and then describes the delays that are **excludable**—that is, those that do not count toward the time limits.

   a. **Time limits [p.308].** The government must file an indictment or information within 30 days of arrest or service with a summons. Trial must start within 70 days of the information or indictment or the defendant's appearance before a judicial officer, whichever occurs last. Trial cannot commence fewer than 30 days after the defendant's first appearance through counsel or election of self-representation. Other time periods apply following a dismissal, mistrial, appeal, or collateral attack.

   b. **Exclusions [pp.308-309].** Some periods of time are **excludable**— they do not count toward the time limits. The Act sets forth several narrowly defined categories of excludable time. It also allows the exclusion of delays caused by continuances, but only if the judge finds that "the ends of justice served by" a continuance outweigh the public's and defendant's interests in a speedy trial.

2. **Sanctions for Violation of the Act [pp.309-310]**

   When the government violates the Act, a judge has discretion to **dismiss with** or **without prejudice.** A judge's choice of sanction must be informed by the seriousness of the offense, the facts and circumstances leading to dismissal, and the impact of reprosecution on the Act and on the administration of justice. On appeal, findings of fact will be reversed only for clear error and a choice of sanction will be overturned only for an abuse of discretion.

   The Act also provides **direct sanctions** for limited circumstances involving culpable actions by counsel.

17   THE RIGHT TO A PUBLIC TRIAL

While the **Sixth Amendment** grants the *accused* the **right to a public trial,** and the **First Amendment** includes a *public* **right of access to criminal proceedings,** the **Due Process Clause** promises a **right to "fundamental fairness"** that can be jeopardized in a variety of ways by "publicity."

A. THE SIXTH AMENDMENT RIGHT TO A PUBLIC TRIAL [pp.314-319]

The **Sixth Amendment right to a public trial** belongs solely to the defendant, providing a nonabsolute right to open criminal proceedings.

1. **Scope of the Right to a Public Trial: To What Proceedings Does the Right Extend? [pp.314-315]**

    The right to a **public trial** extends not only to the **trial,** but to **other phases of the criminal process** if the presence of the public would serve the purposes of the Sixth Amendment right—to ensure responsible performances by the judge and prosecutor, to encourage witnesses to come forward, and to discourage perjury. The more important a phase is to determining the accused's fate, the stronger the case for extending the public trial right.

2. **Nature and Substance of the Right to a Public Trial: What Protection Does the Right Afford? [pp.315-319]**

    The guarantee of a public trial does not mean that every member of the public must be accommodated or that a trial may not be closed for good reason.

    a. **Meaning of "public" [pp.315-316].** The right to a public trial ensures only **public access** to a proceeding. It ensures that a trial will be open and that opportunities to attend will not be unnecessarily restricted, either directly or constructively. It does not require states to make proceedings accessible to every member of the public who wishes to attend.

    b. **The showing needed to close a trial [pp.316-319].** The public trial guarantee is **not absolute.** The **presumption of openness** can be overcome by an **overriding interest** that justifies closure. Closure must serve **higher values** than the fair trial interests of the accused that are promoted by the presence of the public. Moreover, the presence of an overriding interest must be determined **case by case.** Mandatory closure rules and closure orders based solely on the type of case being tried are impermissible.

Moreover, closure must be *essential* **to preserve higher values.** Judges must consider **reasonable alternatives** and must choose a reasonable alternative to closure that will preserve the higher values that are threatened.

In addition, closure must be **"narrowly tailored" to serve the overriding interest.** Denials of or restrictions on public access must be **no broader than necessary** to protect the interest jeopardized by openness.

On all of these matters, **specific findings** are necessary. A judge must specify the nature of the overriding interest, the facts that show a threat to the overriding interest, the basis for concluding that closure is essential and that alternatives would not be reasonable or effective, and the reasons supporting the breadth of closure that is ordered.

3. Remedy for Violation of the Right to a Public Trial [p.319]

If a **trial** is improperly closed, **reversal and a new trial** are required. There is **no need to show prejudice.** Improper closure of another phase of the criminal process does not always necessitate a new trial, but it does require a remedy "appropriate to the violation."

B. THE FIRST AMENDMENT PUBLIC RIGHT OF ACCESS TO CRIMINAL PROCEEDINGS [pp.320-323]

Implicit in the **First Amendment** guarantees of freedom of speech, of the press, to peaceably assemble, and to petition the government for a redress of grievances is the *public's* **constitutional right to have access to criminal trials.**

1. Scope of the Public Right of Access: To What Proceedings Does the Right Extend? [pp.320-322]

The right of access applies to **criminal trials** and to **some other phases of the criminal process.** The determination whether the right extends to a particular phase hinges on (1) whether there is **a history or tradition of public access** to the proceeding and (2) whether **public access plays a particularly significant positive role in the actual functioning of the process.** Public access can play a "positive role" by keeping the participants responsible, by providing an outlet for community reactions and emotions, and by enabling public discussion and improvement of the judicial process.

2. Substance of the Public Right of Access: What Entitlement Does the First Amendment Afford? [pp.322-323]

The First Amendment right of access is **not absolute.** Closure is permissible in **rare cases** in which the **presumption of openness** is overcome by an **overriding interest** and a showing that closure is **essential to preserve higher values.** Any closure must be **narrowly tailored.** If an accused seeks closure because public access poses threats to interest in a fair trial, a proceeding may be closed if a judge makes **specific findings** demonstrating a *substantial probability* that the right to a fair trial will be prejudiced by publicity and that reasonable alternatives to closure cannot adequately protect the fair trial right.

C. PUBLICITY AND THE RIGHT TO A FAIR TRIAL [pp.323-300]

Publicity and public access to criminal proceedings can threaten the accused's overriding **right to a fair trial**—a right that is constitutionally safeguarded by the **Due Process Clause** and specific guarantees in the Bill of Rights.

1. Meaning of the Right to a "Fair" Trial [pp.323-324]

The "**fundamental fairness**" guaranteed by the promise of **due process of law** includes both a "substantive" component—an assurance of **accurate, reliable outcomes**—and a "procedural" component—an assurance of **fair play** in accord with the principles of our **adversarial, accusatorial system.**

2. Potential Risks of Unfairness [pp.324-325]

Both the **publication of information** and the **presence of the media** can threaten the fairness of a trial.

   a. **Potential unfairness caused by publicity before and during trials [p.324].** Publicity before and during trials can compromise the **impartiality of** *potential* **and** *actual* **jurors,** can **influence witnesses** to distort their testimony in ways that undermine the search for truth, and can **put pressures on judges or prosecutors or both** that alter their behavior in ways that may be unfair to the accused.

   b. **Potential unfairness caused by the presence or the conduct of the media at the trial [pp.324-325].** The **presence and conduct of media representatives** may compromise the fairness of trials by **adversely affecting and influencing judges, lawyers, jurors, witnesses, or defendants.** The mere awareness of media interest and scrutiny can alter participants' conduct in unacceptable ways, and disruptive conduct by either media representatives or members of the public can distract participants from their tasks.

3. Safeguards Against the Risks of Prejudicial Publicity [pp.325-329]

If publicity renders a trial unfair, a resulting conviction must be reversed. If threats to fairness arise before or during a trial, preventive steps are available.

   a. **Restricting the disclosure of information [p.325].** Although judges have some authority to **restrict disclosure of information** about a pending case, that authority is tightly restricted. Prior restraints on the release of information by the media and threats of sanctions for disclosure by the media are unlikely to survive First Amendment scrutiny. The same measures are more likely to be permissible when directed toward lawyers and other trial participants.

b.   **Preventing access to proceedings [pp.325-326].**   The **denial of access to courtrooms and files** is another option, but it is tightly limited by the First Amendment right of public access to criminal proceedings.

c.   **Continuances and changes of venue [p.326].**   Prejudicial publicity can be dealt with by means of a **continuance,** which allows passions to subside and memories to fade, or a **change of venue,** which allows trial before an untainted community. *In extreme cases*, a failure to change venue can result in the reversal of a conviction without proof of actual unfairness.

d.   **Measures designed to deal directly with the jurors [pp.326-329].** Prejudice caused by publicity can be addressed by a variety of measures that deal directly with jurors.

First, either before or during trial jurors can be **questioned** to determine whether they are aware of and have been improperly biased by publicity. Prior to trial, a juror can be **stricken for cause** or **removed by a peremptory challenge.** During trial, a juror can be **removed and replaced by an alternate juror** or a **mistrial** can be declared.

Second, judges can **instruct jurors** before trial begins, during the trial, and at the end of trial to put aside matters heard outside the courtroom and any preconceived opinions and to judge the case impartially, based on the evidence at trial. Judges can also **admonish jurors** not to speak to others about the case and not to read or watch media reports.

Third, judges can **sequester jurors** during the trial, insulating them from possible exposure to improper publicity.

4.   **Safeguards Against the Risks of Media Presence [pp.329-330]**

Measures to combat the risks of media presence and conduct are also available.

a.   **Print media [p.329].**   A judge can **limit the number of print media representatives and bar distracting or disruptive behavior** by those individuals but **may not deny access** simply because of the risks of media presence.

b.   **Broadcast media [pp.329-330].**   The risks posed by **broadcast media** are more serious. A judge can **limit the number of representatives, restrict the amount of equipment, and bar distracting or disruptive behavior. Due process does not** *require* **the exclusion of broadcast media** because broadcast coverage does not automatically render a trial unfair. Nonetheless, the First Amendment probably *allows* judges to guard against the peculiar risks posed by such coverage by denying broadcast media access.

18 THE RIGHT TO THE ASSISTANCE OF COUNSEL

In our adversarial system, the Sixth Amendment **right to the assistance of counsel** is probably the most fundamental and essential of all rights. Counsel is the mechanism that ensures the *rough equality* between opponents that is essential to fair outcomes by fair processes. Counsel also enables the accused to enjoy the other rights that ensure fair trials.

A. NATURE OF THE RIGHT TO THE ASSISTANCE OF COUNSEL [pp.336-339]

The Sixth Amendment right to counsel includes a right to retained or appointed legal assistance. All indigents charged with felonies, but only some charged with misdemeanors, are entitled to appointed counsel.

1. The Right to Legal Assistance [p.336]

The right to counsel includes only an entitlement to the **trained, expert assistance of a lawyer.**

2. The Right to Retain Counsel of One's Choice [p.337]

An accused has the right to use her own funds to retain an attorney whom she wants to have represent her. This **right to counsel of choice** is not absolute. Sufficiently weighty interests can justify restricting a defendant's choice.

3. The Right to Appointed Counsel [pp.337-339]

The Constitution **requires the government to provide appointed counsel for indigents.**

   a. **Meaning of indigency [p.337].** Individuals with no or only a modest amount of resources clearly qualify as indigent, but the line between those who are constitutionally eligible for appointed counsel and those who are not is unclear. Typically, statutory provisions for appointed counsel prescribe the criteria for indigency.

   b. **Scope of the right to appointed counsel [pp.337-339].** An indigent defendant charged with **any felony** is constitutionally entitled to **appointed counsel.** An indigent defendant charged with a **misdemeanor** is entitled to **appointed counsel** only if a conviction for the misdemeanor results in a sentence that includes **actual imprisonment.** If counsel is not appointed and a trial results in a conviction, the judge cannot sentence the defendant to actual imprisonment. However, the uncounseled conviction may be a basis for increasing a sentence of imprisonment imposed for *a later conviction* for a different offense.

It is uncertain whether an accused is entitled to **retained counsel** for **misdemeanors that do not result in actual imprisonment.** The right to retain an attorney might apply to all offenses or might be subject to the same limits as appointed counsel.

B. SCOPE OF THE RIGHT TO THE ASSISTANCE OF COUNSEL [pp.340-344]

The right to counsel applies to the trial stage and to some pretrial and post-trial stages of a criminal case.

1. Assistance of Counsel at Trial [p.340]

An accused is clearly entitled to counsel's assistance from the beginning until the end of a trial. An accused is also entitled to counsel for the period of time prior to trial needed **to enable adequate preparation** by counsel and for some period after the verdict—at least for the time during which post-trial motions may be filed and through the end of the sentencing.

2. Assistance of Counsel at Formal Pretrial Proceedings [pp.340-342]

An accused has the right to counsel at any pretrial event that qualifies as a **"critical stage" of the prosecution.** A pretrial adjudicatory stage is critical if the accused is **confronted with the prosecution or the substantive and procedural law** and if **counsel is necessary to preserve the basic right to a fair trial.** Most formal courtroom proceedings prior to trial qualify.

    a. First appearances or arraignments [p.341]. An accused will be entitled to counsel at a first appearance or arraignment if a lack of assistance jeopardizes the fairness of the trial. Whether that is the case depends on the nature of and purposes served by the first appearance.

    b. Preliminary hearings [p.341-342]. Preliminary hearings are used to determine whether there is adequate cause to require an accused to stand trial for an offense. It is likely that there is a right to counsel at **all preliminary hearings.**

3. Assistance of Counsel at Post-Trial Proceedings [pp.342-344]

Post-trial motions and sentencing hearings are parts of the trial itself for purposes of the right to counsel. Appeals and collateral attacks, however, are separate phases of the criminal process.

a. **The right to counsel on appeal [pp.342-344].** Defendants have a right to retained or appointed counsel for a **first appeal as of right.** The right to retained counsel is based on the **Due Process Clause,** while the right to appointed counsel is rooted in both the **Due Process** and **Equal Protection Clauses.** The right to counsel on appeal includes a **right to effective assistance.**

An indigent defendant has **no right to appointed counsel for discretionary state appeals or applications for discretionary review by the United States Supreme Court.** It is unclear whether a state could deny an accused the right to retain counsel for these phases. It is clear that ineffective assistance by retained counsel does not deny due process.

b. **The right to counsel for collateral attacks on criminal convictions [p.344].** In general, indigents have **no constitutional right to appointed counsel for purposes of pursuing collateral relief.** A prisoner **might** be able to show that particular circumstances in his case require a due process right to counsel for purposes of a collateral attack.

C. SUBSTANCE OF THE RIGHT TO THE ASSISTANCE OF COUNSEL: THE RIGHT TO EFFECTIVE ASSISTANCE [pp.344-356]

The Sixth Amendment right to counsel is the **right to effective assistance.** A deprivation of effective assistance can result from government actions or from counsel's failure to provide competent representation.

1. **Ineffectiveness Caused by Governmental Restrictions on Counsel [pp.345-349]**

    Counsel must be allowed **to participate fully and fairly in the adversary factfinding process** and **to defend a criminal prosecution in accord with the traditions of the adversary factfinding process.** Reasonable constraints on counsel are permissible, but restrictions that impair the performance of counsel's adversary system functions can deprive the defendant of effective assistance.

    a. **Restrictions on partisan advocacy by counsel [p.345].** An accused is entitled to have counsel engage in **partisan advocacy.** Limitations that unreasonably impair counsel's efforts to present arguments to the trier of fact can deprive the defendant of effective assistance.

    b. **Restrictions on consultation between the accused and counsel [pp.346-347].** Official interference with the accused's **right to consult** with counsel can also deny effective assistance. The right to consult is **absolute** before an accused begins to testify; any infringement is unconstitutional. While a defendant is testifying, however, a judge *may* deny a request to consult or a request for a recess for that purpose. Moreover, a judge *may* bar consultation during a **brief recess** between direct and cross-examination of the defendant in which it is **virtually certain that any conversation would relate to the ongoing testimony.** The recess must be so **short** that it is **appropriate to assume that nothing but the accused's testimony will be discussed.** During recesses that are not "brief" or "short," it is unconstitutional to prohibit consultation.

c. **Restrictions on counsel's ability to present a defense [pp.347-348].** Because counsel's functioning is essential to enjoyment of the Sixth Amendment "right to make a defense," restrictions on counsel's **ability to present a defense** can deprive the accused of effective assistance.

d. **Other impermissible state restrictions on counsel's abilities to render effective assistance [p.348].** State actions that **impair counsel's loyalty, limit counsel's zeal, interfere with counsel's ability to investigate or prepare for trial,** or otherwise hinder an attorney's efforts to perform the functions expected of counsel in our adversarial system can also deny effective assistance.

e. **Irrelevance of prejudice and harmless error analysis [pp.348-349].** A deprivation of effective assistance is a "structural error" that requires "automatic reversal" of a conviction. There is **no need to show prejudice,** and the state cannot avoid reversal by showing that the deprivation was "harmless."

2. **Ineffectiveness Caused by Counsel's Deficient Performance: The Doctrine of Strickland v. Washington [pp.349-352]**

Either **appointed or retained** counsel can deprive defendants of the Sixth Amendment entitlement to effective assistance by failing to provide competent representation. This type of deficiency is referred to as **"actual ineffectiveness."**

a. **Logical foundations of the "actual ineffectiveness" doctrine: The purpose and role of counsel in an adversarial system [p.349].** The function of counsel is to provide assistance that ensures the "adversarial testing" essential for a **fair trial**—that is, a trial that produces **a just, reliable result.** Incompetent representation can preclude a fair trial.

b. *Strickland* requirements for an "actual ineffectiveness" claim: Deficient performance and prejudice [pp.349-351]. To succeed with an "actual ineffectiveness" claim, a defendant must establish that counsel rendered a **deficient performance** and that **prejudice** resulted.

Deficient performance occurs when an attorney fails to render **reasonably effective assistance.** The representation must fall below an **objective standard of reasonableness** and outside the **wide range of reasonable professional assistance.** A court must indulge a **strong**

presumption that counsel's conduct was reasonable, must **consider all the circumstances,** must be **highly deferential,** and must avoid the distortion of **hindsight.**

To establish **prejudice,** a defendant must demonstrate **a reasonable probability that, but for counsel's unprofessional errors, the result of the proceeding would have been different.** In addition, counsel's deficient performance must have **rendered the result of the trial unreliable or the proceeding fundamentally unfair.** A result is "unreliable" if it is either **factually or legally inaccurate.** A proceeding is "fundamentally unfair" if the defendant has been deprived of some element of **fair process.**

c. **Actual ineffectiveness in guilty plea contexts [p.352].** The deficient performance and prejudice requirements also apply when an accused claims that a guilty plea is the result of actual ineffectiveness. In the guilty plea context, prejudice is defined as a **reasonable probability that, but for the deficient performance, the defendant would not have pleaded guilty and would have insisted on a trial.**

3. **Ineffective Assistance Caused by Conflicts of Interest [pp.353-356]**

A conflict of interest can deprive the defendant of counsel's **undivided loyalty** or **zealous advocacy** and thereby result in the denial of effective assistance. **Joint representation** of codefendants is a common source of conflicts.

a. **Trial judge failures to prevent potential conflicts of interest [pp.353-354].** A trial judge's failure to prevent a potential conflict can be the basis of a successful claim of ineffective assistance caused by conflict of interest.

The judge has an **affirmative duty to inquire** if she is put on either **actual or constructive notice** of a potential conflict—that is, if she **knows or reasonably should know that a particular conflict exists.** If she is put on notice, the judge has the duty either to **remedy the conflict** or to inquire into the situation and **ascertain that the risk of conflict is remote.** A conflict resulting from joint representation can be remedied by appointing separate counsel.

If a judge fails to fulfill the duty, **a conviction must be reversed.** There is no need to show an actual conflict or prejudice, and the error **cannot be harmless.**

b. **Actual conflicts of interest that impair the performance of counsel [pp.354-355].** A defendant can also establish ineffective assistance because of a conflict by demonstrating that **an actual conflict of interest adversely affected his lawyer's performance.** There must be a showing that the accused's interests were **actually in conflict** with other interests of the lawyer **and** that the conflict had **an adverse effect on the lawyer's representation**—that the lawyer resolved the conflict against the defendant's interests. There is **no need to show prejudice**—an impact on the outcome of the trial—and the constitutional deprivation **cannot be harmless.**

c. **Waiver of the right to conflict-free counsel [p.356].** A defendant *may be allowed* to waive the **right to conflict-free counsel** and to choose representation by an attorney who has or may have a conflict. The **right to counsel of choice** means that ordinarily an informed decision to be represented by a particular lawyer **must be honored.** However, if there is either **an actual conflict of interest** or **a serious potential for conflict,** a judge may deprive a defendant of her choice of counsel by declining to accept a waiver of conflict-free representation.

D. **WAIVER OF THE RIGHT TO COUNSEL AND THE RIGHT OF SELF-REPRESENTATION [pp.356-363]**

An accused is **entitled to waive** the right to the assistance of counsel because the Sixth Amendment contains an implicit **right of self-representation.**

1. **Waiver of the Right to Counsel [p.357]**

    An accused **may waive** the right to counsel if the waiver is **knowing, intelligent, and voluntary.**

2. **The Sixth Amendment Right of Self-Representation: The Doctrine of Faretta v. California [pp.357-363]**

    Except in limited circumstances, the **right of self-representation** requires that defendants who wish to conduct their own defenses be allowed to do so.

    a. **Source of and basis for the right of self-representation [pp.357-358].** Implicit in the Sixth Amendment is a **right of self-representation**—an entitlement of the accused personally to conduct the defense. Self-representation might well *detract from* the fairness of a trial. It was included in the Sixth Amendment **to affirm the dignity and autonomy of the accused** and to reflect the importance of **free choice** and **respect for the individual.**

    b. **Restrictions on the exercise of the right of self-representation [pp.358-361].** A defendant who **validly waives** the right to counsel **and is able and willing to comply with the rules of the courtroom** must be allowed to represent himself. The right cannot be denied because the accused **lacks legal skill, knowledge, or expertise.**

       An accused must be able and willing to give a **valid waiver** of the right to counsel. The waiver must be **knowing and intelligent**—that is, the accused must be **aware of the dangers and disadvantages of self-representation.** Moreover, the waiver must be a **voluntary** relinquishment of counsel—that is, the choice must not be the product of official coercion. The validity of a waiver that is "involuntary" solely because of internal forces is uncertain. An accused must be mentally competent to waive the right to counsel—he must have sufficient ability to consult with his lawyer with a reasonable degree of rational understanding and a rational as well as factual understanding of the proceedings.

It is also undecided whether a waiver can be valid without *admonishment* and *inquiry* by the trial judge. While some courts mandate hearings with warnings, advice, and questioning by the judge, others hold that a waiver can be valid so long as the record contains sufficient evidence that a knowing and voluntary choice was made.

A court can **terminate self-representation** if a defendant **deliberately engages in serious and obstructionist misconduct.** Moreover, to exercise the right, the accused must be **able and willing to abide by rules of procedure and courtroom protocol.**

Finally, a judge has the authority to appoint a trained lawyer to serve as **standby counsel.** Standby counsel can aid an accused who wants help or can take over if self-representation is terminated. Over the accused's objections, counsel may help the defendant **overcome routine procedural or evidentiary hurdles** and **comply with basic rules of courtroom protocol and procedure.**

c. **Substance of and deprivations of the right of self-representation [pp.361-363].** The right of self-representation encompasses **specific rights to have one's voice heard**—to control the organization and content of the defense, make motions and arguments, participate in voir dire, question witnesses, and address the court and jury. It does not include a right to **hybrid representation**—representation in part by counsel and in part by oneself.

The right of self-representation guarantees the accused an entitlement to have **actual control over the case** he chooses to present and an entitlement **to have the jury perceive her as representing herself.** An accused has a right to **protection against unsolicited and intrusive participation by standby counsel** that threatens those entitlements. However, when a defendant **expressly approves of** or **invites** standby counsel's participation, she *cannot* later complain about *that* participation and it will be *difficult to challenge other* participation by counsel.

A defendant who chooses self-representation **cannot claim ineffective assistance of counsel.**

If an accused is deprived of the right of self-representation, a resulting conviction **must be reversed.** Violation of the right **cannot be harmless error.**

THE RIGHT TO TRIAL BY JURY

The Sixth Amendment **right to trial by an impartial jury** is a safeguard against arbitrary law enforcement. The protections that juries provide defendants against corrupt or overzealous prosecutors and compliant, biased, or eccentric judges are essential to fundamental fairness.

A. SCOPE OF THE RIGHT TO TRIAL BY JURY [pp.370-373]

Although the Constitution provides that the accused "shall enjoy" the right to trial by jury "in **all** criminal prosecutions," not all criminal defendants are entitled to jury trials.

1. **"Petty-Serious" Crime Dichotomy [pp.370-371]**

   Those accused of **serious crimes** are entitled to juries, while those accused of **petty crimes** are not.

2. **Distinction Between "Petty" and "Serious" Crimes [pp.371-372]**

   Whether a crime is petty or serious depends **solely** on the **maximum authorized penalty.** The **maximum authorized period of incarceration** is the primary criterion. An offense with a maximum of **more than six months is serious,** while an offense with a maximum of **six months or less is presumptively petty.** The presumption can be overcome in *rare* situations where **additional** *statutory* **penalties,** in conjunction with the maximum authorized incarceration, are **so severe they clearly reflect a legislative determination that an offense is serious.** While the **magnitude of the authorized fine** that renders an offense serious is uncertain, an offense with an authorized fine of $5,000 is clearly petty.

   Whether an offense is serious is determined by the authorized penalty **for that offense alone.** There is no right to a jury when multiple petty offenses are joined for a single trial.

3. **Crimes with No Authorized Maximum Penalty: The Special Case of Criminal Contempt [p.373]**

   If there is no legislative penalty specified for an offense, whether it is petty or serious depends on the **penalty actually imposed.** Criminal contempt is an example. An actual sentence of more than six months renders the contempt serious.

   If a judge **summarily** finds an individual guilty of multiple criminal contempts **during a trial,** a sentence of up to six months may be imposed for each contempt and the sentences may be run consecutively without triggering the entitlement to a jury. However, if multiple **nonsummary** contempt charges **arise from a single trial, are charged by a single judge, and are tried in a single proceeding,** the **cumulative punishment** cannot exceed six months unless the accused is afforded a jury trial.

B. MEANING OF THE RIGHT TO TRIAL BY JURY [pp.374-378]

The guarantee of trial by jury raises questions of **size** and **constituency** of the jury.

1. Jury Size: The Number of Persons Needed to Constitute a Jury [p.374]

Juries of **six persons are constitutional;** juries of **fewer than six are not.**

2. "Fair Cross Section" Requirement [pp.375-378]

Implicit in the right to trial by jury is a **fair cross section requirement.**

a. **Textual basis for and purposes of the fair cross section requirement [p.375].** The fair cross section requirement rests on the guarantee of an *impartial* jury. It guards against arbitrary power and ensures the input of community common sense, preserves public confidence in the system, and implements the belief that civic responsibility entails sharing in the administration of justice.

b. **Meaning and content of the fair cross section requirement [pp.375-376].** The fair cross section requirement does not require that either petit juries or the "pools" or "venires" from which they are chosen must "mirror the community." Instead, it demands that the **"pools" or "venires" must not systematically exclude distinctive community groups and thereby fail to be reasonably representative.** While it is unclear whether systematic exclusion from the **petit jury itself** could ever violate the fair cross section requirement, it is clear that systematic exclusion by means of peremptory challenges does *not* violate the requirement.

c. **Elements necessary for a prima facie violation of the fair cross section requirement [pp.376-377].** To establish a prima facie violation of the fair cross section requirement, an accused must show that the allegedly excluded group is **sufficiently numerous and distinctive,** that the group's **representation in venires is not fair and reasonable,** and that the underrepresentation is the result of **systematic exclusion.** An accused need not belong to the excluded group to have **standing** to bring such a claim.

The requirement that the group be **sufficiently numerous** means that it must be of a certain size in the community. The requirement that the group be **distinctive** means that it must bring to the jury *perspectives and values* different from those of other groups.

The requirement that **representation not be fair and reasonable** means that the percentage of a group's members in venires must be significantly lower than the percentage of the group's members in the community.

The requirement that underrepresentation be the result of **systematic exclusion** means that the disproportionate representation in the venires must be the result of some aspect of the jury selection system. A discriminatory purpose or purpose to exclude is not required.

    d. **The government's opportunity to justify systematic exclusion [pp.377-378].** The government can justify systematic exclusion by showing that **a significant state interest** is manifestly and primarily advanced by the aspects of the jury selection process that resulted in the underrepresentation and that those aspects of the process are **appropriately tailored to serve that interest.** If the government does so, the fair cross section requirement is not violated.

C. JURY SELECTION [pp.378-390]

Petit juries are selected from larger venires or pools of prospective jurors. Both voir dire and **challenges** are significant parts of the selection process.

    1. **A Brief Description of the Voir Dire Process [pp.378-379]**

Voir dire involves questioning of prospective jurors by the parties or the judge or both, either as a group or individually. Trial judges have broad discretion to control the process. One object of voir dire is to identify jurors who should be removed for cause. Another is to provide the parties with informed bases for peremptory challenges.

    2. **The Due Process Entitlement to Specific Voir Dire About Racial Prejudice: The Rule of Ham v. South Carolina [pp.379-381]**

In some instances, the **Due Process Clause** and **Sixth Amendment** guarantees of **impartial jurors** require trial judges **to question prospective jurors about racial prejudice** upon the request of the accused.

    a. **The showing necessary to establish an entitlement to voir dire about racial prejudice [p.379].** A defendant is constitutionally entitled to specific questioning about racial prejudice *only* if he shows a **constitutionally significant likelihood** that **racial prejudice might infect the trial** and result in **jurors who would not be impartial.** Interracial violence alone does not give rise to a sufficient likelihood.

    b. **Entitlement to specific questioning about other kinds of prejudice [p.380].** The limited constitutional entitlement to voir dire clearly extends to cases involving a significant likelihood of *ethnic* prejudice. It is uncertain whether it extends to other kinds of prejudice.

c. **The special case of "capital sentencing" proceedings: The rule of Turner v. Murray [pp.380-381].** The fact that an offense involves interracial violence does not trigger a due process entitlement to specific questioning of jurors who will determine guilt or innocence. Interracial violence does give rise to a due process right to specific questioning of jurors who make capital sentencing determinations. If a judge fails to question them about racial prejudice, a death sentence must be set aside.

3. **"Supervisory Power" Standard for Voir Dire in Federal Courts [p.381]**

    By virtue of the "supervisory power," **federal defendants** are entitled to specific questioning of jurors about racial prejudice when the circumstances show a *reasonable possibility* **that racial or ethnic prejudice might influence the jury.**

4. **Challenges for Cause [pp.381-382]**

    A party may challenge a prospective juror **for cause** if there is reason to believe that the juror will not be impartial, competent, qualified, or able to decide a case based on the evidence at trial. Trial judges have broad authority to determine whether there is cause to remove a juror, and their determinations are rarely overturned. While a judge may ordinarily rely on a juror's assertions that she will set aside information or opinions and judge a case impartially, in rare, extreme cases a judge may be required to remove a juror despite such assertions. Moreover, although it is unlikely, the improper removal of a juror for cause at the government's request could be the basis of a valid claim that jury impartiality was compromised.

5. **Nature and Source of Peremptory Challenges [pp.382-383]**

    A **peremptory challenge** permits a party to remove a prospective juror without giving a reason. There is **no constitutional right** to peremptory challenges. Nonetheless, statutorily authorized peremptory challenges remain an integral part of the jury selection process.

6. **Equal Protection Clause Restrictions on the Exercise of Peremptory Challenges: The Doctrine of Batson v. Kentucky [pp.383-390]**

    Although a peremptory challenge is ordinarily uncontestable, the **Fourteenth Amendment Equal Protection Clause** prohibits certain kinds of **intentional discrimination** in the exercise of peremptory challenges.

    a. **A brief history of Equal Protection Clause constraints on peremptory jury challenges [pp.383-384].** In Swain v. Alabama, the Supreme Court held that a defendant could not establish an equal protection violation by relying solely on the prosecutor's use of peremptories in a particular case. Only proof that the **government in** *case after case* had struck jurors of a particular race so that *no juror* of that race had *ever* served in the jurisdiction could suffice.

In Batson v. Kentucky, the Court overruled *Swain*, holding that an accused can establish an equal protection violation based on the use of peremptory challenges in his case. According to *Batson*, **removal of a juror on the assumption that the juror will be partial to a person of her race is unconstitutional.**

b. **Details of the *Batson* doctrine [pp.384-388].** The *Batson* doctrine establishes a three-step framework for analyzing claims of discrimination in the use of peremptories. **First,** the defendant must make a **prima facie case** that the prosecutor has exercised peremptories on the basis of race. **Second,** the government has the burden to **rebut** the case by articulating **race-neutral explanations. Third,** the court must determine **whether the defendant has proven purposeful discrimination.**

The phrasing of the *Batson* doctrine was designed to deal with a *defendant's* claim that the *prosecution* had used its peremptories to remove members of *his race*. Several post-*Batson* developments have eliminated some of the limits implicit in that phrasing. First, a defendant can succeed with a claim that the prosecution has removed members of *any* race. Second, the **prosecution** can successfully object to the **discriminatory use of peremptories by *the defense*.** Third, either side can succeed with a claim that peremptories have been used to discriminate **on account of** *gender*.

In the **first step,** a trial judge must determine whether the defendant has established a **prima facie case of intentional discrimination.** The defendant is entitled to rely on a fact that is always true—that peremptory challenges allow discrimination by those who are of a mind to discriminate. She must then show that the prosecutor has used peremptories to remove members of her race or of another race and that these facts and other relevant circumstances raise an inference that the peremptories were used to exclude jurors on account of their race. Any fact suggesting a discriminatory motive is relevant. If a prima facie case is established, the court proceeds to step two.

In the **second step,** the **burden shifts to the state to provide explanations** for its challenges. The sole concern is **facial validity**—whether the reasons are **race-neutral.** Race-neutral reasons are those based on something other than the race of the juror. A reason is not race-neutral if discriminatory intent is inherent in the explanation. Disproportionate impact alone does not render a reason facially invalid, but some ostensibly race-neutral reasons may be so closely tied to race that they must be deemed facially invalid. A mere denial of discriminatory motives or affirmation of good faith cannot rebut a prima facie case. If the prosecution fails to provide facially valid explanations, the defendant's claim must be sustained. If the reasons offered are race-neutral, the court must proceed to step three.

In the **third step,** the trial court must look at all of the circumstances, including the credibility of the rebuttal explanations, and decide whether it is **more likely than not that the peremptory challenges were in fact used to remove jurors on account of race.** The trial court's determination is entitled to great deference on appeal and should be overturned only if it is clearly erroneous.

c. **Extension of the *Batson* doctrine to defense use of peremptories [p.388].** The Equal Protection Clause also bars **intentional discrimination by the defense in the exercise of peremptories** because the defense qualifies as a state actor and because a discriminatory challenge violates a juror's right to equal protection.

d. **Extension of the *Batson* doctrine to discrimination on account of gender [pp.388-389].** The Equal Protection Clause **forbids intentional discrimination on account of gender** in the exercise of peremptories. It is uncertain whether discriminatory challenges of members of any other group entitled to "heightened" or "intermediate" equal protection scrutiny are unconstitutional, but it is clear that a party *may* strike a member of any group or class normally subject to "rational basis" equal protection review.

e. **Remedies for *Batson* violations [pp.389-390].** If the prosecution makes intentionally discriminatory use of peremptory challenges and the violation is discovered *after trial,* a conviction must be reversed. Whether defense misuse of peremptories requires reversal is uncertain.

If the unconstitutional use of peremptories is discovered *during jury selection,* a judge can either discharge the venire and summon a new pool of jurors or disallow the discriminatory challenges, reinstate the stricken jurors, and continue with the selection process.

D. SUBSTANCE OF THE JURY GUARANTEE DURING TRIAL [pp.390-393]

A defendant is constitutionally entitled to jurors who behave in ways that guarantee fair treatment and a fair outcome.

1. Guarantee of Impartial and Competent Jurors Who Render a Decision Based on the Evidence Presented at Trial [pp.390-391]

An accused has the right to jurors who are impartial, competent, and who decide the case on the evidence. A verdict is infirm if any juror fails to satisfy these criteria.

a. **Requirement of impartiality [p.390].** The Sixth Amendment guarantees trial by an "**impartial** jury"—one that is not biased or prejudiced against the accused. A trial before jurors who are not impartial violates due process.

b. **Requirement of competence [p.391].** A defendant is also entitled to **competent** jurors—jurors who are capable of understanding the evidence and reaching a rational decision. A trial before jurors who have physical or mental impairments that affect their competence is unfair.

c. **Requirement of a decision based on the evidence [p.391].** Due process requires that jurors be **capable and willing to decide the case solely on the evidence** introduced in court. A jury's verdict must be based on the evidence developed at the trial.

2. **Remedies for Deprivations of the Entitlement to Impartial, Competent Jurors Who Render a Decision Based on the Evidence [pp.391-393]**

During the trial, if there is reason to believe that a juror is biased, incompetent, or unwilling or unable to decide based on the evidence, a judge may inquire into the situation and, if warranted, may **remove the juror and replace her with an alternate.** If the jury is irreparably compromised or there are insufficient alternate jurors, a **mistrial** may be required.

After a verdict is rendered, when there is evidence that a juror's performance was constitutionally deficient, the proper remedy is a **post-trial hearing with an opportunity to show actual bias or some other infirmity.** If it is established that a juror did not satisfy the constitutional criteria—for example, that she was biased, incompetent, or improperly influenced—a conviction must be reversed.

E. JURY DELIBERATIONS AND VERDICTS [pp.393-398]

Jury deliberations and verdicts give rise to issues of nullification, unanimity, inconsistency, and impeachment.

1. **Desirability of and Entitlement to Instructions About "Jury Nullification" [pp.393-395]**

Jurors have the "power" or "prerogative" to engage in "nullification"—to acquit an accused despite the fact that the law and facts support a conviction.

a. **The lower courts' attitude toward nullification [p.394].** Typically the courts hold that an accused had **no entitlement to jury nullification instructions** because such instructions might lead to the overuse of a prerogative that is desirable only in rare, compelling cases.

b. **The Supreme Court's attitude toward nullification [pp.394-395].** While Supreme Court opinions suggest that the jury's exercise of the power to nullify is proper in the occasional case in which a result dictated by the law is unjust, references to nullification as a **"power"** that jurors have **"no right to exercise"** suggest that its use ought to be rare and that defendants are not entitled to nullification instructions.

2. **Requirement of Unanimous Jury Verdicts [p.395]**

The **Sixth Amendment guarantees *federal* defendants the right to a unanimous verdict.** The **Fourteenth Amendment Due Process Clause does not guarantee** *state* **defendants a right to a unanimous verdict** when a jury includes **twelve** persons, but it **does require that juries of six be unanimous.**

3. **Constitutionality of "Inconsistent" Jury Verdicts [pp.395-396]**

The Constitution **does not forbid inconsistent verdicts.** A conviction that is logically inconsistent with another verdict returned by the same judge or jury is constitutional.

4. **Inquiry into Deliberations and "Impeachment" of Verdicts [pp.396-398]**

Both the common law and the controlling federal rule restrict the use of juror testimony to impeach verdicts.

a. **Common law prohibition on the use of juror testimony to impeach verdicts [p.396].** An almost universal common law rule flatly prohibits the impeachment of a verdict by juror testimony about "internal" infirmities, but it allows jurors to testify about "external" or "extraneous" matters. The rule can bar the accused from proving matters that would render verdicts invalid.

b. **Federal Rule of Evidence 606(b) [pp.396-397].** Federal Rule of Evidence 606(b) exemplifies a typical, modern "codification" of the common law rule. The rule (1) **only** prohibits testimony **upon inquiry into a verdict;** (2) **only** prohibits testimony about **internal matters,** specifically allowing testimony about **extraneous prejudicial information** or **outside influences;** (3) prohibits testimony **not only** concerning matters occurring **after a jury retires to deliberate but also** concerning matters that arise **during the course of the trial;** and (4) **only** prohibits **juror testimony,** not the testimony of nonjurors about internal matters.

c. **Constitutionality of restrictions on juror testimony to impeach verdicts [p.398].** The federal rule **is constitutional** despite the fact that it can prevent an accused from proving a valid claim that he was deprived of his Sixth Amendment entitlement to an impartial, competent jury.

F. WAIVER OF THE RIGHT TO TRIAL BY JURY [pp.398-399]

The right to jury trial **may be waived** so long as the waiver is **knowing and voluntary.** Most states condition an accused's ability to waive jury trial on the consent of the prosecutor or the approval of the judge or both. Because there is **no constitutional right to waive a jury trial or to have a bench trial,** as a general rule, jurisdictions are free to so restrict an accused's ability to waive the right to jury trial.

 ## 20 THE GUARANTEE AGAINST DOUBLE JEOPARDY

The **Fifth Amendment Double Jeopardy Clause** provides that **no person shall be subject for the same offense to be twice put in jeopardy of life or limb.** This guarantee protects against **successive prosecutions** for the same offense and protects against **multiple punishment** for the same offense.

A. THE PROTECTION AGAINST ''SUCCESSIVE PROSECUTIONS'' FOR THE ''SAME OFFENCE'' [pp.405-418]

The protection of the Double Jeopardy Clause against successive prosecutions applies only when *one* **jeopardy has attached and terminated** and a *second* **jeopardy is contemplated.**

1. ''Attachment'' of Jeopardy [pp.405-406]

Jeopardy attaches in a **criminal trial** only when a person is at risk of conviction and attaches in certain **juvenile adjudicatory hearings** that are analogous to criminal trials.

a. Point of attachment in jury trials [p.405]. In jury trials, jeopardy attaches **when the jury is sworn.**

b. Point of attachment in bench trials [p.406]. In bench trials, jeopardy attaches **when the first witness is sworn** or at the **beginning of the introduction of evidence.**

c. Point of attachment when an accused pleads guilty [p.406]. When a defendant pleads guilty, jeopardy attaches **when the court accepts the plea.**

2. ''Termination'' of Jeopardy [pp.406-412]

Various events can terminate jeopardy, including acquittals, convictions, mistrials, and dismissals.

a. **"Acquittals" [p.407].** An **acquittal** terminates jeopardy even if the acquittal is **egregiously erroneous.** A **verdict of not guilty** is an acquittal. A **verdict of guilty for a lesser included offense** is an acquittal of the greater, inclusive offense. Moreover, a ruling by a judge is an acquittal if it represents a **resolution in the defendant's favor of some or all of the factual elements of the offense** or if it is **based on a defense that establishes a lack of culpability.**

b. **"Convictions" [pp.408-409].** An **unreversed conviction** or a **conviction reversed on grounds of insufficient evidence** terminates jeopardy. A **conviction reversed for trial error or on "weight of the evidence" grounds** does not terminate jeopardy.

c. **"Dismissals" [pp.409-410].** A **dismissal** is a trial court ruling in the defendant's favor **on grounds unrelated to guilt or innocence.** The **"label"** given to the ruling is **not determinative.** The question is whether the court has decided that a defendant cannot be convicted for some reason other than "a lack of criminal culpability."

A dismissal that has been **requested or consented to by the defense** does not terminate jeopardy. A dismissal that has **not** been **requested or consented to by the defense** terminates jeopardy.

d. **Mistrials [pp.411-412].** A **mistrial** is a ruling that a trial cannot or should not continue but is not a ruling in favor of either side.

In general, a mistrial **requested or consented to by the defense** does not terminate jeopardy. However, if the request or consent results from **government conduct intended to goad or provoke the defendant into moving for a mistrial,** the mistrial terminates jeopardy.

In general, a mistrial **granted over the defendant's objection** on the court's initiative or at the request of the prosecutor terminates jeopardy. However, in cases of **manifest necessity** for the mistrial, jeopardy is not terminated. Manifest necessity is a **high degree of need.** Whether it exists depends on all the relevant circumstances, including possible alternative remedies that would allow a trial to continue.

3. **Proceedings That Constitute a "Second" Jeopardy [p.413]**

When a first jeopardy has terminated, the Fifth Amendment bars a second jeopardy. An accused is put in a second jeopardy by **any further proceedings devoted to the resolution of factual issues going to the elements of the offense.** Both an entirely new trial and the resumption of a previous trial qualify as second jeopardies.

Appellate review and reversal of a ruling that terminates jeopardy are not barred by double jeopardy *if* a conviction can be entered without "further proceedings" devoted to resolving factual issues pertaining to the elements. In that case, there is no second jeopardy.

4. **Meaning of the "Same Offense" in Successive Prosecution Contexts [pp.414-416]**

The Fifth Amendment prohibits double jeopardy—successive prosecutions—only for **"the same offense."**

a. **"Same sovereign" requirement [p.414].** Two offenses can be the *same* only if they are crimes against **the same sovereign.** According to the **"dual sovereignty doctrine,"** when offenses are defined, charged, and prosecuted by "separate sovereigns" there is no double jeopardy bar.

b. **"Same act or transaction" requirement [p.415].** Offenses are the *same* only if they are **based on the same act or transaction.** Prosecutions for identical charges based on different acts do not trigger double jeopardy protection.

c. **"Elements" test of Blockburger v. United States [pp.415-416].** To be the *same*, two offenses **need not be identical in elements or in actual proof.** According to the *Blockburger* test, whether two offenses are the same depends on their statutory elements. If **each offense requires proof of an additional fact that the other does not**—that is, if **each has an element that is not included in the other**—the offenses are **not the same.** If **every element of one offense is also an element of the other offense,** the two **are the same.** For some offenses such as felony murder and criminal contempt, a court may have to look beyond the "generic" or "abstract" statutory elements to the elements that actually have been or will be proven.

If two offenses are the same, the bar on "successive prosecutions" applies no matter which is prosecuted first.

5. **Exceptions to the Prohibition on "Successive Prosecutions for the Same Offense" [pp.417-418]**

There are exceptions to the bar on successive prosecutions for two offenses that are the *same* under *Blockburger.* If the government first prosecutes one offense, it may later prosecute a more serious offense *if* it was initially **unable to proceed on the more serious charge** either because the **additional facts necessary to sustain that charge had not occurred** or **had not been discovered despite the exercise of due diligence.** There is an additional exception to the successive prosecutions bar if **the defendant is "solely responsible" for the successive prosecutions.**

6. **The "Collateral Estoppel" Doctrine of Ashe v. Swenson [p.418]**

    According to the **collateral estoppel doctrine**—which may bar a successive prosecution even if two offenses are *not* the same—when **an issue of ultimate fact has once been determined in the defendant's favor by a valid and final judgment,** double jeopardy principles bar **the same government** from relitigating **that same issue** in a criminal proceeding against **the same defendant.**

B. **THE PROTECTION AGAINST "MULTIPLE PUNISHMENT" FOR THE "SAME OFFENSE" [pp.419-428]**

    The Double Jeopardy Clause also prohibits **multiple punishment for the same offense.** The multiple punishment protection contains three separate safeguards. In addition, there is one double jeopardy protection against "punishment" that is actually part of the guarantee against successive prosecutions.

    1. **The General Rule Allowing Sentence Increases and the Requirement of "Credit" for Time Served [pp.419-420]**

        When a defendant is retried following the reversal of a conviction, double jeopardy almost always **allows imposition of a higher sentence** for the second conviction. However, double jeopardy **does require** that the accused be given **credit for time served** because of the initial conviction.

    2. **Prohibition on "Cumulative Punishment" for the Same Offense at a Single Trial [pp.420-421]**

        When an accused is tried at a single trial for separate statutory crimes, double jeopardy bars **cumulative punishment for the same offense.** For purposes of this rule, however, whether two offenses are the *same* depends wholly on legislative intent—**two offenses are the "same" only if the legislature did not intend them to be punished cumulatively.** The *Blockburger* "elements" test is a guide to legislative intent. If two offenses are the same under *Blockburger*, it is presumed that cumulative punishment was not intended; if they are not the same, it is presumed that cumulative punishment was intended. These presumptions are rebuttable.

    3. **Prohibition on Multiple Punishments Imposed After Separate Proceedings [pp.421-426]**

        A legislature may not authorize **multiple punishments** for two offenses that are the same under *Blockburger* if the punishments are imposed **after separate trials**—even if one of the trials is "civil" in nature.

        a. **Standards for determining whether a sanction is punishment for double jeopardy purposes [pp.422-424].**   A civil sanction is subject to this multiple punishment bar only if it is *so punitive* as to constitute **punishment for purposes of the Double Jeopardy Clause.** Relevant criteria include **legislative intent,** the **history** of the sanction, and the **character** of the sanction.

If a **legislature intends** a sanction to be punitive, it is punishment. If the legislature does not intend punishment, a sanction still may be punishment. Legislative intent can be gleaned from the nature and characteristics of a proceeding, the bases for imposing the sanction, and an inconsistency between the legislative label and the sanction's nature.

The historical and traditional understanding of a sanction as civil and remedial rather than criminal or punitive can indicate that the sanction is not punishment.

The **character of the sanction** is probably the most important criterion. If a civil sanction serves the goals of punishment—retribution and deterrence—it constitutes punishment. If it serves remedial purposes, it is not punishment. Compensation is a remedial goal, and even deterrence can qualify as remedial. Sanctions that are not remedial, but serve other "nonpunitive" purposes, are not punishment.

b. **Individualized, case-by-case assessment versus categorical evaluation of sanctions [pp.425-426].**   A **civil, compensatory penalty,** such as a fine, must be **judged on an individualized, case-by-case basis.** In the rare instance in which the magnitude of the sanction is seriously **disproportionate** to its remedial objectives and the sanction can be explained only as also serving **retributive or deterrent purposes,** it will be deemed punitive. The sanction must be **reduced** to a level that is roughly proportionate to remedial goals.

Other kinds of sanctions are **judged categorically**—by looking to the *type* of sanction imposed rather than the individual sanction imposed in a specific case. In United States v. Ursery, the Supreme Court used a "two-part test" for civil, in rem forfeitures. The first inquiry was whether the legislature **intended** the proceedings to be civil or criminal. The second was whether the proceedings were **so punitive** in **fact** that they could not legitimately be viewed as civil in nature.

c. **Possible additional limitations on the scope of the protection against multiple punishment at separate trials [p.426].**   The prohibition on multiple punishment at separate criminal and civil trials applies *only* when the two sanctions are **for the same offense,** *may not* apply if the **civil punishment is imposed before the criminal punishment,** and *may not* apply if the civil and criminal proceedings are not conducted sequentially but are instituted **simultaneously** or **very close in time.**

4. **Exception to the General Rule Allowing Higher Sentences after Retrial: The Doctrine of Bullington v. Missouri [pp.426-428]**

Ordinarily, double jeopardy allows both a second sentencing proceeding and a "higher sentence" when a second conviction follows the reversal of an initial conviction. An "exception" to this rule applies when an accused is put in jeopardy of the death penalty at a **trial-like capital sentencing proceeding** and is **"acquitted" of the death penalty**—that is, sentenced to life imprisonment. In that case, there is **an absolute bar to a second capital sentencing trial.**

a. **Applicability of the** *Bullington* **exception to noncapital sentencing proceedings [p.427].** It is unclear whether the bar on successive sentencing proceedings applies only to capital sentencing trials. It *may* also apply to some trial-like noncapital sentencing proceedings.

b. **Requirements for a "trial-like" sentencing proceeding [pp.427-428].** In *Bullington,* the exception to the ordinary rule allowing second sentencing proceedings rested on the "trial-like" nature of the state's capital sentencing proceedings. Those proceedings were "trial-like" because (1) juries were **not given unbounded discretion** to select a punishment but instead were given a **choice between two alternatives** and **standards to guide the choice;** (2) the prosecution had **the burden** of establishing certain facts **beyond a reasonable doubt;** and (3) the accused had the **opportunity to present additional evidence** and could not be sentenced to death without a **unanimous jury determination.**

c. **Effects of the** *Bullington* **prohibition on successive sentencing proceedings [p.428].** If a sentencing proceeding falls within the *Bullington* exception, an **acquittal or other termination of jeopardy for a sentence bars a second jeopardy for that sentence**—that is, the double jeopardy bar on "successive prosecutions" applies.

21   APPEALS OF CRIMINAL CONVICTIONS

A **direct appeal of a conviction** is the final step in adjudicating guilt or innocence. Most states and the federal system provide a right to appeal to an "intermediate" appellate court, followed by an opportunity for discretionary review by the highest appellate court.

A. THE DEFENDANT'S RIGHT TO APPEAL AND THE GOVERNMENT'S INABILITY TO APPEAL [pp.435-436]

Defendants have the right to seek appellate reversal of flawed convictions. The government is unable to obtain appellate reversal of flawed acquittals.

1. The Defendant's Right to Appeal a Conviction [p.435]

While there is **no constitutional right to appeal a conviction,** all jurisdictions provide defendants with the **statutory right to at least one direct appeal.** There are also opportunities for discretionary review by the highest state court and the United States Supreme Court.

2. The Government's Inability to Obtain Appellate Reversal of an Acquittal [pp.435-436]

While statutes provide the government with some opportunities to seek appellate review of adverse rulings in criminal cases, the Double Jeopardy Clause restricts the availability of appellate relief for the government. The government **may not obtain appellate reversal of an erroneous acquittal in order to retry a defendant.**

B. THE DEFENDANT'S RIGHTS ON APPEAL [pp.436-437]

Both the **Due Process** and **Equal Protection Clauses** provide defendants with certain rights on appeal.

1. Entitlement to Due Process on Appeal [p.436]

The **Due Process Clause guarantees fairness** between the state and the individual. Consequently, a jurisdiction's appellate process must **not be arbitrary** and must **afford a fair opportunity** for adjudication on the merits, **meaningful access to the appellate system,** and **an adequate opportunity to present claims fairly.** Specifically, in a **first appeal as of right** every defendant has a **right to the effective assistance of counsel** and a **transcript,** if one is necessary for meaningful review.

2. Guarantee of Equal Protection on Appeal [pp.436-437]

Because the **Equal Protection Clause** guards against **invidious discrimination,** a state **may not deny one class of individuals meaningful access to the appellate system or an adequate opportunity for review.** A state denies equal protection when it **fails to provide indigents with counsel for first appeals as of right.**

C. GENERAL PRINCIPLES OF APPELLATE REVIEW [pp.437-439]

Certain general principles of appellate review are followed in most jurisdictions.

1. Final Judgment Rule and Its Exceptions [pp.437-438]

Typically, defendants may appeal only **final judgments** or **final decisions.**

They may not appeal prior to conviction and sentencing, but states may authorize **interlocutory appeals** from rulings prior to final judgment.

A **"collateral order" exception to the final judgment rule** permits appeals from orders that are not final judgments *if* the orders conclusively determine a disputed question, resolve an important issue separate from the merits of the case, and would be effectively unreviewable if not appealed before final judgment.

2. The General Bar on Prosecution Appeals and Statutory Allowances [pp.438-439]

Over time, there has been movement away from the general bar on government appeals. Jurisdictions have provided considerable opportunities for the prosecution to appeal final judgments and to pursue interlocutory appeals of certain other rulings.

3. Prohibition on Appeal of Moot Cases [p.439]

In general, an appellate court will not review a case that has become **moot** after trial has ended and before the appeal has been decided. A case is moot when an appellate decision can no longer have any consequences.

4. Rule Against Review of Issues Not Raised at Trial and the "Plain Error" Doctrine [p.439]

In general, a party may not seek appellate correction of an error not brought to the attention of the trial court unless there was a good reason for the failure to do so. However, an appellate court has discretion to reverse a conviction on the basis of **plain error**—error that is **clear or obvious and that affected substantial rights of the defendant**—even though it was not raised at trial.

D. RETROACTIVITY OF RULES OF CONSTITUTIONAL LAW TO CASES ON APPEAL [p.440]

A **new rule** of constitutional law pertaining to the conduct of criminal prosecutions is **to be applied retroactively to all cases pending on direct review or not yet final** at the time the rule is announced. The new rule is to be applied in every subsequent judicial review of such cases.

E. HARMLESS ERROR ON APPEAL [pp.441-442]

Appellate courts will not reverse convictions based on **harmless errors** in the trial court.

1. Nonconstitutional Errors: Federal and State Standards [p.441]

A **nonconstitutional error is harmless** if the court is sure the error **did not influence the jury or had very slight effect.** It is **not harmless** if it had **substantial and injurious effect or influence in determining the jury's verdict.**

2. **Constitutional "Trial Errors": The "Beyond a Reasonable Doubt" Standard [pp.441-442]**

   For a **constitutional** *trial* error—an error that occurs during the presentation of the case to the jury—to be harmless, it must have been **harmless beyond a reasonable doubt.**

3. **Constitutional "Structural Defects": Automatically Reversible Errors [p.442]**

   A **constitutional structural defect**—a defect that affects the framework within which the trial proceeds—**cannot be harmless.** When such a defect is found on appeal, **reversal is automatic.**

F. **CONSTITUTIONAL PROTECTION AGAINST GOVERNMENTAL VINDICTIVENESS BASED ON APPEAL OF A CONVICTION [pp.442-446]**

   Following a successful appeal, the **Due Process Clause** limits prosecutors' authority to charge the defendant with a more serious offense and judges' power to impose a higher sentence upon reconviction.

   1. **Due Process Clause Protection Against Vindictiveness [pp.442-443]**

      Due process requires that **vindictiveness** play no part in the sentence a defendant receives after a new trial following a successful appeal. If a defendant demonstrates that a higher sentence is the product of **actual vindictiveness,** the sentence is unconstitutional.

   2. **Presumption of Vindictive Sentencing: The Doctrine of North Carolina v. Pearce [pp.443-445]**

      According to the doctrine of North Carolina v. Pearce, certain circumstances give rise to a **rebuttable presumption of unconstitutional vindictiveness** in resentencing. The presumption arises only if there is a **reasonable likelihood that an increase is the product of actual vindictiveness.** For a reasonable likelihood of vindictiveness to be found, the following circumstances must be present.

      a. **The sentence must be higher and must be imposed by the same sentencing authority [pp.443-444].**   The second sentence after reconviction must be **higher** and must be **imposed by the same sentencing authority** that imposed the initial sentence. Only then is there a sentence **"increase."**

      b. **The sentencing authority must have had her judgment challenged and overturned [p.444].**   The presumption arises only if **the sentencing authority** imposing the two sentences **had her judgment challenged and overturned** by another authority.

c.   **Both sentencing decisions must be made in essentially the same circumstances [p.444].**   For the presumption to arise, the two sentencing decisions must be made **in similar circumstances on the basis of presumptively similar information.** If the circumstances surrounding the resentencing and the information available to the trial judge are materially different, the likelihood of vindictiveness is insufficient to trigger the presumption.

d.   **Rebuttal of the presumption of vindictive sentencing [p.445].**   Unless the *Pearce* presumption is rebutted, a higher sentence must be vacated. A judge can rebut the presumption of vindictiveness with **new "objective" information that justifies the sentencing increase.**

3.   **Presumption of Vindictive Charging: The Doctrine of Blackledge v. Perry [p.446]**

A presumption of unconstitutional vindictiveness also arises when a **prosecutor files a more serious charge following a successful appeal** of a conviction. For the presumption to arise, a more serious charge must be filed after an appeal and those charges must cover the same conduct as the initial charges. Whether the *same prosecutor* must file the charges in both proceedings is an unsettled question. The presumption of prosecutorial vindictiveness is also rebuttable. A showing that it was initially **impossible to proceed on the more serious charges** will **rebut** the presumption.

 COLLATERAL CHALLENGES AND REMEDIES

Requests for **collateral remedies**—such as writs of habeas corpus or coram nobis or motions to vacate sentences—are civil actions outside the direct channel of criminal case adjudication. When appellate review is no longer available, prisoners may pursue collateral challenges to obtain release from confinement alleged to be unlawful because of serious errors in the process leading to conviction. While both federal and state systems provide collateral remedies, the discussion here focuses on the federal remedy available to state prisoners—the **writ of habeas corpus**—and the federal remedy available to federal prisoners—the **motion to vacate a sentence.**

> **Note:** In 1996, the **Antiterrorism and Effective Death Penalty Act** (the 1996 Act) made several changes to the law pertaining to federal collateral remedies. This outline describes the law *prior* to the 1996 Act, then highlights the areas in which changes were made.

A. THE "SUSPENSION CLAUSE" OF THE UNITED STATES CONSTITUTION [p.451]

Article I, section 9 of the Constitution prohibits **suspension of the writ of habeas corpus.** One view holds that this provision creates **a right to federal habeas corpus.** Another holds that it merely prohibits Congress from making state habeas corpus unavailable to federal prisoners. The Supreme Court has not endorsed either position.

B. FEDERAL COLLATERAL REMEDIES AND THEIR UNDERLYING POLICIES [pp.452-453]

Federal statutes provide collateral remedies for both federal and state prisoners.

1. Current Statutes That Govern Federal Collateral Remedies [p.452]

Under 28 U.S.C. §2254, federal courts are authorized to grant **habeas corpus** relief to those in **state custody** under specified conditions. Under 28 U.S.C. §2255, federal courts are authorized to grant federal prisoners' **motions to vacate sentences.**

2. Competing Policies That Underlie Requests for Collateral Relief [pp.452-453]

The federal statutes and the Supreme Court's interpretations of those statutes reflect attempts to accommodate the competing policies underlying collateral relief. On the one hand, the availability of collateral remedies insures that fundamental rights are observed and guards against unjust imprisonment. On the other hand, collateral remedies entail substantial costs—they undermine finality, upset the federal-state balance, interfere with state criminal justice processes, frustrate efforts to punish the guilty, and drain resources.

C. THE "IN CUSTODY" AND "EXHAUSTION OF REMEDIES" REQUIREMENTS [pp.453-454]

To secure federal collateral relief, an individual must be **in custody** and must first **exhaust other available remedies.**

1. In-Custody Requirement [p.453]

A state or federal petitioner must be **in custody**—either actually confined or otherwise subject to substantial restraints on freedom.

2. Exhaustion of Remedies Requirement [p.454]

A state prisoner must first **exhaust remedies *still* available in state court.** The **1996 Act** permits courts to deny requests for habeas relief "on the merits" despite a failure to exhaust remedies and requires that a waiver of the exhaustion requirement be express.

D. SUBJECT MATTER OF CLAIMS FOR COLLATERAL RELIEF [pp.454-455]

While federal collateral relief is generally available for claims of unconstitutional confinement, not all such claims are cognizable.

1. **General Predicate for Collateral Relief: "Unconstitutional" Custody [pp.454-455]**

   State and federal prisoners may request collateral relief on the grounds that they are being held in custody **in violation of the Constitution or laws of the United States.** Relief is available for a constitutional defect in the process leading to conviction and incarceration.

2. **Exception for Fourth Amendment Exclusionary Rule Claims: The Doctrine of Stone v. Powell [p.455]**

   A state prisoner may not obtain habeas corpus relief on the ground that evidence obtained in violation of the **Fourth Amendment** was used to convict her *if* the state afforded the prisoner **a "full and fair opportunity"** to litigate the claim. Other sorts of claims may be raised even though a state has afforded a full and fair opportunity to litigate.

3. **Inapplicability of "New Rules" of Constitutional Law on Habeas Corpus: The "Retroactivity" Doctrine of Teague v. Lane [pp.456-458]**

   In Teague v. Lane, the Court held that **"new rules"** of constitutional law ordinarily **do not apply in habeas corpus proceedings.**

   a. *Teague* **limitation on cognizable habeas claims [pp.456-457].** A state prisoner ordinarily **may not obtain habeas corpus relief based on a "new rule" of constitutional law** announced after his conviction became final. Except in two rare instances, such **new rules do not apply retroactively to convictions on collateral review.** Habeas petitioners cannot obtain relief based on claims that would require either the application or the announcement of a new rule.

   b. **Meaning of "new rule" [p.457].** A rule of constitutional law is **new** if it breaks new ground, if it imposes a new obligation on state or federal governments, if it leads to a result not dictated by existing precedent, if there have been reasonable contrary conclusions by other courts, or if it was susceptible to debate by reasonable minds.

   c. **Two "exceptions" to the bar on habeas claims resting on "new rules" [pp.457-458].** There are **two exceptions** to the holding that new rules are not retroactive to cases on collateral review.

   First, a new rule will be retroactive if it **places** certain kinds of **conduct beyond the power of the criminal lawmaking power** to proscribe or

prohibits imposition of a certain type of **punishment for** a class of defendants because of their status or offense.

Second, a new rule will be retroactive if it requires the observance of **procedures that are implicit in ordered liberty.** The rule must be a **watershed rule** of criminal procedure **that implicates the fundamental fairness of the trial.** It must involve new procedures without which the **likelihood of an accurate conviction is seriously diminished** and must **alter our understanding of** the bedrock procedural **elements essential to** the **fairness** of a proceeding.

E.   PROCEDURAL IMPEDIMENTS TO COLLATERAL RELIEF [pp.459-468]

Federal collateral relief may also be denied on a variety of "procedural" grounds.

1.   "State Procedural Default" Bar to Collateral Relief [pp.459-463]

When a state has declined to address the merits of a federal claim because a prisoner has failed to meet a state procedural requirement, the **state procedural default** limitation may bar federal habeas corpus review of the prisoner's claim. (A **federal procedural default** also may bar a federal prisoner's motion to vacate a sentence.) Relief should be denied unless the prisoner establishes **cause and prejudice** or shows that a **fundamental miscarriage of justice** will result.

   a.   **Need for an independent and adequate state procedural ground [pp.459-460].**   The "state procedural default" limitation applies only if the state court's judgment is actually based on a procedural default that is **independent** of the merits of the federal claim and **adequate** to sustain the state court's judgment.

   If a state court judgment **fairly appears** to rest primarily on or be interwoven with **federal law** and the court does not include a **clear and express statement** of its reliance on an independent and adequate state ground, there is a **conclusive presumption** that the judgment does not rest on the independent and adequate state ground. Collateral review is not barred.

   b.   **"Cause and prejudice" exception [pp.460-462].**   A prisoner can avoid the "state procedural default" bar to collateral relief if her claim falls within the **"cause and prejudice" exception.**

   The petitioner must establish **"cause for the procedural default"**— some objective factor external to the defense that impeded efforts to comply with the state's procedural rule. Cause is shown if the factual or legal basis for the claim was not reasonably available or if state interference made compliance with the procedural requirement impracticable. The "futility" of presenting an objection is *not cause.* Moreover, counsel's ignorance or inadvertence is *not cause* unless it constitutes "ineffective assistance."

A petitioner must also show **"actual prejudice"** as a result of the constitutional violation. While a petitioner must show **an effect on** the outcome of the trial, she need not show that it is *more likely than not* that she would not have been convicted. A *reasonable probability* of a different outcome is probably sufficient.

c. **"Fundamental miscarriage of justice" or "unjust incarceration" exception [pp.462-463].** A petitioner can also avoid the "state procedural default" bar if her claim falls within the **"fundamental miscarriage of justice" or "unjust incarceration" exception.** To establish that a fundamental miscarriage of justice will result if a claim is not considered, the petitioner must establish that **a constitutional violation has probably resulted in the conviction of one who is actually innocent.** More specifically, she must demonstrate that it is **more likely than not that no reasonable juror would have found her guilty beyond a reasonable doubt.**

2. **Procedural Bars Resulting from "Multiple" Petitions for Collateral Relief [pp.463-468]**

Two doctrines, the **"successive petition" doctrine** and the **"abuse of writ" doctrine,** raise procedural bars to second or subsequent petitions for collateral relief.

a. **Petitions for collateral relief raising claims previously adjudicated: The "successive petition" doctrine [pp.463-464].** Ordinarily a federal court **may not reach the merits of "successive claims"** for collateral relief—claims that rest on grounds that were raised and rejected on the merits in a prior petition. There *may be* a **cause and prejudice exception** to the "successive petition" bar. If there is, presumably a petitioner would have to show some "objective reason" that she should be allowed to raise her claim a second time and a "reasonable probability" of a different outcome.

There *is* an **exception** to the "successive petition" bar if collateral review is necessary to prevent a **fundamental miscarriage of justice.** The exception is identical to the "fundamental miscarriage of justice" exception to the "state procedural default" bar.

b. **Petitions for collateral relief raising claims not previously raised: The "abuse of writ" doctrine [pp.465-466].** An **"abusive petition"** is a second or subsequent petition for habeas relief raising grounds that were available but not relied on in a prior petition. Under the **"abuse of writ" doctrine,** if the petitioner **deliberately withheld the newly asserted ground** in the prior petition **or otherwise abused the** writ, a federal court **should refuse to entertain** the petition unless the petitioner demonstrates either **cause and prejudice** or that a **fundamental miscarriage of justice** would occur.

The **government has the burden of pleading abuse**—that a ground was either deliberately withheld or not raised because of "inexcusable neglect." The petitioner **has the burden of disproving abuse** by showing either (1) **cause for failing to raise the claim** in the earlier petition and **prejudice from the alleged constitutional violation** or (2) that a **fundamental miscarriage of justice** would result from a failure to entertain the claim. The terms have the same meaning as in the "state procedural default" context.

The **1996 Act** made several changes pertaining to "multiple" petitions for collateral relief. Students should consult the full text of the outline for the details of those changes. **[pp.467-468]**.

3. Delay in Seeking Collateral Relief [p.468]

State and federal prisoners' requests for collateral relief may be denied because of a **delay in bringing the claims.** A federal court has "equitable discretion" to dismiss a petition if delay has **prejudiced the state's ability to respond** *and* if the **petitioner failed to exercise "reasonable diligence"** in bringing a claim.

The **1996 Act** creates one-year "statutes of limitation" for the filing of petitions for collateral relief.

F. EVIDENTIARY HEARINGS AND STATE COURT FINDINGS OF FACT AND DETERMINATIONS OF LAW [pp.469-473]

In some circumstances, a federal court *must* hold an **evidentiary hearing** in habeas proceedings; in others, it *may* do so. Moreover, in some circumstances, **findings of fact by state courts** are **presumed to be correct.** Resolutions of **legal questions and mixed questions of law and fact by state courts are not presumed to be correct.**

1. Evidentiary Hearings in Habeas Corpus Proceedings: The Holding of Townsend v. Sain [pp.469-470]

A federal court has "plenary" power to hold an **"evidentiary hearing"** to determine facts pertaining to habeas corpus claims and must do so unless a state court has reliably found the relevant facts after holding a full and fair hearing. An evidentiary hearing is required in six specific situations. In all other cases, a federal court *may* in its discretion hold an evidentiary hearing.

2. State Court Resolutions of Factual and Legal Questions [pp.470-473]

Section 2254(d) of Title 28 of the United States Code prescribes the circumstances in which findings of fact by state courts must be presumed correct and specifies the showing required to overcome that presumption. The presumption limits the power to relitigate factual issues in federal court.

a. **The §2254(d) "presumption of correctness" for state court findings of fact [pp.470-471].** According to §2254(d), **a state court determination of a factual issue** after a hearing on the merits, evidenced in writing, **shall be presumed to be correct.** Rebuttal of the presumption requires convincing evidence that the state factual determination was erroneous. There are eight specific situations in which the **presumption of correctness does not arise.**

b **Federal court authority to determine questions of law [pp.471-472].** The "presumption of correctness" applies only to findings on **questions of fact.** A federal court has a duty to make independent determinations of both **legal questions** and **mixed questions of fact and law;** it may not defer to state court determinations of either.

Questions of law concern the determination of what the law is on a particular subject. **Questions of fact** concern the determination of "basic, primary, or historical facts." **Mixed questions of fact and law** require the application of a legal standard to the historical facts. It is sometimes difficult to determine whether a particular question is a "question of fact" or a "mixed question." In those circumstances, a question is classified as "factual" if the state court seems better positioned to decide it and "mixed" if the federal court seems better positioned to decide it.

The **1996 Act** changed the law in ways that seem to require some deference to state court resolutions of legal questions and to increase the deference that must be accorded state court factfinding.

G. HARMLESS ERROR ON COLLATERAL REVIEW [pp.473-474]

Harmless error standards in federal habeas corpus proceedings are different from those on direct appeal in one significant respect. In habeas proceedings, a **constitutional** *trial* **error** need not be "harmless beyond a reasonable doubt." Instead, it **is harmless if it did not result in actual prejudice**—that is, **if it did not have substantial and injurious effect or influence on the jury.** Presumably, **constitutional** *structural* **errors** are treated the same as they are on direct appeal—that is, they are never harmless and result in automatic reversal.

PART I

INTRODUCTION TO CRIMINAL PROCEDURE

Part I is a brief introduction to criminal procedure. Its purpose is to lay a foundation for the study of the substance of the law of criminal procedure that is covered in Parts II and III.

- **Chapter 1** describes the nature and content of the law encountered in criminal procedure courses and explains the significance of the topics addressed by those courses.

- **Chapter 2** briefly sketches the typical stages through which a criminal case progresses. This sketch provides students with a basis for understanding the contexts in which the law of criminal procedure operates.

- **Chapter 3** discusses a number of general, foundational concepts. The topics include the limited application of the Bill of Rights to the federal government, the regulation of state criminal processes by the Fourteenth Amendment Due Process Clause, the independence of state constitutional provisions, the federal supervisory power, and the assignment and weight of burdens of proof regarding constitutional claims.

THE STUDY OF CRIMINAL PROCEDURE

CHAPTER OVERVIEW

This brief chapter describes the nature of the law that is the focus of courses in criminal procedure, sketches the basic division of criminal procedure into "investigatory" and "adjudicatory" courses, addresses the significance of studying criminal procedure, and highlights the importance of maintaining a larger perspective while learning the vast array of doctrinal standards that have been developed.

More specifically, it discusses:

- **Content of criminal procedure courses.** The law of criminal procedure is almost exclusively **constitutional law.** The Bill of Rights guarantees that restrict the processes of criminal justice are the primary source of the rules and standards encountered.

- **Division between "investigatory" and "adjudicatory" criminal procedure.** Typically, law schools offer two criminal procedure courses. The **"investigatory"** or **"police practices"** course is concerned with Bill of Rights provisions that limit official authority to investigate and prove crimes. The **"adjudicatory"** or **"trial rights"** course addresses constitutional rights accorded the accused in the more formal pretrial, trial, and post-trial phases of criminal cases.

- **Significance of criminal procedure.** The rights that form the core of both courses are vital constituents of the free society designed by the Framers of our Constitution. Every lawyer should have a general understanding of these guarantees and an appreciation of their roles.

- **Doctrinal details and the larger perspective.** Students of criminal procedure should absorb the array of doctrinal standards and details that give content to the general terms of the Constitution; at the same time they should try to keep the bigger constitutional picture in view.

A. CONTENT OF CRIMINAL PROCEDURE COURSES

Early on, most law students take courses in substantive criminal law and civil procedure. One might expect a criminal procedure course to blend the attributes of those two courses—to be analogous to the study of civil procedure but to focus on the rules applicable to criminal trials. That is not the case. For the most part, criminal procedure courses are actually devoted to the study of **constitutional law.** More specifically, the courses focus on constitutional rights that regulate the processes of criminal justice. The modes of reasoning and analysis brought to bear on criminal procedure questions are those generally employed in analyzing other issues of constitutional law.

B. INVESTIGATORY VERSUS ADJUDICATORY CRIMINAL PROCEDURE

Law school curricula typically contain at least two courses devoted to the study of criminal procedure—a **basic "investigatory"** or **"police practices"** course and an **advanced "adjudicatory"** or **"trial rights" course.** This outline is designed for use in **both criminal procedure courses.** It endeavors to address most of the major topics that are addressed in both the "investigatory" and the "adjudicatory" courses. Part II of the outline treats the topics covered in the police practices course. Part III discusses those encountered in the trial rights course.

1. The "Police Practices" Course

Students are often required to take a basic criminal procedure course that covers constitutional guarantees applicable to the **"investigatory" stages** of a criminal case. It treats **Fourth, Fifth, and Sixth Amendment guarantees** that restrict law enforcement officers' authority to investigate crimes and to secure evidence that can be used to prosecute criminals. Specifically, it addresses the constraints on **searches and seizures, government participation** in criminal offenses, methods used to obtain **confessions,** techniques designed to secure eyewitness **identifications,** and the **rules of exclusion** that bar illegally obtained evidence from criminal trials.

2. The "Trial Rights" Course

The advanced criminal procedure course ordinarily addresses rights operative during the **"adjudicatory" phases** of a criminal case—that is, guarantees that come into play during the more formal pretrial, trial, and post-trial stages. This course typically centers on such topics as **discovery** by the defense and prosecution, **bail** and **preventive detention, guilty pleas** and **plea bargaining,** the defendant's rights to a **speedy trial** and **a public trial,** the **public right of access** to criminal proceedings, the **right to counsel** at trial, the **right to trial by jury,** the guarantee against **double jeopardy, appel-**

late review of convictions, and **collateral remedies** for unconstitutional confinement.

C. SIGNIFICANCE OF THE STUDY OF CRIMINAL PROCEDURE

While there are a small number of statutes and rules of procedure that merit consideration, the primary concerns of both criminal procedure courses are fundamental constitutional liberties contained in the Bill of Rights. The Framers of our Constitution considered these liberties essential components of the free society they sought to design. Each Bill of Rights provision governing the processes of criminal justice is a part of the Framers' attempt to strike a balance between individual freedom and societal security. These guarantees define our national character—what we are and what we stand for. They have both substantive and symbolic significance. For these reasons, any well-rounded lawyer should understand and appreciate the content and the functions of the rights encountered in the study of criminal procedure. Indeed, it is arguable that every citizen ought to have a sense of their importance.

D. DOCTRINAL DETAILS AND LARGER PERSPECTIVES

Much of the time, the study of criminal procedure focuses on various narrow rules designed to address specific situations. One objective of the study of criminal procedure is to acquire a working knowledge of the **doctrinal details** that give content to the general, broad terms of the Bill of Rights guarantees. The importance of this objective should not be minimized. The doctrines developed in United States Supreme Court opinions make up the body of law that guides the resolution of criminal procedure claims. An awareness of the controlling standards is essential for intelligent formulation and analysis of those claims.

In the process of learning the important details of the controlling legal standards, students should not lose sight of the **bigger picture.** Each standard or rule that bears on an issue of search and seizure law, for example, tells us something about the balance between personal privacy or physical freedom and the power of law enforcement to detect and capture those who threaten our collective well-being. Each interpretation of the Fourth Amendment—no matter how narrow it may seem—tells us a bit more about how the Constitution resolves the conflict between liberty and security. Without an awareness of this larger perspective, the doctrinal details may seem insignificant, if not absurd. By keeping the big picture clearly in view, students may be able to see that each of these details is an integral part of a fundamental constitutional right. Moreover, they may more fully understand that each of these rights plays a vital role in one of our law's most vital tasks—the creation of an orderly, free society.

THE PROCESSES OF the CRIMINAL JUSTICE SYSTEM

2

CHAPTER OVERVIEW

The rights studied in criminal procedure courses operate against the backdrop of the federal and state criminal justice systems. Many of the cases studied will refer to events or stages that occur during the processing of a criminal case. These events or stages are important because the existence and scope of some of the constitutional rights encountered depend entirely on whether a case has progressed to a particular point in the process. As a result, students should have a general understanding of the functioning processes of criminal justice.

The sketch that follows is a general description of steps that are typical in a criminal case. Those steps include **arrest,** the **initial charge** and **initial appearance,** the **preliminary hearing,** the **formal charge in the trial court, pretrial motions** and **discovery, arraignment** and **trial, post-trial motions, sentencing, appeals of convictions,** and **collateral challenges** by prisoners.

Students should not conclude that the actual systems operating in the various state and federal courts all proceed precisely along the lines described here. In any particular jurisdiction, there may be significant variation in the order of steps, and some stages may be modified or omitted. Moreover, a number of cases will not progress all the way through a system. Many will drop out at various stages of the process. For example, at any step along the way a prosecutor or judge may decide to dismiss charges or a defendant may decide to plead guilty.

A. ARREST

The first formal stage of a case is often the **arrest** of a suspect. A person believed to have committed an offense is physically taken into custody. Police officers sometimes make arrests **pursuant to warrants** issued by magistrates. Other times they make arrests **without warrants** based on their own assessments of probable cause. Sometimes, however, an individual is not arrested until after a **formal charge** of some sort has been filed—for example, a **grand jury indictment** or a **prosecutor's information.**

B.   INITIAL CHARGE AND INITIAL APPEARANCE

Either before or after arrest, a **formal complaint** may be filed. A formal complaint is a document that alleges an offense. Soon after arrest, the suspect makes his or her **initial appearance** in a courtroom. During this appearance, a judge may inform the suspect of the offenses charged and may also apprise her of her rights. One of those rights is the right to the assistance of counsel. For an indigent defendant, the process of appointing a lawyer may begin at this stage. In addition, the judge may prescribe the conditions for a defendant's pretrial release from custody. Some arrestees may be detained prior to trial to ensure their appearance to face the charges or to prevent them from endangering the public prior to trial.

For a less serious charge that is within the jurisdiction of the low-level court in which the initial appearance occurs, a defendant may be asked to enter a plea to the charge during the initial appearance. A guilty plea will result in a conviction. A plea of not guilty will lead to a trial at a later date.

For a serious charge that is not within the jurisdiction of the court, a defendant may well be entitled to a **preliminary hearing.** At the initial appearance, the judge may set a date for the preliminary hearing.

C.   PRELIMINARY HEARING

A **preliminary hearing** (or "prelim") also takes place in the lower court. The object is to determine whether there is a basis for subjecting the accused to a trial for the alleged offense. The standard used for this determination is **probable cause.** Probable cause is much less demanding than the "beyond a reasonable doubt" standard that governs the determination of guilt or innocence at trial. At the preliminary hearing, the judge must decide whether there are grounds from which a reasonable person could suspect that the defendant did commit the crime or crimes charged.

The preliminary hearing is an *adversarial* proceeding. The prosecution presents evidence in support of the charge. The defendant has an opportunity to challenge that evidence and also is entitled to present contradictory evidence to refute the charge. If the court does not find probable cause to support the accusation, it dismisses the charge. If the court finds probable cause, it orders the defendant "bound over" for trial in the higher court with jurisdiction to try the offense.

D. FORMAL CHARGES IN THE TRIAL COURT: INFORMATIONS AND GRAND JURY INDICTMENTS

For a serious criminal case to go forward to trial, the charges must be formalized in writing. Two kinds of documents perform this function: **informations** and **indictments.**

An information is a charging document prepared by a prosecutor. An **indictment** is a charging document returned by a grand jury, a group composed of ordinary citizens. In jurisdictions where an indictment is required for an offense, the prosecutor cannot proceed without first presenting the case to a grand jury. The defendant can be put on trial only if the grand jurors find probable cause and issue a "true bill." If the grand jurors do not find probable cause, they issue "no bill," and the proceedings come to an end. Presentations to grand juries are one-sided and are enveloped in secrecy. The government alone presents evidence in support of the charge; there is no opportunity for a prospective defendant to respond. Moreover, the proceeding is not open to the prospective defendant or any other member of the public. The grand jurors, the prosecution, and the witnesses are the only persons present.

> **Note:** In some jurisdictions, defendants are entitled to either a preliminary hearing before a judge or an indictment by a grand jury, but *not* to both. The prosecutor decides which charging route to pursue.

E. PRETRIAL PROCEEDINGS

Prior to trial, defendants may bring a variety of **pretrial motions.** Some are aimed at securing a dismissal of the charges. For example, a defendant might move to have charges dismissed on grounds that a trial would violate the Double Jeopardy Clause or the Speedy Trial Clause. Others are attempts to have inculpatory evidence excluded from trial. For example, a defendant might move to have narcotics excluded on the ground that they were found as a result of an unreasonable search or might seek to have a confession excluded because it was coerced or because officers failed to comply with the dictates of the *Miranda* doctrine. A judge may rule on these motions at or after holding an evidentiary hearing.

Discovery also occurs during the period prior to trial. At both preliminary hearings and hearings on pretrial motions, each side presents evidence in the presence of the opponent. As a result, those stages serve limited, *informal* discovery functions. Traditionally, *formal* discovery in criminal cases by either side was disfavored. In modern times, however, attitudes have changed. First, the recognition that a defendant has a constitutional entitlement to certain kinds of information in the government's possession has encroached on the antidiscovery tradition. More important, as a matter of policy, most jurisdictions have increasingly required both sides in criminal cases to divulge information to the opponent.

F. THE TRIAL COURT: ARRAIGNMENT AND TRIAL

The **arraignment** is the defendant's **"first appearance"** in the *trial* court. The accused is asked to plead to the charges. A guilty plea results in a conviction and leads to the imposition of a sentence. A plea of not guilty sets the stage for trial.

At the **trial,** the prosecution must prove each essential element of each offense **beyond a reasonable doubt.** For serious charges, the defendant is constitutionally entitled to a jury trial but may waive that right and agree to have a judge serve as the factfinder.

In **jury trials,** selection of the jurors is the first stage. A "venire" or "panel" of potential jurors is summoned to the courtroom and questioned. The questioning of prospective jurors is known as **voir dire.** Depending on the jurisdiction, voir dire may be conducted by the judge alone, by the parties, or by both the judge and the parties. A judge may remove a venireperson on the judge's own initiative or a party may **challenge a juror for cause** if there is reason to believe that he or she cannot serve as an impartial finder of fact. If cause is sufficiently shown, the court must remove the juror. Each side also has a limited number of **"peremptory" challenges** or strikes—challenges that a party may use to remove a juror without providing any reason.

Following jury selection, each side makes an **opening statement** outlining the matters it intends to establish. The **prosecution** then begins to **present its evidence.** After the prosecution has finished its case-in-chief, the **defense may present evidence.** The defense has no obligation to put on a case; it may rest on the claim that the prosecution has failed to sustain its burden of proof. After the defense case concludes, the **prosecution** has a chance to present **rebuttal** evidence. Then, the **defense** has an opportunity to respond with its **rebuttal** evidence.

It is worth noting that at any time during the trial the charges may be **dismissed**— either at the request of the state, on the court's initiative, or upon motion by the defense. Moreover, at the end of the prosecution's case or at the end of all of the evidence, a trial judge may grant a defense motion for **"judgment of acquittal."** In granting such a motion, the judge is ruling in favor of the defendant and preventing the case from reaching the jury. Finally, at all stages of the trial, events can precipitate **mistrials.** A mistrial is a termination of the current trial that contemplates the possibility of a retrial.

In jury trials, the judge is required to **instruct the jurors** on the applicable law. The parties submit the instructions they desire before the judge decides on the instructions to be given. Jury instructions consist of both "standard" instructions applicable to every criminal case and instructions specifically applicable to the case at hand.

After **closing arguments** by each side (sometimes delivered *before* the jury is instructed), the case is submitted to the trier of fact. After deliberations, jurors may return a **verdict** of **guilty** or **not guilty.** If the verdict is not guilty, the defendant is released. Upon a verdict of guilty, the court enters a **judgment of conviction.** Sometimes, despite their best efforts to reach a verdict and further instructions by the court designed to prevent a deadlock, jurors cannot agree. In such "hung jury" cases, a mistrial is declared.

G. POST-TRIAL MOTIONS AND SENTENCING

After trial, post-trial motions may be filed. For example, the defense may request that the court **set aside a guilty verdict** and enter an **acquittal** or may request a **new trial.** Unless such a request is granted, the judge sets a date for **sentencing.** Sentencing schemes vary from jurisdiction to jurisdiction and have changed dramatically over time. Some schemes grant the judge wide discretion to set a term within a statutory range. To make such a decision, the court will receive input from each side both before and during a sentencing hearing. Other schemes prescribe more concrete, restrictive formulas for calculating a defendant's sentence. Still others prescribe by statute the sentence to be imposed—either a specific term of years (10 years in prison) or a set range of years (5 to 10 years in prison).

H. APPEALS AND COLLATERAL CHALLENGES

Ordinarily, a defendant has a limited time within which to file an **appeal** of a conviction. On appeal, the convicted defendant claims that the proceedings below were infected with an error that renders the conviction invalid. Most claims allege that an error tainted the particular proceedings and requires reversal and retrial. A limited number of claims, however, assert error of a kind that requires reversal and precludes retrial for the offense.

After a conviction is final—that is, after an unsuccessful appeal has been pursued or the time for direct appeal has expired—a prisoner still might bring a **collateral challenge.** Such a challenge ordinarily involves a claim that confinement is illegal because of some constitutional infirmity in the process that led to conviction. The word "collateral" refers to the fact that the process invoked and the remedy sought are outside the direct chain of events leading from arrest through trial to conviction and appeal. Federal defendants can bring such challenges in federal courts. State defendants can file collateral challenges both in state and in federal courts. A **writ of habeas corpus** is one type of collateral remedy. Jurisdictions have also created other devices for securing collateral relief. The availability of collateral review is restricted by a number of limitations. Collateral review is the final stage in the formal processes of the criminal justice system.

FOUNDATIONAL CONCEPTS AND PRINCIPLES

CHAPTER OVERVIEW

Each of the following subsections addresses a concept or principle that in some sense is fundamental to the study of criminal procedure. Some of the topics pertain not only to criminal procedure but also to other areas of constitutional law. A basic understanding of these subjects provides a helpful backdrop for the doctrines encountered in criminal procedure. The subjects covered here include the following:

- **Applicability of the Bill of Rights.** The guarantees of the Bill of Rights actually restrict only federal criminal justice processes. Those provisions do not bind the states.

- **The Due Process Clause and state processes.** Although the Bill of Rights does not control state processes, the Fourteenth Amendment Due Process Clause does. By a process of "selective incorporation," the Supreme Court has concluded that almost all of the specific entitlements found in the Bill of Rights are also a part of the "due process" required of state systems.

- **Independence of state constitutions and laws.** States are free to enact "independent" constitutional provisions and laws that provide their citizens with rights that furnish more protection than that afforded by the federal Constitution.

- **The federal supervisory power.** The federal courts have an inherent "supervisory power" over the administration of criminal justice. This power carries an authority to require that the processes and players in the federal criminal justice system satisfy higher standards than those imposed by the Constitution.

- **Burdens of proof on criminal procedure claims.** The issue of who bears the burden of proof on a criminal procedure question has not often been addressed directly by the courts. Ordinarily, the answer can be logically deduced. In most cases, the party with the burden must satisfy the "preponderance of the evidence" standard in order to prevail.

A. APPLICABILITY OF THE BILL OF RIGHTS

As discussed above, criminal procedure courses are primarily concerned with the study of constitutional rights. The rights addressed are specified in the **Bill of Rights.** More specifically, they appear in the **Fourth, Fifth, Sixth,** and **Eighth Amendments** to our Constitution.

According to a long-standing Supreme Court holding in Barron v. Baltimore, 32 U.S. (7 Pet.) 243, 8 L. Ed. 672 (1833), the **Bill of Rights constrains only the federal government.** It does *not* regulate the activities of *state* agents. This means, for example, that the *Fourth Amendment* does not safeguard "the people" against "unreasonable searches and seizures" conducted by *state* law enforcement officers. Nor does the *Sixth Amendment* require *state* court systems to provide counsel, a jury, or a speedy and public trial.

B. THE DUE PROCESS CLAUSE AND STATE CRIMINAL JUSTICE PROCESSES

The **Fourteenth Amendment** provides, in part, that no state shall "deprive any person of life, liberty, or property, without **due process** of law." The Supreme Court has rejected the contention that the drafters of this **Due Process Clause** intended to "incorporate" the Bill of Rights. In other words, the Court has not agreed with the view that those who enacted the guarantee of "due process" literally meant to make the precise guarantees in the first eight amendments applicable directly to the states. Instead, a majority of the Court has endorsed the view that the Due Process Clause requires states to follow procedures and accord rights that are "necessary to an Anglo-American regime of ordered liberty." Duncan v. Louisiana, 391 U.S. 145, 88 S. Ct. 1444, 20 L. Ed. 2d 491 (1968). States must abide by the specific Bill of Rights safeguards that are "fundamental to the American scheme of justice." Id.

The result of this understanding of the Due Process Clause is what has come to be known as a **"selective incorporation"** approach to the relationship between the particulars of the Bill of Rights and the Fourteenth Amendment guarantee. The approach is "selective" in nature because it requires individual analysis and evaluation of each Bill of Rights provision. With regard to each guarantee, the question is whether it is "necessary to an Anglo-American regime of ordered liberty" or "fundamental to the American scheme of justice." For the provisions applicable to the criminal process, however, the practical outcome of this case-by-case approach has been almost complete "incorporation." By virtue of the due process guarantee, the Supreme Court has held that states are obligated to respect every facet of every right found in the Fourth, Fifth, Sixth, and Eighth Amendments **except** the Fifth Amendment **"indictment" requirement,** the Sixth Amendment **jury "unanimity" requirement,** and possibly the Eighth Amendment **safeguard against "excessive bail."** All the other rights in those provisions have been deemed "necessary" and "fundamental" to our "scheme of justice." For students of criminal procedure, this means that with regard to almost every rule and doctrine encountered, the restrictions and obligations imposed on federal and state governments are *identical.*

 # EXAMPLES AND ANALYSIS

1. Barry, a Los Angeles Police Department Detective, unreasonably searched Mick's van. Mick asserts that Barry's actions violate the Fourth Amendment to the United States Constitution. Is he right?

No. Although it is commonly said that a state officer has violated the Fourth Amendment, that statement is incorrect because the Bill of Rights applies only to federal agents. Because the Due Process Clause imposes constraints on state officers identical to those found in the Fourth Amendment, Detective Barry has violated the Fourteenth Amendment, not the Fourth Amendment.

2. Chuck, a legislator, concludes that because the Sixth Amendment does not regulate state practices, the state of Iowa can enact a law banning public trials in order to eliminate prejudicial publicity and speed up the conduct of trials. Is Chuck correct?

No. The "public trial" guarantee of the Sixth Amendment is among the Bill of Rights provisions that have been "selectively incorporated." In other words, the Supreme Court has held that the Fourteenth Amendment guarantee of due process requires states to grant public trials whenever the Sixth Amendment would require a public trial in a federal court. Consequently, Iowa is not free to ban public trials.

C.   INDEPENDENT STATE CONSTITUTIONS AND LAWS

Under Article VI, the United States Constitution is the supreme law of the land. Therefore, states cannot deprive their citizens of any of the rights guaranteed by the Fourteenth Amendment. This means, for example, that states must provide a jury trial and the effective assistance of counsel to every defendant granted those rights by the Due Process Clause.

However, the Constitution does not prohibit states from extending to their citizens "additional" rights—that is, rights not granted by the Fourteenth Amendment. It does not prevent states from giving more expansive versions of the very same rights found in the federal Constitution. A state can provide such rights in its own constitution or by statute. When it does so, the rights provided are **independent** of those found in the federal Constitution. As a result, when a state court is called on to interpret the provisions of a state constitution or statute, it may be guided by but **is not bound by** United States Supreme Court interpretations of the Bill of Rights. See Michigan v. Long, 463 U.S. 1032, 103 S. Ct. 3469, 77 L. Ed. 2d 1201 (1983). Even if the language of a state provision is identical to the language of a Bill of Rights guarantee, the state court is not bound by interpretations of the federal provision.

For example, defendants accused of "petty" offenses do not have a constitutional right to trial by jury under the Fourteenth Amendment. Nonetheless, a state constitutional guarantee of "trial by jury" might be construed to grant every criminal defendant a right to a jury determination. In addition, the Fourteenth Amendment does not provide a right to appointed counsel for indigent state defendants who are charged with misdemeanors unless they are sentenced to "actual imprisonment." A state, however, might provide a statutory entitlement to counsel for all indigent defendants.

If a state court's decision rests on an **"independent and adequate" state legal ground,** it is insulated from reversal on federal law grounds. Even if the decision also rests on an erroneous federal premise, a federal court should not overturn it. However, if a state's decision is ambiguous and could be based on either federal or state law, a reviewing court will not presume that it is based on state law. Michigan v. Long. To insure that a federal court correctly understands that a state court decision actually rests on an independent and adequate state basis and should not be reversed on federal grounds, a state court must include a **"plain statement"** that its conclusion rests upon state law. See id.

The independence of state constitutions and statutes is significant. A defendant's claim under the United States Constitution may be precluded or rendered doubtful by a narrow interpretation of the scope of a federal constitutional right. If state law provides a similar right, a defendant can and should argue for a broader interpretation of the state provision, an interpretation that could validate her claim. Arguments and reasoning to support such a contention can readily be found in overruled or dissenting Supreme Court opinions.

 # EXAMPLES AND ANALYSIS

1. In the interest of saving time and money and freeing citizens from the burdens of jury service, the state of North Dakota has adopted a constitutional amendment requiring bench trials in all criminal cases. Can this amendment be implemented without violating the federal Constitution?

No. A state can extend greater rights to its citizens, but it cannot deny its citizens rights guaranteed by the federal Constitution, which is the "supreme" law of the land.

Defendants have a Fourteenth Amendment–due process right to trial by jury for all "serious" offenses. Insofar as the North Dakota amendment infringes on this due process right to be tried by a jury, it is unconstitutional.

2. The South Dakota Constitution, in language virtually identical to the Fifth Amendment, provides that "no person, in any criminal case, shall be compelled to be a witness against himself." The South Dakota Supreme Court has interpreted that provision to prohibit the use of any confession obtained during custodial interrogation if the warnings set out in Miranda v. Arizona are not recited in the exact language used in the *Miranda* opinion. In an earlier opinion, the United States Supreme Court held that for Fifth Amendment purposes, the *Miranda* warnings do **not** have to track the exact language used in the *Miranda* opinion. Should the South Dakota Supreme Court interpretation be overturned by the United States Supreme Court?

No. The South Dakota court's decision rests entirely on an **independent and adequate** state ground; therefore, it is not subject to reversal on federal grounds. The United States Supreme Court has no authority to interpret the South Dakota Constitution. Moreover, the South Dakota Supreme Court's interpretation does not deprive the citizens of South Dakota of any federal right. Instead, it grants those citizens greater rights than those granted by the Fifth Amendment. South Dakota is free to do so without risk of federal interference.

D. THE FEDERAL SUPERVISORY POWER

The federal judiciary has a "supervisory authority over the administration of criminal justice in the federal courts." McNabb v. United States, 318 U.S. 332, 63 S. Ct. 608, 87 L. Ed. 819 (1943). This inherent **supervisory power** insures that the processes of justice operate fairly and preserves the integrity of the courts. Because the supervisory authority is distinct from the authority to enforce the Constitution and federal statutes, rulings promulgated pursuant to the supervisory power may well be **more demanding** of the government than either constitutional or statutory law.

According to the Supreme Court, the supervisory power serves **three objectives:** (1) "to **implement a remedy for** violation of **recognized rights"**; (2) "to **preserve judicial integrity**"; and (3) "to **deter illegal conduct**." United States v. Hasting, 461 U.S. 499, 103 S. Ct. 1974, 76 L. Ed. 2d 96 (1983).

McNabb v. United States provides an illustration of the operation of the supervisory power. In *McNabb*, the Supreme Court used the supervisory power to reverse a conviction based on a confession that had been secured by officers who had disregarded a statute requiring that arrested persons be promptly taken before a judicial officer. Although neither the Constitution nor the statute required exclusion of the confession, the Court invoked the supervisory power in order to deter officers from ignoring the statute and thereby to insure that convictions would be obtained "by methods that commend themselves to a progressive and self-confident society." See also Rosales-Lopez v. United States, 451 U.S. 182, 101 S. Ct. 1629, 68 L. Ed. 2d 22 (1981) (concluding that the supervisory power requires that federal court jurors be asked questions about racial prejudice in circumstances where the Constitution does not require such questioning).

In theory, the supervisory power is important to the law of criminal procedure because its exercise can effectively restrict federal officers' investigatory methods, federal prosecutors' pretrial and courtroom conduct, and federal judges' prerogatives. The restrictions imposed by rules based on the supervisory power can provide advantages for criminal defendants as effectively as the constitutional rights created specifically for their benefit.

In practice, however, the supervisory power has had limited impact. It is *rarely* invoked to limit the authority of federal actors. Moreover, the Supreme Court has evinced a grudging attitude toward its use in criminal cases, indicating that judges should be cautious in using the supervisory power to reverse criminal convictions. See United States v. Hasting; United States v. Payner, 447 U.S. 727, 100 S. Ct. 2439, 65 L. Ed. 2d 468 (1980). In addition, most criminal law enforcement and prosecution occurs in state courts, and the federal supervisory power is inapplicable to state cases under review in federal court.

 # EXAMPLE AND ANALYSIS

A federal district court granted Mack habeas corpus relief based on its conclusion that the state trial court in which Mack was tried improperly allowed the government to introduce a confession made to an undercover agent. The district court held that a judge must exclude a confession whenever it has been obtained by an undercover agent whose reliability is not established by clear and convincing evidence. The court specifically observed that it was not resting its holding on a constitutional basis, stating that the "spirit of due process informs this holding which is exclusively based on our supervisory power over the administration of criminal justice in the courtroom." If the government appeals, how should the appellate court rule?

The district court's ruling should be reversed. A federal court may use supervisory power to restrict only *federal* authorities. The federal courts have no supervisory power over the administration of criminal justice in the state courts. Because the Constitution is the only source of federal control over state criminal processes, if Mack's confession is constitutionally admissible the federal court cannot order it excluded.

E. BURDENS OF PROOF ON CRIMINAL PROCEDURE CLAIMS

The Supreme Court has not often addressed questions concerning the **burden of proof** regarding claims that constitutional rights pertaining to criminal procedure have been violated. Two questions can arise: **Who bears** the burden of proof on a particular issue? and **What is the magnitude** of that burden?

1.   Who Bears the Burden of Proof?

Few decisions specify which party bears the burden of proof. In most cases, however, the answer to this question can be logically deduced. In general, the law places the burden of proof **on a claimant.** In criminal procedure contexts, the defendant is the claimant. The accused is alleging that the government has deprived her of a constitutional entitlement. Consequently, the defendant ordinarily should be required to establish the **basic elements of such a claim.**

A defendant claiming an unreasonable search under the Fourth Amendment, for example, must establish a basis for concluding that a search occurred and must establish that it was unreasonable. The first component is satisfied by a showing that the government "violated a reasonable expectation of privacy." The second could be satisfied by a showing that the search was performed without a warrant.

This does not mean that the government never has the obligation to persuade the court with regard to any issue raised by a criminal procedure claim. The law sometimes provides a basis for **"justifying" official conduct** or **"rebutting" a defendant's claim** of unconstitutionality. On these sorts of issues, the burden of proof should properly rest **on the government.**

If, for example, a defendant proves that a warrantless search was performed, the government can justify that search (that is, it can prove that the search was not unreasonable despite the lack of a warrant) by establishing **"probable cause"** and **"exigency"** or by proving "**voluntary consent** by a person with authority." In this situation, the government has the burden of proving probable cause and exigency or consent.

 ## EXAMPLES AND ANALYSIS

1. The Equal Protection Clause forbids purposeful race discrimination in the use of peremptory jury challenges. At a trial for rape, Shane alleges that the prosecutor has used the government's peremptory jury challenges in a racially discriminatory manner. The court rules in favor of Shane's claim after concluding that the government did not prove, by clear and convincing evidence, that its peremptory challenges were used in a nondiscriminatory fashion. Is the ruling correct?

No. As the proponent of the Equal Protection claim, Shane must carry the burden of proof of showing that the government engaged in purposeful race discrimination.

2. Billy is on trial for aggravated arson. The government seeks to introduce an identification of Billy that an eyewitness to the fire made at a pretrial lineup. Billy objects

to the identification on the ground that he was denied the assistance of counsel at the lineup. The government asserts that he waived his right to counsel. Who has the burden of proof on the waiver issue?

The government has the burden of proving that Billy waived the right to counsel. It must show that he knowingly, intelligently, and voluntarily relinquished the right to assistance at the lineup.

---

2. What Is the Magnitude of the Burden?

To the extent the Court has spoken to this question, it has concluded that matters determinative of constitutional "criminal procedure" claims must be proven by **"a preponderance of the evidence."** See United States v. Matlock, 415 U.S. 164, 94 S. Ct. 988, 39 L. Ed. 2d 242 (1974) ("the controlling burden of proof at suppression hearings should impose no greater burden than proof by a preponderance of the evidence"); see also Colorado v. Connelly, 479 U.S. 157, 107 S. Ct. 515, 93 L. Ed. 2d 473 (1986) (a waiver of *Miranda* protections needs to be established only by a preponderance of the evidence); Nix v. Williams, 467 U.S. 431, 104 S. Ct. 2501, 81 L. Ed. 2d 377 (1984) (to bring illegally obtained evidence within the "inevitable discovery" exception to the exclusionary rule the government need only satisfy the preponderance standard). Proof "by a preponderance of the evidence" means **"more likely than not."**

Thus, if a defendant claims to have been the victim of an unreasonable search or seizure, he must show the elements of such a claim by a preponderance of the evidence. In addition, an accused presumably must establish by a preponderance that she was deprived of the effective assistance of counsel because her lawyer had an "actual conflict of interest" that "adversely affected" the representation of the defendant. If the government seeks to validate a search by showing consent, it must establish by a preponderance of the evidence that voluntary consent to search was given by a person with authority to consent. See Matlock v. United States. Even a claim that a confession is involuntary and that its use will violate the Due Process Clause is governed by the preponderance norm. Lego v. Twomey, 404 U.S. 477, 92 S.Ct. 619, 30 L. Ed. 2d 618 (1972) (defendant is constitutionally entitled to have the government prove voluntariness of a confession by a preponderance of the evidence).

The only instance in which the Supreme Court has imposed a higher burden of proof is in the area of pretrial identifications. When a defendant shows a deprivation of the Sixth Amendment entitlement to counsel at a corporeal identification process and the state wants the identifying witness to make an "in-court" identification, the state must establish by **"clear and convincing evidence"** that the courtroom identification is from an "independent origin." United States v. Wade, 388 U.S. 218, 87 S.Ct. 1926, 18 L. Ed. 2d 1149 (1967).

Although the Constitution does not usually require more than the preponderance standard, "[s]tates are free, *pursuant to their own law*, to adopt a higher standard." Lego v. Twomey. Some states require clear and convincing evidence with regard to a limited number of issues.

EXAMPLE AND ANALYSIS

Gillian established that the warrant to search her home did not particularly describe the place to be searched and therefore was invalid under the Fourth Amendment. According to controlling doctrine, the prosecution still may use the narcotics they found during a search pursuant to this invalid warrant *if* the searching officers "reasonably relied on" the warrant. If the judge cannot decide whether the officers' reliance on the warrant was reasonable—that is, if the judge is "in equipoise" on the issue—how should he rule?

The judge should rule for the defendant. If a defendant carries the burden of demonstrating that a search was unreasonable, the government has the burden of establishing that any illegally obtained evidence falls within the scope of an "exception" to the exclusionary rule. Here, by showing that the warrant was defective, the defendant proved a constitutional violation. By establishing that the narcotics were found pursuant to that warrant, the defendant showed a basis for exclusion. The government is relying on the "good faith" exception to the exclusionary rule to support its claim that it should be allowed to introduce the narcotics. Consequently, the government must shoulder the burden of showing reasonable reliance on the warrant by a preponderance of the evidence.

REVIEW QUESTIONS AND ANSWERS

Question: Horace was convicted of lewd and lascivious acts with a child. At his trial, the prosecution introduced evidence found in Horace's pocket following his arrest for indecent exposure. Horace appeals, claiming that the evidence was obtained as a result of an illegal search. The Florida Supreme Court agrees, holding that "incident to a lawful arrest" officers may conduct only a patdown of the outer clothing of an arrestee unless there is a "realistic possibility" that a full search of the arrestee will disclose evidence of the crime for which he has been arrested. Because there was no realistic possibility that Horace had evidence of his indecent exposure in his possession at the time of the arrest, the officers who searched his pocket went beyond permissible bounds. The prosecution requests review by the United States Supreme Court, maintaining that the Florida decision is flatly contrary to controlling Fourth Amendment precedent and should be overturned. Is the prosecution correct?

Answer: The validity of the prosecution's argument depends on the basis for the state court's ruling. If the state court's ruling rests on state law, the prosecution's argument lacks merit because a state may grant its citizens greater protection than the Supreme Court's interpretations of the Fourth Amendment afford. If the state court's ruling rests on the Fourth Amendment, however, the prosecution's argument is valid. The Supreme Court has held that officers may always thoroughly search the person of every lawful arrestee. A state court has no authority to modify that holding. It may neither expand nor contract the scope of Fourth Amendment protection. If the state court opinion "fairly appears" to rest on federal grounds and there is no "plain statement" of an independent state law basis, the court's ruling will be presumed to rest on federal grounds and will be subject to reversal.

Question: Suzanne, a federal judge, is concerned with the unfairness that she has seen resulting from federal prosecutors' reluctance to divulge potentially exculpatory evidence to defendants. She has observed that when the prosecutors do decide to disclose such evidence, they frequently wait until it is too late for defendants to make good defensive use of the evidence at trial. Clarence is charged with plotting to bomb a federal facility. Relying on her "supervisory power," Suzanne orders an assistant U.S. attorney "to turn over to the defense, at least two weeks before trial, every potentially exculpatory item in your possession or in the possession of the law enforcement agencies working on this case whether or not you are required to do so by the Constitution." Is the court's order proper?

Answer: Possibly. The prosecutor has a *constitutional* obligation to turn over *"material"* exculpatory evidence. The order here goes beyond the constitutional obligation insofar as it requires *all* "potentially exculpatory" evidence to be disclosed and requires disclosure to be made "at least two weeks before trial." The supervisory power is theoretically available as a basis for the court's order. The order arguably protects the court's integrity and promotes a fair outcome. Still, a federal court should probably hesitate to invoke the supervisory power to upset the adversarial system's balance in a case in which disclosure to the defense is not constitutionally commanded and is not ordered by the discovery rules of the jurisdiction. In light of the Supreme Court's indications that the supervisory power ought to be used sparingly, this invocation of the supervisory power to force the government to assist the defendant might well be reversed on appeal.

PART II

PROCESSES OF INVESTIGATION: RIGHTS AND REMEDIES

Part II addresses rights and remedies pertinent to the **investigatory** stages of criminal cases. The rules and doctrines described restrain governmental efforts to detect crimes, apprehend criminals, gather evidence to prove crimes, and present that evidence in court. This part corresponds to the "basic" or "investigatory" criminal procedure courses.

The topics covered include the following:

- **Searches and seizures.** The **Fourth Amendment** regulates searches and seizures of persons, objects, and places. It prohibits all **unreasonable searches and seizures** and spells out the requirements for valid warrants to search or seize.

- **Government involvement in the commission of crimes.** Federal and state courts have developed **entrapment defenses** that preclude the conviction of those lured into crime by government officials. The constitutional guarantee of fundamental fairness included in the **Due Process Clause** also might preclude conviction in egregious cases of official participation in crimes sought to be prosecuted.

- **Confessions.** Government officials may attempt to secure incriminating statements from individuals suspected or accused of crimes. Three constitutional guarantees—**the Fifth Amendment Due Process Clause, the Fifth Amendment privilege against compulsory self-incrimination,** and **the Sixth Amendment right to counsel**—restrict the techniques that may be used and the admission of confessions that are given.

- **Identifications.** Investigators sometimes seek to secure eyewitness identifications of suspected or accused persons. Both the **Sixth Amendment right to**

counsel and the **Fifth Amendment Due Process Clause** limit the permissible methods and the admission of identifications obtained by unacceptable methods.

- **The exclusionary rules.** According to the **exclusionary rules,** evidence secured in violation of constitutional restrictions on investigatory methods is presumptively excluded from trial. However, there are a number of limitations on the scope of these rules of exclusion. These limitations permit the government to introduce illegally obtained evidence.

Fourth Amendment Regulation of Searches and Seizures

4

Chapter Overview

A course in investigatory criminal procedure will devote considerable attention to the topic of **search and seizure.** The **Fourth Amendment** to the Constitution is the source of the law that regulates official searches and seizures. The text of that amendment provides as follows:

> The right of the people to be secure in their persons, houses, papers, and effects, against unreasonable searches and seizures, shall not be violated, and no Warrants shall issue, but upon probable cause, supported by Oath or affirmation, and particularly describing the place to be searched, and the persons or things to be seized.

The amendment limits search and seizure authority in both general and specific ways. The general limitation in the **"reasonableness clause"** assumes that the government may search and seize but forbids **unreasonable** searches and seizures. The meaning of the term "unreasonable" is the concern of a large majority of the Fourth Amendment doctrines studied in this chapter. The limitations of the **"warrant clause"** specify the conditions required for valid warrants to search and seize: **probable cause, oath or affirmation,** and **particularity of description.** A few of the doctrines discussed in this chapter explain the conditions necessary for valid warrants to search and seize.

More specifically, this chapter addresses:

- **Definitions of searches and seizures.** A government investigatory practice is regulated by the Fourth Amendment only if it qualifies as a **search or seizure.** Highly refined doctrinal standards dictate whether a practice falls within those categories.

- **Probable cause to search or arrest.** For both warrantless and warranted searches and seizures, the normal substantive showing needed to justify a search is **probable cause.** The role of **"hearsay" from informants** in probable cause determinations raises particularly difficult questions.

- **The warrant requirement.** The **warrant requirement** provides that a search is ordinarily unreasonable unless officers obtain a warrant prior to conducting the search. **Public arrests of suspected felons,** however, are constitutional whether or not officers secure a warrant in advance.

- **Issuance and execution of warrants.** There are both explicit and implicit Fourth Amendment restrictions on the authority of judges to **issue** warrants and the authority of officers to **execute** them. The restrictions include **probable cause, oath or affirmation, particularity, a neutral and detached magistrate,** and **the knock and announce principle.**

- **Exceptions to the search warrant rule.** The warrant requirement is qualified by a number of **exceptions** that permit reasonable warrantless searches. Those exceptions include **searches incident to arrest, the *Chrisman* exception, searches for arrestees, exigent circumstances, the "automobile" doctrine, inventories, consent searches,** and **the "plain view" doctrine.** With regard to each exception, it is important to identify (1) its rationale, (2) the showing needed to qualify, and (3) the scope of the warrantless search authorized.

- **The Terry v. Ohio "stop-and-frisk" doctrine.** Under Terry v. Ohio, limited seizures of persons and limited searches of their persons—**stops and frisks**— are permissible on **less than probable cause.** The *Terry* doctrine raises a number of questions: When is a person seized? What is required to justify a limited detention and frisk? and What are the permissible scopes of stops and frisks?

- **Other "interest balancing" contexts.** The *Terry* doctrine rests on a "balancing" of individual and societal interests. In a number of other investigatory contexts, this interest-balancing approach has led to suspension of the probable cause and warrant norms and a lessening of Fourth Amendment protection. The contexts include **sweeps of homes, detentions of persons during searches, school searches, highway checkpoints, drug testing,** and a variety of **"administrative" searches.**

- **Situations that trigger heightened Fourth Amendment standards.** The use of **deadly force** to apprehend suspects and **forcible intrusions into the human body** are not reasonable unless the government satisfies standards that are more demanding than the probable cause norm applicable to ordinary full searches and seizures.

Note: While studying the rights guaranteed by the Fourth Amendment and the doctrines that give content to those rights, students should be mindful of the ordinary *consequences* of violating those rights and the other rights discussed in this outline—the **exclusion from trial of evidence obtained as a result of the violations.** This outline discusses the **exclusionary rules**—the rules that dictate the exclusion of illegally obtained evidence—in Chapter 12, after all the relevant rights have been explained. Because of the close relationship between the constitutional rights and the "sanctions" for violations of those rights, however, some instructors and casebooks prefer to consider the "sanctions" for violations before or in conjunction with the rights themselves. Students whose instructor or casebook addresses the exclusionary rules at an early stage of the course should consult Chapter 12 at that time.

A.   THE THRESHOLD: DEFINITIONS OF SEARCHES AND SEIZURES

The Fourth Amendment regulates only official **"searches"** and **"seizures."** The limitations contained in its terms cannot come into play unless the **governmental conduct** at issue falls into one of these two "threshold" categories.

In most Fourth Amendment cases, there is no serious question that a search or seizure, or both, has occurred. A home is entered. A person is forcibly taken to the police station. A car is towed to a city impound lot. In such cases, the Fourth Amendment clearly applies.

In some cases, however, it is uncertain whether the actions of officials qualify as either a search or a seizure of a person, place, or effect. A listening device is placed on top of a public telephone booth. Police officers fly over a residential backyard surrounded by high fences. A heat-detecting device is aimed at a private home. In such situations, "threshold" search or seizure questions arise. What follows are the standards designed to resolve those questions.

1.   Definition of a "Search": The "Privacy Violation" Approach of Katz v. United States

Whether a particular action qualifies as a search depends on the effect it has on the primary interest safeguarded by the Fourth Amendment—on whether it deprives an individual of a **constitutionally protected privacy interest.** According to the landmark opinion in Katz v. United States, 389 U.S. 347, 88 S. Ct. 507, 19 L. Ed. 2d 576 (1967), an act is a search for Fourth Amendment purposes if it **"violate[s] the privacy upon which [one] justifiably relie[s]."** The act does not have to intrude physically into a protected place, nor does it have to be undertaken for criminal law enforcement purposes.

In Katz v. United States, for example, the government put an electronic device on top of a telephone booth and listened to and recorded the user's half of conversations. Even though there was no physical intrusion, the government's conduct "violated the privacy upon which [the telephone user] justifiably relied" and therefore constituted a search.

a. **"Reasonable expectation of privacy" doctrine.** The *Katz* inquiry has been translated into the specific doctrinal standards originally proposed in Justice Harlan's concurrence in *Katz*. A search is an invasion of a **"reasonable expectation of privacy."** See Smith v. Maryland, 442 U.S. 735, 99 S. Ct. 2577, 61 L. Ed. 2d 220 (1979). (The words **"justifiable"** and **"legitimate"** are used interchangeably with the word **"reasonable."**)

The Supreme Court has also adopted Justice Harlan's two-pronged approach to resolving "reasonable expectation of privacy" inquiries. First, the person alleging that a search took place must demonstrate **"an actual (subjective) expectation of privacy."** Second, that expectation must be one **"that society is prepared to recognize as reasonable."** See Smith v. Maryland.

b. **"Actual (subjective) expectations of privacy."** To establish that the government invaded a *reasonable* expectation of privacy, the person claiming that a search occurred must have **"exhibited an actual (subjective) expectation of privacy."** Smith v. Maryland.

   i. **Actual expectations of the individual or of people in general.** Apparently, the question is not whether **the particular individual** making a claim expected privacy but whether **people in general** who behave in ways that the individual has behaved actually expect privacy. See Smith v. Maryland.

   For example, an individual may sincerely expect that the numbers she dials from her telephone will remain private. However, because telephone users in general know that they are revealing those numbers to a telephone company that has facilities to record and sometimes does record them, the individual does not have an "actual expectation of privacy." Id.

   ii. **Expectations vis-à-vis the government or private parties.** Because the Fourth Amendment is a restraint on government action, the relevant question would seem to be whether people actually expect privacy **vis-à-vis the government.** The little case law that exists, however, suggests that the lack of an actual expectation of privacy vis-à-vis a private entity can preclude the finding that one was the victim of a Fourth Amendment search. See Smith v. Maryland (rejecting a claim that the use of a pen register is a search because telephone users do not expect that the numbers they dial will remain private from the telephone company).

   iii. **The limited influence of actual expectations.** For the most part, determinations of threshold search questions have not hinged on the "actual expectations" prong. In fact, there is no Supreme

Court case in which the actual expectation of privacy criterion has been determinative of the claim that a search occurred.

c. **Expectations "that society is prepared to recognize as reasonable."** The second prong is **whether society is prepared to recognize an actual, subjective privacy expectation as reasonable.** Smith v. Maryland. Almost all of the threshold issues resolved by the Supreme Court have turned on this criterion. The opinions resolving those issues have identified a number of factors relevant to the determination.

i. **Voluntary disclosure to a third party.** Individuals sometimes converse with or otherwise convey information to third parties who, unbeknown to those individuals, are acting for the government. In this situation, there is no search because it is not reasonable to expect that information **voluntarily disclosed to a third party** will remain private from him or from anyone else that he wishes to share it with, including the government. Smith v. Maryland. By choosing to disclose the information, a person sacrifices his own privacy and **"assumes the risk"** that the information is being or will be conveyed to others. United States v. White, 401 U.S. 745, 91 S. Ct. 1122, 28 L. Ed. 2d 453 (1971).

It is important to note that this factor operates only when there is (1) **voluntary disclosure** and (2) **cooperation with the government by the third party** to whom the information is disclosed. It is <u>irrelevant</u> to situations in which the government acquires voluntarily disclosed information without the cooperation of the third party.

For example, if the government enlists someone to associate with a particular individual and to report her conversations, there is no search because the information received is "voluntarily disclosed" to the "false friend." United States v. White. This is true even if the false friend surreptitiously records those conversations and even if he uses a concealed electronic device to transmit the conversations simultaneously to government agents who are listening. Id.

Similarly, when the telephone company, acting at the request of governmental officials, employs a pen register to record the numbers dialed from a private residential telephone, there is no search because the numbers have been "voluntarily disclosed" to the phone company who has willingly conveyed them to the authorities. Smith v. Maryland; see also United States v. Miller, 425 U.S. 435, 96 S. Ct. 1619, 48 L. Ed. 2d 71 (1976) (holding the same for information contained in financial records given to a bank by an individual and passed on to officials by the bank).

[Handwritten margin notes, left side:]
But: might "waiver" be in recognition of an individual 3rd party's abilities - knowledge, memory, is it fair to wire as well?

Limit: what you voluntarily give up to 3rd party - other than that per search search

Test:

White Facts

Jeff:
Friends: can chone
home phone: new Reality

Smith Facts

[Handwritten margin notes, right side:]
before law disclosed..

[Handwritten note, bottom:]
LIMIT: Info must be in cooperation w/ 3rd person not just at tion communicated to 3rd person & independently

ii. **Knowing exposure to the public.** In *Katz*, the Court noted that "[w]hat a person knowingly exposes to the public, even in his own home or office, is not a subject of Fourth Amendment protection." Subsequently, the Court has confirmed that society will not recognize as reasonable an asserted expectation of privacy in information **knowingly exposed to the public.** The police **do not conduct a search** when they take advantage of a public vantage point to gain access to such exposed matters. See California v. Ciraolo, 476 U.S. 207, 106 S. Ct. 1809, 90 L. Ed. 2d 210 (1986).

For "knowing exposure" to render a privacy expectation unreasonable, two conditions must be satisfied: (1) the **vantage point** must be **lawful and routinely occupied** by the public (see California v. Ciraolo; Florida v. Riley, 488 U.S. 445, 109 S. Ct. 693, 102 L. Ed. 2d 835 (1989)) **and** (2) the exposed matters must be **subject to acquisition by the naked, unaided senses.** It does not seem to matter whether members of the public actually take advantage of the opportunity to view the exposed information. The question is whether the public is typically present in the place and *could* gain access. See California v. Ciraolo. Moreover, it does not matter that a technological device is used to aid the senses so long as the same information could have been acquired by the naked senses. United States v. Knotts, 460 U.S. 276, 103 S. Ct. 1081, 75 L. Ed. 2d 55 (1983).

In California v. Ciraolo, officers flew over a double-fenced backyard at an altitude of 1,000 feet and by simply using their eyes were able to see marijuana growing there. Even though the backyard was an area entitled to Fourth Amendment protection (see section A.1.c.iii below, discussing the protection afforded the "curtilage"), the aerial surveillance of that area did not constitute a "search" because the officers stayed in lawfully navigable airspace, public and commercial air travel at that altitude is routine, and the officers used only their naked senses to see the contraband.

In United States v. Knotts, officers used an electronic beeper attached to a drum of chemicals to monitor the travels of an individual along public roadways. They did not "search" because any member of the public standing along the roads could have seen this activity with unaided eyes. In that case, it did not matter that officers "enhanced" their senses with an electronic device. See also United States v. Karo, 468 U.S. 705, 104 S. Ct. 3296, 82 L. Ed. 2d 530 (1984) (holding that use of electronic beeper to learn information concealed behind walls of home, and therefore not obtainable by unaided senses, is a search).

iii. **Lack of societal interest in protecting the privacy of matters.** If activities that take place in a particular area are not of a sort that deserve the privacy protection contained in the Fourth Amendment, official intrusion into that area will not be a search. Any actual expectation of privacy is not reasonable if "[t]here is **no societal interest in protecting the privacy**" of the information that could be learned or the activities that could be intruded on. Oliver v. United States, 466 U.S. 170, 104 S. Ct. 1735, 80 L. Ed. 2d 214 (1984).

The Court relied on this factor to deny Fourth Amendment coverage in Oliver v. United States. In that case, officers physically trespassed on "open fields"—privately owned land not within the immediate vicinity of a dwelling. This physical intrusion was not a Fourth Amendment "search," in large part because open fields "do not provide the setting for those intimate activities that the Amendment is intended to shelter." It did not matter that the defendants owned the land, that the criminal law forbade trespassing, and that the owners had taken precautions to prevent physical intrusion. Because nothing worthy of or in need of constitutional privacy protection occurs in open fields, intrusions upon them **cannot violate reasonable expectations of privacy.**

Note: Not all private lands are "open fields." The area immediately surrounding a private home is designated the **"curtilage"** and is protected by the Fourth Amendment because it is an area to which the intimate activities of the home extend. (An additional reason for affording protection against curtilage invasions could be to provide a sort of "buffer zone" for the privacy of the home.) Consequently, an officer's physical intrusion on the curtilage at ground level is a search. See Oliver v. United States. Moreover, aerial surveillance from an unlawful altitude or from a space that is not routinely occupied by the public is also a search. See Florida v. Riley.

The **scope of the curtilage** is dictated by four factors: whether there is a surrounding enclosure, the uses to which the area is put, whether precautions have been taken to shelter the privacy of the area, and physical proximity to a dwelling. See United States v. Dunn, 480 U.S. 294, 107 S. Ct. 1134, 94 L. Ed. 2d 326 (1987).

The **degree of protection** afforded the curtilage is unclear. The usual showings needed for a reasonable search are probable cause and a search warrant. See Sections B.1 and C.1.a below. The Court has reserved the question of the "degree of . . . protection afforded the curtilage," an indication that searches may be reasonable on less than probable cause or without a warrant. See Oliver v. United States.

iv.   **The fact that nothing, nothing of significance, or nothing "legitimate" will be learned.** The government does not violate a "reasonable" expectation of privacy if its conduct **cannot reveal any information.** Thus, in United States v. Karo, the Court held that the transfer of an object to a person with an electronic beeper attached was not a search because the transfer alone **could reveal nothing at all** to the government.

Likewise, if conduct by government officials can disclose to them **nothing that they do not already know,** it cannot invade a "reasonable" privacy expectation. In United States v. Jacobsen, 466 U.S. 109, 104 S. Ct. 1652, 80 L. Ed. 2d 85 (1984), a federal agent reopened a package after Federal Express workers had privately inspected it and had described to the agents what they had seen inside. The reopening was not a search because it "was a **virtual certainty that nothing else of significance was in the package**" and that the inspection "**would not tell [the federal agent] anything more** than he already had been told." See also Illinois v. Andreas, 463 U.S. 765, 103 S. Ct. 3319, 77 L. Ed. 2d 1003 (1983) (concluding that there was no search because there was no substantial likelihood that the contents of a package already examined by government agents had changed).

Finally, if an act **cannot reveal "significant" or "legitimate" information,** it cannot compromise a "reasonable" expectation of privacy. In United States v. Jacobsen, a chemical "field test" of a powdery substance was not a search because it **could reveal only** that the substance was not contraband—**an insignificant fact**—or that the substance was contraband—**an illegitimate fact.**

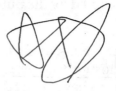

It is critical to note that in all these situations the question is not whether an action in fact failed to disclose information, but whether in advance it can be said that the action **could not disclose information.** According to the Court's reasoning, no deserving interest in secrecy or confidentiality can be compromised if nothing of legitimate significance can be learned.

 EXAMPLES AND ANALYSIS

1. A resident places his trash in opaque plastic bags and puts them at the curb for collection on pickup day. At the request of law enforcement officers, the trash collector

keeps the resident's trash separate and turns it over to them. The officers open the bags and find incriminating narcotics residue.

This difficult situation has been resolved by the Supreme Court. A majority concluded in California v. Greenwood, 486 U.S. 35, 108 S. Ct. 1625, 100 L. Ed. 2d 30 (1988), that there was no search. The opinion rested on two apparently independent and debatable premises.

First, the Court reasoned that the collector was a third party to whom the resident "voluntarily disclosed" his trash. There was no violation of a reasonable expectation of privacy when that third party who was working for the authorities conveyed the disclosed information to them. It is arguable, however, that the contents contained in opaque trash containers are not "voluntarily disclosed" to the trash collector—only the outside of the bags is disclosed.

Second, the Court opined that trash placed at the curb is "knowingly exposed" to members of the public who are known to rummage through it from a lawful vantage point. This premise is also questionable. The contents of closed, opaque containers are hardly "exposed," and it is arguable that the risk of exposure by rummagers is an insufficient basis for finding that a resident has sacrificed his or her privacy interest.

Note that if a particular act is not a search, it is **not subject to Fourth Amendment regulation.** Thus, it is constitutional for the government to engage in that act **without any justification.** A common misconception is that the conclusion that a search has occurred means that the government must refrain from the conduct at issue. In fact, this threshold determination means only that the conduct **is subject to Fourth Amendment regulation.** The government can constitutionally engage in such conduct so long as it does so **reasonably.**

2. Drug enforcement agents patrol the terminals of the city's airport with dogs that are capable of detecting illegal narcotics by their sense of smell. One of the dogs approaches a person's tightly locked suitcase that is sitting on the floor beside him as he waits in line for a boarding pass. The dog alerts the agents that narcotics are present.

The dog's action does not constitute a search because it did not physically intrude into the suitcase and did not expose the contents of the suitcase. Most important, the act could reveal only two things—that no contraband was present, a fact of no significance, or that contraband was present, an illegitimate fact. See United States v. Place, 462 U.S. 696, 103 S. Ct. 2637, 77 L. Ed. 2d 110 (1983).

Note that only the dog-sniff is a "nonsearch." If the agents were to open the suitcase after the dog's alert, that act would be a search and would require justification.

---

2.   Definition of a "Seizure" of Places and Effects

Unlike the threshold "search" question, the question of **when property— places or effects—has been seized** has generated few questions and little law. The constitutional regulation of seizures of places and effects is a safeguard against unjustified interference with **property or possessory interests.** Consequently, a " **'seizure' of property** occurs when there is some **meaningful interference with an individual's possessory interests in that property."** United States v. Jacobsen; United States v. Karo.

Jacobsen
Facts

Thus, a state agent seizes a package by taking it into her custody or by destroying or causing measurable damage to it. See United States v. Jacobsen (taking possession of a package and destroying a "trace amount" of the powder found inside were both seizures although the latter was de minimis); but see United States v. Karo (because the presence of electronic beeper in object was not a meaningful interference with possession but was merely a technical trespass, the transfer of that object to an individual was not a seizure of his property).

A person's home is undoubtedly "seized" for Fourth Amendment purposes when agents "secure" it by taking steps that restrict a person's access to or free use of the premises. Consequently, if officers who wish to search a dwelling for contraband station themselves at the doors and prevent occupants from entering, they have seized the home and must have adequate justification. See Segura v. United States, 468 U.S. 796, 104 S. Ct. 3380, 82 L. Ed. 2d 599 (1984).

3. **Definition of a "Seizure" of a Person**

The question of **when a person has been seized** is very significant. It has been the subject of considerable attention and has given rise to a substantial body of doctrine. Because the question is intimately related to a subset of Fourth Amendment law taken up later—the *Terry* stop-and-frisk doctrine— discussion is postponed until Section G.2 below.

4. **Government Agent Requirement**

The Fourth Amendment regulates only searches and seizures by agents of the sovereign. Burdeau v. McDowell, 256 U.S. 465, 41 S. Ct. 574, 65 L. Ed. 1048 (1921); United States v. Jacobsen. It does not govern the actions of "private parties." Consequently, conduct that clearly constitutes a "search" or a "seizure" under the preceding standards is subject to the commands of the Fourth Amendment only if it is performed by a "government agent." If an individual who has no involvement with the state breaks into a neighbor's home, finds contraband, and takes it to the police, the Constitution is not implicated.

a. **Distinction between "private parties" and "government agents."**
    There is no clearly defined line between private parties and government actors. It is clear, however, that to qualify as a state agent, a person does not have to be a government employee; she need only act for the state. If a government official specifically requests an action by an

otherwise private citizen, that citizen becomes a government agent. See, e.g., Smith v. Maryland, 442 U.S. 735, 99 S. Ct. 2577, 61 L. Ed. 2d 220 (1979) (assuming that the telephone company's attachment of a pen register at the request of government officials was state action).

Questions of government agency do not arise often. When they do, they ought to be resolved by a realistic assessment of whether the person conducting the search or seizure was acting for his own private purposes or instead was acting at least partially on behalf of or at the instigation of government officials.

state actor Test (handwritten)

b. "Extension" of a private party's action by a government agent. Although the Fourth Amendment does not apply to a search or seizure by a private party, if agents of the state go beyond or extend the private party's conduct in ways that infringe upon Fourth Amendment interests, their additional conduct is constitutionally regulated. Walter v. United States, 447 U.S. 649, 100 S. Ct. 2395, 65 L. Ed. 2d 410 (1980); United States v. Jacobsen.

 EXAMPLE AND ANALYSIS

A private party enters another's home, searches it, finds film canisters, and turns them over to the police. The police then open the canisters and examine the contents of the films by screening them. The homeowner objects that his home has been searched in violation of the Fourth Amendment.

The search of the home was by a private actor, and thus is not governed by the Fourth Amendment. Therefore, the possession of the canisters by the police was entirely lawful. However, both the official opening of the canisters and the screening of the films extended the private party's invasion of privacy. They were official searches subject to Fourth Amendment requirements. See Walter v. United States.

REVIEW QUESTIONS AND ANSWERS

Question: Malcolm is concerned about the crisis in illegal narcotics. As a public service, he decides to spend his ample spare time looking through unlocked automobiles found on private property and in public areas. On most occasions, he has taken the contraband he has found to the police. Sometimes, he has called the police, told them that he has found "something of interest" in a vehicle, given them a description of the vehicle and its location, and invited them to "have a look." The police accepted his invitation on some occasions, but on others, they asked Malcolm to go back into the car himself, remove the contraband, and bring it to them. Are any of these activities controlled by the Fourth Amendment? If so, are they unconstitutional?

Answer: Malcolm's initial, unprompted entries are private searches and are not within the scope of the amendment. The police entries upon Malcolm's invitations and Malcolm's reentries after police requests qualify as searches by agents who are acting for the state. They are regulated by the Fourth Amendment, but are unconstitutional only if they are "unreasonable" searches.

Question: During a conversation, Olivia tells Pat that she was involved in a conspiracy to assassinate the president. By means of a listening device attached to Pat's baseball cap, federal agents intercept and record the conversation. Did the federal agents search Olivia?

Answer: It depends on whether the listening device was attached with Pat's knowledge and cooperation. If so, the fact that Olivia voluntarily disclosed the information to someone who was revealing it to the government precludes the claim that the agents violated a reasonable expectation of privacy. If Pat did not knowingly cooperate, there was a search. Olivia's voluntary disclosure to Pat means only that it is not reasonable to expect that Pat will keep the information private. Olivia can and does have a reasonable expectation of privacy against government intrusions into private conversations without the "connivance" of the third party to whom she is conversing. That is the essence of the holding in Katz v. United States.

Question: Burt is conducting a narcotics manufacturing business in his dwelling, which is located near a public road. While standing on the road, police officers see contraband growing near Burt's residence. They also see suspicious activities through an uncurtained window in the home and use a sophisticated heat-detection device to ascertain that abnormal levels of heat are emanating from the outer walls of the home. Did the officers search Burt's home?

Answer: The observations of the contraband within the curtilage and the suspicious activities within the home are not searches. Although both the curtilage and the home are protected, the officers did not invade reasonable expectations of privacy in those places by observing with their unaided senses from a lawful vantage point the information that Burt "knowingly exposed."

The use of the heat detection device may have violated a "reasonable expectation of privacy" and therefore may qualify as a search. On the one hand, the officers did not trespass into a protected area; they only acquired information that was "exposed" on the outside of the home. Moreover, the information they could obtain was limited in content. On the other hand, the officers learned the heat levels emanating from Burt's home. This information was "legitimate"—there was nothing inherently illegal about it. It was arguably "significant"—it was indicative of something happening within a private dwelling. Moreover, because it could not be detected by unaided senses but required a sophisticated device, the information was not "knowingly exposed" to the public.

B. PROBABLE CAUSE TO SEARCH OR ARREST

The Fourth Amendment provides a right against "**unreasonable** searches and seizures." Reasonable searches and seizures are constitutional. For the most part, the substance of Fourth Amendment protection hinges on the meaning of the term "unreasonable." That concept dictates the scope of the constitutional rights granted by the amendment and thereby defines the breadth of governmental authority to search and seize.

1. Probable Cause: A "Norm" of Reasonableness

The second clause of the Fourth Amendment explicitly requires "**probable cause**" as a prerequisite for issuance of a warrant. As will be made clear later, searches and seizures without warrants can be constitutional. As a general rule, these warrantless searches and seizures must also be based on probable cause. See Wong Sun v. United States, 371 U.S. 471, 83 S. Ct. 407, 9 L. Ed. 2d 441 (1963). Therefore, **probable cause is a norm of reasonableness for all searches and seizures.** In the context of criminal investigations, it signifies the level of governmental interest needed to justify official invasions of privacy, liberty, or property interests.

2. Probable Cause to Search

Probable cause to search requires that three things be shown: (1) an item in which the government has a legitimate interest—typically evidence, contraband, fruits of crime, or instrumentalities of crime (2) is currently (3) in the particular place to be searched. These showings must be based on articulable, objective facts.

3. Probable Cause to Arrest

An arrest is a "seizure of a person." Probable cause to arrest an individual requires that two things be shown: (1) a crime was committed (2) by the person to be arrested. Brinegar v. United States, 338 U.S. 160, 69 S. Ct. 1302, 93 L. Ed. 1879 (1949). These showings also must be based on articulable, objective facts.

4. Staleness of Probable Cause to Search

Showings of probable cause to search are sometimes rejected because the supporting information is said to be **stale.** The issue of staleness arises in situations in which the facts at one time supported a finding that an object was in the place to be searched, but the passage of time has diminished the likelihood that the object is **presently** in that place. Time diminishes the likelihood because mobile items tend to change locations and consumable items tend to be consumed. When the diminished likelihood falls below the level required for probable cause, a search is not justified.

For example, an officer's current report that he saw an ounce of cocaine in a specified apartment two weeks earlier may not lead a reasonable person to conclude that the cocaine is still likely to be there. If not, the probable cause showing is stale and no search warrant should issue.

No Stale
Arrest

Probable cause to arrest does **not** go stale. Once it is shown to be sufficiently likely that a person committed an offense, the mere passage of time will not diminish that likelihood. There is no logical reason that one's status as an offender is affected by the passage of time.

5. Level of Probability Required

Probable cause exists when the facts and circumstances would lead a person of reasonable caution to conclude that the predicates necessary to justify a search or seizure have been established. Brinegar v. United States. Probable cause does **not** require **certainty.** It does **not** even require a showing that the required conclusions are **"more likely than not"** to be true—that is, at least 51 percent likely. Instead, the level of likelihood constitutionally required is **"a fair probability"** or a **"substantial chance."** Illinois v. Gates, 462 U.S. 213, 103 S. Ct. 2317, 76 L. Ed. 2d 527 (1983).

Test for
P.C.

Because probable cause does not require certainty, but only a "fair probability," it contemplates the possibility of **"mistake."** The fact that an item was not present in the place searched or the fact that an arrestee did not in fact commit an offense does **not** mean that the officers lacked probable cause to search or arrest at the time they acted. See Hill v. California, 401 U.S. 797, 91 S. Ct. 1106, 28 L. Ed. 2d 484 (1971).

(E&A) EXAMPLES AND ANALYSIS

1. Officers suspect that a man who is renting a car was involved in the bombing of a federal building. They arrest him even though they lack adequate information to support a probable cause finding. The prosecution contends that the Fourth Amendment demands only probable cause to obtain warrants and that in cases of warrantless action, searches and seizures are valid so long as they are not "unreasonable." The prosecution further argues that it was "reasonable" to seize the man in this case because if the officers did not act he could have fled the jurisdiction.

This argument is flawed. As a general rule, probable cause is necessary for searches and seizures whether or not a warrant is needed or obtained. An arrest supported by less than probable cause is unreasonable.

2. While patrolling the city airport, Rex, a drug-detecting dog, alerts officers to the presence of narcotics in a suitcase. On the basis of Rex's reaction, officers secure a warrant to open the suitcase. No contraband is found. Is the warrant valid?

Because warrants require probable cause, the answer depends on whether Rex's behavior is a sufficiently reliable indicator of the presence of narcotics. If his training and expertise are such that a reasonable person would conclude that there is a "fair probability" of contraband in the suitcase, the warrant is valid. The fact that no contraband was found does not change that conclusion.

6. "Objective" Nature of Probable Cause

According to the Supreme Court, **"[s]ubjective intentions play no role in ordinary, probable-cause Fourth Amendment analysis."** Whren v. United States, 517 U.S.—, 116 S. Ct.—, 135 L. Ed. 2d 89 (1996). If the *objective facts* establish probable cause for an arrest or detention, an officer's *subjective motivation* will not defeat a probable cause finding or otherwise render the arrest or detention unreasonable because "the Fourth Amendment's concern with 'reasonableness' allows certain actions to be taken in certain circumstances, whatever the subjective intent." Id. Presumably, this same principle is equally applicable in the context of probable cause to search.

EXAMPLE AND ANALYSIS

In Whren v. United States, officers who had probable cause to believe that a motorist had violated the traffic laws stopped his vehicle and saw narcotics inside. The defendants claimed that the stop should be deemed invalid, despite the existence of probable cause, *if a reasonable police officer would not have made the stop for the traffic violation.* They asserted that the "reasonable officer" standard was necessary to guard against improper "subjective" motivations—to prevent officers from using traffic stops as "pretexts" to investigate other crimes or as a means of concealing their reliance on impermissible factors such as race.

The Supreme Court rejected the defendants' arguments because "[a]s a general matter, the decision to stop an automobile is reasonable where the police have probable cause to believe that a traffic violation has occurred" and because "[s]ubjective intentions play no role in ordinary, probable-cause Fourth Amendment analysis." Adhering to "the traditional common-law rule that probable cause justifies a search and seizure," the Court upheld the stop.

7. Hearsay As a Basis for Probable Cause

Sometimes the facts offered to support findings of probable cause are not known firsthand to an officer who is applying for a warrant or seeking to justify a warrantless search. Instead, they are supplied by some third person, typically an "informant" or "tipster." Such information is said to be **hearsay.** Probable cause showings can be based on hearsay. Draper v. United States, 358 U.S. 307, 79 S. Ct. 329, 3 L. Ed. 2d 327 (1959).

8. Evaluations of Hearsay-Based Probable Cause Showings: The *Aguilar-Spinelli* Two-Prong Test

At one time, when hearsay formed all or an essential part of a probable cause showing, the value or weight of the hearsay had to be judged under the *Aguilar-Spinelli* **two-prong test.** See Aguilar v. Texas, 378 U.S. 108, 84 S. Ct. 1509, 12 L. Ed. 2d 723 (1964); Spinelli v. United States, 393 U.S. 410, 89 S. Ct. 584, 21 L. Ed. 2d 637 (1969).

The two-prong test rested on at least three premises. First, probable cause determinations must be made by judges, not police officers or informants. Second, the probability that an informant's conclusion is true depends on two independent variables—the kind of information underlying that conclusion and the truthfulness of the informant. And third, judges can make independent evaluations of probable cause only if they are provided with facts bearing on both of those variables. Otherwise, they are simply deferring to the conclusions of others.

Under the two-prong test, an informant's conclusion that an object was located in a certain place or that a person had committed an offense could not suffice. Similarly, an officer's conclusion that an informant was "reliable" was inadequate. Instead, the "facts and circumstances" underlying both the informant's conclusion and the officer's conclusion had to be supplied. Put otherwise, officers had to provide judges with information pertaining to the informant's **"basis of knowledge"** and the informant's **"veracity."** Both prongs had to be satisfied for probable cause to be established.

a. **"Basis of knowledge" prong.** The **basis of knowledge prong** is concerned with the "facts and circumstances" underlying an informant's conclusion—that is, with the nature and amount of information that led to that conclusion. Some "bases of knowledge" such as **firsthand observations** justify confidence in the conclusion. Others, such as conjecture or rumor, provide grounds for doubt.

For example, an informant might report that illegal weapons are in a vehicle or that a defendant is in possession of narcotics. If the informant asserted that she had seen the weapons or the narcotics herself, or if there were other grounds for concluding that she had such firsthand information, her basis of knowledge would be reliable. If, however, she claimed that she had heard of the weapons from another individual or believed that the person had narcotics because she "could tell from the odd way he was behaving," the basis for her conclusion would be doubtful.

b. **"Veracity" prong.** The **veracity prong** focuses on and calls for "facts and circumstances" that indicate the **truthfulness** of the informant's report. Both evidence of the informant's general character for honesty and evidence indicative of the truthfulness of the particular report at issue are relevant. (The former is sometimes said to bear on the "veracity of the informant" while the latter is said to support the "reliability of the information.")

For example, an informant's veracity might be established by the fact that she has supplied accurate information on several past occasions. Or the reliability of her information might be bolstered by the fact that it constitutes a statement against her penal or financial interests because it is unlikely that a person would make such a statement if it were not true.

Example:

c. **Application of the two-prong test when hearsay is only a part of the probable cause basis.** In Spinelli v. United States, the Supreme Court prescribed a method for giving proper weight to hearsay that is an essential part of a probable cause showing but is supplemented by other evidence. The object of each stage was the same: to determine whether the showings regarding the informant's basis of knowledge and veracity were sufficient to justify reliance on her conclusion.

In the **first stage,** the **tip or hearsay alone** had to be evaluated according to the two-prong *Aguilar-Spinelli* standards. If probable cause was not established because the showing on either or both of the prongs was deficient, a judge proceeded to the second stage.

In the **second stage,** the tip or hearsay had to be evaluated **in light of the corroborating information.** Again, the two-prong test was applicable. At issue was whether the corroborating information gave grounds for finding that the informant had a sound way of knowing or was telling the truth. Police investigation that confirmed some of what the informant had reported could provide a basis for finding that either or both of the prongs were satisfied.

9. **Abolition of the Federal Two-Prong Test; Continuing Adherence in Some States**

The **two-prong test has been "rejected"** and "abandoned" by the Supreme Court. Illinois v. Gates, 462 U.S. 213, 103 S. Ct. 2317, 76 L. Ed. 2d 527 (1983); Massachusetts v. Upton, 466 U.S. 727, 104 S. Ct. 2085, 80 L. Ed.

2d 721 (1984). Under the Fourth Amendment, showings of probable cause no longer need to satisfy the *Aguilar-Spinelli* standards. Nevertheless, in interpreting their own constitutions, several state courts have continued to follow the two-prong approach to evaluating hearsay-based probable cause showings.

10. **Evaluations of Hearsay-Based Probable Cause Showings: The** *Gates* **"Totality of the Circumstances" Test**

Under the Fourth Amendment, the two-prong test has been replaced by the flexible **"totality of the circumstances"** approach. Illinois v. Gates. This approach requires judges to add up all the facts and decide whether probable cause is established. Hearsay from an informant is not evaluated under "rigid" standards but is instead simply added in as part of the mix of relevant facts. In essence, the question is whether the "totality of circumstances" would lead a reasonable person to conclude that there is a "fair probability" that a certain item is in a particular place or that a certain individual has committed an offense.

a. **Role of the two prongs.** Under the totality approach, the basis of knowledge and veracity prongs are still **"highly relevant"** factors in determining the value of hearsay. Id. Nevertheless, probable cause can be found even though neither prong is satisfied. Moreover, "a deficiency in one may be compensated for, in determining the overall reliability of a tip, by a strong showing as to the other, or by some other indicia of reliability." Id.

b. **Value of independent police corrobortion. Independent official corroboration** of facts reported by an informant can also play an important role under the *Gates* totality approach to probable cause determinations. Such corroboration might suggest either that the informant's information was gained in a reliable way or that the informant was telling the truth. Moreover, even if they do not confirm anything reported by an informant, pertinent facts gathered by law enforcement officers are a part of the totality of circumstances that must be taken into account in evaluating probable cause showings.

c. **Anonymous tips.** Anonymous tips can play a role in the totality of the circumstances analysis. As with hearsay from known informants, facts supportive of anonymous tipsters' bases of knowledge or veracity will give added weight to the information they supply.

d. **Significance and limits of the** *Gates* **totality approach.** The replacement of the "rigid" two-prong test with the more "fluid" totality approach had the effect of freeing judges from strictures that precluded findings of probable cause in situations in which hearsay was a critical part of the showing made. Nevertheless, the *Gates* approach does have some "limits beyond which a magistrate may not venture in issuing a warrant." A judge must have **"a substantial basis** for determining the existence of probable cause. . . . [H]is action **cannot be a mere ratification of the bare conclusions of others."** Illinois v. Gates. This means that if a judge is presented with a " 'bare bones' affidavit[ ]" that contains nothing other than an officer's or informant's "conclusions," he may not find probable cause. Once any additional information is provided, however, there is no "prescribed set of rules" that dictates whether or not probable cause can be found. Id.

For example, probable cause may not be found simply because an officer swears under oath that there are illegal explosives at a given location. Similarly, if an informant alleges that contraband is in a given place and an officer asserts that the informant is reliable, probable cause has not been shown. In both cases, the judge is presented only with others' conclusions.

EXAMPLE AND ANALYSIS

A state appellate court concludes that a probable cause finding is inadequate under the Fourth Amendment because the informant's basis of knowledge was not clearly established. Has the court erred?

Under the **presently controlling** totality analysis, the failure to satisfy either "prong" is not necessarily fatal. The magistrate (in a warrant case) or trial judge (in warrantless situations) must be affirmed if in the totality she had a "substantial basis" for finding probable cause. If the rest of the record provided such a basis, the lower court should be affirmed despite the lack of facts regarding the informant's basis of knowledge.

Note that if the state court were to adopt the two-prong test as a proper interpretation of the **state constitution,** then its decision might well be correct. Under that test, if the hearsay was essential to the finding of probable cause and the showing of the informant's basis of knowledge was inadequate (both on the face of the tip and in light of independent corroboration), probable cause could not be found.

REVIEW QUESTIONS AND ANSWERS

Question: Federal agents search Timothy's home pursuant to a warrant based on an affidavit that states, "I have been informed by a confidential and reliable informant, who has furnished me with information on fifty prior occasions leading to arrests or successful searches on all but two of those occasions, that a ton of chemical explosives is currently in Timothy's garage located at 123 Plum Lane." Was the probable cause showing adequate?

Answer: In this case, the hearsay is the only information supplied. The informant's veracity is strongly established by a "track record" of truthtelling, but there is no evidence of his basis of knowledge—that is, how he knew the explosives were in the garage. *Gates* provides conflicting indications of whether probable cause should be found.

On the one hand, the Court noted that a deficiency in one prong could be compensated for by a strong showing on the other. That would suggest that probable cause could be found in this case. Moreover, the Court specifically precluded hearsay-based probable cause findings in only one situation—when the informant provides a mere conclusion about the "criminality" **and** the officer provides a mere conclusion about the informant's reliability.

On the other hand, the Court emphasized that if an officer swears under oath that contraband can be found in a place, a judge may not rely on the officer's "bare" conclusion. Even though the oath provides good evidence of the officer's veracity, a judge must insist on the facts that underlie that conclusion. It is arguably illogical to hold that the sworn conclusions of a known officer cannot furnish probable cause but that the unsworn conclusions of an unknown informant can do so.

Question: Based on an anonymous phone call reporting that "Colin is selling narcotics from the trunk of a Ford Mustang with California license plate ACB 334, parked at the corner of West 50th Street and Brand Avenue," Officer Murtaugh goes to the location to set up surveillance. He spots a vehicle matching the description exactly. A man is leaning on the rear fender. Ten minutes later, a woman approaches, the two converse, then the woman leaves. Thirty minutes later, she returns and shakes hands with the man leaning on the fender. The man leaning on the fender then opens the trunk, reaches in, and returns to the woman. Shortly thereafter, she walks away again. Murtaugh searches the trunk, finds narcotics, then arrests Colin. If Colin later objects that Murtaugh lacked probable cause, may the trial court find in his favor?

Answer: *Gates* provides flexibility for judges to exercise their judgment. There are limited situations in which hearsay cannot be the basis for a probable cause finding. And there are others in which the facts are so powerful that it would undoubtedly be error not to find probable cause. Many cases, however, probably fall into a middle ground in which magistrates and trial judges are justified in ruling either way.

In this case, the judge is probably acting well within the authority granted by *Gates* if he sustains Colin's claim that Murtaugh lacked probable cause. The totality approach probably would *allow* a finding of probable cause based on the detail in the tip coupled with the corroboration of those details and the suspicious activity that was consistent with a narcotics transaction. However, it does not *mandate* a probable cause finding. Based on the fact that the tip was anonymous, that the detail about the car was not so great or unique that it provided strong evidence of firsthand involvement with the seller, and that the activity witnessed was not highly suspicious and was limited to interaction with one individual, a judge could plausibly conclude that there was not a "fair probability" that contraband was in the trunk.

C. THE WARRANT REQUIREMENT

Warrants are documents that are issued by judicial officers—judges or magistrates—upon application by police officers or other representatives of the executive branch. Upon reviewing the application, the judicial officer is supposed to make an independent determination of whether an adequate showing has been made. A **search warrant** authorizes the search of a place and the seizure of objects. An **arrest warrant** authorizes the seizure of a person. Warrants specify the scope of the search or seizure authority that is granted.

Neither clause of the Fourth Amendment explicitly requires a warrant to search or seize. The first requires reasonableness. The second sets forth the prerequisites for a valid warrant to search. Because the Fourth Amendment is the result of colonial resentment toward searches pursuant to **general warrants** and **writs of assistance,** some argue that a search warrant requirement is directly contrary to history. Others disagree, finding no inconsistency between the Framers' hostility to abusive warrants and a command that searches usually must be performed under the authority of narrowly drawn warrants based on probable cause. In the Supreme Court, the latter view has prevailed.

1. Warrants to Search

This first subsection is concerned with the issue of whether a warrant is necessary to search a place.

a. Search warrant requirement. According to this prevailing view, **warrantless searches are "per se unreasonable."** Katz v. United States, 389 U.S. 347, 88 S. Ct. 507, 19 L. Ed. 2d 576 (1967). This means that to be constitutionally reasonable a search ordinarily requires not only probable cause but also a search warrant. No matter how much cause to search officers have, their failure to secure judicial authorization **in advance** renders a search presumptively unconstitutional.

 # EXAMPLES AND ANALYSIS

1. Officers have ample firsthand evidence that narcotics are being used in an apartment. They enter immediately and seize the contraband. The entry is unconstitutional because it violates the warrant requirement. Johnson v. United States, 333 U.S. 10, 68 S. Ct. 367, 92 L. Ed. 436 (1948).

2. Officers have probable cause to eavesdrop electronically on a conversation being conducted from a public telephone booth. They limit their listening so that it is no

more extensive than a judge could properly have authorized by warrant. After they record incriminating comments, the officers maintain that their actions should be upheld because they were justified, limited, and successful. Their argument should be rejected because the eavesdropping was a warrantless search and consequently was unreasonable. Katz v. United States.

---

b. **Rationales for the search warrant requirement.** The privacy lost as a result of an unjustified search cannot be restored. The primary reasons for imposing a search warrant requirement are to **prevent unreasonable invasions of privacy** and **to guard against hindsight justification** of unjustified searches. See Katz v. United States; Johnson v. United States.

The warrant rule **prevents unreasonable invasions of privacy** in at least three ways. First, neutral judicial officers reject officers' biased or erroneous showings of cause, deny warrants, and thereby prevent unreasonable searches from occurring. Second, the awareness that the facts supporting cause must be sworn to in advance discourages officers from conducting unsupportable searches in the hope that they can rely on "hindsight"—that they can claim to have known in advance what they discovered only after they searched. Finally, the particular descriptions that must be contained in a warrant limit the scope of searches and seizures to what is justified.

The warrant requirement also **insures that unreasonable searches are identified and invalidated.** It does so by requiring officers to document the facts they know before they search, precluding supplementation of probable cause showings by hindsight. As a consequence, a reviewing court can determine whether the search actually was reasonable at the time it was conducted.

c. **Exceptions to the search warrant rule.** The search warrant requirement is a "norm" of reasonableness, but it is not inflexible. In fact, there are many exceptions to the rule. A warrantless search that falls within one of these exceptions is reasonable. The exceptions to the warrant requirement are discussed in detail in section F below.

2. Warrants to Seize Persons

This subsection is concerned with whether warrants are required in order to arrest those suspected of crimes.

a. **Rule for felony arrests.** An arrest is a seizure of a person and is unreasonable unless it is supported by probable cause. However, **no warrant is needed for a public felony arrest.** United States v. Watson, 423 U.S. 411, 96 S. Ct. 820, 46 L. Ed. 2d 598 (1976). Even if there is

Test ✓

VPC: that
committed felony
2) Public Place

ample time to secure an arrest warrant, an officer can reasonably arrest a person in a public place so long as she has probable cause to believe the arrestee committed a felony.

The Supreme Court's rejection of an arrest warrant requirement in this situation rests primarily on two historical facts. First, the common law that predated the Fourth Amendment tolerated warrantless public arrests of felons. Second, since the adoption of the Fourth Amendment both the federal government and the states have consistently adhered to and reaffirmed that common law rule. United States v. Watson.

An arrest warrant requirement could prevent unjustified liberty infringements much like the search warrant rule prevents unjustified privacy invasions. Implicit in the common law rule that has been made a part of the Fourth Amendment is the conclusion that those preventive benefits do not outweigh the government's interest in the immediate apprehension of those suspected of serious crimes.

> **Note:** A search or arrest warrant is needed to enter a dwelling to arrest a felon because the entry is a search that triggers the privacy protection rationales that underlie the **search warrant requirement.** See Section F.3 below.

b. **Rule for misdemeanor arrests.** There is no Supreme Court holding regarding the propriety of warrantless, **public misdemeanor arrests.** The language and reasoning of United States v. Watson, however, suggest that there may well be a Fourth Amendment arrest warrant requirement for **misdemeanors committed outside the presence of the arresting officer.** The common law rule required a warrant unless a misdemeanor was committed in the presence of the officer. Moreover, the balance of interests tips differently in misdemeanor cases. The liberty deprivation suffered by arrestees is still serious, while society's interest in immediate apprehension is considerably less weighty than it is in felony cases.

Test:

E&A EXAMPLE AND ANALYSIS

Detective Vincent has more than adequate cause to believe that Bill, who has just entered a movie theater, sold a small quantity of marijuana to an undercover informant. May Vincent arrest Bill without a warrant?

If the offense is a felony, no warrant is required for such a public-place arrest. If the offense is a misdemeanor and was not just committed in the officer's presence, the Fourth Amendment probably does require a warrant.

D. ISSUANCE OF WARRANTS

The second clause of the Fourth Amendment (the "warrant clause") specifies certain prerequisites for a **valid warrant to search or seize.** Other implicit requirements have been found in the constitutional text.

1. "Probable Cause" Requirement

According to the warrant clause of the Fourth Amendment, "no Warrants shall issue, but upon **probable cause.**" Simply stated, neither a search nor an arrest warrant can ever be valid unless the issuing judge is provided with facts that support a finding of probable cause. (The meaning of probable cause is discussed in section B above.) A warrant is invalid if probable cause is not shown to the magistrate **in advance.** A deficient showing cannot be remedied by later proof that the officers were in possession of adequate information before the search but failed to present it to the magistrate. Aguilar v. Texas, 378 U.S. 108, 84 S. Ct. 1509, 12 L. Ed. 2d 723 (1964).

2. Misrepresentations in Probable Cause Showings

Even though the face of an affidavit presented to a magistrate contains facts adequate to support a finding of probable cause, misrepresentations by the affiant may invalidate the probable cause finding. Franks v. Delaware, 438 U.S. 154, 98 S. Ct. 2674, 57 L. Ed. 2d 667 (1978). A warrant will be voided if the party who is seeking invalidation proves "by a **preponderance of the evidence**" that (1) a **false statement** was included in the affidavit; (2) the false statement was included **knowingly and intentionally or with reckless disregard for the truth;** and (3) with the false statement excised, **the remaining information does not support a finding of probable cause.** Id. While the question remains open, it is probably unlikely that "negligent" misrepresentation (that is, statements that an affiant reasonably should know are false) must be excluded from consideration.

> **Note:** To receive a hearing on allegations of misrepresentation, the party seeking to invalidate the warrant must first make **"a substantial preliminary showing"** of the same facts that he must ultimately prove by a preponderance.

EXAMPLE AND ANALYSIS

On the basis of a paid informant's tip plus a small amount of additional independent investigation, Officer James applied for an arrest warrant. The affidavit did not report how the informant had gained his information, but told of repeated past instances in which the informant had given accurate information. The arrest warrant was issued.

Prior to trial, the arrestee challenges the validity of the warrant, establishing that Officer James neglected to mention a handful of instances in which the informant's past tips had proven inaccurate and omitting facts that could have suggested a strong motive to lie in this case. Should the challenge be sustained?

In this case, the officer has not presented an affirmative falsehood, but has instead omitted truthful information that is important to the accurate determination of cause. Because the distortion of the process and outcome seems similar if not identical, there seems to be no reason to treat the situations differently.

Assuming, therefore, that the doctrine of Franks v. Delaware controls, the challenge should be sustained if the arrestee proves two matters: (1) that the officer's failure to include the information bearing on the veracity of the informant was intentional, knowing, or done with reckless disregard for the truth of the presentation in the affidavit; and (2) that if the omitted information were included, the affidavit would not establish probable cause. With regard to the first matter, it seems unlikely that the officer's omission would have been merely careless. The second matter is less clear. The informant's veracity was an important variable in the equation. No basis of knowledge was shown, and the additional investigative information was limited. Nonetheless, the totality might still have been sufficient to support a finding of probable cause.

---

3.   "Neutral and Detached Magistrate" Requirement

Although the requirement is not expressed in the text of the Fourth Amendment, warrants must be issued by **"neutral and detached" magistrates.** Connally v. Georgia, 429 U.S. 245, 97 S. Ct. 546, 50 L. Ed. 2d 444 (1977). This requirement guarantees accuracy in probable cause determinations and flows logically from the role of warrants as safeguards against biased, potentially mistaken judgments by overzealous law enforcement officers.

The issuing individual **must be neutral,** that is, impartial with regard to whether warrants should be issued. Thus, warrants granted by a magistrate who is compensated for every warrant issued, but is paid nothing if a warrant request is denied, are invalid. See Connally v. Georgia.

The individual **must also be detached** from the executive branch so that she is not biased in favor of requests by officers. Consequently, when the attorney general—the chief law enforcement officer of the state—also acts as a justice of the peace, the warrants she issues cannot survive constitutional scrutiny. See Coolidge v. New Hampshire, 403 U.S. 443, 91 S. Ct. 2022, 29 L. Ed. 2d 564 (1971).

Magistrates **do not have to be lawyers.** A person is qualified to issue warrants so long as she is **"capable of determining whether probable cause exists for the requested arrest or search."** Shadwick v. City of

Tampa, 407 U.S. 345, 92 S. Ct. 2119, 32 L. Ed. 2d 783 (1972). For example, municipal court clerks are constitutionally qualified to issue valid warrants to arrest individuals for municipal ordinance violations. See id.

4. "Oath or Affirmation" Requirement

The text of the Fourth Amendment states that the "probable cause" needed to issue a warrant must be "supported by Oath or affirmation." Individuals applying for warrants must therefore swear or affirm that the information they are providing to the judge is true. This guarantee of veracity provides a further safeguard against unjustified searches or arrests by threatening penalties for dishonesty and impressing on officers the necessity to furnish accurate information.

5. "Particularity" Requirements

The British used "general warrants" to uncover wrongdoing by our colonial ancestors. General warrants granted officials broad authority to determine what places to search and what objects to search for and seize. To eliminate these abusive devices, the Framers of the Fourth Amendment included "particularity" requirements. According to the text, warrants must **"particularly describ[e both] the place to be searched, and the persons or things to be seized."**

a. **Particular description of the place to be searched.** By requiring particular description of the place to be searched, the Fourth Amendment guards against invasions of privacy that are broader than justified by the cause demonstrated. Put otherwise, it prevents searches from extending beyond the place to which probable cause extends. Maryland v. Garrison, 480 U.S. 79, 107 S. Ct. 1013, 94 L. Ed. 2d 72 (1987).

b. **Particular description of the persons or things to be seized.** The Fourth Amendment also requires particular description of the persons or things to be seized. This demand serves two functions. It guards against unjustified deprivations of liberty or property by allowing only seizures of persons or items that are supported by probable cause. It also guards against unjustified invasions of privacy by effectively restricting the places that are subject to search and the duration of the search. Officers may look only in areas where the specified items could be and must terminate their searches when all specified items are found. See Andresen v. Maryland, 427 U.S. 463, 96 S. Ct. 2737, 49 L. Ed. 2d 627 (1976).

c. **Meaning of "particularity."** There is no invariable, bright-line standard of particularity. In general, descriptions of places, persons, and things must be as particular as is reasonable in the circumstances. The degree of particularity required can vary depending on the descriptive information that is available and the scope of the authority needed by law enforcement to conduct an effective investigation. It is unreasonable to demand detailed description when details are not known or accessible or when such a demand could thwart the objectives of the investigation.

For example, if a certain stolen item is the object of a search, officers should be able to describe its characteristics in considerable detail. However, if a quantity of marijuana is sought, the descriptive information available is likely to be limited and little detail should be required. Similarly, if documentary evidence of a complex real estate fraud is the goal, authorization to search for "memoranda and other evidence pertaining to the fraudulent transaction" might be particular enough. Both the limited availability of information about the relevant papers and the need to have ample authority to examine all files to determine which are pertinent militate in favor of that conclusion. See Andresen v. Maryland.

(E&A) EXAMPLE AND ANALYSIS

Videomania, a retailer specializing in television and videotape equipment, was burglarized. Several televisions and VCRs were stolen. Based on probable cause to believe that the stolen items were in the warehouse of a competitor, investigators secured a warrant to search "the blue-gray warehouse on Wagon Court for five color televisions and seven VCRs." Is the warrant valid?

The warrant is probably not particular enough in two respects. First, the description of the place to be searched—the warehouse—should provide an address or details that would pinpoint the building more specifically. As it is, there is a cognizable, and avoidable, risk that another, similar warehouse might be erroneously searched. More clearly, the things to be seized—the televisions and VCRs—should be more particularly described. Brand names, model numbers, and even serial numbers, if available, should be included so that both the search for the stolen items and the seizures of property are kept within proper bounds.

---

d. **Mistaken descriptions and the particularity requirement.** Warrants can contain mistaken descriptions of places, persons, or things. Because of such descriptions, warrants might authorize searches of areas that there is clearly no probable cause to search or seizures of individuals or items that there is clearly no probable cause to seize. Such warrants might violate the probable cause requirement because the search or seizure authorized is not supported by probable cause. They might also violate the particularity requirement insofar as they authorize searches or seizures that are broader than those that are justified. In

Anticipatory warrants
p. 929 Book
Mag. can cut S.W. to issue based on if certain expected to happen events occur

sum, warrants containing mistaken descriptions are potentially unconstitutional.

Nonetheless, a warrant is not necessarily invalid when its description of a place or object turns out to have been **mistaken. If at the time a warrant is issued** it is **reasonable** to believe that probable cause to search or seize extends to the place described or the person or object seized, the warrant **is sufficiently particular and otherwise valid.** A later showing that the description mistakenly included an area that should not have been included "does not retroactively invalidate the warrant." Even though the description was **in fact** mistakenly over-broad, the warrant is valid unless the officers applying for the warrant **knew or "should have known" of the mistake.** Maryland v. Garrison.

Garrison
Facts

In Maryland v. Garrison, a warrant to search the entire third floor of a building was issued based on facts that furnished probable cause to search a particular individual's apartment. Later, it was discovered that there were two apartments on the third floor—the one that the officers had probable cause to search and another, unrelated apartment. The Supreme Court concluded that the warrant "was valid when it issued" because at that time it was reasonable to believe "that there was only one apartment on the third floor of the building." The reasonable mistake made in describing the area to be searched did not render the warrant insufficiently particular.

E. EXECUTION OF WARRANTS

The second clause of the Fourth Amendment does not address the execution of warrants. Nonetheless, if a warrant that is valid when issued is improperly executed, the resulting search and seizure can be "unreasonable."

1. The Fourth Amendment "Knock and Announce" Principle

Book
p. 96 N36
Magistrate probably can issue warrants requiring No Knock

One of "the factors to be considered in assessing the reasonableness of a search or seizure" of a dwelling is the "method of entry." The method of entry may render a search pursuant to a valid warrant unreasonable. The primary constraint upon the method of entry is the **"common-law 'knock and announce' principle."** This principle "forms a part of the reasonableness inquiry under the Fourth Amendment," and, apparently, establishes a "presumption in favor of announcement." Wilson v. Arkansas, — U.S. —, 115 S. Ct. 1914, 131 L. Ed. 2d 976 (1995). As a result, "in some circumstances an officer's unannounced entry" can make the search of a home unreasonable.

The "knock and announce" principle is a safeguard against several harms threatened by unannounced entries. It prevents damage to dwellings, limits the ambit of necessary privacy invasions, and protects the safety of officers and occupants.

2. Reasonable Unannounced Entries: "Specific" versus "Categorical" Justifications

While the Fourth Amendment reasonableness requirement includes the "knock and announce" principle, it does not "mandate a rigid rule of announcement." A demonstration of **"countervailing law enforcement interests"** can "establish the reasonableness of an unannounced entry." Wilson v. Arkansas. In other words, the interests served by announcement can be outweighed, and the presumption in favor of announcement dispelled, by a showing of "contrary considerations" that call for entry without notice.

The **rationale** for this flexibility is clear. In individual cases, the harms presumptively threatened by unannounced entries can be less serious than the particular perils that would be caused by giving notice. When that is the case, it is certainly reasonable to refrain from giving an announcement.

The precise **nature of the interests** that can render an unannounced entry reasonable is not clear. The Court has refused to "attempt a comprehensive catalog of the relevant countervailing" interests. It has indicated that "a threat of physical violence" or a danger "that evidence would likely be destroyed if advance notice were given" would suffice. Moreover, an officer in pursuit of an escaping prisoner who has gone into his dwelling need not pause to give notice. Id.

Categorical exceptions to the "knock and announce" requirement are not valid under the Fourth Amendment. Determinations of whether a "no-knock" entry is justified must be made on a case-by-case basis based on the **specific facts and circumstances** of each case. In Richards v. Wisconsin, —U.S.—, 117 S. Ct. 1416 (1997), a unanimous Court rejected the claim that felony drug cases were a category of crime that justified a per se exemption from the knock and announce demand. Nonetheless, officers do not need **probable cause** to enter premises without knocking and announcing. Instead, "to justify a 'no-knock' entry, the police must have a **reasonable suspicion** that knocking and announcing their presence, under the particular circumstances, would be dangerous or futile, or that it would inhibit the effective investigation of the crime, by, for example, allowing the destruction of evidence."

[handwritten notes in margin:]
1) Futile
2) Dangerous
3) Evidence dest.

EXAMPLES AND ANALYSIS

1. Officers have a warrant to search a home for evidence of land fraud. They have no information indicating that advance notice will defeat their efforts or endanger their persons. May they enter without knocking?

Such an entry would seem to be presumptively unreasonable. By holding that the "knock and announce" principle is a part of the reasonableness equation, and suggesting that the common law rule included "a presumption in favor of announcement," the Court

[handwritten note at bottom:] supp.1 → Excessive damage — violates 4th Amend BUT Remedy in tort compensation not suppression

seemed to indicate that unannounced entries into dwellings would be unreasonable unless the government could provide a legitimate reason for not announcing.

2. Armed with an arrest warrant, officers proceed to Saul's home to arrest him for the shotgun murder of a liquor store owner. When they arrive, they hear a voice from within shout "Get ready!" May they enter without knocking and announcing?

Protecting the officers against physical violence is clearly an adequate reason to permit unannounced entry. The question is whether the showing of that interest is sufficient here. A "no-knock" entry would not be justifiable simply because Saul committed a violent crime. Entry without knocking and announcing would be reasonable if the particular facts of this case—the shotgun murder and the shout—give rise to a "reasonable suspicion" that an announcement would be dangerous.

3. Mistakes in Executing Warrants

Earlier, the subject of mistaken descriptions in warrants was discussed. Mistakes can also occur in the execution of warrants. Such mistakes might take two different forms. An officer might mistakenly interpret the scope of a perfectly valid warrant that itself contains no errors. Or she might err in acting pursuant to the mistaken description contained in a warrant. In either case, the reasonableness of the resulting conduct—the search or seizure—depends on the reasonableness of the mistake.

In the case of **mistaken interpretation of the warrant,** it must be **reasonable at the time of execution** to believe that the warrant authorizes the action taken. Thus, if a warrant validly and particularly authorizes the search of a particular person's home, and an officer reasonably but mistakenly believes that another dwelling is that person's home, a search of that dwelling will be reasonable even though it was not actually authorized by the warrant.

Similarly, when an officer relies on a **mistaken warrant,** it must be **reasonable at the time of execution** not to realize that the warrant description is mistaken. See Maryland v. Garrison. For example, if a warrant description of a home is mistakenly (although not facially) overbroad (that is, it erroneously includes an area that there was no cause to search) and an officer searches the area authorized by the warrant, that search will be valid so long as the officer's failure to realize that the warrant was overbroad is **"objectively understandable and reasonable."** Maryland v. Garrison.

 EXAMPLE AND ANALYSIS

Officer Gordon is asked to execute a warrant that mistakenly authorizes the search of "a home located at 434 Wentworth Avenue." The district attorney informs Gordon

[handwritten margin notes:]
3rd party accompaniment
Supp. p. 2-3
it is a violation of 4th Amend
for police to bring members of
the media or other 3rd parties
into a home during execution of
a warrant when presence of
the third parties in the home
is not in the aid of the execution of the
warrant

that the home being searched belongs to Peter Dornan, a narcotics distributor who has evaded detection for years. When he arrives at the address, Gordon notices that the mailbox has the name "G. Burnett" below the number 434. A child who answers his knock confirms that it is the "Burnett residence." Gordon searches the dwelling anyway. It turns out that Peter Dornan—the subject of the probable cause to search— lived at 443 Wentworth and that a reasonable mistake led to the wrong address in the warrant. Is Gordon's search reasonable?

Although the reasonable mistake in the warrant description means that it was valid when issued, the mailbox and conversation with the child may well have put Gordon on sufficient notice to render his execution unreasonable. It is certainly arguable that once he gained this information it was no longer reasonable for him to believe that the warrant was correct in authorizing the search of 434 Wentworth. If so, the fact that the mistaken warrant in fact described the place he searched will not prevent his search from being deemed unreasonable.

REVIEW QUESTIONS AND ANSWERS

Question: Detectives have probable cause to believe that Marian had sex with an underage boy, a felony under the state's law. While investigating the offense, they had spoken to Robin, Marian's personal assistant. Subsequently, they developed probable cause to believe that Robin had filed a false declaration about Marian's whereabouts at the time in question. Filing such a report is a misdemeanor. Without warrants, Marian and Robin are arrested while having lunch at Le Chique, a favorite dining spot of the Hollywood elite. Are the arrests valid?

Answer: Marian's arrest is valid. Le Chique is a public place and the offense is a felony. Under *Watson*, only probable cause is needed. Robin's arrest is probably not valid. The common law rule did not allow warrantless arrests for misdemeanors unless they were committed in an officer's presence and the officer immediately arrested the suspect.

Question: On August 3, Officer Lutz prepared an affidavit stating that he had seen 400 kilos of heroin in Bonnie's home at 8875 Quince Court on July 28. Lutz took it to a magistrate, who issued a warrant authorizing a search of 8875 Quince Lane for heroin. Lutz asked Officer Flood to execute the warrant for him. Flood proceeded to the address, knocked and immediately entered. He found illegal firearms but no narcotics. It is later discovered that Lutz saw only 40 kilos of heroin at Bonnie's home and that his observations took place on June 28. Was Flood's search unreasonable?

Answer: These facts raise several questions involving the proper issuance and execution of warrants. First, the warrant erroneously specified the address of Bonnie's home. The question is whether a reasonable officer should have been aware of the magistrate's mistake. It is arguable whether Lutz should have seen and noticed the word "Lane" rather than "Court." On the other hand, Officer Flood was merely asked to execute the warrant. His failures to recognize the mistake when he received the warrant and when he executed it hardly seem "objectively unreasonable." (The case would be different if something at the house searched should have alerted Flood to the mistake.)

Second, the affidavit contained two false statements. Both the date of Lutz's observations and the amount of heroin were misstated. If the false statements were intentionally, knowingly, or recklessly made, they must be eliminated from the affidavit. Then it must be determined whether the affidavit would still have supported a finding of probable cause. Both misstatements bear on the issue of "staleness." Forty kilograms is likely to be completely gone from a location sooner than 400 kilograms. Moreover, heroin is much more likely to be gone from the premises after almost five weeks than after only one week. In other words, with the correct information—40 kilograms of heroin seen almost five weeks earlier—one might well conclude that there is no longer a "fair probability" that any heroin is still present. If so, the warrant was void.

Finally, Flood's knock and immediate entry might have violated the "knock and announce" principle, which contemplates giving occupants an opportunity to respond. Flood did not announce that he was a police officer and did not wait before entering. Unless there were specific facts in this case that gave rise to a reasonable suspicion that knocking and announcing would lead to the destruction of the heroin, would endanger the officer, would be futile, or would otherwise inhibit an effective investigation, Flood's execution of the warrant was unreasonable.

F. EXCEPTIONS TO THE SEARCH WARRANT RULE

The requirement that officers obtain warrants before conducting searches is a "cardinal principle" of Fourth Amendment law. California v. Acevedo, 500 U.S. 565, 111 S. Ct. 1982, 114 L. Ed. 2d 619 (1991). Nonetheless, it is a rule qualified by many exceptions. The nature and contours of the primary **exceptions to the warrant rule** are the subjects of this section. Some of the exceptions discussed are also **exceptions to the probable cause norm.** Because a search without a warrant is presumptively unreasonable, the government has the burden of showing that it falls within an exception to the warrant rule.

1. Searches Incident to Arrest

Officers have a limited authority to conduct warrantless searches when they arrest suspects. The authority to perform a **search incident to arrest** is rooted in two justifications—to prevent the arrestee from using a weapon to harm the officers or to escape, and to prevent the arrestee from destroying or concealing evidence. Chimel v. California, 395 U.S. 752, 89 S. Ct. 2034, 23 L. Ed. 2d 685 (1969).

   a. **The showing needed to conduct a search incident to arrest.** To perform a search incident to arrest, officers need only establish that they lawfully arrested a suspect and took him into custody.

    i.   **A lawful arrest.** For officers to have valid authority to search an individual incident to arrest, the arrest must be **lawful.** See Chimel v. California; United States v. Robinson, 414 U.S. 218, 94 S. Ct. 467, 38 L. Ed. 2d 427 (1973). An arrest is lawful if there is probable cause to believe the suspect committed an offense. See section C.2 above. In the case of a misdemeanor committed outside the presence of the officer, an arrest warrant may also be necessary. See section C.2.b above.

    ii.   **A custodial arrest.** The authority to search incident to arrest has been recognized only in cases of **custodial arrest**—when officers actually take a suspect **into custody.** See United States v. Robinson. In some cases, officers have probable cause to arrest a suspect but decide to issue a citation instead. Although the Supreme Court has not addressed the question whether there is any authority under the Fourth Amendment to search "cited" suspects "incident to arrest," it would not seem reasonable to permit officers to do so. The rationales for the search incident to arrest exception are closely tied to the fact of custody.

    iii.   **Probable cause to search not required.** While **probable cause to arrest** is necessary, the authority to conduct a search incident to arrest does **not** require any showing that a weapon or evidence might be present in the area searched. The justifications for searching are presumed to arise from the mere fact of the custodial arrest. See United States v. Robinson.

    iv.   **Discretion to arrest or search allowed.** Depending on the situation, an officer who has probable cause might be **required to arrest** a suspect or might have **discretion to determine whether to arrest** a suspect. Similarly, the search of an arrested suspect might be **mandated** in some or all cases or it might be **discretionary.** In all such cases, the officer may exercise the power to search incident to arrest so long as she makes a lawful, custodial arrest. The fact that the arrest or the search was the product of the officer's discretionary choice does not deprive her of the authority to conduct a warrantless search incident to the arrest. See Gustafson v. Florida, 414 U.S. 260, 94 S. Ct. 488, 38 L. Ed. 2d 456 (1973).

  b.   **Scope of search incident to arrest authority.** A search incident to an arrest is limited to (1) the **person of the arrestee;** (2) the **area within the immediate control of the arrestee;** and (3) for arrests within dwellings, the **areas immediately adjacent to the place of arrest.**

    i.   **Person of the arrestee.** Officers may thoroughly search **the person of the arrestee** and remove any items found there. United States v. Robinson. They may also open **any "containers"** found on the person of the arrestee. Id. They may not "strip search" an arrestee as part of a search incident—that is, there is no automatic authority to remove the arrestee's clothing. See Illinois v. Lafayette, 462 U.S. 640, 103 S. Ct. 2605, 77 L. Ed. 2d 65 (1983).

ii. **Area within the immediate control of the arrestee.** In addition, officers may search the **area " 'within [an arrestee's] immediate control'**—construing that phrase to mean the area from within which he might gain possession of a weapon or destructible evidence." Chimel v. California. Any containers discovered during this search may also be opened.

The authority to search the area within an arrestee's immediate control has both **temporal and spatial limits.** A search incident to an arrest cannot be **remote in either time or place** from the arrest itself. United States v. Chadwick, 433 U.S. 1, 97 S. Ct. 2476, 53 L. Ed. 2d 538 (1977). However, neither the physical nor the temporal boundaries of the authority can be pinpointed with precision. No bright line delineates the space within the arrestee's control, nor is there a precise period of time during which the power to search must be exercised.

(a) **Spatial boundaries.** The question, according to *Chimel*, is whether the area is one from which the arrestee might gain possession of a weapon or evidence. Some courts have concluded that this includes places into which an arrestee could **"lunge."** Moreover, **actual impediments to access,** such as locks, handcuffs, or numerous police officers, might limit or prevent access to an area that otherwise is within an arrestee's reach. Whether such impediments should or do preclude a proper search incident to arrest is debatable. On the one hand, the arrestee might have no realistic opportunity to obtain a weapon or evidence. On the other hand, the Supreme Court has shown an affinity for bright-line fictions and a hostility toward case-by-case adjudication in this area.

(b) **Temporal boundaries.** A search incident to arrest cannot be "remote in time" from the arrest. If it is remote, a search falls outside the scope of the exception. Searches that follow **"immediately upon"** an arrest or are **"contemporaneous with"** an arrest are valid. New York v. Belton, 453 U.S. 454, 101 S. Ct. 2860, 69 L. Ed. 2d 768 (1981). These phrases suggest that any substantial delay **between the arrest and the search** will preclude a legitimate search incident to arrest—unless, perhaps, there is good reason for the delay.

A search performed more than an hour after law enforcement has taken exclusive control of an object is too remote. United States v. Chadwick.

(c) **Automobile interiors: The "passenger compartment" and "recent occupant" rules of New York v. Belton.** In New York v. Belton, the Supreme Court announced a bright-line rule defining the area of immediate control in the context of automobile passenger compartments. According to that rule, the **entire passenger compartment** of an automobile and **every container found inside** is within the "immediate control" of a person in an automobile. Id. Consequently, the entire compartment may be searched incident to that person's arrest. The **trunk** of the vehicle is **not** within the scope.

RULE

Because the arrest is the predicate for a search incident to arrest, logic suggests that the area of immediate control should be determined **at the time of the arrest and search.** Ordinarily that is the case. In the vehicle context, however, a passenger compartment may be subject to search even though the arrestee did not have actual access to it at the time of the arrest or at the time of the search.

BELTON Facts

In *Belton*, the arrestee had been removed from the vehicle and handcuffed. The officer returned to the car, found a jacket on the backseat, and unzipped the pocket, finding narcotics. According to the Court, a search incident to arrest was justified because the arrestee was a **"recent occupant"** who was inside the vehicle **"just before"** the arrest. New York v. Belton. The meaning of "recent" and "just before" are not entirely clear, but the terms suggest that the **time between the arrestee's presence in the vehicle and the search** must be very short.

Whether this authority to search a place that the arrestee occupied **prior to arrest** extends to settings other than the passenger compartments of vehicles is uncertain.

iii. **Areas immediately adjoining the place of arrest.** "[A]s an incident to arrest," officers may "as a precautionary matter and **without any probable cause or reasonable suspicion, look in closets and other spaces immediately adjoining the place of arrest from which an attack could be immediately launched"** by a person other than the arrestee. Maryland v. Buie, 494 U.S. 325, 110 S. Ct. 1093, 108 L. Ed. 2d 276 (1990). The authority to conduct such a search is automatically triggered by an arrest in a home and surely applies to arrests in other buildings. Because the rationale is to prevent attacks, its scope is limited to whatever is necessary to ascertain whether dangerous **persons** are in these "immediately adjoining spaces."

Red limits

> **Note:** When officers make an in-home arrest, they also have the authority to perform a "protective sweep" of other areas in the home **if they have a reasonable suspicion that dangerous persons are present.** See section H below. Unlike the authority to search incident to arrest, the authority to do a protective sweep does not arise *automatically* by virtue of the lawful arrest.

iv.   Searches conducted prior to arrest. A lawful arrest is a necessary predicate for a valid search incident to arrest. The probable cause to arrest cannot be supplied by the search alleged to be incident to that arrest. However, if an officer has probable cause to arrest, she may conduct a valid search incident to arrest **prior to formally taking the suspect into custody.** Rawlings v. Kentucky, 448 U.S. 98, 100 S. Ct. 2556, 65 L. Ed. 2d 633 (1980).

EXAMPLE AND ANALYSIS

Officers arrest Arnie in the study of his home pursuant to an arrest warrant. One officer reaches into Arnie's suit coat pocket and extracts an envelope. He tears open the envelope to examine the contents. Four feet away is a closet door. The other officer opens the closet door and looks inside. He finds a closed briefcase, opens it, and finds a quantity of narcotics. Are the searches valid as incident to Arnie's arrest?

Assuming that the warrant and arrest are valid, the search of Arnie's person and the envelope are valid under the authority to search thoroughly the person of the arrestee. The closet search is arguable. Clearly, the door to this area immediately adjoining the place of arrest can be opened to determine if a dangerous person is present. A further search of the closet, however, hinges on whether the inside of the briefcase is properly considered within the area of Arnie's immediate control. While it seems unrealistic to think he could actually have reached a weapon or evidence there, the possibility that Arnie might "lunge" this distance and the possibility that a court would be willing to ignore actual impediments to access—in this case the closet door and the briefcase—make the resolution of this question debatable.

If the officer had taken the envelope from Arnie, put it in his pocket, then opened it later at the stationhouse, would it have been a proper search incident to arrest? A search incident cannot be remote in time or place from the arrest. In this case, the envelope search would probably be outside the exception.

---

2. The *Chrisman*—"At the Elbow of the Arrestee" Exception

In Washington v. Chrisman, 455 U.S. 1, 102 S. Ct. 812, 70 L. Ed. 2d 778 (1982), the Supreme Court recognized an exception that is related to but distinct from the search incident to arrest exception. The officer is entitled to "stay at the elbow of the arrestee" in order to maintain control over him. Washington v. Chrisman. Under certain circumstances, if the exercise of this authority necessitates an entry into a private place—a search—that entry is reasonable despite the absence of a search warrant. The *Chrisman* exception is rooted in an officer's needs "to ensure his own safety" and to preserve "the integrity of the arrest." An arrestee who is not monitored adequately may escape and may injure or even kill the officer.

a. **The showing needed for the "at the elbow of the arrestee" exception.** The *Chrisman* exception is triggered by two showings: a **lawful custodial arrest** and a **request by the arrestee to enter a private place.**

   i. **A lawful custodial arrest.** The government must demonstrate a **lawful custodial arrest.** The officer must have taken the arrestee into custody based on probable cause to believe he had committed an offense. There is no need to show cause to believe that the arrestee was likely to escape or inflict harm or that there was any cause to search the place that the officer entered.

   ii. **A request by the arrestee to enter a private place.** The exception recognized in *Chrisman* clearly applies to cases in which the arrestee makes a **request to enter a private place**—a home or other building. The officer need not grant the request, but if he does he is empowered to stay with the arrestee and, thus, to enter the place without a warrant.

   Chrisman involved a request by a student to enter his dormitory room. It is not clear whether the exception recognized in that case applies in situations in which the officer **requires the arrestee to enter a private place.** Surely, an officer cannot gain warrantless search authority by demanding for no good reason that an arrestee enter a dwelling. However, if the officer has justifications that make his demand reasonable, the logic of *Chrisman* could support warrantless authority to enter and stay at the arrestee's side.

b. **Scope of the "search."** The officer may enter the private place, may go wherever the arrestee goes, and may observe objects that come into her view. See section F.8 below, discussing the "plain view doctrine." Whether an officer has any authority to search closed spaces in the vicinity of the arrestee is an open question. The time and space limitations of the search incident to arrest exception preclude its direct application to the areas inside a dwelling entered by an arrestee. The logic of that exception, however, could support the conclusion that an officer can look in areas that come within the control of an arrestee who has been allowed to enter a dwelling. If so, the scope of the warrantless search authority granted by the "at the elbow" doctrine would be much broader than that recognized in the *Chrisman* decision.

 # EXAMPLE AND ANALYSIS

Candy is arrested while sunbathing near the pool at her apartment building. Because she is wearing only a thong-type bathing suit, Officer Jones instructs her to get dressed for the trip to the police station. Candy objects to Jones coming into her apartment and insists that she would "rather go dressed like this if you intend to come with me." Jones orders her to enter. Upon entering her bedroom, Jones sees cocaine traces on a mirror on the bureau. Is the entry constitutional?

While this situation is different from *Chrisman* insofar as Candy not only did not request to enter but tried to resist, the government might win with a claim that there was a need to make sure that Candy was dressed properly for transportation to the police station. This argument becomes even more persuasive if Candy was going to spend any time in a cell. Nonetheless, it is still uncertain whether any reason can justify forcing an arrestee to enter her home and, if so, whether *Chrisman*'s at-the-elbow authority extends to such a situation.

3. Searches for Arrestees: The Doctrine of Payton v. New York

Normally, an entry of a private dwelling requires a search warrant. The privacy of the home is the quintessential interest protected by the search warrant rule. Nevertheless, a "partial exception" to the search warrant rule may apply when officers search a private dwelling in order to arrest a felon.

a. **The showing needed to justify entry.** Officers must have a **valid arrest warrant for a felony.** The warrant must be based on probable cause and must meet the other requirements for a valid warrant. In addition, officers must have **probable cause** that the subject of the warrant **is presently in his home.** If both conditions are satisfied, they may enter the home to make the arrest. No search warrant is needed to invade the home privacy interest of the alleged felon. Payton v. New York, 445 U.S. 573, 100 S. Ct. 1371, 63 L. Ed. 2d 639 (1980).

Note: The *Payton* doctrine does require officers to secure a warrant before they enter a private dwelling to arrest a suspected felon. Nevertheless, it is accurate to classify the doctrine as a "partial exception" to the **search warrant** rule because **only an arrest warrant** is required.

To issue a search warrant, a magistrate must determine **both** that the "object" sought is one in which the government has a legitimate interest (for example, that there is cause to believe that it is contraband or evidence) **and** that the item is presently in the place to be searched. An arrest warrant, however, demands **only** a judicial determination that the person is an "object" in whom the government has a legitimate interest (that is, there is cause to believe he committed a felony).

Under the *Payton* doctrine, the second determination essential to justify a **search**—that there is probable cause to believe that the "felon" is presently in his home—does not have to be made **in advance by a judicial officer.** Because *Payton* entrusts that determination to police officers, it is a "partial exception" to the search warrant rule.

b. Scope of the exception. Officers may **enter** the residence of the suspected felon in order to arrest her. They may look **only** in places where the alleged felon could be found. Spaces too small to harbor a person are outside the scope. Moreover, once the arrestee is found or it is determined that she is not present, officers must terminate their search.

i. Entries into the dwellings of "innocent" third parties not included: The doctrine of Steagald v. United States. The partial exception of Payton v. New York justifies invasions of the privacy interests of suspected felons. It does not govern entries that invade only the home privacy interests of "innocent third parties"— persons who are not the subject of a felony arrest warrant.

The home privacy interests of an "innocent third party" are protected by the search warrant requirement. Consequently, if officers wish to enter a third party's home to arrest a suspected felon believed to be there, their invasion of the privacy interest of the third party is unreasonable unless they first secure a **search warrant.** Steagald v. United States, 451 U.S. 204, 101 S. Ct. 1642, 68 L. Ed. 2d 38 (1981). Put otherwise, the innocent home-dweller's constitutional rights are violated by an entry without a search warrant.

Note: According to "standing" doctrine (see Chapter 12, section B.2), the felon can assert only his own privacy interests. Consequently, an arrested felon cannot rely on the violation of an innocent third-party home-dweller's constitutional rights. The arrestee must demonstrate that his own Fourth Amendment rights were violated. This requires both a showing that the entry of the home infringed on his constitutional interests and a showing that it did so unreasonably. The former depends on whether the arrestee had a privacy interest that was invaded by the entry. The latter depends on whether the officers satisfied the constitutional standards for reasonably invading that interest.

ii. **Entries that invade third-party interests in "shared" dwellings.** In some cases, both the suspected felon and an "innocent third party" have privacy interests in a home. The doctrine of Payton v. New York clearly holds that the suspected felon's interest may be invaded if officers secure an arrest warrant and have probable cause to believe that the subject of the warrant is in the home. In other words, it is **reasonable to search the suspected felon's home** without a search warrant.

The interesting question is whether the third party's home privacy interest is entitled to the full protection of a search warrant or to the reduced protection afforded by the *Payton* rule. Because the third party is not the subject of a felony arrest warrant, the holding of Steagald v. United States might control. In that case, the invasion of the third party's privacy would require a search warrant.

On the other hand, *Steagald* involved no claim that the third party had shared his privacy with the subject of the arrest warrant. It is arguable that a person in that position is not wholly innocent and that the act of sharing privacy with a suspected felon diminishes the third party's constitutional entitlement. Thus it would be **reasonable to search the third party's home** on the basis of a felony arrest warrant plus probable cause to believe the subject is in the home.

(E&A) EXAMPLE AND ANALYSIS

Based on credible information that Bernard was involved in an arson at a church more than a year earlier, officers go to his office to arrest him. They have no evidence that Bernard has any intent to flee. They walk past the receptionist, proceed to

Bernard's office, open the door, and walk in. If Bernard objects that the officers' entry violated his Fourth Amendment rights, how should a judge rule?

There are several bases for challenging the reasonableness of the entry. The first question is whether officers had probable cause to arrest Bernard. If so, they would need an arrest warrant to enter his office if the privacy protection goal of Payton v. New York extends beyond homes to offices. That point is arguable. Whether or not a warrant is needed, officers would need cause to believe that Bernard was in his office at the time. And, finally, they might well have violated the "knock and announce" principle by entering without giving notice.

4.   Exigent Circumstances Searches

The exigent circumstances exception to the search warrant requirement is the most open-ended of the exceptions. Any circumstances that qualify as an "exigency"—a sufficient need to search without a warrant—can trigger application of the doctrine.

a.   **The showing needed to invoke the exigent circumstances exception.** There are two things that the government must always show to invoke the exigent circumstances exception: **probable cause to search** and **an exigency.** In at least some cases, **an interest of sufficient importance** must also be shown. A few courts have tried to reduce ambiguity and provide guidance to officers and courts by prescribing lists of specific factors that are relevant to exigent circumstances determinations.

   i.   **Probable cause to search.** The warrantless searches justified by exigency must be based on **probable cause to search.** The exception dispenses only with the need for a search warrant. Although there is no need to demonstrate probable cause in advance, the search will be deemed unreasonable if officers cannot later show that they had probable cause to search prior to their search.

   ii.   **Exigent circumstances.** The government must show **an exigency—a need to search without a warrant.** Normally this entails proof either that the purpose of the search would have been thwarted by the delay involved in seeking judicial approval or that some other sufficiently serious harm would have occurred. The destruction or concealment of evidence or contraband is one sort of exigency. A threat to the safety of an individual also qualifies.

      (a)   **A "need to act" may not constitute a "need to search."** A need to **act** without a warrant does not necessarily translate into a need to **search** without a warrant. For example, if officers have probable cause to believe that a container in a public place holds heroin, they need to do something to prevent the contraband from "escaping." However, they can satisfy the exigency without searching the container. A "less intrusive" seizure will prevent escape by immobilizing the container without violating the privacy of its interior. Because there is no inherent reason that a search warrant cannot be sought before the container is searched, there is no basis for an exception from the warrant rule.

(b) **Degree of likelihood that harm will occur.** Inherent in the notion of exigency is a question of degree. Fourth Amendment reasonableness certainly cannot demand that the government show a **certainty** that a particular harm will occur. The question, therefore, is **how likely** the prospect of harm must be. Although the Supreme Court has not said so, the requisite likelihood is probably similar to that required for probable cause. In that case, an exigency showing would require a **fair probability that some particular interest would be frustrated or harmed** if a warrant were sought prior to searching.

(c) **Specificity of the showing of exigency.** There is room for debate over the **specificity of the exigency showing** necessary to invoke the exception. On the one hand, it is arguable that certain combinations of factors automatically give rise to a sufficient need to search. Under that view, probable cause to believe that easily disposable contraband is in a place where persons are present would trigger the exigent circumstances exception.

On the other hand, a more particularized showing that destruction is likely might be needed. In the situation described, officers would have to point to at least one specific reason to believe that the individuals present are likely to dispose of contraband. See Vale v. Louisiana, 399 U.S. 30, 90 S. Ct. 1969, 26 L. Ed. 2d 409 (1970) (refusing to allow a warrantless search when officers had probable cause to search a home for narcotics, the alleged possessor had been arrested in the front yard of his home, and his mother and brother, also residents of the home, were present and knew of his arrest).

(d) **"Hot pursuit": A recurrent type of exigency.** One common type of exigency, known as **"hot pursuit,"** is created when an officer is actively pursuing a suspect who enters a home or other private place. In such cases, officers do not have to take the time necessary to get a warrant in order to enter to make an arrest. The need to apprehend the alerted, fleeing criminal qualifies as an exigency. Moreover, in hot pursuit situations, a suspect who is armed or has committed a crime of violence may pose a risk of danger to the public if she is not immediately apprehended. This danger also satisfies the exigency requirement.

Although situations that give rise to hot pursuit claims usually involve **actual pursuit by law enforcement officers,** the doctrine can also apply to situations involving **pursuit by others.** In Warden v. Hayden, 387 U.S. 294, 87 S. Ct. 1642, 18 L. Ed. 2d 782 (1967), for example, taxicab drivers followed an armed robber to a home and officers arrived fewer than five minutes later. A "hot pursuit" entry was justified.

No matter who the pursuer is, a hot pursuit entry requires **"immediate and continuous pursuit."** Thus, in Welsh v. Wisconsin, 466 U.S. 740, 104 S. Ct. 2091, 80 L. Ed. 2d 732 (1984), even though there was reason to believe that the defendant had swerved from the road, abandoned his vehicle, and entered his home a short time before officers arrived there, the lack of "immediate [and] continuous pursuit" from the scene of the offense rendered the "hot pursuit" doctrine inapplicable.

Typically, hot pursuit entries involve the immediate pursuit of a person **from the scene of a crime.** Nevertheless, the doctrine also applies when a suspect flees from an officer trying to make an arrest **at a time and place remote from the commission of the offense.** In United States v. Santana, 427 U.S. 38, 96 S. Ct. 2406, 49 L. Ed. 2d 300 (1976), a woman was standing in the threshold of her front door. Officers who had probable cause to believe she had committed an offense came to arrest her. When she saw the officers approaching, the woman turned and ran into the house. The officers' warrantless entry into her dwelling to complete their intended arrest was justified by "hot pursuit."

iii.   **An interest of sufficient importance.** At least in the context of **home privacy invasions,** probable cause to search and a present need to search to prevent frustration of the state's interest in detecting and proving crime will not always justify a warrantless entry. The nature of the interest to be served by a search must be sufficiently important to justify the risk to home privacy posed by a warrantless entry.

In Welsh v. Wisconsin, there was probable cause to believe that defendant had driven his automobile while under the influence of intoxicants and that evidence of his intoxication—his blood alcohol level—was dissipating by virtue of his biological processes. In Wisconsin, driving under the influence was "a noncriminal, civil forfeiture offense" that did not carry any possibility of imprisonment. As a result, a majority held that the state's interest in prosecuting drunken driving was not weighty enough to justify a warrantless home entry. Even though there was an exigency and probable cause to search the home, the governmental interest served by a warrantless entry did not outweigh the risk to home privacy inherent in an officer's determination of probable cause.

According to the Court, "application of the exigent-circumstances [doctrine] . . . should **rarely** be sanctioned when there is probable cause to believe that **only a minor offense** . . . has been committed." The majority stated that **"it is difficult to conceive of** a warrantless home arrest that would not be unreasonable under the Fourth Amendment when the underlying offense is **extremely minor."**

The principle of Welsh v. Wisconsin might be limited to **home privacy invasions.** On the one hand, the importance of the interest might be irrelevant when lesser privacy interests are at stake. On the other hand, the nature and importance of the interest might always be relevant when exigency is the basis claimed to justify a warrantless search.

iv. **"Multifactor" approach to exigent circumstances.** The somewhat amorphous, open-ended nature of the exigent circumstances exception creates uncertainty among officers and judges. Some courts have provided a more concrete framework for analysis by prescribing lists of variables pertinent to deciding whether a warrantless search is justified by exigency.

In Dorman v. United States, 435 F.2d 385 (D.C. Cir. 1970), the court prescribed the following seven considerations relevant to entries made to arrest: (1) the gravity of the offense, (2) whether a suspect is believed to be armed, (3) whether more than the minimum probable cause showing exists, (4) whether there is strong reason to believe the suspect is present, (5) the likelihood the suspect will escape if not swiftly apprehended, (6) whether entry can be made peaceably, and (7) whether the entry is made during the day or at night. The court did not prescribe a formula for determining when these considerations justify an exigent circumstances finding.

The Supreme Court has neither endorsed nor disapproved such multifactor exigency analyses.

b. **Scope of an exigent circumstances search.** The exigent circumstances exception allows a warrantless search because officers have both **cause** to believe that something of government interest is in a place and **need** to search before a search warrant can be obtained. Logically, the scope of the permissible intrusion must be dictated by those two factors. A warrantless intrusion should extend **only to areas where the item that the officers have cause to look for could be** and should last **only so long as the need to search continues.**

For example, a hot pursuit entry to capture a fleeing criminal cannot justify a search through bureau drawers. And, if the feared harm is destruction of contraband, the discovery that no one is present could negate the need to act and terminate warrantless search authority. In the latter case, however, if the mere fact that contraband is easily destroyed is a sufficient basis for an exigency finding, the need to find the contraband would continue despite the absence of specific persons.

EXAMPLE AND ANALYSIS

An anonymous phone tipster calls the police station and reports that a "young child is being held at 421 Windridge Lane, in the basement, and is going to be sexually abused sometime in the next hour." Officers rush to the address, enter, and search the basement. They find nothing. Does the homeowner have a valid claim that her Fourth Amendment rights were violated?

Yes. The need to enter a home to prevent imminent serious harm is a sufficient exigency. However, the entry here was unsupported by probable cause. A completely anonymous tip alone cannot furnish a fair probability that the child was present or that a crime was about to be committed. In addition, the showing of exigency suffers from the same deficiency. The anonymous report is not a solid foundation for a conclusion that there was in fact a need to enter.

While the demand for sufficient showings of cause and need to search does prevent officers from stopping or detecting some crimes, the fact pattern here illustrates why such showings are considered necessary. Without a demand for evidence of cause and need, many unjustified invasions of privacy would occur.

5. The "Automobile" or *Carroll-Chambers* Doctrine

The **"automobile doctrine"** is a "species" of exigency-based exception to the warrant rule. It has been the subject of an extensive and independent body of doctrine. As explained below, the warrantless search permitted by this exception is not based entirely on exigency or need to act. It also rests on the "diminished" Fourth Amendment privacy interest in vehicles. Although the label "automobile doctrine" is a convenient shorthand, it can be misleading. The doctrine clearly applies to other kinds of vehicles. Moreover, it is still uncertain whether it applies to all automobiles.

a. The showing necessary to trigger the automobile doctrine. To come within this exception, the government must prove **probable cause to search a vehicle** and **ready mobility.** These elements might be sufficient to invoke the exception.

Two additional facts that **might** have to be established are that the vehicle was at least partially **in use for transportation** at the time the officers searched it and that it was either **stopped in transit, found stationary in a public place,** or **found stationary on the private property of someone other than the vehicle owner.** Even if they are required, these criteria would disqualify only a limited number of vehicles—those exclusively being used for purposes other than transportation or those found stationary on the private property (or curtilage) of the vehicle owner.

   i. Probable cause to search. Officers must possess **probable cause to search.** This requires a "fair probability" that the vehicle contains an item that the government has a legitimate interest in seizing, such as contraband, evidence, or the fruits or instrumentalities of crime. Only the search warrant requirement is suspended by this doctrine. Chambers v. Maroney, 399 U.S. 42, 90 S. Ct. 1975, 26 L. Ed. 2d 419 (1970).

   ii. A vehicle. The doctrine applies only to **vehicles**—that is, modes of transportation. The vehicle must be **readily mobile** and may have to be at least partially **in use for transportation.**

   (a) All vehicles qualify. Originally, this exception was designed to govern searches of **automobiles.** It has been applied by lower courts to other forms of transportation such as airplanes, boats, and motorcycles. In light of the exigency and diminished privacy rationales of the exception, this extension to **all vehicles** is logical.

   If the criteria necessary to satisfy the automobile doctrine are established, the fact that a vehicle serves more than one purpose does not make a difference. See California v.

Carney, 471 U.S. 386, 105 S. Ct. 2066, 85 L. Ed. 2d 406 (1985) (refusing to distinguish between "worthy" and "unworthy" vehicles based on multiple uses). Thus, "motor homes" fall within the exception even though they serve both transportation and residential functions. Id.

(b) **"Ready mobility" requirement.** One of the essential rationales for the exception is exigency. A vehicle has its own source of locomotion and might well depart before officers can obtain a search warrant, frustrating the government interest in conducting a search. Consequently, to invoke the exception a vehicle must be **"readily mobile by the turn of an ignition key."** California v. Carney. If a vehicle is disabled in some way and not readily mobile, there is insufficient need for warrantless action.

(c) **"Being used for transportation" criterion.** The exception is also rooted in the "diminished expectation of privacy" in a vehicle. United States v. Chadwick, 433 U.S. 1, 97 S. Ct. 2476, 53 L. Ed. 2d 538 (1977). This diminished expectation "stem[s] from its use as a licensed motor vehicle subject to a range of police regulation." California v. Carney. A warrantless search, therefore, is permitted if a vehicle is **licensed** and if there are objective indications that it is **being used, at least in part, for transportation purposes.** Id. The "in use for transportation" criterion does not mean that the vehicle must be actually transporting someone or something **at the moment** the officers seek to search it. The question is whether the vehicle is **generally** serving a transportation function at the relevant time.

Moreover, the doctrine **may apply** even if a vehicle is **not in use for transportation.** In California v. Carney, the Supreme Court reserved the question whether the "vehicle exception [applies] to a motor home that is situated in a way or place that objectively indicates that it **is being used as a residence.**" The "factors that **might** be relevant in determining whether a warrant would be required" include the location of the vehicle, immobility, licensing, connection to utilities, and ease of access to a public road. In sum, whether the exception also applies to readily mobile vehicles that are presently in use solely for residential purposes is an open question.

iii. **Location of the vehicle criterion.** The "automobile" doctrine exempts from the warrant requirement vehicles that are **on the highway**—that is, those that are stopped by officers while in

Chadwick p. 73

Bag → if P.C. can reach
But not gun
W/o warrant
—Not incidat [?] warrant
if arrested don't get to
—then per se
remote in time
place

transit on a public roadway. It also includes vehicles **found stationary in a public place,** California v. Carney, and vehicles **found stationary on the private property of someone other than the vehicle owner.** See Pennsylvania v. Kilgore, 518 U.S. —, 116 S. Ct. 2485, 135 L. Ed.2 d 1031 (1996).

The doctrine *may not* apply to vehicles that are **found stationary on private property (or curtilage) of the vehicle owner.** In Coolidge v. New Hampshire, 403 U.S. 443, 91 S. Ct. 2022, 29 L. Ed. 2d 564 (1971), a plurality of the Court concluded that a vehicle that was parked on the owner's property could not be searched without a warrant. The later opinions in California v. Carney and Pennsylvania v. Kilgore, however, cast serious doubt on the current validity of the *Coolidge* plurality's conclusion. Both *Carney* and *Kilgore* indicated that the automobile doctrine permits the warrantless search of every vehicle that is "readily mobile" and "being used for transportation" because both rationales for the exception—the need to act and diminished privacy expectations—are satisfied.

Privacy interest in containers diminishes when brought into car P. interest of person likewise does not

b.   Scope of an automobile doctrine search. The scope of a search under this exception is limited only by the nature of the probable cause to search.

i.   Areas of the vehicle to which the probable cause extends. A warrantless automobile doctrine search of a vehicle allows officers to search **any part of the vehicle that there is probable cause to search.** See California v. Acevedo, 500 U.S. 565, 111 S. Ct. 1982, 114 L. Ed. 2d 619 (1991).

For example, if the facts supporting probable cause focus on one specific portion of the vehicle such as the trunk, the search must be limited to the trunk. Similarly, if the item being sought is too large to fit within a given space such as the glove compartment, a search of that space is impermissible.

No warrant needed to search passengers' containers either P.C. only —Houghton Book-p.

BUT unless arresting passenger can't search passenger (or clothes on passenger) coat on v. //f passenger

Locked compartments of the vehicle may be searched. A lock would clearly not preclude a search pursuant to a warrant, and the scope of an automobile doctrine search is as broad as would be permitted if officers had a warrant to search. See United States v. Ross, 456 U.S. 798, 102 S. Ct. 2157, 72 L. Ed. 2d 572 (1982).

ii.   Separate containers within the vehicle. Officers are also permitted to search **every separate container** within the vehicle that could contain the object of their search. California v. Acevedo. There is authority to search such a container both when officers have probable cause to search an entire vehicle and when they have probable cause to search only a container that is inside a vehicle.

> **Note:** Officers might have probable cause to search **a container that is not inside a vehicle.** In such cases, the fact that the container might depart while a warrant is being sought creates a need to take action. Nevertheless, **a warrantless search is not permitted.** A seizure of the container will satisfy the need to act and the privacy interest in containers is not diminished. For those reasons, officers **must** take the less intrusive warrantless alternative, a seizure and immobilization of the container pending application for a search warrant. United States v. Chadwick. In sum, searches of moveable containers found outside vehicles **are not exempt from the warrant requirement.** Of course, a specific showing that a seizure would be impractical or dangerous would support an "exigent circumstances" search of such a container.

iii.   **Location of automobile doctrine searches.** Officers may search a vehicle **at the place where it is stopped or found.** They are also permitted to take the automobile **to the police station** (or another place of impoundment) and conduct a warrantless search there. Texas v. White, 423 U.S. 67, 96 S. Ct. 304, 46 L. Ed. 2d 209 (1975); Chambers v. Maroney, 399 U.S. 42, 90 S. Ct. 1975, 26 L. Ed. 2d 419 (1970).

iv.   **Timing of automobile doctrine searches.** Officers may conduct a warrantless search **immediately upon finding the vehicle** or **as soon as they arrive at the police station.** They are also permitted to delay the warrantless search for an undefined period of time. According to the controlling doctrine, a later search is unreasonable if the officers delay **"indefinitely."** It may also be unreasonable if an individual were to prove that the delay in conducting the warrantless search **"adversely affected a privacy or possessory interest."** United States v. Johns, 469 U.S. 478, 105 S. Ct. 881, 83 L. Ed. 2d 890 (1985).

 EXAMPLE AND ANALYSIS

Four days after stopping a car and arresting its driver, officers conduct a warrantless search of a cardboard box taken from the trunk. A judge declares the search unreasonable, even though the officers had probable cause to search the box, because: (1) the trunk was outside the immediate control of the arrested driver; (2) the search was conducted four days after the arrest and therefore was not contemporaneous; and (3) officers had probable cause to search the box before it was put in the trunk, but deliberately delayed their seizure of the box until the box was put in the trunk in order to be able to invoke the automobile doctrine. Did the trial court err?

Yes. The first two grounds reflect confusion of two distinct exceptions to the search warrant rule. If the government were relying on a "search incident to arrest" theory, the judge would be correct since the trunk is outside the area of immediate control of an arrested driver and the search must be contemporaneous with the arrest. Neither of these restrictions, however, applies to the automobile doctrine. Probable cause to search a box in the trunk of a vehicle stopped in transit justifies the opening of the trunk and the search of the box. So long as the delay is not "indefinite" (and four days is not), the search is permissible unless the owner can show harm to possessory or privacy interests caused by the delay.

Care must be taken not to confuse exceptions to the warrant rule. Each exception requires particular showings, and the scope of the search allowed by each exception is distinct. In any situation, the applicability of each exception should be assessed independently.

The judge's third ground is specious. Under the automobile doctrine it does not matter when the probable cause to search arises with respect to a container. If there is probable cause and the container is within a vehicle, a warrantless search is allowed. Officers are entitled to wait for such circumstances to develop. The fact they have done so deliberately does not undermine their authority.

---

6.   Inventory Searches of Vehicles and Arrestees

Another exception to **both the warrant and probable cause requirements** is known as an **"inventory search."** These searches are not conducted to investigate or detect crime, but, rather, to "inventory"—to determine and document the contents of—a particular area. Warrantless inventories are reasonable because they **protect property interests** of vehicle owners or arrestees, **protect officials against false or true claims** of lost or stolen property, and **protect** the police and those in jail **against dangerous instrumentalities.** South Dakota v. Opperman, 428 U.S. 364, 96 S. Ct. 3092, 49 L. Ed. 2d 1000 (1976); Illinois v. Lafayette, 462 U.S. 640, 103 S. Ct. 2605, 77 L. Ed. 2d 65 (1983).

Two kinds of inventories have been approved: inventories of **vehicles** and inventories of **arrestees.** Showing and scope questions must be addressed separately for each kind.

a.   Inventory searches of vehicles. Under certain conditions, warrantless inventory searches of vehicles without probable cause are reasonable.

i. The showing necessary to conduct a vehicle inventory. The prerequisites for a valid vehicle inventory are **a lawful impoundment** and **standard police procedures.** South Dakota v. Opperman.

(a) "Lawful impoundment" requirement. The justifications for conducting an inventory arise only when officers take a vehicle into custody. Without official possession, there is no obligation to protect an owner's belongings, no basis for fearing liability, and insufficient reason for concern about danger. However, when officials take a vehicle into custody, they "seize an effect." The Fourth Amendment demand that such seizures be reasonable gives rise to the **lawful impoundment** requirement for valid inventory searches.

In general, an impoundment is **lawful** if there is **adequate reason to take possession** of the vehicle. The question is whether there is a sufficient state interest in removing the vehicle from where it is and taking it into official custody. There is an adequate interest if a vehicle is "impeding traffic or threatening public safety and convenience." South Dakota v. Opperman. Thus, cars parked in violation of ordinances or broken down in the middle of public streets may be impounded. In addition, vehicles whose drivers are arrested may ordinarily, if not always, be taken into custody.

An impoundment is **not lawful** if the official **decision to impound** is entrusted to the **unfettered discretion** of the officer. Still, impoundment decisions do not have to be guided by rigid policies or inflexible formulas. Some discretion to decide is allowed "so long as [it] is exercised . . . according to **standard criteria** and on the basis of **something other than suspicion of evidence of criminal activity.**" Colorado v. Bertine, 479 U.S. 367, 107 S. Ct. 738, 93 L. Ed. 2d 739 (1987).

(b) "Standard police procedures" requirement. Police departments must have **standard procedures** that guide and regulate their officers' inventory searches. South Dakota v. Opperman. The **decision to inventory** cannot be left to officers' **unfettered discretion.** Florida v. Wells, 495 U.S. 1, 110 S. Ct. 1632, 109 L. Ed. 2d 1 (1990).

Rigid, "all or nothing" policies clearly satisfy the "standard police procedures" requirement. Thus, a departmental policy that commands the search of every vehicle or of only those vehicles that meet certain, objective criteria would be acceptable. Nonetheless, there is no need to take away all discretion from the officers conducting inventories. Officers "may be allowed **sufficient latitude to determine whether a particular container should or should not be opened in light of the nature of the search and characteristics of the container itself.**" A policy that allows the "exercise of judgment **based on concerns related to the purposes of an inventory search** does not violate the Fourth Amendment." Florida v. Wells.

(c) **"Opportunity to make other arrangements" factor.** In South Dakota v. Opperman, the Supreme Court suggested that an inventory might be unreasonable if the owner of the vehicle was "present to make other arrangements for the safekeeping of his belongings." Since *Opperman*, the Court has made it clear that officers **do not have to extend the owner an invitation to make other arrangements.** Colorado v. Bertine.

An owner, however, might **request permission to make other arrangements.** She might seek to have someone else take possession of her vehicle or might ask for the opportunity to remove items before an inventory is performed. It is uncertain whether officers are constitutionally permitted to deny such a request. If officers do grant an owner's request to go through the vehicle prior to an inventory, but still have reason to retain custody of the vehicle, the reasoning of the inventory cases suggests that it would be reasonable to then conduct an inventory of the vehicle.

ii. **Scope of a valid vehicle inventory.** Standard police procedures are one source of limitation on the scope of a proper inventory. The more significant question is what independent restrictions the Constitution imposes. The question should be answered by referring to the justifications for warrantless inventories.

(a) **Scope authorized by the standard procedures.** If the standard procedures regulating an officer's inventory search limit the places where an officer may look, a search beyond those places would be outside the inventory exception. Therefore, the search would violate the Fourth Amendment.

(b) **Scope allowed by the Fourth Amendment.** Assuming that a department's standard procedures authorize an inventory search, the question is whether the search authorized is consistent with the Fourth Amendment.

The Fourth Amendment does allow officers to look thoroughly through **all generally accessible areas of the passenger compartment,** including closed spaces such as glove compartments and consoles. They may also inventory **trunks.** The fact that an area is **locked** probably does not preclude a valid inventory. However, if officers cannot search a locked area without causing significant property damage, it is arguably impermissible to conduct an inventory.

Inventories of some parts of vehicles may be constitutionally forbidden. Generally inaccessible spaces such as the areas beneath rear seats, behind door panels and roof liners, and underneath the dashboard could be outside the scope of a reasonable inventory. Further, the area under the hood of a vehicle, or perhaps some parts of that area, might be outside the scope of a properly limited inventory search. As already mentioned, whether inventories of such areas are constitutional should hinge on a reasoned evaluation of whether the three justifications for inventories are sufficiently at stake.

 Closed containers found inside impounded vehicles may be searched as part of a vehicle inventory. Colorado v. Bertine. Officers **do not** have to take the arguably less intrusive alternative of removing a container as a sealed unit and checking it in a secure storage area. Id. Once again, locks probably make no difference.

b.   **Inventory searches of arrestees.** Under certain conditions, warrantless inventory searches of arrestees without probable cause are reasonable.

   i.   **The showing needed to conduct an inventory of an arrestee.** A valid inventory of an arrestee requires **a lawful arrest** of someone who is **going to be incarcerated** and **standard police procedures.** Illinois v. Lafayette.

   (a)   **"Lawful arrest" requirement.** The justifications for inventories of arrestees arise only because a person has been taken into custody. The Fourth Amendment demands that "seizures of persons" be reasonable. If the seizure is unreasonable, an inventory that follows will be unconstitutional. Consequently, the first requirement for a constitutional inventory of an arrestee is a **lawful arrest.** Illinois v. Lafayette.

   (b)   **"Going to be incarcerated" requirement.** Inventories of arrestees are permitted only when an arrestee is **going to be incarcerated** for some period of time. Illinois v. Lafayette. The property protection, anticlaims, and safety rationales underlying inventories are irrelevant to cases in which arrestees are released without being confined in jail.

(c) **"Standard police procedures" requirement.** An inventory of an arrestee is not reasonable unless the officer conducting it is acting pursuant to **standard procedures.** Once again, an officer cannot have **unfettered discretion** to decide who will be searched. However, discretion is constitutionally acceptable if it is exercised on the basis of **standard criteria** and **not for investigatory purposes.** See Subsection a.i(b) above.

ii. **Scope of an inventory of an arrestee.** Again, both the department's standard procedures and the Fourth Amendment itself should limit the scope of a proper arrestee inventory.

(a) **Person of the arrestee.** Officers may thoroughly search the person of the arrestee, removing all belongings. In circumstances of particular need, officers might be allowed to require an arrestee to remove his or her clothing, but such circumstances would be "rare." Illinois v. Lafayette.

(b) **Personal belongings and containers.** Officers also may open and look through **any article or container found "on the person or in the possession** of an arrested person who is to be jailed." There is no need to take the "less intrusive" alternative of storing closed containers intact in secure facilities. Illinois v. Lafayette.

(c) **Time and place of an inventory of an arrestee.** An inventory of an arrestee will typically occur **at the police station or jailhouse,** prior to the individual's introduction into a jail cell. Nonetheless, there is no obvious reason why it cannot be performed at an earlier time and different place if all the requirements of the exception are satisfied. Moreover, in *Lafayette*, the Court indicated that it could be proper to inventory a belonging just before giving it back to an arrestee who is being released.

EXAMPLE AND ANALYSIS

Boyd was arrested for driving his car under the influence of cocaine. After he was taken in handcuffs to the police station by one officer, another officer went through his van, using the keys to unlock the glove compartment. He also looked in a refrigerator that was located in the rear of the van and removed the lid of a compartment housing the spare tire. Finally, the officer used a master key in his possession to open a suitcase inside the van. He then towed the van to the city impound lot.

At the police station, Boyd was asked to empty his pockets and to place a shoulder bag he was carrying on the counter. Once Boyd was put in his cell, the desk sergeant unzipped every compartment in the shoulder bag and examined its contents.

A trial judge concludes that the search of the van and its contents was unconstitutional because officers lacked probable cause, a prerequisite for a valid automobile doctrine search. He upholds the search of Boyd and his shoulder bag as proper "searches incident to Boyd's valid arrest." Was the trial judge correct?

The trial judge was correct that the automobile doctrine requires probable cause. However, he was wrong to declare the search of the van unconstitutional if the officer was conducting an inventory pursuant to valid "standard police procedures." It was lawful to impound the van because Boyd had been validly arrested. An inventory does not require any cause, and all the areas searched—even the locked areas—are probably within the proper scope of a valid inventory. The fact that a search does not satisfy one exception to the warrant rule does not preclude it from meeting a different exception.

The trial court was probably correct that the searches of Boyd and his shoulder bag were valid, but for the wrong reason. These were not proper searches incident to arrest. They were remote in place and time from the arrest, and the shoulder bag was no longer in Boyd's immediate control. However, assuming that the desk sergeant was following legitimate "standard procedures," both Boyd and the contents of his shoulder bag could be inventoried at the station because he had been lawfully arrested and was being incarcerated. This example again reinforces the point that each exception to the warrant rule must be separately analyzed. While there is some common ground between the "search incident to arrest" and "arrestee inventory" exceptions to the warrant requirement, the two are distinct. They rest on different rationales, require different showings, and permit searches of different scopes.

---

7.   Consent Searches

If a person with authority validly consents, the Fourth Amendment allows an officer to conduct a search without a search warrant and without probable cause. Moreover, even if the person giving consent lacks authority, a warrantless search may still be reasonable.

a.   **The showing needed for a consent search.** To invoke the "consent exception," the government must demonstrate **a voluntary consent by a person with common authority.**

   i.   **Necessity for actual consent.** A consent search requires evidence that consent was actually given. Explicit permission to search is not required for a valid consent. Instead, a person's actions can provide a basis for inferring a grant of such permission. Consent should not be inferred, however, when a person simply acquiesces in or fails to resist an official demand for permission to search.

ii. **Voluntariness requirement.** The government must show, by a preponderance of the evidence, that a consent was **"in fact voluntarily given, and not the result of duress or coercion, express or implied."** Schneckloth v. Bustamonte, 412 U.S. 218, 93 S. Ct. 2041, 36 L. Ed. 2d 854 (1973).

Voluntariness is determined in the **totality of the circumstances.** Schneckloth v. Bustamonte. Relevant circumstances fall into two general categories: the **external coercion or pressure** brought to bear on the individual and **internal, subjective strength of will** possessed by the individual. Therefore, facts that evince coercion (or a lack thereof) are relevant—for example, the nature of the law enforcement conduct preceding the consent and the setting in which it occurred. Likewise, facts that bear on a person's strength of will or vulnerability are also relevant—for example, native intelligence, educational level, maturity, prior experience with law enforcement, intoxication, and knowledge of the right to refuse to give consent. Id.

Some amount of **official coercion** is almost certainly necessary for a consent to be deemed involuntary. A consent that is "involuntary" because of purely subjective forces operating internally within the individual's mind is most probably valid. See Colorado v. Connelly, 479 U.S. 157, 107 S. Ct. 515, 93 L. Ed. 2d 473 (1986) (holding that some amount of coercive police conduct is essential to finding a confession involuntary or coerced under the Due Process Clause). Consent coerced by the conduct of a private party is also probably a valid basis for a search. See id. (observing that a private party's coercion does not render a confession coerced or involuntary for purposes of the Due Process Clause).

iii. **Knowledge of the right to refuse.** While knowledge of the constitutional right to refuse consent is relevant to voluntariness, it is **not a "sine qua non of an effective consent to a search."** Schneckloth v. Bustamonte. Officers do not have to warn a person of the right to refuse. Moreover, a consent given by a person who was ignorant of the right to refuse is not invalid.

iv. **Advice to seized individuals.** The Fourth Amendment does not require that a lawfully seized individual must be advised that he is "free to go" before a consent can be found voluntary. Ohio v. Robinette, — U.S. —, 117 S. Ct. 417, 136 L. Ed. 2d 347 (1996).

A consent that is voluntarily given is not rendered invalid by the failure to provide such advice. This is apparently the case whether the lawful seizure is continuing or has been completed at the time the consent is given.

v. Authority to give consent. A consent is valid only if it is given by a person who has **authority to consent.** "Third parties"—persons other than the person who objects to the search later—may give valid consent if they have **common authority.** United States v. Matlock, 415 U.S. 164, 94 S. Ct. 988, 39 L. Ed. 2d 242 (1974).

To have common authority to consent to the search of a place, an individual need not have a property interest. Moreover, a property interest alone is not sufficient for common authority. Rather, **common authority "rests on mutual use of the property by persons generally having joint access or control for most purposes."** United States v. Matlock. The degree of use and the extent of the access or control that are required to satisfy the *Matlock* standard cannot be specified with precision.

vi. Scope of an individual's authority. The scope of an individual's authority to give a valid consent is determined by the extent of that person's "mutual use" and "joint access or control." A person who uses and has access to some spaces does **not** have authority to consent to the search of related or nearby but distinct spaces. For example, a person does not have authority to consent to a search of every portion of a dwelling simply because he uses certain, limited parts of that dwelling. Similarly, someone with mutual use of and joint access to a room does not necessarily have authority to consent to the search of every distinct private belonging within that room.

This principle, however, has a limit. There are some private spaces that are treated as **"unitary"** for purposes of authority to consent. For such spaces, whenever a person uses and has access to any part he gains authority to consent to a search of the entire space. In Frazier v. Cupp, 394 U.S. 731, 89 S. Ct. 1420, 22 L. Ed. 2d 684 (1969), a young man had permission to possess his cousin's duffel bag and to use some compartments in it. The Supreme Court held that he had authority to consent to the search of the entire duffel bag as a result. The Court pointedly rejected the "metaphysical" distinction urged by the defendant between the compartments his cousin used and those he did not.

For purposes of determining the scope of authority to consent, it is not clear when a court should be willing to accept distinctions and when it should consider them **"metaphysical."** It is arguable that the limitation of Frazier v. Cupp is narrow and that authority distinctions should be recognized in all cases but those involving small containers generally thought of as single units.

b. **Scope of a valid consent search.** If a person with authority has given a valid consent, an officer is entitled to search **any area to which the consent extends.** Because consent searches are reasonable only because officers have secured permission to search, the scope of a reasonable consent search cannot be broader than the scope of the permission granted.

If a consenting party expressly limits the allowable search, officers must abide by that limitation. However, the consenter may well not be explicit about the scope of the permission she intends to grant. In that case, "[t]he standard for measuring the scope of a suspect's consent . . . is that of **'objective' reasonableness—what would [a] reasonable person have understood by the exchange between the officer and the suspect?"** Florida v. Jimeno, 500 U.S. 248, 111 S. Ct. 1801, 114 L. Ed. 2d 297 (1991). If "it is reasonable for an officer to consider a . . . consent . . . to include" a particular area, that area falls within the scope of the consent given. Id. Moreover, if it is reasonable to understand a consent as extending to a particular area, there is no need for an officer to confirm that understanding by inquiring or seeking express permission to search the area. This objective, reasonable person standard for determining the scope of a consent requires each case to be judged on its own facts.

Florida v. Jimeno illustrates the operation of this standard. An officer pulled the defendant over for a traffic infraction, told him he had reason to believe that he was carrying narcotics in his vehicle, and asked for permission to search the car. The defendant granted the officer permission to search the automobile. The officer proceeded to open a folded, brown paper bag on the floorboard and found a kilogram of cocaine inside. In these circumstances, the Supreme Court held that the search was reasonable because "it was objectively reasonable for the police to conclude that the general consent to search [the] car included consent to search containers within that car which might contain drugs."

c. **The "apparent authority" doctrine.** In some cases, officers search based on consent given by a person who, in fact, does not have common authority. In those cases, the searches **do not** fall within the consent exception to the warrant requirement. Because the consenter lacks authority, the consent could not be constitutionally valid.

A warrantless search performed in those circumstances may nevertheless be reasonable under the **apparent authority doctrine.** Although this doctrine is constitutionally distinct from the consent exception, it is discussed at this point because of its factual and logical connections to the consent exception.

The doctrine can be simply expressed: If a person who gives consent does not have authority, the search is still reasonable if officers have an **objectively reasonable belief that the person who has given consent has common authority.** Illinois v. Rodriguez, 497 U.S. 177, 110 S. Ct. 2793, 111 L. Ed. 2d 148 (1990). Officers do not always have to inquire about a person's authority or relationship to the place searched. In some situations, they can have an objectively reasonable belief in authority without inquiring. In others, the circumstances may be such that an officer could not **reasonably believe** that a person had authority without asking. Moreover, even in cases in which a person affirmatively asserts that she has authority to consent (or asserts facts that would clearly be the basis for common authority), it may not be reasonable to believe the assertion. The question is always whether in the particular circumstances a belief in authority is **objectively reasonable.**

Finally, even if an officer conducts a search in circumstances that render it unreasonable to believe that a person has authority to give consent, the search will be constitutional if the person does in fact have **actual authority** to consent. Id.

EXAMPLES AND ANALYSIS

1. A trial judge declares a defendant's consent invalid. The judge found that the police officer who requested consent was polite and used no improper tactics. However, the judge rested his conclusion on the fact that the defendant, who had recently immigrated from an authoritarian regime, believed that a refusal to cooperate could have resulted in a violent beating. Should the ruling be sustained on appeal?

Probably not. Although there is "subjective involuntariness," there is no "objective coercion." The voluntariness standard for judging consents is borrowed from the voluntariness standard for judging confessions. In the latter context, some amount of official coercion is a prerequisite for a finding of involuntariness. Assuming that the same principle applies in the consent context, there is no basis for declaring the defendant's consent involuntary here.

2. Late one night, four officers in two vehicles pull over a car in a high-crime area. With their guns drawn as a safeguard against attack, they ask both of the occupants

for permission to search their persons. Both give consent. A judge later declares one of the consents valid and the other invalid despite the fact that the setting and official conduct were identical. Is the judge's ruling defensible?

Possibly. Assuming that there is sufficient external coercion (late at night, high-crime area, four officers, guns drawn), to allow a finding of involuntariness, it is possible that the subjective states of the two individuals support different outcomes on the voluntariness question. For example, one of the individuals might be young, inexperienced with law enforcement, intoxicated, and ignorant of his rights. The other might be a veteran of police encounters, sober, and well aware of his right to refuse. Therefore, the consent of the first individual might be involuntary and the consent of the second individual voluntary.

3. Officers are summoned to a mobile home. A young woman, disheveled and appearing to be under the influence of some substance, tells them that the occupant of the home is a heroin dealer and that a large stash is inside. Officers knock on the door but receive no answer. When the woman urges them to enter, they ask her if she lives there. She says that she does not but that she sleeps over a lot and has permission to come in whenever she wants. When officers ask for the key, she hesitates, searches in her pocket, then answers that she must have lost it. If the officers enter, will their search be reasonable?

First, the woman might have actual common authority. The question is whether she is telling the truth and, if so, whether her contact with the mobile home qualifies as "mutual use" and "joint access and control for most purposes." While there is some room for argument, if she really has "permission to come in whenever she wants," she may well have common authority. If so, the search would be a reasonable consent search even if it was not reasonable to believe that she had authority. If the facts do not support a finding of actual authority, the search would not be a reasonable consent search.

Second, the search is reasonable under the apparent authority doctrine if it was reasonable for the officers to believe she had authority. The reasonableness of such a belief is certainly questionable here in light of her condition and her conduct. A reasonable person might have questioned the veracity of her statements. If a belief in authority was not reasonable, then the search would not be reasonable under the apparent authority doctrine.

---

8. The Plain View Doctrine

The plain view doctrine has been included among the exceptions to the rule that warrantless searches are per se unreasonable. In fact, the doctrine does not authorize a search of any sort. Rather, it merely allows officers to **seize** effects in certain circumstances without first obtaining a warrant. Horton v. California, 496 U.S. 128, 110 S. Ct. 2301, 110 L. Ed. 2d 112

(1990). The circumstances that justify such warrantless seizures are (1) **lawful arrival at the place from which the object can be plainly viewed,** (2) **lawful access to the object seized,** and (3) **an object whose incriminating nature is "immediately apparent."** Id.

a. **Lawful arrival at the place from which the object can be plainly viewed.** A reasonable plain view seizure requires that officers **lawfully arrive at the place from which they view the object.** Id. If officers violate the Fourth Amendment in arriving at the place that enables them to view an object, the violation will taint a subsequent seizure. The "lawful arrival" criterion reflects the principle that an otherwise lawful seizure of an object will be tainted if it is the product of a prior illegal search.

b. **Lawful access to the object that is seized.** Officers must also have a **"lawful right of access to the object itself."** Horton v. California. This means that they must justify their presence in the place where they **seize** the object. If the item is in a public place, no grounds are needed to justify access to it because the Fourth Amendment does not restrict officers' access to public places. However, if the object is in a private place, officers need either a warrant or an exception to the warrant requirement to justify the entry that gives them access to the object.

The "lawful access" requirement is nothing more than a safeguard against circumvention of the search warrant requirement. According to that requirement, **no amount of probable cause,** not even "[i]ncontrovertible testimony of the senses," **can justify a warrantless search.** Horton v. California. If lawful plain view of an incriminating object permitted intrusion into a private place to seize the object, the plain view doctrine would undermine the search warrant rule.

The "lawful access" criterion insures that a **search** that gives officers access to the item that is seized is not justified on the basis of plain view and probable cause alone. By demanding an independent justification for such a search—a warrant or an exception to the warrant requirement—the "lawful access" demand guarantees that the warrant rule will not be undercut by the plain view doctrine.

c. **An object whose incriminating nature is "immediately apparent."** For an item to be seized, its **incriminating nature must be "immediately apparent."** Id. This criterion reflects a fundamental Fourth Amendment restraint on seizures of effects—the general rule that officers may not seize an object unless they have **probable cause to seize** it. Arizona v. Hicks, 480 U.S. 321, 107 S. Ct. 1149, 94 L. Ed. 2d 347 (1987). (**Note:** A lesser degree of cause will suffice only if the situation presents "special operational necessities" that justify lowering the norm. Id.; see section G.5 below.)

The "immediately apparent" language suggests that this third plain view criterion is meant to reflect more than the probable cause requirement alone. The words "immediately apparent" might mean that officers must *instantaneously* recognize an object's incriminating nature. If that were the case, a seizure would be unreasonable whenever an officer took any time to think about whether there were grounds to seize the object. In fact, it is highly unlikely that a seizure would be deemed invalid simply because officers had to reflect on the nature of the object before concluding that it was "incriminating."

It is much more likely that the "immediately apparent" phrase is intended to capture a different Fourth Amendment limitation. Specifically, it reflects the notion that the probable cause to seize an object **cannot be the product of a search or seizure undertaken to investigate the nature of the object.** Officers who have some level of suspicion about an object in plain view but lack probable cause ordinarily may not conduct a search or seizure for the purpose of determining the character of that object. If they do so and their search or seizure generates probable cause that leads them to seize the object, the seizure cannot be justified by the plain view doctrine because it is tainted by the preceding illegal search or seizure.

 # EXAMPLES AND ANALYSIS

1. In Arizona v. Hicks, an officer legally entered an apartment where he then saw a turntable. He had grounds to suspect that it was stolen but lacked probable cause. To pursue his suspicion, he moved the turntable and examined the serial number. After an investigation of the number provided probable cause to believe the turntable was stolen, the officer seized it.

The Supreme Court reasoned that the movement of the turntable was both a search (an invasion of privacy) and a seizure (an interference with possession) that was not supported by the original reason for entering the apartment. Because this movement was not supported by **probable cause** to believe the turntable was stolen, it was an unreasonable search and seizure that tainted the later seizure based on probable cause.

2. In Minnesota v. Dickerson, 508 U.S. 366, 113 S. Ct. 2130, 124 L. Ed. 2d 334 (1993), an officer was conducting a legal patdown of a suspect for weapons when he felt a lump in a pocket. Suspecting that it could be narcotics, the officer manipulated the object with his fingers. When his sense of touch gave him probable cause to believe the lump was contraband, the officer removed it from the suspect's pocket. Although

Dickerson did not involve the plain view doctrine directly, the Supreme Court's reasoning provides further support for the preceding explanation of the "immediately apparent" criterion.

The Court observed that "the incriminating character of the object [had not been] immediately apparent to" the officer as a result of the patdown. In other words, probable cause to seize it did not arise until he engaged in a further search—the tactile manipulation. Because that search was not based on probable cause it "was constitutionally invalid, [and] the seizure of the cocaine that followed [was] likewise unconstitutional."

---

    d.   Rejection of an inadvertence requirement. In *Coolidge v. New Hampshire*, 403 U.S. 443, 91 S. Ct. 2022, 29 L. Ed. 2d 564 (1971), the plurality opined that the plain view doctrine cannot justify the seizure of an object unless **the discovery of that object is inadvertent.** A discovery is inadvertent when it is not "anticipated, where the police [do not] know in advance the location of the [item] and intend to seize it." Id.

    In *Horton v. California*, the Court rejected the "inadvertence" requirement, holding that an object is subject to seizure under the plain view doctrine whether or not it has been inadvertently discovered. This means that even though officers have probable cause to seize an item in advance and have time and opportunity to secure a search warrant for that object, they do not have to obtain a warrant. So long as the other requirements for a plain view seizure are satisfied, they may reasonably seize the item.

 # EXAMPLE AND ANALYSIS

While walking in the common area of an apartment building, an officer sees contraband narcotics through an uncurtained window of an apartment. The officer hesitates, debating whether it is necessary to apply for a warrant to enter. At that point, the resident comes into the room. In a panic, he begins to grab all the narcotics. The officer then forces her way through the front door and pursues the resident into a rear bedroom. After apprehending the resident, the officer notices three expensive-looking fur coats lying on the bed. She opens the coats to examine the labels, finds the name of a high-class department store, calls the store, and learns that the coats were stolen. The officer seizes the coats and the contraband. Are the seizures justified by "plain view"?

The contraband was properly seized. The officer had a lawful view of the contraband—there is no invasion of privacy involved in occupying a common area and looking through an uncurtained window. There was "lawful access" to the contraband—the entry of the apartment and pursuit of the resident were justified by probable cause plus exigent circumstances. And there was probable cause to seize the contraband. (Note that if the officer had entered the apartment prior to the resident's arrival, she would have violated the warrant rule. Despite clear probable cause, she could not search without a warrant. Because her access to the contraband would have been unlawful, a plain view seizure could not be sustained.)

It is unlikely, however, that the seizure of the coats should be sustained. Both the view of the coats and access to the coats were lawful. The problem is that it was probably not "immediately apparent" that the coats were "incriminating." Assuming that there was no probable cause to believe that the coats were stolen prior to opening them, that act was an unconstitutional search. Because the probable cause that developed from the phone investigation was the product of the unlawful search of the coats, the seizures based on that cause were not constitutional.

REVIEW QUESTIONS AND ANSWERS

Question: Barton was arrested for felonious sexual abuse of a minor. Officers had information that several hours earlier he had engaged in sexual relations with a young boy in exchange for money. When Barton was arrested, he was standing in the lobby of a hotel conversing with the bellman. Just prior to arresting him, officers had seen him set his suitcase on the counter of the registration desk. After arresting and handcuffing Barton, the officers took possession of his suitcase.

After putting the suitcase in the backseat of the police car, the officers asked Barton if they could search it. He asked if they had a warrant. The officers replied that they probably didn't need to get a warrant, but that if he refused to give them permission, they would probably be able to get a warrant. They mentioned that his refusal was "awfully suspicious, if you are innocent." Barton then allowed them to open the case. What exceptions to the warrant rule, if any, justify the warrantless opening of the suitcase?

Answer: At least three different exceptions are potentially applicable, but it is not certain that any of them is satisfied.

First, the search incident to arrest exception might permit the search. There would have to be probable cause to arrest Barton. In addition, the suitcase would have to be within the area of his "immediate control." The facts do not say how close the case was to the place of arrest. Moreover, it is arguable that the handcuffs would have prevented Barton's access and therefore should preclude a search incident to arrest. Finally, the search was not conducted immediately after the arrest. To be incident to an arrest, a search cannot be "remote in time" but must be contemporaneous with the arrest. Whether the time that passed in this case was too long to allow a search incident is not clear.

Second, a consent search claim is possible. The problem is that there were indicia of coercion—an arrest, handcuffing, placement in a police car, and the officers' statements that they probably do not need a warrant and that Barton's refusal would be suspicious. Moreover, Barton's reticence and his grant of permission only after the officers' words would provide further support for a conclusion that the consent was not voluntarily given. In sum, there is serious question about whether the government could prove voluntariness by a preponderance of the evidence.

Finally, this search could be an inventory of an arrestee. The arrest would again have to be lawful—based on probable cause. The officers would also have to be following "standard procedures." The facts do not speak directly to this issue, although the request for consent suggests that the officers may not have been conducting an inventory. Finally, an inventory would be permissible only if Barton was going to be incarcerated at least for a short time—a likely event considering the nature of the offense. The fact that the search took place in the police car before arrival at the station should not preclude a valid inventory search.

Question: Mary snatched an old woman's purse and fled from a crowd of angry witnesses. She ran into an old frame home two blocks away. While some of the witnesses stood guard, others called the police. Officers arrived ten minutes later, knocked on the front door, then entered. They found Mary hiding in the basement and arrested her. They seized a purse that she was holding. Mary objects to the officers' warrantless entry of her home. Is her objection valid?

Answer: Clearly, this seems to be a case in which the officers had probable cause to believe that a criminal had fled into a house shortly before they arrived. The continuous pursuit by others and the short time between the pursuit and the entry suggest that the "hot pursuit" variation of the "exigent circumstances" doctrine is applicable.

There is one potential problem, however. In Welsh v. Wisconsin, the Supreme Court suggested that a warrantless entry of a home to apprehend an individual who has committed an "extremely minor" offense might never be reasonable. Moreover, the *Welsh* Court refused to allow officers to enter without a warrant to prevent the destruction of evidence concerning a "minor offense."

The offense in *Welsh* was driving under the influence, a noncriminal, civil forfeiture offense for which no imprisonment was possible. The offense committed here, purse snatching, might well be more serious. After all, while purse snatching is a relatively petty kind of theft and probably is classified as a misdemeanor, it does pose some risk of harm to another person. Moreover, it is undoubtedly a "criminal offense" and probably is punishable by imprisonment. For these reasons, the *Welsh* principle may not be controlling.

Question: Officers have probable cause to believe that Betty is trafficking in illegal explosives. A knowledgeable informant who has been reliable in the past tells them that Betty stores the explosives in an old school bus parked on her ranch. Without a warrant, officers go to the ranch. They enter the property and find the bus parked 500 yards from Betty's home. Its appearance suggests that the bus has not moved in some time. All windows but the front one are painted black and the two rear tires are almost flat. Officers call for a tow truck, have the bus taken to the city impound lot, and search it thoroughly there. Is the search valid under the automobile doctrine?

Answer: It is uncertain whether the automobile doctrine justifies the search. Probable cause to search is needed, but it seems to be satisfied. In addition, the vehicle must be readily mobile—that is, it must be capable of moving by the turn of a key. There are indicia here that suggest the bus was not mobile. Those same facts suggest that the officers could not have reasonably believed that it was mobile. In those circumstances, the automobile doctrine would not apply. Moreover, the bus was parked on the owner's private property. While the Court's opinions in California v. Carney and Pennsylvania v. Kilgore suggested that such cars might fall within the doctrine, no case has so held.

If there was probable cause to search, the vehicle was readily mobile, and the private property location does not preclude application of the doctrine, it was permissible for officers to have the bus towed and to search it later at the impound lot. The automobile doctrine, when satisfied, always allows vehicles to be taken to the police station and searched.

G. STOPS AND FRISKS: THE DOCTRINE OF TERRY v. OHIO

The doctrines treated in this section and in several sections that follow are also exceptions to both the warrant and probable cause requirements. They are discussed separately from the doctrines addressed in the preceding section because of their broader Fourth Amendment significance. They are more than mere warrant rule exceptions. Moreover, all of them share a common thread: They evaluate the reasonableness of a search or seizure by balancing the **magnitude of an intrusion on the individual** against the **government interests claimed to justify that intrusion.**

This section addresses the "stop and frisk" doctrine of Terry v. Ohio, 392 U.S. 1, 88 S. Ct. 1868, 20 L. Ed. 2d 889 (1968). When investigating individuals suspected of imminent, ongoing, or past criminal activity, officers sometimes approach them in public places, make inquiries, and pat them down to determine whether they are in possession of a dangerous weapon. In its landmark decision in *Terry*, the Supreme Court for the first time considered the appropriate Fourth Amendment treatment of such "stops and frisks."

1. The Holding of Terry v. Ohio

The first question in *Terry* was whether the Fourth Amendment imposes any regulation on "stops and frisks." The Court determined that it does. Although it is not an "arrest," a "stop" is a seizure of a person. And even though it may not be a "full-blown search," a frisk is a serious invasion of privacy that does qualify as a search. Therefore, the Fourth Amendment, which requires seizures and searches of persons to be reasonable, applies.

The next question was what the Fourth Amendment required to render a stop and frisk reasonable. The Court concluded that neither a warrant nor probable cause is necessary for a stop and frisk. However, an "inarticulate hunch"—an officer's unfounded, subjective suspicion that an individual is involved in crime—is not sufficient. Instead, the officer needs "specific and articulable facts which, taken together with rational inferences from those facts, reasonably warrant [the] intrusion." More specifically, the officer must demonstrate facts that "lead[ ] him **reasonably to conclude** in light of his experience that **criminal activity may be afoot** and that the persons with whom he is dealing may be **armed and presently dangerous.**" Id.

Test

In numerous subsequent opinions, the Court has developed the meaning and limitations of this Fourth Amendment stop-and-frisk doctrine sketched in *Terry*. The following subsections outline the standards that have emerged from *Terry* and those later decisions.

2.   The "Threshold" Question: When Is a Person "Seized"?

The Fourth Amendment regulates only encounters in which law enforcement officers **seize** individuals. "[N]ot all personal intercourse between policemen and citizens involves 'seizures' of persons." Terry v. Ohio. In other words, some interactions do not amount to seizures.

The distinction between encounters that **are seizures** and those that **are not seizures** is very important. Because seizures are regulated by the Fourth Amendment, they are unconstitutional unless the government can show reasonableness. Because encounters that are not seizures are not governed by the Fourth Amendment, they can be undertaken for no reason—that is, there is no need to justify them as reasonable. The Court has paid considerable attention to the doctrine designed to distinguish seizures from nonseizures.

a.   **"Intent" requirement.** A seizure cannot be effected accidentally; it "requires **an intentional acquisition of physical control.**" Brower v. County of Inyo, 489 U.S. 593, 109 S. Ct. 1378, 103 L. Ed. 2d 628 (1989). A "Fourth Amendment seizure does not occur whenever there is a governmentally caused termination of an individual's freedom of movement . . . , but only when there is **a governmental termination of freedom of movement through means intentionally applied.**" Id.

In essence, a seizure requires that an officer act with the intent of terminating the freedom of the individual. "[I]f a parked and unoccupied police car slips its brake and pins a passerby against a wall," the

Fourth Amendment is not implicated. Id. But if officers set up a roadblock in order to stop a fleeing offender and that offender crashes into the roadblock, a seizure has occurred. Id.

b. **"Physical force" or "show of authority" requirement.** An officer cannot seize a person unless he **either** applies **physical force** to the person or displays **a show of authority.** California v. Hodari D., 499 U.S. 621, 111 S. Ct. 1547, 113 L. Ed. 2d 690 (1991).

   i. **Seizure by physical force.** Any actual physical contact with a person will qualify as "physical force." California v. Hodari D. Consequently, an officer satisfies the physical force criterion whenever she merely touches a person with her hand, another part of his person, or an object.

   In addition, the use of physical force is apparently **sufficient** in itself **to complete a seizure**—at least when the officer's purpose is to detain the suspect. The suspect does not have to submit to the force, although flight will end the seizure. Id.; see subsection ii(b) below (describing the "submission" requirement for seizures resulting from shows of authority). Moreover, the *Hodari D.* Court strongly indicated that the "reasonable person" requirement applicable to seizures by shows of authority has no application when physical force is used.

   ii. **Seizure by a "show of authority."** For a show of authority by an officer to result in a seizure, two things are necessary: (1) **a show of authority that would make a reasonable person feel not free to leave** and (2) **submission by the suspect.**

     (a) **The *Mendenhall* standard: Whether a reasonable person would feel free to leave.** A person can be "seized" by a show of authority "only if, in view of all of the circumstances surrounding the incident, **a reasonable person would have believed that he was not free to leave.**" United States v. Mendenhall, 446 U.S. 544, 100 S. Ct. 1870, 64 L. Ed. 2d 497 (1980). Unless the show of authority displayed by the officer is of such a character that it satisfies this objective, "reasonable person" test, the infringement on liberty is insufficient to amount to a Fourth Amendment seizure.

     Sometimes an individual does not feel free to leave a location because of **self-imposed restraints** on her liberty. In that situation, the doctrinal inquiry is modified. "[T]he appropriate inquiry is whether **a reasonable person would feel free to decline the officers' requests or otherwise terminate the encounter.**" Florida v. Bostick, 501 U.S. 429, 111 S. Ct. 2382, 115 L. Ed. 2d 389 (1991).

Bostic
Facts

In Florida v. Bostick, a bus had stopped at a place along the route from its point of departure to its ultimate destination. During this stopover, officers boarded the bus and approached a seated passenger. The Supreme Court rejected the claim that the passenger was seized simply because a reasonable person in that setting would not feel free to leave. That feeling, according to the Court, was the result of his own decision to travel on the bus. In such circumstances, a seizure occurs only if the officers' conduct would make a reasonable person feel not free to decline their requests or otherwise terminate the encounter.

EXAMPLE AND ANALYSIS

If an officer blocks a person's route with his car or points a gun at a person and commands her to stop, the authority displayed is such that a reasonable person would not feel free to leave. Suppose, instead, that an officer approaches a person in a public place, asks to see her identification, asks a few investigatory questions, and asks for consent to search a personal belonging. Does a seizure occur?

There undoubtedly is a show of authority in such circumstances. Nevertheless, unless the officer "convey[s] a message that compliance with [his] requests is required," the authority shown is insufficient to satisfy the *Mendenhall* standard. Florida v. Bostick. Because such conduct does not qualify as a seizure, officers do not need grounds for suspicion.

The conclusion would not change if officers had directed the same conduct toward a passenger seated on a bus during a temporary stopover. While the "cramped confines of a bus are one relevant factor," such an approach on a bus is not a seizure per se. Unless officers engage in some additional, "coercive" behavior, the Fourth Amendment is not triggered. Florida v. Bostick.

(b)   **Submission by the suspect.** Satisfaction of the *Mendenhall*–reasonable person standard is a *"necessary,* **but not a** *sufficient,* **condition for seizure . . . effected through a 'show of authority.' "** California v. Hodari D. For a seizure to be completed, the individual must also **submit** to the show of authority. If the suspect flees or walks away, no seizure has occurred. Id.

Hodari
Facts

In *Hodari D.*, a young man began to run upon seeing law enforcement officers. One officer pursued him and eventually tackled him to the ground. Even though the officer's pursuit may have satisfied the "reasonable person" standard, the suspect did not submit. Consequently, there was no Fourth Amendment seizure until the officer tackled him.

 # EXAMPLE AND ANALYSIS

On a mere hunch that a young man loitering near a corner might be involved in narcotics trafficking, an undercover officer approaches. He introduces himself and asks for permission to search the young man's shoulder bag. After standing silent for a short time, the young man begins to walk away, the officer calls to him, pulls his gun, and orders the young man to "Stop!" The young man begins to run, whereupon the officer catches him and wrestles him to the ground. Did the officer violate the Fourth Amendment?

When the officer approached and asked for permission to search, no seizure occurred because the officer's conduct was not sufficient to make a reasonable person feel not free to leave. This is true even though the suspect "submitted" by standing silently in place for a short time. When the officer pulled a gun and issued an order to stop, his behavior satisfied the *Mendenhall*–reasonable person standard. However, the suspect failed to submit. Consequently, he was not seized at that point either. Only when the officer gained physical control was there a seizure.

It is uncertain whether the seizure that did occur was reasonable. On the one hand, the young man's flight arguably gave the officer grounds to seize him at least temporarily. See California v. Hodari D. (suggesting that flight may be a basis for adequate suspicion). On the other hand, the flight here might well be an insufficient indicator of criminal activity. It was in response to a pulled weapon and a command to stop, following the young man's assertion of his right to walk away (the officer had only a hunch—an insufficient ground for a detention) and his right not to give consent.

Conduct such as walking away and refusing consent—the mere assertion of one's rights—is clearly distinguishable from conduct such as flight—which goes beyond the assertion of rights. The former **cannot** support a reasonable suspicion. See Florida v. Bostick. At least in some circumstances, the latter may be suspicious enough to justify a stop.

3. Justification for Stops and Frisks: A "Reasonable Suspicion"

The opinion in Terry v. Ohio suggested that a stop and frisk requires more than a hunch but less than probable cause. It described the necessary showing in somewhat vague terms. Since *Terry*, the showing needed has been further explained and described as a **"reasonable suspicion."** The reasonable suspicion needed to stop or detain a suspect is different and distinct from that needed to conduct a frisk.

a. **The showing needed for a stop or temporary detention of a person.** Stops or temporary detentions are permissible in order to detect and prevent ongoing or imminent crimes. In those situations, officers must have a **"reasonable suspicion" that "criminal activity is afoot" or that the suspect is "engaging in criminal activity."** See Alabama v. White, 496 U.S. 325, 110 S. Ct. 2412, 110 L. Ed. 2d 301 (1990); United States v. Mendenhall. Such stops or detentions are also permissible in order to detect and apprehend those who have engaged in past, completed crimes. In those situations, an officer must possess a **"reasonable suspicion" that an individual "was involved in or is wanted in connection with a completed felony."** United States v. Hensley, 469 U.S. 221, 105 S. Ct. 675, 83 L. Ed. 2d 604 (1985). It is undecided whether a stop for a completed offense is permissible for any "past crimes" that are less serious than felonies. Id.

[handwritten margin notes: "Test:", "Test:", "Past Felony"]

b. **The showing needed for a frisk or weapons patdown of a person.** To conduct a limited patdown of the outer clothing of a suspect for weapons—a frisk—an officer must have a **"reasonable suspicion" that the suspect who is being detained "is armed and presently dangerous."** Terry v. Ohio; Minnesota v. Dickerson, 508 U.S. 366, 113 S. Ct. 2130, 124 L. Ed. 2d 334 (1993). The authority to frisk does not follow automatically from the authority to detain, but instead requires this independent showing of objective grounds for believing that the suspect could pose a danger to the officer during a detention.

c. **Definition of a "reasonable suspicion."** Probable cause is not required for a stop and frisk, but an " 'inchoate and unparticularized suspicion or "hunch" ' " will not suffice. See United States v. Sokolow, 490 U.S. 1, 109 S. Ct. 1581, 104 L. Ed. 2d 1 (1989) (quoting Terry v. Ohio); Alabama v. White. A **reasonable suspicion** is required—that is, a level of likelihood somewhere between that engendered by a hunch and that required for probable cause. To establish such a suspicion, an officer must point to **"articulable"** and **"objective"** facts.

Because "[r]easonable suspicion is a **less demanding standard** than probable cause," Alabama v. White, "the required degree of suspicion [is] not as high." Id. The level of likelihood that must be shown to establish probable cause is a "fair probability." Officers need not establish that their conclusions are "more likely than not" true. See section B.5 above. Consequently, the level of likelihood required to establish a reasonable suspicion is somewhat **less than a fair probability.**

Reasonable suspicion differs from probable cause insofar as both the **"quantity"** of the facts that give rise to a reasonable suspicion and the **"quality"** of those facts can be **"lesser."** In other words, the information that establishes grounds to stop or frisk "can be **different in quantity or content** than that required to establish probable cause" and also can be "**less reliable** than that required to establish probable cause." Alabama v. White.

Judges must make their own, **independent determinations of reasonable suspicion** and cannot simply defer to the judgments of officers or to officers' reliance on "profiles" prepared by law enforcement agencies. United States v. Sokolow. On the other hand, "the fact that . . . factors may be set forth in a 'profile' does not somehow detract from their evidentiary significance as seen by a trained agent." Id. Thus, judges must not discount factors simply because they appear in profiles. Moreover, although they must not simply defer to officers' judgments, courts should make an effort to credit the experience and training of the officers in evaluating the significance of factors.

Finally, even though no single fact directly describes **"ongoing criminal activity,"** the totality of the facts can still support a reasonable suspicion of criminal activity. Id. What this means is that none of the individual facts relied on to establish a reasonable suspicion need be inherently suspicious or indicative of criminal activity when judged in isolation.

(E&A) EXAMPLE AND ANALYSIS

An anonymous caller telephones the police station and reports that "George, a blond man who is six feet seven inches tall and has a crewcut, is dealing narcotics from a booth at the Four Tops Diner." Officer Jones goes immediately to the diner and sees a large blond man with a crewcut sitting in a corner booth. As the man gets up to leave, Jones grabs him by the arm. In response to the officer's inquiries, the man admits that his name is "George" and that he has been selling cocaine. Did Jones's conduct violate the Fourth Amendment?

Officer Jones clearly seized George—grabbing his arm was physical force. The question is whether he had a "reasonable suspicion" that the man was engaged in criminal activity. While the reasonable suspicion standard is not particularly demanding, George has a strong argument that the officer had insufficient facts for a forcible detention.

An anonymous tip can provide a foundation for a reasonable suspicion finding, but if nothing is known about the "reliability" of the tipster or her information, the tip "standing alone" is not enough to support a reasonable suspicion finding. Alabama v. White. Something more is needed. In Alabama v. White, officers corroborated not only certain extant details provided by an anonymous caller but also the caller's predictions about a woman's future conduct. The fact that the caller had told truths provided some evidence of veracity. The fact that the caller knew about future conduct by the woman furnished evidence of inside knowledge about her life. For these reasons, the Court found a sufficient basis for "reasonable suspicion," but noted that *White* was "a close case."

In this situation, nothing was known about the anonymous caller's basis of knowledge or veracity. The details corroborated were not extraordinary and did not indicate that the caller had access to information about "George's" life. They could have been obtained by anyone in the diner. Because the corroboration in this case provides significantly less support for the caller's reliability, there is a strong argument that Officer Jones lacked reasonable suspicion. If so, the stop was invalid and the statements made were illegally obtained.

---

4. Scope of *Terry*-Stops: Limits on Temporary Detentions of Persons

The reason that "stops" are reasonable despite the absence of probable cause is that they are not as intrusive as "arrests"—they are not "full seizures" but are limited, temporary deprivations of freedom. The line between a temporary detention and an arrest is not clearly defined. In general, to qualify as a "stop" the intrusion on a suspect's freedom of action must be markedly less than that ordinarily associated with an arrest. Several factors are relevant.

a. **Temporal factor: How long may a temporary detention last?** Investigative stops cannot "continue[ ] indefinitely." At some point, they become "de facto arrest[s]." United States v. Sharpe, 470 U.S. 675, 105 S. Ct. 1568, 84 L. Ed. 2d 605 (1985). That point, however, is not defined by a fixed period of time. While *Terry* detentions should be brief, there is no hard and fast "brevity" limit—that is, no per se or bright-line time limit.

Instead, a detention is reasonable in duration when "the police **diligently pursue[ ] a means of investigation that [is] likely to confirm or dispel their suspicions quickly,** during which time it [is] necessary to detain the" suspect. United States v. Sharpe. If they are "**dilatory** in their investigation," or "**unnecessarily prolong[ ]**" the detention, the stop is unreasonable in scope. Id.

This "sliding scale" approach to the temporal limitation on *Terry*-stops is a two-edged sword. On the one hand, a stop can usually last as long as is reasonably necessary to conduct the investigation. On the other hand, even a very brief stop can be unreasonable if officers delay unnecessarily and do not diligently pursue their suspicions.

b. **Locational factor: May a suspect be moved during a *Terry* detention?**

A suspect **may not be transported to the police station** on the basis of a mere reasonable suspicion. "[T]he line [between an investigative detention and an arrest] is crossed when the police . . . **forcibly remove a person from his home or other place in which he is entitled to be and transport him to the police station,** where he is detained, **although briefly,** for investigative purposes." Hayes v. Florida, 470 U.S. 811, 105 S. Ct. 1643, 84 L. Ed. 2d 705 (1985).

To be reasonable, transportation of a suspect to a police station requires more than a reasonable suspicion alone. The transportation is reasonable if the officer has **probable cause to arrest** the suspect. It *may* also be permissible for certain limited purposes, such as fingerprinting, if the officers obtain **judicial authorization for "the seizure of a person on less than probable cause."** Hayes v. Florida. Put otherwise, an officer *may* be able to transport a suspect to a police station for limited investigatory purposes if he secures a detention order from a judge on the basis of "reasonable suspicion."

Can't Move to Station

Limited movements of a suspect during a stop are probably allowed if they are reasonably necessary to accomplish the purposes of the stop. See Florida v. Royer, 460 U.S. 491, 103 S. Ct. 1319, 75 L. Ed. 2d 229 (1983). It is unclear whether a suspect can ever be moved a substantial distance during an investigative detention. An eyewitness may be at the scene of the crime several miles away from the point of detention or a victim may be hospitalized across town from the site. In those cases, whether it is reasonable to take a properly detained suspect to the scene or hospital is arguable.

Can order out / car

During the lawful detention of a vehicle, an officer may as a matter of course order both the driver, see Pennsylvania v. Mimms, 434 U.S. 106, 98 S. Ct. 330, 54 L. Ed. 2d 331 (1977), and passengers, see Maryland v. Wilson, — U.S. —, 117 S. Ct. 882, —137 L. Ed. 2d 41 (1997), to exit the vehicle pending completion of the stop. The incremental intrusion on liberty caused by the order to get out of the vehicle is *per se* reasonable. It requires no additional justification.

c. **Other relevant factors: How much may official conduct intrude on a suspect's liberty?** The general question is whether law enforcement conduct is sufficiently limited to be considered a temporary *detention* or so intrusive that it ought to be treated as a *de facto arrest.* Duration and the movement of the suspect are relevant because they increase the infringement on a suspect's liberty. Other actions by officers that intrude on or restrict a suspect's liberty are also relevant and can turn a detention into an arrest.

An officer might, for example, ask a large number of questions, ask questions of an accusatory nature, or use a demanding tone. She might administer a sobriety test or initiate an encounter in an isolated or threatening setting. All such factors can increase the intrusiveness of an encounter.

Fingerprints can be ok

Taking fingerprints during an investigative stop is permissible if there is reason to believe that the fingerprinting will confirm or dispel a suspicion. Hayes v. Florida. Nevertheless, fingerprinting and similar investigative techniques bear on the intrusiveness of an encounter and could contribute to a finding that the border between detentions and arrests was crossed.

Handcuff No

Handcuffing might in and of itself support a conclusion that a de facto arrest has occurred. Even if it is permissible to use handcuffs during a detention, they will significantly increase the infringement on a suspect's liberty.

5.   Scope of *Terry*-Stops: Temporary Detentions of Effects

When an individual is detained based on a reasonable suspicion of criminal activity, the personal effects that he is carrying are necessarily detained. No independent justification is required to detain those effects. An officer, however, might wish to detain personal effects **independently** of the seizure of a person. The question considered here is the constitutionality of such an independent seizure on less than probable cause.

a.   Permissibility of and grounds for seizing effects. In United States v. Place, 462 U.S. 696, 103 S. Ct. 2637, 77 L. Ed. 2d 110 (1983), the Supreme Court concluded that a limited, independent detention of an effect is permissible in some circumstances. At least where an officer "reasonably . . . believe[s] that . . . [an effect] contains narcotics," he may seize the effect in order to conduct an investigation designed to confirm or dispel that suspicion. Id.

Because the *Place* Court dealt only with seizures of containers suspected of harboring contraband, it did not address the permissibility of detentions based on reasonable suspicion that an object is involved in or is concealing evidence of some other sort of crime. Later, in Arizona v. Hicks, 480 U.S. 321, 107 S. Ct. 1149, 94 L. Ed. 2d 347 (1987), the Court made it clear that limited seizures of effects are not always reasonable when officers have a reasonable suspicion that the effect is somehow involved in criminality.

Hicks Facts

In *Hicks*, an officer suspected that a turntable was stolen. He lifted it to examine the serial number. The Court held that this limited seizure (and search) **could not be justified on less than probable cause.** The majority observed that a limited seizure of an inanimate object on less than probable cause is allowable only when **"the seizure is minimally intrusive and [special] operational necessities** render it the only practicable means of detecting certain types of crime.'' Id. Temporary seizures of objects suspected of containing narcotics satisfy both of these criteria; limited seizures of objects suspected of being stolen do not meet the ''special operational necessities'' requirement.

It is unclear whether any ground other than a reasonable suspicion of the presence of contraband can justify the independent, temporary detention of an effect. Both the seriousness of the offense at issue and the difficulty of detecting that offense would be relevant variables.

b.   Allowable scope of seizures of effects. The question here is what an officer can do with an object that she has seized based on a reasonable suspicion. As in the case of detentions of persons, there is no bright-line answer to this question.

   i.   Variable intrusiveness of seizures of effects. The question of the permissible scope of the temporary seizure of an inanimate object is complicated by ''the fact that seizures of property **can vary in intrusiveness.**'' See United States v. Place. A piece of luggage **seized from a person** not only intrudes on the person's **possessory interest** in the item, it also impinges on that person's **liberty.** If, however, a container were seized from a shipment, the only harm might be a limited deprivation of a **possessory interest** in the item. Consequently, to determine whether the seizure of an effect is sufficiently confined in scope one must first determine **the character of the seizure and the ''nature and extent'' of the intrusions** that result. See id.

   ii.   Temporal factor: How long may a seizure of an effect last? If an object is seized **from the custody of an individual,** the seizure may last **no longer than a seizure of the person.** See United States v. Place. Consequently, such a seizure may not last ''indefinitely'' and may not exceed the time that it takes for the diligent pursuit of a course of investigation likely to confirm or dispel the official suspicion. See subsection 4.a above.

   If the effect is **not in a person's custody** and therefore does not restrict personal liberty, **a longer seizure might well be permissible.** In other words, a seizure that was longer than reasonably necessary for the diligent pursuit of suspicions might still be reasonable because of the limited infringement of constitutionally protected interests caused by the unnecessary delay.

EXAMPLE AND ANALYSIS

If officers seize a shoulder bag from a traveler at an airport and delay subjecting that bag to a drug-detecting dog for no good reason, the lack of diligence renders the seizure unreasonable because it resulted in an unjustified restriction on the traveler's freedom of movement. But if officers seize the same shoulder bag from an air freight shipment, a similar unnecessary delay might cause no cognizable harm to possessory interests. The only result of the delay might be that the bag remains for an additional period of time in the possession of law enforcement rather than in the possession of the air freight company. From the standpoint of an owner's possessory interests, it is arguable that no additional harm results from the official lack of diligence.

---

      iii.   **Other factors: What can be done with the seized effect?** Officers are allowed to subject an effect to a "canine sniff" designed to determine whether it contains contraband narcotics. Such a sniff of a container sitting in a public place is not a "search." United States v. Place. Officers may also request consent to search.

However, officers may not open a container based on a reasonable suspicion. Moreover, they are probably barred from performing even a "less intrusive search"—such as manually manipulating the exterior of a soft container, as a means of pursuing their suspicion. Cf. Minnesota v. Dickerson, 508 U.S. 366, 113 S. Ct. 2130, 124 L. Ed. 2d 334 (1993) (holding that the manual manipulation of an object in the pocket of a detainee on the basis of suspicion that it was contraband was a search that required probable cause).

> **Note:** A lesser search of a container taken from a detainee, and perhaps even the opening of such a container, might be permissible as an "extended frisk of the person" if officers have a reasonable suspicion that the container is harboring a dangerous weapon. See subsection 6 below, discussing the permissible scope of frisks.

Whether and when officers may **transport an effect to another location** in order to carry out an investigation is unclear. If the object has been seized from the custody of a person, it is arguable that "the limitations applicable to investigative detentions of the person should define the permissible scope of an investigative detention" of the object on less than probable cause. United States v. Place. If so, an effect could **not** be taken to a police station (see subsection 4.b above) but might properly be taken to another location if necessary for an effective investigation.

However, except to the extent that it extends the duration of the seizure, movement of an object does not necessarily increase the harm to the liberty interests of the individual from whom it is taken. Moreover, movement of an object to a police station might be no more intrusive than movement to any other location. In sum, it is arguable that officers can transport an inanimate object to a police station and any other place so long as they diligently pursue and do not unnecessarily prolong the investigation.

For objects that have not been taken from the custody of a person, the argument in favor of allowing officers to transport them to other locations is even more compelling. The possessory deprivation involved may not be increased at all by the movement of the effect. Suppose that officers seize a carton from the mail based on a reasonable suspicion that it contains marijuana. Suppose further that it would take an hour to have a drug-sniffing dog brought to the post office. It would be more cost-efficient and would take the same amount of time if the carton were taken to the dog at the police station or at a halfway point between the police station and post office. The movement of the carton to either location would arguably cause no greater intrusion on possessory interests than would be the case if the dog were summoned to the carton at the post office.

6. Scope Of *Terry*-Frisks

During an investigative detention, if an officer has a reasonable suspicion that a suspect is armed and presently dangerous, she is authorized to conduct a **patdown of his outer clothing** to detect large weapons such as "guns, knives, [and] clubs." Terry v. Ohio. While the officer may **thoroughly explore all areas of the person,** she must stay on the outer surface of the suspect's clothing. If she intrudes beneath the surface—into a pocket, for example—the frisk will be deemed unreasonable in scope, see Sibron v. New York, 392 U.S. 40, 88 S. Ct. 1889, 20 L. Ed. 2d 917 (1968), unless perhaps it is impractical for the officer to pursue the suspicion by remaining on the outer surface. See Adams v. Williams, 407 U.S. 143, 92 S. Ct. 1921, 32 L. Ed. 2d 612 (1972) (reaching directly to the waistband of the suspect seated in a car to remove a weapon held permissible when the officer had reason to fear for his safety and the suspect refused to comply with the officer's request to get out of the car).

If the officer feels a weapon during a proper limited frisk, it is reasonable to reach below the surface of the suspect's clothing to extract it. But if the officer ascertains that the suspect is not in possession of a weapon, the frisk must end. Even if he has a reasonable suspicion that an object felt during a frisk is contraband, the officer may not manipulate it with his fingers in an effort to determine its identity. See Minnesota v. Dickerson.

Officers may also conduct **limited weapons searches of vehicles** ("vehicle frisks") based on a reasonable suspicion that a "suspect is dangerous and . . . may gain immediate control of weapons" from the vehicle. Michigan v. Long, 463 U.S. 1032, 103 S. Ct. 3469, 77 L. Ed. 2d 1201 (1983). The suspect need not be inside the vehicle at the time of the search. Id. (upholding search of car conducted when driver was standing outside).

However, a vehicle weapons search must be **"restricted to those areas [over] which [the suspect] would generally have immediate control, and that could contain a weapon."** Id. It is a limited **"area search"** of the **passenger compartment** and includes the authority to search accessible **containers found within the passenger compartment** if they could hold a weapon such as a gun, club, or knife.

E&A   EXAMPLE AND ANALYSIS

Gerry is pulled over in his car based on a reasonable suspicion that he robbed a bank. When he is asked to step out of his vehicle, Gerry becomes belligerent and begins to complain of "harassment" by the police. While one officer stands between Gerry and his car, another officer enters the car. Under the front seat he sees a bag of narcotics. In the trunk, he finds a firearm. Were the discoveries constitutional?

For purposes of the vehicle frisk doctrine of Michigan v. Long, it does not seem to matter that Gerry was "outmanned" and was being guarded by one officer. He could have broken away or he might have been permitted to reenter his vehicle after the detention. In either case, a weapon would pose a threat to the officers.

To look for weapons in the passenger compartment, the officer had to have a reasonable suspicion that Gerry was dangerous and could gain immediate control of a weapon from the car. The language in *Terry* suggested that a frisk requires objective indicia of both danger and the presence of a weapon. In *Long*, however, ambiguity in the Court's phrasing suggests that there may be no need to point to facts that indicate the presence of a weapon in a vehicle.

In this case, Gerry's belligerence could be the basis for a finding of "dangerousness." However, there were no facts indicating the presence of a weapon in the vehicle. If such facts are required, as they probably should be, the entry of the vehicle in this case was invalid. If such facts are not required, it was permissible to look under the seat. If the requirements for a "plain view" seizure were satisfied (see section F.8 above), then it was proper to take the bag. Although the purpose and scope of a vehicle frisk hinge on the need to "disarm" the car, officers do not have to ignore contraband that comes into plain view.

Finally, even when grounds for a weapons frisk of a vehicle do exist, the trunk of the vehicle is not within the scope of such a frisk. The *Long* Court specifically limited its "area search" to the "passenger compartment." Therefore, the discovery of the firearm in the trunk was not constitutional.

REVIEW QUESTIONS AND ANSWERS

Question: Officer Jackson is patrolling downtown when he receives a radio report that an anonymous person just called the police station and reported that a blond man in a black leather jacket had just attempted to rape a woman at knifepoint near the corner of Third and Main. Jackson sees Ringo, a blond man in a black leather jacket, standing near the corner of Fifth and Main. A tattered backpack is sitting on the ground near his feet.

Jackson approaches Ringo and informs him that he would like to ask a few questions. Ringo says, "I'm not sure I want to talk to you," whereupon Jackson puts his hand on his weapon and says he would "really appreciate it if you would cooperate." In response to a question about whether he had "been at Third and Main in the last hour," Ringo gets angry and yells that he's "tired of being harassed by the police." At that point, Jackson grabs hold of Ringo, pats him down for weapons, and handcuffs him. He then picks up the backpack and feels its entire outer surface. Upon feeling a "brick-like" shape, Jackson opens the backpack and finds narcotics. Were Jackson's actions reasonable?

Answer: Probably not. The question depends on the resolution of a number of issues:

First, when did Jackson seize Ringo? The initial approach was not a seizure because a mere approach and request to answer questions does not pass the *Mendenhall*–reasonable person standard. When Ringo hesitated and Jackson asked again with his hand on his weapon, the additional facts might well make a reasonable person feel not free to leave. If so, the seizure must be justified at this point. If not, then there is no need to have justification until Jackson grabs Ringo.

Second, did Jackson have a reasonable suspicion of criminal activity? The completely anonymous tip does not give rise to a reasonable suspicion. The fact that a blond man in a leather jacket is two blocks from the alleged rape attempt would not seem to be significant corroboration. When Jackson put his hand on his weapon and asked a second time, it is very unlikely he had a "reasonable suspicion." Ringo's hesitance or refusal to cooperate would not provide additional grounds. He was merely exercising his constitutional rights. If a seizure did not occur until Jackson grabbed Ringo, then Ringo's belligerent behavior should also be considered.

Even with this added, Jackson may well not have had a reasonable suspicion. If Jackson lacked reasonable suspicion when he seized Ringo, that invalid detention would taint everything that follows.

Third, even if the detention was constitutional, was the frisk reasonable in its inception and scope? If there were reasonable grounds to suspect Ringo of attempting a rape at knifepoint a short time before, there would seem to be a basis for a reasonable suspicion that he was still "armed." Moreover, his conduct could support a reasonable suspicion that he was dangerous. A frisk of his person might be justified. Since the officer found nothing, however, he did not have grounds to arrest Ringo. The handcuffing might well have turned the stop into a de facto arrest, exceeding the bounds of a permissible detention. It is unclear whether a dangerous detainee may be handcuffed during a *Terry*-stop.

Next, was Jackson's manual examination of the backpack justifiable? If he did have a reasonable suspicion that Ringo was armed and dangerous, a backpack at Ringo's feet that harbored a weapon would arguably be as accessible as the passenger compartment of a nearby car. A backpack might be a "higher privacy" area than a vehicle, but Jackson merely palpated the exterior, so the intrusion was limited. Still, it is not certain that belongings not on the accused are subject to a *Terry*-frisk. The doctrine of Michigan v. Long might be limited to vehicles.

Finally, could the backpack be opened without a warrant? Even if the frisk of the backpack was acceptable, it could not be opened unless Jackson felt a weapon or, during a permissible frisk, gained probable cause to arrest Ringo. Jackson did not feel a weapon. If his experience in detecting drugs coupled with his sense of touch gave rise to a fair probability that the brick-like shape was contraband, Jackson could open the backpack as an incident of Ringo's arrest. The formal arrest would not have to precede the search incident so long as the probable cause did. It is worth noting that the opening of the backpack could not be justified on probable cause alone. No amount of probable cause can justify a warrantless search. Some exception to the warrant rule is necessary.

Question: Marie is traveling on a train from Boston to Chicago. In Pittsburgh, during a one-hour stop, narcotics officers enter the train with a narcotics-sniffing canine. While Marie is having a meal in the train depot, the dog sniffs the carry-on luggage she has placed under a seat. The dog responds ambiguously. Uncertain what to do, the handler takes possession of the luggage and leaves a note in its place informing Marie that he has taken it to the Pittsburgh police station for further investigation. The note includes the phone number of the station and informs Marie that she may reclaim the bag if nothing is found after the investigation is complete. Is the officer's conduct constitutional?

Answer: The constitutionality of the officer's conduct is uncertain. Preliminarily, the dog-sniff of the luggage on the train does not qualify as a search. The only difference from the sniff in United States v. Place is that Marie's luggage was on the train rather than in a public airport terminal. That factual difference should not lead to a different constitutional outcome on the question of whether a dog-sniff is a search.

The next question is whether the seizure was valid. According to *Place,* the officer could seize the luggage independently of any seizure of Marie if he had a reasonable suspicion that it contained contraband. It is uncertain whether the ambiguous reaction of the dog provides such a suspicion. If not, the seizure was invalid from the start.

Furthermore, the officer may detain the luggage only temporarily. Because he seized it from the custody of a person who was in transit, the temporal restrictions that govern the seizure of persons apply. According to United States v. Sharpe, the detention must not be "indefinite." So long as the officer does not act in a dilatory manner or unnecessarily prolong the seizure of the luggage, it will be reasonable in scope. The question here is whether the officer diligently pursued an investigative means likely to confirm or dispel his suspicion quickly. That would depend on the investigatory means that were available to the officer and on the investigatory steps that he followed after he left the train.

For example, if he had no other means of determining the contents of the bag, and simply took it because he was concerned that he might never find it again, his seizure would be unreasonable. If, however, he seized the bag with the intent of giving a second canine an opportunity to sniff it, and if he acted with dispatch in subjecting the suitcase to the second dog, the seizure could be reasonable.

If the latter were true and the dog failed to signal the presence of contraband, Marie might argue that the officers were bound to return the suitcase to her. That argument probably should fail. If the officer had a reasonable suspicion that contraband was present in the suitcase and if he acted with diligence, he could have detained Marie herself in Pittsburgh for the time it took to pursue his suspicion.

H. "PROTECTIVE SWEEPS" OF HOMES: THE DOCTRINE OF MARYLAND v. BUIE

In certain circumstances, arresting officers are empowered to look through or "sweep" a home in order to protect themselves against dangers that might arise from others who are present in the home. Maryland v. Buie, 494 U.S. 325, 110 S. Ct. 1093, 108 L. Ed. 2d 276 (1990).

1. The Showing Needed to Conduct a "Protective Sweep" of a Home

The first thing that must be shown to justify a protective sweep of a home is **a lawful arrest.** A lawful arrest requires **probable cause to arrest** and possibly a warrant. In addition, the arrest must occur **in a home.** Arrests **outside homes** do not trigger the "protective sweep" authority recognized in *Buie.* Finally, officers must have **"a reasonable, articulable suspicion that the house is harboring a person posing a danger to those on the** arrest scene.'' Maryland v. Buie. The authority to sweep is "decidedly not 'automati[c]' '' but requires **"a reasonable belief based on specific and articulable facts"** that others are present in the home and that they pose a danger. Id. (**Note:** Officers do have "automatic" authority to search areas "immediately adjoining the place of arrest" whenever they arrest a person in a home. See section F.1.b.iii above.)

2. Scope of a Sweep of a Home

The authority to sweep is limited in at least three ways:

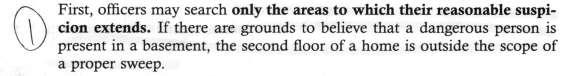 First, officers may search **only the areas to which their reasonable suspicion extends.** If there are grounds to believe that a dangerous person is present in a basement, the second floor of a home is outside the scope of a proper sweep.

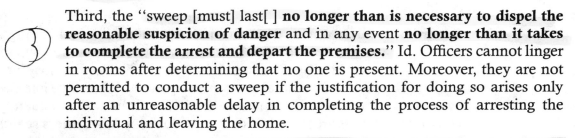 Second, the sweep may not be a "full search of the premises, but may extend only to a **cursory inspection of those spaces where a person may be found.**" Id. Thus, officers may not look in spaces too small to harbor a person and may not continue to examine spaces after ascertaining that no person is present.

Third, the "sweep [must] last[ ] **no longer than is necessary to dispel the reasonable suspicion of danger** and in any event **no longer than it takes to complete the arrest and depart the premises.**" Id. Officers cannot linger in rooms after determining that no one is present. Moreover, they are not permitted to conduct a sweep if the justification for doing so arises only after an unreasonable delay in completing the process of arresting the individual and leaving the home.

I. DETENTIONS AND SEARCHES OF INDIVIDUALS PRESENT DURING SEARCHES OF PREMISES

During the search of a place, officers may have an interest in investigating the involvement of individuals present at the time either by detaining them or searching their persons. In some instances, the constitutionality of doing so is clear. In others, it remains subject to question.

1. Detentions of Individuals During Searches of Premises: The Doctrine of Michigan v. Summers

An officer is allowed to detain an **occupant** of premises while she conducts a **search** of those premises pursuant to a **valid warrant** to search for **contraband.** Michigan v. Summers, 452 U.S. 692, 101 S. Ct. 2587, 69 L. Ed. 2d 340 (1981).

a. **"Occupant" or "resident" limitation.** The person detained must be an **occupant** or **resident** of the premises being searched. Id. Mere casual visitors or guests may not be detained. It is not clear whether the authority to detain extends to longer-term guests, such as friends or relatives staying in a home for a week or two. Some but not all of the reasons that underlie the authority to detain an occupant do pertain to such guests.

Usually, a resident who is detained will be found on the premises during the search. Nonetheless, the doctrine does permit an officer to require a resident **found outside his home** to enter and remain during the pendency of the search. In *Summers*, when the officers arrived the resident was just leaving. The officers met him on the sidewalk outside his home and escorted him back inside. While it is likely that the authority to detain occupants does not extend to those found any substantial distance from their homes, it is uncertain where the boundary lies.

Summers involved a private dwelling. Whether occupants of offices or other commercial establishments could be detained in analogous circumstances is unsettled. If there is authority to detain in such situations, it is restricted to individuals with a clear connection to the premises being searched. In other words, only those whose relationship to the premises is analogous to that of a resident to a private dwelling could be held.

b. **Potential "search warrant" limitation.** If officers are conducting a search pursuant to **a valid search warrant,** detention of an occupant is clearly allowable. The *Summers* Court neither endorsed nor "preclude[d] the possibility that [a] comparable [detention] may be justified by exigent circumstances in the absence of a warrant." Consequently, whether occupants are subject to detention during **a warrantless search based on exigency** is an open question.

c. **Possible "contraband" limitation.** A detention is reasonable if the object of the search is **contraband.** It is uncertain "whether the same result would be justified if the search warrant merely authorized a search for **evidence."** Michigan v. Summers.

d. **Permissible scope of a *Summers* detention.** Occupants or residents may be properly detained **"while a proper search is [being] conducted."** Id. For that duration, the detention is presumptively reasonable. If a detention lasts longer than the time it takes for a "proper search," it is unreasonable.

Even if a detention lasts no longer than a proper search, "**special circumstances, or possibly a prolonged detention,** might lead to [the] conclusion" that the detention is unreasonable **"in an unusual case."** Id. In other words, in some situations a detention that lasted no longer than the search could be too long or otherwise too intrusive to be considered reasonable. One can only speculate about the circumstances that "might" lead to that conclusion. Perhaps if the premises were so extensive that a proper search would last the better part of a day, a detention during that time would be too "prolonged." Or perhaps an occupant's special need to depart the premises—a doctor's appointment or important meeting, for example—could render an otherwise reasonable detention unreasonable.

2. Searches of Individuals During Searches of Premises

If a valid warrant were to authorize the search of a particular person for an item properly subject to seizure, a search of that person would be constitutional. The search of a person found in a particular place pursuant to a warrant that authorized the search of "all occupants" or "all persons present" in the specified place might also be reasonable. It is arguable, however, that such a warrant would be invalid because the phrases "all occupants" or "all persons present" do not "particularly describe the place to be searched." See section D.5 above.

The question raised here is whether a person can ever be searched simply because she is present in a place that is subject to search by virtue of a valid warrant or sufficiently exigent circumstances.

a. **Persons present in commercial establishments.** A customer or client who is present in a commercial establishment at the time of a warranted search for contraband **may not be searched** simply because he is within the confines of the area that may legitimately be searched. Such an individual is a **separate and distinct place** "clothed with [his own] constitutional protection." Ybarra v. Illinois, 444 U.S. 85, 100 S. Ct. 338, 62 L. Ed. 2d 238 (1979).

Such a search is valid only if officers acquire **probable cause** to search the particular person for contraband. Nothing less will justify such a search. Thus, even if officers have information that gives rise to a reasonable suspicion that the contraband that is the object of the warrant will be found on the person, they may not search him. Even a frisk is forbidden. Id.

Although there is no Supreme Court holding on the subject, it seems very likely that this holding would be extended to analogous situations in private dwellings. Consequently, a guest or visitor in a home would not automatically be subject to search when the home is the subject of a search warrant for contraband.

b. **Occupants of private dwellings and individuals with analogous connections to commercial establishments.** The *Summers* doctrine authorizes only the **detention** of an occupant. The Court did not address the propriety of a **search** of such a person. The *Ybarra* opinion bars only the search of individuals who happen to be present in commercial establishments at the time of a valid search for contraband. It did not discuss the propriety of searching a person with a stronger connection to the premises.

Consequently, it is uncertain whether individuals with sufficiently strong connections to premises being searched are subject to search simply because they are present at the time of an authorized search of those premises. Occupants of dwellings, business owners, and employees of businesses could all qualify. On the one hand, such persons might be considered separate and distinct "places," and the searches might require individualized probable cause. On the other hand, the individuals' connections to the places might justify treating them as integral parts of the places being searched. In that case, they would be subject to search like any other closed space within the premises.

 # EXAMPLES AND ANALYSIS

1. Officers have a valid warrant to search Cheever's home for evidence of an assassination attempt. When they are a block away, they notice that Cheever is backing his car out of the driveway. They turn on their lights and siren, pull Cheever over, and take him inside his home. During a four-hour search of Cheever's home, the officers detain him. They refuse to allow him to use the telephone and require that he be accompanied to the bathroom. Was the detention constitutional?

There are several reasons why the detention might be invalid. First, the warrant authorized a search for evidence. The *Summers* holding extends only to searches for contraband. It did not, however, rule out detention authority in other cases. The reasons underlying the authority recognized in *Summers* were (1) to prevent flight, (2) to prevent harm to the officers, and (3) to facilitate the orderly completion of the search. All three reasons might well support a detention when the target of the search is evidence of a serious, violent crime such as an attempted assassination.

Second, Cheever had left his property. He was backing his car out of the driveway and was pulled over in the street. While *Summers* permitted the detention of an occupant found on his front sidewalk, it might not allow the detention of one who has physically left his property. The Court noted that seizing Summers "on the sidewalk outside was **no more intrusive** than the detention of [a] resident[ ] of the house . . . found inside." The *Summers* doctrine might, however, permit the detention of an occupant who has just left his property. Any additional intrusion in that situation could be deemed minimal.

Finally, the detention here might be too extensive because of its length and restrictiveness. The four-hour length of the detention could be objectionable as too "prolonged." But unless the police officers delayed the search unnecessarily, it seems unlikely that such an argument would succeed. Because the Court said that a detention could last "while a proper search is conducted," it seems unlikely that four hours would trouble the Court. The refusal to let Cheever use the telephone and the refusal to allow him to go to the bathroom in private certainly increased the intrusiveness of his detention. This alone could tip the balance of interests against the government. On the other hand, the interest in preventing harm to the officers and flight by the detainee might support these additional restrictions.

2. Fawn lives in a townhouse in the center of town. Armed with a valid warrant to search for cocaine, Detective Arnold knocks at her door. He introduces himself and shows the warrant. Fawn tells Arnold that she is on her way out and that he should lock the door when he's finished. Arnold steps into Fawn's path as she tries to leave and tells her she must remain for a short time. He takes her purse from her arm, opens it, and empties the contents. He then orders her to remove her coat and jacket. When she does, Arnold turns the pockets inside out. Has Arnold violated Fawn's rights?

The answer to this question is uncertain. On the one hand, as the resident of the townhouse Fawn has a strong relationship to it. Her purse and pockets are places that could harbor the contraband that is the subject of the warrant. If those places could not be searched, the object of the officer's mission might be defeated. These facts distinguish this case from *Ybarra*, which prohibited the search of a patron in a bar. Perhaps Fawn should not be regarded as a separate and distinct private space.

On the other hand, the warrant did not particularly describe Fawn as a place to be searched. Even residents of dwellings might have separate and distinct privacy interests in their persons—which arguably include personal belongings such as Fawn's purse. Because the warrant did not authorize the search of Fawn and because the officer lacked particularized probable cause to search her, the searches of Fawn's clothing and purse might be considered as unreasonable as the search of Ybarra's person.

J. SCHOOL SEARCHES

The Fourth Amendment does apply to searches of schoolchildren conducted by school officials. Because of the **special relationship** between officials and their students and the **special need** to maintain order and control in schools, properly limited searches can be reasonable without a search warrant or probable cause. New Jersey v. T.L.O., 469 U.S. 325, 105 S. Ct. 733, 83 L. Ed. 2d 720 (1985).

1. Conditions Necessary to Conduct a School Search

In New Jersey v. T.L.O., the Court recognized that **school officials** may conduct **warrantless** searches of **schoolchildren** on **less than probable cause.** The official must have a **reasonable suspicion** to support such a search.

a. Primary or secondary school setting requirement. The school search doctrine of *T.L.O.* applies only to "schoolchildren"—students enrolled in **primary and secondary schools.** It has no application at the college level because neither the special relationship nor the special need underlying the school search doctrine is present in that setting. Normal Fourth Amendment requirements govern searches at that level.

b.   **School official requirement.** School searches may be conducted only by **school officials.** Thus, teachers or administrators may perform them, while law enforcement officers may not. Moreover, school officials must be acting in the interest of the school—that is, to serve the objectives of the educational institution. Searches by school officials acting **"in conjunction with or at the behest of law enforcement agencies"** are not authorized by the school search doctrine. *New Jersey v. T.L.O.* They are probably subject to the Fourth Amendment requirements that govern other law enforcement searches.

c.   **"Reasonable suspicion" requirement.** School officials do not have unfettered authority to search students. To conduct a school search, the official must have **"reasonable grounds for suspecting** that the search will turn up evidence that the student has violated or is violating **either the law or the rules of the school."** *New Jersey v. T.L.O.* Two things are noteworthy about this standard. First, the level of likelihood required is the same as that demanded for a *Terry* stop-and-frisk. See section G.3 above. Second, a suspected violation of **any law** or of **any school rule** can be the basis for a search. No rule of the institution is too trivial to support a search.

2.   Scope of an Authorized School Search

The *T.L.O.* doctrine authorizes a search of the student's person. Searches of other areas in which students have privacy interests are not authorized by the Court's holding.

a.   **The school setting.** A school search must be performed **in the school setting.** The authority granted does not extend to other places. Consequently, if a teacher sees one of her students in a supermarket and has a reasonable suspicion that the student has shoplifted, the teacher is not empowered to conduct a search to discover the stolen item.

b.   **The "person" of the student.** In general, school officials who satisfy the showing described above may search **the person of the student.** This includes **all personal belongings** carried by the student at the time of the search.

The authority to search a schoolchild's person, however, is not unlimited. A school search is "permissible in its scope when the measures adopted are **reasonably related to the objectives of the search and not excessively intrusive in light of the age and sex of the student and the nature of the infraction."** Although the meaning of this limitation on scope is not entirely clear, it suggests at least two constraints.

First, the scope of the search must be **limited by the nature of the "reasonable suspicion"** possessed by the official. A teacher may look only in places where the object that is the basis of her reasonable suspicion could be located. For example, a search for a gun or knife could not extend to a small shirt pocket. And if a teacher were informed that a student always kept cigarettes in her purse in violation of a school rule, a search of that student's coat pocket would be unreasonable.

The second constraint is more complicated. An official may have grounds for conducting a search beyond the private areas of the student's clothing and the effects carried by the student. Such a search may involve disrobing by the student or touching of the student's person by the official, or both. Clearly, this type of search effects a more serious invasion of personal privacy. Moreover, two factors can further exacerbate the intrusion—age and gender. An adolescent is presumably more vulnerable and has a greater concern for bodily privacy than a younger child and therefore would suffer a more severe deprivation of privacy. The intrusion can be further increased if the searching official is of the opposite gender. Thus, a teenage girl would suffer an even greater infringement if a male teacher were to require her to disrobe.

The *T.L.O.* Court's standard does not categorically prohibit these more intrusive searches. Instead, it suggests that when the intrusion goes beyond that effected by an "ordinary" search of the person of a student, its reasonableness depends on the interest being served by the search— that is, on the "nature of the infraction" suspected. To be reasonable, more severe intrusions require more weighty interests.

 # EXAMPLE AND ANALYSIS

Janine, a junior high school teacher, was told by one of her students that Matt, a 14-year-old pupil in her homeroom, is distributing cocaine at school and that he keeps his supply tucked inside a special pouch sewn inside his undershorts. Janine observes Matt engaged in "suspicious" conversation in the hallways with a number of other students. Some of these students are generally suspected of being drug abusers. At lunchtime, Janine takes Matt into the faculty restroom, locks the door, and orders him to take his pants off. Is her action constitutional?

Janine's action is questionable in two respects. In the first place, Janine may not have an adequate basis for a reasonable suspicion. Unless there is some basis for crediting the student's tip, there is little reason to rely on it. Matt's conversations with others who are suspected of drug use would seem to provide very little additional objective information supporting a reasonable suspicion that he is in possession of narcotics.

Even if Janine did have a reasonable suspicion that Matt had narcotics in his under-shorts, the scope of her search may well be unreasonable. Cocaine possession and distribution in a junior high school is a very serious offense and, therefore, one that may justify requiring a student to disrobe. However, the invasion of Matt's privacy was particularly severe—he is a teenager and was ordered to disrobe in the presence of a *female* teacher. The severity of the intrusion could easily have been lessened by having a male official conduct the search. The government could plausibly contend that an offense of this magnitude justifies an intrusion this severe and that there is no need to pursue the less intrusive alternative. Matt could contend that no matter how serious the offense, a strip search of a teenager by a teacher of the opposite gender is not permitted unless it is necessitated by an emergency of some sort.

---

c. **Automobiles and other belongings not on the person of the student.** The opinion in *T.L.O.* did not address the constitutionality of school searches of student automobiles or other personal effects not found on the person of the student. The same interest-balancing that led the *T.L.O.* Court to allow searches of students' persons could easily lead to the conclusion that searches of vehicles and other effects without warrants and on the basis of a "reasonable suspicion" are reasonable.

d. **Lockers, desks, and other school property.** In *T.L.O.*, the Court stated that it was "not address[ing] the question . . . whether a schoolchild has a legitimate expectation of privacy in **lockers, desks, or other school property** provided for the storage of school supplies." It specifically declined to "express any opinion on the standards (if any) governing searches of such areas." If the Court were to conclude that schoolchildren have no legitimate privacy expectations in such areas, official searches could be conducted without any showing of cause. If students do have protected Fourth Amendment interests, a "reasonable suspicion" may be required to justify searches of these spaces.

3. **Possibility of Random Searches of Schoolchildren**

As will be seen in the following sections, some governmental searches and seizures have been deemed reasonable despite the lack of any "individualized suspicion." Officials are allowed to conduct these searches even though they have no objective basis for suspicion about the particular person or place that is being searched or seized.

In *T.L.O.*, the Court held out the possibility that there are "circumstances that **might** justify school authorities in conducting **searches [of students] unsupported by individualized suspicion.**" The cases that permit such

random searches and seizures have identified three variables that would be relevant to an assessment of the reasonableness of random searches of students: (1) the degree of intrusion on privacy—that is, whether the intrusion is "limited"; (2) the presence of "special needs"—that is, whether a weighty interest beyond ordinary law enforcement is being served; and (3) restrictions on official discretion—that is, whether the searching official is deprived of discretion to select the individuals to be searched. See sections K, L, and M below.

 # EXAMPLE AND ANALYSIS

Becker High School has had a serious weapons problem. In the past year, one student was wounded by a gun and three were injured in knifing incidents. The school board has concluded that the authority to search students suspected of possessing weapons has been inadequate to eliminate the problem. Consequently, it has adopted the following protocol:

> At the beginning of each school day, the principal shall draw three letters from a bowl containing each letter of the alphabet. Students whose last names begin with the letters drawn shall be asked to report immediately to the principal's office. Each student will then be thoroughly patted down by an official of the same gender. If a weapon is detected, it will be removed and disciplinary proceedings will be instituted immediately.

Several parents sue the school district, alleging that the program is unconstitutional. How should the court rule?

It is unclear whether "random" searches pursuant to such a protocol are ever constitutional in the school setting. If so, this program seems potentially defensible when assessed against the criteria that are relevant. First, the intrusion is limited to an outer clothing frisk by a person of the same gender. *Terry* doctrine would support classifying this as a serious but limited privacy intrusion. Moreover, the relationship between students and school officials may render it even less intrusive than a *Terry*-frisk.

Second, Becker High School has an arguably serious problem with weapons. The interest being served—protecting students and teachers against violence—is weighty. The program may well detect weapons and lead to their removal from the community. Alternatively, it may deter students from bringing weapons to school more effectively than the threat of being searched only when officials have a reasonable suspicion. Moreover, courts should pay considerable deference to officials' judgments regarding the need for random search and seizure programs, which are considered effective even though only a small percentage of searches or seizures are "successful." See sections K and L below.

Finally, there is no discretion to choose the students to be searched. All students are eligible and those searched are selected by random drawing. No discrimination or harassment is possible under such a scheme and the students know, if they are informed of the program, that every student is equally at risk of being searched.

K.   PERMANENT AND TEMPORARY CHECKPOINTS OR ROADBLOCKS

Ordinarily, any seizure of a person requires at least a "reasonable suspicion" that the particular person is or has been involved in criminal activity. In certain circumstances, **seizures effected at traffic checkpoints** are reasonable even though officers possess no individualized suspicion with respect to the person seized. Such "random" seizures at both permanent (or "fixed") and temporary (or "mobile") checkpoints can be constitutional.

1.   Cases Upholding Permanent and Temporary Checkpoints

The Supreme Court has upheld one type of permanent checkpoint and one type of temporary checkpoint. In United States v. Martinez-Fuerte, 428 U.S. 543, 96 S. Ct. 3074, 49 L. Ed. 2d 1116 (1976), the Court held that **permanent checkpoints designed to detect illegal aliens** were constitutional. In Michigan Department of State Police v. Sitz, 496 U.S. 444, 110 S. Ct. 2481, 110 L. Ed. 2d 412 (1990), the Court concluded that a **temporary checkpoint conducted to detect drunken drivers** was reasonable.

In both cases, the Court agreed that a driver who is stopped at a checkpoint is **"seized"** for purposes of the Fourth Amendment even though the infringement on her liberty is brief and modest. The *Martinez-Fuerte* opinion concluded that neither individualized suspicion nor a warrant was needed to support seizures at the permanent immigration checkpoints at issue. Likewise, the *Sitz* Court endorsed suspicionless seizures of all drivers passing through the temporary sobriety checkpoint.

2.   Criteria for Judging the Constitutionality of Checkpoints

The holdings in *Martinez-Fuerte* and *Sitz* were carefully limited to the particular checkpoints involved in those cases. The opinions did not provide bright lines for determining the constitutionality of random stops at other permanent or temporary checkpoints. However, they did furnish three criteria by which to judge checkpoint stops.

a.   **Magnitude of the seizure.** The first relevant variable is the **magnitude of the seizure** occurring at the checkpoint. The intrusion on the liberty interests of the detained motorist must be limited or minimal. The intrusion is measured both objectively and subjectively.

The **objective magnitude** of the intrusion is measured by the **"duration of the seizure and the intensity of the investigation."** Michigan Department of State Police v. Sitz. In *Martinez-Fuerte*, the "initial" stops of all motorists probably lasted less than a minute. "Secondary" stops of a limited number of motorists lasted from three to five minutes. Both kinds of stop were deemed **"brief."** In *Sitz*, the "average delay for each vehicle [of] approximately 25 seconds" was also considered **"brief."**

In addition, motorists passing through the checkpoint in *Martinez-Fuerte* were briefly questioned, might be asked to produce documentation of citizenship, and were subjected to visual inspection by the officer operating the checkpoint. The *Sitz* checkpoint also entailed brief questioning and visual inspection. These kinds of investigatory measures were thought to cause "limited" or "slight" objective intrusions on the motorists.

The **subjective magnitude** of the intrusion is measured by a checkpoint's **"potential to generate fear and surprise in motorists."** Michigan Department of State Police v. Sitz. The potential to generate fear and surprise can be diminished by ① **visible signs of the officers' authority,** the fact that ② **other motorists are being stopped,** and ③ **restrictions on the officers' discretion** to select the site of the checkpoint and to choose the investigatory methods to be used during a stop. It is clear, however, that these three intrusion-limiting factors do not always have to be present. In *Martinez-Fuerte*, the Court upheld secondary inspection referrals without reasonable suspicion despite the fact that only a small percentage of motorists were subjected to them.

b. **Nature of the interest served by the checkpoint.** The nature of the interest served by the checkpoint is also a highly relevant variable. The permanent checkpoint in *Martinez-Fuerte* was established to serve the **"important** law enforcement interests" in preventing illegal immigration, and the temporary checkpoint in *Sitz* was conducted to combat "drunken driving," a **"serious** public danger" of considerable "magnitude" that states have a substantial "interest in eradicating." It is arguable that random stops at checkpoints are *never* reasonable unless the interest being served qualifies as "important" or "serious."

c. **"Need" for suspicionless stops and "effectiveness" of the checkpoint.** The *Martinez-Fuerte* Court relied, in part, on the **"need"** for suspicionless stops as a means of effectively detecting illegal aliens. Moreover, both the *Martinez-Fuerte* and the *Sitz* opinions suggest that **"effectiveness"** or "the extent to which [the checkpoint] system can reasonably be said to advance [the public] interest" is relevant to its reasonableness.

These statements might suggest that "need" and "effectiveness" should play significant roles in evaluating the reasonableness of a checkpoint. There are two reasons, however, why that is not the case.

First, relatively **small percentages of detection** are considered sufficiently **effective**. A 1.5 percent drunken-driver arrest rate in *Sitz* and a 0.5 percent illegal-alien detection rate in *Martinez-Fuerte* were deemed "effective."

Second, the *Sitz* majority made it clear that courts should hesitate to invalidate checkpoints based on their assessments of need or effectiveness. According to the *Sitz* Court, "the decision as to which among reasonable alternative law enforcement techniques should be employed to deal with a serious public danger" is entrusted to "politically accountable officials." Courts should not substitute their judgments for the judgments of those officials.

 # EXAMPLE AND ANALYSIS

Brandon was stopped at a temporary "drug interdiction" checkpoint set up on a two-lane road 30 miles from the border between the United States and Mexico. When the officer who stopped his vehicle informed Brandon that he was engaged in an effort to stop the flow of narcotics into the United States, Brandon panicked and began to speed away. After a short chase, he was apprehended and arrested and his car was searched. A kilogram of cocaine was found under the front seat. Prior to trial, a judge suppressed the cocaine, reasoning that the government failed to show that temporary drug-interdiction checkpoints were "any more effective than less intrusive stops based on articulable, particularized suspicion" because the evidence showed "that stops of as long as 10 to 15 minutes occurred" and that "the checkpoint was operated to find illegal narcotics and was simply an effort to enforce the criminal laws by unconstitutional means." Should this ruling be sustained on appeal?

The ruling is arguably supportable, but on only one of the three grounds cited by the trial judge. First, the government does not have to demonstrate that the checkpoint intrusions were more effective than less intrusive, suspicion-based stops. While the dissent in *Sitz* relied on that argument, it is fair to say that the majority rejected it. Moreover, the judge seems to have ignored the majority's exhortation not to substitute her judgment for that of the responsible officials.

Second, the fact that a checkpoint is used to enforce criminal laws does not seem to render it unconstitutional. Immigration checkpoints and sobriety checkpoints are used to enforce criminal laws. So long as the interest being promoted is sufficiently important, the checkpoint is sustainable. The interest in stopping the flow of narcotics and all the harms caused by that flow certainly seem weighty enough to justify checkpoint stops.

The finding regarding the duration of the stops, however, may support the judge's ruling. The stops in *Sitz* averaged 25 seconds and those in *Martinez-Fuerte* were no longer than three to five minutes. Ten- to fifteen-minute random stops at a temporary checkpoint might be too intrusive to be reasonable and could render the entire checkpoint unconstitutional.

For analytical purposes, keep in mind that the Court has not declared all checkpoints reasonable. Case-by-case analysis is required. In evaluating any checkpoint, all aspects that bear on both sides of the balance should be examined. Additional facts concerning the drug interdiction checkpoint in this example could change the conclusion regarding its constitutionality.

L. DRUG TESTING

Ordinarily, reasonable searches require both probable cause, see Arizona v. Hicks, 480 U.S. 321, 107 S. Ct. 1149, 94 L. Ed. 2d 347 (1987), and a search warrant, see Johnson v. United States, 333 U.S. 10, 68 S. Ct. 367, 92 L. Ed. 436 (1948). Even when those norms are suspended, some amount of individualized suspicion typically is essential. There are a small number of instances, however, in which **searches** pass Fourth Amendment muster despite the lack of any particularized justification. **Random drug testing** is one of those instances. It has been approved by the Supreme Court in three distinct contexts: tests of certain railroad employees following specified incidents, see Skinner v. Railway Labor Executives' Association, 489 U.S. 602, 109 S. Ct. 1402, 103 L. Ed. 2d 639 (1989); tests of certain Customs Service employees, see National Treasury Employees Union v. Von Raab, 489 U.S. 656, 109 S. Ct. 1384, 103 L. Ed. 2d 685 (1989); and tests of student athletes, see Vernonia School District 47J v. Acton, — U.S. —, 115 S. Ct. 2386, 132 L. Ed. 2d 564 (1995). The reasonableness of random drug testing must be judged case by case under the criteria delineated in these three opinions.

1. The Cases Upholding Random, Suspicionless Drug Testing

In Skinner v. Railway Labor Executives' Association, the Court approved blood, urine, and breath tests for drugs or alcohol that were administered to certain "covered" railroad employees following specified train "accidents" or "incidents." In National Treasury Employees Union v. Von Raab, the Court sanctioned urine tests for drugs that were given to employees who sought transfer or promotion to positions that entailed drug interdiction or required the individual to carry a firearm. And in Vernonia School District 47J v. Acton, the Court permitted a school system to condition student participation in primary or secondary school athletics upon a student's submission to mandatory urine testing for drugs.

Although the holding in each case was confined to the particular drug testing at issue, the Court's opinions establish a few general principles applicable to all drug tests. First, blood, urine, and breath tests for alcohol or drugs are **searches** and therefore must satisfy the Fourth Amendment reasonableness requirement. Second, **random drug testing**—tests administered without a warrant or any particularized suspicion about the individual—**can be reasonable.** Finally, the way to determine whether a particular drug testing scheme is constitutional is to **balance the nature and extent of the test's intrusion on the individual's constitutional interests against the legitimate government interests promoted by the test.**

2. **Nature and Extent of the Privacy Intrusion**

In evaluating any drug test search, the first relevant concern is the **nature and extent of the intrusion on an individual's privacy interests.** Drug testing invades privacy by both revealing confidential information about the person and infringing on personal dignity. To be reasonable, the "intrusions on privacy" caused by random drug tests must be "limited." See *Skinner.* Two distinct factors can support a conclusion that the intrusion effected by a drug test is limited: diminution of the individual's privacy interest and restrictions on the government's conduct.

a. **Factors that diminish an individual's expectation of privacy.** Each case in which the Supreme Court sanctioned random drug testing involved individuals with **diminished expectations of privacy.** In other words, the privacy interests of those tested were lower than "normal." Those privacy interests were thought to be diminished because the individuals were (1) employees in an industry that was pervasively regulated by the government, see *Skinner*; (2) public employees whose jobs required fitness, probity, judgment, and/or dexterity, see *Von Raab*; (3) schoolchildren committed to the temporary custody of state officials, see *Acton*; or (4) participants in school athletics, see id. Therefore, in any case of random drug testing, the first question is whether there are comparable factors that reduce the privacy expectations of those tested.

b. **Factors that restrict the intrusiveness of the government's conduct.** Ordinarily, governmental intrusions into the human body, such as blood and breath tests, are considered to be very serious deprivations of privacy. Moreover, official monitoring of bodily functions such as urination is thought to be a severe affront to human dignity. Nevertheless, the magnitude of such intrusions can be lessened by various aspects of drug testing processes.

The schemes approved by the Supreme Court involved the following features that **restricted the intrusiveness of the government's conduct:** the tests revealed only information pertaining to illicit drug or alcohol use, see, e.g., *Skinner*; the testing process was relatively commonplace and was performed by medical personnel, see, e.g., id.; disrobing was not required, see, e.g., *Acton*; there was no direct visual observation of the process of urination, see, e.g., id.; the information learned from the tests was disclosed to only a limited number of individuals and was not disclosed to law enforcement personnel, see, e.g., id.; and the testing process was standardized and not subject to discretionary variation by the individual administering it, see, e.g., *Skinner.* Therefore, in evaluating the constitutionality of random drug testing, the second question is whether similar factors restrict the intrusiveness of the government's conduct.

3. Government Interests Promoted by the Tests

To be reasonable, the intrusion effected by a drug testing procedure must be outweighed by the government interests promoted by that procedure. The **nature of the interests** promoted, the **need for random testing,** and the **effectiveness of such testing** are all important variables.

a. **Nature of the government interests promoted by the tests.** In *Skinner* and *Von Raab*, the government interests served by random drug testing were deemed **"compelling."** In *Acton*, however, the Court stated that an interest does not have to be compelling to justify random drug testing. Instead, the nature of the interest need only "appear[ ] *important enough* **to justify the particular search at hand."** Nevertheless, a drug testing scheme is unlikely to be found reasonable unless the government interest sought to be promoted is "important" when judged in the abstract.

Interests that have qualified include promoting the safety of railroad travel, ensuring the physical fitness and integrity of public employees involved in drug interdiction or handling firearms, and preventing drug use by primary or secondary school students involved in interscholastic athletics.

It is significant that each of these interests qualified as a **"special need[ ] beyond the normal need for law enforcement."** In arriving at the conclusion that the tests were reasonable, the Court stressed that the testing programs were **not designed to further the enforcement of criminal laws** against drug possession or use and that the information learned by the drug tests **could not be used for criminal prosecution purposes.** It is uncertain whether a random drug-testing program that was either designed or used to enforce the criminal laws could ever be constitutional. In the absence of "special needs," the government might be precluded from invoking the balancing process that supports random drug testing.

b. **Proof of a drug use problem in the particular case.** Even if the interest claimed to be served by a drug testing program is adequate in the abstract, it is arguable that the government's interest in conducting the program is insufficient unless there is evidence that a drug use problem in fact exists in the population to be tested. The Court has rejected this argument, concluding that proof of the existence of a drug use problem in the group subject to testing is **relevant but not essential.** In *Skinner,* the Court relied on evidence of drug and alcohol use by railroad employees and the contribution of that use to railroad accidents. In *Acton,* there was evidence that alcohol and drug abuse by students, particularly student athletes, had grown and was contributing to rebellion within the schools. The *Acton* Court mentioned that there was proof that the problem facing the schools was "immedia[te]." In *Von Raab,* however, a drug testing program was upheld even though there was no evidence of drug abuse by Customs Service employees or of any impairment of their functioning.

c. **Extent to which government interests are promoted by the tests: Need and effectiveness.** The **need for random, suspicionless drug testing** is also **relevant** to assessments of the government interest. There is a need for random testing if a particularized suspicion requirement would impede the government's efforts to further the interest at stake.

A particularized suspicion requirement can hinder the government's efforts in a variety of ways. First, in some situations it may be exceedingly difficult to detect signs of drug use by a particular individual. If so, many individuals using drugs may go undetected. Second, efforts to gather specific evidence might delay the administration of the tests. The result will be a loss of evidence in some cases. Third, some individuals who would be deterred by the threat of random testing may be inclined to risk drug use if they know that particularized suspicion is needed before they can be tested. Fourth, those who are responsible for developing the grounds for suspicion may not be adequately schooled in detecting drug use. Moreover, the effort expended in doing so may distract them from more important tasks.

The **effectiveness** of random, suspicionless testing is also relevant. Nevertheless, the government does not have to provide empirical proof of efficacy. In the three cases in which the Court approved programs there was no evidence of the number of drug users detected or the number of individuals deterred from drug use. As a matter of common sense, the Court decided that random testing was sufficiently effective because it would detect a certain number of users and deter use by an additional number who feared detection.

It is arguable that there is a **"less intrusive alternative"** to random testing—namely, testing only those whose behavior gives rise to an articulable suspicion of drug use—and that the government should be compelled to employ that alternative. This argument has been rejected for two reasons. First, as stated in *Acton,* "the 'least intrusive' search practicable'' is not the only search that ''can be reasonable.'' Second, it makes sense to force officials to pursue a less intrusive alternative only if that alternative is effective. Suspicion-based drug testing is thought to be an insufficiently effective means of dealing with drug use by those who have been targeted for random testing.

4. A Case Rejecting Random, Suspicionless Drug Testing

In Chandler v. Miller, — U.S. —, 117 S.Ct. 1295 (April 15, 1997), the Supreme Court applied the criteria developed in its three prior drug testing cases to a novel situation and concluded that the balance of interest tipped against the drug testing program involved. Consequently, the Court found the ''searches'' effected by the program to be ''unreasonable.''

Chandler involved a unique enactment by the Georgia Legislature. Under the law, candidates for state office had to certify that they had tested negative for illegal drugs. More specifially, ''to qualify for a place on the ballot, a candidate [had to] present a certificate . . . reporting that the candidate submitted to urinalysis drug tests within 30 days prior to qualifying for nomination or election and that the results were negative.'' Nominees of the Libertarian Party sought declaratory and injunctive relief barring enforcement of the statute. The trial court and Eleventh Circuit denied relief, concluding that under *Skinner, Von Raab,* and *Acton* the drug testing requirement was constitutional.

An 8-1 majority of the Supreme Court reversed. The Court agreed that the testing method was ''relatively noninvasive'' because it ''invoke[d] the drug-testing guildelines'' applicable to the programs upheld in *Skinner* and *Von Raab,* ''permit[ted] a candidate to provide a urine specimen in the office of his or her private physician,'' and provided that the ''results of the test [be] given first to the candidate, who controls further dissemination of the report.''

According to the majority, a ''special need for drug testing must be substantial—important enough to override the individual's acknowledged privacy interest, sufficiently vital to suppress the Fourth Amendment's normal requirement of individualized suspicion.'' Georgia had provided no evidence ''of a concrete danger''—i.e., no demonstration that drug abuse by state officials was a problem. In addition, its program was neither ''well designed to identify candidates who violate antidrug laws'' nor ''a credible means to deter illicit drug users from seeking state office.'' Moreover, there was no good reason to conclude that suspicion-based searches would not suffice to combat drug use by candidates for public office who are ''subject to relentless scrutiny.'' The Court concluded that what was at stake was ''the image the State [sought] to project''—''it's commitment to the struggle against drug abuse.'' This need was ''symbolic,'' but not ''special.''

Because Georgia had "diminishe[d] personal privacy for a symbol's sake" and "public safety [was] not genuinely in jeopardy," the majority held that "the Fourth Amendment preclude[d] the suspicionless search" occasioned by Georgia's ballot-access drug-testing statute.

M. OTHER ADMINISTRATIVE SEARCHES

The drug testing programs approved by the Supreme Court opinions discussed in the previous section were not designed to enforce the criminal laws. They were developed to promote distinct governmental interests. For that reason, the testing programs fall into the more general category of **"administrative" or "regulatory" searches.**

A number of other types of "administrative" or "regulatory" searches have also reached the Supreme Court. In a variety of contexts—sometimes described as "situations of **'special need,'** " New York v. Burger, 482 U.S. 691, 107 S. Ct. 2636, 96 L. Ed. 2d 601 (1987)—the Court has held that administrative searches can be reasonable without satisfying the probable cause or search warrant requirements of the Fourth Amendment. Before outlining the general doctrines that govern administrative searches, a few preliminary observations are in order.

First, a search can qualify as "administrative" or "regulatory" even though it has some connections to criminal law enforcement. More specifically, a search may be "administrative" if the ultimate objective of the government's regulatory scheme is also an objective of criminal law enforcement, if evidence discovered is later used to prosecute a crime, or if the agent conducting the search is a police officer. The relevant question is **whether the search is *designed* to enforce a regulatory scheme or the criminal law.**

Second, the reasonableness of an "administrative search" must be determined by balancing the government interests served by the search against the invasion of privacy caused by the search. The appropriateness of suspending the probable cause and search warrant requirements will depend on the results of that balance.

The following section sketches the general terms of the controlling principles. While the important considerations and distinctions will be highlighted and illustrative contexts will be described, there is no attempt to be comprehensive. Students wishing to explore the nuances of this complicated area of Fourth Amendment law should examine the Court's opinions.

At least three general categories of reasonable administrative or regulatory searches can be identified: those that require search warrants based on "area-wide" showings of cause; those that require neither a warrant nor any showing of cause; and those that do not require a warrant but do require a showing of justification less than probable cause.

1. **"Administrative" or "Regulatory" Searches That Are Reasonable If Supported by Search Warrants Based on Unparticularized, "Area-wide" Showings of Cause**

In some settings, the Court has concluded that administrative searches **require search warrants.** The warrants required, however, do not have to be supported by particularized showings of probable cause with respect to the place to be searched. Instead, judges may grant warrants based on general considerations bearing on the particular objectives of the search or inspection to be conducted.

For this category of administrative searches, warrants have been deemed necessary because the searches at issue involve **significant (although limited) intrusions on privacy** and the requirement of **advance judicial approval will not frustrate the purposes** of the regulatory scheme. Particularized showings of cause have not been required because (1) regulatory inspection programs have a **long history of acceptance;** (2) the important **public interests** served by these programs **could not be effectively promoted** if the government had to make particularized showings of cause; and (3) the searches performed effect only **limited invasions of privacy.**

 # EXAMPLES AND ANALYSIS

1. City inspectors entered private dwellings as part of a scheme designed to detect housing code violations. The scheme's purpose was "to prevent . . . the . . . development of conditions which are hazardous to public health and safety." A lessee challenged the reasonableness of the inspectors' entries.

In Camara v. Municipal Court, 387 U.S. 523, 87 S. Ct. 1727, 18 L. Ed. 2d 930 (1967), a landmark administrative search case, the Supreme Court held that the inspectors needed search warrants but that the warrants did not have to be based on a showing of "probable cause to believe that a particular dwelling contain[ed] violations of" the housing code. Instead, the probable cause necessary for a warrant could be based on a showing that "**reasonable legislative or administrative standards for conducting an area inspection** [were] satisfied with respect to a particular dwelling." More specifically, adequate cause to conduct a housing inspection search could "be based upon [such factors as] the passage of time, the nature of the building . . . , or the condition of the entire area." See also See v. City of Seattle, 387 U.S. 541, 87 S. Ct. 1737, 18 L. Ed. 2d 943 (1967) (holding that a "routine" entry of business premises to determine compliance with the city fire code had to be based on the same kind of "area" search warrant required in *Camara*).

2. A statute authorized warrantless searches of business premises to look for safety hazards and violations of the federal Occupational Safety and Health Act (OSHA).

In Marshall v. Barlow's, Inc., 436 U.S. 307, 98 S. Ct. 1816, 56 L. Ed. 2d 305 (1978), the Supreme Court concluded that the warrantless entries were unreasonable and therefore declared the statute violative of the Fourth Amendment. As in *Camara*, however, a warrant could issue without a showing "that conditions in violation of OSHA exist[ed] on the premises" to be searched. A warrant would be valid if it was shown "that a specific business had been chosen for an OSHA search on the basis of a general administrative plan for the enforcement of the Act derived from neutral sources such as, for example, dispersion of employees in various types of industries across a given area, and the desired frequency of searches in any of the lesser divisions of the area."

2. "Administrative" or "Regulatory" Searches That Require Neither a Warrant nor Any Showing of Cause

In some situations, "administrative" searches are reasonable despite the absence of either a warrant or a particularized showing of cause to search the place that is searched.

Administrative searches have qualified for this category when the following factors have been present: the business searched was subject to **close or pervasive governmental regulation;** there was a **substantial government interest** underlying the regulatory scheme involved; **warrantless inspection was necessary** to further that scheme; and the statutory inspection provisions served some of the functions of a search warrant by **providing notice to individuals that the searches were pursuant to law** and by **limiting the discretion** of searching agents, particularly **with regard to time, place, and scope** of the search. See New York v. Burger. A **long** *history* **of close governmental regulation** of the particular type of business subject to inspection is also a relevant consideration. Regulation of the enterprise by the government is important because the choice to engage in a regulated enterprise **limits one's justifiable expectations of privacy.**

 EXAMPLES AND ANALYSIS

1. A federal agent conducted a warrantless search of the business premises of a caterer who served liquor. The agent was acting pursuant to a statute that authorized him to inspect both the records that the business was required to keep and the liquor on the premises. The purpose of the statute was to ensure proper revenue collection.

In Colonnade Catering Corp. v. United States, 397 U.S. 72, 90 S. Ct. 774, 25 L. Ed. 2d 60 (1970), the Supreme Court held that the controlling statute did not contemplate warrantless searches, but left no doubt that if Congress had authorized searches without warrants or particularized showings of cause, those searches would have been reasonable.

2. A federal agent inspected the premises of a pawnshop operator who was federally licensed to deal in sporting weapons. The governing statute authorized entry to inspect required records, firearms, and ammunition on the premises. Its purpose was to regulate traffic in firearms. In United States v. Biswell, 406 U.S. 311, 92 S. Ct. 1593, 32 L. Ed. 2d 87 (1972), the Court sustained the warrantless, causeless entry.

3. Police officers inspected an automobile junkyard as part of a regulatory scheme that permitted the inspection of required records, vehicles, or vehicle parts. The scheme was designed to prevent automobile theft.

In New York v. Burger, the Court held that even though the officer had neither a warrant nor any cause to search the junkyard, his search was reasonable. Moreover, it did not matter that **police officers conducted the search** or that the **defendant was prosecuted** for possession of stolen property found during the inspection.

3. "Administrative" or "Regulatory" Searches That Do Not Require Warrants but Do Require a Showing of Justification Less Than Probable Cause

For some "administrative" or "regulatory" searches, the Fourth Amendment does not require a warrant but does require a showing of cause to conduct the search. While probable cause is not required, the precise level of suspicion or cause needed to justify these searches is unclear. There are statements in the cases that suggest an individualized "reasonable suspicion" requirement, but the opinions never clearly endorse that standard. Instead, they endorse a vague "standard of reasonableness under all the circumstances." See O'Connor v. Ortega, 480 U.S. 709, 107 S. Ct. 1492, 94 L. Ed. 2d 714 (1987).

These opinions reason along the following lines. Insistence on **a warrant requirement would seriously frustrate the interests served by the particular regulatory scheme at issue.** Likewise, **a probable cause demand would substantially interfere with the state's objectives.** Because the regulatory schemes serve **"special needs" other than criminal law enforcement** and the normal Fourth Amendment requirements would frustrate the effort to serve those needs, warrantless searches based on less than probable cause are reasonable.

 ## EXAMPLES AND ANALYSIS

1. In O'Connor v. Ortega, hospital officials searched a state hospital employee's office. The search served the state's "special need" to ensure the efficient and proper operation of the workplace. The Court held that when such a search is conducted for "work-

related purposes" or as part of an investigation into "work-related misconduct," neither a warrant nor probable cause is necessary. A showing of "reasonableness under all the circumstances" is sufficient.

2. In Griffin v. Wisconsin, 483 U.S. 868, 107 S. Ct. 3164, 97 L. Ed. 2d 709 (1987), a probation officer searched a probationer's home. A regulatory scheme authorized the officer to conduct such a search without a warrant if he had "reasonable grounds" to believe that contraband was present. The "regulatory" searches pursuant to that scheme served the "special need" of guaranteeing that restrictions essential to the probation system were being observed. The Court found that those searches satisfied the Fourth Amendment reasonableness requirement.

N. ELEVATED STANDARDS OF FOURTH AMENDMENT REASONABLENESS

Sections G through M above have discussed a number of situations in which issues of Fourth Amendment reasonableness have been decided by balancing the interests of the individual against those of the government. In most of the cases, that balancing process has led to the conclusion that a search or seizure could be reasonable without satisfying the two basic Fourth Amendment requirements—probable cause and a search warrant. In other words, it has led to lowered standards of Fourth Amendment reasonableness. Interest balancing can also lead to the opposite conclusion—that is, a particular search or seizure may require **more than** probable cause and a search warrant. In other words, the balancing process can lead to **elevated** standards of Fourth Amendment reasonableness. The settings in which standards have been elevated involve **more severe intrusions** on Fourth Amendment privacy or liberty interests than those occasioned by ordinary "full" searches or seizures.

1. Use of Deadly Force to Arrest

The use of deadly force to apprehend a suspect is a Fourth Amendment **seizure.** Tennessee v. Garner, 471 U.S. 1, 105 S. Ct. 1694, 85 L. Ed. 2d 1 (1985). Ordinarily, probable cause to believe that a person has committed a felony is sufficient to render a full seizure of a person—an arrest—reasonable. Because it is more intrusive than an ordinary arrest, a seizure by means of deadly force is not reasonable every time an officer has probable cause to believe a suspect has committed a felony. Such seizures are only reasonable in a limited category of cases. See id.

a. Official conduct that is regulated: Any use of deadly force or only deadly force that kills? Traditionally, deadly force has included more than force that actually results in death. The definition adopted by the drafters of the Model Penal Code provides an example. According to that definition, deadly force is "force which the actor uses with the

purpose of causing or which he knows to create a substantial risk of causing death or serious bodily harm." Model Penal Code §3.11(2).

There is some dispute concerning the proper scope of the Fourth Amendment "deadly force" standard developed in Tennessee v. Garner. One view holds that the *Garner* standard governs only situations in which an officer **uses deadly force that kills** (or at least inflicts serious harm on) a suspect. The other view maintains that *Garner's* restrictions apply whenever an officer **uses deadly force,** whether or not he actually inflicts harm. The traditional definition of deadly force, the "use of deadly force" language of *Garner,* and the balancing test underlying the *Garner* Court's reasoning all suggest that the latter is the better view. Under that view, if an officer uses deadly force in any circumstances other than those that satisfy the *Garner* standards, she violates the Constitution.

Even if the standards limiting the use of deadly force are not restricted to situations in which an officer apprehends a suspect by actually killing or injuring him, they would seem to be limited to cases in which the use of deadly force **either strikes the suspect or results in apprehension.** According to California v. Hodari D. (discussed in section G.2.b.iii(b) above), any "physical force" affects at least a temporary seizure, but an officer's "show of authority" does not effect a seizure at all unless a suspect submits to it. Under that principle, if an "untouched" suspect flees from the use of deadly force there is no Fourth Amendment activity and therefore no possible Fourth Amendment violation.

b.   The showing needed to seize a suspect by means of deadly force. Deadly force may be used only when it is **necessary** to apprehend a limited category of suspects who pose **risks of serious physical harm.** In some cases, a **warning** is also a prerequisite to the use of deadly force.

   i.   A present threat or a past offense involving or threatening serious physical harm. An officer may use deadly force to apprehend a suspect if the "suspect **threatens the officer with a weapon or there is probable cause to believe that he has committed an offense involving the** *infliction or threatened infliction of serious physical harm.*" Tennessee v. Garner. According to this standard, deadly force is constitutionally reasonable in only two instances. An officer may use deadly force to protect herself against a threat from a suspect wielding a weapon. An officer may also use deadly force to capture a suspect who is believed to have committed an offense that caused or threatened serious physical harm. The common thread in both instances is the need to prevent **serious physical harm.** In the first instance, the risk of harm is **immediate** and apparent, while in the second instance, the suspect's past conduct provides evidence of a **future risk** of serious physical harm.

To qualify for the use of deadly force, an offense must have resulted in or threatened serious **physical** harm. The Court clearly precluded offenses that inflict or threaten other kinds of harm no matter how serious they may be. What is unclear is *how serious* the physical harm must be in order to qualify.

In addition, while it is clear that offenses involving the **threatened** infliction of serious physical harm do meet the standard, there is an inherent ambiguity in the word "threatened." If read narrowly, it could include only suspects who **intentionally threaten** harm to others—such as a bank robber who points a gun at a teller or an assaulter who jabs at a victim with a knife. If read more broadly, the word could include a suspect whose criminal conduct **created a substantial risk** of harm to others—such as a grossly intoxicated driver or a distributor of extremely dangerous drugs. The first would seem to be a more natural reading of the *Garner* language.

Note that when an officer uses deadly force to capture a suspect believed to have committed an offense that caused or threatened serious physical harm, the officer needs only **probable cause** to believe that the suspect committed a qualifying offense. She does not have to establish that it is "more likely than not" that the suspect committed the offense. Instead, she has to establish only a **"fair probability"** that the suspect committed the offense. See section B.5 above, discussing the meaning of probable cause.

If a suspect's offense does not fit within the categories described by *Garner*, an officer may not use deadly force **even if he is certain** that the suspect committed the offense. For example, an officer may not use deadly force to apprehend a suspect who he **knows** is stealing an expensive automobile loaded with expensive property even if doing so is necessary to prevent the suspect's escape.

ii.   **Necessity to use deadly force and the issuance of a warning.** Even in situations involving suspects who pose risks of serious physical harm, "deadly force may be used **[only] if necessary to prevent escape, and if, where feasible, some warning has been given."** Tennessee v. Garner. Because the intrusion on an individual is so serious—the potential loss of life—deadly force may be used only "as a last resort." An officer must have no reasonable alternative means of preventing the suspect's escape.

Both the "necessity" and "warning" requirements are designed to guarantee that the use of deadly force is really justifiable in the circumstances.

In some instances, a suspect may be threatening a third person with immediate serious physical harm. An officer might be confident that he could apprehend the suspect without using deadly force but might reasonably believe that it is necessary to use deadly force **to prevent serious physical harm to the third person.** Although the Court's standard does not explicitly extend to that situation, it seems most unlikely that the use of deadly force in that situation would be unreasonable.

EXAMPLE AND ANALYSIS

An officer has a warrant to arrest Chip for violating the following statute: "Anyone who engages in sexual intercourse with another person without the freely given consent of that person shall be guilty of sexual assault, a class three felony." When the officer tells Chip that he is under arrest, Chip pushes him down and runs toward his motorcycle. Fearing that Chip will escape, the officer warns him and then shoots him in the arm. Chip bleeds to death. Did the officer violate Chip's Fourth Amendment rights?

There is a good chance that the officer did violate Chip's rights. First, it is not at all clear that the crime is one that could justify the use of deadly force. If the offense requires merely intercourse in the absence of consent, as the language suggests, then it does not seem to satisfy the *Garner* "serious physical harm" requirement. While sexual assault involving physical force or violence would seem to involve the "infliction or threatened infliction" of such harm, sexual assault that only requires intercourse without consent does not seem to qualify.

Second, it is arguable that it was not necessary to use deadly force. The officer's subjective belief that Chip would get away is surely not enough. The necessity to use deadly force should be judged by an objective standard. Moreover, even if the officer was reasonable in believing that Chip would escape, one might contend that he should have tried to disable the motorcycle before shooting at Chip's person.

Suppose that the bullet had missed Chip but that Chip had surrendered immediately after being fired at by the officer. Would the Fourth Amendment analysis change? Chip was seized when he submitted to the officer's use of deadly force—a show of authority. The only question is whether deadly force that does not harm the suspect is governed by the *Garner* standard. Although the question has not been settled by the Supreme Court, the better view is that such a use of deadly force is subject to

Garner. The risk to human life created by the use of deadly force would seem to tip the balance of interests in that direction.

---

2. Intrusions into the Human Body

A search inside a human body—drawing blood or performing surgery, for example—may be more intrusive than a normal full search. Evaluation of the intrusiveness of such a search must be done on a case-by-case basis, taking into account the threats to privacy, dignity, and health interests. See *Winston v. Lee,* 470 U.S. 753, 105 S. Ct. 1611, 84 L. Ed. 2d 662 (1985). Searches of human bodies that prove to be sufficiently more intrusive must satisfy higher than normal Fourth Amendment standards.

a. **Magnitude of the intrusion: Threats to privacy, dignity, and health.** Like searches of other places, searches inside human bodies can intrude on legitimate expectations of privacy by revealing confidential information. They can be more intrusive than ordinary searches in three respects. First, the nature of the **information that is revealed might be more intimate or private.** The search could disclose particularly personal facts about an individual's life. Second, a bodily intrusion can infringe on an "individual's **dignitary interests in personal privacy and bodily integrity**"; it can deprive her of constitutional interests in "**personal privacy and bodily integrity.**" *Winston v. Lee.* Third, bodily intrusions "may threaten the **safety or health**" or may even "**endanger[ ] the life**" of the individual. Procedures that invade a person's body may well entail risks of physical harm.

The first step in evaluating the reasonableness of a human body search is to determine the severity of the intrusion by measuring the infringement on the person's privacy, dignity, and health and safety interests.

b. **The showing needed to justify a "more intrusive" search inside the body.** Some bodily intrusions are no more intrusive than ordinary full searches of persons, homes, and effects. In those cases, Fourth Amendment norms govern. Probable cause and a search warrant will render the intrusion reasonable, and the warrant may be dispensed with if an exception to the warrant requirement applies.

For example, in *Schmerber v. California,* 384 U.S. 757, 86 S. Ct. 1826, 16 L. Ed. 2d 908 (1966), the Court decided that the drawing of blood by medical authorities to determine alcohol content was no more intrusive than an ordinary search. Because it was based on probable cause plus the exigency created by the ongoing dissipation of the blood alcohol level, the blood drawing was reasonable despite the lack of a warrant. A warrant would have been needed if the objective had been to determine whether a more enduring characteristic was present in the person's blood. Thus, a test to determine a person's blood type or DNA makeup would require a search warrant.

If a search within a human body is **extensive** or **substantial**—that is, if it intrudes on constitutional interests **more severely than an ordinary search**—officials must have **"a more substantial justification,"** perhaps **"a compelling need."** Winston v. Lee. A **search warrant** is presumptively required. Moreover, it is necessary to show **more than probable cause** to believe that evidence will be found.

For example, in Winston v. Lee, the government wanted a doctor to probe surgically for a bullet thought to be lodged beneath the skin of a suspect. In an adversarial hearing, the government had shown ample probable cause to believe that the bullet was present and that it would provide evidence of the suspect's involvement in an attempted robbery. The Court concluded that the "medical risks," though "not extremely severe," were disputed and uncertain and that the harm to privacy interests occasioned by drugging the man " 'into a state of unconsciousness' " and "search[ing] beneath his skin for evidence" was "severe." The state could not "demonstrate a compelling need for" the evidence because it already had "substantial evidence of the origin of the bullet." Consequently, the proposed surgery was deemed unreasonable.

EXAMPLE AND ANALYSIS

Officers arrested Remo for driving under the influence. Believing that Remo was under the influence of cocaine when arrested, one of the officers used a syringe to extract a quantity of blood during the booking process. Did the officer comply with the Fourth Amendment?

Assuming that the officers had probable cause to believe that Remo's blood would provide evidence of his offense and that the evidence was being destroyed, it would be permissible to have blood drawn without seeking a search warrant. However, it is very likely to be unreasonable for an officer to draw the blood during booking.

In Schmerber v. California, the Court stressed that the taking of blood was done in a reasonable manner because it was done by medical personnel. Moreover, such a test was deemed commonplace—the kind of intrusion to which individuals are accustomed. The drawing of blood by an officer in a stationhouse may be unreasonable. It is not "commonplace," it seems more harmful to dignitary interests than the drawing of blood by trained medical personnel, and it may well pose a greater health risk. If the intrusion is sufficiently more severe, a greater justification than probable cause would be required. Put otherwise, officers would need a "more substantial" or a "compelling" reason to search in this manner—perhaps a need for the evidence and a good reason that medical personnel could not draw the blood.

3. Newsroom Searches and Nighttime Searches

In *Zurcher v. Stanford Daily*, 436 U.S. 547, 98 S. Ct. 1970, 56 L. Ed. 2d 525 (1978), a university newspaper argued that the search of a newsroom should require a higher than normal showing of justification because of the potential harm to First Amendment "free press" interests posed by such searches. The Court rejected the claim that the newsroom search was sufficiently more intrusive to require heightened Fourth Amendment standards and held that the probable cause and search warrant norms governed.

Searches of private dwellings during nighttime hours arguably pose greater threats to personal privacy. A resident might be found in a state of undress or might be engaged in "intimate" activities. Moreover, a resident's interest in quiet repose might well be greater at night. See *Gooding v. United States*, 416 U.S. 430, 94 S. Ct. 1780, 40 L. Ed. 2d 250 (1974). The Supreme Court has not yet decided whether the standards for nighttime residential searches are more demanding than the Fourth Amendment norms.

REVIEW QUESTIONS AND ANSWERS

Question: Acting on information that Jared, the subject of a valid arrest warrant, was in a local motel room, officers went to the motel and set up surveillance. Two hours later, Jared came out of the room, leaving the door ajar, and went to his truck, which was parked about 50 feet away. The officers moved in and arrested him as he reached his truck. They were aware that Jared had been arrested twice before in the presence of individuals possessing firearms. Two officers then went to his motel room and entered. An illegal weapon was found in plain view in an open suitcase on the end of a bed. Jared was charged with possession of the weapon. In response to his motion to suppress the gun, the officers claimed that they had entered the room to "protectively sweep" it. Should the trial court uphold the entry as a "protective sweep"?

Answer: Probably not. A motel room is a temporary abode entitled to the protection of the search warrant requirement. Maryland v. Buie authorized warrantless sweeps after **in-home arrests** when officers are aware of facts that give rise to **a reasonable suspicion that the home harbors a person posing a danger.** In this case, the arrest occurred 50 feet from the room. While it is arguable that the doctrine of *Buie* should extend to such cases because dangerous persons could cause harm to officers and would be motivated to do so by virtue of the arrest, the better view would confine protective sweep authority to those cases in which officers are present in the unfamiliar and particularly dangerous confines of a dwelling (or other private space).

Moreover, even if authority to conduct a protective sweep were to be expanded to include arrests near dwellings, officers clearly must have a particularized reasonable suspicion that others are present and dangerous. The two prior arrests of Jared in the presence of persons with firearms should not be considered sufficient to support a reasonable suspicion that a dangerous person was currently in the motel room. Thus, while a plain view seizure of the weapon would be permitted if the entry was valid, the invalidity of the warrantless entry taints the discovery and seizure of the weapon.

Question: Officers received a tip that an "Arabic" woman and her associates were getting ready to move drugs from an apartment where the police had previously purchased narcotics. Officers hurried to the apartment building where they saw an "Arabic-looking woman" sitting on the front steps. They asked if she lived in the building and she replied that she did. The officers then ordered her to accompany them into the apartment they were about to search. They detained her during the warrantless search of the apartment. When they were finished searching the apartment the officers opened the woman's purse and found a substantial quantity of narcotics inside. Did the officers' detention of the woman and search of her purse violate the Fourth Amendment?

Answer: Probably. The doctrine of Michigan v. Summers authorizes the detention of occupants of dwellings under certain circumstances. Those circumstances are not present here. First, the search of the apartment would have to be valid. If the officers lacked either probable cause or exigency, the search is invalid.

Second, even if a warrantless search was justified here, *Summers* authorizes a detention when officers are searching for contraband **pursuant to a warrant.** The Court did not address the validity of detentions during warrantless searches such as this one.

In addition, even if a detention is permissible during a valid warrantless search, only **occupants**—those with a connection to the premises to be searched—may be detained. Here, the officers did not have evidence that the woman was an occupant or resident of the apartment they intended to search. For that reason, the detention should be invalid.

Moreover, even if the officers did have a sufficient basis for believing that the woman was an occupant of the apartment, the search of her purse would have been highly questionable. *Summers* authorized a *detention* but not a *search* of the person. The government could argue that the probable cause to search the apartment allows the search of an occupant and that *Ybarra* precludes only the search of persons with limited connections to business premises. The defense could argue that specific probable cause to search a person is required and that the officers did not have probable cause to search this woman. The latter argument seems more persuasive.

Question: A patrol officer received a late night report of a break-in at a residence. The officer arrived at the home and noticed a broken window on the front porch. The door was ajar. The officer knocked and then heard footsteps along the side of the house. She looked down the side of the house, saw a young man running toward the alley in the rear, and shouted "Halt!" When the young man continued to run, the officer pursued. Concluding that she would not be able to catch up, the officer drew her weapon and fired once. The bullet struck the young man in the right shoulder and knocked him to the ground. The young man got up and continued to run. Once more, the officer yelled "Halt!" whereupon the young man turned around. Believing that the young man was pointing a gun at her, the officer fired one shot at his chest, killing him. Did the officer's actions violate the Fourth Amendment?

Answer: This fact pattern raises questions about the propriety of using deadly force. It is very likely that the officer violated the Fourth Amendment when she fired her weapon the first time. The second shot, the one that killed the suspect, may have been constitutional.

First, according to Tennessee v. Garner, an officer may seize a suspect by means of deadly force only when the suspect threatens her with a weapon or the officer has probable cause to believe the suspect committed an offense involving the threat or infliction of serious physical harm. Neither of these predicates existed when the officer first shot the suspect. There was no direct threat, and the nighttime break-in is not an offense that meets the *Garner* criterion. While there is an argument that *Garner* regulates only the killing of a suspect, the better view is that it controls situations in which officers seize suspects by the *use* of deadly force. In this case, the government might argue that no seizure ever occurred because the suspect continued to flee—that is, he did not submit. Thus, while the officer used deadly force, she did not effect a seizure. The flaw is that the officer "physically touched" the suspect with her bullet. That touching resulted in at least a temporary seizure by means of unjustified deadly force. Such a seizure is unreasonable.

The second time the officer fired her weapon she killed the suspect. Whether this use of deadly force was constitutional depends on whether it was tainted by the earlier use of deadly force and on whether it was an independently justified use of deadly force. When the suspect continued to flee, the initial seizure ended. There does not seem to be any clear connection between the initial, illegal use of deadly force and the later use. If there is no connection, then no taint of illegality can carry over to the second seizure. Independently, the second seizure *may* be justifiable. In *Garner*, the Court said a seizure by means of deadly force is reasonable if the suspect threatens the officer with a weapon. Presumably, an officer need not be certain that she is being threatened. It is likely that probable cause to believe that the suspect is threatening the officer is sufficient to justify the use of deadly force.

5 GOVERNMENT INVOLVEMENT IN THE COMMISSION OF CRIMES

 CHAPTER OVERVIEW

There are two potential defenses to criminal charges based on excessive involvement by governmental agents in the commission of the offenses charged—the **entrapment defense** and the **due process defense.** The defense of entrapment, by far the more prominent of the two, is not rooted in any constitutional command. Instead, courts base the defense on either their interpretation of legislative intent or their own disapproval of improper governmental methods of investigation and prosecution. Consequently, each jurisdiction is free to recognize or reject an entrapment defense and to formulate the standards for the defense as it sees fit.

There are two general versions of the entrapment defense. The **''subjective'' version** is based on a judicial perception that the legislators responsible for defining offenses did not intend to punish ''entrapped'' individuals. It is concerned in part with the nature of the government's conduct, but its primary focus is the **predisposition of the defendant** to commit the crime.

The **''objective'' version** of entrapment is rooted in a judicial desire to discourage unacceptable kinds of law enforcement conduct. It is concerned **solely** with the **conduct of the government agents.** The availability of the objective version of the defense is not affected by the particular defendant's willingness to commit the offense.

The following discussion focuses on Supreme Court precedents that explain the two basic approaches to the entrapment defense. There is no effort to capture the various nuances of state entrapment law.

Excessive government involvement in the commission of an offense also might give rise to a defense based on the **Due Process Clause** of the **Fifth** or **Fourteenth Amend-**

ment. The **due process defense** is based on the premise that in some circumstances the government's participation in the accused's offense can render a conviction for that offense "fundamentally unfair." The Supreme Court's support for a due process defense has been so tentative and equivocal that its legitimacy is uncertain. What is certain is that if a due process defense is available at all, it is reserved for a narrow range of situations involving egregious governmental misconduct. Because the due process defense is grounded in the Constitution, every jurisdiction would be bound to respect it.

A. THE ENTRAPMENT DEFENSE

A claim of entrapment is basically an assertion that government agents engaged in inappropriate conduct that lured the defendant into committing a crime. A successful entrapment claim provides a complete defense to a criminal charge.

1. "Subjective" Version of the Entrapment Defense

Supreme Court decisions have fashioned a **"subjective" version** of the entrapment defense that is available in **federal** proceedings. It is deemed "subjective" because its primary concern is whether the particular defendant deserves to be punished for the crime charged. It rests on the premise that an individual who is lured into criminal conduct by government agents is not truly culpable. That individual does not deserve or need to be punished for his conduct. The subjective version of entrapment is apparently the **majority view.**

    a. Doctrinal standards for the subjective version of entrapment. According to the subjective version of the defense, a defendant has been entrapped when the "alleged offense . . . **[was] the product of the creative activity of [government] officials.**" Sorrells v. United States, 287 U.S. 435, 53 S. Ct. 210, 77 L. Ed. 413 (1932); Sherman v. United States, 356 U.S. 369, 78 S. Ct. 819, 2 L. Ed. 2d 848 (1958). Whether an offense is the product of governmental creative activity depends on two variables: the **nature of the government's conduct** and the **willingness of the defendant to commit the offense.** More specifically, it hinges both on whether the government **"instigated"** and whether the defendant was **"predisposed."**

        i. Sufficient instigation by government officials. Because governmental misconduct is not the prime focus of the subjective version of entrapment, the doctrine pertinent to that element is sparse. It is clear that a defendant cannot succeed with an entrapment defense unless she demonstrates a certain amount of "creative" conduct by government officials. More specifically, the "act for which the defendant [is being] prosecuted [must be] **instigated by**" a government agent who **"lured [the] defendant"** into committing it. It must be the **"creature of [the agent's] purpose."** Sorrells v. United States. The **"criminal design [must] originate[ ]** with the officials of the government." Id.; Sherman v. United States. If the government agents "**merely afford opportunities or facilities** for the commission of [an] offense," then the conduct will not be sufficient to support an entrapment defense. Sorrells v. United States.

ii. **Predisposition of the defendant.** "The principal element in the defense of entrapment [is] **the defendant's predisposition to commit the crime.**" United States v. Russell, 411 U.S. 423, 93 S. Ct. 1637, 36 L. Ed. 2d 366 (1973). An individual who is **predisposed** to commit an offense cannot succeed with an entrapment claim. Predisposition is dispositive because the subjective version of the defense extends protection to the **"unwary innocent,"** not the **"unwary criminal,"** Sherman v. United States; it is designed to identify individuals who are not suitable objects of criminal punishment. No matter how extensive the government participation or instigation, a crime is not the "product of [governmental] creative activity" if the defendant was predisposed to commit it.

The prosecution has the **burden of proving predisposition beyond a reasonable doubt.** Jacobson v. United States, 503 U.S. 540, 112 S. Ct. 1535, 118 L. Ed. 2d 174 (1992). This means that to defeat an entrapment claim the prosecution must satisfy the trier of fact beyond a reasonable doubt that it did not "implant in the mind of an **innocent person** the disposition to commit the [crime]," Sherman v. United States, but rather that the defendant had a **"previous disposition to commit"** the offense. Sorrells v. United States.

The government must show "that the defendant was disposed to commit the criminal act **prior to first being approached by Government agents.**" A showing merely that the accused was disposed **prior to the time the government agent first suggested the criminal act** will not suffice. Jacobson v. United States. For example, the government could prove that a defendant was disposed to purchase illegal child pornography prior to the time that its agents solicited him to make a purchase and still fail to carry its burden of proof. Unless the prosecution showed that the defendant's disposition was "independent [of] and not the product of the attention that the Government directed at" him prior to the solicitation to purchase the material, it would not prevail on the issue of predisposition.

In addition, "[e]vidence of **predisposition to do what once was lawful is not, by itself, sufficient to show predisposition to do what is now illegal.**" Id. For example, if a defendant sought to acquire child pornography at a time when it was lawful to do so, that conduct is relevant but not sufficient to prove that he was predisposed to engage in the same conduct after it had been criminalized. Id.

To carry its burden of proof on the issue of predisposition, the government is allowed to subject the accused to a "searching inquiry into his own conduct and predisposition." Sorrells v. United States. An accused's character, her past acts, and the amount of inducement required to get her to commit the acts charged are all relevant to the determination.

b. Legal foundation of the subjective approach. The Supreme Court has grounded the federal version of the entrapment defense on its perception of a legislative intent not to criminalize individuals whose acts are the product of government instigation and creative activity. According to the Court, "Congress could not have intended that its [criminal] statutes were to be enforced by tempting innocent persons into violations." Sherman v. United States. This view holds that the definitions of federal criminal offenses implicitly exclude persons who have been entrapped into engaging in the proscribed conduct.

2. "Objective" Version of the Entrapment Defense

The objective version of the entrapment defense focuses exclusively on the conduct of the government. It is deemed "objective" because it is not concerned with the predisposition of a particular defendant. Instead, objective entrapment is concerned solely with the risk that the government's conduct would instigate a criminal offense by a person who is not otherwise inclined to commit one. Its aims are to condemn and prevent government misconduct, to safeguard the processes of criminal justice from taint, and to preserve public confidence in the criminal justice system. See Sherman v. United States (Frankfurter, J. concurring).

a. Doctrinal standards for the objective version of entrapment. The dispositive question under the objective approach is whether government agents have engaged in **"lawless means or means that violate rationally vindicated standards of justice."** Id. The government stays within acceptable bounds if its conduct is "likely to induce to the commission of crime . . . **only those ready and willing to commit crime."** Officials violate standards of justice if their actions would be "likely to induce . . . **others who would normally avoid crime and through self-struggle resist ordinary temptations."** Id. In other words, an objective entrapment defense requires conduct so extreme that it is likely to instigate a crime by an individual who is **not ready and willing to commit it.** See also Model Penal Code §2.13 (allowing an entrapment defense if government agents use "methods of persuasion or inducement **which create a substantial risk that . . . an offense will be committed by persons other than those who are ready to commit it**").

b. Legal foundation of the objective approach. The precise legal basis for the objective formulation of the entrapment defense is not entirely clear. Because the defense is designed to prevent law enforcement excesses, to protect the judicial process from the taint of unfair methods, and to preserve public confidence in the criminal justice system, an appropriate source would seem to be the judiciary's "inherent supervisory power over the administration of criminal justice." See Chapter 3, section D.

 # EXAMPLES AND ANALYSIS

1. Undercover agent James offers to supply Luther with classified government documents if Luther will sell them to foreign agents and split the profits. Luther agrees to the plan. After he attempts to sell one of the documents, Luther is arrested and charged with a federal offense. Should his entrapment defense succeed?

No. The federal courts follow the subjective version of entrapment. That defense first requires government instigation sufficient to lure an individual into crime. Conduct that "merely afford[s] opportunities or facilities for the commission of a crime" is not sufficient. Therefore, the defense would fail here. The same result would follow under an objective approach because this kind of conduct is the sort that is likely to induce only those "ready and willing to commit crime." It is not the kind of behavior that creates a "substantial risk" of inducing offenses "by persons other than those who are ready" to commit them.

2. Barney had sexual relations with a 16-year-old girl. He is charged with statutory rape under a statute that prohibits sexual relations "with anyone under the age of 18." Six months earlier, the legislature had amended this statute, raising the age limit from 16 to 18. At trial, Barney establishes that the girl was working for the government and proves that over the course of several months she repeatedly enticed him to have sex with her. The prosecution offers evidence that Barney has a history of having sexual relations with young women. Three girls testify that prior to the amendment of the statutory rape law Barney had sex with them when they were 17 years old. If the jury finds that the conduct of the alleged victim was sufficient to create a substantial risk that a person who was not ready and willing to have sex with a person under 18 would do so, should it find that Barney was entrapped?

The jury should sustain an entrapment defense if the jurisdiction follows the objective approach. An objective entrapment defense succeeds if the kind of conduct employed by the government agent is likely to induce crime by a person who would normally avoid crime and resist ordinary temptations—that is, if it creates a substantial risk of inducing an offense by a person "not ready and willing." The jury's finding would meet those standards.

If the jurisdiction follows a subjective approach, the result is less clear. Despite the victim's conduct, if the prosecution proved that Barney was predisposed to have sex with someone under the legal age, the jurors should reject Barney's entrapment defense. If the nuances of the federal version of the subjective defense are applicable, the fact pattern sketched above provides insufficient evidence for a predisposition finding. Evidence that Barney was willing to engage in the same conduct at a time when it was legal to do so is *relevant* to predisposition, but it is *not sufficient* to carry the government's burden of proving predisposition beyond a reasonable doubt. It is not clear, however, that a jurisdiction adhering to the subjective form of the entrapment defense would be required to impose the same burden of proof as that imposed by the Supreme Court.

B. THE DUE PROCESS DEFENSE

It is unclear whether the Due Process Clause can support a valid defense based on excessive official involvement in the commission of a criminal offense. In United States v. Russell, 411 U.S. 423, 93 S. Ct. 1637, 36 L. Ed. 2d 366 (1973), a Supreme Court majority observed that "we **may** someday be presented with a situation" that would justify recognition of a due process defense to criminal charges. Thus, the Court has held out the possibility of a due process defense without clearly endorsing it. The defense has been successfully employed in only a very small number of cases.

1. Nature of the Potential Due Process Defense

Because a due process defense would be dictated by the Fifth and Fourteenth Amendments to the Constitution, it would apply in both federal and state courts. The concern of the defense would be governmental misconduct. It would be premised on the view that it is "fundamentally unfair" to convict a defendant whose acts are the product of certain kinds of egregious misconduct by law enforcement agents, and thus would preclude prosecutions and convictions based on such misconduct.

Because the Constitution's concern is with unfair methods of enforcing the criminal law, a particular defendant's predisposition or willingness to commit an offense should not be relevant. Consequently, a due process defense based on the government's role in bringing about the commission of an offense would be similar to the objective version of the entrapment defense. Because it would be more difficult for a defendant to establish than an objective entrapment defense, the due process defense would be superfluous in jurisdictions that recognize objective entrapment. In subjective entrapment jurisdictions, however, a due process defense might be successful in cases in which predisposition would defeat an entrapment claim.

2. Doctrinal Standards of a Due Process Defense

The potential due process defense has been the subject of minimal doctrinal development. In raising the possibility of such a defense, the *Russell* Court sketched vague standards that would define the scope of a due process defense. "[T]he conduct of law enforcement agents [would have to be] **so**

outrageous that due process principles would absolutely bar the government from invoking judicial processes to obtain a conviction." It would have to "violate 'fundamental fairness' " or be "shocking to the universal sense of justice." United States v. Russell.

The only thing clear from these standards is that the scope of a due process defense would be very narrow; it would bar convictions in only a limited number of extreme cases. The degree and character of the official involvement in the alleged offense would have to be "sufficiently offensive" (see Hampton v. United States, 425 U.S. 484, 96 S. Ct. 1646, 48 L. Ed. 2d 113 (1976) (Brennan, J., dissenting)) to make it fundamentally unfair for a state or the federal government to convict any person—even a willing participant—whose criminal acts were the product of the government's actions.

REVIEW QUESTIONS AND ANSWERS

Question: In early 1990, Mark sold a small amount of narcotics for Melanie. At the time, Melanie was a narcotics user. In 1995, Mark became a paid government informer. In 1997, he moved in with Melanie at her home on a ranch. Two months later, Melanie asked Mark to leave because he had used drugs in the home and encouraged other women who lived there—including recovering addicts—to use drugs. Mark had also threatened Melanie's son. Mark grew belligerent when Melanie asked him to leave, making various threats against her.

One month after he moved out, Mark asked Melanie to put him in touch with people who could sell him drugs. She resisted, but Mark called frequently, came to the house without invitation, and made threats against Melanie, her son, and her horses. Eventually, Melanie introduced Mark and his friend (a narcotics officer) to a methamphetamine supplier. Later, Mark, Melanie, and the supplier met in Melanie's front yard. The supplier showed Mark three pounds of narcotics. Narcotics agents moved in and arrested both Melanie and the supplier. Melanie was charged with possession of narcotics with intent to distribute. Should her entrapment defense succeed?

Answer: Probably. Under either version of entrapment, the government's conduct must be examined. Mark's threats, requests, and persistence would certainly seem to be sufficient "government inducement" to satisfy the first element of subjective entrapment. Moreover, there is a very good claim that it satisfied the sole criterion for objective entrapment because it constitutes the sort of conduct that would cause a person who was not ready and willing to commit a narcotics offense to do so. After all, Mark was both threatening and persistent. He aimed his threats at Melanie and her son and would not accept her refusals. The nature of his conduct and the continuing attempts to get Melanie to participate would seem to satisfy the demand of the objective version of entrapment.

Predisposition must also be examined if the subjective version of entrapment is applicable. If, as under the federal version, the government must prove predisposition to commit the offense, the proof here seems insufficient. The only proof of predisposition was Melanie's past drug use and Mark's sale of drugs for her. On the other hand, Melanie showed an antidrug attitude by making Mark leave for using drugs and by opening her home to recovering addicts. Mark proposed the criminal transactions in this case, repeated the proposal several times, and threatened Melanie and her son. Melanie repeatedly refused to help and only set up the transaction after Mark persisted and threatened her. All these facts militate against a finding that she was predisposed to participate in a narcotics transaction prior to Mark's first approach. A court might well conclude on these facts that no reasonable juror could find predisposition beyond a reasonable doubt—that is, that the evidence was insufficient as a matter of law. If so, Melanie has a valid entrapment defense.

Question: Zed sold two undercover police officers a package containing sugar instead of cocaine. One week later, after drinking heavily, the officers came to Zed's apartment at 2 A.M. They knocked and demanded to be let in and then accused Zed of "ripping us off." Displaying a loaded gun, the officers demanded that Zed either give them money or drugs. Zed offered them $100 and a small package of cocaine. After he gave them the drugs, the officers arrested him for distributing narcotics. Does Zed have a defense to a charge of narcotics distribution?

Answer: Zed might have a valid entrapment defense. If the jurisdiction follows an objective approach, he might well succeed with the claim that the officers' late-night visit, accusation, and implicit threat were the sort of conduct that would trigger the commission of an offense by a person who was not ready and willing to do so. The government would argue, however, that tactics such as these could only succeed with someone who was capable of selling narcotics.

Zed's defense might well fail under the subjective version of entrapment. There would be sufficient government inducement, but Zed's past conduct and the fact that he responded with the narcotics relatively quickly could sustain the prosecution's burden of showing "predisposition." If a trier of fact found that he was predisposed to sell the drugs, his entrapment defense would be invalid.

Zed might succeed with a claim that the officers' conduct here was sufficiently flagrant to give rise to a due process defense. Their late-night arrival in an intoxicated condition, demand, and implicit threat with a loaded weapon could be deemed "outrageous," "offensive," and "shocking to our sense of justice." It might well be deemed fundamentally unfair to prosecute here when the crime was manufactured by the officers, the behavior of the officers violated standards of decency, and the defendant might well have been coerced by a threat of physical harm. See People v. Shine, 187 A.D.2d 950, 590 N.Y.S.2d 965 (1992) (finding that the egregious misconduct of the police officers who went to defendant's home at night and demanded drugs violated due process).

6 DUE PROCESS CLAUSE REGULATION OF CONFESSIONS

 CHAPTER OVERVIEW

The Constitution does not explicitly address the subject of **confessions**—extrajudicial inculpatory statements secured from suspects by law enforcement agents—or the **methods used to obtain them.** Nonetheless, the Supreme Court has found that more than one provision of the Constitution contains implicit restrictions on law enforcement "interrogation" methods and on the confessions they produce. One of these provisions is the Fourteenth Amendment command that no state shall "deprive any person of life, liberty, or property, without due process of law." (See United States Constitution, Amendment 5, for an identical restriction on the federal government.)

In Brown v. Mississippi, 297 U.S. 278, 56 S. Ct. 461, 80 L. Ed. 682 (1936), the Supreme Court for the first time held that the Due Process Clause limits states' ability to convict defendants based on confessions obtained by law enforcement officers. According to the Court, due process forbids convictions based on confessions "obtained by violence" because violence is a law enforcement "method[that is] revolting to the sense of justice." Since 1936, the Court has decided numerous cases involving claims that the admission of a "coerced" confession at trial violated a defendant's right to due process of law. The result is a relatively simple, yet quite vague, doctrine.

Today, two other constitutional guarantees—the Fifth Amendment privilege against compulsory self-incrimination (see Chapter 7) and the Sixth Amendment right to counsel (see Chapter 9)—also restrict law enforcement methods designed to secure confessions and limit the admissibility of confessions. Nonetheless, the restrictions imposed by the Due Process Clause continue to play an important role.

Those restrictions are the subject of this relatively brief chapter. Specifically, the chapter discusses:

- **The common law rule.** The common law had a rule that foreshadowed the Due Process Clause guarantee against coerced confessions. That rule rested primarily on a concern with the untrustworthiness of such confessions.

- **The Due Process Clause "involuntary" or "coerced" confession doctrine.** Due process is offended by "involuntary" or "coerced" confessions. This section explains the meaning of those terms and the variables that are relevant to deciding whether a particular confession offends due process. The section also discusses the underlying rationale for concluding that the Due Process Clause guards against coerced confessions and the point in time at which due process is offended.

A. THE COMMON LAW RULE

Prior to the advent of constitutional regulation in 1936, the common law provided a basis for objecting to the use of a confession. According to the **common law rule,** "a confession forced from the mind by the flattery of hope, or the torture of fear, comes in so questionable a shape when it is to be considered as evidence of guilt, that no credit ought to be given to it; and therefore it is rejected." The King v. Warickshall, 1 Leach 263, 168 Eng. Rep. 234 (K.B. 1783).

On its face, this rule would seem to be concerned only with confessions that have been coerced from an individual ("forced from the mind") by one of two methods: (1) holding out a desirable inducement of some sort ("the flattery of hope") or (2) threatening or inflicting some unpleasant consequence ("the torture of fear"). The rule barred the use of such a confession ("it is rejected") because of a concern that it might well lead the trier of fact to an erroneous conclusion of guilt ("so questionable a shape . . . as evidence of guilt . . . that no credit ought to be given to it"). In other words, the common law prohibition was based on the **untrustworthiness** of the confession.

B. DUE PROCESS DOCTRINE

An outline of the Due Process Clause's regulation of confessions must address the following questions: What confessions are inconsistent with due process? How does one determine whether a confession falls into the proscribed category? Why does the use of such a confession violate the guarantee of due process? As the discussion below explains, the Due Process Clause prohibits confessions **coerced by government officials.** The determination of which confessions violate due process must be made based on the **totality** of relevant circumstances—including both external pressures and internal weaknesses. Coerced confessions are barred because of their potential for **unreliability** and their inconsistency with principles of **accusatorial fair play,** and, possibly, because of a desire to **deter** coercive methods.

1.   Due Process Prohibition of "Involuntary" or "Coerced" Confessions

The Due Process Clause is not concerned with all questionable confessions. Its sole concern is **involuntary** or **coerced** confessions. The dispositive question is whether an individual confessed because his **"will was overborne."** *Arizona v. Fulminante*, 499 U.S. 279, 111 S. Ct. 1246, 113 L. Ed. 2d 302 (1991).

2.   "Totality of the Circumstances" Approach: External Pressures and Internal Attributes

The determination whether a confession is involuntary or coerced depends on an assessment of the **"totality of the circumstances."** See *Fikes v. Alabama*, 352 U.S. 191, 77 S. Ct. 281, 1 L. Ed. 2d 246 (1957). Any factor that is relevant to establishing whether the particular individual's will was "overborne" is relevant and must be taken into account. The relevant factors include **external pressures** brought to bear on the suspect—the tactics and practices used by the police and the setting in which they are used. They also include the **internal attributes** of the suspect—any permanent or transient variables that indicate either weakness or strength of will. See *Spano v. New York*, 360 U.S. 315, 79 S. Ct. 1202, 3 L. Ed. 2d 1265 (1959).

The relevance of both external pressures and internal attributes means that the amount of coercion needed to render a confession "involuntary" varies. The stronger the suspect, the greater the coercion needed to make a confession inadmissible. The more vulnerable the suspect, the less the coercion needed to render a confession involuntary. The very same police methods might yield an acceptable confession when used on a strong-willed suspect, but an unacceptable confession when used on a more vulnerable suspect. Moreover, a vulnerable individual might confess involuntarily in response to one set of tactics but might give a voluntary statement in response to less coercive methods.

3.   Official Coercion Requirement

Two noteworthy features of the Supreme Court's due process opinions are the repeated use of the term "involuntary" to describe the proscribed confessions and the strong emphasis on the individual weaknesses of each suspect. These features could suggest that a confession that is solely the product of internal variables that deprive a suspect of her "free will" is barred by the Due Process Clause. In *Colorado v. Connelly*, 479 U.S. 157, 107 S. Ct. 515, 93 L. Ed. 2d 473 (1986), the Supreme Court rejected that position, holding that **"coercive police activity is a necessary predicate** to the finding that a confession is not 'voluntary' within the meaning of the Due Process Clause." According to the Court, "while mental condition is surely relevant to an individual's susceptibility to police coercion, **mere examination of the confessant's state of mind can never conclude the due process inquiry.**" Id.

In Colorado v. Connelly, a psychotic man told a police officer that he had killed a woman because the "voice of God" told him he must either confess to the killing or commit suicide. These "command hallucinations" impaired his "volitional abilities" and interfered with "his ability to make free and rational choices." Nonetheless, the confession was not prohibited by due process because the officer to whom he confessed used no coercion whatsoever.

Connolly Facts

Arguably, in the case of an extremely vulnerable suspect the most minimal official pressure, such as one simple question, could constitute "coercive police activity." It seems quite unlikely, however, that the Court would accept that position. It is more likely that there is a "threshold" level of coercion necessary to trigger due process concern. No matter how vulnerable the suspect, that amount of official coercion would always be essential. The exact amount of coercion needed to satisfy the threshold requirement is far from clear.

In addition, due process is not violated unless the source of the coercion is a **state agent.** "The **most outrageous behavior by a private party** seeking to secure evidence against a defendant does **not** make the evidence inadmissible under the Due Process Clause." Id. There is no bright-line standard for determining when an individual's involvement with the state is sufficient to render her a "state agent." The question is whether the person is acting for the state or solely for her own private purposes. Formal government employment is not necessary.

(E&A) EXAMPLE AND ANALYSIS

Jorge is a refugee from an authoritarian regime in which police brutality is the norm. Late one evening, after fortifying himself with alcohol, Jorge burglarizes a store. Shortly thereafter, he is arrested for driving while intoxicated. When an officer asks him for the third time what he had been doing that evening, Jorge admits to the burglary. Is his confession admissible under the Due Process Clause?

The confession is likely to be admissible. While an arrest and questions about the suspect's whereabouts create some pressure to confess, it seems unlikely that there is sufficient "coercive activity" to satisfy the threshold requirement of the Due Process Clause. Jorge's weaknesses—his experience with and expectations about police conduct, his intoxication, the lateness of the hour—would all be relevant once sufficient official coercion were brought to bear. Alone, however, such internal variables cannot support a due process claim. Without sufficient official pressure, a confession cannot be considered coerced.

4. "Inherently Coercive" Situations

Some actions in certain settings can generate so much pressure to confess that they are deemed **"inherently coercive."** Such situations give rise to an "irrebuttable presumption" of coercion. As a result, examination of the particular attributes of the individual—her physical or mental condition—is unnecessary. No matter how strong-willed the person is shown to have been, any statement made will be considered "involuntary." See Ashcraft v. Tennessee, 322 U.S. 143, 64 S. Ct. 921, 88 L. Ed. 1192 (1944). Physical brutality or torture create inherent coercion. Psychological pressures that subject an individual to "mental torture" can also qualify. For example, in Ashcraft v. Tennessee, officials conducted a 36-hour uninterrupted and incommunicado custodial interrogation by using relays of interrogators. The subject of the interrogation, a man whose wife had been murdered, had no sleep or rest during the period. According to the majority, the situation was "so inherently coercive that its very existence [was] irreconcilable with the possession of mental freedom by a lone suspect against whom its full coercive force was brought to bear." Consequently, despite considerable government evidence that the man "appeared normal"—that is, that he did not seem to be in a physically or mentally weakened state—the Supreme Court rejected the claim that his confession was voluntary.

5. Relevance of Promises and Trickery

Both true and false government promises and deception or trickery by government agents can be relevant factors in the "totality of circumstances" that bear on the "involuntariness" of a confession. A promise or deception might create pressure to confess or might weaken the resistance of the suspect. In Spano v. New York, for example, the Court relied, in part, on the fact that an officer who was an acquaintance of the suspect made false representations to the effect that the suspect's telephone call had gotten the officer into "trouble," that "his job was in jeopardy, and that loss of his job would be disastrous to his three children, his wife, and his unborn child." This deceptive effort at gaining sympathy added to the other pressures brought to bear and contributed to a finding that the suspect's confession was involuntary.

Nevertheless, the fact that a promise was used to secure a confession does not necessarily render the confession involuntary. See Arizona v. Fulminante (rejecting statement in earlier opinion that promises make confessions inadmissible). Even if the government fails to keep its promise, a confession that results will not always be coerced. The same is true of trickery. A statement produced by deceptions, misrepresentations, or other dishonest ploys is not automatically inadmissible under the Due Process Clause.

By focusing solely on "coercion" or "involuntariness," the Court's due process doctrine suggests that the sole relevant question is whether a particular promise or trick engendered pressure that "overbore the will" of a suspect. A promise or trick is pertinent only insofar as it "forces" a confession from a suspect. If it merely induces the suspect to speak or deceives him into deciding to speak, the Due Process Clause is not offended.

It is arguable, however, that coercion is not the only fundamentally unfair way of securing confessions and that convictions based on confessions obtained by other improper means can violate our sense of fair play. See Moran v. Burbine, 475 U.S. 412, 106 S. Ct. 1135, 89 L. Ed. 2d 410 (1986) (Stevens, J., dissenting) (maintaining that due process was violated when officers deceived the suspect's lawyer about their intent and then proceeded to interrogate the suspect and secure a confession in the absence of the attorney). While the extant "*coerced* confession" doctrine does not provide the basis for such a claim, it does not preclude the possibility that there are other unfair interrogation methods that could violate due process.

6. Rationales for the Due Process Bar on Involuntary or Coerced Confessions

One reason that due process or "fundamental fairness" is violated by the use of a coerced confession is the **risk of untrustworthiness.** See Spano v. New York. In an effort to escape undue pressure, an individual may make unreliable statements that could lead to the **conviction of an innocent person.** See Ashcraft v. Tennessee (Jackson, J., dissenting). Such an erroneous conviction would offend **substantive due process.**

Another justification for barring involuntary confessions is that the use of coercion to extract a statement and secure a conviction **"offend[s] an underlying principle in the enforcement of our criminal law: that ours is an accusatorial and not an inquisitorial system."** Rogers v. Richmond, 365 U.S. 534, 81 S. Ct. 735, 5 L. Ed. 2d 760 (1961). The Constitution guarantees not just substantively fair outcomes but also that those outcomes will be the product of **fair methods and procedures.** It assures **procedural due process**—that is, **fair play** by the government. In an accusatorial system, it is considered unfair for the government to force an individual to assist its efforts to convict by admitting her guilt.

One *effect* of excluding involuntary confessions is to **deter the use of coercion** by law enforcement officials. It is also arguable that deterrence is an additional *reason* for such exclusion. The deterrence of coercion could serve due process values in two ways. First, it could reduce the chance that a coerced confession would go undetected and result in an unjust conviction. Second, it could reduce the personal harms inflicted by the coercion itself. Of course, the latter would be a reason for due process exclusion only if the personal injuries inflicted by coercion are concerns of the Due Process Clause.

7. Timing of the Due Process Violation

Due process is violated when a coerced confession is introduced at trial. The **use of the confession** to obtain a conviction deprives the accused of "life, liberty, or property, without due process of law." See Spano v. New York (referring to "the abhorrence of society to the **use** of involuntary confessions").

It is unclear whether the **coercive methods** themselves violate the due process rights of the individual subjected to them. Some, if not all, out-of-court coercion does seem to deprive its victims of constitutionally protected interests. When law enforcement officers use physical violence or brutality, for example, the suffering of the individual would seem to qualify as a loss of "liberty" whether or not that individual makes a statement that is introduced at trial. The same reasoning would seem to apply to at least some kinds of psychological coercion.

EXAMPLES AND ANALYSIS

1. Angie is believed to have drowned her baby in a lake. Officers tell her that if she tells the truth they will recommend that she be sentenced to the minimum term allowed by law. Angie confesses. Is her confession admissible?

Probably. The Supreme Court has rejected the position that promises always render confessions involuntary. While the promise here created some pressure to admit her responsibility, it was not enough to "overbear" Angie's will and "coerce" her confession. Without additional facts probative of involuntariness, the confession should be admissible.

2. Marco is suspected of a rape and murder of a young woman. He adamantly denies the crime. Officers beat his head on the wall of an interrogation room and threaten to put lit cigarettes in his eyes. Marco confesses but later recants. Before trial, it is proven that another man committed the crimes. Were Marco's constitutional rights violated?

Probably. The confession was not used to convict Marco, so there was no judicial deprivation of liberty without due process. However, the physical and mental suffering inflicted on Marco might well qualify as official, extrajudicial deprivations of "liberty." If so, these deprivations were imposed "without due process of law" because such coercion is not a permissible method of law enforcement.

REVIEW QUESTIONS AND ANSWERS

Question: Connie agreed to submit to a "computer stress voice analyzer" (CSVA). During the test, she made a statement denying involvement in a felony. An officer then told her that the stress analyzer showed her denial to be false. In fact, the results of such a test cannot be conclusive with regard to whether a person has told the truth. After the officer made the statement, Connie confessed to her involvement in the felony. A judge rejected Connie's claim that due process required suppression of her confession. Should the judge's ruling be upheld on appeal?

Answer: While not indisputable, the judge's ruling is sustainable. The officer's statement to Connie, although somewhat deceptive and likely to create some pressure to confess, could be found not to have "overborne her will" in the totality of the circumstances. The Supreme Court has rejected the claim that an officer's use of the results of a polygraph test to secure a confession is "inherently coercive." See Wyrick v. Fields, 459 U.S. 42, 103 S. Ct. 394, 74 L. Ed. 2d 214 (1982). The facts here do not indicate additional coercive tactics by the officer, nor do they suggest that Connie had any internal vulnerabilities that would support an involuntariness finding.

Question: Frances was 12 years old when her younger sister was found suffocated to death. Three months later, Frances's mother had her admitted to the mental health wing of a county hospital. Frances was kept in a locked ward for adolescents. As part of her treatment program, she was encouraged to talk and write about her problems. The program involved rewards for talking with staff members and a loss of certain privileges for those who refused to answer questions or write in their journals.

Staff members knew that Frances was suspected in the death of her sister. They informed her on more than one occasion that they were required to report to the authorities any information about "hurting or killing a child." Thereafter, Frances was encouraged to speak openly about physical harm she caused others and was asked several times to write the names of persons she had harmed.

Approximately one year after she first entered the hospital, Frances admitted "spontaneously" during a group therapy session that she had killed her sister. She later said that the secret had been "eating her up." Subsequently, she confessed eight more times. Staff members reported these confessions. Frances was charged with murder. The trial judge suppressed her confessions, and the government has appealed, arguing (1) that the confessions were the result of "internal pressure rather than official coercion" and, alternatively, (2) that the source of any official pressure was hospital staff, not the police. How should the appellate court rule?

Answer: The ruling should be upheld. First, there would seem to be enough "external pressure" here to support a finding of coercion. The staff encouraged Frances to speak and asked her to list the people she had hurt. Moreover, disclosure was rewarded, while silence was met with the loss of privileges. This coercive activity must be added to Frances's vulnerabilities. She was a young adolescent with mental health problems who had been committed to the hospital for a year. In sum, while a judge might have concluded that her confession was a "spontaneous" response to her own feelings of guilt, the court's finding of involuntariness is supported by the totality of the circumstances.

Second, county hospital staff members are state employees. When they act on behalf of the state, their conduct should be subject to the Due Process Clause. See *Estelle v. Smith,* 451 U.S. 454, 101 S. Ct. 1866, 68 L. Ed. 2d 359 (1981) (holding that a confession made to the state psychiatrist appointed to examine the defendant for competency purposes was subject to the dictates of the *Miranda* doctrine). The use of confessions coerced by state agents to convict suspects violates due process. There is no reason to conclude that the Constitution tolerates convictions based on such confessions simply because the coercing agent is not a law enforcement officer. At least one federal court, however, has held that Due Process Clause regulation applies only when the state agent's questioning "is of a nature that reasonably contemplates the possibility of criminal prosecution." If that limitation were applied to these facts, it would seem to be satisfied because of the fact that the staff members were required to report to the authorities.

THE PRIVILEGE AGAINST COMPULSORY SELF-INCRIMINATION AND CONFESSIONS: THE DOCTRINE OF MIRANDA V. ARIZONA

CHAPTER OVERVIEW

The Fifth Amendment provides that **"[n]o person . . . shall be compelled in any criminal case to be a witness against himself."** On its face, this **"privilege against compulsory self-incrimination"** seems to be the most logical source of constitutional control over police interrogation practices and the admissibility of confessions. Historically, however, this guarantee pertained only to legal compulsion—that is, "compulsion" brought to bear on a "witness" involved in "legal proceedings."

It was not until 1966, in Miranda v. Arizona, 384 U.S. 436, 86 S. Ct. 1602, 16 L. Ed. 2d 694 (1966), that the Supreme Court concluded that the privilege also applied to extrajudicial custodial interrogation. This conclusion meant that law enforcement's efforts to secure confessions would be regulated not only by the general requirement of due process but also by the specific dictates of the Fifth Amendment privilege.

While this revolutionary extension of the Fifth Amendment's scope was significant as a matter of constitutional theory, its practical impact would have been negligible if the Court had concluded that the prohibition on "compelling" any person "to be a witness against himself" was virtually identical to the Due Process Clause prohibition on "coercing" confessions of guilt. In fact, the Court concluded that the two restrictions are very different. According to the *Miranda* Court, the Fifth Amendment privilege affords suspects greater protection and, consequently, restricts law enforcement conduct more severely. This conclusion was not surprising because the *Miranda* decision was prompted by the perception that the due process doctrine was not effectively controlling undesirable interrogation methods.

First, due process prevents only coercion that **overbears the will** of an individual, whereas the Fifth Amendment privilege seeks to insure that a confession is "**truly the product of his free choice.**" Miranda v. Arizona. The privilege clearly does not tolerate as much pressure to confess guilt as the Due Process Clause.

Second, and perhaps more important, determinations of coercion and of the admission of a statement under the Due Process Clause hinge on somewhat open-ended evaluations of the totality of relevant circumstances. Determinations of compulsion and of the admissibility of a statement under the Fifth Amendment privilege depend on much more focused, discrete inquiries such as whether a suspect was in custody, whether she was subjected to interrogation, whether she was adequately warned of and chose to waive her rights, and whether officers respected her desire to remain silent or be assisted by a lawyer.

This chapter is concerned solely with the *Miranda* doctrine—both its general rules and the detailed doctrinal standards that have been developed to give content to those rules. More specifically, this chapter discusses:

- **The constitutional foundations of Miranda v. Arizona.** The Supreme Court's original explanation of the logical connections between the Fifth Amendment's command and *Miranda*'s rules is addressed. The Court's subsequent modification of that explanation is also sketched.

- **The elements of the *Miranda* doctrine.** The threshold requirements that trigger the applicability of *Miranda* are **custody** and **interrogation.** When both are present, a suspect is protected by the specifics of *Miranda*'s procedural safeguards. Those safeguards always include adequate **warnings** and a knowing and voluntary **waiver.** When a suspect makes an adequate request to remain silent or be assisted by a lawyer, **additional protections** are triggered.

- **The public safety exception.** Unlike the Fourth Amendment warrant rule, the *Miranda* doctrine is not riddled with exceptions. The sole exception to the *Miranda* requirements in cases of custodial interrogation is the "**public safety**" **exception** recognized in New York v. Quarles.

A. CONSTITUTIONAL FOUNDATIONS OF THE *MIRANDA* DOCTRINE

This section discusses the constitutional foundations of Miranda v. Arizona. First it describes the original premises on which the doctrine rested. Then it explains the modified understanding of *Miranda*'s roots that is now endorsed by a majority of the Court and how that understanding differs from the original premises.

1. The *Miranda* Court's Explanation

The *Miranda* Court specifically dealt with the admissibility of statements made during "**custodial interrogation**" under the Fifth Amendment privilege not to be compelled to incriminate oneself. According to the majority's reasoning, because "compulsion [is] inherent" in custodial interrogation settings, statements made in these settings "can[not] truly be the product of . . . free choice." The use of such statements to obtain convictions would violate the constitutional command against compelling a person to be a witness against himself. Unless "adequate protective devices are employed to dispel the compulsion inherent in custodial surroundings," statements obtained from suspects are not admissible at trial. The various "procedural safeguards" prescribed by *Miranda* are "adequate protective devices." If they are employed, compulsion is dispelled and any statement obtained is admissible.

In sum, statements made during a custodial interrogation that is not conducted according to the *Miranda* rules (or equally effective alternatives) had to be excluded from trials **because the use of such a statement to convict was a violation of the Fifth Amendment rights of the accused.**

2. Explanation in Opinions Subsequent to *Miranda*

In subsequent opinions, the Court has explained *Miranda* differently. Statements made during custodial interrogation that do not comply with the rules of *Miranda* are **presumed to be compelled** but are **not actually compelled.** See New York v. Quarles, 467 U.S. 649, 104 S. Ct. 2686, 81 L. Ed. 2d 550 (1984); Oregon v. Elstad, 470 U.S. 298, 105 S. Ct. 1285, 84 L. Ed. 2d 222 (1985). The Fifth Amendment explicitly commands the exclusion of statements that are actually compelled; it does not require the exclusion of the presumptively compelled products of custodial interrogation.

According to the currently controlling understanding of *Miranda*, the *Miranda* Court recognized this presumption of compulsion and required exclusion of the products of improper custodial interrogation in order to provide "enlarged protection for the Fifth Amendment privilege." New York v. Quarles. Both the **procedures** that the *Miranda* decision prescribed for custodial interrogations **and** the **prohibition on the use** of statements are **"prophylactic"** measures—that is, they are designed to guard against potential violations of the Fifth Amendment. Id. When the *Miranda* rules are not followed, statements are excluded for two reasons: (1) to avoid the <u>risk</u> that the statements are compelled and, therefore, would violate the Fifth Amendment, see Withrow v. Williams, 507 U.S. 680, 113 S. Ct. 1745, 123 L. Ed. 2d 407 (1993); and (2) to encourage officers to comply with the *Miranda* rules, thereby lessening the future likelihood of compelled self-incrimination, see Michigan v. Tucker, 417 U.S. 433, 94 S. Ct. 2357, 41 L. Ed. 2d 182 (1974). <u>In sum, the *Miranda* Court ordered the exclusion of a statement made in response to custodial interrogation **because exclusion lessens the risks of compelled self-incrimination, not because the admission of such a statement would violate the Constitution.**</u>

B.   ELEMENTS OF THE *MIRANDA* DOCTRINE

There are two essential requirements for any aspect of the *Miranda* doctrine to be applicable—custody and interrogation. Once those prerequisites are satisfied, the *Miranda* scheme imposes a number of different procedural safeguards. Unless those safeguards are respected, a suspect's inculpatory statements will be inadmissible.

1.   Applicability of *Miranda* to All Crimes

At one time, some lower courts concluded that the *Miranda* doctrine did not apply to relatively minor offenses. In Berkemer v. McCarty, 468 U.S. 420, 104 S. Ct. 3138, 82 L. Ed. 2d 317 (1984), the Supreme Court rejected the state's argument that *Miranda* should not govern the admissibility of statements pertaining to a misdemeanor traffic offense. According to the Court, a suspect "is entitled to the procedural safeguards enunciated in *Miranda*, **regardless of the nature or severity of the offense** of which he is suspected or for which he was arrested."

2.   Threshold Requirements for *Miranda* Protection: "Custody" and "Interrogation"

None of the protective devices prescribed by the *Miranda* doctrine have any application unless a person is in **custody and** is subjected to official **interrogation.** Since *Miranda*, both of these threshold requirements have been explained in considerable detail.

a.   **Definition of "custody."** Custody requires a significant deprivation of physical freedom. More specifically, a person is in custody only if she is subjected to either **formal arrest or its functional equivalent.** Berkemer v. McCarty. A lesser infringement on a suspect's liberty, such as a mere "traffic stop" or *Terry*-type detention, see Chapter 4, section G, does not constitute custody.

A **formal arrest** occurs when a person is explicitly told that she is being placed under arrest. The **functional equivalent of a formal arrest** occurs when "a suspect's **freedom of action is curtailed to a 'degree associated with a formal arrest'** " or, in other words, when he is "subjected to **restraints comparable to those associated with a formal arrest.**" This determination must be made from the standpoint of **"a reasonable [person] in the suspect's position."** Berkemer v. McCarty.

Intentions or plans in the mind of an officer that are neither explicitly nor impliedly manifested to the suspect "have no bearing on the [custody] question." This premise has two consequences. The unexpressed intent to arrest will not support a custody finding. See id. By the same token, the absence of intent to arrest or the fact that an officer does not consider an individual a suspect will not militate against a finding of custody. Stansbury v. California, 511 U.S. 318, 114 S. Ct. 1526, 128 L. Ed. 2d 293 (1994).

An individual suspect's subjective belief regarding his status does not determine whether he is in custody. The question is whether a "reasonable person in the suspect's position" would believe that his freedom of action has been curtailed to a degree associated with a formal arrest. It is possible, though not certain, that the language "in the suspect's position" means that the "reasonable person" standard must be informed by particular relevant characteristics of the individual suspect—at least those that officers know and perhaps those they *should know*. See subsection b below (in determining whether official conduct constitutes "interrogation," at least those characteristics of which an officer is aware must be taken into account).

A suspect can be in custody under the definition prescribed in Berkemer v. McCarty even though she **is not in a police station.** See Orozco v. Texas, 394 U.S. 324, 89 S. Ct. 1095, 22 L. Ed. 2d 311 (1969). By the same token, the fact that a person **is in a police station** does not necessarily mean that she is in custody. Oregon v. Mathiason, 429 U.S. 492, 97 S. Ct. 711, 50 L. Ed. 2d 714 (1977).

⬢ E&A   EXAMPLE AND ANALYSIS

After an extensive investigation, federal agents assigned to investigate a number of mail bombings have focused their investigative efforts on Teddy. They are confident that he is responsible for the crimes. Two agents call on him at his remote cabin and ask if he would be willing to accompany them to their office to answer some questions. When Teddy asks if he is "under arrest," the officers assure him that he is not and that they are "merely asking for his willing cooperation." Teddy agrees to go with them. While at headquarters, he makes incriminating statements in response to direct questions. Must those statements be excluded from Teddy's trial by virtue of the *Miranda* doctrine?

The statements do not have to be excluded because Teddy was not in custody. The fact that an investigation has focused on a suspect does not satisfy the "custody" requirement. See Beckwith v. United States, 425 U.S. 341, 96 S. Ct. 1612, 48 L. Ed. 2d 1 (1976) (*Miranda* requires custody, and official "focus" on a suspect is not a substitute for custody). Moreover, not every police station interrogation is custodial. See Oregon v. Mathiason. Only if a reasonable person would believe he was under arrest or equivalent restraints is the custody requirement satisfied. In this case, Teddy went to the police station voluntarily. Because the custody requirement was not satisfied, the requirements of *Miranda* were simply inapplicable.

b.   Definition of "interrogation." *Miranda* applies only if a person in custody is subjected to **interrogation.** The interrogation requirement is satisfied if officers employ either **"express questioning or its functional equivalent."** Rhode Island v. Innis, 446 U.S. 291, 100 S. Ct. 1682, 64 L. Ed. 2d 297 (1980). The functional equivalent of express questioning includes **"words or actions on the part of the police** (other than those normally attendant to arrest and custody) **that the police *should know* are *reasonably likely to elicit an incriminating response from the suspect.*"** Id.

An officer's **intent to elicit** an incriminating response may be relevant, but it is not determinative of the interrogation issue. The dispositive question is whether the officer should have known that his conduct was reasonably likely to elicit an incriminating response. An officer's intent to elicit does not necessarily establish that the officer *should have known* that her actions *were reasonably likely to succeed.* Id.

Police **knowledge of** "the **unusual susceptibility** of a [suspect] to a particular form of persuasion" **is a relevant factor** in determining whether the police "should have known that their words or actions were reasonably likely to elicit an incriminating response *from the suspect.*" Id. The same would seem to be true with regard to police knowledge of other characteristics that could make a suspect more likely to respond with incriminating statements. It is unclear whether characteristics of which the police *should be aware* are also relevant. Individual traits that officers neither know of nor should know of are **not relevant.**

Miranda safeguards are triggered only when "interrogation" is conducted by a state agent who is **known to the suspect to be a state agent.** Consequently, even express questions by undercover government agents are not within the scope of the activities governed by the *Miranda* doctrine. Illinois v. Perkins, 496 U.S. 292, 110 S. Ct. 2394, 110 L. Ed. 2d 243 (1990). There is no basis for a *presumption of compulsion* unless a suspect in custody is subjected to interrogation by a known state agent. Of course, if an undercover state agent uses **actual coercion** to obtain a statement from a suspect, that statement is barred by both the Due Process Clause and the privilege against compulsory self-incrimination. See Arizona v. Fulminante, 499 U.S. 279, 111 S. Ct. 1246, 113 L. Ed. 2d 302 (1991).

(E&A) EXAMPLE AND ANALYSIS

Pete was arrested for manufacturing contraband narcotics after officers found a field of marijuana on his family's farm. Officers put him in an interrogation room with a copy of the front page of the local newspaper. A highlighted story regarding his arrest stated that his mother and brother were suspected of conspiring with him to grow the marijuana and that they might be arrested or questioned soon. It also told of how neighbors were shunning the family. Pete is extremely close to his mother and younger brother and is exceptionally protective of them. After reading the story, Pete called in the officers and told them that "the idea and operation were all mine. My family had no knowledge of it and nothing to do with it." Officers admit that they intentionally left the highlighted story in the room in the hope that it might motivate Pete to speak. Was Pete interrogated?

It is uncertain. The question is whether officers should have known that their actions were "reasonably likely to elicit an incriminating response from the suspect." The officers' intent to get a statement is not dispositive of this issue. Pete's closeness to and protectiveness of his family would be relevant to this determination if the officers knew of them. The officers should know that those attributes would make it more likely that the suspect would make an incriminating response to the newspaper story. Pete's particular attributes *might* also be relevant if the officers *should have known* of them. They are irrelevant if the officers neither knew nor should have known of them.

---

3. The First *Miranda* Safeguard: Adequate Warnings

The *Miranda* majority prescribed four warnings that must be given to a suspect subjected to custodial interrogation. The suspect must be told that (1) he has **the right to remain silent;** (2) anything he says **can and will be used against him;** (3) he has the **right to consult with a lawyer and to have the lawyer with him during interrogation;** and (4) if he cannot afford one, **a lawyer will be appointed to represent him.** The first three of these warnings are **"absolute prerequisites."** They must be delivered **in all cases,** no matter what the proof regarding the suspect's knowledge. The final warning might be omitted in a case where the suspect is clearly not indigent.

Although the warnings must always be given, they need not be given in the **exact form or language** prescribed in *Miranda* so long as the warnings that are given **"reasonably convey"** the rights that are expressed in the four original warnings. California v. Prysock, 453 U.S. 355, 101 S. Ct. 2806, 69 L. Ed. 2d 696 (1981). In other words, if the adequacy of the warnings is at issue, "substance" will govern over "form."

The type and extent of variation allowable by virtue of the "reasonably convey" standard are not entirely clear. In general, if the language used is different, the warnings are probably acceptable if a reasonable person would hear the same essential messages as those contained in the original warnings. If the warnings delivered contain additional information, they are apparently valid so long as the entire message conveyed is consistent with *Miranda*.

For example, in Duckworth v. Eagen, 492 U.S. 195, 109 S. Ct. 2875, 106 L. Ed. 2d 166 (1989), an officer gave the four required warnings and then added, "[W]e have no way of giving you a lawyer, but one will be appointed for you, if you wish, if and when you go to court." The Court found these warnings unobjectionable. First, they accurately described the state's procedure. More important, that procedure was consistent with *Miranda* because officers **do not have to provide a suspect with a lawyer unless they subject him to custodial interrogation.** Apparently, the Court believed that a reasonable indigent suspect who heard the four warnings plus the additional information would understand that he was entitled to an appointed attorney and that if he wanted such assistance he would **not be interrogated.**

EXAMPLES AND ANALYSIS

1. Mel is arrested for child abuse. Officers tell him that he has "the right not to talk and the right to an attorney." Mel responds by saying that he "has nothing to hide and certainly doesn't need a lawyer because I was well within my rights in beating my own kid as much as I damn well please." Did the officers' failure to deliver adequate warnings render Mel's statement inadmissible under *Miranda*?

No. The warnings clearly did not contain all the information that is required by the four *Miranda* warnings. However, the officers did not interrogate Mel. The inadequacy of the warnings is irrelevant because the *Miranda* requirements only apply to custodial interrogations.

2. Suppose that Mel had not responded to the officers' warning. The officers then asked him if he wished to waive his rights. Mel said that he did. The officers then asked, "What did you do?" Mel gave a full confession to beating his child. Later, he admits that he knew all his *Miranda* entitlements because he had served as a police officer for a short time. Is the confession admissible under *Miranda*?

No. *Miranda* warnings are "absolute prerequisites." A suspect's knowledge is not a substitute for delivering them. The warnings here were deficient—they did not inform Mel that anything he said could and would be used against him, and they did not tell him of his right to appointed counsel. Mel was in custody and was interrogated by the single express question asked by the officers. His statement must be excluded because of the violation of the *Miranda* warnings requirement.

4. The Second *Miranda* Safeguard: A Knowing and Voluntary Waiver

After adequate warnings are delivered, officers must secure a valid waiver from the suspect. In order to introduce at trial a statement secured by custodial interrogation, the government has the "heavy burden" of demonstrating that the suspect made a **knowing and voluntary waiver** of the *Miranda* entitlements. Miranda v. Arizona; North Carolina v. Butler, 441 U.S. 369, 99 S. Ct. 1755, 60 L. Ed. 2d 286 (1979).

a. **"Waiver" requirement.** The government must first show that the suspect in fact **waived** her rights. There must be a basis for concluding that she made a choice to relinquish or forgo the right to remain silent and, unless counsel is present, the entitlement to a lawyer.

Although a waiver can be established by the suspect's express oral or written statement, Miranda v. Arizona, an **express waiver is not required,** North Carolina v. Butler. To determine whether a suspect waived her rights, a court must examine the totality of relevant circumstances. In the absence of an express waiver, a suspect's **"actions and words"** can furnish a basis from which it can be **"clearly inferred"** that a suspect wished to relinquish her rights. Mere silence in the face of warnings cannot prove a waiver, but **"silence, coupled with an understanding of rights and a course of conduct indicating waiver,"** can support a finding of waiver.

b. **"Knowledge" requirement.** A valid waiver of *Miranda* "rights" must be **"knowing."** Miranda v. Arizona; North Carolina v. Butler. The government must show **only** that a suspect knew **the matters contained in the basic *Miranda* warnings**—that he has the right to remain silent, that anything he says can be used against him, and that he has the right to retained or appointed counsel before and during interrogation. To validly waive *Miranda*'s protections, a suspect needs no other knowledge, and a suspect's ignorance of any other matters, including "the full consequences of his decisions," will not render his waiver insufficiently "knowing." See Connecticut v. Barrett, 479 U.S. 523, 107 S. Ct. 828, 93 L. Ed. 2d 920 (1987).

For example, in Colorado v. Spring, 479 U.S. 564, 107 S. Ct. 851, 93 L. Ed. 2d 954 (1987), the Court upheld a waiver by a suspect who was not aware of all the crimes that were to be the subject of official questioning. And in Moran v. Burbine, 475 U.S. 412, 106 S. Ct. 1135, 89 L. Ed. 2d 410 (1986), a waiver by a suspect who was not informed of his attorney's attempts to speak with him was found to be valid. In both situations, the individuals had been warned and were aware of the essential *Miranda* entitlements. The additional "knowledge" that each suspect lacked—in *Spring*, the topics of the interrogation, and in *Burbine*, his attorney's efforts to contact him—was superfluous and not essential for a sufficiently knowing waiver.

Normally, proof that a suspect was aware of the minimum facts needed for a knowing waiver is supplied by the recitation of adequate *Miranda* warnings. In a case where a suspect could not understand English or had mental impairments that precluded a basic understanding of the content of the warnings, a waiver should probably be considered insufficiently knowing to satisfy *Miranda*'s standards. Even if an officer was not aware of the suspect's limitations, the actual lack of the minimal knowledge needed should render the suspect's waiver invalid.

It is sometimes said that a waiver must be "intelligent." See *Miranda v. Arizona*. Nonetheless, the fact that a suspect's decision to forgo *Miranda* protections is unwise, contrary to the suspect's best interests, or illogical is "irrelevant" and does not render the waiver invalid. See *Connecticut v. Barrett* (the fact that a suspect's "decision was illogical is irrelevant" to the validity of his waiver).

c. **"Voluntariness" requirement.** The government must also show that a waiver was **"voluntary."** *Miranda v. Arizona; North Carolina v. Butler.* When determining whether a waiver was voluntary, the first question to ask is whether the waiver was the product of some amount of **official coercion.** If there was no official coercion brought to bear on the suspect, the waiver is voluntary. *Colorado v. Connelly*, 479 U.S. 157, 107 S. Ct. 515, 93 L. Ed. 2d 473 (1986). A suspect's subjective characteristics—that is, internal impairments of her free will—cannot alone render a waiver "involuntary." *Id; see also* Chapter 6, section B.3, for a discussion of the identical qualification on the meaning of "involuntary" for purposes of the due process–coerced confession doctrine. "Absent evidence that [a suspect's] 'will [was] overborne and his capacity for self-determination critically impaired' because of **coercive police conduct,** his waiver of his Fifth Amendment privilege [is] voluntary under . . . *Miranda.*" *Colorado v. Spring.*

[handwritten margin notes: Voluntary, due process—coerced confession same]

Once there is sufficient official coercion, the voluntariness of a waiver is determined by examining the totality of relevant circumstances. This includes not only the coercive conduct employed by the police but the setting in which the waiver was obtained and the subjective attributes of the suspect. See *Colorado v. Spring; Fare v. Michael C.*, 442 U.S. 707, 99 S. Ct. 2560, 61 L. Ed. 2d 197 (1979).

(E&A) EXAMPLE AND ANALYSIS

Harv, who had not slept in 47 hours and was slightly intoxicated, was subjected to custodial interrogation and confessed his guilt after twice being fully informed of his *Miranda* entitlements and signing a written waiver that said that he "knowingly and voluntarily" wished to waive his rights and make a statement. Before Havr signed this waiver, an officer told him that "those in charge want to hear the truth and would not be happy if a lawyer got in the way of the truth coming out." At the time, three other armed officers were in the room. Unbeknown to any of them, Harv had once been beaten by the police and had an abiding fear of the authorities as a result. Is Harv's confession admissible under *Miranda*?

It is quite arguable that Harv did not "voluntarily" waive his rights. An express waiver, even one that purports to be "voluntary," is not valid if in fact it was not voluntary. Here, there would seem to be sufficient official coercion because of the presence of three armed officers and the officer's statement that put pressure on Harv to tell the truth and not rely on counsel. Moreover, Harv's subjective vulnerabilities are factors that must be taken into account in the totality assessment of voluntariness. His fatigue, intoxication, and fear of authorities all make him more likely to have his will overborne by official pressure. In determining the voluntariness of a waiver, it does not matter whether the officers were or should have been aware of the suspect's weaknesses.

5. Additional *Miranda* Safeguards Based on Invocation of the Right to Remain Silent

The first *Miranda* warning informs a suspect of "the right to remain silent." A suspect's **invocation of this entitlement to remain silent** gives rise to **additional *Miranda* safeguards.**

a. The necessary predicate: An invocation of the right to remain silent. Additional procedural safeguards arise only when a suspect actually invokes her right to remain silent. The suspect must express a desire not to speak with the authorities. Although the Supreme Court has not directly addressed the standard for determining whether a suspect's conduct is adequate to invoke the right to silence, it has dealt with that issue in the context of requests for counsel. The Court has held that **only a clear request** for counsel qualifies as an assertion of the *Miranda* entitlement. It seems highly likely that the identical standard governs assertions of silence. See subsection 6.a below for further explanation of the governing standards.

b. Additional safeguards triggered by an invocation of the right to remain silent. Once a suspect adequately expresses a desire to remain silent, **custodial interrogation must cease.** Miranda v. Arizona. It may be "resumed," however, if officers **"scrupulously honor" the suspect's "right to cut off questioning."** Michigan v. Mosley, 423 U.S. 96, 96 S. Ct. 321, 46 L. Ed. 2d 313 (1975). Put otherwise, "authorities must respect a person's exercise of th[e] option" to terminate questioning. Id. If they "scrupulously honor" the invocation of the right to remain silent and then obtain a valid waiver, statements made in response to custodial interrogation will be admissible.

The "scrupulously honored" standard does not provide a bright line for determining when a resumption of custodial interrogation is permissible. Any circumstance that indicates respect or a lack of respect for the suspect's expressed desire to remain silent should be taken into account. The Court has identified several relevant factors:

i.   **Passage of sufficient time between the invocation and the resumption of interrogation.** Time is the only factor that can be dispositive. If there is no more than a **"momentary respite [or] cessation"** of the interrogation process before the officer attempts to restart the interrogation session, the right to cut off questioning **has not been scrupulously honored.** No waiver can be considered valid, and statements that are the product of custodial interrogation will be inadmissible. Michigan v. Mosley. While "an interval of more than two hours" is sufficient (see id.), the minimum amount of time that must pass before officers may resume custodial interrogation is uncertain.

ii. **Subject of the resumed interrogation: The different crime criterion.** After a suspect invokes his right to silence, the authorities might resume interrogation about a **"different crime"** from the one that was (or would have been) the subject of an initial interrogation. That factor will weigh in favor of a finding that the suspect's right to silence was scrupulously honored. Michigan v. Mosley. Some lower courts have found that a change of topic is essential—that officers may **never** resume interrogation about the same crime. Other courts have held that it is possible to "scrupulously honor" a suspect's invocation of silence even though the topic of the resumed interrogation is the same crime. The later view seems more consistent with the *Mosley* opinion. The *Mosley* Court indicated that a change of subject is an important factor but did not say that it is a prerequisite to the resumption of interrogation.

iii. **Different locations, different officers, and the delivery of fresh *Miranda* warnings.** The *Mosley* Court cited other factors that weigh in favor of a finding that an assertion of silence was scrupulously honored. These include the facts that the invocation occurred in one place while the resumption of interrogation occurred in a **different place,** the assertion of silence was made to one officer and the resumption was by a **different officer,** and a **second set of *Miranda* warnings** was given prior to the resumption.

 # EXAMPLE AND ANALYSIS

Ruth is arrested for attempted murder. She is taken to an interrogation room where a detective is waiting. After the detective gives her the requisite warnings, Ruth says she "isn't inclined to speak with" the detective. The detective leaves. Fifteen minutes later, he returns, again recites the warnings, then asks Ruth if she "would consider answering some questions about an arson committed last month" at her place of business. If Ruth now agrees to answer questions and waives her rights, can her waiver be valid?

It is arguable. First, Ruth probably invoked the right to silence, but her statement that she wasn't *inclined* to speak could be considered ambiguous. If her invocation was clear enough, the next question is whether 15 minutes is a sufficient respite or is simply too brief to allow resumption of interrogation. On the one hand, it is more than a "momentary respite." On the other hand, it is not a very substantial period of time. If the time is adequate to allow a finding that the officer "scrupulously honored" Ruth's assertion, then the fresh *Miranda* warnings and the change of interrogation topics would militate in favor of such a finding. The brevity of the break, the same identity of the officer, and the same location would support a contrary finding. In sum, a judge's finding that Ruth's assertion was not "scrupulously honored," and therefore that a waiver was invalid, should be sustained. A finding to the contrary might be supportable, but it also might be erroneous based on the short time span between assertion and resumption.

---

6. Additional *Miranda* Safeguards Based on Invocation of the Right to Counsel

The third and fourth *Miranda* warnings inform suspects of their right to the presence of retained or appointed counsel. Assertions of the *Miranda* entitlement to the presence of an attorney also trigger additional procedural safeguards. These safeguards are different from those applicable when a suspect asserts the right to remain silent.

a.   The necessary predicate: An invocation of the right to counsel. To invoke the *Miranda* entitlement, a suspect's request for counsel must be **clear and unambiguous.** Davis v. United States, 512 U.S. 452, 114 S. Ct. 2350, 129 L. Ed. 2d 362 (1994). More specifically, a suspect "must articulate his desire to have counsel present **sufficiently clearly that a reasonable police officer in the circumstances would understand the statement to be a request for an attorney.**" Id.

A reference to an attorney that is "**ambiguous or equivocal** in that a reasonable officer . . . would have understood only that the suspect *might* **be invoking the right to counsel**" does not qualify as an assertion of the right to counsel. Moreover, an ambiguous expression concerning the suspect's wishes with regard to counsel has no effect—that is, it poses no additional impediments to custodial interrogation. An officer does not have to stop questioning or even seek clarification of the suspect's wishes regarding counsel.

Once a suspect invokes his right to counsel with sufficient clarity to satisfy the *Davis* standard, however, his *"post-request* responses to further interrogation may not be used to cast retrospective doubt on the clarity of the initial request." Smith v. Illinois, 469 U.S. 91, 105 S. Ct. 490, 83 L. Ed. 2d 488 (1984).

A suspect's **request to have the assistance or presence of any individual other than a lawyer** has no effect on the *Miranda* inquiry. It raises no additional safeguards against custodial interrogation other than those that are ordinarily applicable. Fare v. Michael C., 442 U.S. 707, 99 S. Ct. 2560, 61 L. Ed. 2d 197 (1979). Moreover, a request for some other person does not automatically constitute an invocation of the right to remain silent. Id.

b. **Additional safeguards triggered by an invocation of the right to counsel.** Once a suspect clearly requests an attorney, interrogation must cease. Interrogation may continue **only if** an **attorney is present or the suspect initiates further communications** with the authorities. Edwards v. Arizona, 451 U.S. 477, 101 S. Ct. 1880, 68 L. Ed. 2d 378 (1981). If neither of these conditions is satisfied, **no waiver can be valid** and any statements that are the product of custodial interrogation will be presumed to be compelled.

   i. **Presence of an attorney.** The assistance of counsel is an adequate device to protect against the compelling atmosphere of custodial interrogation. Miranda v. Arizona. If a suspect expresses the need for counsel's assistance, the presence of counsel to assist the suspect during custodial interrogation will furnish sufficient protection to satisfy the Fifth Amendment. However, the fact that a suspect has **consulted with an attorney** following a request for counsel is **not** a basis for permitting the authorities to initiate further interrogation of a suspect who has invoked counsel. Only the presence of counsel will suffice. Minnick v. Mississippi, 498 U.S. 146, 111 S. Ct. 486, 112 L. Ed. 2d 489 (1990).

   ii. **Suspect's initiation of further communications.** If an attorney is not present, the authorities may not custodially interrogate a suspect following a request for counsel **"unless the accused himself initiates further communication, exchanges, or conversations with the police."** Edwards v. Arizona. If the *authorities initiate* the communications, any statements that are the product of custodial interrogation are inadmissible. It does not matter that the suspect gives what would otherwise qualify as a valid waiver because any waiver is presumed invalid.

   The critical question, therefore, is whether the suspect or the authorities "initiated" further communications. In part, this depends on the **meaning of "initiation."** Inquiries or statements that "relat[e] to the routine incidents of the custodial relationship"—such as requests for a drink of water or to use the telephone—do **not** constitute initiation. **Initiation by a suspect** occurs only if the suspect demonstrates **"a desire . . . to open up a more generalized discussion relating directly or indirectly to the investigation."** Oregon v. Bradshaw, 462 U.S. 1039, 103 S. Ct. 2830, 77 L. Ed. 2d 405 (1983). Put otherwise, initiation occurs when a suspect **"evince[s] a willingness and a desire for a generalized discussion about the investigation."** Id.

Initiation by the authorities does not occur when an officer makes an inquiry or statement relating to the "routine incidents of the custodial relationship." On the other hand, statements that satisfy the *Bradshaw* standard—those that evince a desire to discuss the investigation—clearly will constitute official initiation. What is not certain is whether a statement that is neither "routine" nor indicative of a desire to discuss the investigation should be considered official initiation even though a similar statement by a suspect would not constitute initiation.

iii. **Irrelevance of the officer's identity, or the officer's unawareness of the assertion, and the topic of the interrogation.** When the right to silence is asserted, a change in the identity of the interrogator and a change in the subject matter of the proposed interrogation bear on the question of whether the suspect's assertion of his right has been respected. However, when the right to counsel is asserted and officials initiate further communications with the suspect, the fact that the later interrogation was conducted by a **different officer is irrelevant.** The fact that the interrogating officer was **wholly unaware of the suspect's request for counsel is also irrelevant.** Officials have the responsibility to insure that they learn of requests for counsel. Arizona v. Roberson, 486 U.S. 675, 108 S. Ct. 2093, 100 L. Ed. 2d 704 (1988). In addition, the fact that the topic of the later interrogation is a **different offense** from the one that was or would have been the subject of an earlier interrogation usually does not matter. Id. Unless a suspect makes it clear that her desire for counsel is "offense specific"—that is, that she wants assistance only for a particular offense—the presumption is that she desires assistance with all custodial interrogations.

 # EXAMPLE AND ANALYSIS

Manny is being held in the county jail after having been arrested for knifing a member of a rival gang. After hearing the *Miranda* warnings, Manny states, "I want a lawyer." After Manny spends two hours visiting with an appointed attorney in his cell, officers ask him if he "still needs a lawyer." Manny hesitates, then says that he has changed his mind and will answer questions without assistance. He signs a written waiver and makes statements in response to the officers' questions. Are his statements admissible under *Miranda*?

No. Manny has clearly asserted his right to counsel. A waiver and further custodial interrogation are permitted only if a lawyer is present or Manny initiates communications. The two-hour consultation with a lawyer will not suffice. Moreover, the officers "initiated" communications when they inquired about whether he still needed counsel. That inquiry seems to suggest a desire for communication about the subject matter of the investigation. The officers' initiation of communications rendered the waiver invalid and the statements inadmissible.

---

7. **The New York v. Quarles "Public Safety" Exception to the *Miranda* Doctrine**

There is only one exception to the restrictions *Miranda* imposes on custodial interrogations—the **public safety exception** recognized in New York v. Quarles, 467 U.S. 649, 104 S. Ct. 2626, 81 L. Ed. 2d 550 (1984). Even though a suspect is in custody, if officers wish to ask "questions **reasonably prompted by a concern for the public safety,**" they do not have to recite the *Miranda* warnings or secure a waiver of the suspect's rights. Any statements made in response to such questions are **not subject to exclusion** under *Miranda*.

a. **Objective, "reasonable officer" standard.** An officer's **subjective motivation is irrelevant** to the applicability of the public safety exception. The exception may apply even though it is not shown that the officer was in fact motivated by a concern for the public safety. So long as the questions are **"reasonably prompted"** by a public safety concern, the exception is applicable. Apparently, the relevant question is whether a reasonable officer could have been motivated to ask the questions in order to protect the public safety.

b. **Nature and magnitude of the public safety interest.** One question is what constitutes a sufficient public safety interest to justify application of the exception. Serious risks to the life or health of one or more individuals are certainly sufficient. Whether other sorts of potential harm suffice and what those harms might be are unanswered questions.

c. **Immediate and future threats to the public safety.** If the threat of harm is immediate and can be prevented only by swift action, the public safety exception is clearly applicable. If there is no need to act quickly because the threatened harm will not occur until some future time, it is uncertain whether the public safety exception applies. The primary rationale for the public safety exception is that the delivery of *Miranda* warnings in public safety situations could deter a suspect from speaking, thereby frustrating the interest in ensuring public safety. Arguably, that rationale supports a public safety exception even when the threatened harm is not immediate.

d. Applicability of the "public safety" exception to other *Miranda* doctrine requirements. The *Quarles* Court dealt with a **failure to warn** a suspect prior to custodial interrogation and held that there was **no need to give warnings** (and secure a waiver) when a public safety need is present. The *Miranda* doctrine also requires a voluntary waiver, requires that assertions of the right to silence be "scrupulously honored," and demands that officers not "initiate" custodial interrogation following requests for counsel. The *Quarles* opinion did not address the question whether there is a public safety exception to these other *Miranda* requirements.

Suppose that a suspect clearly requests an attorney. An officer then initiates further communications because of a public safety concern and asks "questions reasonably prompted by a concern for the public safety." The suspect's answers to those questions will be admissible only if the *Quarles* public safety exception is expanded to situations in which officers violate the rule against official initiation of communications following requests for counsel. Whether that expansion or any other expansion of the public safety exception is warranted remains an open question.

e. Actual compulsion and the public safety exception. The public safety exception is justifiable only because the current constitutional explanation of the *Miranda* doctrine holds that it is merely a "prophylactic" scheme. Statements that are the product of custodial interrogation do not have to be excluded because they are "actually compelled" and would violate the Fifth Amendment if used at trial. Instead, they are "presumed compelled" and are excluded to enforce *Miranda*'s prophylactic scheme and to guard against the risks of compulsion inherent in custodial interrogation. See section A.2 above.

In cases of **actual compulsion** there can be **no public safety exception.** The privilege against compulsory self-incrimination commands in absolute terms that "no person shall be compelled to be a witness against himself." This "constitutional imperative" contained in the Fifth Amendment bars the state from using compelled statements and does not allow an exception for even the most pressing needs. See New York v. Quarles.

REVIEW QUESTIONS AND ANSWERS

Question: Two officers who believed that Champ might be involved in the strangulation murder of his acquaintance went to see him at his place of work. When the officers said they wanted "to talk about the victim's murder," Champ asked if they could talk elsewhere. He then agreed to go to the "homicide office" with the officers. At the office, Champ answered some questions about his relationship to the victim and then was allowed to leave.

Three weeks later, one of the officers went to find Champ at a bar, but found him sitting at the back of the bus. When the officer entered the front door of the bus, Champ immediately exited the rear door, walked to the police car, and got into the front seat. The officer got in the driver's seat and asked if it was okay to go to his office. When Champ expressed concern about "getting home," the officer said he would make sure Champ got home.

At 1:30 A.M., without giving any warnings, the officer began to question Champ about the victim's death. Over the next hour, Champ took three "breaks," during which he left the interrogation room to smoke, use the restroom, or get water. He was unescorted during these breaks. After his third break, around 2:30 A.M., Champ began to sob. When the officer asked why, Champ responded by admitting that he had put his hands around the victim's neck. After 90 minutes of additional questioning during which additional incriminating statements were made, the officer placed Champ under arrest. Were Champ's statements obtained in violation of *Miranda*?

Answer: The issue is arguable. The facts provide no evidence of *Miranda* warnings and do not provide the basis for an inference that Champ waived his rights. Clearly, the officer did not comply with *Miranda*'s requirements. The question is whether *Miranda* applied to the session. Clearly, the questions asked by the officer qualify as "interrogation." The only question is whether Champ was in custody when he made the statements.

Custody requires a formal arrest—which did not occur until all statements were made in this case—or its "functional equivalent." The question is whether a reasonable person in the suspect's position would have believed at any relevant time that he was under restraints comparable to those associated with a formal arrest. On the one hand, it does not seem that Champ was forced to go to the police station on either occasion. Rather, in both instances he made what is arguably a free choice to accompany the officers. On the other hand, the officers twice sought his cooperation, coming to his place of work and then coming onto a bus he was riding. Each time they demonstrated interest in the strangulation of a victim with whom Champ was acquainted. Although these factors are relevant, they are probably insufficient to render Champ "in custody" for purposes of *Miranda*. A reasonable person would not feel sufficiently restrained by the officer's actions to trigger *Miranda* application. This finding is supported by the fact that Champ was allowed freedom to leave the interrogation room without being accompanied by the officer.

It is arguable, however, that after Champ made his initial admission that implicated him in the murder, a reasonable person would have felt that he was being restrained to a degree associated with a formal arrest. He might reasonably have believed that he was not going to be allowed to leave the police station because he was going to be formally arrested. If so, he was in "custody," and his subsequent statements would be inadmissible. See State v. Champion, 533 N.W.2d 40 (Minn. 1995). While some judges think that a noncustodial situation is automatically made custodial when a suspect admits to serious wrongdoing, others hold that the admissions are simply one more factor to be taken into account in applying the Berkemer v. McCarty standard for custody. It seems likely that the Supreme Court would prefer the latter view.

Question: Shawn was arrested for murder. Detective Young advised her of her rights and asked, "Understanding these rights, do you wish to talk to me now?" Shawn said, "No." Young then escorted Shawn to her cell.

Not long afterward, Detective Treadwell came to Shawn's cell. Treadwell had known her since she was a young girl and had been a friend of her family. The two belonged to the same church. According to Treadwell's later report of his visit with Shawn, "I gave her the *Miranda* warnings and she waived her rights. I spoke words of encouragement, telling her we all make mistakes and that she shouldn't feel bad about the situation. I told her it wasn't a good situation she was in, but I wasn't going to judge her and I felt no one else—meaning other church members—would judge her. I basically told her that based on our teachings we don't judge each other, that she should keep her head up, should be strong and remember what we believe in." Treadwell then left. Four hours later, Shawn summoned Treadwell to her cell and made a confession. Should the confession be excluded under the *Miranda* doctrine?

Answer: The case is arguable, but there is a good claim for exclusion of the confession. The first question is whether Shawn invoked her right to remain silent when she said "No." Assuming that the United States v. Davis standard for invocations of counsel is applicable, the question is whether a reasonable officer would understand that her statement was an assertion of her desire not to talk. A simple "No" in response to the question "Do you wish to talk to me now?" would certainly seem to be sufficiently clear to constitute an invocation of the right to remain silent. If so, later events—in this case, her statement that she wanted to talk—cannot be used to cast "retrospective doubt" on the clarity of her wishes.

If the suspect effectively invoked her right, the officer's authority to "resume interrogation" was limited by the "additional safeguard" explained in Michigan v. Mosley. The next question, therefore, is whether Officer Treadwell's conduct constituted "interrogation." Here, the officer was an acquaintance and fellow church member of the suspect. His lengthy remarks were related to the suspect's "situation" and to the significance of their religious beliefs in that situation. It is entirely possible that the officer was intending to secure a statement from Shawn. In light of this intent, what the officer knew about the suspect, the officer's bonds with the suspect, and the length and content of his remarks, there is a strong argument that he "should have known that his words were reasonably likely to elicit an incriminating response from this suspect." Moreover, although there was a break of four hours, the confession to this same officer would seem to be the product of the officer's words rather than a spontaneous act of conscience.

If Officer Treadwell did "resume interrogation" following an assertion of the right to remain silent, the next question is whether he "scrupulously honored" the suspect's right to cut off questioning and secured a waiver of rights. Here, the officer secured a waiver. The question, however, is whether he satisfied the "scrupulously honored" standard. To answer that question requires a determination of the amount of time between Shawn's "No" and Treadwell's "resumption." If the time is too short, no waiver by Shawn can be valid. Assuming that sufficient time passed, the factors weighing in favor of finding that Treadwell honored Shawn's right are that he gave fresh warnings, that he was a different officer, and that the visit occurred in a different place. Two factors supporting a contrary conclusion are that the officer came to the cell "not long after" Shawn asserted her right and that he interrogated Shawn about the same crime. In sum, if the passage of time is sufficient to satisfy the minimum period required, a trial court could plausibly support either conclusion.

Finally, with regard to assertions of the right to counsel, it does not matter that an officer does not in fact know of a suspect's invocation. The same ought to be true with regard to assertions of the desire to remain silent. Consequently, even if Treadwell was unaware of what Shawn said to Officer Young, the *Mosley* standard has to be satisfied.

Question: Officers went to Mack's home pursuant to a warrant to arrest him for conspiracy to distribute crack cocaine and a search warrant for narcotics. After Mack was placed under arrest, Officer Martin read him his rights and Mack said he wanted a lawyer. Officer Martin then asked him if "there were in the apartment any weapons or other items that could pose a danger to the officers who would be searching it for narcotics." Mack led her to a weapon on the shelf in his bedroom closet. Did the officer violate *Miranda*?

Answer: On the facts provided, the officer did violate *Miranda*. Mack clearly asserted his right to counsel. After he did so, Officer Martin not only "initiated" further communications, her initiation by means of an "express question" also constituted custodial interrogation. Officer Martin violated the Edwards v. Arizona branch of the *Miranda* doctrine **unless** the New York v. Quarles "public safety" exception is applicable. There are two problems with applying *Quarles* to this case.

First, New York v. Quarles recognized a public safety exception to the requirement that an officer issue warnings to a suspect. Here the officer's violation was not a mere "failure to warn" but a transgression of the *Edwards* bar on officer-initiated interrogations following requests for counsel. Whether the public safety exception should be extended to this situation is debatable.

The second problem is more serious. Even assuming that the public safety exception can be applied to this sort of *Miranda* violation, the facts do not seem to support its application in this case. The officer's question must be "reasonably prompted by a concern for the public safety." The facts do not demonstrate a basis for an objectively reasonable concern for the public safety. The facts that Mack was being arrested for a narcotics offense and that the officers had grounds to search the apartment for narcotics do not seem sufficient to support a reasonable belief that there was a danger to the officers who were going to search the apartment. Narcotics offenders may be dangerous, even violent, but there is no logical basis for automatically assuming that their homes harbor dangers to searching officers.

8

THE SIXTH AMENDMENT RIGHT TO COUNSEL: A FOUNDATION

CHAPTER OVERVIEW

The entitlement to counsel discussed in Chapter 7—the "implicit" *Miranda* entitlement—is rooted solely in the Fifth Amendment and is nothing more than a procedural safeguard against compelled self-incrimination. The entitlement to counsel discussed in this chapter is the explicit **Sixth Amendment right of the "accused . . . to have the assistance of Counsel for his defence."**

Although this Sixth Amendment guarantee was originally a right to assistance **at trial,** it has been extended to certain **pretrial stages** of the criminal process. Chapter 9 discusses the extension of counsel to government agents' pretrial efforts to elicit inculpatory statements from defendants. Chapter 10 treats the extension of counsel to official pretrial efforts to secure identifications from witnesses. As a foundation for understanding those two pretrial extensions of the Sixth Amendment right, this chapter explores the nature and scope of the right to assistance at trial and the basic reasons that it has been extended to pretrial stages. A complete discussion of the right to the assistance of counsel at trial is included in Chapter 18.

A. THE RIGHT TO COUNSEL AT TRIAL

1. Purpose of the Right to the Assistance of Counsel

The American system of criminal justice is **adversarial.** In large part, this means that it functions by means of a contest between two opposing sides—the state and the accused. In an adversarial system, fundamental fairness requires, among other things, rough equality between the two sides. The assistance of counsel is "indispensable to the fair administration of our adversary system of criminal justice," Brewer v. Williams, 430 U.S. 387, 97

S. Ct. 1232, 51 L. Ed. 2d 424 (1977), because counsel is essential to ensuring this equality. Without the assistance of counsel, the state could use its superior strength to overpower the accused. With counsel, the accused has a means of defending against the state's efforts.

2. Nature and Substance of the Right to the Assistance of Counsel

The accused has a Sixth Amendment right to retain a lawyer or, if indigent, to have a lawyer appointed at state expense. Gideon v. Wainwright, 372 U.S. 335, 83 S. Ct. 792, 9 L. Ed. 2d 799 (1963). See Chapter 18, section A.2 and A.3. However, the Sixth Amendment does not require states to appoint counsel to represent an indigent defendant charged with a misdemeanor if the defendant is **not subjected to actual imprisonment** for the offense. Scott v. Illinois, 440 U.S. 367, 99 S. Ct. 1158, 59 L. Ed. 2d 383 (1979). It is unclear whether the state could deny representation by a **retained** attorney in the same situation. See Chapter 18, section A.3.b.iii.

Both retained and appointed lawyers must provide effective representation. If a defense attorney's performance constitutes **ineffective assistance,** the defendant is deprived of the Sixth Amendment entitlement. Strickland v. Washington, 466 U.S. 668, 104 S. Ct. 2052, 80 L. Ed. 2d 674 (1984). See Chapter 18, section C.2, for a full discussion of the standards for determining ineffectiveness.

The pretrial entitlements to counsel discussed in Chapters 9 and 10 are outgrowths of the guarantee of assistance at trial. Consequently, the preceding standards regarding appointment and effectiveness also govern those entitlements.

B. PRETRIAL EXTENSIONS OF THE RIGHT TO COUNSEL

The Supreme Court has not confined the Sixth Amendment right to counsel to the trial itself. It has extended that right to a limited number of pretrial stages of the criminal process. Those events include formal courtroom proceedings, such as preliminary hearings and arraignments. See Chapter 18, section B.2. They also include two informal investigatory processes—certain efforts to elicit statements and certain processes designed to secure eyewitness identifications.

1. Rationales for Extending Counsel to Pretrial Stages

The conclusion that the right to counsel must be available at certain pretrial stages of the criminal process is based on the following reasoning. At the time the Bill of Rights was adopted, the adversarial contest was essentially confined to trial. Later, our system of criminal justice developed a number of pretrial steps that expanded the adversarial contest. See United States v. Ash, 413 U.S. 300, 93 S. Ct. 2568, 37 L. Ed. 2d 619 (1973). If the right to counsel did not extend to at least some of these pretrial events, the constitutional goal of a fair trial contest between "equal adversaries" might well be undermined. By using its superior strength against an unassisted defendant before trial, the government would be able to gain advantages that could render the right to counsel at trial and the other trial rights empty promises. See United States v. Wade, 388 U.S. 218, 87 S. Ct. 1926, 18 L. Ed. 2d 1149 (1967) (pretrial counsel is necessary "if the guarantee is not to prove an **empty right**"). Equal strength at trial would be pointless if unequal pretrial encounters had already sealed an accused's fate. Id. ("[T]oday's law enforcement machinery involves critical confrontations of the accused by the prosecution at pretrial proceedings where the results might well **settle the accused's fate and reduce the trial itself to a mere formality.**"). In sum, a right to pretrial counsel is essential to ensure "meaningful" assistance at trial and thereby to preserve the fairness of the trial. See United States v. Ash.

2. Scope of Pretrial Counsel

The right to counsel does not extend to every pretrial phase, but only to those in which the absence of assistance would pose serious threats to the fairness of the trial itself. As a matter of doctrine, an accused has a Sixth Amendment right to counsel only at " **'critical stages' of the prosecution.**" United States v. Henry, 447 U.S. 264, 100 S. Ct. 2183, 65 L. Ed. 2d 115 (1980). If a pretrial event does not qualify as a "critical stage," there is no Sixth Amendment right to counsel.

The two chapters that follow discuss two kinds of pretrial investigatory activities—efforts to secure inculpatory statements from defendants and attempts to obtain identifications by witnesses—that in certain, limited circumstances are considered "critical stages" of the prosecution.

9 THE RIGHT TO COUNSEL AND CONFESSIONS

CHAPTER OVERVIEW

By the mid-1960s, the Supreme Court had become increasingly frustrated with the ineffectiveness of the "involuntary confession" doctrine of the Due Process Clause as a means of regulating law enforcement efforts to obtain confessions from suspects. In 1964, in *Massiah v. United States,* 377 U.S. 201, 84 S. Ct. 1199, 12 L. Ed. 2d 246 (1964), the Court found additional protection in the **Sixth Amendment right to counsel.** The Court held that in some circumstances accused individuals have a Sixth Amendment entitlement to the assistance of counsel when the government seeks to secure inculpatory statements. If a statement is obtained in the absence of a lawyer and without a waiver of the right to counsel, it cannot be used to convict the defendant. The Court's holding placed additional constitutional restrictions on government efforts to secure confessions and thereby establish guilt.

Miranda v. Arizona was decided just two years after *Massiah.* In large part, *Miranda*'s Fifth Amendment–based doctrine was also the product of the Court's frustration with the involuntary confession doctrine. In the years following *Miranda,* some thought that the *Massiah* Court's interpretation of the Sixth Amendment had actually been replaced by the *Miranda* doctrine. They suspected that the right to counsel no longer afforded any independent protection against official efforts to secure incriminating admissions. That has proven not to be the case. Today, while its scope is narrowed by restrictive criteria, the right to counsel recognized in *Massiah* continues to limit "interrogation" practices and the admissibility of confessions.

Students should note that the **elements** of the *Miranda* and *Massiah* doctrines **are very different** "since the **policies** underlying the two constitutional guarantees [on which each doctrine is based] **are quite distinct.**" *Rhode Island v. Innis,* 446 U.S. 291, 100 S. Ct. 1682, 64 L. Ed. 2d 297 (1980). Consequently, although there are times when both doctrines govern official efforts to obtain statements, there are many cases in which only the restrictions imposed by *Miranda* or only the limitations dictated by *Massiah* are applicable.

This chapter discusses:

- **The "initiation of adversary proceedings" and "deliberate elicitation" requirements.** The two essential components of a valid *Massiah* doctrine claim are **an initiation of formal adversary proceedings** and **deliberate elicitation by a government agent.** This chapter explores the meaning and details of each of these independent components. It explains that *Massiah* governs both **direct** and **surreptitious** elicitation and discusses the somewhat elusive, additional requirement of a **basis for attributing** the activities of a state informant to the regular officers of the state.

- **The possibility of waiver.** In undercover agent contexts, waiver of the right to counsel is not a possibility. When known officers seek to elicit information directly, however, an accused can waive the entitlement to counsel held out by the *Massiah* doctrine.

- **Invocation of the right to counsel.** Under the *Miranda* doctrine, invocation of counsel is a significant event. Under the *Massiah* doctrine, an invocation of the right is equally significant. It poses a substantial barrier to the government's ability to secure a valid waiver.

A. THE THRESHOLD REQUIREMENT: A FORMAL INITIATION OF ADVERSARY PROCEEDINGS

The Sixth Amendment right to counsel **does not attach** until the **"formal initiation of adversary judicial proceedings."** Moran v. Burbine, 475 U.S. 412, 106 S. Ct. 1135, 89 L. Ed. 2d 410 (1986). Prior to **"the first formal charging proceeding,"** an individual is not an "accused," has no constitutional right to the assistance of counsel, and cannot base a claim on the denial of that right. Id.

The right to counsel **does not attach** upon arrest, issuance of an arrest warrant, the acquisition of sufficient evidence to prove an offense, or the decision to file charges. Instead, there must be a **"formal charge, preliminary hearing, indictment, information, or arraignment."** Kirby v. Illinois, 406 U.S. 682, 92 S. Ct. 1877, 32 L. Ed. 2d 411 (1972).

The point of attachment applies to both **appointed** and **retained** counsel. An individual cannot create a constitutional right to counsel prior to the initiation of proceedings by forming a relationship with an attorney. Moran v. Burbine. Put simply, the right to counsel cannot be violated, because it does not come into existence, prior to the formal initiation of proceedings.

The **attachment** of the right to counsel is **"offense specific."** If an individual is formally charged with one offense and is merely arrested for or suspected of a second offense, he has an entitlement to counsel for the former but not the latter offense. Maine v. Moulton, 474 U.S. 159, 106 S. Ct. 477, 88 L. Ed. 2d

481 (1985). When a charged and an uncharged offense are similar and both grow out of the same conduct, it is *arguable* that the attachment of the right to counsel for the charged offense carries over to the uncharged offense. But when offenses are distinct, the right to counsel attaches only for formally charged offenses.

 ## EXAMPLES AND ANALYSIS

1. Marco is arrested for racketeering. He is taken to an interrogation room and questioned about his offense. He later claims that statements he made should be excluded because the interrogating officers violated his right to counsel. Is his claim valid?

No. While Marco may have a valid *Miranda* claim, he has no Sixth Amendment claim because formal adversary proceedings have not yet been initiated. His right to counsel has not attached.

2. If Marco had been the subject of a secret, sealed indictment at the time of the questioning, would the result change?

Yes. Even though it is not yet public, Marco has been formally charged. The indictment, which shows that the government is committed to prosecute Marco, triggers the attachment of his right to counsel. Marco's claim is valid if he did not validly waive his Sixth Amendment entitlement.

B. NATURE OF THE CRITICAL STAGE DEFINED BY *MASSIAH*: "DELIBERATE ELICITATION" BY A GOVERNMENT AGENT

Even after the right to counsel has attached, it extends only to **"critical stages of the proceedings."** United States v. Henry, 447 U.S. 264, 100 S. Ct. 2183, 65 L. Ed. 2d 115 (1980). According to the *Massiah* doctrine, a "critical stage" of the criminal process that requires the assistance of counsel is reached when a government agent **deliberately elicits** incriminating information from an accused. Id.; Kuhlmann v. Wilson, 477 U.S. 436, 106 S. Ct. 2616, 91 L. Ed. 2d 364 (1986).

1. Government Agent Requirement

To trigger the right to counsel, the individual engaging in the regulated activity—that is, in the deliberate elicitation—must be working for the government. The individual does not have to be an official employee, nor does she have to be compensated for the work. The question is whether the person is acting for—at the instigation, behest, or request of—the government. See Chapter 4, section A.4 (discussing the "government agent" requirement for purposes of Fourth Amendment application).

For example, in United States v. Henry, two cellmates of the accused obtained inculpatory statements from him. One of them was working with the FBI, but the other was not involved with the government. The defendant raised a valid claim that his right to counsel had been violated by the activities of the first cellmate. He could make no such claim regarding the activities of the second cellmate.

2. "Deliberate Elicitation" Requirement

According to Massiah v. United States, the government violates the right to counsel when it uses against an accused statements **"deliberately elicited from him . . . in the absence of his counsel."** For a defendant to be entitled to the assistance of counsel, there must be **"deliberate elicitation"** by the government. Massiah v. United States; United States v. Henry. There is no controlling definition of "deliberate elicitation." Some aspects of the requirement are clear; others are ambiguous.

a. **An "intent" to elicit information is apparently required.** The word "deliberate" and other language used by the Court to describe the conduct that gives rise to a counsel entitlement suggest that the person eliciting the information from the accused must intend to elicit inculpatory information. The Court, however, has never discussed this question, and no case has turned on the presence or absence of intent by the elicitor.

b. **Active elicitation is required.** The government agent must **actively elicit** incriminating statements. The right to counsel does not apply unless a government agent takes **"some action, beyond merely listening,** that was designed deliberately to elicit incriminating remarks." Kuhlmann v. Wilson. The mere passive reception of information cannot qualify as a "critical stage." Consequently, there is no right to counsel if an official listens in on an accused's revelations by means of an "inanimate" listening device or if an in-person agent passively receives an accused's disclosures.

In Kuhlmann v. Wilson, for example, the Supreme Court affirmed a lower court conclusion that there had been no *Massiah* violation based on its finding that the government's informant had not actively elicited the statements that were used against the defendant.

Affirmative, direct questioning will qualify as deliberate elicitation, but it is not necessary. United States v. Henry. Merely **"engaging in conversation"** with an accused or **"having some conversations"** with an accused satisfies the deliberate elicitation requirement. See Massiah v. United States; United States v. Henry. In addition, the fact that an accused was "first [to] raise[ ] the subject of the crime under investigation" or was the one who "instigated the meeting" with the government agent is irrelevant. See United States v. Henry; Maine v. Moulton. So long as a government agent engages in "deliberate elicitation" and the statements are the product of that conduct, *Massiah*'s right to counsel doctrine applies.

c. **Both direct and surreptitious elicitation are included.** Both **direct elicitation by a known government agent**—such as a police officer or prosecutor—and **surreptitious elicitation by an undercover agent**—such as a cellmate or acquaintance—fall within the scope of the conduct that is governed by the *Massiah* right to counsel. See Brewer v. Williams, 430 U.S. 387, 97 S. Ct. 1232, 51 L. Ed. 2d 424 (1977).

Thus, in *Massiah*, *Henry*, and *Moulton*, undercover agent elicitation in the absence of counsel was deemed unconstitutional, while in Brewer v. Williams and Michigan v. Jackson, 475 U.S. 625, 106 S. Ct. 1404, 89 L. Ed. 2d 631 (1986), the violations of the Sixth Amendment were based on elicitation by known police officers.

EXAMPLE AND ANALYSIS

Hector is arrested for arson. The prosecutor files an information against him. While he is out on bail, Hector visits with Arnelle. Unbeknown to Hector, Arnelle has been asked by detectives to find out what she can about the arson from Hector. During a conversation about the arson charges that is initiated by Hector, Arnelle periodically makes comments that keep the conversation going. Hector makes incriminating statements that Arnelle reports to the detectives. Prior to trial, Hector moves to suppress those statements, claiming that he was entitled to counsel during the conversations with Arnelle. The trial judge refuses to suppress the statements because "the defendant raised the subject of the crime himself, was not questioned by the government informant, and never asked for a lawyer." Is the court's ruling correct?

No. Hector was formally charged and Arnelle's conversations with him are sufficient to satisfy the deliberate elicitation requirement. It does not matter that Hector initiated the conversations about his alleged offense, that he was not directly questioned, or that he never asked for a lawyer. When a government agent deliberately elicits statements after formal charges, the right to counsel is violated unless the accused validly waives his right. The accused has no duty to assert his right. The state has the obligation to respect that right or secure a waiver.

3. **Requirement of a "Basis for Attributing" the Elicitation to the Government**

In United States v. Henry, a cellmate of the accused was "engaged to provide confidential information to the Federal Bureau of Investigation as a paid informant" and was operating under instructions from an FBI agent. The cellmate, who clearly was a state agent, "had some conversations" with the accused and obtained inculpatory statements. That activity clearly constituted "deliberate elicitation." The Supreme Court upheld the defendant's *Massiah* claim, but **not** simply because a "state agent" had "deliberately elicited" incriminating statements. Instead, the Court reasoned that "the **Government** violated" the defendant's right to counsel "[b]y **intentionally creating a situation likely to induce [the accused] to make incriminating statements** without . . . counsel."

This reasoning suggests that in cases involving undercover agents, more is needed to trigger the right to counsel than active elicitation by a person who is working for the state. There must also be an adequate **basis for attributing that conduct to** *the Government*—that is, to "regular" law enforcement agents. The "Government" is responsible only if it **"intentionally creates"** or **"knowingly exploits"** a situation that it **knows** or **should know** is likely to involve active elicitation by its undercover operatives. Maine v. Moulton; United States v. Henry.

In evaluating whether the Government "intentionally created" or "knowingly exploited" a situation "likely to induce" the accused to make incriminating statements, no single factor is dispositive. The question is whether, under all the relevant circumstances, it is fair to say that law enforcement officers **"intended," "knew,"** or **"must have known"** that their **undercover agent was "likely" to elicit actively.** Maine v. Moulton. The Court has identified some of the factors relevant to the determination:

a.   **Custody and undercover status.** An accused who is in **custody** is more vulnerable and therefore is **more likely to disclose** incriminating information to an undercover agent than one who is free of official confinement and its inherent pressures. United States v. Henry. Moreover, an accused is **more likely to trust an undercover agent**—a cellmate or friend—with inculpatory information that he would not share with a known police officer. Id. In United States v. Henry, the Court relied on the facts that the defendant was in custody and that he was unaware that his cellmate was working for the authorities in deciding that the cellmate's elicitation should be attributed to the Government.

b.   **Compensation of the agent.** An agent who is **compensated only if he gains information** is **more likely to elicit actively.** Id. The contrary would seem to be true if law enforcement officers have made it clear that no compensation will be paid if the agent actively elicits. Thus, in United States v. Henry, the Court also thought it important that the defendant's cellmate had an arrangement that called for payment only if he secured information.

   c.   **Instructions to the agent.** If there are no instructions regarding how
        the agent should conduct himself or if the instructions forbid the agent
        only from engaging in specific kinds of active elicitation, it is more likely
        that an undercover agent will actively seek information. See United
        States v. Henry; Maine v. Moulton. On the other hand, clear instructions
        that prohibit any active elicitation should make it less likely.

        In United States v. Henry, the Court stressed that the FBI agent had
        instructed the cellmate not to "question or initiate conversations"
        with the accused but left the cellmate "free to discharge his task of
        eliciting the statements in myriad less direct ways." And in Maine v.
        Moulton, the Court concluded that the instructions given to the infor-
        mant were "necessarily inadequate" because they told him only to "be
        himself," to "act normal," and "not [to] interrogate" the defendant.
        Again, he was left free to engage in other sorts of active elicitation.

4.   Good Faith Investigations of Different, Uncharged Offenses

   Inculpatory statements regarding a charged offense may be acquired in the
   course of a **good faith investigation** of a different, uncharged offense. Because the defendant's right to counsel has not attached regarding the latter
   offense, see section A above, the *Massiah* doctrine poses no bar to the use
   of statements to prove that offense. See Maine v. Moulton. However, if the
   "deliberate elicitation" standards set out above are satisfied, the statements
   may not be used to prove the charged offense. The government's "good
   faith" investigation of the uncharged crime is **not** the basis for an exception
   to the right to counsel provided by the *Massiah* doctrine. Maine v. Moulton.

   For example, in Massiah v. United States, the defendant's codefendant,
   while working for the government, sought to elicit information to determine
   the identities of others involved in the defendant's narcotics transactions.
   While it did not condemn the government's legitimate investigatory efforts,
   the Court nonetheless held that the defendant's statements could not be
   used against him without violating his right to counsel. And in Maine v.
   Moulton, the government allegedly was seeking to investigate a plan to
   harm witnesses to the defendant's offense. Despite this legitimate goal, the
   Court held that statements elicited from the accused could not be used to
   prove the offense with which the defendant had already been charged.

C.   WAIVER OF THE RIGHT TO COUNSEL

The right to counsel recognized by the *Massiah* doctrine **may be waived.** As a
practical matter, waiver issues can arise only when the elicitation is by known
law enforcement officers. See United States v. Henry (observing that "the concept
of a knowing and voluntary waiver . . . does not apply in the context of communications with an undisclosed undercover informant"). To establish a waiver,
the state must prove " 'an intentional relinquishment or abandonment of a

known right or privilege.' " Brewer v. Williams. There must be a **knowing and voluntary** choice to forgo one's entitlement to the assistance of counsel. Id.

1. An "Actual Relinquishment" That Need Not Be "Express"

An **express oral or written waiver** of the Sixth Amendment right to counsel can be sufficient but is **not required.** A waiver can be inferred from a defendant's conduct, considering all the surrounding circumstances. However, the state must prove that the accused actually made **a choice to relinquish** her constitutional entitlement. Without such proof, no waiver can be found. See id. Thus, in Brewer v. Williams, a bare majority of the Court rejected a claim that the accused had waived his right to counsel because the prosecution did not provide adequate proof from which it could be inferred that he had in fact "relinquished" his right.

2. A "Knowing" Waiver

A waiver must be **knowing**—that is, an accused must have adequate knowledge of her entitlement to counsel. As a general rule, the information contained in the *Miranda* warnings provides sufficient information for a valid waiver of the Sixth Amendment right to counsel. Patterson v. Illinois, 487 U.S. 285, 108 S. Ct. 2389, 101 L. Ed. 2d 261 (1988). Consequently, if the government shows that the defendant received *Miranda* warnings and there is no impediment to understanding those warnings, a waiver will probably be sufficiently knowing. It is possible that the government also needs to show that an accused was aware that he had been formally charged with a crime. Id. Because the accused in *Patterson* clearly knew he had been charged, the Court did not need to resolve that issue.

There is one instance, however, in which additional knowledge must be proven. If the defendant has a lawyer and that lawyer attempts to speak with the defendant, a valid waiver cannot be established unless the authorities tell the defendant or he is otherwise made aware of the attorney's efforts. Put simply, **a waiver made by an accused who "was not told that his lawyer was trying to reach him during questioning . . . would not be valid."** Id. Recall that a waiver of *Miranda* counsel in similar circumstances would be valid. See Moran v. Burbine, discussed in Chapter 7, section B.4.b. This distinction in the knowledge needed for a valid waiver of *Miranda*'s Fifth Amendment counsel and *Massiah*'s Sixth Amendment counsel reflects a premise stated in the introduction to this chapter: The *Miranda* and *Massiah* rights to counsel are rooted in different constitutional guarantees that further different policies.

3. A "Voluntary" Waiver

As under *Miranda*, a waiver of the *Massiah* right must be **voluntary.** A waiver of rights that is coerced by some amount of official pressure is invalid. Once adequate official coercion is established, the determination of voluntariness is made in the totality of circumstances, including the individual, subjective attributes of the accused that are relevant to the question whether she made a "free" choice. For further discussion of this requirement, see Chapter 7, section B.4.c.

D.   INVOCATION OF THE RIGHT TO COUNSEL

In Vocation

Cite
Miranda
Silence

When an accused effectively **invokes** his Sixth Amendment right to counsel, **no waiver can be valid unless the accused initiates further communications** with law enforcement. If the authorities initiate communications, statements that are the product of deliberate elicitation are inadmissible. Michigan v. Jackson, 475 U.S. 625, 106 S. Ct. 1404, 89 L. Ed. 2d 631 (1986) (specifically adopting the *Miranda* doctrine rule of Edwards v. Arizona for Sixth Amendment counsel invocations).

1.   What Constitutes an Invocation?

The limitation imposed by the holding of Michigan v. Jackson is virtually identical to that imposed by the *Miranda* doctrine holding of Edwards v. Arizona. For a discussion of the standards used to determine whether an individual has effectively invoked her right to counsel, see Chapter 7, section B.6.a.

Miranda different

One important distinction needs to be mentioned. An accused can effectively invoke the Sixth Amendment *Massiah* right to counsel by making a general request for appointed counsel when she appears in court. See Michigan v. Jackson. It is also arguable that the mere appearance in court with counsel amounts to an adequate invocation of the Sixth Amendment right. See McNeil v. Wisconsin, 501 U.S. 171, 111 S. Ct. 2204, 115 L. Ed. 2d 158 (1991) (assuming a valid invocation based on the defendant's representation at an initial court appearance by a public defender). The defendant does not have to request counsel in the context of an "interrogation" session.

Miranda different

However, if a defendant does effectively assert the Sixth Amendment right to counsel by requesting counsel in court or appearing with counsel in court, he has **not** invoked his *Miranda* entitlement to the assistance of counsel for purposes of custodial interrogation regarding a different, uncharged offense. McNeil v. Wisconsin.

 EXAMPLE AND ANALYSIS

Suppose that a defendant is charged with murder. He appears at his arraignment and asks for an appointed attorney. An officer subsequently approaches the accused, asks if he wants to talk, obtains a waiver of the right to counsel, and deliberately elicits statements. Those statements will be barred because the officer violated the rule of

Michigan v. Jackson. The officer initiated communications following the suspect's invocation of counsel. Doing so rendered the purported waiver invalid.

If the same officer approached the suspect following his arraignment, issued the *Miranda* warnings, secured a waiver, and conducted a custodial interrogation regarding an uncharged rape, the suspect's statements regarding that rape would not be barred by the *Miranda* doctrine rule of Edwards v. Arizona because the suspect's request for counsel was **not** an invocation of his *Miranda* entitlement. Consequently, the officer's initiation of communications was not improper.

---

2.   What Constitutes "Initiation" of Communications by the Suspect or the Authorities?

Michigan v. Jackson holds that once a suspect invokes his Sixth Amendment right, official "initiation" of communications will render a subsequent waiver of counsel invalid. The "initiation" criterion endorsed by *Jackson* is **identical** to the "initiation" criterion imposed by Edwards v. Arizona and its progeny. For a full discussion of that doctrine, see Chapter 7, section B.6.b.ii.

E.   DIFFERENCES BETWEEN THE *MIRANDA* AND *MASSIAH* DOCTRINES

Miranda is based solely on the **privilege against self-incrimination.** *Massiah* is grounded solely on the **right to counsel.** These distinct constitutional foundations have led to distinct doctrinal requirements. Those distinctions must be kept in mind in analyzing *Miranda* and *Massiah* issues:

1.   Custody

Miranda requires custody; *Massiah* does not.

2.   Formal Charges

Massiah requires the "initiation of formal adversary proceedings"; *Miranda* does not.

3.   Interrogation and Deliberate Elicitation

The applicability of *Miranda* hinges on interrogation. While *Massiah* is satisfied by "interrogation," it requires only "deliberate elicitation."

4.   Undercover Agents

Miranda does not apply to activities by unknown government agents. *Massiah* does govern deliberate elicitation by such agents.

5.   Waivers

The entitlements under both doctrines can be waived knowingly and voluntarily. The information in the *Miranda* warnings is generally sufficient "knowledge" for valid waivers under either doctrine. However, in contrast to *Miranda*, waiver of the *Massiah* right may require that the defendant know that he has been charged and does require that he be aware if his attorney has tried to contact him.

6.   Invocations of Counsel

A general request for counsel during a courtroom appearance constitutes an "invocation of counsel" under *Massiah* doctrine, but does not for purposes of *Miranda*. Under both *Miranda* and *Massiah*, when a suspect effectively invokes counsel, a waiver cannot be valid unless the suspect or accused "initiates" further communications.

REVIEW QUESTIONS AND ANSWERS

Question: Barbara was arrested for attempted murder and was taken to the police station. Later that afternoon, while she was in a holding cell, Barbara made incriminating statements to Minnie. Unbeknown to Barbara, Minnie was an undercover police officer who had a concealed tape recorder on her person. Sometime that same afternoon, the prosecutor had filed an information against Barbara. The prosecution intends to introduce Barbara's statements at her trial. Barbara raises a Sixth Amendment objection. How should the judge rule?

Answer: Before the judge can rule properly, two questions need to be answered. First, did the prosecution file the information prior to the time Barbara made the statements to Minnie? If not, Barbara's Sixth Amendment right to counsel had not attached. If so, it had attached. Even if the right attached, there is a second question: Did Minnie engage in any active elicitation? Assuming the recorder was running the entire time, the tape should indicate whether Minnie questioned Barbara or had conversations with her that produced her incriminating statements. Of course, it is also possible that Minnie actively elicited the statements in "silent" ways—by gestures or written inquiries, for example. If she actively elicited the statements, Barbara was entitled to counsel. If she passively received the statements, the encounter was not a critical stage and Barbara had no entitlement to counsel's assistance.

In sum, Barbara's statements are barred by the *Massiah* doctrine **only** if the information was filed before she made them **and** Minnie actively elicited them. Note that there is no need in this case to ask whether there is a basis for attributing Minnie's conduct to the "regular Government." Because Minnie is an "undercover police officer," she **is** the regular Government.

Question: Parker was released on bail pending his trial for lewd and lascivious acts with a minor. On the morning before his trial was to begin, Parker went golfing. He was paired up with Ralph. During the day, Parker, who was nervous about his upcoming trial, made a number of inculpatory remarks. The prosecutor now wishes to have Ralph testify to the content of those remarks. Parker objects on Sixth Amendment grounds. May Ralph testify?

Answer: Parker made his statements the day before trial was to start, clearly after the initiation of adversary proceedings. Therefore, his right to counsel had attached. Nevertheless, the statements are admissible unless: (1) Ralph was working for the state; (2) Ralph actively elicited Parker's remarks; and (3) regular Government agents intentionally created or knowingly exploited a situation in which it was likely that their undercover operative would elicit incriminating statements. Parker must show all three elements to succeed with his Sixth Amendment objection.

THE RIGHT TO COUNSEL AND IDENTIFICATION METHODS

10

CHAPTER OVERVIEW

Prior to 1967, the Supreme Court had not recognized any *constitutional* safeguards against government efforts to secure eyewitness identifications of suspects. To attack the reliability of in-court or out-of-court identifications, a defendant had to rely on cross-examination of witnesses and argument to the jury. In three important opinions issued on the same day in 1967, United States v. Wade, 388 U.S. 218, 87 S. Ct. 1926, 18 L. Ed. 2d 1149 (1967); Gilbert v. California, 388 U.S. 263, 87 S. Ct. 1951, 18 L. Ed. 2d 1178 (1967); and Stovall v. Denno, 388 U.S. 293, 87 S. Ct. 1967, 18 L. Ed. 2d 1199 (1967), the Supreme Court concluded that there are, in fact, two distinct constitutional guarantees that regulate the obtainment and use of identification evidence. One of those guarantees, **the Sixth Amendment right to counsel,** is the topic of this chapter. The other guarantee, **the Due Process Clause,** is the topic of Chapter 11.

Some pretrial identification sessions qualify as "critical stages of the prosecution." At those sessions, defendants have a Sixth Amendment right to the assistance of counsel. (The foundation of the right to counsel is discussed in Chapter 8.) This chapter discusses the criteria used to determine which identification methods give rise to the right to counsel.

More specifically, this chapter addresses:

- **The initiation of adversary proceedings requirement.** As is always the case with the Sixth Amendment right to counsel, the right does not attach at any identification session prior to an initiation of formal proceedings.

- **The nature of the critical identification stage.** Currently, to be a critical stage at which counsel is required, an identification session must involve an accused's

193

physical presence at a "trial-like confrontation" with the government and must not be capable of accurate reconstruction.

- **Waiver of the right to counsel.** The right to counsel for identification processes can be waived. The accused must make a knowing and voluntary decision to relinquish his entitlement.

- **The exclusion of identification evidence.** Identifications secured during un-counseled, critical identification stages must be excluded from trial. Later identifications by the same witness are presumptively excluded, but they may be admitted if the government demonstrates that they have an "independent origin."

A. THE THRESHOLD REQUIREMENT: AN INITIATION OF ADVERSARY PROCEEDINGS

As discussed in Chapter 9, the right to counsel **attaches only** at the **"initiation of adversary judicial criminal proceedings—whether by way of formal charge, preliminary hearing, indictment, information, or arraignment."** Kirby v. Illinois, 406 U.S. 682, 92 S. Ct. 1877, 32 L. Ed. 2d 411 (1972). A suspect **never** has an entitlement to counsel at an identification proceeding held prior to the time that he is formally charged and thereby becomes an "accused." For a full explanation of this requirement, see Chapter 9, section A.

 EXAMPLES AND ANALYSIS

1. A defendant is arrested on probable cause to believe he committed a robbery. At the police station, the robbery victim is asked to take a look at the defendant. The victim identifies the defendant as the man who robbed him. Because mere arrest does not trigger the right to counsel and the defendant was not formally charged at the time the victim made the identification, there was no violation of the right to counsel.

2. A defendant appears without counsel at a "preliminary hearing" to determine whether there is adequate cause to bind him over for trial on charges of rape and other related offenses. A witness identifies the defendant at the hearing. The right to counsel has attached because the preliminary hearing qualifies as an "initiation of formal adversary proceedings." Moore v. Illinois, 434 U.S. 220, 98 S. Ct. 458, 54 L. Ed. 2d 424 (1977). The identification was obtained in violation of the right to counsel and therefore must be excluded from trial.

B. NATURE OF THE CRITICAL STAGE: A "TRIAL-LIKE CONFRONTATION" FOR PURPOSES OF IDENTIFICATION

Even after the initiation of formal proceedings, an accused is not entitled to counsel at all identification processes. The defendant has a Sixth Amendment right to counsel only when the session qualifies as a **"critical stage of the prosecution."** United States v. Wade.

1. "Trial-Like Confrontation" Requirement

An identification procedure cannot qualify as a critical stage unless it involves the **physical presence of the accused at a "trial-like adversary confrontation."** United States v. Ash, 413 U.S. 300, 93 S. Ct. 2568, 37 L. Ed. 2d 619 (1973). The stage is critical if the **defendant is actually present** at a **government-arranged confrontation with a witness** for identification purposes. The session does not have to resemble a "trial" in any other way. Nor must it have any additional "adversarial" aspects.

Consequently, a defendant has a right to counsel at a "corporeal" lineup—a procedure in which he stands with others and a witness attempts to select the perpetrator of an offense. United States v. Wade. A defendant has no right to counsel, however, when his photograph is included in an array shown to an identifying witness. United States v. Ash.

2. "Accurate Reconstruction" Criterion

Even though a method of identification qualifies as a "trial-like confrontation," it can **"cease to be 'critical' "** if it is capable of **"accurate reconstruction"** at the trial and thereby provides the accused with **"the opportunity to cure defects at trial."** United States v. Ash. If that is the case, there is no right to counsel.

Thus, for example, the authorities might take and analyze an accused's blood or handwriting for purposes of identification. That procedure does involve the "physical presence" of the accused at a "trial-like adversary confrontation." Nevertheless, such a confrontation is not a critical stage because "accurate reconstruction" of the identification process is possible and any defects in that procedure can be identified and "cured" at trial. According to the Court, **"knowledge** of the techniques of science and technology **is sufficiently available,** and the **variables** in techniques **few enough,** that the accused has **the opportunity for meaningful confrontation [of the results of such an identification process] at trial."** Id. (quoting United States v. Wade).

EXAMPLE AND ANALYSIS

The Supreme Court has never used the "accurate reconstruction" criterion as a basis for concluding that an "eyewitness identification" process is not a critical stage. It is uncertain whether such a process could ever "cease to be critical" on this basis. Take, for example, a fully videotaped and audiotaped corporeal lineup. On the one hand, it is arguable that counsel could use the tapes to "accurately reconstruct" the identification and "confront" the witness and the identification at trial. Therefore, counsel would not be needed at the pretrial identification session. See United States v. Ash (Stewart, J., concurring) (making a similar argument with regard to a photographic identification).

On the other hand, eyewitness identification processes are not as "scientific" as blood tests or handwriting analysis and they have a greater number of variables. Perhaps most important, once a witness's perceptions and memories have been "tainted" by suggestion at an identification, the witness may "freeze" on the identification. A subsequent attempt to have the witness make an identification may be irreparably and imperceptibly influenced by the uncounseled identification. Furthermore, at trial the witness may insist that the person she identified at the session is the culprit even though that impression was created by the identification session. See United States v. Wade. In sum, it may be difficult, if not impossible, for counsel to "cure" the defects in the initial process at trial.

C. WAIVER OF THE RIGHT TO COUNSEL

As with all Sixth Amendment entitlements to counsel, the right to assistance in identification settings **can be waived.** The government has the burden of proving that the accused actually waived the right to the assistance of counsel. The general requirements for waiver of counsel in identification contexts are the same as those that govern the waiver of *Miranda* and *Massiah* rights to counsel. The waiver must be sufficiently **"knowing"** and **"voluntary."** For a full discussion of the meaning and significance of these two requirements, see Chapter 7, sections B.4.b and B.4.c.

Clearly, an accused must "know" that she is entitled to a lawyer's assistance. It is not at all clear, however, whether any additional knowledge is required for a valid waiver. It is arguable, for example, that an accused must have some awareness of the risks of misidentification, the dangers of government overreaching, and the protection that a lawyer can provide in order to make an " 'intelligent waiver' " of this entitlement to counsel. United States v. Wade.

D. EXCLUSION OF EVIDENCE OBTAINED IN VIOLATION OF THE RIGHT TO COUNSEL

When the state secures an identification in violation of the right to counsel described in this chapter, that identification is **"per se"** barred from the trial. United States v. Wade. It may **never** be used against the defendant at trial.

Any **subsequent identification** by the same witness—usually, but not necessarily, an in-court identification—is **presumptively barred.** That later identification **is admissible,** however, if the government proves **"by clear and convincing evidence"** that it had an **"independent origin."** United States v. Wade. A subsequent identification has an independent origin when it is "based upon observations of the suspect other than [those at] the [uncounseled] identification" session. More specifically, the independent origin standard is satisfied by evidence that the witness's later identification is based on observations at the scene of the crime rather than observations at the unconstitutional identification session. Id.

Various factors are relevant to the "independent origin" inquiry. They include the following:

1. Extent and Quality of the Witness's Opportunity to Observe the Crime

The better the witness's **opportunity to observe** the perpetrator at the scene of the crime, the more likely the subsequent identification has an origin that is independent of the identification session. A weak opportunity to observe will militate against an independent origin finding.

2. Discrepancies Between Any Pre-identification Description by the Witness and the Defendant's Actual Appearance

If the witness gives a **description** after the crime and it is consistent with the **actual appearance** of the defendant, the case for an "independent origin" is enhanced. If there are significant discrepancies between the description and appearance, the case for an independent origin is weakened.

3. Prior Identifications or Failures to Identify the Accused

If the witness made an untainted identification of the accused prior to the uncounseled identification session, that fact will weigh in favor of an "independent origin" finding. If the witness failed to identify the accused when given an earlier opportunity, that fact will count against an independent origin finding.

4. Time Periods Between the Crime and the Two Identifications

Memories fade over time. The longer the period between a witness's observations at a crime scene and the witness's identification of an individual, the less likely it is that the identification is based on those observations. For purposes of determining whether an identification has an independent origin, two time spans would seem pertinent—the time from the crime to the uncounseled session and the time from the crime to the later identification claimed to have an independent source. The longer these periods are, the less supportable an "independent origin" finding will be. Conversely, shorter time periods improve the case for an independent origin finding.

5. Facts About the Uncounseled Identification Session

Any facts that indicate that the uncounseled session was conducted in an unfair or suggestive manner or that the witness's identification was otherwise weak or unreliable will count against an "independent origin" conclusion. Facts indicating a fair session or a reliable identification should provide support for an independent origin conclusion.

The preceding list of factors includes those that have been highlighted by the Supreme Court. It is not necessarily exhaustive. Anything else that tends to suggest that a subsequent identification was actually the product of observations at the crime scene rather than observations at an uncounseled identification session could support an "independent origin" finding. Anything suggesting the contrary should count against an "independent origin" conclusion.

REVIEW QUESTIONS AND ANSWERS

Question: Arnold was arrested for bank robbery. He was later indicted by a grand jury. Subsequently, Arnold participated in a lineup that was videotaped by the authorities. He did not ask for nor did the police offer him counsel. At the lineup, a teller identified Arnold. Later, the bank vice president was shown the videotape. She also identified Arnold. Are the witnesses' identifications admissible at Arnold's trial under the Sixth Amendment?

Answer: The teller's identification must be excluded; the vice-president's is admissible. Arnold's right to counsel attached upon indictment for the robbery. The corporeal lineup at which the teller identified him was a "trial-like confrontation" at which he was physically present. It was, therefore, a "critical stage of the prosecution." The showing of the tape to the vice president, however, was not a critical stage because Arnold was not present. Under the doctrine of *Ash*, Arnold had no entitlement to counsel when the vice president viewed the tape. It should also be noted that if a defendant has the right to counsel, he need not request assistance. If no lawyer is present, the burden is on the government to prove a waiver of the right to counsel. In Arnold's case, there is no evidence that he waived his right.

Question: The 10-year-old son of a wealthy publisher was kidnapped and held for ransom for seven days. After the ransom demand was paid, the child was released. He reported that during his captivity he had not been blindfolded and had spent many hours just a few feet from the woman who had kidnapped him. The child gave a relatively detailed description of the kidnapper. By following a number of leads and relying heavily on the boy's description of his captor, FBI agents arrested Nadine two days later. A week later, Nadine was indicted for kidnapping. The agents immediately brought the kidnap victim to her cell and asked him if Nadine was "the lady who kidnapped you." The boy stared hard at her, then said that Nadine "looks like the lady who held me." Nadine did not have counsel present and had not waived the assistance of counsel. At Nadine's trial, six months after her indictment, the prosecution intends to introduce the boy's identification of Nadine and to have the boy identify her in court. Nadine objects on Sixth Amendment grounds. How should the judge rule?

Answer: The judge must exclude the out-of-court identification but could allow the boy to make an in-court identification. The out-of-court identification is subject to the per se rule of exclusion announced in *Wade* and *Gilbert*. Nadine was indicted, and she was physically present at a "trial-like confrontation." The boy's later identification in court is presumptively excludable, but it may be admitted if the government shows by "clear and convincing evidence" that it has "an independent origin."

The judge *could* find an "independent origin" here. That conclusion could be supported by the following facts: the boy had a chance to observe his kidnapper's face at close range for a considerable period of time; his description matched Nadine's actual appearance; and the initial identification was made just 10 days after the kidnapping.

The judge, however, is not compelled to find an independent origin for the courtroom identification. A finding that the government failed to sustain its clear and convincing evidence burden could be supported by the following facts: at the cell the boy did not seem certain that Nadine was his captor; there will be six months between his kidnapping and the courtroom identification; and the identification session was very suggestive—the boy had one choice, Nadine was in a cell, and the agents asked him if she looked like "the lady who kidnapped you."

In sum, the out-of-court identification is barred. A judge could either admit or exclude the proposed courtroom identification.

DUE PROCESS AND IDENTIFICATION METHODS

CHAPTER OVERVIEW

The Fifth and Fourteenth Amendments prohibit federal and state governments from "depriv[ing] any person of life, liberty, or property, without due process of law." These **Due Process Clauses** guarantee defendants that criminal proceedings will be conducted in accord with principles of **"fundamental fairness."** See *Lisenba v. California*, 314 U.S. 219, 62 S. Ct. 280, 86 L. Ed. 166 (1941). On the same day in 1967 that it decided in *United States v. Wade* and *Gilbert v. California* that the right to counsel imposes limitations on identification processes, the Supreme Court, in *Stovall v. Denno*, 388 U.S. 293, 87 S. Ct. 1967, 18 L. Ed. 2d 1199 (1967), concluded that identification processes could compromise the fundamental fairness of criminal trials. As a result, the Court held that the Due Process Clauses also impose limitations on governmental identification processes and on the admissibility of eyewitness identifications. The due process doctrine first announced in *Stovall v. Denno* and developed by a small number of subsequent opinions is the Court's effort to identify the circumstances in which government-generated identification evidence offends our notion of "fundamental fairness." That relatively simple doctrine is the focus of this short chapter.

Specifically, this chapter addresses:

- **The Due Process Clause concern with "unnecessarily suggestive" identification processes.** Due process is not concerned with questionable eyewitness identification evidence unless that evidence is the product of government "suggestion" that could improperly influence a witness. Moreover, due process is offended only by suggestion that is "unnecessary."

• **The Due Process Clause restrictions on the admissibility of identification evidence.** In identification contexts, the sole concern of the Due Process Clause is the introduction of unreliable evidence. Defendants do not have a "process right" to be treated fairly during identification processes; they do have an "evidentiary right" not to be convicted on the basis of misidentifications caused by governmental suggestion. Consequently, due process prohibits only the introduction of "unreliable" eyewitnesses' identifications. A number of factors are relevant to the reliability of an eyewitness' identification made at a suggestive identification session.

A. THE CONCERN OF THE DUE PROCESS CLAUSE: "UNNECESSARILY SUGGESTIVE" IDENTIFICATION METHODS

From the time the Due Process Clause was first brought to bear on eyewitness identification methods in Stovall v. Denno until today, its concern has been limited to methods that are **suggestive** to the witness in ways that are **not necessary.** An identification procedure threatens due process if it is **"unnecessarily suggestive and conducive to irreparable mistaken identification."** Id. If a process either is not suggestive or is suggestive only in ways that are necessary, it cannot violate due process.

1. Government "Suggestion" Requirement

The Due Process Clause is concerned not with unreliable evidence alone but with unreliability generated by the conduct of government officials. See Colorado v. Connelly, 479 U.S. 157, 107 S. Ct. 515, 93 L. Ed. 2d 473 (1986) (noting that the coerced confession doctrine requires "official coercion" because unreliability alone is a matter that the Constitution leaves to state evidentiary laws). No matter how unreliable an identification is, if its unreliability is not the result of improper governmental identification procedures its use cannot violate due process.

Consequently, to trigger due process scrutiny of an eyewitness identification, the identification must be the product of an official process that is **suggestive.** There must be something about the identification method that could have improperly influenced the witness to select the defendant as the person who committed an offense. The fact that a witness is offered only one choice, that the accused was physically distinguishable from other lineup participants, that the accused's picture was the only mugshot in a photo array, or that officers verbally cued the witness to select the defendant are all examples of suggestive influences.

The Due Process Clause is probably not concerned with the slightest amount of suggestion. There is presumably some "threshold" amount necessary to give rise to a plausible due process claim. See Chapter 6, section B.3 (suggesting that the coerced confession doctrine must require more than a small amount of official coercion). The minimum amount required, however, is not clear. It is arguable that there must be sufficient suggestion to give rise to **"a very substantial likelihood of . . . misidentification."** See Simmons v. United States, 390 U.S. 377, 88 S. Ct. 967, 19 L. Ed. 2d 1247 (1968).

2. "Lack of Necessity" Requirement

The Due Process Clause is concerned only with identification methods that are "**unnecessarily** suggestive." Stovall v. Denno. No matter how suggestive a process is, if there is a need for its suggestive aspects—that is, if there are good reasons why they cannot be eliminated—no due process claim is possible. The logically relevant question is whether *the suggestion* is necessary, not whether *an identification* is necessary.

EXAMPLE AND ANALYSIS

In Stovall v. Denno, an injured victim of an attack was in the hospital. Because she had life-threatening injuries, the police quickly brought a suspect that they had apprehended to the victim's hospital room. The suspect was the only black man in the room and was handcuffed to a police officer. When the police asked the victim if the suspect " 'was the man,' " she identified him as her attacker. Although the identification process was extremely suggestive, the Court rejected the defendant's due process claim because "an immediate . . . confrontation [with the suspect for identification purposes] was imperative" in these circumstances.

The Court's conclusion seems to gloss over a critical distinction. It may well have been necessary to arrange an immediate presentation of the suspect to the victim. Moreover, that necessity to act quickly may have made it impossible to conduct a perfectly fair, nonsuggestive process. Nonetheless, it is still quite arguable that the process that was used was "unnecessarily suggestive." There was no showing that the degree of suggestion present in the actual confrontation was necessary. Officers might have had adequate time to give the victim a choice of more than one black man, they surely could have removed the suspect's handcuffs, and they certainly didn't need to ask whether the suspect was "the man."

B. DUE PROCESS CLAUSE RESTRICTIONS ON THE ADMISSIBILITY OF IDENTIFICATION EVIDENCE

When the government conducts an unnecessarily suggestive identification session, the identification obtained may be excluded from trial by the Due Process Clause. This subsection discusses the criteria for determining which identifications are barred by principles of fundamental fairness and which identifications may be constitutionally used to secure convictions. Put simply, due process is violated only when an **unreliable** eyewitness identification **is introduced.**

1.   Due Process Clause Bars the Use of Tainted Identification Evidence

The government does not violate due process when it subjects a suspect to an unnecessarily suggestive identification method and secures an identification from a witness. A violation of fundamental fairness can occur only **when the product of such a session—a suggested identification—is used at trial to obtain a conviction.** See Manson v. Brathwaite, 432 U.S. 98, 97 S. Ct. 2243, 53 L. Ed. 2d 140 (1977). (For a discussion of the point when due process is violated in the "coerced confession" context, see Chapter 6, section B.7.)

Suggestive identification processes are constitutionally questionable because they give rise to "substantial likelihood[s] of **irreparable misidentification.**" Simmons v. United States. They create a risk that an eyewitness will erroneously identify a person at the identification session and that this initial error will lead the same witness to later misidentifications of the same person. Consequently, when the government engages in unnecessary suggestion, **both an identification made at the session and any subsequent identification are presumptively inadmissible** at trial. Because the use of either the initial identification or a later identification by the witness could lead to an erroneous conviction in violation of due process, both are presumptively excluded from trial.

2.   The Government May Use Any Identification Evidence If It Demonstrates "Reliability"

The presumption of inadmissibility for identifications obtained by means of unnecessarily suggestive methods is rebuttable. A pretrial **identification made at an unnecessarily suggestive session** is admissible if the state establishes its **"reliability."** Manson v. Brathwaite. Moreover, any **subsequent identification** by the same witness is also admissible if it is shown to be **reliable.** See Coleman v. Alabama, 399 U.S. 1, 90 S. Ct. 1999, 26 L. Ed. 2d 387 (1970); Simmons v. United States. See Chapter 10, section D, for a discussion of the different rules governing the admissibility of identifications that are made at or after identification processes conducted in violation of the right to counsel.

The "reliability" inquiry used to determine the admissibility of identifications made at or after suggestive processes is analogous to the "independent origin" inquiry used to determine the admissibility of an identification made subsequent to an uncounseled lineup. See Chapter 10, section D. Despite its label, it is not designed to determine whether a particular identification is likely to be "correct" or "accurate" in some abstract sense. Instead, the reliability inquiry is designed to determine whether an identification "stems from" the witness's observations at the crime scene or from improper official suggestion at the identification session. In the former case, it is "reliable" and its use at trial does not violate due process. In the latter case, the identification is unreliable and is barred by due process.

To overcome the presumption of inadmissibility, the government has the burden of proving reliability by a **preponderance of the evidence.** The "totality" of relevant circumstances should be taken into account. According to the Manson v. Brathwaite Court, relevant factors include:

a. **Witness's opportunity to view the offender at the crime scene.** The better the witness's opportunity to see the offender at the time of the offense, the more likely it is that her identification is the result of observations at the crime scene. A weak opportunity to observe makes it more likely that the government's suggestion prompted the identification.

b. **Witness's degree of attention.** The greater the witness's attention at the time of the crime, the stronger the likelihood that the identification is reliable. If the witness paid limited attention, her identification is less likely to be reliable.

c. **Accuracy of a witness's prior description.** If a witness gives a description of an offender prior to making an identification and that identification is consistent with the identified individual's actual characteristics, it is more likely that the identification by the witness was the product of observations at the crime scene. Material differences between a description and a person's actual appearance indicate that the government's suggestion influenced the witness's identification.

d. **Witness's level of certainty.** The more certain the witness is that the person she is identifying is the person she saw commit the offense, the more likely it is that her identification is based on recollections from the crime. Tentativeness or uncertainty indicates susceptibility to suggestion and, therefore, a greater likelihood that an identification was produced by governmental suggestion.

e. **Time between the crime and the identification confrontation.** The Court assumes that memories fade continuously over time. Consequently, the longer the time between the original viewing of the offender and the identification of an individual, the weaker the case for that identification's reliability. Shorter time periods enhance the case for reliability.

f. **Degree of suggestiveness in the identification process.** The more suggestive the identification process—that is, the greater its potential for influencing a witness to select a particular individual—the less likely it is that the government will be able to establish that an identification was the product of observations made at the crime scene rather than the product of improper suggestion. Consequently, the suggestiveness of an identification procedure is relevant at two stages. First, a minimum amount of suggestion is required to trigger due process scrutiny. Second, the degree of suggestion is an important factor in the reliability calculation. The relevance of suggestion to the reliability of an identification means that the defendant should emphasize every suggestive facet of a process while the government ought to maintain that the suggestiveness of a process was actually quite limited.

REVIEW QUESTIONS AND ANSWERS

Question: Approximately one hour after an attempted rape, Markus was found in an alley two blocks from the scene of the crime. Officers immediately hurried him to the hospital where the victim was receiving outpatient treatment for minor injuries. When the officers brought Markus into the treatment room, the victim said that she was "fairly sure he's the man, but it was dark and I didn't get a real good look." Must this identification be excluded from Markus's trial on due process grounds?

Answer: The answer is uncertain. The government might successfully argue that even though the officers' showing of a single suspect to the victim was highly suggestive, it was necessary to obtain a quick identification so that they could determine whether a dangerous criminal was still at large. The court should require a showing of insufficient time to give the victim a choice of possibilities. If the court finds "necessity" for the suggestive identification process, the Due Process Clause does not call for exclusion.

If the court rejects the necessity claim, then it must determine whether the "reliability" of the identification has been proven by a preponderance of the evidence. The government should maintain that the witness was "fairly sure" and that the time between the crime and the identification was very short. The defendant should argue that the witness had a poor opportunity to see her attacker, that she was not certain that Markus was the man, and that the single person showup was a highly suggestive method of identification. The defendant would seem to have the better side of the "reliability" argument, but the case does not seem so one-sided to require a court to find in his favor.

Question: Two women wearing stocking masks robbed the First Federal Bank. Only one of them spoke. According to the teller who heard her, the robber's voice was "distinctive, very high-pitched." Mirna was arrested eight months later, based on an anonymous tip. Investigators had her speak the words used by the robber into a tape recorder. They also recorded four other women speaking the same words. They then played the audiotape for the teller. She was "almost sure" that Mirna's voice was the one she had heard. It had a high pitch, the highest of any of the voices on the tape. Prior to trial, Mirna moves, on due process grounds, to exclude the out-of-court voice identification and to prohibit the teller from identifying Mirna's voice at trial. How should the judge rule?

Answer: The first question is whether the voice array was "unnecessarily suggestive." The judge would first have to determine whether Mirna's voice was sufficiently distinguishable from the others to render the array too suggestive or if there were other ways in which the session suggested to the witness that she should select Mirna's voice. If so, there appears to be no necessity that would preclude the assembly of a nonsuggestive array.

If the voice identification session was sufficiently suggestive, the next question concerns the reliability of the teller's out of court and in court identifications. To determine reliability, the judge must examine the relevant factors. On the one hand, the teller was "fairly sure" and Mirna's voice was "high-pitched," matching the description given by the teller. These facts would weigh in favor of "reliability." On the other hand, eight months had passed since the teller had heard the voice. This cuts against reliability. The balance in this case could be tipped by facts that are unknown, including whether the teller had a good opportunity to hear the robber's voice and whether the voice array was mildly or extremely suggestive.

Note that both the out-of-court and the in-court identifications are likely to be treated the same—that is, both found reliable or both found unreliable. It is possible, however, for a court to distinguish between an identification made at a suggestive session and one made later. The witness's degree of certainty could differ markedly. Moreover, the time between the crime and the two identifications will certainly be different.

12 THE EXCLUSIONARY RULES

CHAPTER OVERVIEW

The preceding chapters have concentrated on the substance of the constitutional rights that restrict law enforcement's investigatory efforts. In a few instances, the law's responses to official illegalities have been considered. See Chapter 6, sections B.6 and B.7 (due process bar to coerced confessions); Chapter 10, section D (right to counsel bar to identification evidence); Chapter 11, section B (due process bar to identification evidence). For the most part, however, the discussion of *consequences* has been delayed until this, the concluding chapter in Part II. The sole focus of Chapter 12 is **the exclusionary rules,** the rules that define the primary legal consequences for violations of the Fourth, Fifth, and Sixth Amendment doctrines discussed in Chapters 1 through 11.

As will be seen, these exclusionary rules are not all of one kind. Not only are they based on **violations of different constitutional guarantees,** but their **natures and purposes differ.** Some of the rules mandate that evidence be excluded in order **to deter future violations of constitutional rights.** Others require exclusion because **rights would be violated by the use of the excluded evidence.** Some arguably command exclusion for both of these reasons. Moreover, some of the rules are designed to promote the **search for truth** while others are designed to serve other ends and clearly impede the search for truth.

This chapter is divided into two main sections. The first section explains each exclusionary rule and the **rationales** for the various rules. The second section addresses the **operation** of those rules.

A.   THE EXCLUSIONARY RULES AND THEIR RATIONALES

The tendency to refer to **"the exclusionary rule"** suggests that there is only one rule. In fact, there are a number of different rules rooted in different constitutional guarantees. Because the rationales that underlie each of these rules are not identical, they must be considered individually.

An appreciation of each rule and its rationale is very important. First, the legitimacy of an exclusionary rule depends on whether its rationale is defensible. Second, the appropriateness of any limitation on the operation of an exclusionary rule must turn on the rationale that supports that rule. This section explains each exclusionary rule and its rationales.

1.   Fourth Amendment Exclusionary Rule

The Fourth Amendment exclusionary rule originated in Weeks v. United States, 232 U.S. 383, 34 S. Ct. 341, 58 L. Ed. 652 (1914), a federal case. Forty-seven years later, in Mapp v. Ohio, 367 U.S. 643, 81 S. Ct. 1684, 6 L. Ed. 2d 1081 (1961), it was made applicable to the states. The basic command of the Fourth Amendment rule is quite simple: **Evidence acquired by means of an unreasonable search or seizure must be excluded from court.**

At one time, defendants were thought to have a Fourth (or Fourteenth) Amendment **right** to have evidence excluded. See Weeks v. United States; Mapp v. Ohio. According to that view, Fourth Amendment rights were violated when illegally obtained evidence was admitted at trial. Later, two *additional* rationales for Fourth Amendment exclusion were developed: **deterrence** of future Fourth Amendment violations and the preservation of **judicial integrity.** See Mapp v. Ohio.

Today, the Fourth Amendment exclusionary rule no longer rests on these three separate premises. According to the prevailing view, the primary **purpose of the rule is deterrence**—to safeguard constitutional rights in the future by removing officers' incentives to disregard Fourth Amendment restrictions. United States v. Calandra, 414 U.S. 338, 94 S. Ct. 613, 38 L. Ed. 2d 561 (1967). The "rule is **[not] a personal constitutional right** of the party aggrieved" by an illegal search or seizure because the admission of illegally obtained evidence **does not** effect a further violation of the Constitution. Id. The violation of Fourth Amendment rights has been "fully accomplished" by the unreasonable search or seizure. Id. Moreover, the exclusion of evidence does not "repair" a past wrong or compensate the victim of an illegal search.

This exclusionary rule is thought to deter official misconduct by " **'removing the incentive** to disregard' " constitutional restrictions. Mapp v. Ohio. The "profits" of illegality are taken away and officials are put "in the **same [evidentiary] position** they would have occupied if no violation [had] occurred." Murray v. United States, 487 U.S. 533, 108 S. Ct. 2529, 101 L. Ed. 2d 472 (1988). Official illegalities could probably be further deterred if courts went beyond the mere "removal of profit" and "punished" government officials by putting them in a **worse position** than they would have occupied had they not violated the Constitution. The Supreme Court, however, has specifically rejected such a "punitive" approach. See Nix v. Williams, 467 U.S. 431, 104 S. Ct. 2501, 81 L. Ed. 2d 377 (1984). According to the deterrence reasoning that underlies Fourth Amendment exclusion, "while the government **should not profit** from its illegal activity, **neither should it be placed in a worse position** than it would otherwise have occupied." Murray v. United States.

The **judicial integrity** rationale for Fourth Amendment exclusion has not been completely disavowed. Nevertheless, it "has limited force as a justification" for excluding probative evidence. Stone v. Powell, 428 U.S. 465, 96 S. Ct. 3037, 49 L. Ed. 2d 1067 (1976). Moreover, it adds nothing to the deterrence rationale. Judicial integrity is offended only when a court admits evidence in a situation in which exclusion would have a significant deterrent effect. United States v. Leon, 468 U.S. 897, 104 S. Ct. 3405, 82 L. Ed. 2d 677 (1984).

2. Due Process Clause Exclusion of "Coerced Confessions"

The Due Process Clause bars the government from using coerced confessions to obtain convictions. One clear rationale for this "exclusionary rule" is that the **use of such a confession is fundamentally unfair**. See Lisenba v. California, 314 U.S. 219, 62 S. Ct. 280, 86 L. Ed. 166 (1941). It is "substantively" unfair because coerced statements are potentially **untrustworthy** and therefore risk the conviction of innocent persons. Moreover, it is "procedurally" unfair because the use of an involuntary confession **offends a basic principle of fair play inherent in our accusatorial system.** See Spano v. New York, 360 U.S. 315, 79 S. Ct. 1202, 3 L. Ed. 2d 1265 (1959). Consequently, coerced confessions **must** be excluded because their use would violate defendants' **due process rights.** See Mincey v. Arizona, 437 U.S. 385, 98 S. Ct. 2408, 57 L. Ed. 2d 290 (1978).

The exclusion of coerced confessions undoubtedly has the **effect** of **deterring** some official coercion. Officers are less likely to resort to coercion when they know they will be deprived of its fruits. Whether deterrence is a **purpose** of the due process exclusionary rule is uncertain. At least in egregious cases that involve physical or psychological harm to the victim of the coercion, it is arguable that deterrence is another objective sought by due process exclusion.

3. The *Miranda* Exclusionary Rule

The *Miranda* exclusionary rule bars the government from introducing statements acquired in violation of *Miranda*'s safeguards against custodial interrogation. The *Miranda* Court held that "the government **may not** *use* statements" obtained in violation of the "procedural safeguards" it had prescribed.

The rationale for excluding evidence secured in violation of *Miranda* is not entirely clear. As is the case under the Fourth Amendment, an accused clearly has **no constitutional right to exclusion.** See Michigan v. Tucker, 417 U.S. 433, 94 S. Ct. 2357, 41 L. Ed. 2d 182 (1974); New York v. Quarles, 467 U.S. 649, 104 S. Ct. 2626, 81 L. Ed. 2d 550 (1984). A failure to comply with *Miranda* gives rise to a presumption of coercion but **does not constitute "actual compulsion."** New York v. Quarles. In the absence of actual compulsion, there is no reason to conclude that statements obtained are in fact untrustworthy or that their use would undermine principles of fair play. See Michigan v. Tucker. Consequently, the use of a statement secured in violation of *Miranda's* requirements does not violate the Fifth Amendment entitlement of an accused.

One goal of the *Miranda* exclusionary rule is **deterrence.** By barring the use of *Miranda*-violative statements, courts seek to discourage officers from failing to comply with the *Miranda* safeguards. When officers do comply with *Miranda's* scheme, the risks of compelled self-incrimination are diminished.

Deterrence, however, is not the only reason for excluding statements secured in violation of *Miranda.* By prohibiting the introduction of statements made in response to the undispelled pressures of custodial interrogation, *Miranda's* exclusionary rule **"safeguards a 'fundamental trial right' "—the right not to be compelled to be a witness against oneself.** Withrow v. Williams, 507 U.S. 680, 113 S. Ct. 1745, 123 L. Ed. 2d 407 (1993). It "serves to guard against" the possibility that compelled statements—statements that are potentially unreliable and contrary to accusatorial fair play—will be used at trial in violation of the constitutional command. Id.

In sum, the *Miranda* exclusionary rule decreases the risks of unconstitutional compulsory self-incrimination in two ways: (1) it promotes compliance with the *Miranda* safeguards; and (2) it keeps statements that might be compelled from being used at trial to convict.

> **Note:** In cases in which **actual compulsion** is demonstrated, the privilege against self-incrimination grants a **right to exclusion.** The use of a truly compelled statement violates a defendant's explicit Fifth Amendment right. The reasons underlying this exclusionary right are the same as those supporting the right to exclusion granted by due process. See Chapter 6, section B.6.

4.   The *Massiah* Exclusionary Rule

The *Massiah* exclusionary rule provides that "incriminating statements, obtained by [government] agents" in violation of the accused's Sixth Amendment entitlement to counsel, "[can]not be constitutionally used . . . as evidence against *him* at his trial." Massiah v. United States, 377 U.S. 201, 84 S. Ct. 1199, 12 L. Ed. 2d 246 (1964). According to the Court, an accused is "denied the basic protections of [the Sixth Amendment] guarantee **when [the prosecution] use[s] against him at his trial evidence of his own incriminating words.**" Id. These words clearly indicate a rationale for *Massiah*-based exclusion. They suggest that the *Massiah* exclusionary rule is constitutionally required because the **use** of statements obtained in violation of *Massiah* doctrine **violates an accused's Sixth Amendment right to counsel.**

The clarity of the *Massiah* Court's statements has, however, been undercut by later opinions. In Nix v. Williams, the Court merely *assumed for the sake of argument* that the *Massiah* exclusionary rule was part of the defendant's constitutional entitlement, but refrained from endorsing that view. Moreover, the Court did indicate that **deterrence** of future *Massiah* violations **is** an objective of exclusion. At least in part, the *Massiah* rule is designed to insure that officers respect the right to counsel in future situations governed by *Massiah*. See Nix v. Williams. In addition, the Court has held that the Michigan v. Jackson "branch" of *Massiah* doctrine is purely "prophylactic" and that the exclusion of evidence obtained in violation of Michigan v. Jackson is **solely deterrent.** Michigan v. Harvey, 494 U.S. 344, 110 S. Ct. 1176, 108 L. Ed. 2d 293 (1990). See Chapter 9, section D, for a discussion of the *Jackson* holding.

In sum, the *Massiah* exclusionary rule is a **deterrent** device designed to discourage officials from denying counsel. With the exception of violations of the *Jackson* doctrine, the exclusion of statements obtained as a result of *Massiah* violations **may** *also be a constitutional right*.

5. Exclusion of Identification Evidence Under the Fifth and Sixth Amendments

The rules governing the exclusion of identification evidence under the Fifth and Sixth Amendments have been discussed in detail elsewhere in this outline. See Chapter 10, section D; Chapter 11, section B. Here they are reviewed and their rationales are explained.

a. **Identifications obtained in violation of the Sixth Amendment *Wade-Gilbert* right to counsel.** When an identification is made in the absence of counsel in violation of an accused's Sixth Amendment entitlement to the assistance of counsel, that identification is per se excluded and subsequent identifications by the same witness are presumptively excluded. United States v. Wade, 388 U.S. 218, 87 S. Ct. 1926, 18 L. Ed. 2d 1149 (1967); Gilbert v. California, 388 U.S. 263, 87 S. Ct. 1951, 18 L. Ed. 2d 1178 (1967). One clear reason for exclusion is **to deter** officials from denying counsel at future identification sessions. It is also *possible* that the products of uncounseled sessions are excluded because their use would violate the Constitution. It is unclear whether defendants have a constitutional **right** to exclude pretrial and at-trial identifications secured in violation of their Sixth Amendment entitlement.

   b. Identifications obtained in violation of the due process clause safe-guard against "unnecessarily suggestive" identification processes. The Due Process Clause presumptively excludes from trial identifications that are the result of "unnecessarily suggestive" identification processes, but allows the government to introduce any identification that is shown to be reliable. See Chapter 11, sections B.11 and B.2. The clear rationale for excluding identification evidence under this due process doctrine is that its **use** would be fundamentally unfair and would **violate the Due Process Clause.** Consequently, defendants have a **constitutional right** to have the unreliable fruits of unnecessary suggestion excluded. See Manson v. Brathwaite.

B. OPERATION OF THE EXCLUSIONARY RULES: THE SCOPE OF EXCLUSION AND LIMITATIONS ON EXCLUSION

The exclusionary rules all erect a presumptive bar to the use of evidence acquired in violation of the Fourth, Fifth, and Sixth Amendment doctrines discussed in Part II. The presumption of exclusion extends **both** to the **immediate products** of those violations **and** to the **evidence derived from** those immediate products. However, there are many limitations on the operation of these exclusionary rules. Because of these limitations, in many cases evidence that is acquired as a direct or indirect result of official illegality is admissible at trial. This section describes the nature of these limitations and the showings needed to satisfy each of them.

1. General Scope of the Exclusionary Rules: Immediate and Derivative Evidence

The exclusionary rules presumptively exclude evidence acquired **immediately from,** that is, as a **direct result** of, an illegality. In some cases, the presumption is conclusive—the evidence may **never** be used against the accused for any purpose. Thus, for example, there are no exceptions to the rule that coerced confessions may not be used to prove a defendant's guilt. See section A.2 above. In other cases, the state can overcome the presumption of exclusion and introduce the immediate fruits of an illegality. For example, narcotics obtained during an unreasonable search pursuant to an invalid warrant are admissible if officers "reasonably relied on the warrant." See subsection 3.d.iii below.

At least some, if not all, of the "exclusionary rule[s] also prohibit[ ] the introduction of **derivative evidence,** both tangible and testimonial, that is the product of the primary evidence." Murray v. United States, 487 U.S. 533, 108 S. Ct. 2529, 101 L. Ed. 2d 472 (1988). According to the **"fruit of the poisonous tree" doctrine,** evidence that is **derived from** the evidence that is the immediate product of an illegality is also presumptively excludable. Thus, for example, if officers arrest a suspect illegally and immediately obtain a statement that in turn furnishes probable cause to search the suspect's automobile for narcotics, the narcotics are presumptively inadmissible because they were derived from the statements acquired as a direct result of the illegal arrest.

This derivative evidence principle clearly applies to Fourth Amendment violations and to violations of the *Massiah* doctrine. Its application to other kinds of official illegality is not entirely clear. It is uncertain, for example, whether evidence derived from a coerced confession or from a statement obtained in violation of the *Miranda* doctrine is presumptively excludable. In dictum, the Supreme Court has stated that "tangible" evidence derived from compelled statements is **not** barred by the privilege against compulsory self-incrimination. See Oregon v. Elstad, 470 U.S. 298, 105 S. Ct. 1285, 84 L. Ed. 2d 222 (1985) (stating that the "Fifth Amendment . . . is not concerned with nontestimonial evidence"). (Of course, **due process** may bar the use of such evidence.) In addition, the Court has strongly hinted that the *Miranda* exclusionary rule might be restricted solely to the immediate products of illegalities. If so, only the statements obtained by *Miranda*-violative custodial interrogation would be excludable. Every evidentiary product gained as a result of those statements would be admissible.

2. Standing to Raise Exclusionary Rule Claims

To assert an exclusionary rule claim, an individual must have **"standing."** A person has standing only if her rights have been violated by the methods used to obtain evidence or if her rights would be violated by the use of the evidence in court.

a. Fourth Amendment standing limitation. An individual can assert Fourth Amendment exclusion **only if the unreasonable search or seizure** that led to the acquisition of the disputed evidence **violated her Fourth Amendment rights.** Rakas v. Illinois, 439 U.S. 128, 99 S. Ct. 421, 58 L. Ed. 2d 387 (1978); Alderman v. United States, 394 U.S. 165, 89 S. Ct. 961, 22 L. Ed. 2d 176 (1969). To establish a violation of her rights, the individual must show **not only that the search or seizure was unreasonable but also that she was the "victim" of that search or seizure.** To be a "victim," she must show that the search or seizure **infringed on her** Fourth Amendment interests. Rakas v. Illinois.

To determine if an individual has been deprived of a Fourth Amendment interest, the *nature* of the alleged unconstitutionality must be ascertained. If evidence was allegedly acquired by means of an **unreasonable search,** the individual must show a **"legitimate expectation of privacy" in the place searched.** Rakas v. Illinois. If the claim is based on an **unreasonable seizure of the person—an arrest or detention**—the individual must show a deprivation of her own **physical freedom.** If the claimed violation involves a **seizure of property,** the individual must show an **ownership or possessory interest in the item seized.**

i.   **Standing to object to the search of a place.** The most frequently litigated and difficult questions arise in connection with **standing to object to the search of a place.** The sole question is whether the individual has a **legitimate expectation of privacy in the place searched.** Rakas v. Illinois; Rawlings v. Kentucky, 448 U.S. 98, 100 S. Ct. 2556, 65 L. Ed. 2d 633 (1980). The answer depends on all the factors bearing on the individual's connection to the place.

Typically, **ownership of a place that is searched** gives rise to a legitimate expectation of privacy in that place. Rakas v. Illinois. The owner, therefore, has standing to object to a search. Nonetheless, ownership is not conclusive. If other circumstances indicate that the owner lacks a legitimate expectation of privacy in the place owned, she will not have standing to object to a search of the place.

The following factors all *support* an individual's claim that she has a legitimate expectation of privacy in a place that is searched: **legitimate presence in the place, guest status, and an ownership or possessory interest in the item seized during the search.** However, **none** of these **is alone sufficient** to establish a legitimate expectation of privacy. See Rakas v. Illinois; Rawlings v. Kentucky.

 Proof that one was an **overnight guest** in a home will establish a legitimate expectation of privacy in the home. Consequently, an overnight guest has standing to object to a search of the home. Minnesota v. Olson, 495 U.S. 91, 110 S. Ct. 1684, 109 L. Ed. 2d 85 (1990).

property interest matter Other factors relevant to whether one has a legitimate expectation of privacy in a place include the amount of **prior use of** or **time spent in** a place, one's **relationship to the owner,** and whether one has the **right to exclude** others.

ii.   **Standing to object to seizures of persons or of effects.** Issues of standing to claim the exclusion of evidence acquired by means of an allegedly **illegal seizure of a person or effect** are more easily resolved. To object to the seizure of a person, an individual must show that **his freedom of action** was infringed on by the seizure. Put simply, only the person arrested or detained can object to evidence acquired by means of such a seizure. To object to the seizure of an effect, one must demonstrate **a property interest in**

the item—that is, either an ownership or possessory interest of some sort.

EXAMPLE AND ANALYSIS

Federal agents correctly conclude that a bank's customers do not have legitimate expectations of privacy in the area inside the banker's briefcase. As a result, the agents deliberately conduct unjustifiable searches of the banker's briefcase in order to discover records of illegal transactions by the bank's customers. A court concludes that because the searches were deliberate Fourth Amendment violations designed to take advantage of the "standing" limitation the evidence must be suppressed from the bank customers' trials. Is the court correct?

No. The court failed to recognize that a successful exclusionary rule claim rests on two showings: that the search or seizure was unlawful **and** that it violated the rights of the objecting party. No matter how egregiously or deliberately unconstitutional a search or seizure may be, the evidence obtained will not be excluded unless the person asserting exclusion had a Fourth Amendment interest that was intruded on. "Standing" to object is an independent and essential predicate for exclusion. See Payner v. United States, 447 U.S. 727, 100 S. Ct. 2439, 65 L. Ed. 2d 468 (1980).

b. **Standing to raise other kinds of violations.** The Supreme Court's standing cases have all involved Fourth Amendment claims. Nonetheless, the same principles that govern standing to raise Fourth Amendment exclusionary rule claims almost certainly apply to most, if not all, other kinds of constitutional violations discussed in Part II. Equivalent standing limitations should apply whether the exclusionary rule is a deterrent safeguard or a constitutional right or both.

For example, only the individual subjected to custodial interrogation has standing to seek the exclusion of a statement based on an alleged *Miranda* violation. Only the accused whose statements have been deliberately elicited in the absence of counsel can raise an exclusionary claim based on *Massiah* doctrine. And only the person identified can seek to exclude an identification on the basis of a violation of the *Wade-Gilbert* right to counsel.

The due process–coerced confession doctrine raises an interesting standing issue: Must a defendant be the victim of coercion in order to claim the exclusion of a coerced confession? It is arguable that any defendant should be able to object to the use of a coerced confession because the introduction of the confession will itself violate his due process right to a fair trial. Because that trial right belongs to the defendant, he should have standing to seek exclusion even though he was not the victim of the coercion. With regard to a different due process claim, however, the Supreme Court has held that only the victim of the government's out-of-court conduct had standing to raise an exclusionary rule claim at trial. See United States v. Payner (even if a deliberate and egregious violation of the Fourth Amendment also violates due process, only the victim of the search can raise a due process–based exclusionary claim).

EXAMPLE AND ANALYSIS

Maddie is taken into custody in connection with the highly suspicious death of her infant. After she asks for a lawyer, officers initiate communications with her about the infant's death and obtain a waiver of rights. During custodial interrogation, Maddie incriminates herself and her live-in boyfriend in the death of the child. Should a court exclude the statements from Maddie's and the boyfriend's trials?

Maddie has a valid claim for exclusion under *Miranda*. Officers violated the rule of *Edwards v. Arizona* by initiating communications. The waiver is invalid and the statements are inadmissible at her trial. The boyfriend, however, has no standing to assert the violation of Maddie's *Miranda* "rights."

---

3.   Exceptions to the Exclusionary Rules

The doctrines discussed in this subsection are typically referred to as the **"exceptions" to the exclusionary rules.** When evidence falls within an exception to an exclusionary rule, the government may introduce it at trial even though it is the product of an illegality and the person claiming exclusion has standing to object. Some exceptions apply only to **derivative evidence,** while others pertain also to the **primary products** of illegal conduct.

Before discussing the exceptions, a significant distinction in terminology must be explained. As noted earlier, the "derivative evidence principle" means that the products of illegalities are "presumptively excludable." If evidence that is the product of an illegality falls within an exception to an exclusionary rule, however, it is admissible. The phrase **"fruit of the poisonous tree"** does **not** refer to **all products of illegalities,** but **only** to **products that must be excluded.** Consequently, illegally acquired evidence that is admissible under an exception to an exclusionary rule is **not** the "fruit of the poisonous tree." See Wong Sun v. United States, 371 U.S. 471, 83 S. Ct. 407, 9 L. Ed. 2d 441 (1963) (not all of the "but for" products of Fourth Amendment violations must be excluded as "fruit of the poisonous tree").

a. **"Independent source" doctrine.** Sometimes evidence is acquired both by means of illegal conduct and also by means of independent legal conduct. When that is the case, the evidence that was legally discovered is admissible by virtue of the **"independent source" doctrine.** See Murray v. United States, 487 U.S. 533, 108 S. Ct. 2529, 101 L. Ed. 2d 472 (1988); Silverthorne Lumber Co. v. United States, 251 U.S. 385, 40 S. Ct. 182, 64 L. Ed. 319 (1920).

Although the independent source doctrine is typically referred to as an exception to the exclusionary rules, in fact it is not. The exclusionary rules apply only to evidence that is derived immediately or secondarily from an illegality. Only evidence that has been obtained by illegal means is presumptively excludable and, therefore, needs to come within an exception in order to be admissible. Evidence derived from an independent source is admissible not because it qualifies for an exception to the exclusionary rules but because it has not been acquired by means that make it subject to exclusion. Put otherwise, because evidence gained from an independent source is not governed by the exclusionary rules, there is no need for an "exception."

The independent source doctrine applies in two somewhat different situations. In one situation, certain information is first learned in an illegal way and then the **very same information** is learned by independent legal methods. Even though the information acquired legally is identical to the information gained illegally, it is nonetheless admissible because it was derived from a source independent of the illegality.

Suppose that federal agents illegally arrest an accountant and search his briefcase. They find records probative of large-scale tax fraud. Other agents, following other leads, develop probable cause to search the accountant's office. They find duplicates of the records that were illegally discovered in the briefcase. Even though the same information that was illegally found in the first search was discovered in the independent and lawful second search, the information contained in the second set of records is admissible under the independent source doctrine.

In the other situation, the **very same item of evidence** is discovered twice, once illegally and once legally. So long as the legal means of discovery is truly independent of the illegal means of discovery, the evidence will fall within the independent source doctrine. The fact that the very same item was found illegally does not matter so long as the evidence that the government seeks to introduce has been found by wholly legal means.

Suppose that an officer is suspicious of a particular vehicle. Without probable cause, he opens the passenger's door and looks in the glove compartment, where he discovers contraband. Without touching the contraband he closes the compartment and the car door and sets up surveillance on the car. A second officer, acting wholly independently and on the basis of a reliable informant's tip, arrests the driver of the automobile after he pulls away from the curb. Pursuant to a valid search incident to this arrest, he opens the glove compartment and finds the contraband. Both the information about the contraband's location in the car and the contraband itself are admissible under the independent source doctrine.

Government conduct will not qualify as an independent source if there is a causal connection between the illegality and the allegedly legal conduct. If information gained from illegal conduct is used to justify otherwise legal conduct or if officers decide to take a legal action because of what they learned from an illegality, the independent source doctrine will not apply. If the illegal action enables or facilitates the success of the legal conduct, the legal conduct should not qualify as an independent source.

The Supreme Court has applied the independent source doctrine to Fourth Amendment violations. Logically, it should apply to every kind of illegality discussed in Part II.

 # EXAMPLE AND ANALYSIS

Murry Facts

In **Murray v. United States,** officers illegally entered a warehouse and saw bales of marijuana. They left the marijuana in place and obtained a warrant to search the warehouse. On executing the warrant, they saw the marijuana a second time. This time they seized the bales. The Supreme Court held that both the officers' knowledge that the marijuana was in the warehouse and the marijuana itself would be admissible under the independent source doctrine if (1) no facts learned in the illegal entry were used to establish probable cause for the warrant **and** (2) the decision to seek the warrant was not "prompted by what the[officers] had seen during the initial [illegal] entry." If the officers had either relied on what they saw during the initial entry to establish probable cause for the warrant or made up their minds to secure a warrant because of their discovery during the initial entry, the warranted search would **not** have been an independent source. The allegedly legal search would have been "dependent on," not "independent of," the illegal search.

b.   **"Inevitable discovery" exception.** Sometimes evidence that **could have** been acquired by legal means available to the authorities has **in fact** been acquired by illegal means. Because the evidence can be traced to illegal governmental conduct, it is presumptively excludable. The government, however, may be able to introduce the evidence by relying on the **inevitable discovery exception** to the exclusionary rules. See Nix v. Williams, 467 U.S. 431, 104 S. Ct. 2501, 81 L. Ed. 2d 377 (1984).

i. **The showing required to establish inevitable discovery.** To rely on the inevitable discovery exception, the government must show "by a **preponderance of the evidence** that the [item sought to be introduced] **ultimately or inevitably would have been discovered by lawful means.**" Nix v. Williams. Although the government may demonstrate that the lawful avenue was already being pursued at the time of the illegal acquisition, the inevitable discovery exception has not been restricted to cases in which the officers have actually begun to employ the legal means.

    The government does **not** have to show either **good faith or an absence of bad faith** on the part of the officers who used the illegal method. The exception applies even if the officers knew that their actions were unlawful, knew that there was a lawful alternative, and deliberately chose the unlawful route because it would expedite the discovery of the evidence. Nix v. Williams.

ii. **Differences between the independent source doctrine and inevitable discovery exception.** An item gained from an independent source is not the product of government illegality. It is admissible because it is outside the scope of the exclusionary rules. The inevitable discovery doctrine is "closely related to" the independent source doctrine and is sometimes referred to as the "hypothetical independent source" exception. Id. The critical difference, however, is that evidence admissible under the inevitable discovery doctrine **was in fact the product of an illegality.** An independent, lawful means is hypothesized but was not actually used to acquire the evidence. The inevitable discovery doctrine is a true exception to the presumptive exclusion of illegally obtained evidence.

iii. **Exclusionary rules that are subject to the inevitable discovery exception.** In Nix v. Williams, the Supreme Court held that inevitable discovery **is** an exception to the exclusion of evidence based on violations of the Sixth Amendment right to counsel defined by the *Massiah* doctrine. Although the body of a murder victim was in fact found because of an official's deliberate elicitation of incriminating statements from an accused in the absence of his counsel, the Court allowed admission of the evidence because of an ongoing legal search for the body that would inevitably have discovered the very same evidence. The *Nix* Court concluded that insofar as *Massiah*-based exclusion was designed to **deter** future misconduct, inevitable discovery did not undermine that objective. Furthermore, even if *Massiah*-based exclusion is a **constitutional**

right of the accused, admitting evidence that would inevitably have been discovered did not infringe on that right. In sum, the Court held that the inevitable discovery exception is consistent with the two rationales that underlie *all* exclusionary rules. That strongly suggests that inevitable discovery is an exception to all such rules—that is, that evidence that would inevitably have been discovered is admissible no matter what kind of illegality led to the actual discovery of the evidence.

It is arguable that inevitable discovery should not apply to at least one Fourth Amendment context. Suppose that officers have probable cause to search but fail to obtain a warrant without good reason. They later claim that the evidence obtained as a result of their unreasonable, warrantless search would have inevitably been discovered during the warranted search that they would have conducted had they not acted without a warrant. Admission of the evidence under the inevitable discovery exception would seem to be in tension with the policies that underlie the "cardinal rule" that "warrantless searches are per se unreasonable." See Chapter 4, sections 1.a and 1.b.

   iv.   **Applicability of the inevitable discovery exception to both primary and derivative evidence.** In *Nix*, inevitable discovery was applied to admit **derivative evidence**—facts learned from a body that was found from statements that were the primary product of an official illegality. The logical premises of the inevitable discovery exception, however, suggest that it is **equally applicable to primary products** so long as the requisite showing of inevitability is made.

E&A EXAMPLE AND ANALYSIS

Officers suspect that Willy murdered a female acquaintance. Knowing that they lack probable cause, they pull him over and search his vehicle. In the trunk, they find traces of the victim's hair and skin and a piece of clothing that is stained with blood matching the victim's. At trial, the prosecutor seeks to prove that other officers were engaged in a separate investigation that would have led to a witness who would have placed the victim in Willy's car shortly before her death. Should the evidence found in the car be admitted under the "inevitable discovery" exception?

The evidence may be admissible by virtue of inevitable discovery. The fact that the evidence is primary rather than derivative should not matter. Nor should the fact that the officers discovered the evidence by violating the Fourth Amendment. The inevitable discovery exception is consistent with the solely deterrent purposes of Fourth Amendment exclusion. Moreover, the officers' knowledge that they lacked probable cause is irrelevant to the application of the inevitable discovery exception.

The only thing that needs to be shown, by a mere preponderance of the evidence, is that **the officers inevitably would have discovered the same evidence.** The government would have to satisfy the court that it is more likely than not that they would have pursued the legal investigation and that it would have led to a search of Willy's car at a time when the evidence of the murder was still present in the car. If there is no showing that the officers would have followed the legal course or if the risk of removal or destruction or deterioration of the evidence is too high, a court could not find that it is more likely than not that the evidence would have been discovered. In that situation, the court should not admit the evidence.

---

c.   **Attenuation exception.** The presumption is that every item of evidence derived from an official illegality must be excluded. Nonetheless, there comes a "point at which the connection [between the item and] the unlawful [conduct] becomes 'so attenuated as to dissipate the taint.' " Murray v. United States. At that point, the **"attenuation exception"** to the exclusionary rules applies and permits introduction of the item.

   i.   **The showing required to establish the attenuation exception.** There is no bright doctrinal line for determining whether illegally obtained evidence—evidence that would not have been acquired "but for" official misconduct—falls within the attenuation exception. A court must decide " 'whether . . . the evidence to which instant objection is made has been **come at by exploitation of that illegality or instead by means sufficiently distinguishable to be purged of the primary taint.' "** Wong Sun v. United States, 371 U.S. 471, 83 S. Ct. 407, 9 L. Ed. 2d 441 (1963).

   More specifically, the primary object of an attenuation inquiry is to determine the nature and strength of the **connection between the illegality and the acquisition of an item of evidence.** At some point, this connection is so weak or protracted that the deterrent value of exclusion is thought to be outweighed by the cost of exclusion. See Brown v. Illinois, 422 U.S. 590, 95 S. Ct. 2254, 45 L. Ed. 2d 416 (1975). At that point, the evidence falls within the attenuation exception.

   ii.   **Factors relevant to attenuation determinations.** Any circumstance that bears on the connection between the illegality (the "poisonous tree") and the evidence (the alleged "fruit") is relevant. Those circumstances include:

   (a)   **Time between the illegality and the acquisition of the evidence.** The longer the time period between the misconduct and the discovery of the evidence, the stronger the case for attenuation. Id.

(b)   Intervening circumstances between the illegality and the acquisition of the evidence. Any "significant event" in the chain of events leading from the illegal conduct to the discovery of the disputed evidence weakens the connection between the two. Id. A defendant's arraignment in court, the receipt of *Miranda* warnings, or some independent action of a third person—such as a visit by a family member—could qualify as an "intervening circumstance" that enhances the case for attenuation.

(c)   An excerise of "free will" by an accused or other person. Free will is a specific kind of "intervening circumstance" that can weaken the causal chain between an illegality and the acquisition of evidence. Wong Sun v. United States; United States v. Ceccolini, 435 U.S. 268, 98 S. Ct. 1054, 55 L. Ed. 2d 268 (1978). An illegality may create an opportunity for official interaction with an individual such as a defendant or witness. Evidence may be discovered as a result of an exercise of free will by that individual. Although the intervention of the individual's free will does not sever the connection between the illegality and the discovery of the evidence, it can support the application of the attenuation exception to that evidence.

A *sufficient* **exercise of free will** can be enough by itself to support a finding of attenuation. Wong Sun v. United States; Brown v. Illinois. The mere fact that an individual was **not forced to act,** however, is not a sufficient exercise of free will to attenuate automatically a connection between any earlier illegality and the evidence discovered through that individual.

EXAMPLES AND ANALYSIS

1. In Wong Sun v. United States, a defendant was arrested without probable cause. After he was "released on his own recognizance," he "returned several days later to make a statement." The Court held that this statement was "sufficiently an act of free will" to be attenuated from the taint of the illegal arrest.

2. In Brown v. Illinois, the accused was also arrested without probable cause. He made inculpatory statements after receiving *Miranda* warnings and waiving his rights. The lower court adopted a per se rule, concluding that the official compliance with *Miranda* automatically attenuated the connection between the unlawful arrest and the defendant's statements. The Supreme Court rejected the per se rule and held that compliance with *Miranda* alone did not make the accused's decision to confess **"suffi-**

Wong Sun
Facts

Brown
Facts

ciently an act of free will'' to attenuate the taint of the illegal arrest. While compliance with *Miranda* does demonstrate an *absence of compulsion* that is *relevant* to the attenuation inquiry, it does not establish a *sufficient exercise of free will* to weaken the causal connection between the illegality and the acquisition of the evidence.

> **(d) Nature and character of the official misconduct.** Although it is not directly related to the strength of the causal connection between an illegality and an item of evidence, the **"purpose and flagrancy of the misconduct"** is relevant to attenuation inquiries. Brown v. Illinois. Evidence that is the product of an intentional or egregious illegality is less likely to fall within the attenuation exception than evidence that is the product of carelessness or a reasonable mistake about the legality of a particular act. Put otherwise, the more "culpable" or "extreme" the misconduct, the weaker or more extended the causal chain that is needed to qualify for attenuation.

[handwritten margin note: u. inentable doctrine]

iii. Applicability of the attenuation exception to derivative evidence only. The basis for invoking the attenuation exception is a showing that the connection between official illegality and the acquisition of evidence is weakened or protracted in some way. Consequently, the exception cannot apply to primary evidence that is found as an immediate result of illegality. Only derivative evidence—evidence that is not immediately connected to the unlawful conduct but is acquired at some remove—can qualify.

iv. The special case of "live-witness testimony." All kinds of evidence acquired by illegal means are subject to exclusion. At one time, no distinctions were made between tangible items and verbal evidence. See Wong Sun v. United States. Today, **"live-witness testimony"** is treated differently from other kinds of evidence. Specifically, courts should more readily find attenuation when the illegally obtained evidence is live-witness testimony. United States v. Ceccolini. A causal connection that would be too strong or too direct to allow the admission of a tangible piece of evidence may be sufficiently attenuated to permit the admission of "live-witness testimony" under the attenuation exception. Id.

EXAMPLE AND ANALYSIS

Officers illegally search Max's office without a warrant. They find a reference to Sally and information that gives them probable cause to search Sally's home. After looking up Sally's address, officers secure a search warrant for her home. In Sally's home they find illegal weapons that they connect to Max's illegal enterprises, and a visitor who is willing to answer the officers' questions and testify in court about Max's illegal activities. The government acknowledges that the search of Max's office was unreasonable, but argues that the weapons and the witness's statements and testimony should be considered attenuated.

In this case, the evidence that the government seeks to fit within the attenuation exception derives from the initial violation of Max's rights. The time and number of steps needed to find the derivative evidence count in favor of attenuation. The character of the illegality—whether it was deliberate or flagrant—needs to be examined. Moreover, a court might well make a distinction between the weapons and the witness's evidence. Not only is there an "intervening free will" in the case of the witness's testimony, but, as a general rule, courts should be more receptive to finding a connection attenuated in the case of live-witness testimony.

---

v. The doctrine of Oregon v. Elstad: A case of "presumptive attenuation." In Oregon v. Elstad, 470 U.S. 298, 105 S. Ct. 1285, 84 L. Ed. 2d 222 (1985), officers custodially interrogated a suspect without giving *Miranda* warnings or obtaining a waiver. The suspect made incriminating remarks. Shortly afterward, the officers again conducted a custodial interrogation, this time after warning the suspect and securing a waiver. The suspect again incriminated himself. The Oregon Supreme Court held that the second incriminating statement was a presumptively inadmissible product of the first statement because the suspect was aware that he had "let the cat out of the bag." That awareness presumably made him more willing to make the second statement. According to the Oregon court, the government could introduce the second statement only if it demonstrated that the connection between the initial failure to comply with *Miranda* and the second statement was "attenuated."

The Supreme Court rejected the "cat out of the bag" premise and held that **any connection** between an initial failure to warn and a subsequent statement made after compliance with *Miranda* was **"speculative and attenuated at best."** In essence, the Court presumed that in situations like that in *Elstad*, **either no connection exists** between the *Miranda* violation and the second statement **or any connection** that does exist **is always sufficiently attenuated.** Consequently, although the first statement had to be excluded because of the failure to warn the suspect, the second statement, made after compliance with *Miranda*, was not excludable. Contrary to the Oregon court's holding, there was no need for the government to establish that the causal connection between the *Miranda* violation and the second statement was attenuated.

The *Miranda* violation at issue in *Elstad* was a failure to warn the suspect (and secure a waiver). It is unclear whether the *Elstad* doctrine is applicable when an initial *Miranda* violation is of a different sort—for example, a failure to honor a suspect's request for counsel or a failure to honor scrupulously a suspect's wish to remain silent.

Clearly, if the authorities use **actual coercion** to obtain an initial statement, a later statement is presumed to be inadmissible even if the authorities have complied with *Miranda*. If the government wishes to introduce a subsequent statement, it has the burden of showing that the "coercive impact" of the first encounter "dissipated" prior to the making of the second statement and, consequently, that the "coercion [did not] carr[y] over into the second confession." Id. Relevant factors include "the time that passes between confessions, the change in place of interrogations, and the change in the identity of the interrogators." Id.

Note: As mentioned in subsection 1 above, dictum in *Oregon v. Elstad* hints that the *Miranda* exclusionary rule might be restricted to statements that are the immediate product of *Miranda* violations. If that were truly the case, all derivative evidence would be admissible. There would never be a need to justify the introduction of derivative evidence by establishing that it falls within an exception to the exclusionary rule. The *Elstad* doctrine itself would be superfluous since statements obtained after compliance with *Miranda* would be outside the presumptive scope of the *Miranda* exclusionary rule. After the Court's favorable treatment of *Miranda* exclusion in *Withrow v. Williams*, see section A.3 above, it seems less likely that this dictum will become a holding.

EXAMPLE AND ANALYSIS

Kory was handcuffed and put in a police car after being found hiding near the scene of an attempted sexual assault. Officer Dean approached him and said, "It's best if you come clean now." Kory admitted that he had attacked a woman. Minutes later, while he was being transported to the jail, Officer Dean read Kory the *Miranda* warnings and asked him if he understood them. Kory said he did. Dean then asked if he would sign a written waiver. Kory did so. Following the waiver, Dean asked Kory if he would please make a statement of the facts into a tape recorder. Kory then repeated his admission of guilt and added details that he had not related the first time.

Prior to Kory's trial, his attorney moved to suppress both of his statements because of the initial failure to warn him. The judge found that Officer Dean's failure to warn Kory was a deliberate attempt to secure an admission of guilt in violation of *Elstad* and that the time between the first and second statements was so short that Kory had to feel that there was no point in remaining silent the second time. Because "the connection between the *Miranda* violation and the second admission was not attenuated," the judge suppressed both statements. The government appealed the ruling.

The appellate court should reverse the suppression of the second statement. The first statement was obtained in violation of *Miranda* because the officer custodially interrogated Kory without warnings. The second statement, however, is admissible under the *Elstad* doctrine because the connection between the failure to warn and that statement is "speculative and attenuated, at best." Under *Elstad*, the bad faith of the officer is irrelevant, and the prosecution does not have to demonstrate attenuation.

---

vi. **Exclusionary rules that are qualified by the attenuation exception.** The attenuation exception was developed in connection with the Fourth Amendment exclusionary rule. Assuming that evidence derived from *Miranda* violations is presumptively inadmissible (see subsections 1 and 3.c.v. above), the attenuation exception almost certainly is available to justify its admission.

The Fourth Amendment and *Miranda* exclusionary rules are not constitutional rights of the defendant. It is not entirely clear whether the attenuation exception applies to exclusionary rules that are at least in part personal, constitutional rights of the accused. It is arguable that the **right to exclude** logically extends to every item derived from governmental misconduct. Nonetheless, there are some indications in the Court's opinions that it would recognize an attenuation exception for exclusionary rules that enforce constitutional rights. For example, in Oregon v. Elstad the Court stated that if officials coerce a confession from an accused and the accused later makes a second statement in noncoercive circumstances, the second statement could be admitted if the government were to show that the " 'coercive impact' of the inadmissible statement" had been "dissipated." Moreover, when the Court first endorsed the attenuation exception to the Fourth Amendment exclusionary rule, the prevailing view was that defendants had a constitutional right to exclusion.

EXAMPLE AND ANALYSIS

Officers twist Natalie's arm until she confesses to robbing a bank and tells them who her accomplice was. By questioning the accomplice, officers find the proceeds of the robbery. Assuming that the government can establish an "attenuated connection" between the coerced confession and the proceeds of the robbery, could they be admitted at Natalie's trial?

The answer is uncertain. On the one hand, Natalie could argue that the proceeds of the robbery are clearly the product of coercion and that the use of any product of coercion is fundamentally unfair. Her right to exclusion under the Due Process Clause mandates exclusion. She could distinguish the case in which the disputed evidence is a second confession that follows an initial, coerced confession. In that case, if the government demonstrates that the coercion did not "carry over" to the second statement, there is arguably no causal link between the violation and that statement. In this case, a causal link between the coercion and the tangible proceeds is clearly present.

The government should argue that the absolute prohibition on use imposed by the Due Process Clause applies only to the statements that are coerced. If evidence derived from those statements is sufficiently "attenuated," it is not fundamentally unfair to use the evidence to obtain a conviction.

---

   d. **"Good faith" exception.** The attenuation exception depends in part on the "character" of the official violation—that is, on the extent of its departure from acceptable conduct and the culpability of government officials. The **"good faith" exception** to the exclusionary rule rests *entirely* on the character of the official transgression.

   The label "good faith exception" can be misleading. In fact, the doctrine is not concerned with the actual "good faith" of anyone and can apply even when officers act in total "bad faith." See United States v. Leon, 468 U.S. 897, 104 S. Ct. 3405, 82 L. Ed. 2d 677 (1984). Moreover, the exception is not as broad as its name might suggest. So far, it has been confined to a limited number of situations in which the Fourth Amendment violations are the fault of someone other than the police officer who has conducted an illegal search or seizure. See United States v. Leon (exception held applicable to errors made by magistrates issuing warrants); Illinois v. Krull, 480 U.S. 340, 107 S. Ct. 1160, 94 L. Ed. 2d 364 (1987) (exception held applicable to errors made by legislators); Arizona v. Evans,—U.S.—, 115 S. Ct. 1185, 131 L. Ed. 2d 34 (1995) (exception held applicable to errors made by court employees).

    i. **Applicability of the good faith exception to Fourth Amendment violations.** The current good faith exception applies only to the **Fourth Amendment exclusionary rule.** All three of its variations have been developed for evidence that is the product of an unreasonable search or seizure. Analogous exceptions could be developed for other exclusionary rules. It is possible, for example, that a good faith exception to *Miranda*-based exclusion might be recognized. For the present, however, the good faith exception justifies only the admission of evidence obtained in violation of the Fourth Amendment.

    ii. **Admissibility of both primary and derivative products under the good faith exception.** The good faith exception allows the government to use **both primary and derivative evidence** that has been acquired by illegal means. It is the first exception to allow the government to use the immediate, primary products of illegalities as substantive evidence against the person whose Fourth Amendment rights have been violated. But see subsection 3.b.iv above (suggesting that the logic of the inevitable discovery exception leads to the conclusion that it applies to both primary and derivative evidence).

ⓔⓐ EXAMPLE AND ANALYSIS

Officers apply for a warrant to search an apartment. After questioning whether the showing of cause is adequate, the magistrate decides to issue the warrant. In the apartment, officers find incriminating notes and information that leads them to a locker where contraband is found. The search of the apartment is determined to have been unreasonable because the officers did not furnish probable cause for the warrant. Under the attenuation exception, there is no possibility that the notes found in the apartment could be admitted. They are the direct, primary products of the illegality found during the search. Only the contraband is arguably admissible. In contrast, if the good faith exception is satisfied here, both the notes and the derivative contraband could be admitted.

    iii. **Doctrinal requirements and limitations of the *Leon-Sheppard* good faith exception.** The primary good faith exception was recognized and explained in United States v. Leon and in Massachusetts v. Sheppard, 468 U.S. 981, 104 S. Ct. 3424, 82 L. Ed. 2d 737 (1984).

    (a) **"Objectively reasonable reliance on a warrant" standard.**

The *Leon-Sheppard* good faith exception applies **only** when officers search or seize on the basis of a warrant. It does not permit the admission of evidence acquired as a result of a warrantless search or seizure. When a warrant is invalid for any reason, a search or seizure is unreasonable. Nevertheless, the government may introduce the evidence obtained if the officers conducting the search or seizure acted in **"objectively reasonable reliance on a subsequently invalidated . . . warrant."** United States v. Leon. The controlling question is whether a reasonable officer could have believed that the search or seizure authorized by the warrant was constitutional.

[handwritten margin note: Text:]

(b) Irrelevance of actual, subjective good faith or bad faith. An officer's actual, subjective good faith or bad faith is irrelevant to the objective inquiry mandated by the *Leon-Sheppard* good faith exception. If an officer has a bona fide belief that she is acting constitutionally, but that belief is objectively unreasonable, the exception is not available. If, however, the officer correctly recognizes that a warrant is invalid, but a reasonable officer could have believed that the warrant was valid, the exception is applicable.

(c) Need for adequate training in the law. In making the objective determination required by the *Leon-Sheppard* exception, the **"reasonably well-trained officer"** is the benchmark. "The objective standard" adopted in those opinions "requires officers to have a **reasonable knowledge of what the law prohibits."** United States v. Leon. If an officer is actually ignorant of what the law prohibits, but a reasonable officer would have been aware, the exception does not apply.

(d) Four instances in which the good faith exception does not apply. The Supreme Court listed four instances in which evidence obtained pursuant to a warrant-authorized search or seizure would not be admissible under the *Leon-Sheppard* exception. In each of the four situations described below, the officers conducting the search or seizure could not "reasonably rely" on the warrant.

[handwritten margin note: Examples of No Good Faith!]

- **Knowing or reckless falsehood.** In cases in which a warrant is invalid because officers have knowingly or recklessly provided false information to the issuing magistrate (see Chapter 4, section D.2), the government cannot rely on the good faith exception.

- **A magistrate's abandonment of the judicial role.** The *Leon-Sheppard* exception presumes a "neutral and detached" magistrate. See Chapter 4, section D.3. The exception cannot be invoked when the issuing magistrate "**wholly abandon[s] his judicial role.**" United States v. Leon. The exception may be available, however, when an issuing magistrate fails to qualify as "neutral and detached" but does not "wholly abandon" his role. The Court's language suggests that the exception is unavailable **only** in *egregious* cases—those in which a reasonable officer ought to realize that a warrant is invalid.

- **Seriously deficient probable cause showings.** An officer also cannot rely on a warrant that is "based on an affidavit **'so lacking in indicia of probable cause as to render official belief in its existence entirely unreasonable.'** " Id. When the facts provided to a magistrate fall so short of furnishing probable cause that "reasonable minds" cannot "differ on the question of whether a particular affidavit establishes probable cause," the good faith exception is not available. Id.

- **Seriously facially deficient warrants.** Warrants must meet certain constitutional "form" requirements. Most notable is the "particularity" demand. See Chapter 4, section D.5. If a search is unreasonable because a warrant does not contain a sufficiently particular description of the place to be searched or the things to be seized, the *Leon-Sheppard* "good faith" exception is applicable unless the warrant is "**so facially deficient . . . that the executing officers cannot reasonably presume it to be valid.**" See United States v. Leon; Massachusetts v. Sheppard. If the lack of particularity in a warrant is so serious or extreme that a reasonable officer could not believe that the warrant is constitutionally satisfactory, the good faith doctrine is not available.

The Supreme Court identified these four instances as situations that would not justify application of the good faith exception. The Court did not describe the list as exhaustive. Other situations in which it is not "objectively reasonable" for officers to rely on a warrant should be treated similarly.

iv. Two variations of the good faith exception. The most prominent and frequently relied-on variety of good faith exception is the *Leon-Sheppard* doctrine. Two other variations of the good faith exception, however, are built on the same logical foundation.

(a) The Illinois v. Krull "legislative authorization" variation. A legislature may pass a statute that authorizes a specific search or seizure. If officers act pursuant to such legislative authorization and it is later determined that the authority granted by the legislature is inconsistent with the Fourth Amendment, there is an "exception to the exclusionary rule." The officers must act in **"objectively reasonable reliance upon [the] statute authorizing"** their search or seizure. *Illinois v. Krull*, 480 U.S. 340, 107 S. Ct. 1160, 94 L. Ed. 2d 364 (1987). In other words, the exception applies if a reasonable officer could believe that the legislatively authorized search was constitutionally reasonable. Both primary and derivative products of the unreasonable search or seizure are admissible under the *Krull* variation of the good faith exception.

(b) The Arizona v. Evans "court employee error" variation. If officers conduct an unreasonable search or seizure as a result of **objectively reasonable reliance on a "clerical error[ ] of [a] court employee[ ],"** any evidence obtained will be admissible under "a categorical exception to the exclusionary rule" that is supported by "the *Leon* framework." *Arizona v. Evans*,—U.S.—, 115 S. Ct. 1185, 131 L. Ed. 2d 34 (1995). Thus, for example, if a person who works in a court clerk's office fails to remove a cancelled arrest warrant from the computer records of the clerk's office and an officer arrests an individual in reliance on those computer records, any evidence acquired is admissible so long as it was objectively reasonable for the officer to rely on the records. Id.

It is not at all clear what the result would be "if police personnel were responsible for [a similar clerical] error" that led an officer to conduct an unreasonable search or seizure. Id. In *Evans*, the Court reserved judgment on that question.

v. Applicability of the good faith exception to warrantless searches. The good faith exception recognized in United States v. Leon and Massachusetts v. Sheppard is explicitly limited to searches or seizures **based on warrants.** The extensions endorsed in Illinois v. Krull and Arizona v. Evans apply to **very narrow categories of warrantless searches or seizures**—those authorized by legislative action and those resulting from court employee clerical mistakes. The current good faith exceptions do **not** apply to the vast majority of situations in which officers acquire evidence by means of unreasonable **warrantless searches or seizures.** In such situations, the Fourth Amendment violations are the result of mistakes by the police themselves rather than other individuals. The **undecided question** is whether there should be a good faith exception for evidence obtained by means of **warrantless searches or seizures that officers reasonably but mistakenly believe are constitutionally valid.** The premises underlying the current good faith exceptions point in both directions.

On the one hand, the good faith exceptions recognized in *Leon*, *Sheppard*, *Krull*, and *Evans* rest in large part on the premise that the Fourth Amendment exclusionary rule is designed *only* to deter police officers. When someone other than a police officer makes an error that leads to a constitutional violation, there is no reason to seek deterrence and therefore no reason to exclude evidence. In cases that involve unreasonable warrantless searches or seizures, however, police officers make the mistakes that result in constitutional violations. Because police officers are the proper object of the deterrence sought by Fourth Amendment suppression, it is arguable that there should be no good faith exception for evidence acquired by unreasonable warrantless actions.

On the other hand, the current good faith exceptions also rest on the notion that police officers should not be expected to be "more than reasonable." If they are "penalized" when they make *reasonable* mistaken judgments, officers may be hesitant to do their jobs. See United States v. Leon. If that were to happen, effective law enforcement would be undermined and society would be less secure. To avoid that consequence, it is arguable that there should be a good faith exception that applies to evidence acquired by warrantless searches and seizures that officers reasonably, but mistakenly, believe to be constitutional.

EXAMPLES AND ANALYSIS

1. Detectives apply for and receive a warrant to search Francine's mobile home. They find contraband weapons while executing the warrant. The warrant is later determined to be invalid because it was not supported by probable cause and did not particularly describe the items to be seized. The trial judge correctly concludes that the officers who secured and executed the warrant could reasonably have believed that the warrant was based on an adequate showing of cause and was particular enough. She issues a ruling "admitting the contraband weapons because the officers' reasonable belief

rendered the search reasonable and, therefore, not violative of the Fourth Amendment." Is her ruling correct?

The result is correct, but the reasoning is faulty. The warrant was invalid; therefore, the search was unreasonable and violative of the Fourth Amendment. The officers' reasonable belief about the warrant's validity does not make it valid. However, because they acted in reasonable reliance on a warrant, the evidence falls within the *Leon-Sheppard* good faith exception to the exclusionary rule and is therefore admissible. The judge's reasoning confuses the issue of the reasonableness (i.e., constitutionality) of the search with the issue of the reasonableness of the officer's belief that the warrant was valid. The latter belief cannot render an unreasonable search constitutional, but it can justify the admission of evidence that has been illegally obtained.

2. Delores is arrested for attempted murder. She is taken to the police station, is given *Miranda* warnings, and waives her rights. In response to questions, she confesses to the crime. Prior to her trial, Delores moves to have her confession excluded. The trial judge agrees that Delores's arrest was illegal because the arresting officer lacked probable cause to believe that Delores had attempted to kill the victim. The government argues that the judge should admit the statements because the officer acted in "objective good faith." How should the judge rule?

The judge could decide this issue for either side. The officer did not act in reasonable reliance on a warrant, did not act on the basis of legislative authorization, and did not act pursuant to a clerical error by a court employee. Consequently, none of the current good faith exceptions applies to his unreasonable, warrantless arrest. The judge could plausibly rule that no good faith exception applies to reasonable mistakes by officers in conducting warrantless arrests. Alternatively, the judge could decide that warrantless arrests are subject to a good faith exception analogous to that recognized in *Leon* and *Sheppard*. If so, and if a reasonable officer could have believed that he had probable cause to arrest Delores, the weapons should be admitted.

---

e. **Impeachment use of illegally obtained evidence.** Impeachment is the process of casting doubt on the credibility of a witness's testimony. When evidence is admitted for impeachment purposes, the jury is instructed that it may not use the evidence for its substantive value but only for purposes of evaluating a witness's credibility. Illegally obtained evidence may have value not only as proof of a defendant's guilt but also to **impeach** the witness.

Illegally obtained evidence can impeach a witness in at least two ways. First, when a person has said two things that cannot be reconciled, there is good reason to question that person's credibility. Evidence that has been unlawfully acquired might consist of a statement by the witness that is *inconsistent with her trial testimony*. Thus, for example, in response to custodial interrogation without *Miranda* warnings a defendant might admit that she was at the scene of a crime. At trial, she may testify that she was not at the scene. The statement to the police is inconsistent with her testimony and casts doubt on her credibility.

Second, illegally acquired evidence might simply *contradict* a witness's trial testimony. Contradiction of a person's statements can certainly undermine that person's credibility. Thus, for example, an officer might search an automobile without probable cause and discover contraband. If the car owner were to testify at trial that she did not have contraband in her automobile, her testimony could be contradicted by the contraband that the officer states he found in the vehicle. Such contradiction would raise doubts about the owner's veracity.

The Supreme Court has recognized an **impeachment use exception** to the exclusionary rules. This subsection explains the circumstances in which that exception is available.

i. **Exclusionary rules that are subject to the impeachment use exception.** In part, the availability of the impeachment use exception depends on the nature of the violation that produced the disputed evidence. Evidence obtained in violation of the *Miranda* doctrine, the Fourth Amendment, or the *Michigan v. Jackson* branch of *Massiah* doctrine (see Chapter 9, section D) **may be admissible under the impeachment use exception.** See Harris v. New York, 401 U.S. 222, 91 S. Ct. 643, 28 L. Ed. 2d 1 (1971) (recognizing exception to *Miranda* rule); United States v. Havens, 446 U.S. 629, 100 S. Ct. 1912, 64 L. Ed. 2d 559 (1980) (recognizing exception to Fourth Amendment rule); Michigan v. Harvey, 494 U.S. 344, 110 S. Ct. 1176, 108 L. Ed. 2d 293 (1990) (recognizing exception to *Massiah* rule for *Michigan v. Jackson* doctrine violation). All of these situations involve exclusionary rules that serve *deterrent* purposes; none of them involves a *constitutional right to exclusion.*

Statements that are **actually coerced from suspects, however, are not admissible for impeachment purposes.** The Due Process Clause prohibits *any* use of a coerced confession. Mincey v. Arizona, 437 U.S. 385, 98 S. Ct. 2408, 57 L. Ed. 2d 290 (1978). Even if a defendant's coerced confession of guilt is directly contradictory to his trial testimony, it may not be used to cast doubt on his credibility. Like substantive use of a coerced confession, impeachment use would violate the defendant's right to due process of law. Id.

The Court has reserved the question whether evidence obtained in violation of the other branches of *Massiah* doctrine may be used for impeachment purposes. The resolution of this question should depend on whether the *Massiah* exclusionary rule is a part of the right to counsel or is purely a deterrent device. See section A.4 above. If exclusion is a right, impeachment use should be prohibited; if it is solely a deterrent, impeachment use should be allowed.

ii. **Testimony that is subject to impeachment by illegally obtained evidence.** Evidence acquired by means of an unreasonable search or seizure may be introduced to impeach a **defendant's direct testimony** and a **defendant's responses to the prosecution's cross-examination** so long as the cross-examination stays within the scope allowed by the rules of evidence. United States v. Havens.

Similarly, evidence acquired in violation of the *Miranda* safeguards, see Harris v. New York; Oregon v. Hass, 420 U.S. 714, 95 S. Ct. 1215, 43 L. Ed. 2d 570 (1975), and evidence acquired in violation of the Michigan v. Jackson branch of *Massiah*, see Michigan v. Harvey, may be introduced to impeach a **defendant's direct testimony.** Although there are no holdings on point, it is likely that a **defendant's answers to proper cross-examination** could also be impeached by both kinds of illegally obtained evidence.

iii. **Testimony that is not subject to impeachment by illegally obtained evidence.** The impeachment use exception to the Fourth Amendment exclusionary rule does not extend to the testimony of witnesses other than the defendant. Consequently, evidence that has been obtained in violation of the **Fourth Amendment may not be used to impeach a defense witness's testimony.** James v. Illinois, 493 U.S. 307, 110 S. Ct. 648, 107 L. Ed. 2d 676 (1990). The same is probably also true of the *Miranda* and *Massiah* exclusionary rules.

iv. **Kinds of illegally obtained evidence that may be used to impeach.** Both tangible and verbal evidence may be used to impeach a defendant. See United States v. Havens (T-shirt that was the product of an illegal search used to impeach a defendant); Harris v. New York (defendant's responses to custodial interrogation used to impeach him). Moreover, when the impeachment use exception is applicable, both **primary and derivative products** of the illegal conduct are admissible.

4. Types of Proceedings in Which the Exclusionary Rules Apply

All the exclusionary rules apply at the **trial** stage of criminal prosecutions. They do not necessarily apply at other stages of the criminal process or in noncriminal proceedings. (**Note:** All but one of the Supreme Court cases resolving issues of exclusion at proceedings other than criminal trials involve the Fourth Amendment exclusionary rule. Consequently, there is some uncertainty about the applicability of other exclusionary rules in such proceedings.)

a. **Grand jury proceedings.** The Fourth Amendment exclusionary rule does **not** apply to grand jury proceedings. United States v. Calandra, 414 U.S. 338, 94 S. Ct. 613, 38 L. Ed. 2d 561 (1974). Consequently, the government may use evidence acquired by means of an illegal search as a basis for posing questions to a grand jury witness who was the victim of an illegal search. Id.

b. **Habeas corpus review of state convictions.** So long as a state has accorded a defendant a "full and fair" opportunity to litigate a Fourth Amendment unreasonable search or seizure claim, the defendant **may not raise that claim** in a collateral, habeas corpus attack on his conviction in federal court. Stone v. Powell, 428 U.S. 465, 96 S. Ct. 3037, 49 L. Ed. 2d 1067 (1976). The bar to such claims is based on the conclusion that the Fourth Amendment exclusionary rule **does not apply** at the habeas corpus stage. Id.

In Withrow v. Williams, 507 U.S. 680, 113 S. Ct. 1745, 123 L. Ed. 2d 407 (1993), however, the Court held that the *Miranda* exclusionary rule **is applicable** upon federal habeas corpus review of a state conviction. Even if a state has afforded a full and fair review of a defendant's claim that a statement was obtained in violation of *Miranda*, federal habeas review of that claim is still available.

The basic reason for the different treatment of the Fourth Amendment and *Miranda* exclusionary rules in the habeas corpus context is that the Fourth Amendment rule is *purely* a deterrent safeguard against future unreasonable searches and seizures while the *Miranda* rule *also* provides trial protection against the risks of compelled self-incrimination. See section A.3 above.

c. **Forfeiture proceedings.** In One 1958 Plymouth Sedan v. Pennsylvania, 380 U.S. 693, 85 S. Ct. 1246, 14 L. Ed. 2d 170 (1965), a state sought forfeiture of an automobile on the grounds that it had been used for illegal transportation or possession of liquor. The Supreme Court held that evidence acquired from the unlawful search of the automobile was subject to exclusion. The government could not use the evidence to prove the illegal use that was the predicate for forfeiting the vehicle. In holding that the Fourth Amendment exclusionary rule was applicable to that kind of proceeding, the Court relied on the conclusion that the "proceeding [was] quasi-criminal in character." It "requir[ed] a determination that the criminal law ha[d] been violated" and resulted in a "forfeiture [that was] clearly a penalty for the criminal offense." The Court noted that the vehicle to be forfeited in the case was distinguishable from contraband narcotics, which are inherently criminal to possess. The vehicle was "contraband" only because of the use to which it had allegedly been put.

The holding of *One 1958 Plymouth Sedan* is limited to proceedings for the forfeiture of property used in connection with a crime. The Fourth Amendment exclusionary rule probably does not apply in proceedings for the forfeiture of "true" contraband—items that it is inherently criminal to possess. Moreover, it is unclear whether the exclusionary rule applies in proceedings instituted for the forfeiture of "fruits" of crime, such as profits made from illegal activities.

d. Civil proceedings. In United States v. Janis, 428 U.S. 433, 96 S. Ct. 3021, 49 L. Ed. 2d 1046 (1976), the Supreme Court held that the Fourth Amendment exclusionary rule did not bar from a **federal civil tax proceeding** evidence that was unlawfully seized in good faith by a **state police officer.** Relying on *Janis*, the Court held in Immigration and Naturalization Service v. Lopez-Mendoza, 468 U.S. 1032, 104 S. Ct. 3479, 82 L. Ed. 2d 778 (1984), that the Fourth Amendment exclusionary rule is also inapplicable in a **civil proceeding seeking deportation** of an individual who is not eligible to remain in the United States. As a result, the government was not barred from introducing statements made by the prospective deportee after he was illegally arrested.

Some of the *Janis* Court's reasoning suggests a general rule that the Fourth Amendment exclusionary rule is inapplicable in **all civil proceedings.** The Court noted, for example, that it **"never ha[d] . . . applied [the rule] to exclude evidence from a civil proceeding."** The holdings in both *Janis* and *Lopez-Mendoza,* however, are limited by the facts before the Court. *Janis* held that the exclusionary rule is inapplicable to a **federal civil tax proceeding** when the evidence sought to be introduced has been illegally obtained by a **state officer.** *Lopez-Mendoza* held that the exclusionary rule has no application in **civil deportation proceedings.** Neither opinion dispositively answers the more general question whether the Fourth Amendment (or any other) exclusionary rule is ever applicable in civil cases in which the government is a party.

REVIEW QUESTIONS AND ANSWERS

Question: Nell was pulled over for speeding. Walt was sitting in the front passenger seat. After Officer Max cited Nell, he noticed that she and Walt seemed nervous. Max asked for permission to search the car. Nell refused. Max then ordered Nell and Walt out of the car and conducted a search. He found several pounds of marijuana in the trunk. Prior to their trial for possession of marijuana, Nell and Walt moved to suppress the evidence. The judge found that Officer Max had "grossly inadequate cause" to search the car and was operating on a "mere hunch." The judge also found that neither Nell nor Walt owned the car, that Nell had borrowed it from her cousin, and that Walt was "simply a passenger." Should the judge grant the motions to suppress?

Answer: The judge should not grant Walt's motion. It is not clear whether the judge should grant Nell's motion. Officer Max violated the Fourth Amendment. However, only those with "standing" to object to his unlawful search can have the evidence excluded. Mere passengers in vehicles do not have legitimate expectations of privacy in areas such as the glove compartments or trunks. See Rakas v. Illinois. Because Walt can establish nothing other than his passenger status and legitimate presence in the car, he cannot establish that he had a Fourth Amendment interest violated by the search of the car.

Nell might well have standing. She had borrowed the car from her cousin, was in control of the vehicle, and had the authority and ability to exclude others. An ownership or other property interest is unnecessary. A judge could conclude that she had a legitimate expectation of privacy in the vehicle.

The government should contend that Nell had no legitimate expectation in the trunk. If Nell was not using the trunk on this occasion and had not used it in the past, a judge could conclude that she lacked a legitimate privacy interest in the trunk.

The fact that Nell had a "possessory" interest in the effect seized is not sufficient to establish a reasonable privacy expectation in the place searched. See Rawlings v. Kentucky. Nonetheless, that fact is *relevant,* and if the marijuana was in the trunk because Nell had stored it there a judge could conclude that she did have a Fourth Amendment privacy interest in the trunk. If so, the marijuana should be excluded from Nell's trial.

Question: Federal agents searched Connie's home pursuant to consent given by her 16-year-old daughter. During the search they found cocaine in Connie's kitchen cabinet. They left the home and secured a warrant to search Connie's home for cocaine. The affidavit in support of the warrant included the fact that the officers had seen cocaine in the home. It also detailed extensive surveillance and information from reliable third persons who had been in the home recently and had seen Connie dealing in cocaine. Upon executing the warrant, the agents found the cocaine they had seen during the earlier search. Connie was charged with possession of cocaine with intent to distribute. She moved to suppress the cocaine, alleging that the officers' first search of her home was unreasonable because her daughter's consent had been coerced. The judge found the consent invalid. What arguments should the government make to justify introduction of the cocaine? Should the court exclude the cocaine?

Answer: The government should contend that the cocaine was obtained from an independent source—the search pursuant to the warrant. According to this argument, the second search for and seizure of the cocaine were not the product of the earlier illegality. According to Murray v. United States, a warranted search is not an independent source if the government's decision to obtain the warrant is "prompted" by what it learned during an illegal search. It is unclear in this case whether the government's decision to seek the warrant was independent of the first entry.

In addition, a warranted search does not qualify as an independent source if information learned during an illegal search is presented to the magistrate and "affect[s] his decision to issue the warrant." Id. Here, illegally obtained information was presented to the magistrate. According to one interpretation of *Murray*, the warranted search is not an independent source if the magistrate **in fact relies on the unlawfully obtained information.** According to another interpretation, even if the magistrate does rely on the tainted information, a warranted search is independent **if the legally obtained information in the affidavit is sufficient to support a finding of probable cause.** Although the first interpretation seems more consistent with the literal language in *Murray*, it is not certain that the Supreme Court would reject the second interpretation.

Question: A police informer called Jerry's girlfriend and arranged to buy illegal weapons from Jerry at the girlfriend's apartment in the afternoon. When the informer went to the room, the transmitter he was wearing malfunctioned. Jerry arrived shortly thereafter. Because they feared for the informer's safety, officers forcibly entered the apartment despite the fact that the weapons transaction had not yet occurred. The officers arrested Jerry. Incident to the arrest, they found weapons in a case Jerry was carrying. Jerry was charged with possession of illegal weapons. He moved to suppress the weapons prior to trial. The government conceded that the entry of the apartment was unlawful but argued that the weapons were admissible under the "inevitable discovery" exception. How should the judge rule?

Answer: The judge should suppress the evidence unless the government demonstrates by a preponderance of the evidence that it would inevitably have discovered the weapons. The government could rely on the fact that its informer had arranged a "controlled buy." The prosecution could argue that he either would have bought the weapons and turned them over to the police or would have seen enough to give the police probable cause to conduct a legal search of Jerry or the apartment. The defendant should argue that the government cannot show that it is *more likely than not* that the informer would have either purchased the weapons or seen enough to furnish probable cause to justify a legal search at a time when the weapons were still present. The defendant's argument seems quite persuasive.

Two other points merit mention. In discussing the independent source exception in *Nix*, the Supreme Court did not state that the government must be actively pursuing the independent legal means of investigation at the time of its illegality. Some lower courts, however, have imposed such a requirement. In this case, such a requirement could pose an additional impediment to the government's inevitable discovery claim. In addition, the evidence here is *primary*—that is, it is the immediate product of the illegality. The *Nix* Court endorsed inevitable discovery in a case that involved *derivative* evidence. Nonetheless, the logic of the independent source exception strongly suggests that it *does* extend to primary products of illegalities.

Question: Neighbors reported a disturbance in an apartment and a sound that "could have been gunfire." Officers hastened to the apartment, knocked, then pried the door open. Inside, they found Olive sitting on a couch. After talking to her for 10 minutes, the officers secured a written consent to search the apartment. Minutes later, in the bedroom closet, they found the body of Olive's estranged husband. He had been shot twice through the head. The officers returned to the living room, arrested Olive, and gave her *Miranda* warnings. She waived her rights. During questioning, Olive told the officers that her sister, Justine, was "to blame" for the death.

While one officer took Olive to the police station, the other went to Justine's home. He told Justine that Olive had implicated her in a killing and asked if she "wanted to help straighten things out." Justine began to cry, then said, "She asked for my gun, and, you know, she's my sister. He deserved it, but I didn't kill him. Olive did." Upon being asked, Justine told the officers that she had thrown the gun "into the pond out back." Two days later, officers dredged the pond and found the weapon. At her murder trial, Olive moved to suppress the body, Justine's statement, and the gun. The trial judge found that the entry of Olive's apartment was "wholly lacking in probable cause" but that Olive's consent to the search of the apartment was "voluntary and uncoerced." The government contends that the "attenuation" exception justifies admission of all of the items. Should the evidence be admitted?

Answer: There is a plausible claim with regard to each item of evidence that it is "attenuated." The claim is weakest for the body and strongest for the gun. A judge should probably suppress the body but admit the statement and gun.

First, attenuation analysis must take into account the *nature of the illegality*. Here, the warrantless entry of Olive's home was "wholly lacking in probable cause." It was not the result of a reasonable or even a merely negligent mistake. This fact should count against an attenuation finding.

Second, the *time between the illegality and the discovery* is important. The body was found soon after the illegal entry. In that sense, it was closely connected to the illegality. The officer went immediately to Justine's home. Although a bit more time passed before Justine made her statement, the time between the illegal entry and that statement was not long. The gun, however, was uncovered two days later. That time period should weigh in favor of the prosecutor's attenuation claim.

Third, there were some *intervening circumstances* between the illegality and each discovery. Olive's voluntary consent came between the entry and the search that led to the body. Some courts suggest that if a consent is voluntary, it insulates evidence from the taint of a prior illegal search. Others take the better view that a voluntary consent that is the *product* of the illegal search does not automatically sever or attenuate the connection between the preceding and the subsequent searches. Here, a court probably should conclude that the mere fact of a voluntary consent is insufficient to dissipate the taint between the clearly illegal entry and the discovery of the body a short time later. The consent and the body were closely connected products of the illegal entry.

The officers obtained Justine's statement after they arrested Olive, *"Mirandized"* her, heard Olive blame Justine, and then spoke to Justine. All these "intervening circumstances" could contribute to a finding that the taint of the illegal entry had been dissipated. Moreover, when the evidence acquired as a result of an illegal search is live-witness testimony, a court should more readily find attenuation. See United States v. Ceccolini. Because the degree of free will exercised by the witness is an important factor in the attenuation determination, the trial court should evaluate whether Justine spoke freely or as a result of pressure generated by the officer and the situation. If Justine's statement was the product of her free choice to speak, that would enhance the case for attenuation. If it was not the product of her free will, the case for attenuation would be undermined.

A similar analysis should apply to the gun. Whether Justine's decision to reveal its location was an exercise of her free will or of official pressure is important. In addition, the dredging of the pond is an intervening link in a fairly protracted causal chain leading from the illegal entry of Olive's apartment to the gun.

In sum, the discovery of the body probably does not fit within the attenuation exception. Justine's statement and the gun *might well* be found admissible under that exception.

Question: Winfro was arrested for an attempted arson at the governor's mansion. When he received the *Miranda* warnings, he replied, "I want a lawyer." The interrogating officers continued to question him. In response to the questioning, Winfro made incriminating statements and gave the officers the name of his accomplice, Marty. The officers immediately arrested Marty. After he was given proper *Miranda* warnings and waived his rights, Marty made a statement incriminating both himself and Winfro. He also turned over combustible materials that the two men had used in the arson attempt. Should any or all of the evidence be excluded from the trial of Winfro and Marty?

Answer: None of the evidence should be excluded from Marty's trial. Winfro's statements should be excluded from his trial. It is unclear whether Marty's statements and the tangible evidence should be excluded from Winfro's trial.

First, assuming that the only violation is the officers' disregard of Winfro's request for counsel, Marty cannot have any evidence suppressed. He lacks standing to assert Winfro's *Miranda* violation. The fact that Marty was the source of his own statement and the tangible evidence is irrelevant unless those items are traceable to a violation of *his* "rights."

Second, Winfro's statements cannot be used against him. When the officers interrogated him despite his clear request for counsel, they violated the *Miranda* doctrine. According to *Miranda*, the statements Winfro made **must** be suppressed.

Finally, there is room for debate over the admissibility of Marty's statements and the combustible material at Winfro's trial. Winfro should argue that they are both the "fruits" of the *Miranda* violation. Clearly, there is a causal connection linking the items to his statement, and it is a relatively close connection. Violation of the *Miranda* doctrine was patent, and the time between the violation and the subsequent discoveries was short. Moreover, while Marty was not "coerced" into speaking, he made his revelations after being arrested for attempted arson. The revelations can hardly be considered the product of a truly free will.

The government has two arguments in response. First, it should claim that there is **no fruits doctrine** under *Miranda*. The Court suggested that possibility in *Oregon v. Elstad*, and some lower courts have so concluded. If so, there is no need to undertake attenuation analysis because *products* of statements obtained in violation of the *Miranda* doctrine are always admissible. Second, the government should contend that even if there is a fruits doctrine, the disputed evidence is attenuated by the "free-willed" statement and action of Marty. A court should be reluctant to exclude the voluntary statement of a live witness. *United States v. Ceccolini*. By extension, a court should also be hesitant to exclude tangible evidence that is voluntarily revealed by such a witness.

While a court could plausibly accept either of the government's arguments, it could also accept Winfro's assertion that there is a fruits doctrine under *Miranda* and that the evidence here was insufficiently attenuated to dissipate the taint of the illegality.

Question: Based on an anonymous tip, officers suspected that Terrence was involved in illegal narcotics transactions and that there was a stash of narcotics in his residence. Detective Solo approached Terrence as he stood on the sidewalk in front of his home. Without restraining him in any way, Solo began to talk to Terrence. Terrence grew nervous. When Solo asked if he had narcotics in his home, Terrence grew "loud and aggressive," saying that he would not help the officer "put me in jail." He refused to consent to a search of his home and stated that he wanted a lawyer. Based on the anonymous tip and Terrence's behavior, Solo obtained a warrant to search the residence. He discovered large amounts of cocaine in a rear bedroom. Prior to trial, Terrence moved to suppress the narcotics. The trial court specifically found that the warrant was not supported by probable cause. The government contends that the narcotics are admissible by virtue of the good faith exception to the exclusionary rule. How should the judge rule?

Answer: If Solo acted in "reasonable reliance" on the invalid warrant, the evidence should be admitted. The question here is whether the affidavit was so lacking in indicia of probable cause that it was "entirely unreasonable" to believe that probable cause existed. Put otherwise, could a reasonable officer have concluded that there was probable cause?

The first question is whether a reasonable officer would give any weight to Terrence's assertions of his rights and of the ways he asserted those rights. Assertions of rights alone clearly cannot be the basis for even a reasonable suspicion, much less probable cause. See *Florida v. Bostick*, 501 U.S. 429, 111 S. Ct. 2382, 115 L. Ed. 2d 389 (1991). It is unclear whether assertions of rights or the manner of a suspect's assertions can count *at all*. If they cannot count, and if a reasonably well-trained officer should know that they cannot count, then the assessment of good faith should take only the anonymous tip into account. It seems "entirely unreasonable" to believe that such a tip could be the basis for a probable cause finding. In that case, the good faith exception should not apply.

If the assertions of rights are pertinent or if a reasonably well-trained officer could conclude that they would add weight to the probable cause showing, the next question is whether it was "entirely unreasonable" to believe that the tip **plus** Terrence's conduct furnished probable cause to search the home. On the one hand, a court might conclude that such a belief was not "entirely unreasonable." On the other hand, a judge still might plausibly conclude that this combination of factors was so deficient that a reasonable officer could not have believed that the search warrant was supported by probable cause. If so, the exception should not apply.

PART III

PROCESSES OF ADJUDICATION: RIGHTS AND REMEDIES

Part III discusses primarily constitutional and some statutory rights and remedies pertinent to the **adjudicatory** stages of criminal cases. Most of the rules of law addressed here are **essential elements of a fair trial** in our accusatorial, adversarial system of criminal justice. They grant substantive and procedural entitlements to those accused of criminal offenses and, as a result, restrict judges' authority to conduct trials and prosecutors' efforts to secure convictions. The topics covered in this part are ordinarily the focus of advanced criminal procedure courses.

The topics discussed include:

- **Discovery and disclosure.** Most of the law of "criminal discovery" is the product of state statutes and court rules that define each side's entitlements. The **Due Process Clause,** however, does require the government to disclose some exculpatory information to defendants. Moreover, both that clause and the **privilege against compulsory self-incrimination** pose some impediments to states' efforts to require the defense to reveal information to the government. Finally, the **Sixth Amendment Compulsory Process Clause** allows only limited use of evidentiary preclusion as a sanction for defense violations of discovery rules.

- **Bail and preventive detention.** The **Eighth Amendment** provides a constitutional guarantee against **excessive bail.** In most cases, it requires judges to prescribe reasonable conditions under which a defendant can secure release prior to trial and conviction. In some circumstances, however, both the Eighth Amendment and the Due Process Clause tolerate **preventive detention** of criminal defendants. Statutes in each jurisdiction establish the processes and set out the criteria for releasing or detaining defendants prior to trial and

247

while convictions are on appeal. The **Federal Bail Reform Act** governs release and detention decisions in the federal system.

- **Plea bargaining and guilty pleas.** While there is a wide range of constitutionally permissible methods of **plea bargaining,** there are some limits that prosecutors may not exceed. Moreover, when a guilty plea is entered in reliance on a plea bargain, a breach by the prosecutor violates **due process.** A **guilty plea** must be voluntary, knowing, and intelligent. In a petition seeking a writ of habeas corpus, a defendant ordinarily may not challenge a guilty plea based on an ''antecedent'' constitutional violation.

- **Speedy prosecution.** The **Due Process Clause** provides a very limited safeguard against **pre-accusation delay**—that is, official delay in the filing of criminal charges. The **Sixth Amendment** guarantees the right to a **speedy trial** once a defendant has been arrested for or formally accused of an offense. The **Federal Speedy Trial Act** and similar state statutes supplement constitutional guarantees and seek to insure that defendants are brought to trial expeditiously.

- **Public trials and pretrial publicity.** The **Sixth Amendment** grants the accused a right to a **public trial.** The **First Amendment** provides a **public right of access** to criminal proceedings. The **Due Process Clause** furnishes protection against the potential for unfairness inherent in prejudicial publicity about a criminal case.

- **Counsel.** The **Sixth Amendment** provides that the ''accused shall enjoy'' the **''right to the Assistance of counsel for his defence.''** This guarantee prevents the state from denying counsel, failing to appoint counsel for indigents, and unreasonably restricting counsel's ability to defend. It also prevents convictions based on deficient performance by defense counsel. The Sixth Amendment also provides an implicit **right of self-representation.**

- **Jury trial.** The **Sixth Amendment** includes an entitlement to **trial by an impartial jury.** Juries provide the common sense of the community as a safeguard against arbitrary and oppressive governmental prosecutions. In addition, the **Equal Protection Clause** guards against certain kinds of discrimination in the selection of jurors, and the **Due Process Clause** provides some assurance that jurors who serve on a case will at all times be impartial and competent and will render their decisions based on the evidence presented in court.

- **Double jeopardy.** The **Fifth Amendment Double Jeopardy Clause** states that no person shall ''be subject for the same offense to be **twice put in jeopardy of life or limb.''** This guarantee against double jeopardy furnishes criminal defendants with protection against both **successive prosecutions** and **multiple punishment** for the same offense.

- **Appeals.** There is no constitutional right to appeal a conviction, but when an appeal is allowed the **Due Process Clause** and **Equal Protection Clause** require fair and nondiscriminatory appellate procedures. The **Double Jeopardy Clause** restricts, but does not forbid, all government appeals in criminal cases. The final judgment rule, the mootness doctrine, the general rule barring consideration of issues not raised at trial, and the exception for "plain error" all regulate appellate court processes. Retroactivity principles dictate the law that will govern on appeal, while harmless error standards determine whether an error will result in "reversal" on appeal. Finally, **due process** forbids the government from vindictively punishing an individual for appealing a conviction.

- **Collateral remedies.** Federal statutes prescribe and restrict the collateral remedies available for state and federal prisoners in federal court. Restrictions on those remedies include the "in custody" and "exhaustion of remedies" requirements, the bar to Fourth Amendment claims, the general nonretroactivity of "new rules" of constitutional law, the state procedural default doctrine, the successive petition doctrine, the abuse of the writ doctrine, the presumption of correctness for state court factfinding, and the harmless error doctrine.

13 DISCOVERY AND DISCLOSURE

 CHAPTER OVERVIEW

Discovery is the process by which the parties in litigation disclose to their opponents information about the case. Parties in criminal cases might disclose, for example, the names of prospective witnesses, statements made by those witnesses, the results of tests or examinations, tangible items of evidence, the nature of a potential defense, or other information pertinent to the case.

Originally, the Anglo-American common law barred discovery in criminal cases. Today, American jurisdictions have abandoned the prohibition on criminal case discovery and have increasingly favored more generous disclosure. The law of discovery is mainly the product of state statutes, court rules, or common law development by courts. As a result, jurisdictions vary widely in the amount of discovery they afford. Some have edged away from the common law tradition in limited, discrete ways; others have veered sharply from the past, opening wide the doors to criminal case discovery. Moreover, while some jurisdictions require roughly equal disclosure by both sides, many are more generous to the defendant, requiring greater disclosure from the prosecution.

Such state variation is possible because the Constitution has relatively little to say about discovery in criminal cases. Still, in some instances the Constitution requires the government to reveal information to the defendant. In those cases, states can neither prohibit disclosure nor permit concealment. Moreover, the Constitution imposes limited constraints on the kinds of disclosures that an accused can be forced to make. States may not command revelation when the Constitution grants a right not to reveal. The primary concerns of this chapter are the constitutional mandates and restrictions.

More specifically, this chapter treats:

- **The sources and content of the law of criminal discovery.** Very briefly, the chapter discusses the laws that provide for discovery in criminal cases and the various ways in which jurisdictions have formulated their laws.

- **The prosecution's constitutional duties to disclose.** When the prosecution possesses exculpatory evidence, the **Due Process Clause** guarantee of "fundamental fairness" sometimes requires disclosure to the defendant. The standards for determining when a state has the constitutional duty to divulge information and when the failure to divulge invalidates a conviction are outlined in this section.

- **The defendant's protections against disclosure.** The **Fifth Amendment privilege against compulsory self-incrimination** and the **Due Process Clause** provide defendants with limited protection against being forced to disclose information to the state. The nature and extent of those protections are explored here. Moreover, the **Sixth Amendment right to present evidence in one's defense** restricts states' power to sanction discovery violations by barring an accused from introducing evidence. This restriction is sketched here.

A. SOURCES AND CONTENT OF THE LAWS THAT GOVERN DISCOVERY IN CRIMINAL CASES

This section briefly describes the sources and the content of the law of criminal case discovery. Because of the great variation among jurisdictions, there is no attempt to be comprehensive. Instead, a very general description of possibilities is provided.

1. Sources of Discovery Law

Most jurisdictions have statutory provisions or rules of court that regulate discovery. Jurisdictions frequently have both general discovery provisions that cover most categories of evidence or information and more specific provisions that address the discovery of material regarding narrow topics such as alibi defenses. See, e.g., Federal Rule of Criminal Procedure 16 (providing the rules for discovery in general) and FRCrP 12.1 (prescribing discovery with regard to an alibi defense). Some statutes or rules do not permit judges to order discovery over and above that which the laws specifically prescribe, while others do allow judges some latitude. A small number of jurisdictions still have "common law" systems in which the courts develop the law that governs criminal case discovery.

2. Content of Discovery Law

The law of criminal case discovery varies from jurisdiction to jurisdiction. This subsection sketches possible variations but is not intended as a comprehensive description. The approach of the federal system will serve as an illustration. For a more detailed treatment of state laws, students should refer to LaFave and Israel, Criminal Procedure (2d ed. 1992). To determine a particular jurisdiction's approach, students should consult the law of that jurisdiction.

a. **Material subject to discovery.** A majority of jurisdictions provide for discovery by both the defense and the prosecution. Most of them require more liberal disclosure from the prosecution.

   i. **Defense discovery.** Discovery rules might require the prosecution to disclose any or all of the following sorts of material in its possession: written, recorded, or oral statements by witnesses, by defendants, or by codefendants; criminal records; the results of tests or examinations; documents and other tangible items; and lists of prospective witnesses.

   Federal Rule of Criminal Procedure 16, for example, provides that "[u]pon request of a defendant the government shall disclose" written or recorded statements made by the defendant, written records containing oral statements made by the defendant in response to interrogation, recorded testimony by a defendant before a grand jury relating to the offense, and oral statements made in response to interrogation if there is an intent to use them at trial. See FRCrP 16(a)(1)(A). Upon request, the government must (1) give the defendant a copy of her prior criminal record (FRCrP 16(a)(1)(B)); (2) permit the defendant to inspect and/or copy books, papers, documents, photographs, tangible objects, buildings or places, if they are "material" to the defense or are "intended for use" in the case-in-chief or were "obtained from or belong to the defendant" (FRCrP 16(a)(1)(C)); and (3) permit the defendant to inspect and copy results or reports of physical or mental examinations and scientific tests or experiments (FRCrP 16(a)(1)(D)).

   ii. **Prosecution discovery.** Provisions might require a defendant to disclose any or all of the following to the government: witness lists or statements, documents and tangible items, and the results of tests or examinations. Some jurisdictions make the prosecution's discovery entitlements dependent on initial requests by the defendant. Others afford unconditional government discovery—that is, the prosecution is entitled to material whether or not the defendant has sought discovery.

   Federal Rule of Criminal Procedure 16 makes prosecution discovery from the defendant **conditional** on the defendant's request for discovery from the government. If the defendant asks to inspect and copy **either** books, papers, and so on **or** the results or reports of examinations, tests, or experiments, the government is entitled to inspect and/or copy books, papers, documents, photographs, or tangible objects that the defendant intends to introduce in her case-in-chief. FRCrP 16(b)(1)(A). Similarly, if the defendant asks for the aforementioned kinds of items, the government may inspect and copy results or reports of physical or mental examinations and of scientific tests or experiments which the defendant intends to introduce as evidence in chief or which were prepared by a witness the defendant intends to call when such documents relate to the testimony of that witness. FRCrP 16(b)(1)(B).

Specific provisions can require a defendant to inform the state whether she intends to raise a particular defense. The most popular provisions pertain to alibi or insanity defenses; some require notification of other kinds of defenses. These provisions also require disclosure of a list of the witnesses who will support the particular defense.

Federal Rule of Criminal Procedure 12.1(a) provides that when the federal prosecutor makes a written demand, the defendant must "serve . . . a written notice of [his or her] intention to offer a defense of alibi" and must include "the specific place or places at which the defendant claims to have been at the time of the alleged offense and the names and addresses of the witnesses upon whom the defendant intends to rely to establish such alibi." The prosecutor then has an obligation to notify the defendant of names and addresses of witnesses who will "establish the defendant's presence at the scene of the alleged offense and any other witnesses to be relied on to rebut testimony of any of the defendant's alibi witnesses." FRCrP 12.1(b). A court can sanction a failure by either party to comply by excluding evidence, but cannot bar a defendant from testifying. FRCrP 12.1(d). Moreover, if the defendant decides not to rely on an alibi defense, his earlier expression of an intention to do so cannot be used against him. FRCrP 12.1(f).

b. **Continuing duties to disclose.** Typically, rules impose "continuing duties to disclose." If additional material that is subject to discovery comes to a party's attention or into a party's possession after that party has fully responded to an initial request, the party has a duty to disclose the additional material.

According to **FRCrP 16(c),** "[i]f, prior to or during trial, a party discovers additional evidence or material previously requested or ordered, which is subject to discovery or inspection," that party must notify the opponent or the court of its existence.

c. **Protection from discovery.** A party may typically seek a "protective order" from a court to prevent, limit, or delay an opponent's discovery of some item that is discoverable under the applicable rules. The grounds that justify such protection from discovery may be set out specifically or left to the determination of the court.

Federal Rule 16 provides that "[u]pon *a sufficient showing* the court may at any time order that the discovery or inspection be denied, restricted, or deferred, or make such other order as is appropriate." FRCrP 16(d)(1).

d.   Sanctions for violations of discovery rules. Courts are authorized to respond to violations of rules providing for discovery with a variety of measures, including ordering the immediate disclosure of the material, continuing a trial, precluding a party from introducing evidence that was not disclosed, ordering mistrials, holding parties in contempt of court, or dismissing charges.

Federal Rule 16 authorizes judges to order a party that has failed to comply "to permit the discovery or inspection, [to] grant a continuance, [to] prohibit the party from introducing the evidence not disclosed or [to] enter such order as it deems just under the circumstances." FRCrP 16(d)(2).

B.   THE GOVERNMENT'S CONSTITUTIONAL DUTY TO DISCLOSE

The Constitution **does not grant the accused a general right to discover evidence** or other material in the possession of the prosecution. See Weatherford v. Bursey, 429 U.S. 545, 97 S. Ct. 837, 51 L. Ed. 2d 30 (1977) ("There is no general right to discovery in a criminal case"). The **Due Process Clause,** however, does impose on the government a limited duty to disclose information to the defendant. See Brady v. Maryland, 373 U.S. 83, 83 S. Ct. 1194, 10 L. Ed. 2d 215 (1963). This subsection explains the scope of that duty and the consequences of a violation.

1.   Duties Not to Use and to Correct False or Perjured Testimony by a Government Witness

The **Due Process Clause** is violated when the government **deliberately or knowingly introduces false or perjured testimony** or knowingly **"allows [false testimony] to go uncorrected when it appears."** Napue v. Illinois, 360 U.S. 264, 79 S. Ct. 1173, 3 L. Ed. 2d 1217 (1959). The prosecution is charged with "knowledge" **if any prosecutor** in the office **is aware** of a falsehood. Giglio v. United States, 405 U.S. 150, 92 S. Ct. 763, 31 L. Ed. 2d 104 (1972). Known falsehoods must be disclosed. If the government deliberately or knowingly uses or fails to correct false testimony, a resulting conviction "is fundamentally unfair, and must be [reversed] **if there is any reasonable likelihood that the false testimony could have affected the judgment of the jury."** United States v. Agurs, 427 U.S. 97, 96 S. Ct. 2392, 49 L. Ed. 2d 342 (1976).

In contrast, if the government is **unaware** of false testimony during trial but **discovers it only after the trial has ended,** a conviction will be upheld

unless the disclosure of the falsehood at trial "probably would have resulted in an acquittal." See United States v. Agurs (describing the standard for reversal in cases of "newly discovered evidence").

2. **Duty to Disclose "Exculpatory" Evidence: The Doctrine of Brady v. Maryland**

In Brady v. Maryland, the Supreme Court relied on the due process duty to correct false evidence as a basis for holding that **"suppression by the prosecution of evidence favorable to an accused upon request violates due process where the evidence is material either to guilt or to punishment."** Moore v. Illinois, 408 U.S. 786, 92 S. Ct. 2562, 33 L. Ed. 2d 706 (1972). This holding—the *Brady* doctrine—imposes a prosecutorial duty to disclose and requires reversal of a conviction when that duty is violated. Its "elements" are discussed here.

a. **"Suppression" of evidence by the prosecution. A failure to disclose exculpatory evidence to the defense** is sufficient to violate due process; affirmative "suppression" or concealment is not necessary. Moreover, the government's good or bad faith in failing to disclose evidence to the defense does not matter. See Brady v. Maryland; Kyles v. Whitley,— U.S.—, 115 S. Ct. 1555, 131 L. Ed. 2d 490 (1995). Finally, the prosecution need not be in actual possession of the undisclosed evidence. If law enforcement agents or others acting on the government's behalf in the case are aware of the evidence, the prosecutor has a duty to learn of and disclose it. Kyles v. Whitley.

b. **The evidence must be "favorable to an accused" and "material" to guilt or punishment.** The *Brady* doctrine applies to evidence that is **"favorable to an accused"**—that is, to evidence with potential exculpatory value. It does not require disclosure of incriminating or unfavorable evidence.

   Moreover, to violate due process the undisclosed evidence must be **material to guilt or punishment.** Evidence "is material **only if there is a reasonable probability that, had the evidence been disclosed to the defense, the result of the proceeding would have been different."** United States v. Bagley, 473 U.S. 667, 105 S. Ct. 3375, 87 L. Ed. 2d 481 (1985); Kyles v. Whitley. The defendant **need not show** that a different outcome would **"more likely than not"** have occurred. Kyles v. Whitley. (In contrast, if exculpatory evidence that was not in the government's possession is discovered after trial, a defendant is entitled to relief only if the evidence "probably would have resulted in an acquittal." See United States v. Agurs.)

   If multiple items of evidence are not disclosed, materiality is judged by considering the evidence **"collectively, not item-by-item."** Kyles v.

Whitley. A court must evaluate the **"cumulative effect of suppression"** under the "reasonable probability" standard. Id.

A failure to disclose evidence that is **material to guilt** requires a **new trial.** A failure to disclose evidence that is only **material to punishment** requires only a **new punishment proceeding.** See Brady v. Maryland (granting only a new sentencing hearing because evidence was material to punishment but not to guilt).

c. **Significance of a "request" for the evidence.** Although *Brady* dealt with a situation in which the defense had made a "specific request" for a favorable item of evidence, the prosecution has a duty to disclose material evidence **whether or not a request is made.** Moreover, the "reasonable probability" materiality standard governs both request and nonrequest situations. See United States v. Bagley. The fact that the defense has made a **specific request** for the particular piece or kind of undisclosed evidence is, however, relevant to the materiality assessment. A failure to respond to a specific request for evidence may be more likely to affect the outcome of the trial by misleading defense counsel about the existence of evidence and altering the preparation or presentation of the defendant's case. See id.

d. **The timing of the disclosure required by the *Brady* Doctrine.** The duty to disclose material evidence **may, but does not necessarily, require pretrial disclosure.** A prosecutor can satisfy the constitutional requirement to disclose by revealing the evidence during trial **unless** the delay significantly impairs the defense's ability to derive its exculpatory value.

e. **Inapplicability of "harmless error" analysis.** When the government breaches the duty to disclose favorable, material evidence, it violates the defendant's right to due process. Because a showing of "materiality" requires a "reasonable probability" of a different outcome, the violation cannot be "harmless beyond a reasonable doubt." Kyles v. Whitley. See Chapter 21, sections E.2 and E.3 (discussing the concept of harmless constitutional error). Consequently, a conviction **must be reversed.**

 # EXAMPLE AND ANALYSIS

A jury convicted Floyd of conspiracy to import heroin. Prior to trial, Floyd's counsel requested "all *Brady* material." The government turned over some potentially favorable material in its possession. After trial, Floyd learns that the prosecutor did not disclose the fact that a key government witness was a paid informant who had once been convicted of "false pretenses." Floyd also learns that the Drug Enforcement Administration had illegally wiretapped the home of Floyd's alleged co-conspirator and had recorded one conversation in which there was a conspicuous failure to refer to Floyd during discussion of the importation scheme. Floyd moves for a new trial. The prosecutor responds by claiming that he had "innocently and inadvertently forgotten to turn over information about the informant" and that the DEA "did not inform [him] of the recording." Is Floyd entitled to a new trial?

Very possibly. First, neither response by the prosecutor carries any weight. Whether the government's failure to disclose violates due process does not depend on whether the failure is "culpable"—that is, whether the evidence was intentionally suppressed or inadvertently overlooked. Moreover, evidence in the possession of law enforcement officers involved in a case is within the scope of the government's duty to disclose whether or not the prosecutor knows of it. The sole question is whether the evidence is material—that is, whether there is a reasonable probability that the result of the trial would have been different if the evidence had been disclosed. The "cumulative effect" of all the evidence must be evaluated. There may well be a "reasonable probability" that the jurors would have had a "reasonable doubt" about Floyd's guilt if they had known that a *key witness* was a *paid* informant, that he had been convicted of a *crime of dishonesty*, and that a co-conspirator had *failed to mention Floyd's involvement* during a conversation that he did not know was being overheard by the government. In resolving Floyd's claim, it would be important to know how strong the rest of the case was, how important a witness the informant was, whether the "false pretenses" conviction could have been used to impeach the informant, and how unnatural it would have been for the co-conspirator not to mention Floyd in the context of the conversation that was wiretapped.

C. CONSTITUTIONAL RESTRICTIONS ON REQUIRED DEFENSE DISCLOSURE

Certain of the defendant's constitutional rights can restrict the government's power to require defense disclosure or to sanction the defendant for failing to comply with discovery requirements. Those rights include the guarantee of **due process,** the **privilege against compulsory self-incrimination,** and the **entitlement to present evidence in one's defense.**

1. Protection Against Discovery Afforded by the Due Process Clause

The **Due Process Clause** guarantees a fundamentally fair trial. Fairness within an "adversarial" system does not require that defendants always be allowed to withhold what they know from the government. Williams v. Florida, 399 U.S. 78, 90 S. Ct. 1893, 26 L. Ed. 2d 446 (1970) (parties do not "enjoy an absolute right always to conceal their cards until played"). It is not "unfair" to require defense disclosure *if* it serves the state's "legitimate" interest in "enhanc[ing] the search for truth." Id.

Due process is violated if a state requires a defendant to disclose information about a particular subject without granting the defendant a "reciprocal" right to disclosure from the government. The Due Process Clause "speak[s] to the balance of forces between the accused and the government" and, "in the absence of a strong showing of state interests to the contrary, [requires that] **discovery must be a two-way street.**" Wardius v. Oregon, 412 U.S. 470, 93 S. Ct. 2208, 37 L. Ed. 2d 82 (1973). It undermines the adversary system and is "fundamentally unfair to require a defendant to divulge the details of his own case while at the same time subjecting him to the hazard of surprise concerning refutation of the very pieces of evidence which he disclosed to the State." Id.

 EXAMPLES AND ANALYSIS

In Williams v. Florida, a defendant challenged Florida's "notice of alibi" rule that required a defendant who wanted to raise an alibi defense to notify the state and provide the names of alibi witnesses. The state had to notify the defendant of witnesses it intended to call to rebut the alibi claim. The Supreme Court held that the rule **did not violate due process** because it was "carefully hedged with reciprocal duties requiring state disclosure to the defendant," served an "obvious and legitimate" state interest in "protecting itself against an [easily fabricated] eleventh-hour defense," and was "designed to enhance the search for truth."

In Wardius v. Oregon, however, the Court agreed with a defendant's claim that the state's "notice of alibi" rule **violated the Due Process Clause.** The approach taken by the rule was "fundamentally unfair" because it required a defendant to divulge his defense and identify supportive witnesses but did not require the state to inform the defense of prospective rebuttal witnesses. According to the Court, "the Due Process Clause . . . forbids enforcement of alibi rules unless reciprocal discovery rights are given to criminal defendants."

   2. **Protection Against Discovery Afforded by the Privilege Against Compulsory Self-Incrimination**

   The **Fifth Amendment** guarantees that **no person "shall be compelled in any criminal case to be a witness against himself."** A mandate that the accused reveal information to the government can violate this constitutional guarantee. To establish a violation, the matter disclosed must be **testimonial,** it must be **incriminating,** and the defendant must be improperly **compelled** to disclose it. Fisher v. United States, 425 U.S. 391, 96 S. Ct. 1569, 48 L. Ed. 2d 39 (1976).

   a. **Requirement of a "testimonial" disclosure.** The Fifth Amendment prohibits the government only from compelling **testimonial** self-incrimination. See Schmerber v. California, 384 U.S. 757, 86 S. Ct. 1826, 16 L. Ed. 2d 908 (1966). Discovery rules may not compel a person to "be a witness"—to *testify*—against himself. In other words, a defendant may not be required to reveal incriminating thoughts or knowledge orally, in writing, or by conduct. Discovery rules that command a defendant to produce *nontestimonial* evidence cannot violate the privilege.

An individual may be forced to provide incriminating tangible evidence such as blood, see id., or written statements by witnesses, see United States v. Nobles, 422 U.S. 225, 95 S. Ct. 2160, 45 L. Ed. 2d 141 (1975). These sorts of evidence are not testimonial—they do not contain the defendant's thoughts. The privilege is not implicated unless the very **act of producing** a nontestimonial item reveals incriminating thoughts or knowledge and the government seeks to use **those thoughts or that knowledge** to incriminate the defendant.

b.   **Requirement that the disclosure be "incriminating."** The Fifth Amendment prohibits compelling a person "to be a witness **against himself.**" Only compulsory **self-incrimination** is forbidden. The privilege bars the state from using incriminating evidence that is the product of required discovery. The government, however, may enforce discovery rules that require a defendant to furnish evidence that is not itself incriminating and does not lead to incriminating evidence. See Doe v. United States, 487 U.S. 201, 108 S. Ct. 2341, 101 L. Ed. 2d 184 (1988) (recognizing the "incrimination element" of the privilege).

c.   **Requirement that the defendant be "compelled."** The Fifth Amendment bars the government from **compelling** self-incrimination. Nothing in the Constitution, however, prohibits a defendant from incriminating himself. Voluntary disclosures to the prosecution before or during a trial cannot violate the Fifth Amendment privilege.

   i.   **Testimonial disclosures that are not compelled.** Discovery rules might require an individual to produce papers that contain his own thoughts. Even though the thoughts contained in the papers are both "testimonial" and "incriminating" in nature, they may be used against the individual without violating the Fifth Amendment because the government has **only compelled the production of the "testimony," it has not compelled the testimony itself.** Fisher v. United States. Put otherwise, the defendant's **thoughts have not been forced from his mind—they were voluntarily expressed by the defendant.** Id. Because the defendant **has,** however, **been compelled to produce** the papers, any testimonial, self-incriminating content contained in this **"act of production" may not be used** against the accused. United States v. Doe, 465 U.S. 605, 104 S. Ct. 1237, 79 L. Ed. 2d 552 (1984).

EXAMPLE AND ANALYSIS

Frances kept extensive records of the prostitution ring she operated. To prosecute her successfully, the government requested that she produce those records and a judge ordered her to comply. Frances objected, asserting her Fifth Amendment privilege. The judge ruled that her claim was invalid. Did the judge rule correctly?

Yes. Although the records contain testimonial, self-incriminating content, the Fifth Amendment allows the government to force Frances to turn them over and to use the content against her because the "testimony" in the records is not being forced from her mind. However, because the act of producing the records is being compelled, the government may not use any "testimonial" content expressed in that act to incriminate her. In other words, anything that the act of production reveals about Frances's thoughts or knowledge may not be used against her. Thus, if the fact that Frances produced the records in response to the government's request shows that she was aware of their existence and if that awareness is probative of guilt, the government may not use Frances's compelled response to the request to prove her awareness.

---

        ii.   **"Acceleration" of legitimate compulsion.** When an accused discloses information at trial as a result of the "legitimate pressures" created by the "force of historical fact" and "the strength of the State's case" against him, he has effectively been "compelled" to reveal that information. Williams v. Florida. Even if the information is "testimonial" and "self-incriminating," the Fifth Amendment is not violated because such compulsion is "legitimate"—that is, it is not the sort of government-generated pressure forbidden by the privilege. If the state does not *add* to these legitimate pressures to disclose, but simply requires the disclosures to occur at an earlier time, the constitutional result is the same. There is no "compelled self-incrimination transgressing the Fifth . . . Amendment." Id. Consequently, discovery rules **may properly require** the disclosure of testimonial, self-incriminating information if their effect is merely to **"compel[the individual] to accelerate the timing of his disclosure, forcing him to divulge at an earlier date information that"** he plans to divulge at trial. Williams v. Florida.

EXAMPLE AND ANALYSIS

In Williams v. Florida, a discovery rule required the accused to disclose an intent to raise an alibi defense, to provide specific information about the place the defendant claimed to have been at the time of the crime charged, and to furnish the names and addresses of alibi witnesses. The defendant complied, but claimed that the required disclosure violated his Fifth Amendment right. The Court did not dispute that the defendant had incriminated himself and was willing to assume that he had been required to provide testimonial evidence. Nonetheless, it concluded that the discovery rule did not "require[ ] the defendant to rely on an alibi or prevent[ ] him from abandoning the defense." Moreover, it had "in no way affected [the defendant's] crucial decision to call alibi witnesses or added to the **legitimate pressures**" to disclose this information at trial. Its only effect was to compel an accelerated disclosure of the information.

One reading of *Williams* finds it essential that the defendant could decide to abandon the alibi defense prior to trial without having his expression of intent to raise an alibi used against him. Some courts, however, have upheld rules that do allow a defendant's change of heart regarding an alibi to be used against him. In addition, some interpret the *Williams* holding as not authorizing the government to "accelerate" pressures to reveal other kinds of evidence. They read the holding as limited by the alibi context and as confined to other situations that, like alibi, have a limited potential for incrimination. Others, however, have concluded that *Williams* allows states to compel defendants to accelerate the disclosure of any information that they intend to reveal at trial. According to that interpretation, discovery rules may constitutionally require a defendant to disclose any defense that he intends to use and may even require the disclosure of lists of every witness that the defendant intends to call.

---

3. Protection Against Discovery Sanctions Provided by the Sixth Amendment Right to Compulsory Process

The **Sixth Amendment** explicitly provides a **right "to have compulsory process for obtaining Witnesses in [the defendant's] favor."** Taylor v. Illinois, 484 U.S. 400, 108 S. Ct. 646, 98 L. Ed. 2d 798 (1988). Because this guarantee "embrace[s] the right to have the witness' testimony heard by the trier of fact," it affords a constitutional entitlement "to offer testimony." Id. This entitlement "may . . . be offended by the imposition of a discovery sanction that . . . excludes the testimony of a material defense witness." Id.

The **right** to offer testimony is **not absolute;** it may be outweighed by "countervailing public interests." Id. Consequently, **states are not categorically prohibited from** enforcing discovery rules with the sanction of **"evidence preclusion."** In some circumstances, state interests in sanctioning discovery violations are sufficient to justify barring a defendant from presenting evidence in his defense. Id.

There is no "comprehensive set of standards" for determining when the "preclusion sanction" comports with the Sixth Amendment. It is clear, however, that only "serious" and "willful" violations may result in preclusion. There are at least two situations in which the sanction is valid. First, if "a pattern of discovery violations is explicable only on the assumption that the violations were **designed to conceal a plan to present fabricated testimony,** it [is] entirely appropriate to exclude the tainted evidence." Id. Second, if the "explanation" for a failure to disclose a witness's identity shows that the failure was "**willful and motivated by a desire to obtain a tactical advantage** that would minimize the effectiveness of [the government's] cross-examination," a court may exclude the testimony of that witness. Id. In these circumstances, a court may exclude evidence even though alternative sanctions that do not infringe on the right to offer evidence are available. Id.

REVIEW QUESTIONS AND ANSWERS

Question: After Angie is convicted of first-degree theft, she learns that a store detective who testified for the state lied when she said that she had seen Angie leaving the store on the day of the alleged theft. Moreover, Angie also discovers that the investigating officer took a statement from a saleswoman on the day of the theft in which she said that she had seen another woman handling the jewelry that Angie had allegedly stolen that day. According to the statement, the other woman "looked an awful lot like" Angie. Angie moves for a new trial. Should her motion be granted?

Answer: It is uncertain. If the government intentionally introduced the false testimony by the detective or knowingly allowed the falsehood to go uncorrected, Angie is entitled to a new trial if there is "any reasonable likelihood" that the false testimony could have affected the jury's judgment. In addition, the government's failure to disclose the potentially exculpatory statement of the saleswoman provides the basis for a possible due process entitlement to a new trial. The failure to disclose requires a new trial if the evidence is "material"—that is, if there is a "reasonable probability" that Angie would not have been convicted if the evidence had been disclosed for use at trial.

Question: Carrie is charged with child abuse after her stepchildren are found locked in small dark closets. Prior to trial, the government asks, pursuant to an applicable discovery rule, whether Carrie intends to raise any defense related to her mental capacity and requests a list of any witnesses, including experts, and any documents, including health records, that Carrie intends to introduce in support of such a defense. Carrie asserts a constitutional right not to reply. Does she have a valid claim?

Answer: It is unlikely that Carrie has a valid claim. A due process claim would be valid only if the discovery rule does not grant "reciprocal" discovery to the defense. A Fifth Amendment privilege claim would not be valid because, like notice-of-alibi rules, a rule requiring a defendant to disclose a "mental impairment" defense only "accelerates" the timing of a disclosure. The rule does not exert any impermissible compulsion on the defendant.

Question: Before trial, Benjy responded to the state's pretrial request for documents he intended to introduce at his felony tax-evasion trial. During the trial, after the state had rested, Benjy notified the state that he had "overlooked three crucial documents" and offered to furnish them to the state immediately. The state asked the court to prohibit Benjy from using the three documents in his defense. Benjy objected. May the court grant the state's request?

Answer: The court must make certain findings to grant the state's request. Evidence preclusion threatens a defendant's Sixth Amendment right to offer evidence in his defense. The right is not absolute, but preclusion requires a "serious" and "willful" discovery violation. If the judge finds that Benjy held the documents back in an effort to conceal a plan to present fabricated evidence or that his failure to comply was willful and motivated by a desire for tactical advantage over the government, the court may grant the government's requested sanction. If Benjy's explanation that he "overlooked" the documents is the truth—that is, if his failure was inadvertent or negligent, at worst—preclusion is not consistent with the Constitution.

14 BAIL AND PREVENTIVE DETENTION

CHAPTER OVERVIEW

This chapter is primarily concerned with **release on bail** and **"preventive detention"** of accused individuals **prior to trial.** It also briefly addresses **release and detention pending appeal** of a conviction. Accused individuals have interests in gaining release. Both pretrial and postconviction detentions can cause unjustified losses of liberty and can impair the defendant's ability to prepare and present an adequate defense. Moreover, a detained individual may lose a job, may become alienated from family and friends, and may even be victimized by others in jail. At the same time, society has strong interests in regulating pretrial release. Accused persons may frustrate efforts to enforce the criminal laws by fleeing the jurisdiction or by destroying evidence or tampering with witnesses. Moreover, they may commit additional crimes while they are released and may inflict irreparable damage on the community.

Both constitutional provisions and legislative enactments attempt to strike a proper balance between individual and societal interests. The **Eighth Amendment prohibition of "excessive bail"** and the **Fifth and Fourteenth Amendment guarantees against deprivations of "life, liberty, or property, without due process of law"** restrict governmental power to detain accused persons. Within the constraints of those provisions, state and federal "bail statutes" prescribe the processes and conditions for obtaining release as well as the substantive criteria that must guide release decisions.

More specifically, this chapter discusses:

- **The Eighth Amendment right against "excessive bail."** It is unclear whether the "Excessive Bail Clause" of the Eighth Amendment regulates both legislatures and courts or only courts. What is clear is that the clause prohibits **only**

265

"excessive bail." The meaning of the term "excessive" and the consequent restrictions on governmental authority to detain those awaiting trial are addressed here. A brief sketch of potential constraints on detention pending appeal is also included.

- **Indigents and money bail.** Indigent defendants have claimed that the Eighth Amendment, the Equal Protection Clause, and the Due Process Clause provide protection against monetary bail conditions that they are unable to satisfy. They have asserted an entitlement to release on alternative, nonfinancial conditions that will serve the interests of the system. The issues raised by such claims are considered briefly.

- **The Federal Bail Reform Act of 1984.** Subject to constitutional limitations, each jurisdiction makes policy choices regarding bail and detention that are designed to strike a balance between the accused's "liberty" interests and the state's concerns with enforcing the law and protecting the community. These policies are reflected in the bail statutes of each jurisdiction. The Federal Bail Reform Act of 1984 governs pretrial and postconviction release in the federal system and provides a useful vehicle for discussion and illustration.

- **Preventive detention.** An individual might be detained to prevent flight, to prevent interference with the processes of the court, or to prevent further harm to the community. Of these kinds of "preventive detention," the most controversial is the last. First, the constitutionality of the practice of preventive detention is considered. Then, the federal "preventive detention" scheme is described in detail.

A. THE EIGHTH AMENDMENT RIGHT AGAINST "EXCESSIVE BAIL"

"**Bail**" refers to the conditions under which an accused person may gain release from official confinement prior to trial or pending appeal. Frequently, but not always, the conditions are financial—for example, the deposit of money or property with the court or the provision of a "bail bond" in a specified amount. The **Eighth Amendment** limits official authority to set bail conditions by providing that "**[e]xcessive bail shall not be required.**" Two main questions arise in connection with the Excessive Bail Clause: (1) **whether it speaks at all to the authority of legislatures** to regulate release on bail, and (2) **what is meant by the term "excessive."**

1. Nature of the Eighth Amendment Right

There is dispute over the nature of the Eighth Amendment guarantee. One view holds that the provision **does not grant a constitutional right to bail.** It imposes **no restrictions on legislative authority** to grant or deny release on bail, but **merely precludes courts from requiring "excessive bail"** when the legislature has granted a statutory right to bail. See United States v. Salerno, 481 U.S. 739, 107 S. Ct. 2095, 95 L. Ed. 2d 697 (1987). According to this view, a legislature could deny bail to all or select classes of defendants without running afoul of the Eighth Amendment. A violation can occur only if a judge demands excessive bail from an accused who has a legislatively granted right to bail.

The contrary view holds that the Excessive Bail Clause **contains an implicit constitutional right to nonexcessive bail** and **governs both legislatures and courts.** Neither can deprive a defendant of the right to have bail set at a level that is not excessive. Under this interpretation, a legislature could not deny bail to all defendants because in many cases the consequence would effectively be "excessive bail."

The Supreme Court has refrained from endorsing either view. See United States v. Salerno ("We need not decide today whether the Excessive Bail Clause speaks at all to Congress' power to define the classes of criminal arrestees who shall be admitted to bail"). The issue will be raised again in the discussion of "preventive detention."

2.   Meaning of "Excessive" Bail

The constitutional command that "[e]xcessive bail shall not be required" prohibits courts, and possibly legislatures, from setting bail conditions that are "excessive." At one time, the Supreme Court suggested that bail is "excessive" **whenever it is set at a level "higher than an amount reasonably calculated" to assure "the presence of [the] accused" for trial.** Stack v. Boyle, 342 U.S. 1, 72 S. Ct. 1, 96 L. Ed. 3 (1951). Today, however, it is clear that bail conditions are **not** constitutionally **excessive** if they are **set at a level reasonably calculated to serve any "compelling interest."** United States v. Salerno. Thus, bail conditions reasonably calculated to prevent flight, to safeguard the integrity of court processes, or to prevent an accused from further endangering the safety of those in the community are not excessive. See id.

 # EXAMPLE AND ANALYSIS

Cleo is charged with lewd acts with a minor. A judge concludes that Cleo is likely to appear for trial if released on her own recognizance, but sets bail at $1,000 in order to "send a message about the seriousness of the offense." Cleo appeals the ruling, claiming that the $1,000 bail is "excessive."

The appellate court should agree with Cleo. Under the Eighth Amendment, a court cannot set bail at a level higher than is reasonably needed to serve a legitimate purpose of pretrial release conditions. Sending a message about the seriousness of an offense is **not** a legitimate objective of bail conditions.

On remand, the judge conditions Cleo's release on "reporting daily to the marshal." Cleo appeals this condition on Eighth Amendment grounds. Again, the appellate court should probably reverse the trial judge's order. Unless the reporting requirement is reasonably calculated to ensure Cleo's appearance or prevent some cognizable danger, its imposition on Cleo's freedom is "excessive."

a. **Necessity for individualized determinations of bail.** The Eighth Amendment requires that bail conditions be set on an individualized basis. Each accused is entitled to have a bail determination made based on the facts of her particular case. Stack v. Boyle. For each defendant, there must be "evidence" and a specific "showing" that the conditions of release are no more than are reasonably necessary to ensure her presence or serve some other compelling interest. Id. Consequently, the nature and seriousness of an alleged offense cannot be the sole determinant of the conditions necessary to ensure a defendant's appearance. To decide what is needed to ensure a particular defendant's appearance, the judge should consider all the factors relevant to the likelihood of that defendant's flight—for example, the weight of the evidence against the accused, her financial ability, her ties to the community, and her character and trustworthiness. See id. Similarly, to ascertain the conditions needed to prevent danger to the community, the judge must evaluate the nature of any potential danger, the likelihood that the particular defendant will cause harm, and the measures needed to minimize or eliminate the risk in the particular case.

 EXAMPLE AND ANALYSIS

Judge James has devised a "bail schedule" that prescribes a fixed amount of bail for each offense. The amounts are graded according to the seriousness of and the punishment authorized for each offense. The schedule establishes a presumptive minimum amount necessary to ensure any defendant's appearance for each offense. That presumption is irrebuttable. Is the judge's scheme constitutional?

No. The Eighth Amendment demands individualized determinations of the amount of bail reasonably necessary in each case. All relevant facts must be taken into account in setting that figure. By making the seriousness of the offense and the authorized punishment the sole considerations, the judge has ignored this demand and has created a risk that the amount set for a particular defendant will be more than is needed to ensure appearance at trial.

b. **Constitutionality of denying release on bail.** The prohibition on "excessive" bail does not preclude either legislatures (if the Eighth Amendment governs their actions) or courts from explicitly denying release on bail or from implicitly denying release by deliberately setting unreachable bail conditions. A complete denial of bail will not be "excessive" **if** it is no more than is reasonably calculated to serve one of the "compelling" interests that are proper bases for imposing bail conditions. Although such instances are likely to be rare, if the facts establish that detention is the only way to ensure an accused's presence or prevent a serious threat to the integrity of the judicial process, a judge may deny release without violating the Eighth Amendment.

 # EXAMPLE AND ANALYSIS

A state legislature proposes a bail scheme that prohibits release on bail in all capital cases. Opponents contend that the proposal is unconstitutional. Does the scheme violate the Eighth Amendment?

If the Eighth Amendment does not restrict legislative power, then the proposed scheme cannot violate that provision because lawmakers are free to deny bail to all or certain classes of defendants. If the Excessive Bail Clause does govern legislatures, the provision is arguably constitutional *either* because the penalty facing a capital defendant is so severe that no conditions could reasonably ensure presence *or* because capital defendants pose such serious dangers to society that no release conditions could adequately ensure community safety.

On the one hand, "presumptions" based solely on the nature of an offense or a penalty arguably are unjustifiable and violate the principle that requires individualized bail determinations. On the other hand, the unique severity of the death penalty may justify a presumption that there are simply no conditions that could sufficiently counteract the incentive to flee. In addition, the extreme danger posed by a capital defendant may justify a presumption that the only way to adequately ensure community safety is "preventive detention."

State provisions precluding the release of capital defendants "when proof is evident and the presumption great" have survived constitutional challenges. Moreover, in United States v. Salerno, the Supreme Court repeated its earlier declaration that "in criminal cases bail is not compulsory where the punishment may be death."

3. The Eighth Amendment and Bail on Appeal

Bail provisions typically make some provision for release on bail pending the appeal of a conviction. See, e.g., section C.2 below. The question here is whether the Eighth Amendment regulates the practice of granting bail on appeal. The answer is uncertain.

One possibility is that the **Eighth Amendment** guarantee against excessive bail **has the same force on appeal** that it has prior to conviction. See Sellers v. United States, 89 S. Ct. 36, 21 L. Ed. 2d 64 (1968) (Black, J.) (suggesting that the "command of the Eighth Amendment" regarding excessive bail does regulate release pending appeal). If so, the provision precludes courts (and perhaps legislatures) from setting bail conditions "higher" than reasonably necessary to serve compelling interests and requires individualized, case-by-case assessments.

Assessments of the excessiveness of bail conditions pending appeal would clearly have to take into account the increased risks of both flight and interference with court processes following conviction. Conditions that might be excessive if imposed to ensure appearance *for trial* might well be reasonable when used to guarantee that a defendant will submit to imprisonment following affirmance of a conviction on appeal.

Another possibility is that the **prohibition on excessive bail** governs only release on bail prior to conviction and **does not apply to bail on appeal.** If so, it does not prevent courts or legislatures from denying or setting excessive bail on appeal. Conditions could not violate the Eighth Amendment even if they were more restrictive than reasonably necessary to serve a compelling interest. The Supreme Court has not determined which view of the relationship between the Excessive Bail Clause and bail on appeal is correct.

B. CONSTITUTIONALITY OF MONEY BAIL FOR INDIGENTS

Bail systems have traditionally relied heavily on financial conditions for release. Although there has been considerable movement away from that model in recent years, monetary conditions of release are still frequently used. Indigent defendants who have not been able to gain release because they lack resources have challenged financial release conditions on three constitutional grounds: (1) the Eighth Amendment prohibition on excessive bail, (2) the Fourteenth Amendment Equal Protection Clause, and (3) the Fourteenth Amendment Due Process Clause. See Gonzalez v. Warden, 21 N.Y.2d 18, 233 N.E.2d 265, 286 N.Y.S.2d 240 (1967). A few courts have been receptive to the constitutional challenges to bail raised by indigents. Most courts, however, have not agreed with their claims and have upheld reasonable financial conditions for indigent defendants despite the availability of alternative, nonfinancial release conditions. See, e.g., Gonzalez v. Warden; Pugh v. Rainwater, 572 F.2d 1053 (5th Cir. 1978). These three claims are briefly described below.

1. The Eighth Amendment Challenge to Financial Bail Conditions

Indigents have argued that if there are nonfinancial bail conditions that will accomplish the state's goals, money bail that results in detention is "excessive" because it restricts an indigent's liberty more than is necessary to serve the legitimate purposes of society. In other words, the Eighth Amendment requires the state to permit release on nonfinancial conditions that will serve its purposes.

2. The Equal Protection Clause Claim

Indigent defendants have claimed that they are discriminated against on account of financial status in violation of the **Fourteenth Amendment Equal Protection Clause** when they must remain in jail pending trial while those with resources gain pretrial release. See Bandy v. United States, 81 S. Ct. 197, 5 L. Ed. 2d 218 (1960) (Douglas, J.) ("to demand a substantial bond which the defendant is unable to secure raises considerable problems for the equal administration of the law"). To eliminate this unconstitutional discrimination, courts must prescribe nonfinancial conditions that will serve the state's purposes.

3. The Due Process Clause Claim

Indigents have asserted that pretrial detention resulting from an inability to meet financial conditions is "fundamentally unfair" because it undermines the "presumption of innocence" and interferes with their opportunities to prepare defenses. Both kinds of unfairness arguably violate the guarantee against deprivations of liberty "without due process of law."

C. FEDERAL BAIL REFORM ACT OF 1984: RELEASE BEFORE TRIAL AND PENDING APPEAL

Subject to the constitutional limitations discussed in this chapter, state and federal systems have authority to prescribe conditions and provide mechanisms for release on bail pending trial and appeal. The governing statutes vary dramatically in both substance and degree of detail. No attempt is made here to survey the various statutory provisions. Instead, a brief sketch of the influential and highly detailed **Federal Bail Reform Act of 1984,** 18 U.S.C. §§3141-3156, is provided.

1. Bail Pending Trial

The Act presumes that a defendant will be released on bail conditions pending trial. Although detention is authorized, **a judge must order pretrial release** *unless* the government establishes one of the limited bases justifying detention. See sections E.1 and E.3 below.

a. **Release on personal recognizance or an unsecured bond.** The Act requires judges to impose the **least restrictive** release conditions that will prevent flight and protect the community. Judges **"shall order the pretrial release of the person on personal recognizance, or upon execution of an unsecured appearance bond** in an amount specified by the court . . . **unless the [judge] determines that such release will not reasonably assure the appearance of the person or will endanger the safety of any other person or the community."** 18 U.S.C. §3142(b).

    b. **Release on conditions.** The state has the burden of justifying additional release conditions. If the state carries its burden, the judge **"shall order the pretrial release** of the person . . . **subject to the** *least restrictive . . . condition,* or *combination of conditions,* **that [the judge] determines will reasonably assure the appearance of the person . . . and the safety of any other person and the community."** 18 U.S.C. §3142(c)(1)(B). Possible conditions include, inter alia, remaining in the custody of a person, maintaining employment, restricting associations or travels, refraining from the use of drugs or alcohol or from the possession of a firearm, undergoing treatment, executing an agreement to forfeit money or property, or providing a bail bond. 18 U.S.C. §3142(c)(1)(B)(i)-(xiv).

    c. **Factors to be considered.** In determining the appropriate release conditions, a judge "shall . . . take into account the available information concerning" (1) "the **nature and circumstances of the offense,"** (2) "the **weight of the evidence,"** (3) "the **history and characteristics of the person,"** and (4) "the **nature and seriousness of the danger** . . . that would be posed by . . . release." 18 U.S.C. §3142(g).

    d. **Financial conditions that result in pretrial detention.** The Act specifies certain substantive and procedural prerequisites for pretrial detention. See section E below. To prevent circumvention of these prerequisites— that is, to prevent judges from effectively detaining individuals **without complying with the substantive and procedural requirements**—the Act provides that a judge **"may not impose a financial condition that results in the pretrial detention of the person."** 18 U.S.C. §3142(c)(2). This provision does **not require** a judge to **release** an individual who cannot satisfy a financial condition that has been imposed. Instead, if a judge prescribes a financial condition after deciding that it is the least restrictive condition needed to reasonably ensure a defendant's appearance and if the defendant cannot meet that condition, a judge is supposed to **"proceed with a detention hearing** . . . and order the defendant detained, if appropriate." United States v. McConnell, 842 F.2d 105 (5th Cir. 1988).

2. **Bail Pending Appeal**

Following conviction, there is a **strong presumption in favor of detention.** Pending appeal, a judge **"shall order that a person . . . be detained unless** the [judge] finds" (1) **"by clear and convincing evidence** that the person **is not likely to flee or pose a danger to the safety of any other person or the community** if released" under the provisions that regulate pretrial release **and** (2) "that the **appeal is not for purpose of delay and raises a substantial question of law or fact likely to result in—(i) reversal, (ii) an order for a new trial, (iii) a sentence that does not include . . . imprisonment, or (iv) a reduced sentence to a term less than the total of the time already** served plus the expected duration of the appeal process." 18 U.S.C. §3143(A), (B).

In essence, a convicted defendant has the burden of showing clearly and convincingly that there are conditions that will render him not likely to flee or endanger the community, that he is not appealing to delay the process, that his appeal raises a debatable claim, and that if he is detained and the claim on appeal is decided in his favor he will have served unjustified time in jail.

D. CONSTITUTIONALITY OF PREVENTIVE DETENTION

"Preventive Detention" is the practice of **denying an accused any opportunity for pretrial release** in order **to prevent either flight or danger.** While no state currently has a "full-scale preventive detention scheme" to prevent threats to the public safety, both the District of Columbia and the federal government have such provisions. See LaFave and Israel, Criminal Procedure 606-607 (2d ed. 1992); see also section E below (describing the preventive detention provisions of the Federal Bail Reform Act of 1984).

Preventive detention is subject to challenge on both **Fourteenth Amendment–Due Process** and **Eighth Amendment–Excessive Bail** grounds. In United States v. Salerno, the Supreme Court upheld the constitutionality of the federal provisions that authorize pretrial detention to prevent community danger. The *Salerno* opinion sheds considerable light on the constitutionality of preventive detention.

1. Preventive Detention and "Substantive" Due Process

Under the **Due Process Clause,** punishment may be imposed only for past offenses. To satisfy **substantive due process,** preventive detention must be **regulatory, not punitive.** Id. Detention can be "regulatory" if (1) it is **not intended as punishment;** (2) it is **not excessive in relation to an alternative, regulatory purpose that it is designed to serve;** and (3) the **interest** served by detention is **sufficiently important to "outweigh the individual's liberty interest."** Id. (suggesting that the interest furthered may have to be **"both legitimate and compelling"**).

   a. **Whether detention is "intended" as punishment.** Whether a detention scheme is **"intended"** **to be punitive** depends on the purpose of the legislature. Pretrial detention schemes aimed at preventing danger to the community, guaranteeing that an accused appears for trial, or insuring that a defendant does not threaten the integrity of judicial processes by threatening witnesses or engaging in other obstructive behavior are intended **not** to be punitive but to serve "legitimate regulatory goals." See id.

   b. **Whether detention is excessive in relation to its "regulatory" purpose.** Detention must not be excessive in relation to its regulatory purpose. The question here is whether the imposition on the detainee's freedom is proportionate to, and no greater than what is required to serve, the regulatory purpose of the detention. Relevant criteria include whether the class of potential detainees is limited to those posing serious threats, whether a prompt detention hearing is required, whether the period of pretrial detention is limited, and whether the "conditions of confinement" reflect the purported regulatory objectives.

c. **Whether the regulatory interest is sufficiently important.** Preventive detention schemes seek to prevent harm to the community, ensure defendants' appearances at trials, and/or prevent interference with or disruption of judicial processes. Each of these interests is sufficiently important to outweigh an arrestee's "strong interest in liberty." Thus, a preventive detention scheme can be consistent with substantive due process if it is designed to **prevent "crime by arrestees"** or **"identified and articulable threat[s] to . . . individual[s] or the community."** Moreover, detention designed to restrain individuals who **"present[] a [sufficient] risk of flight or a [sufficient] danger to witnesses"** can comport with substantive due process. Id.

 # EXAMPLE AND ANALYSIS

In United States v. Salerno, the defendants contended that the Federal Bail Reform Act provision allowing detention when a judge "finds that no condition or combination of conditions will reasonably assure the safety of any other person and the community," 18 U.S.C. §3142(e), violated substantive due process. The Court rejected the due process challenge because Congress did not intend punitive detention, because the "incidents of pretrial detention" were not "excessive in relation to the regulatory goal Congress sought to achieve" (preventing danger to the community), and because the "government's interest in preventing crime by arrestees is both legitimate and compelling." It was also important that the provision allowed the detention only of those accused of "extremely serious offenses" and required the government to make a specific showing, by clear and convincing evidence, that there were "no conditions of release [that could] reasonably assure the safety of the community."

2. Preventive Detention and "Procedural" Due Process

Due process also requires sufficient *procedural* **protections** to guard against unjust deprivations of liberty—that is, deprivations based on unreliable findings. In *Salerno*, the Supreme Court also rejected the defendants' procedural due process challenge because the Federal Bail Reform Act contained the following "extensive safeguards": a special detention hearing with the right to the assistance of counsel; the rights to testify in one's own behalf, to present information, and to cross-examine witnesses; statutorily enumerated factors to guide the judge's determination; a burden of proof on the government by "clear and convincing evidence"; requirements of written findings of fact and a written statement of reasons supporting a detention decision; and immediate appellate review. While the *Salerno* Court held these safeguards adequate, it did not identify the *minimum* procedural protections necessary to comply with due process.

3. Preventive Detention and the Guarantee Against "Excessive Bail"

Assuming that the Excessive Bail Clause restrains legislative action, it clearly allows legislatures to prescribe "conditions of release **or detention** [that are] **not . . . 'excessive.'** " **Detention** is **not excessive** if it is "mandated on the basis of a **compelling interest.**" Id. Put otherwise, if the state can establish a need to detain an individual to serve a compelling interest, "the Eighth Amendment does not require release on bail." In *Salerno*, the Court held that pretrial detention based on the "compelling" interest in assuring community safety is not excessive. The Court also indicated that detention designed to assure an accused's presence or prevent damage to the processes of justice would be consistent with the Eighth Amendment.

E. FEDERAL BAIL REFORM ACT OF 1984: PREVENTIVE DETENTION

The following section contains a thumbnail sketch of the preventive detention scheme contained in the Federal Bail Reform Act of 1984.

1. Limited Classes of Defendants Subject to Detention Hearings

The Act authorizes detention only after a detention hearing **and** authorizes detention hearings only for certain individuals. A hearing may be held if there is "a serious risk that the person will flee, . . . obstruct or attempt to obstruct justice, or threaten, injure, or intimidate, or attempt to threaten, injure, or intimidate, a prospective witness or juror." A hearing may also be held if the case involves "a crime of violence," "an offense for which the maximum sentence is life imprisonment or death," any of a number of narcotics offenses that carry a maximum term of 10 years, or "any felony if the person has been convicted of two or more" of the kinds of offenses already described. 18 U.S.C. §3142(f)(1), (2).

2. Detention Hearing Requirement

To detain an individual who falls into one of the enumerated categories, a judge must promptly hold a "detention hearing" at which the accused has a right to retained or appointed counsel, and "an opportunity to testify, to present witnesses, to cross-examine witnesses who appear at the hearing, and to present information by proffer or otherwise." 18 U.S.C. §3142(f).

3. Finding Required for Detention

Detention can be justified to prevent either flight or danger. To order pretrial detention, a judge must find "that **no condition or combination of conditions will reasonably assure the appearance of the person as required and the safety of any other person and the community.**" Id. The facts used to support the finding must "be supported by **clear and convincing evidence.**" Id. Moreover, in deciding whether any conditions will ensure the accused's appearance and community safety, the court must "take into account" the same factors relevant to prescribing appropriate release conditions—that is, the nature and circumstances of the offense, the weight of the evidence, the history and characteristics of the person, and the nature and seriousness of any danger posed.

REVIEW QUESTIONS AND ANSWERS

Question: Renee was arrested for and charged with selling narcotics within 500 feet of a school. At her arraignment, the prosecution asks that the judge set bail at $500,000 to insure that the defendant does not flee. Renee opposes the request, claiming that $500,000 would be "excessive." How should the court determine whether to grant the prosecution's request?

Answer: The court must look at all the relevant factors to determine whether the amount requested is "reasonably calculated" to ensure Renee's presence. If it is more than is needed to make sure that Renee does not flee, the amount is excessive. The judge must make an individualized determination based on the nature of the offense, the potential penalty, the strength of the government's case, the defendant's financial resources, her ties to the community, her character, and any other factors that bear on the question of whether less onerous conditions will provide adequate assurance that Renee will show up for trial.

Question: As part of an effort to combat crime by defendants who are released pending trial, a state legislature passes the following law: **"No person shall be entitled to bail pending trial for any felony charge."** On what grounds should this law be challenged? Should a challenge be sustained?

Answer: The statute might be challenged as violative of the implicit right to bail contained in the Eighth Amendment "Excessive Bail Clause" and as violative of the Due Process Clause. It is unclear whether the Eighth Amendment challenge should be sustained. The due process challenge has considerable merit.

It is unclear whether the Eighth Amendment contains a "right to bail" that restricts legislative action. If the Eighth Amendment is addressed only to courts and not to legislatures, the statute should survive an attack on that ground. If legislative action is subject to the Eighth Amendment, then the question is whether a denial of bail for all alleged felons is "excessive." The argument that such a denial is excessive is similar, if not identical, to the argument that a denial of bail violates substantive due process.

The Due Process Clause clearly controls legislative action. It forbids punishment before trial, requires that "regulatory" detentions not be "excessive in relation to" their purposes, and requires that the interests served by such detentions be sufficiently important to justify the serious infringements on liberty effected by pretrial detention. There is a strong argument that the statute will result in many deprivations of liberty that are excessive in relation to the legislature's regulatory purpose and unsupported by sufficiently weighty societal interests. It seems hard to believe that every person charged with a felony poses a sufficient threat of flight or danger to justify a total deprivation of liberty pending trial. There are probably many persons accused of felonies who pose minimal risks if released. When applied to those defendants, the statute at issue here is almost certainly unconstitutional.

The decision in United States v. Salerno provides support for this conclusion. In rejecting the defendants' substantive due process challenge to the federal preventive detention scheme, the Supreme Court stressed that the federal provision focused narrowly on a class of individuals who were shown to pose serious risks of harm. The Court pointedly observed that the federal statute was not a "scattershot attempt to incapacitate those who are merely suspected of . . . serious crimes."

Question: Max was indicted for federal mail fraud. A judge set bail at $100,000. Because he is indigent, Max cannot come up with the funds needed to gain release. What constitutional arguments should he raise regarding the validity of his bail? Are those arguments valid?

Answer: Max should claim that because he does not have the resources to satisfy this financial bail condition, the bail prescribed violates the Eighth Amendment, the Equal Protection Clause, and the Due Process Clause. To have any chance for success, Max should show that there are nonfinancial conditions available that will serve the legitimate purposes of bail. Even with such a showing, however, he is unlikely to prevail. See section B above (discussing these constitutional arguments and their general treatment by lower courts).

Max should also argue that the bail set does not comport with the requirements of the Federal Bail Reform Act. First, he should argue that the $100,000 is not the "least restrictive" condition that will ensure his presence and prevent danger. This argument could have merit. Under the Act, a judge must choose the "least restrictive" condition(s) that will ensure the accused's appearance at trial and will not endanger the community. The $100,000 bail is permitted only if the judge can support a determination that it is the least restrictive condition that will accomplish these purposes.

If the judge can support such a determination, Max should contend that by setting a financial condition that he is unable to meet the judge violated §3142(c)(2) of the Act. That section provides that a judge "may not impose a financial condition that results in the pretrial detention of the person." While this argument has merit, Max is not necessarily entitled to release or to different release conditions. Instead, because Max is being effectively detained by the condition prescribed, the judge must hold a detention hearing. If the conditions that justify "preventive detention" are satisfied, the judge may order that Max be detained.

15 PLEA BARGAINING AND GUILTY PLEAS

CHAPTER OVERVIEW

This chapter discusses the legal regulation of two related and "important components of this country's criminal justice system"—**plea bargaining** and **guilty pleas.** Bordenkircher v. Hayes, 434 U.S. 357, 98 S. Ct. 663, 54 L. Ed. 2d 604 (1978). **Plea bargaining** is the process by which the government and the defense negotiate a resolution of criminal charges without trial. For quite some time, it was a behind-the-scenes, unacknowledged part of the criminal justice system. More recently, the significance of plea bargaining and the benefits it affords both defendants and society have been recognized. See Santobello v. New York, 404 U.S. 257, 92 S. Ct. 495, 30 L. Ed. 2d 427 (1971) (plea bargaining is "highly desirable" and "an essential component of the administration of justice"); Corbitt v. New Jersey, 439 U.S. 212, 99 S. Ct. 492, 58 L. Ed. 2d 466 (1978) (states have legitimate interests in "facilitating plea bargaining").

A **guilty plea**—"the defendant's own solemn admission 'in open court that he is in fact guilty of the offense,' " Henderson v. Morgan, 426 U.S. 637, 96 S. Ct. 2253, 49 L. Ed. 2d 108 (1976) (White, J., concurring)—is often the product of plea bargaining. It is "more than a confession . . . it is itself a conviction." Boykin v. Alabama, 395 U.S. 238, 89 S. Ct. 1709, 23 L. Ed. 2d 274 (1969). Like a trial and verdict by a judge or jury, a guilty plea provides the foundation for a valid conviction and sentence. It is one of the "two ways under our system of criminal justice in which the factual guilt of a defendant may be established such that he may be deprived of his liberty consistent with the Due Process Clause." Henderson v. Morgan (White, J., concurring). A trial court's power to accept a guilty plea is " 'traditional and fundamental. Its existence is necessary for the . . . practical . . . administration of the criminal law.' " United States v. Jackson, 390 U.S. 570, 88 S. Ct. 1209, 20 L. Ed. 2d 138 (1968).

Both the Constitution and laws adopted by each jurisdiction regulate the practice of plea bargaining and the acceptance of guilty pleas. This chapter focuses primarily on the constitutional restrictions on plea bargaining and guilty pleas and also sketches the additional limitations in the federal system prescribed by Federal Rule of Criminal Procedure 11.

Specifically, this chapter discusses:

- **The permissible kinds of bargaining by the prosecution.** Prosecutors have broad discretion to employ various methods of encouraging defendants to plead guilty. Nonetheless, there are some limitations on the bargaining methods they are constitutionally entitled to use. Threats or promises can exceed the bounds of propriety and undermine the validity of a guilty plea.

- **Breaches of plea bargains by the prosecutor or the defendant.** When a guilty plea has been entered in reliance on a plea bargain and the prosecution fails to honor the terms of the deal, the defendant is constitutionally entitled to relief. A court must either order "specific performance" of the agreement or allow the accused to withdraw the guilty plea induced by the breached bargain.

- **Federal Rule of Criminal Procedure 11 and plea bargaining.** Federal Rule of Criminal Procedure 11(e) regulates plea bargaining in the federal system. It approves the practice, describes the roles of the parties and the court, and sketches the sorts of agreements that might be reached.

- **The requirements for valid guilty pleas.** Guilty pleas must be voluntary, knowing, and intelligent. All guilty pleas must be supported by a "record" that establishes their voluntary, knowing, and intelligent character. A guilty plea can be constitutionally acceptable even though the accused will not admit guilt or is asserting innocence.

- **Challenges to guilty pleas.** A guilty plea may be challenged on appeal or on collateral attack on the ground that it was not voluntary, knowing, and intelligent. Moreover, a guilty plea is invalid and may be successfully overturned if it is the result of "ineffective assistance of counsel." An "independent" constitutional claim—an alleged violation of constitutional rights occurring "antecedent" to the entry of a guilty plea—generally may not be relied on as a basis for a collateral attack on a guilty plea. However, constitutional claims that the state lacked power to prosecute a charge may be the basis for a collateral challenge to a guilty plea.

- **Federal Rule of Criminal Procedure 11 and guilty pleas.** Federal Rule of Criminal Procedure 11 details the requirements for a valid guilty plea in federal court. The advice and inquiries demanded by FRCrP 11 go beyond the minimum constitutional requisites for a valid guilty plea.

A.   THE PLEA BARGAINING PROCESS

Plea bargaining, a frequent part of the resolution of criminal charges, takes different forms. A prosecutor may agree to dismiss a serious charge in exchange for a plea to a lesser offense or may agree, when multiple charges are pending, to dismiss some charges in exchange for a plea to others. The prosecutor might agree to make a particular sentencing recommendation to the judge or not to oppose a defendant's request for leniency. A prosecutor might even warn an accused that if a guilty plea is not entered, more serious charges will be filed. See FRCrP 11(e)(1); Bordenkircher v. Hayes.

Plea bargaining has advantages for both the state and the defendant. These advantages include the "prompt and largely final disposition" of many cases, avoidance of "the corrosive impact of idleness" resulting from confinement pending trial, protection of the public from accused persons who are released pending trial, and the enhancement of "rehabilitative prospects" by shortening the time between charge and disposition. Santobello v. New York.

While the Supreme Court has acknowledged the constitutionality and legitimacy of plea bargaining, see id.; Brady v. United States, 397 U.S. 742, 90 S. Ct. 1463, 25 L. Ed. 2d 747 (1970), an accused has **no constitutional right to have the government engage in plea bargaining.** Weatherford v. Bursey, 429 U.S. 545, 97 S. Ct. 837, 51 L. Ed. 2d 30 (1977).

1. Permissible Kinds of Plea Bargaining by the Prosecution

The interest of the state in plea bargaining is "to persuade the defendant to forego [the] right to plead not guilty." Bordenkircher v. Hayes. In part because a guilty plea provides "substantial benefits" to society, Brady v. United States, and in part because it provides a basis for leniency, Corbitt v. New Jersey, the government may encourage guilty pleas by offering the accused "substantial benefits" or "a proper degree of leniency." Id.

The prosecution has broad discretion to select a bargaining method that will provide ample encouragement to plead guilty. The government, for example, can offer to dismiss charges or can promise to make a favorable sentencing recommendation. A prosecutor may even "threaten" to indict a defendant for a more serious offense if he refuses to plead guilty so long as the threat is part of the give and take of a negotiation process in which the accused remains "free to accept or reject the prosecutor's offer." See Bordenkircher v. Hayes. Moreover, the prosecutor may properly carry out such a threat if an agreement is not reached. Id.

 # Example and Analysis

In Bordenkircher v. Hayes, during plea negotiations over a charge of uttering a forged instrument the prosecutor offered to recommend a sentence of five years in prison in exchange for a guilty plea. He also said that if the accused did not plead guilty, "he would return to the grand jury and seek an indictment" under the state's "habitual criminal" provision—which would subject the defendant to a "mandatory sentence of life imprisonment.'' The defendant refused to plead guilty, whereupon the prosecutor carried out the threat. The defendant was convicted and sentenced to life in prison.

The Supreme Court noted that it was undisputed that the "habitual criminal" charge had been justified by the evidence, that the prosecutor had been in possession of that evidence at the time of the original indictment, and that the defendant's refusal to plead had led to the more serious charge. The Court observed that while the Due Process Clause prohibits a prosecutor from "punishing" a defendant for exercising his rights, the prosecutor in this case had not done so. Instead, "the prosecutor . . . no more than openly presented the defendant with the unpleasant alternatives of forgoing trial or facing charges on which he was plainly subject to prosecution." The plea bargaining and the execution of the threat were constitutionally legitimate.

---

2. Limitations on the Prosecutor's Plea Bargaining Methods

The prosecution's authority to bargain has the potential for abuse and is subject to certain constitutional limitations. Id. In general, the **Due Process Clause** requires "**[f]airness in securing agreement.**" Santobello v. New York. The specific requirements of "fairness" in the bargaining process are far from clear.

A prosecutor **may not punish an accused for exercising her constitutional rights. Retaliation** against a defendant **or vindictiveness** because of a refusal to plead guilty and insistence on a trial **violates due process.** Bordenkircher v. Hayes; Corbitt v. New Jersey. There is no constitutional violation, however, if the prosecution merely "discourage[s the] . . . assertion of [the defendant's] trial rights" by confronting the defendant with the threat of more serious charges if no plea is entered. Bordenkircher v. Hayes. A prosecutor should not bring additional or more serious charges after plea negotiations have failed unless the defendant has been given notice of that possibility. Id. Moreover, a prosecutor should not threaten to bring **unwarranted** charges against a defendant. See id.; Brady v. United States.

Plea bargaining practices that deprive a defendant of the "**free[dom] to accept or reject the [government's] offer**" are constitutionally impermissible. Bordenkircher v. Hayes. Whether a particular "inducement" or "encouragement" goes too far and unacceptably impairs a defendant's freedom to choose depends on the circumstances. There is no bright line between permissible and impermissible practices.

A prosecutor **may not make threats or promises during plea negotiations for improper reasons.** A desire to induce a guilty plea is a constitutionally permissible reason for appropriate threats of more serious consequences or offers of more lenient treatment. Threats or promises based on race, religion, or other factors that have no relevance to the bargaining or charging processes are unacceptable. See id.

A legislature may enact statutes that hold out substantial benefits for defendants who forgo trial and plead guilty. Corbitt v. New Jersey. Nevertheless, statutes that **"needlessly encourage[ ]" guilty pleas and the waiver of constitutional rights** impermissibly burden the exercise of those rights and are invalid. United States v. Jackson, 390 U.S. 570, 88 S. Ct. 1209, 20 L. Ed. 2d 138 (1968). In theory, prosecutorial plea bargaining techniques are subject to this same limitation. In practice, however, it is most unlikely that a prosecutor's methods would ever be found to have "needlessly encouraged" a guilty plea and waiver of rights.

 # EXAMPLE AND ANALYSIS

Arno is charged with first-degree murder. He is obsessively devoted to his wife, Monique, who is charged with second-degree murder in connection with the same homicide. During plea negotiations, the prosecutor tells Arno that if he pleads guilty to first-degree murder, the state will make a favorable sentencing recommendation for Monique. If he refuses to plead, the state will seek to raise the charge against her to first-degree murder. The evidence could support that charge. Did the offer and threat by the prosecutor exceed legitimate bounds?

Possibly. In Bordenkircher v. Hayes, the Court noted that a prosecutor's offer of adverse or lenient treatment for someone other than the defendant "might pose a greater danger of inducing a false guilty plea by skewing the assessment of the risks a defendant must consider." This would seem to be particularly true in this case because of Arno's devotion to his wife.

3. Remedies for Improper Plea Bargaining by the Prosecutor

If a defendant pleads guilty in response to improper bargaining by the government, a **plea may be declared involuntary and therefore invalid.** See sections B.1.a and B.2.a below. A conviction based on such a plea **must** be reversed. It is conceivable that a bargaining method could be improper but the plea that results not be "involuntary." In that situation, an accused *might* still successfully claim that a conviction violates due process because it is the invalid product of a plea secured by "fundamentally unfair methods."

If a defendant resists improper bargaining methods and insists on a trial, and the state subsequently brings **improper charges**—charges that are unwarranted, vindictive, retaliatory, or designed as punishment for going to trial—**a conviction must be reversed.** If the bargaining methods used by the government were impermissible but the charges tried were not improper, it is unclear whether a conviction after trial must be overturned.

4. Breaches of Bargains by the Prosecutor

The Due Process Clause guarantees "fairness" in the plea bargaining process. Santobello v. New York. When a guilty plea **"rests in any significant degree on a promise or agreement of the prosecutor,** so that it can be said to be part of the inducement or consideration," **fundamental fairness demands that the government fulfill its promise or agreement.** Id. A defendant is entitled "to what is reasonably due in the circumstances" even if the prosecutor's breach is inadvertent and not culpable. Id. A claim that a guilty plea rests on a breached bargain requires a court to ascertain whether there was a promise or agreement, the nature of that promise, whether the defendant's guilty plea rested "in any significant degree" on that promise, and whether the prosecution failed to perform.

A breach requires a **remedy.** In *Santobello*, the defendant claimed that the government had breached and sought to withdraw his guilty plea as a result. Upon finding a breach, the Supreme Court did not order that the defendant be allowed to withdraw his plea. Instead, the Court remanded the case to the lower court to determine whether **withdrawal of the guilty plea** or **specific performance by the prosecutor** was the appropriate remedy. The *Santobello* majority's decision to remand the question of remedy makes it **unclear** whether an accused **ever has a constitutional entitlement to withdraw a plea or to demand specific performance.** A later description of *Santobello* as a case in which the conviction was inconsistent with due process because the defendant had pleaded "guilty on a false premise" seems to suggest that the defendant is entitled to withdraw a guilty plea when the prosecution breaches the bargain. See Mabry v. Johnson, 467 U.S. 504, 104 S. Ct. 2543, 81 L. Ed. 2d 437 (1984) (noting also that the *Santobello* court had "expressly declined to hold that the Constitution compels specific performance of a broken prosecutorial promise").

5. Unexecuted Bargains and Withdrawn Offers

Unlike the breach of an executed bargain, a "plea bargain standing alone is without constitutional significance." Mabry v. Johnson. Until the defendant pleads guilty and the bargain is "embodied in the judgment of a court," a plea bargain "does not deprive an accused of liberty or any other constitutionally protected interest." Id. Consequently, the acceptance of a prosecutor's proposed plea bargain **does not give rise to a right to have the bargain specifically enforced.** Id. Moreover, if the defendant accepts an offer, is made fully aware of the prosecutor's withdrawal of that offer, and then, with the advice of competent counsel, pleads guilty pursuant to another, less advantageous bargain, the resulting guilty plea is valid. Id. The prosecutor's negligence or culpability in making and withdrawing the earlier offer is irrelevant. Id.

6. Federal Rule of Criminal Procedure 11 and Plea Bargaining

Federal Rule of Criminal Procedure 11(e) governs plea bargaining in the federal system. It specifically **authorizes** the government attorney and defense counsel or the pro se defendant to "engage in **discussions with a view toward reaching an agreement** that, upon the entering of a plea of guilty or nolo contendere . . . , the attorney for the government will . . . move for dismissal of other charges; . . . make a recommendation, or agree not to oppose the defendant's request for a particular sentence . . . ; or . . . agree that a specific sentence is the appropriate disposition of the case." Judges may not participate in plea bargaining discussions.

Any agreement that is reached ordinarily must be disclosed on the record in open court at the time a plea is entered. A **judge is not bound to accept the agreement.** If a judge does accept the agreement, she must advise the defendant that the disposition agreed to will be embodied in the judgment and sentence of the court. If the judge rejects the agreement, she must inform the parties, advise the defendant personally that the court is not bound by the agreement, give the defendant the opportunity to withdraw the plea, and advise the defendant that if the plea is not withdrawn the disposition may be less favorable than that contemplated by the rejected agreement.

B. GUILTY PLEAS

A criminal defendant may plead not guilty, guilty, or nolo contendere. The latter two pleas result in convictions. A guilty plea may be the product of a plea bargain or of the realization that the evidence of guilt is so strong that a trial would be pointless. For essentially the same reasons as plea bargaining, guilty pleas are advantageous to both the defendant and the state. See Brady v. United States; see also section A above (for a discussion of the advantages of plea bargaining). A trial court's power to accept a guilty plea is "traditional and fundamental," United States v. Jackson, but must be exercised "with care and discernment." Brady v. United States. Nonetheless, an accused has **no "absolute right under the Constitution to have his guilty plea accepted** by the court." North Carolina v. Alford, 400 U.S. 25, 91 S. Ct. 160, 27 L. Ed. 2d 162 (1970).

1. Requirements for a Valid Guilty Plea

A guilty plea involves more than an admission of guilt that will support a conviction and sentence. It also entails the **waiver of several fundamental constitutional rights.** Boykin v. Alabama, 395 U.S. 238, 89 S. Ct. 1709, 23 L. Ed. 2d 274 (1969) (noting that a defendant who pleads guilty waives the Fifth Amendment privilege against compulsory self-incrimination and the Sixth Amendment rights to trial by jury and to confront witnesses). Consequently, a guilty plea must be **voluntary, knowing, and intelligent.** Id.; Brady v. United States; North Carolina v. Alford. A guilty plea that is not voluntary, knowing, and intelligent **violates due process and is void.** Boykin v. Alabama; McCarthy v. United States, 394 U.S. 459, 89 S. Ct. 1166, 22 L. Ed. 2d 418 (1969).

a. **A guilty plea must be "voluntary."** A guilty plea must be "the **voluntary** expression of [the defendant's] own choice." Brady v. United States. An **improperly coerced** plea is invalid. Id. Actual or threatened physical harm or mental coercion that overbears the defendant's will renders a guilty plea involuntary. Id. Threats, promises to discontinue improper harassment, misrepresentations (including unfilled or unfulfillable promises), or promises that have no proper relationship to a prosecutor's business (such as bribes) can also make a guilty plea involuntary. Id. A guilty plea produced by coercion is an unreliable admission of guilt and an invalid surrender of constitutional rights.

To evaluate the voluntariness of a plea, a court must consider "all of the relevant circumstances surrounding it." Id. These circumstances include both the pressures applied by state officials and the internal weaknesses of the defendant.

A state may use relatively powerful inducements or threats to "encourage" a guilty plea. See section A.1 above. Guilty pleas resulting from acceptable inducements offered by statute or during plea bargaining are not involuntary. See Bordenkircher v. Hayes; Brady v. United States. Thus, a guilty plea induced by the prosecutor's threat to file more serious, justified charges if the defendant refuses to plead is not involuntary. See Bordenkircher v. Hayes. Moreover, a guilty plea entered because of a statutory provision making the death penalty available only after a jury trial and the defendant's fear of and desire to avoid any risk of death is not involuntary. Brady v. United States. In sum, a guilty plea is not compelled simply because it is motivated by a defendant's fear of a more severe sanction after trial. Id.

 # EXAMPLES AND ANALYSIS

1. Ned was charged with manufacturing methamphetamine after DEA investigators discovered an extensive manufacturing enterprise in his barn. He pleaded guilty because the prosecutor warned him that a failure to enter a plea could well result in serious conspiracy charges being filed against his wife and children, who were apparently aware of the enterprise. There is credible evidence suggesting that Ned's wife and children may have been co-conspirators. Is Ned's plea valid?

Probably not. The prosecutor's threat to file serious charges against Ned's wife and children created inordinate pressure and may well have overborne his will and compelled him to enter the guilty plea. Threats of adverse consequences for family members have a special potential for compulsion.

2. If the prosecutor promised Ned that he would recommend a minimum sentence of "one year in jail" if Ned pleaded guilty but that he would seek the maximum sentence if Ned went to trial, would Ned's guilty plea be valid?

Probably. The state is entitled to use powerful inducements to encourage a guilty plea. The offer of a dramatically different sentencing recommendation is very unlikely to be seen as improper compulsion and very likely to be deemed a permissible part of the negotiating process.

> **Note:** Although the Supreme Court has said that a guilty plea that results from constitutionally ineffective assistance from counsel is invalid because its "voluntariness" is compromised, see Hill v. Lockhart, 474 U.S. 52, 106 S. Ct. 366, 88 L. Ed. 2d 203 (1985), it is appropriate to treat the potential impact of "ineffective assistance" on guilty pleas as a discrete subject, separate from the issue of "voluntariness." See subsection 2.b below (discussing challenges to guilty pleas based on claims of ineffective assistance).

b. **A guilty plea must be "knowing and intelligent."** A guilty plea is valid only if it is **knowing and intelligent.** Brady v. United States. A defendant must be **aware** of certain things **and** must be **mentally competent** to understand and to make the choices entailed in pleading guilty.

First, a defendant must have a **"full understanding of the charges against him."** Id. Due process requires that the accused receive "real notice of **the true nature of the charge[s].**" Henderson v. Morgan. Notice of the "true nature" of a charge requires an awareness of its essential elements, see id., and an **"understanding of the law in relation to the facts,"** McCarthy v. United States. The totality of the surrounding circumstances must be examined to determine whether the defendant received adequate information regarding "the **substance of the charge.**" Henderson v. Morgan.

Second, the accused must understand **"the direct consequences"** of **pleading guilty.** Brady v. United States. Direct consequences surely include the nature and extent of the **sentences that might be imposed** and "the **actual value of any commitments** made" to the defendant by the judge, prosecutor, or her own counsel. Id. Whether there are other "direct consequences" that the defendant must understand is uncertain.

Third, because a guilty plea is a "waiver" of fundamental constitutional rights, a defendant must know the **"nature of the protections" that are being waived.** Henderson v. Morgan. At a minimum, a defendant should understand that she is entitled to a trial, to an impartial jury, and to confront witnesses against her at trial, and should be aware that she is not required to admit her guilt. See Boykin v. Alabama.

A guilty plea is **not invalid** simply because a state's case turns out to be weaker than the defendant thought or because the maximum penalty for an offense turns out to be less than the defendant thought at the time of the plea. See Brady v. United States. Even if the defendant's beliefs are the result of defense counsel's misapprehensions about the state's case or the law, a guilty plea is constitutionally sound unless counsel's assistance was constitutionally "ineffective." See id.; See also subsection 2.b below (discussing the requirements for successful ineffective assistance challenges to guilty pleas).

 # EXAMPLE AND ANALYSIS

In Henderson v. Morgan, the defendant was indicted for first-degree murder but pleaded guilty to second-degree murder, an offense that required an intent to cause death. Defendant challenged his guilty plea on the ground that he was not informed and was not aware that intent to cause death was an element of the offense.

The Supreme Court upheld a lower court decision that found the guilty plea invalid and overturned the judgment of conviction. According to the Court, "the plea could not be voluntary in the sense that it constituted an intelligent admission that [the defendant] committed the offense unless [he] received 'real notice of the true nature of the charge against him.' " Real notice in this case included the fact that "intent" was an essential element of second-degree murder. Even though the prosecutor may well have had ample evidence of intent, the record contained nothing that could "serve as a substitute for either a finding after trial, or a voluntary admission, that respondent had the requisite intent." Defense counsel did not stipulate that the defendant had the intent and did not explain to him that his plea would be an admission of intent. Moreover, the defendant "made no factual statement or admission necessarily implying that he had such intent." In those circumstances, the Court found it "impossible to conclude that his plea to the unexplained charge of second-degree murder was voluntary." It should be noted that the *Henderson* Court was using the word "voluntary" as a term of art. The problem with the guilty plea was not that the defendant was compelled to make it but rather that he was unaware of information that was critical to render his plea a true choice to admit guilt.

---

c. **An accused must be "competent" to enter a guilty plea.** An accused must be **competent to plead guilty.** Godinez v. Moran, 509 U.S. 389, 113 S. Ct. 2680, 125 L. Ed. 2d 321 (1993). The defendant must have "the capacity to understand the proceedings and assist counsel." Id. The constitutional standard for competency to plead guilty is the same as that for competency to stand trial: "whether the defendant **has** 'sufficient present ability to consult with his lawyer with a reasonable degree of rational understanding' and a 'rational as well as factual understanding of the proceedings against him.' " Id. Clearly, a defendant must have the ability to understand the matters essential to a knowing guilty plea—that is, the nature of the charges, the direct consequences, and the rights being waived.

d. **Validity of a guilty plea by a defendant who asserts innocence: The doctrine of North Carolina v. Alford.** An admission of guilt is not a constitutionally required basis for imposition of a criminal penalty. North Carolina v. Alford. Consequently, a guilty plea can be **valid even if** the defendant accompanies the plea with a **refusal to admit guilt or** with **protestations of innocence.** Id. The guilty plea of a defendant who asserts innocence is constitutionally acceptable if (1) the accused **voluntarily, knowingly, and understandingly consents to the imposition of punishment** and (2) the record contains **a strong factual basis of guilt.** Id.

Although states are not constitutionally required to reject guilty pleas from defendants who claim innocence, they do not have to accept such pleas. States remain free to prohibit guilty pleas unless they are accompanied by an admission of guilt.

 # EXAMPLE AND ANALYSIS

In North Carolina v. Alford, the defendant was indicted for first-degree murder, a capital offense. Pursuant to an agreement with the prosecutor, he pleaded guilty to second-degree murder. Before it accepted the plea, the trial court heard the testimony of a police officer, who summarized the state's case, and the testimony of two other state witnesses. The defendant "took the stand and testified that he had not committed the murder but that he was pleading guilty because he faced the threat of the death penalty if he did not do so." In response to the trial judge's inquiry, he affirmed his desire to plead guilty. Later, the defendant claimed that his plea was invalid.

The Supreme Court concluded that "an express admission of guilt . . . is not a constitutional requisite" for a valid guilty plea and that "an individual . . . may voluntarily, knowingly, and understandingly consent to the imposition of a prison sentence even if he is unwilling or unable to admit his participation in the acts constituting the crime." In addition, the Court observed that "a plea containing a protestation of innocence" can be valid "when . . . a defendant intelligently concludes that his interests require entry of a guilty plea and the record before the judge contains strong evidence of actual guilt." In sum, a guilty plea by a defendant who professes belief in his innocence is constitutionally acceptable when there is a "strong factual basis for the plea" and the defendant has "clearly expressed [the] desire to enter" the plea.

---

e. **Need for an adequate record to support a guilty plea.** A guilty plea involves the waiver of fundamental rights. In general, it is "impermissible" to presume the "waiver [of constitutional rights] from a silent record." Carnley v. Cochran, 369 U.S. 506, 82 S. Ct. 884, 8 L. Ed. 2d 70 (1962). Therefore, a guilty plea is invalid unless the record contains an "affirmative showing" that it was "voluntary, knowing, and intelligent." Boykin v. Alabama. The Constitution does not necessarily require judges expressly to instruct or question the accused; other evidence of voluntariness and understanding can suffice. Nonetheless, if the record does not include adequate evidence, a court's failure to inform and inquire will preclude a valid guilty plea.

2. **Challenges to the Validity of Guilty Pleas**

An accused may contest the validity of a guilty plea either on direct appeal of a conviction or by means of a collateral challenge. The potential for a successful attack on a guilty plea depends, in large part, on the context and nature of the defendant's claim.

a. **Claims that a plea was not voluntary, knowing, and intelligent.** A defendant may challenge a guilty plea by claiming that it was not entered voluntarily, knowingly, and intelligently. Such a fundamental attack on the validity of the plea may be made on appeal or on collateral review.

b. **Claims that a plea was based on "ineffective assistance" of counsel.** All defendants, including those who plead guilty, have the Sixth Amendment right to the effective assistance of counsel. See McMann v. Richardson, 397 U.S. 759, 90 S. Ct. 1441, 25 L. Ed. 2d 763 (1970); Hill v. Lockhart. To succeed with an ineffective assistance claim, the defendant must establish "deficient performance" and "prejudice." See Chapter 18, section C.2.c, for a full discussion of the requirements for ineffective assistance claims in guilty plea contexts.

An ineffective assistance challenge to the validity of a guilty plea may be brought either on direct appeal or on a collateral attack in federal court. See Tollett v. Henderson, 411 U.S. 258, 93 S. Ct. 1602, 36 L. Ed. 2d 235 (1973); Blackledge v. Perry, 417 U.S. 21, 94 S. Ct. 2098, 40 L. Ed. 2d 628 (1974). According to the Supreme Court, a challenge based on deficient legal assistance and advice is an attack on the voluntary and intelligent nature of the plea. Tollett v. Henderson.

c. **Claims of "antecedent" constitutional violations.** In general, "a voluntary and intelligent plea of guilty made by an accused person, who has been advised by competent counsel, may not be collaterally attacked." United States v. Broce, 488 U.S. 563, 109 S. Ct. 757, 102 L. Ed. 2d 927 (1989). Thus, in **federal habeas corpus proceedings,** a state defendant who pleaded guilty **may not** attack the validity of a conviction on the basis of an **"antecedent" constitutional violation.** Tollett v. Henderson; Blackledge v. Perry. The accused may not raise a claim that is **"independent"** of the validity of the guilty plea itself—that is, a "claim[ ] **relating to a deprivation of constitutional rights that occurred prior to the entry of the guilty plea.**" Tollett v. Henderson. Habeas corpus relief based on "antecedent" constitutional violations is unavailable; by pleading guilty, defendants effectively "waive" or "forfeit" such claims.

 # Examples and Analysis

In Tollett v. Henderson, a defendant who had pleaded guilty claimed that the grand jury that indicted him was unconstitutionally selected. The Supreme Court held that he could not raise his "antecedent" constitutional claim "to gain release through federal habeas corpus." Likewise, in McMann v. Richardson, a defendant claimed that his guilty plea was motivated by a "coerced confession." The Supreme Court held that a coerced confession claim was not a valid basis for a federal habeas corpus petition challenging a guilty plea that was voluntarily and intelligently made and based on "reasonably competent advice" from counsel.

A defendant with a potentially meritorious claim based on an "antecedent" constitutional violation might be able to succeed with a habeas corpus petition alleging that counsel's failure to present the antecedent claim before or at trial constituted ineffective assistance of counsel. See Blackledge v. Perry (in federal habeas corpus, antecedent violations may be the basis of "ineffective assistance" challenges to guilty pleas). In McMann v. Richardson, the Court concluded that an attorney's advice to plead guilty did not amount to "ineffective assistance" simply because counsel had erroneously assessed the admissibility of the defendant's confession. The defendant could not translate a barred coerced confession claim into a valid ineffective assistance claim because his lawyer's advice was not outside "the range of competence demanded of attorneys in criminal cases."

There is an **exception** to the general prohibition on habeas corpus challenges to guilty pleas based on antecedent constitutional violations. An antecedent violation may be raised if it **contests "the very power of the state to bring the defendant into court to answer the charge against him,"** Blackledge v. Perry, or if it would **"preclude[ ]" a state "from haling a defendant into court on a charge,"** Menna v. New

York, 423 U.S. 61, 96 S. Ct. 241, 46 L. Ed. 2d 195 (1975). An "antecedent" claim that **the State may not constitutionally prosecute** a charge
is not barred on collateral review. Id.; United States v. Broce.

 ## EXAMPLES AND ANALYSIS

Two Supreme Court cases illustrate this exception to the bar on claims of "antecedent"
violations. In Menna v. New York, the Supreme Court held that the defendant could
raise a double jeopardy violation in a federal collateral attack on a guilty plea because
a valid double jeopardy claim would "preclude[ ]" the state "from haling [him] into
court on [the] charge" to which he had pleaded guilty. A meritorious double jeopardy
claim bars the state from trying a defendant for an offense. And in Blackledge v. Perry,
the Court held that the defendant could challenge his guilty plea collaterally on the
ground that the prosecutor had responded "vindictively" to his successful appeal
by charging him with a more serious offense. A valid "due process–prosecutorial
vindictiveness" claim would deprive the state of "power . . . to bring the defendant
into court to answer the charge against him."

In United States v. Broce, however, the Court held that the defendant *could not* raise
an "antecedent" double jeopardy challenge when his claim could not be established
on the face of the current record but would have required a hearing "to expand the
record with new evidence." For "antecedent" claims that cannot be "judged on [the]
face" of the existing record, the "exception" invoked in *Menna* and *Blackledge* "has
no application."

3. **Federal Rule of Criminal Procedure 11 and Guilty Pleas**

Subject to the constitutional limitations discussed above, each jurisdiction
is free to fashion rules regulating the entry and acceptance of guilty pleas.
Federal Rule of Criminal Procedure 11 governs the guilty plea process in
federal courts. Many of the details of this rule are clearly designed to insure
compliance with the constitutional requirements outlined in the preceding
sections. The main features of Rule 11 are sketched below.

FRCrP 11(c) requires a court to "address the defendant personally in open
court and **inform the defendant of, and determine that the defendant
understands,**" the nature of the charge, the mandatory minimum penalty,
and the maximum penalty. An unrepresented defendant must be told of the
right to retained or appointed counsel. The accused must be informed of
the rights to plead not guilty, to be tried by a jury with the assistance of
counsel, to confront and cross-examine witnesses, and not to be compelled

to incriminate herself. In addition, the court must inform the accused that a guilty plea "waives the right to a trial."

FRCrP 11(d) prohibits a judge from accepting a plea "without first, by addressing the defendant personally in open court, **determining that the plea is voluntary** and not the result of force or threats or of promises apart from a plea agreement." The judge "shall **inquire** as to whether the defendant's willingness to plead guilty" is the result of plea discussions.

FRCrP 11(f) requires a court to **make "such an inquiry** as shall satisfy it that there is **a factual basis** for the plea," and FRCrP 11(g) requires a "**verbatim record** of the" guilty plea proceedings that "shall include . . . the court's advice to the defendant, the inquiry into the voluntariness of the plea . . . , and the inquiry into the accuracy of a guilty plea."

REVIEW QUESTIONS AND ANSWERS

Question: Marlo was charged with reckless endangerment, a felony, for leaving her eight-year-old son home alone. During plea negotiations, the prosecutor offered to reduce the charge to child neglect, a misdemeanor, if Marlo pleaded guilty. Marlo was reluctant to accept the offer, insisting that she didn't think she was guilty of anything. The prosecutor warned Marlo that if she refused to accept the offer, he would consider filing two additional reckless endangerment charges based on his belief that Marlo had left her son home alone on at least two other occasions. He also informed her that if she was convicted of all three felony charges he would seek to have her sentenced to life imprisonment based on the state's "three strikes" law. Are these constitutionally permissible bargaining methods? If Marlo pleads guilty, will the plea be valid? If she does not plead guilty, no additional charges are filed, and Marlo is convicted of reckless endangerment, is she entitled to any relief?

Answer: The prosecutor's offer to reduce the charge to a misdemeanor is certainly permissible. The threat to file two additional felony charges and to seek a life sentence is probably permissible under *Bordenkircher* if the two additional felony charges are justifiable. A prosecutor may use strong inducements to encourage a guilty plea—even the threat of serious additional charges—if they are justified. A prosecutor should not, however, threaten to bring unjustified charges in order to induce a guilty plea. If the two additional felony charges here were not justified, the threat was an impermissible bargaining technique.

If the threat was proper, a guilty plea or a conviction would be valid. If the threat was improper and Marlo pleaded guilty to the misdemeanor, she would have a strong argument that the plea was involuntary—that is, that the unjustified threat of two more felony charges and a potential life sentence overcame her will to stand trial. She could also argue that whether or not it was involuntary, the plea was the product of unfair methods and ought to be invalid under the Due Process Clause. The merits of this argument are uncertain.

Finally, if Marlo did not plead guilty in response to the threat of unjustified felony charges and was convicted of the one proper count originally filed, it seems unlikely that she would have any remedy for the impermissible attempt by the prosecutor to secure a guilty plea.

Question: Hector was indicted for two counts of murder. He pleaded guilty to both counts. The prosecutor then recommended and the judge imposed two sentences of life without possibility of parole. Hector has appealed the sentences, claiming that the prosecutor breached a bargain not to request life without possibility of parole if he pleaded guilty. The prosecutor claims that during plea negotiations, she initially said that she would not seek such sentences if Hector pleaded guilty to both counts, but that she retracted that offer and told Hector that she would not deal with him. She claims that his guilty pleas were entered pursuant to the advice of Hector's counsel. How should the appellate court rule? If Hector's appeal is successful, to what remedy is he entitled?

Answer: The court must determine who is telling the truth. If the offer was withdrawn and Hector pleaded guilty for other reasons, his appeal lacks merit. If there was a bargain and Hector pleaded guilty in reliance on it, the prosecutor's breach violates due process, and Hector is entitled to relief.

Assuming his appeal is successful, Hector is entitled either to withdraw his plea and to go to trial on the murder charges or to specific performance of the bargain— that is, to a resentencing at which the prosecutor does not seek life without possibility of parole. It is unclear whether Hector is entitled to his choice of remedy.

Question: Rita pleaded guilty to driving while intoxicated based on her attorney's recommendation that she so plead. After she is sentenced and has exhausted her opportunities for appeal and for state collateral relief, Rita learns that if she had gone to trial she might well have been acquitted because the confession she made to the authorities upon arrest was excludable due to a *Miranda* violation. Alleging that she pleaded guilty because she believed she would clearly be convicted based on her confession, Rita files a petition for a writ of habeas corpus in federal court. Should the petition be granted?

Answer: No. A defendant cannot successfully challenge a guilty plea in a federal habeas corpus proceeding on the basis of an "antecedent" constitutional violation unless the violation challenges the very power of the state to bring the charge. Rita's claim that she pleaded guilty because of her belief that the statement obtained in violation of *Miranda* was admissible is an allegation of an "antecedent" constitutional violation. The habeas court should not entertain this claim because it does not challenge the power of the state to bring the charge.

Rita's only hope for success in her request for collateral relief in federal court would be to claim that her guilty plea was "involuntary" because of ineffective assistance of counsel. She would have to show that her counsel failed to inform her about the *Miranda* claim or otherwise provided bad advice about the admissibility of her confession, and that the failure or advice constituted deficient performance under the standards prescribed in Strickland v. Washington, 466 U.S. 668, 104 S. Ct. 2052, 80 L. Ed. 2d 674 (1984). In addition, she would have to show that but for counsel's errors she would not have pleaded guilty and would have gone to trial. See Hill v. Lockhart.

16 THE RIGHT TO A SPEEDY PROSECUTION

 CHAPTER OVERVIEW

Delay in investigating a criminal offense and bringing charges or in prosecuting those charges can impair the fairness of a trial by hindering the accused's ability to present an adequate defense. Moreover, an individual's life might be disrupted in a variety of serious ways by a prolonged public investigation or the pendency of a formal accusation. Finally, pretrial restraint following arrest or onerous bail conditions can result in substantial deprivations of liberty.

To guard against these kinds of harm, two constitutional guarantees mandate government expedition in the pursuit of criminal charges. The **Due Process Clause** guarantee of "fundamental fairness" forbids some official pre-accusation delays that cause damage to an accused's ability to defend against criminal charges. The **Sixth Amendment Speedy Trial Clause** explicitly provides a **"right to a speedy . . . trial."** Moreover, statutes like the **Federal Speedy Trial Act** provide detailed schemes for the expeditious resolution of criminal charges.

This chapter discusses:

- **Due process protection against pre-accusation delay.** The Due Process Clause is the only constitutional provision that guards against **pre-accusation delay.** Two elements are essential to a due process claim: **government fault** and **prejudice.** In the rare cases in which defendants successfully establish both elements, criminal charges cannot be pursued.

- **The Sixth Amendment speedy trial guarantee.** The first topic is **attachment of the right** to a speedy trial. The right does not come into play until either arrest or formal charge. In addition, it is inoperative during periods when charges are dismissed and a defendant is released. The second topic is the **content of the right** to a speedy trial. Under this heading, the meaning of the term "speedy" and the standards for determining whether the government has moved too slowly are discussed. The Barker v. Wingo "balancing test" is the focus of the discussion.

• **The Federal Speedy Trial Act.** To supplement the constitutional protections, Congress has passed legislation that sets specific **time periods** that apply in federal court cases and prescribes the **remedies** available when the government exceeds those periods. A brief sketch of the substance of the Act concludes this chapter.

A. THE DUE PROCESS CLAUSE AND PRE-ACCUSATION DELAY

The Fifth and Fourteenth Amendments prohibit **deprivations of "life, liberty, or property, without due process of law."** These guarantees ensure **"fundamental fairness"** in criminal trials. Government delay in investigating offenses, filing charges, or prosecuting cases can result in the death or disappearance of witnesses, the loss of evidence, and the fading of memories, all of which can unfairly impair an accused's **ability to present a defense.** Consequently, the **Due Process Clause** provides a certain amount of protection against official **pre-accusation delay.** See United States v. Lovasco, 431 U.S. 783, 97 S. Ct. 2044, 52 L. Ed. 2d 752 (1977).

1. Elements Necessary to Establish a "Due Process–Pre-Accusation Delay" Claim

A defendant must show three things to succeed with a "due process–pre-accusation delay" claim: (1) **delay** (2) for **an insufficient reason** and (3) **prejudice.**

    a. Delay element. The basis of a due process claim is that **undue delay** has harmed a defendant's ability to defend. The "delay" requirement gives rise to two questions: What is the **relevant time period?** and What is the **minimum amount of delay** needed?

    Although the guarantee of due process is said to provide protection against "pre-indictment" or "pre-accusation" delay, see United States v. Lovasco, delay following accusation can also count. The ability to defend can be impaired by any delay prior to the resolution of the charges. Consequently, for due process purposes the **relevant period begins when an offense is completed and continues until a defendant is tried.**

    The **minimum time period** needed to raise a due process claim is uncertain. Some periods are undoubtedly too short to trigger due process scrutiny, but any "substantial" delay should suffice. Once sufficient delay is established, two other requirements must be met.

    b. Insufficient reason element. The "due process inquiry must consider **the reasons for the delay.**" United States v. Lovasco. A defendant must show that the government had insufficient reason to justify the delay. Some reasons are clearly insufficient, others are clearly sufficient, and still others are of unclear significance.

i. **Insufficient reasons.** A defendant can succeed with a due process claim by showing that officials **"intentionally delayed to gain some tactical advantage over . . . or to harass the [defendant]."** United States v. Marion, 404 U.S. 307, 92 S. Ct. 455, 30 L. Ed. 2d 468 (1971). This standard requires **culpable governmental intent**—that is, a **purpose** either to secure a "tactical advantage" (some benefit for the prosecution's case) or to "harass" the defendant (to inflict some kind of unjustified suffering).

Lesser official fault **may** suffice. In United States v. Lovasco, the government apparently conceded that "prosecutorial delay incurred in **reckless disregard of circumstances, known to the prosecution, suggesting . . . an appreciable risk that delay would impair the ability to mount an effective defense**" might support a due process claim. "Reckless" disregard would require both an awareness of the risk of harm to the defendant and a refusal to go forward without good reason.

ii. **Sufficient reasons.** No matter how long it lasts, **good faith investigative delay is permissible** and cannot support a successful due process claim. United States v. Lovasco. If delay results from a prosecutor's *good faith* judgment that further time is needed for a full investigation, a court may not second-guess that judgment. Id. More generally, if a delay is the result of any good faith effort to serve a legitimate governmental objective, a due process claim should fail. Therefore, even if a decision to delay is objectively unreasonable, "fundamental unfairness" cannot be found if the decision is made in good faith.

iii. **Reasons of unclear significance.** Between the two extremes of culpable intent and good faith lie a number of possible reasons. Two general categories can be identified. The first is **"negligent unjustified delay."** Without good reason, officials might fail to pursue an investigation under **circumstances that would have made a reasonable person aware of an appreciable risk of harm to the defense.** The second is **"non-negligent unjustified delay."** The prosecution might have no reason to postpone its pursuit in **circumstances that provide no objective notice of risk to the defense.** It seems likely that the Supreme Court would find that neither of these categories of delay can support a due process claim. Official "recklessness" is probably the minimum fault required to establish fundamental unfairness.

c. **Actual prejudice element.** Even if the reason for delay supports a due process claim, **"proof of prejudice is generally a necessary element."** United States v. Lovasco. There must be **"actual prejudice to the conduct of the defense."** United States v. Marion. Moreover, the actual prejudice **might** also have to be **"substantial."** Id.

"Actual prejudice to the conduct of the defense" means some tangible harm to the opportunity to avoid conviction. Other forms of "prejudice" from delay—such as anxiety, damage to a reputation, financial losses, or injury to one's associations—do not qualify.

In an egregious case, proof of actual prejudice *might* not be required. The *Lovasco* majority noted that "prejudice is *generally* a necessary element," and, for Speedy Trial Clause purposes, an exceptionally long delay can raise a **presumption of prejudice to the defense.** Doggett v. United States, 505 U.S. 647, 112 S. Ct. 2686, 120 L. Ed. 2d 520 (1992) (eight-and-a-half-year delay raises a "presumption of evidentiary prejudice").

2. **Remedy for a Due Process Violation**

If delay, an insufficient reason, and prejudice are established, it is fundamentally unfair to try a defendant. The only remedy for a due process violation is **dismissal of the charges and a permanent bar to conviction.**

 # EXAMPLE AND ANALYSIS

Federal prosecutors have ample evidence to charge Jonas with possession of cocaine with intent to distribute. Drug Enforcement Administration agents persuade the prosecutors to postpone arresting or charging Jonas because they believe that his drug activities could be part of a large narcotics distribution network. The agents fear that if Jonas is arrested or charged, his partners will be alerted and efforts to identify them will be frustrated. Five years later, the agents inform the prosecutors that they have turned up no evidence that Jonas was involved in a large-scale operation and have been unable to identify any other offenders. Prosecutors seek and obtain an indictment against Jonas.

Prior to trial, Jonas moves to dismiss the charges, claiming that the delay violated due process. The judge finds that the five-year delay "must have prejudiced" Jonas's defense and that the prosecutors "should have realized that such a delay would harm his ability to defend." She dismisses the charges. The government appeals. How should the appellate court rule?

The dismissal should *probably* be reversed. The court's presumption of prejudice is debatable. Actual prejudice is ordinarily required for a due process claim, but a five-year delay might support a presumption of prejudice. The ruling is not necessarily reversible on lack of prejudice grounds.

However, the reason for the delay probably does not justify dismissal. First, it is unlikely that "official negligence" with regard to harm to the defense is ever a sufficient foundation. More important, if the prosecutors and the DEA agents were engaged in a "good faith" investigation of other perpetrators, dismissal is unjustified even *if* they "should have known" of the potential harm to Jonas's defense. Judges are not supposed to second-guess official good faith decisions even if such decisions are "unreasonable." The trial judge here did not address the government's good faith.

B.   THE SIXTH AMENDMENT RIGHT TO A SPEEDY TRIAL

The Sixth Amendment provides that **"[i]n all criminal prosecutions, the accused shall enjoy the right to a speedy" trial.** Literally, these words could be read to require trials to progress at a rapid pace once they are commenced. Alternatively, they could be interpreted to demand that every trial be commenced within an absolute, inflexible time period. In fact, however, the clause has been read to require **"speed" in bringing a defendant to trial** and to be **far from absolute.** The speedy trial guarantee is " 'necessarily relative. It is consistent with delays and depends upon circumstances.' " Barker v. Wingo, 407 U.S. 514, 92 S. Ct. 2182, 33 L. Ed. 2d 101 (1972). The " 'essential ingredient' " of the guarantee is " **'orderly expedition and not mere speed.'** " United States v. Marion. In sum, the Sixth Amendment requires as much speed as is "reasonable" in each case.

The fundamental right to a speedy trial serves three objectives. It prevents undue and oppressive pretrial deprivations of liberty, minimizes the anxiety and concern that accompany public accusation, and limits the possibilities of harm to the accused's ability to defend himself. Id.

Assessments of speedy trial claims first require inquiry into **attachment of the right.** Before the right *attaches,* the government has no obligation to provide a speedy trial. Assuming that the right has attached, a second inquiry into the **content of the right** is necessary. The question here is whether the government has brought the defendant to trial with sufficient speed to satisfy the constitutional promise.

1.   Attachment of the Speedy Trial Right: The Time That Counts

Whether a Trial has been "speedy" necessarily requires a threshold determination of the amount of time that counts. For any time to count, the right must **attach and not be suspended.**

a.   **Initial attachment of the right: When the speedy trial clock begins to run.** The right to a speedy trial **attaches only when an individual is either arrested or formally charged with an offense.** Id. "The Speedy

Trial Clause . . . does not apply to the period before a defendant is indicted, arrested, or otherwise officially accused." United States v. MacDonald, 456 U.S. 1, 102 S. Ct. 1497, 71 L. Ed. 2d 696 (1982). Consequently, any time prior to either an arrest or a formal charge **does not count.**

If a formal charge has been made public, the speedy trial right **does attach** even though the defendant is unaware of the formal accusation and has not been arrested or subjected to any other actual restraints on liberty. Doggett v. United States, 505 U.S. 647, 112 S. Ct. 2686, 120 L. Ed. 2d 520 (1992). Formal public accusation alone triggers attachment of the right.

b. **Suspension of the right: When the speedy trial clock stops running.** If **formal charges are dismissed** and the **accused is released from custody** and **is not subject to bail conditions,** the Speedy Trial Clause has no application. Any time that passes **does not count.** United States v. MacDonald; United States v. Loud Hawk, 474 U.S. 302, 106 S. Ct. 648, 88 L. Ed. 2d 640 (1986).

The guarantee does not apply and the time ceases to count **both** when **the prosecution dismisses charges in good faith,** United States v. MacDonald, **and** when **a court dismisses charges against the will of the prosecution,** United States v. Loud Hawk. If a defendant is "not incarcerated or subjected to other substantial restrictions on [his] liberty," the time period following a dismissal of charges is treated like the time prior to an initial arrest or formal charge. Id.

If a prosecutor, in order **"to evade the speedy trial guarantee,"** dismisses charges **"in bad faith"** and later reinstates them, the time between dismissal and refiling **may** count toward a speedy trial claim. United States v. MacDonald. If a prosecutor **does not dismiss charges** but merely **suspends** a formal prosecution with the intent not to pursue the charges further at the present time, the speedy trial guarantee **continues to apply and the time counts.** Klopfer v. North Carolina, 386 U.S. 213, 87 S. Ct. 988, 18 L. Ed. 2d 1 (1967).

c. **Speedy trial right protection for prisoners.** Prisoners have speedy trial rights. If an individual is incarcerated for one offense and is formally charged with another offense, the **right to a speedy trial for the latter offense attaches when the formal charge is filed.** See Dickey v. Florida, 398 U.S. 30, 90 S. Ct. 1564, 26 L. Ed. 2d 26 (1970); Smith v. Hooey, 393 U.S. 374, 89 S. Ct. 575, 21 L. Ed. 2d 607 (1969).

This principle applies whether or not the jurisdiction with custody has filed the later charges. Any state with a pending formal accusation "has a duty to make a diligent and good-faith effort to secure the presence

of the accused from the custodial jurisdiction and afford him a trial.''
Dickey v. Florida.

 ## EXAMPLE AND ANALYSIS

The FBI has clear evidence linking Michael to a string of bank robberies. Agents have been unsuccessful in efforts to identify other participants. To avoid giving notice to unidentified accomplices, the U.S. Attorney requests that the indictments against Michael be kept "sealed." (A sealed indictment is not publicized.) Two years later, when accomplices are found and charged, the indictment against Michael is unsealed. Does the two-year period during which the indictment was sealed count toward a speedy trial claim?

Lower courts have divided over this issue. On the one hand, Michael is formally charged on the day the indictment is returned. In Sixth Amendment terms, he is an "accused." United States v. Marion, which held that the right to a speedy trial is triggered by either arrest or a formal charge, supports attachment in this case.

On the other hand, the *Marion* Court reasoned that losses of liberty and tangible and intangible harms inflicted by public accusation are the "major evils" that prompted the Speedy Trial Clause and that harm to the defense is insufficient to trigger attachment. This reasoning does not support attachment in this case because a defendant who is the subject of a sealed indictment cannot suffer either "major evil."

The more recent opinion in Doggett v. United States supports attachment in the case of a sealed indictment. In *Doggett*, the indictment was made public but the accused was not aware of it. The Court assumed, therefore, that the defendant could not have suffered either of the two "major evils." Still, the Court held that his speedy trial right *had attached.* The *Doggett* Court's reasoning suggests that once a grand jury hands down an indictment, the Sixth Amendment right applies.

2. The Content of the Speedy Trial Right: The Barker v. Wingo Balancing Test

In Barker v. Wingo, 407 U.S. 514, 92 S. Ct. 2182, 33 L. Ed. 2d 101 (1972), the Supreme Court held that the Speedy Trial Clause prescribes no "fixed-time period," no "specific number of days or months" within which the government must bring an accused to trial. Speedy trial claims must be resolved by applying a **"balancing test"** that "compels courts to approach each case[ ] on an ad hoc basis." **Four factors** must be balanced: (1) the **length of delay,** (2) the **reason for the delay,** (3) the defendant's **assertion of his speedy trial right,** and (4) **prejudice** to the defendant. "None of the four factors . . . [is] either a necessary or sufficient condition" for a speedy trial violation. All four factors must be "considered together with such other circumstances as may be relevant."

This "difficult and sensitive balancing process" requires courts to place on the accused's side those factors that suggest the deprivation of a speedy trial and on the government's side those that indicate adequate speed. Factors that are "neutral" should not tip the scales either way. A judge must first **ascertain the facts** pertaining to each of the four factors, then must **determine the side of the balance** on which the factor should be placed, and finally must **determine how much weight** to give the factor. The ultimate question is whether the balance tips in favor of or against a defendant's speedy trial claim.

a. **Length of the delay.** "The **length of the delay** is to some extent **a triggering mechanism.**" Id. There are some periods of time between arrest or charge and trial that are simply **too short** to violate the speedy trial right. Consequently, delay of a certain length is, in fact, **a necessary condition** for a valid speedy trial claim. The minimum length of time necessary to trigger the balancing process is uncertain. Lower courts have found postaccusation periods **approaching one year** to be **sufficient.** Doggett v. United States. **Five months** has generally been considered **too short.**

If the time period is long enough to trigger speedy trial analysis, it is uncertain whether the "length of delay" factor plays a further role in the balance. An exceptionally long delay might, in and of itself, add weight to the defendant's side. What is clear is that the length of the delay is related to the other three factors. The length of delay plays a role in determining whether a reason is adequate, whether and how a defendant should have asserted her right, and whether prejudice should be presumed.

b. **Reason for the delay.** The **reason for the delay** is very important. It is "the flag all litigants seek to capture." United States v. Loud Hawk. The question is "whether the government or the criminal defendant is more to blame for th[e] delay." Doggett v. United States. Different reasons might apply to different periods of delay, and "[d]ifferent weights should be applied to different reasons." Barker v. Wingo. A judge must identify the reason for each period of delay, determine the side of the balance on which it falls, and decide how much weight to give it.

"**[A] valid reason should serve to justify an appropriate delay.**" Barker v. Wingo. A legitimate objective that requires the government to postpone a trial should weigh on the state's side of the balance. Delay that is attributable to "**negligence or overcrowded courts,**" however, should weigh on the defendant's side. And "**a deliberate attempt to delay the trial in order to hamper the defense should be weighted heavily against the government.**" Id.

A trial might be delayed because a party has taken an interlocutory appeal from a trial court ruling. Delay arising from a **government appeal "ordinarily is a valid reason that justifies delay."** United States v. Loud Hawk. Such appellate delay can count against the government, however, if the appeal is taken in **"bad faith or [for a] dilatory purpose,"** if the delay results from **"overcrowded [appellate] courts,"** or if it was **unreasonable to delay the case** by appealing the issue. Id. Unreasonableness depends on the strength of the government's position, the importance of the issue, and the seriousness of the crime. Id.

Delay arising from a **defense appeal "ordinarily will not weigh in favor of a defendant's speedy trial claim."** Even if the appeal is "meritorious," the accused has to show either **"an unreasonable delay caused by the prosecution . . . or a wholly unjustifiable delay by the appellate court."** *Id.* Delay resulting from a defense appeal without merit might *never* count in the defendant's favor.

c. **Defendant's assertion of the right to a speedy trial.** The Barker v. Wingo Court rejected a **"demand-waiver rule"** under which a defendant could never claim the denial of a speedy trial for any period during which he had not demanded a speedy trial. Instead, the Court held that a **defendant's assertion of his right** is one of the factors to be included in the balance.

An **assertion is "entitled to strong evidentiary weight,"** while a **failure to assert "will make it difficult for a defendant to prove that he was denied a speedy trial."** Id. Assertions provide substantial weight to a defendant's side of the balance, while failures to assert provide substantial weight to the government's side.

In evaluating the assertion factor, substance governs over form. Pro forma requests will not help a defendant whose pattern of conduct indicates that he really did not want a speedy trial. See United States v. Loud Hawk (observing that the defendants' conduct that hindered speed contradicted their formal request for speedy trial). A failure to ask for a speedy trial, however, should not weigh against a defendant if there is good reason for the failure. See Barker v. Wingo (suggesting different treatment for failures when attorneys have not been appointed or when attorneys acquiesce in delay without informing clients); Doggett v. United States (not counting failure to assert against an accused who was not aware of the pending charges). Moreover, in determining the appropriate weight for this factor, judges should examine "the frequency and force of [an accused's] objections." Barker v. Wingo.

In sum, to determine which side of the balance the "assertion" factor falls on and how much weight to give it, judges must consider the defendant's conduct and the surrounding circumstances and try to ascertain whether the defendant **in fact desired** a speedy trial and **how strong that desire** was.

    d. **Prejudice to the accused.** Because **prejudice** counts on a defendant's side of the speedy trial balance, an accused should show as much prejudice from delay as possible. In the unlikely event that no prejudice *of any kind* is established, the prejudice factor should probably weigh on the government's side of the balance. Nonetheless, a defendant **does not have to show prejudice** to succeed with a speedy trial claim. Moore v. Arizona, 414 U.S. 25, 94 S. Ct. 188, 38 L. Ed. 2d 183 (1973).

The Speedy Trial Clause protects against three kinds of "prejudice." It serves "(i) **to prevent oppressive pretrial incarceration; (ii) to minimize anxiety and concern of the accused;** and (iii) **to limit the possibility that the defense will be impaired.**" Barker v. Wingo. Because **impairment of the defense** "skews the fairness of the entire system," it is **"the most serious" form of prejudice.** Id. Nonetheless, harm to the other two interests does count in the speedy trial balance.

"Oppressive pretrial incarceration" refers to both **actual incarceration** and **restrictions on freedom resulting from bail conditions. "Anxiety and concern of the accused"** includes the psychological suffering caused by a criminal accusation and the resulting "public obloquy," the "anxiety [caused] to friends and family," and tangible harms such as the disruptions of family life or employment, the curtailments of associations, and the depletions of financial resources that result from criminal charges. United States v. Marion; Barker v. Wingo.

"Impairment of the ability to make a defense" can result from the loss of evidence caused by delay. A defendant should try to show, for example, that helpful witnesses have died or become unavailable, that memories have faded, and/or that tangible items have been lost. Generally, only **"affirmative proof of [actual,] particularized prejudice" to the defense** will count. In cases of excessive delay, however, a **presumption** of defense impairment arises; the presumed prejudice counts on the defendant's side of the balance. The amount of delay necessary to give rise to any "presumptive prejudice" is uncertain, but once the threshold is crossed the "presumption of evidentiary prejudice grows" over time. Doggett v. United States.

3. **Remedy for Violation of the Right to a Speedy Trial**

The **"only possible remedy"** for a speedy trial violation is "the unsatisfactorily severe remedy of **dismissal.**" Barker v. Wingo. A pretrial determination that the balance tips in favor of the defendant precludes the government from seeking a conviction for the offense. The reversal of a conviction on speedy trial grounds prevents retrial.

EXAMPLES AND ANALYSIS

1. Internal Revenue Service investigators present a federal prosecutor with ample proof that Douglas, a prominent lawyer, is guilty of a relatively minor tax fraud based on representations made about domestic workers who cleaned his mansion. A formal charge is filed on March 3, 1997. Douglas immediately asks for an early trial date, hoping to clear his name. He repeats his request weekly. The assistant U.S. attorney handling the case gives it low priority because other cases are more interesting and because Douglas has beaten him in litigation on several occasions. On August 4, 1997, just prior to trial, Douglas moves for dismissal on speedy trial grounds. His motion is denied. Trial commences that day and ends in a conviction August 5. Douglas appeals the denial of his speedy trial claim. Was the trial court ruling correct?

Yes. The five-month delay is probably too short to trigger speedy trial analysis. If the threshold for length is not crossed, the other factors are not pertinent.

2. Suppose instead that Douglas's trial did not begin until May 17, 1999. The trial judge denied his pretrial speedy trial motion on the ground that he was not subjected to restraints at any time, could show no actual prejudice to his defense, and was not entitled to a presumption of prejudice. Should that ruling be overturned on appeal?

Probably. The trial court seems to have struck the wrong balance. A delay of more than 26 months is sufficient to trigger the balancing analysis. The prosecution's failure to pursue the case because it was not "interesting" is a reason that should count against the government. Delay motivated by a desire to retaliate against Douglas should weigh *heavily* against the government. In addition, Douglas sought a speedy trial by his weekly requests, and nothing in the record contradicts the sincerity of his requests. Finally, prejudice to the defense is not necessary for success, and a certain amount of anxiety and concern should be presumed because Douglas was the subject of public accusation for more than two years. The balance here would seem to tip in Douglas's favor.

3. Suppose that Douglas did not demand a speedy trial, but instead acquiesced on every occasion that the government sought a continuance. Should the trial court's rejection of his speedy trial claim be reversed?

No. If a record shows that a defendant truly does not want a speedy trial and no specific prejudice is shown, a trial judge can plausibly find that the speedy trial balance does not tip in the defendant's favor. In Barker v. Wingo, the Court rested its denial of a speedy trial claim primarily on these same two factors. *Barker* could be distinguished from this case because one reason here—bad faith retaliation—weighs more heavily for the accused than the reasons provided in that case. It is doubtful, however, that a bad faith delay of slightly more than two years is enough to alter the balance. The *Barker* majority suggested that it would take "extraordinary circumstances" to justify a ruling for an accused when the record strongly shows that he did not want a speedy trial.

C.   THE FEDERAL SPEEDY TRIAL ACT

The Due Process Clause, Sixth Amendment, and state constitutional speedy trial provisions have not in fact resulted in expeditious criminal justice processes. To protect both defendants' and society's interests in speedy trials, Congress and state legislatures have enacted laws designed to promote the swifter resolution of criminal charges. This section sketches the basic contours of the **Federal Speedy Trial Act,** 18 U.S.C. §§3161-3174 (1982).

1.   Section 3161: Time Limits and Exclusions

The Federal Speedy Trial Act promotes speed by demanding that certain steps be taken within fixed **time limits.** It builds flexibility into those periods, however, by prescribing delays that are **"excludable"**—periods that do not count in determining whether a time limit has been exceeded.

a.   Time limits. Like the Sixth Amendment, the Act does not deal with pre-accusation delays. Its provisions are inapplicable prior to an arrest or summons. The government must file an **indictment or information within 30 days of an individual's arrest or service with a summons.** §3161(b). It must then **commence trial within 70 days of filing (and making public) the information or indictment, or the date the defendant has appeared before a judicial officer, whichever occurs last.** §3161(c)(1). Thus, the Act ordinarily limits the time period from arrest to trial to no more than 100 days.

A prosecution that moves **too quickly** might impair a defendant's ability to prepare a defense. To guard against that harm, the Act prohibits commencement of trial **fewer than 30 days from the date of an accused's first appearance through counsel or waiver of counsel and election to represent himself or herself.** §3161(c)(2).

Sections 3161(d) and (e) specify the time limits applicable when various events occur prior to, during, or after a trial. These events include the refiling of charges after a dismissal requested by the accused, the reinstatement of charges by an appellate court following dismissal by a trial court, and the recommencement of a trial after a mistrial or a new trial is ordered or after the reversal of a conviction on appeal or collateral attack. As a general rule, it provides that the 30- and/or 70-day periods specified in §3161(b) and (c) are applicable.

b.   Exclusions. All delays are presumed to count toward the specified time limits, but some periods are "excludable." See §3161(h). Excludable time does not count against the government in calculating whether the Act's limits have been exceeded. No attempt to describe the various exclusions will be made here. Students interested in their details should consult subsection (h).

For the most part, the numerous excludable time categories are narrowly defined. They refer to delays resulting from particular "events" such as an "interlocutory appeal," a "pretrial motion," or "consideration by the court of a proposed plea agreement." Because Congress realized that it could not contemplate every occurrence that would justify delay, the Act includes a "catchall" of sorts. Section 3161(h)(8)(A) allows the exclusion of "delay resulting from *a continuance granted by any judge.*" For such delay to be excluded, however, the continuance must be granted "on the basis of . . . findings that the ends of justice served by taking such action outweigh the best interest of the public and the defendant in a speedy trial." A judge must consider a prescribed set of factors and must set forth the reasons for her finding orally or in writing. §3161(h)(8)(A), (B).

The Act does not allow the prosecutor, the accused, or both parties to waive its limits. In addition, it specifically prohibits a continuance under §3161(h)(8) "because of general congestion of the court's calendar, or lack of diligent preparation or failure to obtain available witnesses on the part of the attorney for the Government." §3161(h)(8)(C).

In sum, the Act provides fairly short time limits that require the expeditious bringing of charges following arrests and the expeditious start of trials following the filing of charges. The excludable time provision builds flexibility into the Act by setting forth the additional delays that are justifiable.

2. Sanctions for Violation of the Act

Section 3162(a) prescribes the sanctions for exceeding the time periods in §3161. It provides two possibilities: **dismissal with prejudice** and **dismissal without prejudice.** Dismissal with prejudice means the government is permanently barred from bringing charges for the particular offense. Dismissal without prejudice permits the refiling of charges so long as the statute of limitations is not exceeded. Section 3162 is the product of a compromise between those who believed that dismissal with prejudice ought to be the only sanction and those who thought that dismissal with prejudice should never be the consequence of a violation. See United States v. Taylor, 487 U.S. 326, 108 S. Ct. 2413, 101 L. Ed. 2d 297 (1988).

While the sanctions provision gives trial judges a certain amount of discretion in choosing between the two options, this discretion must be guided by three congressionally specified factors: **"the seriousness of the offense; the facts and circumstances of the case which led to the dismissal; and the impact of a reprosecution on the administration of the [Speedy Trial Act] and on the administration of justice."** §3162(a).

a. **Seriousness of the offense.** The more serious the offense, the less inclined a judge should be to order dismissal with prejudice. The less serious the offense, the more inclined a judge should be to order dismissal with prejudice.

b. **Facts and circumstances leading to dismissal.** A judge should assess the "culpability" of the parties—who is to blame and whether the violation was deliberate, careless, or inadvertent. A judge should also consider the number of days by which the government exceeded the applicable time limit.

c. **Impact of reprosecution on the Act and on the administration of justice.** A judge must try to determine whether allowing the government to pursue the case would undermine the goals and purposes of the Act and would be unjust. Once again, the question of "culpability," the seriousness of the crime, and the amount of excess delay ought to be taken into account. The potential "prejudice" to the accused from a prosecution following the violation is also pertinent. See United States v. Taylor.

A judge's choice of sanction will not be overturned unless there is an **abuse of discretion.** A trial court's factual findings "are entitled to substantial deference and will be reversed only for **clear error.**" Id. If the findings are sustainable and support the sanction chosen, an appellate court should not reverse. However, if there are no factors that support the type of dismissal chosen or if the balance clearly tips against that type of dismissal, a trial judge's decision will be reversed. See id. (reversing a dismissal with prejudice because the court lacked evidentiary support for some findings, did not take some factors into account, and reached a conclusion that was not supported by the factors that did have evidentiary support).

The Act also provides limited direct sanctions for particularly culpable actions by attorneys that undermine the Act's objectives. Punishments include monetary penalties, denial of the right to practice, and the filing of reports with disciplinary committees. §3162(b).

REVIEW QUESTIONS AND ANSWERS

Question: Guy and Mike were accused of bank fraud. Government investigators first noticed their activities in 1985, but the indictment charging them with fraud was not returned until 1993. Guy and Mike moved to dismiss the indictment, claiming that the government delay had led to unavailable defense testimony as a result of the death of one witness, losses of memory by other witnesses, and the disappearance of particular exculpatory records. The government explained that the delays in pursuing the investigation and indictment were caused by a "lack of personnel coupled with the low priority of the case." The trial judge dismissed the indictment, finding that Guy and Mike had suffered both "actual and presumptive prejudice" and that the "government had not given good enough reasons to justify this harm to the ability to make a defense." The government appealed the dismissal. How should the appellate court rule?

Answer: The appellate court should probably reverse the decision. The Due Process Clause pre-indictment delay doctrine requires delay for insufficient reasons and prejudice. Here there is an eight-year delay and actual prejudice. Moreover, a presumption of prejudice might well be justified after that period of time. See Doggett v. United States (presuming prejudice to defense after eight-and-a-half-year delay for Speedy Trial Clause purposes). The problem here is that the government's reason for delay probably will not support a due process claim. While there is some lower court authority requiring the government to justify delay whenever defendants suffer prejudice of these kinds, the Supreme Court would probably reject a due process claim without greater government fault or culpability than is evident here. There was no bad faith and no intentional delay to prejudice or harass the accused; nor was there a showing of "reckless disregard" for the risk of harm to the defense.

Question: Marilyn was indicted by a grand jury in March 1993 for 55 counts of Medicare fraud. The indictment was sealed by the court on request of the prosecutor and was not made public until May 1996. For a portion of the three years that the indictment was sealed, the government pursued leads suggesting that others were involved in a large conspiracy with Marilyn. For the last year, the case was delayed because the evidence seemed weak and the prosecutors hoped they might somehow bolster their case. Between 1996 and 1999, Marilyn's trial was postponed on request of the government. Marilyn objected to each postponement. In November 1999, on the day before trial was to begin, Marilyn moved for dismissal of the indictment, alleging a violation of her right to a speedy trial. How should the judge rule?

Answer: The judge could probably support a ruling for the defendant, but probably would not commit error by ruling for the government. The Barker v. Wingo test is controlling. First, as to the length of the delay, the period is clearly sufficient to "trigger" balancing analysis. It is unclear, however, whether the time while the indictment was sealed counts at all toward Marilyn's speedy trial claim. There was an accusation, but it had not been made public and therefore could not be the source of the primary harms that the Sixth Amendment guards against. Whether the time counts could be important. If it does count, the government delay was more than six and a half years. If not, the delay was three and a half years.

Second, the reasons for the delay must be assessed. Assuming that the period when the indictment was sealed does count, the attempt to find co-conspirators was probably a good reason that justified perhaps as much as two years of delay while the indictment was still sealed. The final year of delay seems to be the result of an unsupported "hope" that the weak case for conviction would get stronger. This reason could count against the government—although probably not heavily. The three and a half years that clearly count are unexplained. The prosecution would have to provide justifying reasons to avoid having this period counted against it.

Third, because the defendant could not assert the right to a speedy trial when the indictment was sealed, the failure to do so does not count against her. Moreover, she objected to each delay once it was made public. Unless there is evidence that these were not sincere assertions of her right, this factor places considerable weight on Marilyn's side of the balance.

Finally, there is no mention of specific prejudice. Marilyn presumptively suffered anxiety from the public accusation. She could provide further support for her claim if she proved any tangible prejudice in terms of pretrial restraint or consequences from public accusation. A showing of actual prejudice to her defense would be helpful, but Marilyn could plausibly claim (assuming the entire period counts) that a presumption of prejudice must arise from the delay of six and a half years. While it is not clear that the prejudice factor would tip the scales much, if at all, in Marilyn's direction, in these circumstances it would not seem sensible to conclude that it weighs on the government's side of the balance.

In sum, the issue concerning the time while the indictment is sealed seems critical. If it counts, the balance probably tips in Marilyn's favor. If not, a court could very plausibly conclude that the government should prevail.

Question: Nell was arrested on June 6, 1990, for conspiracy to murder a government official. She was held without bail. On July 16, the grand jury refused to indict her and Nell was released. After further investigation by the FBI, an indictment was returned on January 11, 1991. On February 20, 1991, the trial judge dismissed the indictment because the grand jury had been discriminatorily selected. The government appealed the ruling. On May 29, 1992, the court of appeals upheld the dismissal. The government then decided to wait to reindict Nell, preferring to investigate the case more thoroughly. On October 3, 1994, Nell was indicted once again. Trial was set for November 16. On the morning of November 16, the trial court granted Nell's motion to dismiss for lack of a speedy trial. The government again appealed the dismissal. How should the appellate court rule?

Answer: The appellate court should reverse. Nell was not "an accused" for a long enough period to trigger speedy trial analysis. The right first attached upon arrest on June 6, 1990, but the clock stopped running when no indictment was returned and Nell was released on July 16. The right again attached on January 11, 1991, but the clock stopped running when the indictment was dismissed on February 20. Finally, the right again attached on October 3, 1994, but Nell was to be tried on November 16. The total time was approximately four months, an insufficient period for a valid speedy trial claim.

17 THE RIGHT TO A PUBLIC TRIAL

 CHAPTER OVERVIEW

The **Sixth Amendment** guarantees that **"the accused shall enjoy the right to a . . . public trial."** The right to a public trial is an **essential component of a fair trial** and is a **personal right that belongs to the accused alone.** See Gannett Co. v. DePasquale, 443 U.S. 368, 99 S. Ct. 2898, 61 L. Ed. 2d 608 (1979); Waller v. Georgia, 467 U.S. 39, 104 S. Ct. 2210, 81 L. Ed. 2d 31 (1984). The right to a public trial promotes fairness by "ensuring that the judge and prosecutor carry out their duties responsibly," encouraging "witnesses to come forward," and "discourag[ing] perjury" on the witness stand. Waller v. Georgia.

The **First Amendment** provides rights to freedom of speech, to freedom of the press, to assemble peaceably, and to petition the government for redress of grievances. Implicit in these constitutional rights, the Supreme Court has found a **public right of access to criminal proceedings.** See Richmond Newspapers v. Virginia, 448 U.S. 555, 100 S. Ct. 2814, 65 L. Ed. 2d 973 (1980); Globe Newspaper Co. v. Superior Court, 457 U.S. 596, 102 S. Ct. 2613, 73 L. Ed. 2d 248 (1982). This right belongs to the public, is wholly independent of the defendant's Sixth Amendment entitlement, and can be exercised when the accused is opposed to a public proceeding.

Finally, the **Fifth and Fourteenth Amendments** guarantee defendants the right not to be deprived "of life, liberty, or property without **due process of law.**" In a criminal proceeding, this due process right to "fundamental fairness" can be jeopardized by "publicity." Jurors might be biased or may become aware of inadmissible evidence. Witnesses may be influenced in ways that distort the truthfinding process or undermine procedural entitlements. Judges and prosecutors may be affected in ways that undermine defendants' interests in fair processes that produce fair outcomes.

This chapter discusses three general topics:

- **The Sixth Amendment right to a public trial.** The discussion first focuses on the scope of the public trial right. The accused's right extends beyond the trial to other phases of the criminal process. This section then addresses the nature and substance of the guarantee afforded. Because the right to a public trial is not absolute, in certain circumstances a proceeding can be *closed* over the defendant's objections.

- **The First Amendment right of public access.** Similar questions of scope and substance arise in connection with the First Amendment right of public access to criminal proceedings. The answers to those questions have been similar to those given in the Sixth Amendment context. The public's right extends to proceedings other than the trial itself, and even when the right is applicable, it is not absolute—public access can be denied in certain situations.

- **The accused's due process entitlement to fundamental fairness.** Publicity causes a variety of threats to a defendant's due process right to a fair trial. This section addresses some of those threats and the measures that may be necessary to protect against them.

A. THE SIXTH AMENDMENT RIGHT TO A PUBLIC TRIAL

The **Sixth Amendment** provides a **right to a public trial.** This right belongs to the accused alone and may be waived. The issues that arise pertain to three areas: the **scope** of the right, the **nature and substance** of the right, and the **remedy** for violation of the right.

1. Scope of the Right to a Public Trial: To What Proceedings Does the Right Extend?

While the Sixth Amendment right to a public trial governs only federal court proceedings, the Fourteenth Amendment due process guarantee extends an **identical** right to defendants involved in **state court trials.** Gannett v. DePasquale. Although the Sixth Amendment text refers only to a public **trial,** the guarantee extends to other phases of the criminal process. See Waller v. Georgia (right to public trial applicable to pretrial suppression hearing). The Supreme Court has used a "functional" approach to determine whether the right extends to a particular kind of proceeding. An accused has the right to have a public proceeding if public access to and presence at the proceeding will serve the functions that it serves at trial—**ensuring responsible performances by the judge and prosecutor, encouraging witnesses to come forward,** and **discouraging perjury.** See Waller v. Georgia.

The more important a phase is to determining the defendant's fate, the stronger the case for extending the public trial right. See id.

 # EXAMPLE AND ANALYSIS

In Waller v. Georgia, the defendants moved to have evidence suppressed from their trial, alleging that the government acquired the evidence by unconstitutional means. Over the defendants' objections, the trial court closed the entire suppression hearing. The defendants were ultimately convicted.

The Supreme Court held that the defendants had a constitutional right to a public suppression hearing for the following reasons. First, suppression hearings are often as important to the defendant as the trial and may be "the only trial." Second, suppression hearings often resemble bench trials—they include testimony from witnesses and argument by counsel, and their outcomes often hinge on factual questions. Consequently, public access to and presence at suppression hearings will serve the three objectives of the public trial right. Finally, the extension of the right to suppression hearings is supported by the fact that the public in general has a "strong interest in exposing substantial allegations of police misconduct to the salutary effects of public scrutiny."

The Supreme Court has not addressed other questions involving the scope of the Sixth Amendment right; consequently, the breadth of the right is not entirely clear. The Court has, however, held that the First Amendment right of public access applies at adversarial preliminary hearings (Press-Enterprise Co. v. Superior Court, 478 U.S. 1, 106 S. Ct. 2735, 92 L. Ed. 2d 1 (1986)), and during the voir dire of jurors, (Press-Enterprise Co. v. Superior Court, 464 U.S. 501, 104 S. Ct. 819, 78 L. Ed. 2d 269 (1984)). Undoubtedly, the explicit Sixth Amendment right of the accused also extends to these phases of the criminal process.

2. **Nature and Substance of the Right to a Public Trial: What Protection Does the Right Afford?**

   If the right to a public trial extends to a proceeding, two questions of substance can arise. First, what is meant by **"public"?** Second, does the accused have an **absolute** right to public presence or **can the proceeding sometimes be closed?**

   a. **Meaning of "public."** The right to a public trial does not grant an entitlement to insist on accommodation of every member of the public who wishes to attend. Instead, it accords a **right of public access** to the proceeding. In other words, the Sixth Amendment insures that trials will be open and that the opportunity of the public to attend will not be restricted.

A judge might directly deny access by barring members of the public from attending a proceeding or by locking the courtroom doors. Constructive restrictions on access are also possible. If an inmate is tried in a prison courtroom situated in a remote location, the effective impediments to access may be sufficient to infringe on Sixth Amendment interests. See Commonwealth v. Vescuso, 360 S.E.2d 547 (Va. Ct. App. 1987). Or a constructive denial of access can result if people who wish to attend a trial are allowed to do so only if they submit to intrusive impositions such as full-body searches.

b.   The showing needed to close a trial. The right to a public trial is **not absolute.** Waller v. Georgia. In "rare" circumstances, **a judge can deny or restrict access** to a proceeding without violating the accused's constitutional right. Id.

Nevertheless, because the right to a public trial is a fundamental component of a fair trial, there is a **"presumption of openness."** This "presumption of openness may be overcome **only** by an **overriding interest** based on findings that **closure is essential to preserve higher values** and is **narrowly tailored to serve that interest.**" Id. Moreover, a trial court must "articulate[ ]" the overriding interest that justifies closure and must make "findings specific enough that a reviewing court can determine whether the closure" was justified. Id. Unless these standards are satisfied, a denial of or substantial restriction on access for all or part of a proceeding is unconstitutional.

i.   Need for an "overriding interest" and "higher values." Because a fundamental right of the accused is involved, closure requires an **overriding interest.** In deciding whether there is an interest that outweighs the accused's constitutional entitlement, a judge must act "with special care." Id. The reason for closing the trial must be sufficiently weighty to justify depriving the accused of the presumptive benefits of an open proceeding. In other words, closure must serve **higher values** than the fair trial interests that are served by public access and presence.

Interests that can qualify as overriding include a vulnerable witness's interest in avoiding physical peril or psychological harm; a juror's, witness's, or other person's interest in not suffering a serious invasion of privacy; and the state's interest in a fair trial or in maintaining the secrecy of classified information.

An open proceeding might also threaten the defendant's interest in a fair trial. Publicity could bias jurors or taint witnesses. Nevertheless, if the accused has made "an informed decision to object to the closing of the proceeding," a court probably should not close a trial in order to protect the defendant's fair trial interests.

If the accused prefers openness, the interest in avoiding danger to her fair trial interests is "largely absent." Id.

The presence of an "overriding interest" must be determined on a **case-by-case** basis. Mandatory closure rules or discretionary closure decisions that are based solely on the type of case being tried are not consistent with the presumption of openness. A judge must make specific findings that are based on the particular facts of the proceeding being closed.

 # EXAMPLE AND ANALYSIS

To protect the minor victims of sex offenses, a state adopts a rule closing all trials involving sex crimes against minors. For the same purpose, another state enacts a rule mandating the closure of such trials only during the testimony of the victims. Are these rules valid?

No. To justify closure, the judge *in each case* must hear evidence regarding the harms that could result to the particular minor from having to testify publicly. The trial may be closed only if the evidence demonstrates that there is an overriding interest in protecting the welfare of the particular victim. See Globe Newspaper Co. v. Superior Court, 457 U.S. 596, 102 S. Ct. 2613, 73 L. Ed. 2d 248 (1982) (holding that a rule mandating closure during trial testimony of minor victim violates First Amendment public right of access).

ii. **Closure must be "essential to preserve higher values."** A trial cannot be closed merely because closure **will** serve higher values. To close a proceeding, the judge must find that "closure is **essential** to preserve higher values." Waller v. Georgia. The judge must have a factual basis for concluding that if the trial remains open, higher values will be harmed.

Because closure is not essential if there are **"reasonable alternatives"** that will preserve the higher values, a "trial court **must consider reasonable alternatives to closing the proceeding.**" Id. A judge may reject a proposed alternative if it is not reasonable or practicable. For example, an alternative may be too costly or may inflict more harm than it prevents. A judge may also reject an alternative solution that is insufficiently effective. For example, an alternative may not provide sufficient protection for the higher values threatened by openness. If a workable, effective alternative to closure exists, a judge must employ it.

Example and Analysis

A judge is persuaded that the publicity that will result from an open proceeding will pose a serious risk that the jury will be privy to highly prejudicial, inadmissible matters that will harm the state's ability to secure a conviction. An order to the jurors not to read newspapers or view news broadcasts or a sequestration of the jury will minimize or eliminate the risk. Before ordering closure, the judge must consider these options. If they are reasonable—neither impractical nor too harmful—and effective, the judge may not close the trial.

   iii. **Closure must be ''narrowly tailored to serve'' the overriding interest.** Even if there is an overriding interest that is threatened by openness and there is no reasonable alternative to closure, closure is unconstitutional unless it is **''narrowly tailored to serve that interest.''** Id. In other words, ''closure must be **no broader than necessary to protect that interest.''** Id.

   A court may not close an entire proceeding when the overriding interest is jeopardized only during certain portions of the proceeding. Each period of closure must be justified. For periods during which openness poses no threat to ''higher values,'' there is no interest to outweigh the accused's public trial interests and the presumption of openness controls.

 ## Examples and Analysis

A court finds that the public exposure of conversations intercepted by government wiretaps will seriously damage the privacy interests of innocent persons. This finding does not justify closing an entire hearing held to determine the admissibility of the intercepted conversations. The hearing can be closed only for those portions of the evidence that would expose the contents of the wiretaps. See Waller v. Georgia (holding that the closure of an entire suppression hearing was invalid because any interests that could have justified closure were at risk only during limited portions of the hearings).

Similarly, if it is shown that a rape victim would suffer serious trauma from having to testify in the public eye, an order closing the entire rape trial or even the entire government case would be unconstitutional. A judge could close the trial only during the victim's testimony.

iv. **Requirement of specific findings.** To support a closure order, a court must make **specific findings** concerning the requirements for closure; "broad and general" findings will not suffice. Id. This requirement ensures that judges take care in depriving defendants of the interests in a public trial and provides assurance that each deprivation is in fact justified.

A judge must specify the **nature of the overriding interest** that justifies closure so that it can be determined whether a "higher value" is in fact at stake. A judge must specify facts that demonstrate **a threat to the overriding interest** in the specific proceeding. A judge must have a factual basis for concluding that **closure is essential** and that **alternatives will not be reasonable or effective.** Moreover, a judge must have **reasons that support the breadth of the closure** that is ordered.

3. Remedy for Violation of the Right to a Public Trial

If a **trial** is closed in violation of the Sixth Amendment, a **conviction must be reversed** and a **new trial held.** The defendant **does not have to demonstrate particular prejudice** from the closure. Waller v. Georgia. The error is automatically reversible; it cannot be harmless. The government cannot avoid a retrial even by showing that a violation was "harmless beyond a reasonable doubt."

This does not mean that every time *any proceeding* is closed in violation of the Sixth Amendment a new trial is required. The "remedy" for violation of the right must be "appropriate to the violation." If the violation occurs at a hearing that is separate and distinct from the trial, the accused is presumptively entitled *only to a new hearing*. The defendant is entitled to a new trial only if the outcome of the new "open" hearing differs from the outcome of the original "closed" hearing in ways that would have a "material" impact on the trial itself.

 # EXAMPLE AND ANALYSIS

In Waller v. Georgia, a suppression hearing was closed in violation of the accused's Sixth Amendment right. The Supreme Court granted a new suppression hearing and held that a new trial should be held **"only if** [the] new, public suppression hearing result[ed] in the suppression of material evidence not suppressed at the first trial, or in some other material change in the positions of the parties." If a public suppression hearing would have had no impact on the ultimate trial, a new trial would be an unjustified "windfall" for the defendant.

**B.   THE FIRST AMENDMENT PUBLIC RIGHT OF ACCESS
TO CRIMINAL PROCEEDINGS**

The **First Amendment** provides that "Congress shall make no law . . . abridging the freedom of speech, or of the press; or the right of the people peaceably to assemble, and to petition the Government for a redress of grievances." A core purpose of these rights is " 'to protect the free discussion of governmental affairs' " so "that the individual citizen can effectively participate in and contribute to our republican system of self-government." Globe Newspaper Co. v. Superior Court, 457 U.S. 596, 102 S. Ct. 2613, 73 L. Ed. 2d 248 (1982). To serve its purposes, the " 'discussion of governmental affairs' [must be] informed." Id. Discussion can be informed only if citizens have "access" to proceedings in which governmental affairs are conducted.

In Richmond Newspapers v. Virginia, 448 U.S. 555, 100 S. Ct. 2814, 65 L. Ed. 2d 973 (1980), this reasoning led the Supreme Court to recognize "that **the press and general public have a constitutional right of access to criminal trials . . . embodied in the First Amendment.**" Globe Newspaper Co. v. Superior Court. This implicit right of access raises two basic questions. First, to what phases of the criminal process does the public's right of access extend? Second, what does the right of access guarantee and when, if ever, may it be denied?

1.   Scope of the Public Right of Access: To What Proceedings Does the Right Extend?

The public clearly has a right of access to **criminal trials.** See Richmond Newspapers v. Virginia; Globe Newpaper Co. v. Superior Court. Two factors determine whether the public has a right of access to other phases of the criminal process. The **first** is whether there is **a history or tradition of public access** to the particular proceeding. The **second** is **whether "public access"** to the proceeding **"plays a particularly significant positive role in the actual functioning of the process."** Press-Enterprise Co. v. Superior Court, 478 U.S. 1, 106 S. Ct. 2735, 92 L. Ed. 2d 1 (1986) (*Press-Enterprise II*).

a.   **A history or tradition of public access. A history or tradition of public access** to a particular kind of proceeding militates in favor of a constitutional right of access. The fact that a proceeding has historically or traditionally been conducted in private weighs against a First Amendment right of access. In Press-Enterprise Co. v. Superior Court, 464 U.S. 501, 104 S. Ct. 819, 78 L. Ed. 2d 629 (1984) (*Press-Enterprise I*), the Court held that the public right of access extended to the **voir dire of jurors** in part because of the historical openness of that process. And in *Press-Enterprise II*, the Court held that the tradition of access to **preliminary hearings** of the type conducted in California supported recognition of a First Amendment right.

The Court has never relied on history or tradition to deny a public right of access. However, the historical secrecy of grand jury proceedings would presumably lead to that outcome.

b. **A significant positive role in the functioning of the process.** One reason for the right of access to *trials* is that the presence of the public is thought to improve the actual functioning of the trial process. To decide whether the First Amendment right extends to another phase, it is necessary to determine whether **"public access . . . plays a particularly significant positive role in the actual functioning of the process."** *Press-Enterprise II.*

Public access can play a "positive role" in a variety of ways. Public presence can increase the fairness of a proceeding by keeping all the participants honest and responsible. See Globe Newspaper Co. v. Superior Court. An awareness that citizens can attend enhances public confidence and the appearance of fairness—both of which contribute to the proper functioning of a process. *Press-Enterprise I.* Moreover, by providing an outlet for public "reactions and emotions" and "vindicat[-ing] the concerns of victims and the community in knowing that" justice is being done, openness has " 'community therapeutic value.' " Id. Finally, by keeping the public informed about the processes of criminal justice, access enables the community to discuss and to improve those processes—that is, to engage in the process of self-government contemplated by the First Amendment. See Globe Newspaper Co. v. Superior Court.

To decide whether access plays a "significant positive role" in any particular process, the nature of the process must be examined. The specific procedures that are followed and the objectives of the phase are relevant. The ultimate question must be whether public access makes the sort of contributions described above.

In *Press-Enterprise I*, the Supreme Court concluded that public access to the voir dire of jurors "gives confidence that standards of fairness are being observed," provides an "assurance that established procedures are being followed," and has " 'community therapeutic value.' " In *Press-Enterprise II*, the Supreme Court recognized a First Amendment right of access to a "preliminary hearing" in part because the "preliminary hearing is often the final and most important step in the criminal proceeding." The Court also observed that the absence of a jury heightened the need for the presence of the public as a safeguard against official overreaching and that closure would frustrate the " 'community therapeutic value' of openness."

> **Note:** The Supreme Court has never denied a right of access because the public would not play a "significant positive role" in

a particular process. It is fair to assume, however, that access to a proceeding would be denied if it would undermine rather than promote the effective functioning of the process. The historical secrecy of grand jury proceedings is based, in part, on the need not to alert suspects that they are the objects of governmental interest and the need not to notify them too far in advance of the evidence and witnesses against them. Suspects might flee and investigations could be thwarted if information were made public at the grand jury stage.

2.   **Substance of the Public Right of Access: What Entitlement Does the First Amendment Afford?**

Like the Sixth Amendment right to a public trial, the First Amendment public right of access is **not absolute.** Closed proceedings are possible. Although proceedings are presumptively open and access can be denied only in **rare** cases, closure can be constitutional. See *Press-Enterprise I.*

The standard that dictates when closure is permissible is **identical** to the one that controls closure decisions under the Sixth Amendment. In fact, the Sixth Amendment closure standard was borrowed directly from *Press-Enterprise I,* a First Amendment case. Under this standard, the party seeking closure must overcome the **"presumption of openness"** by showing that an **overriding interest** is at stake, that closure is **essential to preserve higher values,** and that any closure ordered is **narrowly tailored.** For detailed discussion of this standard, see section A.2.b above.

There is one potentially significant difference between First Amendment and Sixth Amendment closure decisions. "No right ranks higher than the right of the accused to a **fair trial.**" *Press-Enterprise I.* Public access can seriously threaten that right. If the defendant is asserting his **Sixth Amendment right** to a public trial, closure in order to protect his fair trial rights should rarely, if ever, be granted. The defendant has expressed a preference for the fair trial interests served by the presence of the public. See section A.2.b.i above. In a **First Amendment case,** however, a defendant may demand closure to protect the right to a fair trial. When this right is endangered by public access, a judge may close the proceeding based on **"specific findings** . . . demonstrating . . . **a substantial probability** that the defendant's **right to a fair trial will be prejudiced by publicity** that closure would prevent." *Press-Enterprise II.* Mere allegations or **"conclusory assertion[s]** that publicity **might** deprive the defendant of "** a fair trial will not suffice. Nor will a demonstrable possibility be enough. The facts must show **"a substantial probability"** of prejudice to the fairness of the trial. Moreover, the court must also specifically find that **"reasonable alternatives to closure cannot adequately protect the defendant's fair trial rights."** Id. If closure is not essential to avoid the substantial probability of prejudice, access may not be denied.

EXAMPLE AND ANALYSIS

In *Press-Enterprise II*, a nurse was charged with murdering 12 patients. He asked for closure of a "preliminary hearing" designed to determine whether he should stand trial, arguing that the threat of publicity would impair his right to a fair and impartial judgment at trial. The trial court granted the request and closed a hearing that lasted 41 days. The California Supreme Court upheld the closure.

The Supreme Court reversed because the "standard applied by the California Supreme Court failed to consider the First Amendment right of access to criminal proceedings." First, the statutory standard for closure required only "a **reasonable likelihood** of substantial prejudice" to the defendant's right to a fair trial. This standard "place[d] a lesser burden on the defendant than the **'substantial probability'** test which" is required by the First Amendment. "Moreover, the court failed to consider whether **alternatives** short of closure would have protected" the defendant's fair trial interests. Voir dire of prospective jurors, although "cumbersome," was a distinct possibility. Finally, "closure of an entire 41-day proceeding would rarely be warranted" and almost certainly violated the requirement that "any limitation" on access " 'must be **narrowly tailored** to serve' " an overriding interest.

C. PUBLICITY AND THE RIGHT TO A FAIR TRIAL

In our judicial system, "[n]o right ranks higher than the **right of the accused to a fair trial**." *Press-Enterprise I.* That right is safeguarded and given content by the general terms of the Due Process Clauses and by the more specific entitlements provided by the Fifth and Sixth Amendments. Publicity about and public access to criminal proceedings can render those proceedings unfair. When the adverse risks or effects of publicity or access are identified before or during the trial, a judge should take steps to prevent or eliminate them. When a conviction results from a proceeding rendered unfair by publicity or access, a defendant is entitled to a new trial.

This section discusses the potential adverse effects that publicity and access can have on the right to a fair trial. It also sketches the measures that are available to remedy those effects.

1. Meaning of the Right to a "Fair" Trial

The Fifth and Fourteenth Amendments guarantee that neither the federal nor any state government shall deprive "any person . . . of life, liberty, or property without **due process of law.**" This guarantee translates into a general right to **"fundamental fairness."** Lisenba v. California, 314 U.S. 219, 62 S. Ct. 280, 86 L. Ed. 166 (1941). Fundamental fairness has both "substantive" and "procedural" components.

Substantive fairness means **accurate, reliable outcomes**—convictions of the guilty and acquittals of the innocent. Procedural fairness means that these outcomes are the product of processes that comport with principles of **fair play.** In part, those principles are dictated by our commitment to a system that is **adversarial** and **accusatorial.** In addition, trials must not only **be fair,** they must **appear fair.** See Offutt v. United States, 348 U.S. 11, 75 S. Ct. 11, 99 L. Ed. 11 (1954) ("Justice must satisfy the appearance of justice"); Wheat v. United States, 486 U.S. 153, 108 S. Ct. 1692, 100 L. Ed. 2d 140 (1988).

The Sixth Amendment guarantees a right to trial "by an impartial jury" that will decide a case without prejudice or bias and on the basis of the evidence properly admitted at trial. See Chapter 19, section D.1. Publicity and public access frequently jeopardize this entitlement and thereby threaten both substantive and procedural fairness.

2. **Potential Risks of Unfairness**

Both the **publication of information** and the **presence of the media** can compromise the fairness of a trial in several ways.

a. **Potential unfairness caused by publicity before and during trials.** **Publicity** can undermine the right to a fair trial by influencing potential or actual jurors. Pretrial publication of information can **impair the impartiality of** *potential* **jurors** by leading them to form opinions about guilt or innocence or exposing them to inadmissible evidence. See, e.g., Irvin v. Dowd, 366 U.S. 717, 81 S. Ct. 1639, 6 L. Ed. 2d 751 (1961). Publicity during a trial can **improperly influence** *actual* **jurors** in the same ways.

Prejudicial publicity might also **adversely affect witnesses,** influencing them to distort their testimony, intentionally or otherwise, and thus undermining the search for truth. The fairness of the trial can also be jeopardized if publicity puts pressures on judges or prosecutors to alter their behavior to satisfy the public.

b. **Potential unfairness caused by the presence or conduct of the media at the trial. Public access** to a trial can also generate risks of unfairness. The very **presence of the media** can have adverse impacts on all participants, including the defendant. **Conduct by** members of **the public or** by **media representatives** also might improperly influence the judge, lawyers, jurors, or witnesses. See Estes v. Texas, 381 U.S. 532, 85 S. Ct. 1628, 14 L. Ed. 2d 543 (1965); Sheppard v. Maxwell, 384 U.S. 333, 86 S. Ct. 1507, 16 L. Ed. 2d 600 (1966).

An awareness that a proceeding is the subject of media interest can lead some participants to alter their behavior in inappropriate ways. The judge might treat the defendant more harshly or the prosecutor might resort to tougher tactics. The quality of the defendant's representation could suffer if her counsel is tempted to play to the press. Jurors might be averse to the public eye or distracted by the awareness that they are in the spotlight. Witnesses might embellish or alter their testimony and distort the search for truth. Finally, the accused might suffer greater anxiety and humiliation from the knowledge that she is the focus of media interest.

In addition, media representatives might conduct themselves in ways that draw attention. Noise, movement, and the presence of equipment can distract the participants—judges, jurors, attorneys, and witnesses— from their tasks.

In sum, media presence can create risks of unfair outcomes from unfair processes. If it does, due process values are undermined.

3. Safeguards Against the Risks of Prejudicial Publicity

If a trial is rendered unfair by publicity, a resulting conviction must be overturned and a new trial held. If threats from publicity arise or become apparent before or during a trial, a judge can take a variety of steps to *prevent* unfairness.

a. **Restricting the disclosure of information.** Trial judges have limited authority to **restrict the disclosure of information** about a pending case. See Sheppard v. Maxwell (observing that the important role played by the press has made the Court "unwilling to place any direct limitations on the freedom traditionally exercised by the news media, for 'what transpires in the court room is public property' "). While the breadth of a judge's authority is not entirely clear, the authority to regulate the release of information by lawyers (and probably other participants such as police officers) is greater than the authority to restrict the media. Prior restraints against the release of information by the press are possible in extreme cases but are very unlikely to survive First Amendment scrutiny. See Nebraska Press Association v. Stuart, 427 U.S. 539, 96 S. Ct. 2791, 49 L. Ed. 2d 683 (1976). Trial participants and members of the media might also be restricted by the threat of after-the-fact sanctions for disclosure, but the special First Amendment protection of the media means that such sanctions are also unlikely to be constitutional.

b. **Preventing access to proceedings.** Another way to minimize the risk of tainting jurors or witnesses is to deny access to the courtroom and the court's files. If information is not available, it cannot be publicized, and if it is not publicized, jurors and witnesses cannot be influenced.

The First Amendment also places tight limits on the availability of this option. Even limited closures require specific showings of a "substantial probability" that the right to a fair trial will be prejudiced and findings that no reasonable alternatives to closure are available. For full discussion of the standards regulating closure, see section B.2 above.

c. **Continuances and changes of venue.** Prejudicial publicity can infect a community to such an extent that a fair trial is impossible. If jurors have been exposed to information that precludes fair, impartial judgments based on the evidence, the delay of the trial by means of a **continuance** might allow passions to subside or memories to fade sufficiently. Alternatively, a **change of venue** might remedy the problem. If the taint is confined to or is only severe in a particular community, moving the trial to another community could eliminate or minimize the prejudice. *In extreme cases,* if the trial judge fails to move the trial, a conviction may be reversed even without proof of actual unfairness at the trial.

 # EXAMPLE AND ANALYSIS

In Rideau v. Louisiana, 373 U.S. 723, 83 S. Ct. 1417, 10 L. Ed. 2d 663 (1963), a "moving picture film with a sound track" of the defendant's detailed confession to bank robbery, kidnapping, and murder was broadcast by television on three successive days. In a parish with a population of 150,000, audiences of 24,000, 53,000, and 29,000 saw and heard the broadcasts. Two weeks later, defendant's motion for change of venue was denied and he was tried, convicted, and sentenced to death for murder.

The Supreme Court held "that it was a denial of due process of law to refuse a request for a change of venue after the people of [the community] had been exposed repeatedly and in depth to the spectacle of Rideau personally confessing in detail to the crimes with which he was later charged." According to the Court, the trial in court was "but a hollow formality." The "real" trial had already occurred when the defendant "pleaded guilty" before "the tens of thousands of people who saw and heard" the broadcasts. There was no need "to examine . . . the voir dire examination of the members of the jury" because "due process of law . . . required a trial before a jury drawn from a community of people who had not seen and heard [the] televised" confession. In essence, the extreme likelihood of irreparable prejudice from pretrial publicity rendered a change of venue the only constitutionally acceptable remedy.

d. **Measures designed to deal directly with the jurors.** A number of safeguards against the prejudice of publicity directly involve the jurors. These include questioning and screening, admonishing, sequestering, and removing jurors.

     i. Questioning and removing jurors during voir dire or during trial. The most prominent alternative for dealing with prejudicial publicity is to **question the jurors.** If the problem is **pretrial publicity,** the questioning is done by voir dire of the jurors during the selection process. If the problem arises **during the trial,** a recess can be declared to allow examination of the jurors. The objects of questioning are to determine whether the jurors have been exposed to any bias or inadmissible evidence, to ascertain the nature of that exposure, and to inquire into the effects on the jurors' abilities to decide the case impartially and based solely on the evidence presented at trial. Prior to trial, a prejudiced juror can be **stricken for cause.** A juror who has been exposed but has not been proven to be prejudiced might be the object of a **peremptory challenge.** During a trial, an improperly influenced juror can be **removed and replaced by an alternate** juror. When the taint is widespread, a **mistrial** might be declared.

     Mere exposure to prejudicial publicity or inadmissible evidence before or during a trial does not render a juror disqualified. See Irvin v. Dowd, 366 U.S. 717, 81 S. Ct. 1639, 6 L. Ed. 2d 751 (1961). Even jurors with preconceived opinions regarding guilt or innocence may be eligible for jury service. Id. In most cases, if the juror expresses a willingness to ignore information, to put aside opinions about the case, and to be impartial and decide the case based on the evidence, the juror may serve. Patton v. Yount, 467 U.S. 1025, 104 S. Ct. 2885, 81 L. Ed. 2d 847 (1984).

     In rare, extreme cases, jurors' statements that they can ignore information and set opinions aside cannot be accepted. If the risk of taint is high enough, a "presumption of prejudice" arises and another remedy is needed to safeguard the defendant's right to a fair trial. See Irvin v. Dowd. In deciding whether to presume prejudice from publicity despite jurors' protestations to the contrary, several factors are relevant: the nature and amount of publicity, its pervasiveness in the community, the number of jurors exposed, the jurors' answers concerning the kind of information to which they were exposed, and the character of the jurors' opinions. A presumption of prejudice will arise only when the inability of the jurors to perform their duties is made "manifest" by the circumstances of the case. Id.

EXAMPLES AND ANALYSIS

1. In Irvin v. Dowd, six murders in a community were "extensively covered by news media in the locality [and] aroused great excitement and indignation throughout" the

county. Shortly after the defendant's arrest, the prosecutor and police issued press releases stating that he "had confessed." Prior to trial, a motion for a change of venue was granted, but the trial was moved to an adjoining county that had also been exposed to the publicity. A second motion for a change of venue was denied and the defendant was convicted of one murder and sentenced to death.

The Supreme Court reversed the conviction. First, the Court found proof in the "popular media" that "the build-up of prejudice [was] clear and convincing." The coverage was extensive and detailed and included many highly incriminating facts, not the least of which were the defendant's confession to six murders, his indictment for four, and his offer to plead guilty in order to avoid the death penalty. This publicity had to cause "a sustained excitement and foster[ ] a strong prejudice among the people." Second, of 430 persons summoned for jury service, 268 were excused for cause because they had "fixed opinions as to the [defendant's] guilt." Ninety percent of the jurors asked "entertained some opinion as to guilt—ranging in intensity from mere suspicion to absolute certainty." Eight of the twelve jurors who were seated "thought [the defendant] was guilty," and some said it would take evidence to overcome their belief.

Under these circumstances, the jurors' "sincere" claims that they "would be fair and impartial" could not be the basis for a finding of impartiality that satisfied the Constitution. For a defendant whose life was at stake, due process required a trial "in an atmosphere undisturbed by so huge a wave of public passion and by a jury other than one in which two-thirds of the members admit, before hearing any testimony, to possessing a belief in his guilt."

2. In Patton v. Yount, the Court upheld a first-degree murder conviction, distinguishing *Irvin* on two grounds. First, the inflammatory media accounts and resulting arousal of public passion had occurred long before the start of the defendant's second trial. By the start of the trial, the passage of time had diminished the likelihood of prejudice due to publicity. Second, the voir dire of the prospective jurors revealed that "the great majority" remembered the case, but did not disclose that the jurors "had such fixed opinions that they could not judge impartially the guilt of the defendant." In those circumstances, there was no basis for a constitutional "presumption of partiality or prejudice" and the trial judge could find, based on the jurors' answers during voir dire, that those seated were in fact impartial.

---

     ii. **Admonishing and instructing jurors.** Jurors can be **instructed at the outset** that they have a duty to put aside anything they have heard and any preconceived opinions and to judge the case on the basis of the evidence admitted at trial. Moreover, if there is reason, a judge can deliver the same **instruction** to an individual juror or to all jurors **during the trial.** Finally, in the **instructions at the end of trial,** jurors can be reminded of their obligations.

In addition, they can be **admonished** not to speak to anyone about the case and not to read or watch media coverage about the case. These steps provide some protection against ongoing publicity.

iii. **Sequestration of the jury.** To guarantee that publicity does not reach the jurors, they can be **sequestered** during the trial. If the risks of prejudicial taint are high, sequestration might be the most, or only, effective measure. Stories about a case can be excised from the newspapers and magazines given to the sequestered jurors and the media broadcasts they see can be monitored to avoid exposure to publicity about the case.

4. Safeguards Against the Risks of Media Presence

The presence and conduct of media representatives at trial can generate some risks of unfairness. While such risks can result from the presence of any media representative, they are most apparent in cases of *broadcast media* coverage of a proceeding.

a. **Print media.** A trial judge may deal with the risks of unfairness created by **print media** presence by limiting the number of media members that may attend. The judge may also closely regulate the conduct of representatives of the press, ordering them not to behave in distracting or disruptive ways.

Media members have a First Amendment right of access. While a judge may close a criminal trial in rare circumstances, the risks posed by the mere presence of print media representatives do not pose a sufficient threat of unfairness to justify closure. A judge **may not deny access** to the print media because of the risks of unfairness caused by media presence.

b. **Broadcast media. Broadcast media** presence poses a much greater threat to the fairness of a trial. A trial judge can regulate the conduct of broadcast media to minimize the distractions. The amount of equipment can be limited and it can be concealed. The number of broadcasters can be limited and they can be instructed not to engage in disruptive behavior during the proceeding—such as talking, changing tapes, and moving equipment. Broadcasters can also be instructed not to direct cameras toward the jurors or the defendant. In sum, a judge can take steps to insure that the presence of the broadcast media does not substantially distract trial participants.

It was once thought that trial judges might be constitutionally obligated to prohibit all broadcast coverage because the high risks of unfairness rendered such coverage per se violative of due process. In Chandler v. Florida, 449 U.S. 560, 101 S. Ct. 802, 66 L. Ed. 2d 740 (1981), the Court rejected that position, holding that **broadcast coverage of a trial**

does not necessarily deny a defendant due process of law. The Court acknowledged that there are special risks generated by broadcast media coverage, but concluded that the existing evidence did not show that unfairness *always* resulted. Without such evidence, the Due Process Clause could not provide the basis for a rule barring broadcast coverage in all cases.

Under *Chandler*, states are free to allow broadcast coverage. To succeed with a due process claim, a defendant must show specific ways in which his trial was rendered unfair by the presence or participation of the broadcast media. Id.

Courts probably **can deny broadcast media access** to trials. The *Chandler* Court held only that states **may permit** broadcast coverage without violating the Due Process Clause. It did not hold that states **must permit** such coverage. The Court has never held that there is a First Amendment right of access for broadcast media. If anything, the *Chandler* Court indicated that there is no such right; it observed that Florida had "the right . . . to bar all broadcast coverage and photography in court-rooms." As a result, a trial judge who fears the risks posed by broadcasting or simply prefers to avoid the burdens of managing a broadcast trial can probably deny requests from the broadcast media without furnishing specific reasons.

REVIEW QUESTIONS AND ANSWERS

Question: Alice is the subject of a grand jury inquiry. She is subpoenaed to give testimony. Alice's attorney requests a trial judge to open the proceeding to the public during Alice's testimony, asserting that Alice has a Sixth Amendment right to have her testimony given in public in order to prevent prosecutorial overreaching. How should the judge rule?

Answer: The trial judge should deny the request for two reasons. First, Alice has not yet been charged with an offense. Because she is not accused, the Sixth Amendment right to a public trial, which belongs personally to "the accused," has almost certainly not attached. Second, grand jury proceedings are traditionally conducted in secret. While it is arguable that the secrecy has given rise to abuses, the tradition of private grand jury proceedings has continued because of a belief that privacy serves legitimate goals during this phase of the criminal process. Both history and policy support the same conclusion—that there is no Sixth Amendment right to a public grand jury hearing.

Question: Ron, the reputed head of a large organized crime syndicate, has been charged with a variety of offenses. The government has requested that Ron's trial be closed because it fears that witnesses will either suffer retaliation from Ron's associates if they testify against him or will be unwilling to testify against Ron in an open proceeding. Ron has opposed any closure of his trial. May the trial judge grant the government's request?

Answer: On the current state of the record, closure of the trial would violate the accused's Sixth Amendment right to a public trial. The first question is whether either of the two interests posited by the government is "overriding." A genuine danger to a witness's well-being would seem to be sufficient to justify closure. The other interest—insuring that witnesses will testify—is debatable. On the one hand, if a witness will not come forward to give probative testimony, the government's ability to protect society could suffer. On the other hand, if a witness's unwillingness to testify could always justify closure for that witness's testimony, the very objectives of the public trial guarantee could be defeated. This tension should probably be resolved by allowing closure only in cases in which a witness's refusal to testify in public is based on concern about some substantial harm that could result from public testimony. A witness in an organized crime case might be at risk of sufficient harm to justify a refusal to testify that, in turn, would justify closure.

Even if an interest is abstractly sufficient, it must be shown to be present in the actual case. The judge must have evidence that each particular witness is in danger or is unwilling to testify before closing that witness's testimony. To close a trial during a witness's testimony, a judge must make specific, supportable findings with regard to that witness. Moreover, the judge must try to determine whether closure will actually provide substantial protection. Because witnesses' identities will not remain private from the defendant or his counsel, it is *arguable* that closure is not justified because it will not in fact provide much protection for the higher values that are at stake.

Closure must be **essential** to serve the overriding interests. In this case, a court should consider alternative means of protecting the witnesses and encouraging them to come forward. Protection by law enforcement officers might be an option. Nonetheless, one might plausibly contend that only closure can provide adequate protection and adequate assurances of privacy for the witnesses.

In sum, closure during the testimony of a witness could be justifiable, but only if further evidence of potential harm is provided and any closure that is ordered is narrowly tailored. The public could be barred only during the testimony of witnesses who need the protection of a closed proceeding.

Question: Herald News, Inc. is interested in providing full coverage of a particularly lurid criminal trial. The defendants are all prominent public officials who were ensnared in a large-scale sting operation designed to detect those trafficking in child pornography. The defendants have made a motion to have the names of several undercover government informants disclosed to the defense. The judge has scheduled a hearing in camera at which she intends to interview each informant. Only the judge, the informant, and the attorney for the government will be present. Herald News, Inc. has requested access to the hearing. Must the request be granted?

Answer: No. The government has a strong interest in the effective use of undercover agents. Secrecy is essential to that interest. In some circumstances, the defendant's right to a fair trial requires that the secrecy be breached by disclosure of an informant's identity. The tradition is to question the informant in camera in order to determine whether the informant's identify must be disclosed. That tradition is soundly premised. If a "public" hearing was required, the government's interest in keeping informants' identities confidential would be defeated before a court could determine whether that interest should give way to the defendant's interest in a fair trial. No right of access should apply to a process if public exposure would thwart significant interests. That is clearly the case in this situation.

Question: Rod is charged with several acquaintance rapes. Prior to trial he moved to have a confession suppressed on the ground that detectives coerced it. Rod's counsel requested that the hearing on the motion to suppress be closed so that potential jurors did not become privy to his statements to the police. Moreover, counsel also requested that the press and public be barred from the courtroom during the testimony of Rod's alleged victims at trial. The latter request was based on a "risk of irreparable damage to Rod's reputation." The court granted both closure requests. Was the court correct?

Answer: Probably not. The judge might be able to close parts of the suppression hearing, but probably cannot close the trial at all.

First, the First Amendment right of access undoubtedly extends to pretrial suppression hearings that are trial-like in format and are very important to the outcome of trial. There is a tradition of openness, access will play a "significant positive role" in the functioning of the process, and the public has a strong interest in allegations of police misconduct. See Waller v. Georgia (Sixth Amendment right to public trial extends to suppression hearings).

Rod's claim that the suppression hearing should be closed rests on the "overriding interest" in a "fair trial" by jurors who are not tainted by exposure to inadmissible and highly prejudicial information such as a coerced confession. A judge might properly find a "substantial probability" of prejudice to the defendant's fair trial right. The question is whether the judge could plausibly find that there are no reasonable alternatives to closure. Voir dire concerning a juror's knowledge of and ability to disregard a suppressed confession might be an adequate and feasible option. A change of venue to a climate where jurors have not been exposed might also be possible if voir dire is inadequate or proves that the community has been irreparably tainted. A judge would have to make "specific findings" that these alternatives were not "reasonable" or would not be "effective" to protect Rod's fair trial right. If such findings are sustainable, only the portions of the hearing that would reveal the confession can be closed.

With regard to the request to close the victims' trial testimony, it seems unlikely that an accused's interest in avoiding harm to his reputation could qualify as "overriding." In the first place, it may simply be insufficient harm to counterbalance the public's interests in access. Moreover, it could lead to closure in a wide array of serious cases. In many kinds of cases a victim's testimony could harm a defendant's reputation. Perhaps a reputation interest might be sufficient in an extreme case—for example, where there is concrete evidence that reputation is of peculiar importance to a defendant and concrete evidence that the damage from testimony would be particularly severe. However, it is hard to imagine many cases in which closure could be justified on this ground.

Suppose that the prosecution and judge both agreed with Rod that closure was for the best. Would the analysis change?

No. The parties and the judge cannot agree to "waive" or deny the right of access because it belongs to members of the press and the public. If a member of the press or public asserts the First Amendment right, closure is valid **only** if the *Press-Enterprise I* standard is satisfied.

Question: Heather is on trial for hiring a man to kill her husband. The prosecution alleges that Heather, who is 30, wanted to be free to pursue an ongoing relationship with an 18-year-old delivery boy. The small rural community in which Heather lives has been inundated with media coverage of the investigation and pretrial proceedings. The judge has declared that he will not ask prospective jurors about their exposure to publicity "so as to avoid reinforcing any impressions they might have gotten." The defense objects. Is the trial judge correct?

Answer: No. With extensive publicity regarding a sensational case, the chances of bias and/or the receipt of improper evidence are high. The judge has an obligation to find out whether the prospective jurors have been too tainted to be impartial and judge the case based on the evidence at trial. Without questioning the jurors, that obligation cannot be satisfied.

Question: The judge in the preceding situation asks all the prospective jurors what they have seen, read, or heard. Each tells of substantial exposure to potentially prejudicial news accounts. Fifteen say that they can put the information aside and be impartial. Twenty say that they could try to put it aside, but that they are not sure they can. Thirty admit that they are biased and could not be impartial to the defendant. The judge decides to go forward, concluding that if six of the fifteen jurors who claim they can be impartial are otherwise qualified they will hear the case. The defense objects. Is the trial judge correct?

Answer: In light of the amount of publicity, the fact that all jurors have been exposed to substantial amounts, the fact that 50 either cannot or are not sure they can put aside opinions and biases, and the sensational nature of the case, the defendant has a strong argument that the claims of the 15 jurors should not be accepted. While jurors who have seen prejudicial publicity and even those who have formed opinions are not necessarily disqualified, when the evidence shows a very high risk of irreparable bias the claims of a small number of jurors that they can be fair probably should not be believed. The judge should at least postpone the trial until passions subside. And perhaps a change of venue is the only effective means of ensuring a fair and impartial jury.

THE RIGHT TO THE ASSISTANCE OF COUNSEL

CHAPTER OVERVIEW

The Sixth Amendment provides that "[i]n all criminal prosecutions, the accused shall enjoy **the right . . . to have the Assistance of Counsel for his defence.**" This guarantee of counsel for criminal defendants is "fundamental and essential to fair trials." Gideon v. Wainwright, 372 U.S. 335, 83 S. Ct. 792, 9 L. Ed. 2d 799 (1963). Because our systems of criminal justice are **adversarial,** the assistance of counsel is probably the most important of all rights guaranteed by the Constitution.

In an adversarial system, a trial is a *contest* between the state and the accused. The fairness of such a contest depends in large part on at least *rough equality* between the opponents. Counsel promotes equality by providing the skill, expertise, knowledge, experience, and advice essential to defending against the government's efforts to convict.

Counsel also insures that the accused is able to take advantage of her other rights. See Gideon v. Wainwright (without counsel, the "noble ideal" of a fair trial that includes various "procedural and substantive safeguards . . . cannot be realized"). An unaided defendant, for example, might forfeit the opportunity to confront witnesses, might fail to preserve her entitlement to an impartial jury, or might succumb to the state's efforts to compel self-incrimination. In sum, the enjoyment of other rights that are necessary for fundamentally fair trials may well depend on the assistance of counsel.

Chapters 9 and 10 addressed the right to counsel during *investigatory* phases of the criminal process. This chapter is concerned with the right to counsel during *adjudicatory* proceedings. The focus is on trial, but the formal pretrial and post-trial stages of a criminal case are also considered.

Specifically, this chapter discusses:

- **The nature of the right to counsel.** The Sixth Amendment right to counsel includes a basic **right to retain a lawyer.** It also includes a **right to appointed counsel** for indigent criminal defendants. The right to appointed counsel, however, does not extend to every trial. Only those accused of felonies and those actually imprisoned for misdemeanors have a Sixth Amendment right to appointed assistance.

- **The scope of the right to counsel.** The primary role of counsel is at **trial.** Nevertheless, the Sixth Amendment also guarantees assistance at **critical pretrial stages** of the adjudicatory process that have an impact on the fairness of the trial. Moreover, the **Due Process** and **Equal Protection Clauses** guarantee counsel on appeal of a conviction.

- **The right to effective assistance.** The Sixth Amendment guarantees a **right to "effective" assistance of counsel.** Denials of effective assistance can be the result of either **state interference** or **incompetent performance.** A state might interfere with and thereby impair a lawyer's performance of her functions, for example, by prohibiting argument, hindering consultation, or restricting the presentation of evidence. Alternatively, without any state interference, an attorney might render a deficient performance as a result of incompetence. In addition, a **conflict of interest** that may or may not be attributable to state "inaction" can result in constitutionally inadequate assistance.

- **Waiver of the right to counsel and the right of self-representation.** An accused **can waive** the right to counsel. In fact, an accused has an **entitlement to waive** the right to counsel and exercise the implicit Sixth Amendment **right of self-representation.** There are some limitations on the availability and exercise of that right.

A.   NATURE OF THE RIGHT TO THE ASSISTANCE OF COUNSEL

This section discusses the *general nature* of the Sixth Amendment right to the assistance of counsel. The *scope* of the right to counsel is sketched in section B, and the more specific aspects of the guarantee of counsel are considered in section C.

1.   The Right to Legal Assistance

The Constitution guarantees a right to the assistance of **counsel.** The defendant is entitled to the **trained, expert assistance of a lawyer.** There is no constitutional entitlement to assistance from another layperson—that is, one who lacks legal training and expertise. See Wheat v. United States, 486 U.S. 153, 108 S. Ct. 1692, 100 L. Ed. 2d 140 (1988) (defendant is not entitled to advocate who is not a member of the bar).

2.   The Right to Retain Counsel of One's Choice

The Sixth Amendment guarantees that accused individuals may use their funds to retain a lawyer. See Scott v. Illinois, 440 U.S. 367, 99 S. Ct. 1158, 59 L. Ed. 2d 383 (1979). This right certainly extends to all felony trials and to all misdemeanor trials that result in actual imprisonment. It is unclear whether it extends to misdemeanor trials that do not result in actual imprisonment. See subsection 3.b.iii below for further discussion of this question.

Implicit in this guarantee is a **right to counsel of choice.** See Wheat v. United States. This presumptive entitlement to choose one's lawyer is not absolute. Countervailing interests that are sufficiently weighty can justify restricting the accused's choice. Id. For example, a defendant may not insist on representation by a lawyer he cannot afford, one who declines to represent him, or one who has a relationship with an opposing party. Id. In addition, the systemic interest in avoiding representation by attorneys with conflicting interests can support a judge's decision to prohibit a defendant from choosing a particular lawyer. See subsection 3.c below for further discussion of this subject.

3.   The Right to Appointed Counsel

Unlike other Sixth Amendment rights, the cost of enjoying the right to the assistance of counsel must be borne by the accused unless she is indigent. The Constitution **requires the government to provide appointed counsel for indigents** to ensure fair trials. Gideon v. Wainwright.

a.   **Meaning of indigency.** The Supreme Court has not defined indigency. Individuals who have no resources or only a modest amount of money or property that could be used to pay a lawyer clearly qualify as indigent. The amount of assets that separates the indigent from the nonindigent, however, is not clear. Moreover, it is uncertain whether and when a defendant is required to sell items of property in order to pay for counsel. While there are no clear *constitutional* answers to these questions, *statutes* that provide for the appointment of counsel do address them.

b.   **Scope of the right to appointed counsel.** Not all indigent criminal defendants are entitled to appointed counsel. The constitutional right extends **only** to those charged with **felonies** and those charged with **misdemeanors that result in sentences of imprisonment.**

    i.   **The right to appointed counsel for felony charges: The holding of Gideon v. Wainwright.** Typically, a felony is a crime punishable by more than a year in prison, while a misdemeanor is an offense punishable by no more than a year in the county jail. An indigent defendant is entitled to the appointment of counsel for **all felony charges.** Gideon v. Wainwright; see Nichols v. United States, 511 U.S. 738, 114 S. Ct. 1921, 128 L. Ed. 2d 745 (1994). The seriousness of the felony and the extent of the statutorily authorized sentence do not matter; every indigent accused of a felony has a right to appointed representation.

ii. **The right to appointed counsel for misdemeanor charges: The holding of Scott v. Illinois.** An accused is also entitled to appointed counsel for **any misdemeanor charge that results in actual imprisonment.** There is no entitlement to counsel if the misdemeanor sentence does not involve any actual imprisonment. Scott v. Illinois. This standard requires a trial judge to consider sentencing prospects before trial begins. If the judge does not wish or intend to sentence an indigent misdemeanant to any jail time, there is no constitutional need to appoint an attorney. If the judge intends to sentence a misdemeanant to *any* actual time in jail or wishes to keep that option open, counsel must be appointed. If a trial is held without appointed counsel, a sentence involving actual imprisonment is constitutionally forbidden.

The holding of *Scott* prohibits actual imprisonment only for *the conviction that is the result of the uncounseled trial.* It does not bar the government from using an uncounseled misdemeanor conviction as a basis for "enhancing" the punishment for a *later conviction.* An uncounseled misdemeanor conviction may be used to justify an increase in the period of imprisonment imposed for a subsequent conviction even though the additional time in prison would not have been an available sanction but for the uncounseled conviction. Nichols v. United States.

 # EXAMPLE AND ANALYSIS

In Nichols v. United States, an accused was convicted of a felony narcotics charge. His prior misdemeanor conviction for driving under the influence was the product of a trial without the assistance of counsel. Under the Federal Sentencing Guidelines, this misdemeanor conviction made him eligible for a sentence for his narcotics conviction that was 25 months longer than the maximum sentence he otherwise could have received. Before the Supreme Court, the defendant claimed that because the 25-month increase resulted from the uncounseled misdemeanor conviction, it could not be imposed without violating the Sixth Amendment.

The Supreme Court rejected his argument, holding that a misdemeanor conviction that is "valid under *Scott* because no prison term [is] imposed, is also valid when used to enhance punishment [for] a subsequent conviction." Id.

Although the holding in *Nichols* is limited to the enhancement of a sentence for a subsequent conviction, the Court's reasoning suggests that uncounseled convictions that are valid under *Scott* can almost certainly be used for **any subsequent purpose.** Undoubtedly, a trial judge could take such a conviction into account in exercising discretion to select a sentence within a prescribed range. Moreover, she could allow the government to impeach a testifying defendant with his prior uncounseled misdemeanor.

iii. **The right to retain counsel and the holding of Scott v. Illinois.** *Scott v. Illinois* held that the "Constitution require[s] **only** that no **indigent** criminal defendant be sentenced to a term of imprisonment unless the State has afforded him the right to assistance of an **appointed counsel** in his defense." It is uncertain whether a jurisdiction could deny any alleged misdemeanant the right to retain a lawyer.

The right to retain counsel might extend to all criminal trials. In a decision rendered before *Gideon*, the Supreme Court suggested that no state could deprive a defendant of the right to retain a lawyer. See Chandler v. Fretag, 348 U.S. 3, 75 S. Ct. 1, 99 L. Ed. 4 (1954). *Scott* does not preclude the recognition of this absolute right to hire legal assistance. The "actual imprisonment" standard of *Scott* could, however, apply with equal force to the right to retain counsel. The constitutionality of denying appointed assistance was premised on the conclusion that if no actual imprisonment results, **a misdemeanor trial without counsel can be fair.** It is certainly arguable that a denial of retained assistance would not deprive an unimprisoned misdemeanant of a fair trial. Further support for this position might be found in Moran v. Burbine, 475 U.S. 412, 106 S. Ct. 1135, 89 L. Ed. 2d 410 (1986). In that case, the right to counsel had not yet attached because formal adversarial proceedings had not been initiated by the government. As a result, the Court rejected the suspect's claim that he had a Sixth Amendment entitlement to retained assistance at a pretrial interrogation. That decision indicates that an accused cannot create a constitutional right to counsel when counsel is not essential to the fairness of the proceeding.

 # EXAMPLE AND ANALYSIS

Ronny is charged with indecent exposure, a misdemeanor. He denies the charge, claiming that the witness is fabricating the story out of revenge. Although Ronny qualifies as indigent, the trial judge denies his request for appointed counsel. When Ronny's older sister offers to pay for a lawyer to represent him, the judge rules that she may not do so "because the defendant is not entitled to legal assistance." Ronny is convicted following a trial at which he quite ineffectively cross-examines the sole witness for the state. The judge then orders him to pay a $500 fine and do 48 hours of community service. Has Ronny's Sixth Amendment right been violated?

It is uncertain. Ronny is not entitled to appointed counsel for a misdemeanor trial that does not result in actual imprisonment, so the judge's first ruling is correct. Whether *Scott* permits a court to deny representation by retained counsel is undecided.

B. SCOPE OF THE RIGHT TO THE ASSISTANCE OF COUNSEL

When an accused has a Sixth Amendment right to counsel, that right clearly extends to trial. The central question here is whether that right extends to proceedings before and after the trial. If there is no right to appointed counsel at the trial of a charge, no right will extend to any pretrial or post-trial proceeding. If there is a right to counsel at a pretrial or post-trial proceeding, an indigent will have the right to appointed assistance.

1. Assistance of Counsel at Trial

An accused clearly is entitled to a lawyer's assistance from the point at which jury selection begins (or, in a bench trial, the point at which a judge begins to hear evidence) to the point at which a verdict is rendered. An accused is also entitled to assistance for a sufficient period prior to the formal commencement of trial **to enable adequate preparation** for the trial. See Powell v. Alabama, 287 U.S. 45, 53 S. Ct. 55, 77 L. Ed. 158 (1932). Presumably, this entitlement includes an adequate period of time to enable counsel to research and make pretrial motions and requests.

An accused is undoubtedly entitled to assistance for some period following the verdict. Logically, the guarantee of trial counsel must extend to the period during which appropriate post-trial motions—such as a motion for judgment notwithstanding the verdict or a motion for a new trial—might be made. Moreover, because a sentencing hearing is ordinarily considered a part of the trial itself, the right to assistance extends to such a hearing. See Mempa v. Rhay, 329 U.S. 128, 88 S. Ct. 254, 19 L. Ed. 2d 336 (1967).

2. Assistance of Counsel at Formal Pretrial Proceedings

The right to the assistance of counsel extends to **all "critical stages" of criminal prosecutions.** Whether a defendant has the right at a particular pretrial proceeding depends on whether it is a "critical stage." Chapters 9 and 10 discussed two informal "critical stages" that are part of the investigatory phase of a criminal case—"deliberate elicitation" of inculpatory statements by government agents and "trial-like identification procedures." This subsection discusses formal, adjudicatory "critical stages."

A stage of the prosecution will be "critical" if the accused is **confronted with "the prosecutorial forces of organized society, and immersed in the intricacies of substantive and procedural criminal law,"** Kirby v. Illinois, 406 U.S. 682, 92 S. Ct. 1877, 32 L. Ed. 2d 411 (1972), and if counsel is "necessary to preserve the defendant's basic right to a fair trial." Coleman v. Alabama, 399 U.S. 1, 90 S. Ct. 1999, 26 L. Ed. 2d 387 (1970). In other words, a stage is "critical" and counsel is required if the failure to have assistance would in some way undermine the fairness of the trial itself.

After the filing of charges, an accused may be brought into court on more than one occasion prior to trial. See Chapter 2 for a discussion of these stages. Under the standards explained above, most of these formal courtroom proceedings qualify as critical stages.

a.   **First appearances or arraignments.** First appearances or arraignments are not of one kind; they are used for different purposes in different jurisdictions. A typical first appearance might involve, among other things, informing the defendant of the charges and his rights, appointment of counsel, the setting of release conditions, and determination of whether the defendant wants a preliminary hearing. The right to counsel clearly extends to first appearances if the lack of assistance would threaten the fairness of defendant's trial. A state can deny counsel, however, even though a prosecutor is present and legal questions are posed, if the nature of the appearance is such that the lack of assistance will not jeopardize the fairness of the trial.

 EXAMPLES AND ANALYSIS

In Hamilton v. Alabama, 368 U.S. 52, 82 S. Ct. 157, 7 L. Ed. 2d 114 (1961), the Supreme Court held that a defendant was entitled to counsel at an arraignment because there was a risk that a defendant would lose a defense if it was not raised at that point. In White v. Maryland, 373 U.S. 59, 83 S. Ct. 1050, 10 L. Ed. 2d 193 (1963), the Court recognized a Sixth Amendment entitlement at a first appearance at which a defendant was asked to plead. Although a guilty plea could be withdrawn later, it could still be used against the defendant at the trial. In both of these cases, because the ability to defend at trial could have been seriously impaired at the first appearance, counsel was required.

b.   **Preliminary hearings.** At the preliminary hearing the judge decides whether there is adequate cause to require an accused to stand trial for the offenses that have been charged. In Coleman v. Alabama, the Supreme Court held that the right to counsel extended to a preliminary hearing because (1) a lawyer's skills could lead a judge to refuse to find adequate cause and to dismiss the charges; (2) counsel's examination of witnesses could generate impeachment evidence for use at trial and could insure that favorable testimony was preserved for use at trial; (3) counsel could insure better preparation for defending at trial by effectively "discovering" the state's case against the defendant; and (4) counsel could make arguments pertinent to other matters of significance—matters such as bail or the need for a psychiatric examination.

The *Coleman* holding probably signifies an entitlement to counsel at **all preliminary hearings** because they will inevitably involve the kinds of functions relied on by the *Coleman* Court. Moreover, the Court's reasoning provides useful guidance concerning the kinds of risks and advantages that can render any stage critical.

3. Assistance of Counsel at Post-Trial Proceedings

As noted above, post-trial motions and sentencing hearings should be considered part of the trial itself. Appeals and collateral attacks on convictions, however, are distinct phases of the criminal process that occur only after trial has ended. The question here is whether defendants and prisoners have a right to counsel during those phases.

a.   The right to counsel on appeal. Criminal defendants are entitled to legal assistance at some, but not all, stages of the appellate process.

   i.   First appeals as of right. The Constitution does not require states "to provide any appeal at all for [convicted] criminal defendants." Ross v. Moffitt, 417 U.S. 600, 94 S. Ct. 2437, 41 L. Ed. 2d 341 (1974). Nonetheless, every jurisdiction does afford convicted defendants the opportunity to appeal. For **a "first appeal as of right," an accused is entitled to the assistance of counsel.** Douglas v. California, 372 U.S. 353, 83 S. Ct. 814, 9 L. Ed. 2d 811 (1963). This right is **not** contained in the Sixth Amendment. Indigent criminal defendants have a right to appointed counsel grounded in both the **Due Process** and the **Equal Protection Clauses.** See Douglas v. California; Ross v. Moffitt. Those who can afford to pay for a lawyer have a **due process** right to retain legal assistance. See Evitts v. Lucey, 469 U.S. 387, 105 S. Ct. 821, 83 L. Ed. 2d 821 (1985).

   Due process requires counsel on appeal because the appellate process would be fundamentally unfair without the assistance of counsel. See Evitts v. Lucey; Ross v. Moffitt. Equal protection also ensures legal assistance for indigents because without such aid there would be a "lack [of] equality" between the "indigent," who would have "only the right to a meaningless ritual, [and] the rich," who would have "a meaningful appeal." Douglas v. California.

ii. **Discretionary review of convictions.** Every state grants criminal defendants a first appeal as of right. In some states higher appellate courts have the *discretion* to provide further appellate review. Likewise, the Supreme Court, in its *discretion*, can review convictions on petition for writ of certiorari. Indigents have **no constitutional right to appointed "counsel for discretionary state appeals and for applications for [discretionary] review in" the United States Supreme Court.** Ross v. Moffitt. The failure to afford assistance violates neither due process nor equal protection principles.

It is unclear whether a state could deny a person with funds to hire an attorney the opportunity to **retain** legal assistance for purposes of seeking and pursuing discretionary review of a conviction.

 # EXAMPLES AND ANALYSIS

In Ross v. Moffitt, the defendants claimed that they were entitled to appointed counsel for purposes of seeking discretionary review by a state supreme court and the United States Supreme Court. The Court rejected the claims for the following reasons. First, discretionary review follows a first appeal with legal assistance, which includes the opportunity to have counsel prepare an initial brief. Second, the criteria for granting discretionary review are such that the court itself "should be able to ascertain" whether they are met without further assistance from a lawyer. As a result, due process is not offended because the processes of discretionary appellate review can be fairly conducted without further legal assistance. Equal protection is not offended because "the relative handicap" suffered by an indigent—that is, the difference between the process enjoyed by those with funds and those without funds—is insufficient. Indigents have "an adequate opportunity to present [their] claims fairly" despite the lack of counsel's assistance. Id.

Suppose that an indigent defendant who was sentenced to death was entitled to a second appeal as of right in the state supreme court after a first appeal as of right to the intermediate court of appeals. Would he be entitled to appointed counsel? The answer is unclear. Ross v. Moffitt dealt only with "discretionary review," and its reasoning rested, in part, on the criteria for granting such review. Moreover, the defendants in those cases were not facing the ultimate penalty. Still, the fact that the defendant has already had legal assistance at the first appeal and, presumably, has a brief prepared by counsel could support a conclusion that there is no entitlement to further assistance.

iii. **The right to effective appellate assistance.** The right to counsel on a first appeal as of right includes an entitlement to **effective** assistance. Whether counsel is appointed or retained, ineffective assistance on appeal constitutes a deprivation of due process. Evitts v. Lucey. However, because a defendant has no right to counsel for discretionary appellate review, she is not entitled to effective assistance at that stage. If counsel performs ineffectively, there is no denial of due process. Wainwright v. Torna, 455 U.S. 586, 102 S. Ct. 1300, 71 L. Ed. 2d 475 (1982). A defendant's entitlement to "effective" assistance of counsel at trial is discussed in section C below.

   b. The right to counsel for collateral attacks on criminal convictions. Defendants can challenge criminal convictions outside the process of direct appellate review. In these "collateral" attacks on convictions, defendants seek "postconviction remedies." See Chapter 22 for a thorough discussion of the processes of collateral review.

   In general, indigent defendants **do not have a constitutional right to appointed counsel for purposes of pursuing collateral relief** in a state postconviction process. See Pennsylvania v. Finley, 481 U.S. 551, 107 S. Ct. 1990, 95 L. Ed. 2d 539 (1987). However, a prisoner **might** be able to establish that in the particular circumstances of her case due process requires the appointment of counsel for purposes of a collateral attack.

 EXAMPLE AND ANALYSIS

In Murray v. Giarratano, 492 U.S. 1, 109 S. Ct. 2765, 106 L. Ed. 2d 1 (1989), a divided Court rejected the claims of prisoners facing death sentences that in the particular circumstances of their cases the appointment of counsel for purposes of seeking collateral relief was required by due process. A majority of the Court, however, did not foreclose the possibility that in a case with more compelling facts the appointment of counsel could be essential to fundamental fairness.

C. SUBSTANCE OF THE RIGHT TO THE ASSISTANCE OF COUNSEL: THE RIGHT TO EFFECTIVE ASSISTANCE

This section is concerned with the substance of the Sixth Amendment right—that is, the specific entitlements included in the guarantee of counsel. In general, the Constitution requires something more than that "a person who happens to be a lawyer is present at trial alongside the accused." Strickland v. Washington, 466 U.S. 668, 104 S. Ct. 2052, 80 L. Ed. 2d 674 (1984). The Sixth Amendment "right to counsel is the **right to effective assistance of counsel.**" McMann v. Richardson, 397 U.S. 759, 90 S. Ct. 1441, 25 L. Ed. 2d 763 (1970). An accused can be deprived of "effective assistance" in two basic ways. The state might deny counsel outright or impede counsel's ability to function. Or a lawyer might simply fail to provide competent representation. Those two sources of ineffectiveness are discussed separately below. Because ineffectiveness caused by a conflict of interest can be either the state's or counsel's fault, it is treated at the end of this section.

1. Ineffectiveness Caused by Governmental Restrictions on Counsel

In general, counsel must be assured **"the opportunity to participate fully and fairly in the adversary factfinding process."** Herring v. New York, 422 U.S. 853, 95 S. Ct. 2550, 45 L. Ed. 2d 593 (1975). The right to effective assistance "mean[s] that there can be **no restrictions upon the function of counsel in defending a criminal prosecution in accord with the traditions of the adversary factfinding process."** Id. Any restriction that impairs counsel's performance of the functions that are essential to fairness in our adversary system deprives the accused of effective assistance.

This does not mean that states may not impose any constraints on defense attorneys. Reasonable restrictions that serve legitimate interests such as order and expedition are permissible. There is no bright-line standard for determining when a state-imposed limitation is reasonable and when it is incompatible with the constitutional guarantee of counsel. The nature of the restriction, the character and extent of its impact on legitimate interests of the defendant, and the governmental objectives it serves are all relevant to the determination.

a. **Restrictions on partisan advocacy by counsel.** "[T]he very premise of our adversary system . . . is that **partisan advocacy** on both sides of a case will best promote the ultimate objective that the guilty be convicted and the innocent go free." Id. An accused is entitled to have a lawyer who zealously advocates his cause. State limitations that unreasonably impair counsel's efforts to present arguments to the trier of fact can deprive an accused of effective assistance.

 ## EXAMPLE AND ANALYSIS

In Herring v. New York, a state statute granted judges the authority to deny counsel any opportunity to make a closing argument at the end of a bench trial. Relying on this statute, a judge did not permit any summation by the defendant's lawyer. The Supreme Court found the statute violative of the right to counsel.

According to the Court, closing argument "serves to sharpen and clarify the issues for . . . the trier of fact" and is the only opportunity for the parties "to present their . . . versions of the case as a whole." For the defense it "is the last clear chance to persuade the trier of fact that there may be a reasonable doubt of the defendant's guilt." Id. Partisan advocacy is a critical part of counsel's role, and "no aspect of such advocacy could be more important than the opportunity finally to marshal the evidence for each side before submission of the case to judgment." The state's countervailing interest in "expediency" was not substantial enough to justify depriving the accused of assistance that "could spell the difference . . . between liberty and unjust imprisonment." Consequently, the judge's decision to deny all closing argument violated the defendant's right to effective assistance.

Two implications of *Herring* merit mention. First, the denial of closing argument in a jury trial would clearly be unconstitutional. Partisan advocacy is even more important when untrained laypersons will decide the defendant's fate. Second, closing argument can be limited. Trial judges have "great latitude [to] control [ ] the duration of and [to] limit [ ] the scope of closing summations." Id. Counsel can be limited to "a reasonable time" and may be barred from "repetitive or redundant" arguments or those that "otherwise impede the fair and orderly conduct of the trial." Id. Finally, the Court's holding governs only "final argument or summation at the conclusion of . . . evidence." Id. Whether denial of the opportunity to engage in other kinds of partisan advocacy would violate the Sixth Amendment remains an open question. It is not clear, for example, whether a court could prohibit opening argument or argument on evidentiary objections.

b. **Restrictions on consultation between the accused and counsel.** The right to effective assistance of counsel includes a **"right to consult."** Perry v. Leeke, 488 U.S. 272, 109 S. Ct. 594, 102 L. Ed. 2d 624 (1989). This entitlement to consult with one's attorney insures that the accused receives expert advice and has an opportunity to develop and present a defense to the state's charges. Official actions that interfere with counsel's ability to consult with the defendant may threaten the Sixth Amendment guarantee. Before the accused begins to testify, that right to consult is "absolute." Id. Any state infringement violates the Constitution. When the defendant is testifying, some restriction on consultation is permissible.

A judge may deny a request to confer while the client is actually giving testimony, and may deny a recess for that purpose. In addition, when a defendant is on the witness stand, the trial judge may prohibit consultation "during a **brief recess** [between direct testimony and cross-examination] in which there is a **virtual certainty that any conversation between the witness [the accused] and the lawyer would relate to the ongoing testimony.**" Perry v. Leeke. If the recess is **short** enough that "it is **appropriate to presume that nothing but the testimony will be discussed,**" the judge can prohibit consultation because a defendant "has [no] constitutional right to discuss [his] testimony [with counsel] while it is in process." Id. However, if a recess is not brief and it is not appropriate to presume that only the client's ongoing testimony will be discussed, a prohibition on consultation violates the guarantee of effective assistance. See Geders v. United States, 425 U.S. 80, 96 S. Ct. 1330, 47 L. Ed. 2d 592 (1976). During such a break, the accused has important interests in talking to his lawyer about matters that might assist his defense. Those interests are paramount and cannot be outweighed by countervailing concerns.

It is not clear when a break is sufficiently "brief" to allow a prohibition of consultation. Is an hour too long? A two-hour lunch break? Moreover, it is uncertain whether a court may ever bar consultation when a defendant is not testifying. The key premises of Perry v. Leeke—that a defendant has no right to discuss his ongoing testimony and that it is virtually certain that he will only discuss his testimony during a brief recess while he is on the stand—would not support a ban on consultation at any other time. Moreover, the Court's declaration that an accused has an "absolute" right to consult prior to his testimony casts serious doubt on the constitutionality of any ban on consultation when a defendant is not testifying.

EXAMPLES AND ANALYSIS

In Geders v. United States, a trial judge ordered defense counsel not to consult with the defendant during a 17-hour, overnight recess between a defendant's direct testimony and cross-examination. The Supreme Court held that the order violated the defendant's right to effective assistance because during the recess the accused had powerful interests in being able to discuss a host of matters with his attorney. The state's fears of inappropriate consultation about ongoing testimony or unethical coaching could be served in other ways and, in any case, could not justify depriving the defendant of his interest in speaking with counsel.

In contrast, the trial court in Perry v. Leeke prohibited discussion during a 15-minute break between a defendant's direct testimony and cross-examination. The Supreme Court upheld the prohibition, concluding that it was appropriate to presume that only the defendant's testimony would be discussed and that a defendant had no right to discuss his testimony with his attorney while it was in progress.

---

    c. **Restrictions on counsel's ability to present a defense.** The Sixth Amendment constitutionalizes the "right to make a defense." See Faretta v. California, 422 U.S. 806, 95 S. Ct. 2525, 45 L. Ed. 2d 562 (1975). Because counsel plays the central role in making a defense, restrictions that hinder an attorney's ability to present a defense can deprive the accused of the Sixth Amendment right to effective assistance.

 EXAMPLES AND ANALYSIS

In Ferguson v. Georgia, 365 U.S. 570, 81 S. Ct. 756, 5 L. Ed. 2d 783 (1961), a state law allowed the defendant to make an unsworn statement but barred defense counsel from eliciting the accused's testimony by means of direct examination. In Brooks v. Tennessee, 406 U.S. 605, 92 S. Ct. 1891, 32 L. Ed. 2d 358 (1972), a state law limited counsel's ability to decide whether and when the accused should take the stand. Both laws were declared unconstitutional because they deprived the accused of "the opportunity to [have his lawyer] participate fully and fairly in the adversary factfinding process," Herring v. New York, and thereby impeded the effort to present a defense.

   d.   **Other impermissible state restrictions on counsel's abilities to render effective assistance.** Restrictions on advocacy, consultation, and the actual presentation of a defense are surely not the only kinds of state interference that can deprive an accused of effective assistance. If a court order, legislative enactment, or other state action were to **impair counsel's loyalty, limit counsel's zeal, interfere with counsel's ability to investigate or prepare for trial,** or infringe on the proper functioning of counsel in some other way, its action could deprive the defendant of effective legal assistance.

   e.   **Irrelevance of prejudice and harmless error analysis.** Because of "the fundamental importance of the . . . right," an accused who demonstrates either an outright denial of counsel or a lesser deprivation of effective assistance **need not show prejudice** to her defense in order to have a conviction reversed. See Perry v. Leeke. In Herring v. New York, the Court reversed a conviction because the judge denied the opportunity for closing argument. The Court did not demand a showing that closing argument would or could have made any difference to the outcome. In Geders v. United States, a prohibition on consultation led to a reversal "without pausing to consider the extent of the actual prejudice, if any, that resulted from the defendant's denial of access to his lawyer." Perry v. Leeke.

   The government cannot avoid reversal of a conviction by showing that a restriction on counsel was "harmless beyond a reasonable doubt." Violations of the right to effective assistance are "structural errors" and are therefore "automatically reversible." See Arizona v. Fulminante, 499 U.S. 279, 111 S. Ct. 1246, 113 L. Ed. 2d 302 (1991). For a discussion of the harmless error doctrine and constitutional errors that cannot be harmless, see Chapter 21, sections E.2 and E.3.

2.   **Ineffectiveness Caused by Counsel's Deficient Performance: The Doctrine of Strickland v. Washington**

A defendant can be deprived of the effective assistance of counsel if an attorney simply fails to provide competent assistance. Strickland v. Washington, 466 U.S. 668, 104 S. Ct. 2052, 80 L. Ed. 2d 674 (1984). The *Strickland* standards for judging **"actual ineffectiveness"** apply to both **appointed and retained** counsel. See Cuyler v. Sullivan, 446 U.S. 335, 100 S. Ct. 1708, 64 L. Ed. 2d 333 (1980) (discussing why a conflict of interest that causes counsel to render inadequate assistance provides the basis for a Sixth Amendment claim even though counsel is retained).

a.   **Logical foundations of the "actual ineffectiveness" doctrine: The purpose and role of counsel in an adversarial system.** The right to counsel "is needed, in order **to protect the fundamental right to a fair trial.**" Strickland v. Washington. According to the Supreme Court, a fair trial is a trial that "produce[s] **a just result,**" a trial "whose **result is reliable.**" Counsel provides the "skill and knowledge" needed to subject the prosecution's evidence "to adversarial testing." Counsel's "role . . . is critical to the ability of the adversarial system to produce just results." Id.

b.   *Strickland* **requirements for an "actual ineffectiveness" claim: Deficient performance and prejudice.** The role and purposes of counsel in the adversarial system give rise to two independent requirements for a valid claim of "actual ineffectiveness." The defendant must show (1) **deficient performance** by counsel **and** (2) **prejudice.** Id. A showing of deficient performance demonstrates that "counsel was not functioning as the 'counsel' guaranteed the defendant by the Sixth Amendment." Id. A showing of prejudice establishes that "counsel's errors were so serious as to deprive the defendant of a fair trial." Id. Without **both** showings, a defendant cannot establish that she was deprived of the substance of the Sixth Amendment entitlement.

i.   **Definition of "deficient performance."** "[T]he proper standard for attorney performance is that of **reasonably effective assistance.**" Id. To establish a Sixth Amendment violation, the accused "must show that counsel's representation was below an **objective standard of reasonableness,**" that it fell outside "the **wide range of reasonable professional assistance.**" Id. These standards are deliberately vague and open-ended because "[m]ore specific guidelines" or "detailed rules for counsel's conduct" could interfere with counsel's independence, restrict counsel's freedom to make tactical decisions, and detract from the vigor of counsel's advocacy.

A lawyer does have basic duties—the duty of loyalty, the duty to avoid conflicts of interest, the duties to advocate zealously for the accused, to investigate, to consult with the defendant, to keep the defendant apprised of developments, and to bring expert skill and knowledge to bear on the case. Nonetheless, these "basic duties neither exhaustively define the obligations of counsel nor form a checklist for judicial evaluation of attorney performance." Id.

A judge must determine whether counsel's assistance "was **reasonable considering all the circumstances.**" Id. A judge's "scrutiny of counsel's performance must be **highly deferential,**" must "eliminate the distorting effects of **hindsight,**" and "must indulge **a strong presumption that counsel's conduct**" was reasonable. Id. These demanding standards make it difficult to establish that an attorney rendered "deficient performance."

ii. **Definition of prejudice.** To establish "ineffective assistance," a defendant must also show that **prejudice** resulted from counsel's deficient performance. Id. "[A]ny deficiencies in counsel's performance **must be prejudicial to the defense** in order to constitute ineffective assistance under the Constitution."

While prejudice requires **more than "some conceivable effect on the outcome** of the proceeding," it is **not necessary to "show** that counsel's deficient conduct **more likely than not altered the outcome.**" Id. The defendant must demonstrate **"a reasonable probability that, but for counsel's unprofessional errors, the result of the proceeding would have been different.** A reasonable probability is a probability sufficient to undermine confidence in the outcome." Id. With regard to **trials,** there must be a "reasonable probability" that "absent the errors the **factfinder would have had a reasonable doubt respecting guilt.**" Id.

A "reasonable probability of a different outcome" is **necessary,** but is **not always sufficient,** to establish prejudice. "[A]n analysis focusing on *mere* outcome determination . . . is defective." Lockhart v. Fretwell, 506 U.S. 364, 113 S. Ct. 838, 122 L. Ed. 2d 180 (1993). A defendant suffers prejudice only if "counsel's deficient performance [also] **renders the result of the trial unreliable or the proceeding fundamentally unfair.**" Id. If the result yielded by counsel's errors is **more reliable** than the "different result" that could have been produced by adequate performance **and** if counsel's errors did not undermine the **fundamental fairness of the proceeding,** a claim of prejudice will fail even if the result would have been different.

> A result is "unreliable" if it is either **factually** or **legally inaccurate.**
> A result is the product of a "fundamentally unfair" proceeding if
> the defendant has been deprived of some element that is essential
> or important to a **fair process.**

 # EXAMPLES AND ANALYSIS

Incompetent performance by counsel can produce a "more reliable" result by preventing a defendant from giving perjurious testimony, see Nix v. Whiteside, 475 U.S. 157, 106 S. Ct. 988, 89 L. Ed. 2d 123 (1986), or by preventing a court's reliance on legal precedent that is later determined to have been erroneous, see Lockhart v. Fretwell.

In Nix v. Whiteside, the Court hypothesized a situation in which an attorney's unreasonable performance stopped a defendant from lying on the witness stand. Every member of the Court agreed that in that situation **prejudice could not be established** "as a matter of law" even if it were assumed that the false testimony would have led to an acquittal. Although the result of the trial would have been "different," it would have been based on a falsehood. Consequently, it would have been **less reliable** than the conviction that actually resulted from the attorney's deficient performance. According to the Court's logic, a defendant cannot suffer prejudice if a lawyer's performance leads to a result based on "truth" and prevents a result that would have been based on perjury. See Nix v. Whiteside; id. (Blackmun, J., concurring). Under the reasoning of *Nix*, attorney incompetence that suppressed any other kind of "false" evidence (such as perjury by a defense witness, a fraudulent document, or a grossly misleading exhibit) clearly could not result in prejudice.

In Lockhart v. Fretwell, an attorney neglected to raise a potentially controlling precedent that would have precluded a death sentence. After capital punishment was imposed, the precedent was overruled—that is, it was found to be "legally erroneous." Under the "correct" law, defendant's death sentence was proper. Even though the attorney's failure to raise the precedent was egregiously deficient performance and would have produced a dramatically different result (a life sentence), a majority concluded that the defendant was not prejudiced. Because the life sentence would have been based on erroneous law, it would have been **less reliable** than the death sentence that was imposed. According to *Fretwell*, deficient performance that prevents an outcome based on "erroneous" law cannot prejudice the defendant unless it renders the proceeding "fundamentally unfair."

Deficient performance by a lawyer that does not produce a "less reliable outcome" can still be **prejudicial if it renders the proceeding "fundamentally unfair."** Id. Although the Court has not elaborated on the meaning of that phrase, it probably had in mind a case like Kimmelman v. Morrison, 477 U.S. 365, 106 S. Ct. 2574, 91

L. Ed. 2d 305 (1986). In Kimmelman v. Morrison, an attorney's deficient performance might have deprived the accused of a valid claim that probative evidence of guilt should be suppressed from his trial because it was obtained in violation of the Fourth Amendment. Even though the failure to suppress "truthful" evidence of guilt could hardly have resulted in a "less reliable" outcome, see Kimmelman v. Morrison (Powell, J., concurring), the Court concluded that the defendant **could** establish prejudice by showing both **deficient performance** that deprived him of a **valid Fourth Amendment suppression claim** and **a reasonable probability that the outcome of the trial would have been different** if the claim had been raised. According to the majority, all defendants, not only those who are factually "innocent," are entitled to effective assistance. Id. A deficient failure to pursue a constitutional exclusionary remedy apparently can render an ensuing trial "fundamentally unfair." The same conclusion would follow whenever a lawyer's error deprives a defendant of any entitlement that is a part of fundamental *procedural fairness*.

---

      c.   Actual ineffectiveness in guilty plea contexts. The *Strickland* standards also govern situations in which an accused alleges that a guilty plea is based on "actual ineffectiveness." Hill v. Lockhart, 474 U.S. 52, 106 S. Ct. 366, 88 L. Ed. 2d 203 (1985). The defendant must show both deficient performance and prejudice. To demonstrate prejudice, the accused must establish a "reasonable probability that, but for counsel's errors, he would not have pleaded guilty and would have insisted on going to trial." Id. It is arguable, though by no means certain, that a defendant would also have to establish a reasonable probability that the result of the trial (or of a sentencing proceeding) would have been different from the result that followed the guilty plea.

 EXAMPLE AND ANALYSIS

Mack pleads guilty to federal narcotics charges. He later appeals his conviction, claiming that counsel failed to advise him that his confession was subject to suppression because officers violated his entitlements under the *Miranda* doctrine. Should the court reverse the conviction based on the guilty plea?

The appellate court should probably reverse his conviction and remand the case for trial if Mack establishes (1) that his attorney's failure to advise him about the *Miranda* claim was "outside the wide range of reasonable professional assistance" and (2) that he would not have pleaded guilty if counsel had advised him properly. The government should argue that Mack's conviction should not be reversed unless he also establishes (1) that his *Miranda* claim would have succeeded and (2) a reasonable probability that with his confession suppressed the outcome of a trial would have been different from the outcome of his guilty plea. The merits of the government's argument are uncertain.

3. **Ineffective Assistance Caused by Conflicts of Interest**

A defendant is entitled to **undivided loyalty** and **zealous advocacy**—to counsel who puts the defendant's interests first and seeks to promote those interests. If counsel has interests that call on her to do something contrary to the defendant's best interests or to fail to do something to further the defendant's interests, she is said to have a **conflict of interest.** By interfering with counsel's loyal, zealous representation, a conflict of interest can result in ineffective assistance. A common source of such a conflict is **joint representation** of two or more codefendants.

Conflicts of interest are treated separately because there are two different grounds for a conflict claim. One is premised on governmental responsibility for the ineffectiveness—more specifically, on the trial judge's failure to prevent a potential conflict. The other is premised on counsel's deficient performance in resolving an actual conflict against the defendant. The doctrinal elements of these two claims are distinct.

a. **Trial judge failures to prevent potential conflicts of interest.** A trial judge who is put on notice that an attorney has a potential conflict of interest must replace the lawyer or "take adequate steps to ascertain whether the risk [of a conflict is] too remote." Holloway v. Arkansas, 435 U.S. 475, 98 S. Ct. 1173, 55 L. Ed. 2d 426 (1978). If the judge neglects this obligation, a conviction must be reversed. Id.

i. **Requirement that the judge be put on notice.** The "affirmative duty to inquire" into a potential conflict of interest arises only when the trial judge **"knows or reasonably should know that a particular conflict exists."** Cuyler v. Sullivan, 446 U.S. 335, 100 S. Ct. 1708, 64 L. Ed. 2d 333 (1980). Typically, an attorney will provide **actual notice** by informing the judge of a potential conflict. Alternatively, the circumstances before or at trial may provide **actual or constructive notice** of a possible conflict. A judge who in fact is unaware of a conflict is on sufficient notice if he **"reasonably should know"** of it.

ii. **Requirement that the judge remedy the conflict or ascertain that the risk of conflict is remote.** A judge who is put on notice must pursue one of two options. The judge can remedy the conflict by relieving the attorney of conflicting responsibilities. In the case of "joint representation of codefendants" the court can **"appoint separate counsel."** Holloway v. Arkansas. A judge can also examine the situation to determine the likelihood of an actual conflict arising. If the judge determines that the risk is "remote," there is no need to take further remedial action. As a practical matter, the first option is much more likely to be taken.

iii. **Remedy of automatic reversal.** If a judge fails to take action in response to notice of a potential conflict, the accused suffers a Sixth Amendment deprivation and is **entitled to have a conviction reversed.** There is no need to show prejudice from a conflict. In fact, there is no need even to show that an actual conflict existed or impaired the attorney's performance. A judge's failure to respond is constitutional error that **cannot be harmless.** See Holloway v. Arkansas; Cuyler v. Sullivan. A new trial is required.

 # EXAMPLE AND ANALYSIS

Pete, a public defender, is appointed to represent Harv and Milt on charges of bombing a federal building. Shortly after being appointed, Pete writes to the trial judge, informing her that he is "afraid that the vigorous representation of each client almost certainly requires me to cast blame on the other." The judge responds that Pete "should develop another tactic." Harv and Milt are convicted. Harv can show that Pete resolved all conflicts in favor of Milt, harming Harv's chances for acquittal. Were Harv and Milt deprived of effective assistance?

Yes. Both codefendants have valid claims because the trial judge was put on notice and failed to respond adequately by either appointing separate counsel or inquiring into the remoteness of the possible conflict. By making that showing, an accused establishes an entitlement to a new trial. It does not matter that one defendant suffered no harm due to the conflict that existed. There is no need to show actual conflict or prejudice to one's defense, and an error cannot be deemed harmless.

b. **Actual conflicts of interest that impair the performance of counsel.** A judge who neither knows nor should know of a potential conflict has no constitutional duty to inquire. Joint representation of codefendants alone does not provide notice. Cuyler v. Sullivan. When there is no "affirmative duty to inquire," an accused can still establish ineffective assistance of counsel by demonstrating that "**an actual conflict of interest adversely affected his lawyer's performance.**" Id. The defendant **must show** that his "**counsel actively represented conflicting interests**" but "**need not demonstrate prejudice**" to his defense as a result of the conflict. Id.

   i. **An actual conflict that adversely affected the lawyer's performance.** The defendant needs to show that his interests were **actually in conflict** with other interests of the attorney. In addition, the defendant must show that this conflict **"adversely affected" the lawyer's performance**—that is, that counsel's actions were somehow inconsistent with his interests. Conflict alone is not enough; the lawyer must have resolved the conflict against the defendant claiming a Sixth Amendment deprivation.

   ii. **No need to demonstrate prejudice.** A defendant **does not have to show resulting "prejudice."** There is no need to show that the lawyer's actions or inactions harmed the defendant's chances for a favorable verdict. The defendant need show only an adverse effect on performance, not an adverse impact on the outcome. Moreover, when a conflicted attorney fails to render an adequate performance, the constitutional error that results "is **never harmless.**" Cuyler v. Sullivan. Deprivations of effective assistance are "automatically reversible."

 # EXAMPLE AND ANALYSIS

Carol and Matty are accused of conspiracy to commit murder. Both are represented by Pearl, a lawyer that Matty has retained. Both are convicted and claim ineffective assistance caused by a conflict of interests. Carol proves that Pearl single-mindedly pursued Matty's interests because Matty was paying her. On several occasions, Pearl failed to cross-examine witnesses who had implicated Carol because of a fear that such cross-examination could harm Matty's chances for acquittal. Carol is unable, however, to demonstrate that cross-examination would have improved her chances for acquittal. Is Carol or Matty entitled to a new trial?

Carol is entitled to a new trial, but Matty is not. It does not matter that Pearl was retained. Defendants are **entitled to conflict-free representation from both appointed and retained lawyers.** Cuyler v. Sullivan. Carol can show that Pearl had a conflict that led to inaction adverse to Carol's interests. Pearl refrained from cross-examination when zealous advocacy of Carol's interests would have called for it. Matty can show a conflict. However, because Pearl's actions favored her, she cannot show an adverse effect on Pearl's representation of her interests.

   Note: If Carol had been complaining of deficient performance for any reason other than a conflict of interests, the doctrine of Strickland v. Washington **would** require her to show prejudice—"a reasonable probability that the result would have been different." Because her claim of deficient performance is rooted in an actual conflict of interest, she can prevail despite an inability to demonstrate prejudice to her defense.

   c.   **Waiver of the right to conflict-free counsel.** Because conflicts of interest lead to ineffective assistance, defendants have a right to representation by conflict-free counsel. Wheat v. United States, 486 U.S. 153, 108 S. Ct. 1692, 100 L. Ed. 2d 140 (1988). A court may allow a defendant to waive the right to conflict-free counsel and choose to be represented by an attorney who has or may have a conflict of interest. Because defendants have the **right to counsel of choice,** an informed decision to be represented by a particular lawyer—even one who may have a conflict—"**presumptively should be honored.**" Id. Nonetheless, the right to counsel of choice is not absolute. A trial judge may deprive a defendant of the right to choose by declining a waiver of conflict-free counsel, if there is either **"an actual conflict of interest"** or **"a serious potential for conflict of interest."** Id.

 # EXAMPLE AND ANALYSIS

Margaret is a highly successful defense attorney known for her ability to secure acquittals in the face of powerful evidence. Fred and Lorraine have been jointly charged with racketeering. They retain Margaret to represent them. The prosecution objects, claiming that Fred and Lorraine have potentially conflicting interests. Fred and Lorraine inform the court that their interests do not conflict and that they are willing to take whatever risk might exist. After looking into the matter, the trial judge decides that Margaret cannot represent both Fred and Lorraine. Lorraine secures separate representation and is convicted. She appeals, challenging the judge's decision that Margaret could not engage in joint representation. Should the appellate court reverse Lorraine's conviction?

The appellate court should find a denial of Lorraine's Sixth Amendment right to counsel of choice and should reverse her conviction *unless* the record shows either an actual conflict or a serious potential for conflict. Neither the mere assertion by the prosecutor nor the possibility for conflict that "inheres in almost every instance of multiple representation," Cuyler v. Sullivan, is sufficient to justify denial of the right to counsel of choice. If the record sustains a finding of at least a serious potential for conflict, then the court acted properly in refusing to allow Margaret to represent both Fred and Lorraine.

D.   WAIVER OF THE RIGHT TO COUNSEL AND THE RIGHT OF SELF-REPRESENTATION

Although a defendant may be **permitted to waive** most constitutional rights, as a general rule, an accused has **no right to waive** those rights. She may be compelled to "enjoy" them. The right to counsel is an exception to that general rule. Because the Sixth Amendment contains an implicit **right of self-representation,** criminal defendants are **constitutionally entitled to waive the right to counsel.**

1. Waiver of the Right to Counsel

An accused **may be allowed to waive the right to counsel.** See Adams v. United States ex rel. McCann, 317 U.S. 269, 63 S. Ct. 236, 87 L. Ed. 268 (1942). Such a waiver is valid if it is **knowing, intelligent, and voluntary.** Id.; Johnson v. Zerbst, 304 U.S. 458, 58 S. Ct. 1019, 82 L. Ed. 1461 (1938). If the defendant validly waives the right to counsel, a trial without assistance is constitutional. For a discussion of the prerequisites for valid waivers, see subsection 2.b.iii below.

2. The Sixth Amendment Right of Self-Representation: The Doctrine of Faretta v. California

The accused has a Sixth Amendment **right of self-representation.** Faretta v. California, 422 U.S. 806, 95 S. Ct. 2525, 45 L. Ed. 2d 562 (1975). Except in limited circumstances, a defendant who wishes to conduct his own defense has a constitutional right to waive the assistance of counsel and represent himself.

     a. Source of and basis for the right of self-representation. The right of self-representation is not explicitly set out in the Sixth Amendment, but it is implicit in the "structure" and "spirit" of that provision. Id. According to the *Faretta* Court, the Sixth Amendment "grants to the accused personally the right to make his defense." That right can be fully enjoyed only if the defendant is entitled to conduct that defense himself—that is, to serve as his own "legal" representative.

     All the rights expressly granted by the Sixth Amendment are fundamental components of fair trials. The right to counsel is probably the most "essential" to fairness. The right of self-representation stands in stark contrast to other Sixth Amendment rights. Its exercise might well *undermine* the fairness of a trial. A defendant's lack of legal knowledge and expertise can preclude the presentation of an effective defense. See Faretta v. California ("It is undeniable that in most criminal prosecutions defendants could better defend with counsel's guidance than by their own unskilled efforts.").

     Despite the potential for "unfairness," the Framers included "the right to appear pro se to affirm the **dignity and autonomy of the accused.**" McKaskle v. Wiggins, 465 U.S. 168, 104 S. Ct. 944, 79 L. Ed. 2d 122 (1984). They constitutionalized the right of self-representation because they "understood the **inestimable worth of free choice**" and the importance of " 'respect for the individual,' " Faretta v. California, and because on occasion the right of self-representation "allow[s] the presen-

tation of what may . . . be the accused's best possible defense."
McKaskle v. Wiggins; see also Faretta v. California ("in rare instances"
the accused may present a better defense than a lawyer would).

b. **Restrictions on the exercise of the right of self-representation.** The right
of self-representation cannot be denied because the defendant lacks "legal
abilities." Nonetheless, it is not absolute. The right to represent oneself
depends on a **valid waiver** of the right to counsel and on the defendant's
ability and willingness to comply with certain rules of the courtroom.

    i.   **Irrelevance of a defendant's legal abilities.** To represent himself
at trial, "a defendant need not himself have the skill and experience
of a lawyer." A **lack of technical legal knowledge, skill, or expertise is not relevant** to the defendant's decision to exercise the right
and cannot be the basis for denying pro se representation. Faretta
v. California.

    ii. **Prerequisite of a valid waiver of the right to counsel.** Because
an exercise of the right of self-representation entails surrender of
the assistance of counsel, an accused who wishes to appear pro se
must waive the right to counsel. Faretta v. California; McKaskle v.
Wiggins. A defendant who fails to provide a valid waiver of counsel
is not entitled to represent herself. A failure to assert the right to
counsel is not sufficient to demonstrate a waiver. Valid waivers of
fundamental constitutional rights are never presumed from silence.
There must be affirmative evidence that a defendant has made a
constitutionally acceptable choice to relinquish the right to counsel. If a judge allows a defendant to represent herself without
securing a valid waiver, a conviction will be subject to reversal for
violation of the defendant's right to the assistance of counsel.

    "[I]n order to represent himself, the accused must **'knowingly and
intelligently'** " waive the right to counsel. Faretta v. California. A
decision to waive counsel does not have to be "smart" or "wise."
For a waiver to be "knowing and intelligent," the accused must
be **"aware of the dangers and disadvantages of self-representation."** He must " 'know[ ] what he is doing and [make] his choice
. . . with eyes open.' "

    The *amount of information* necessary to render a waiver **knowing** is
uncertain. The Supreme Court has not specified the precise things
that an accused must be "aware of" in order to make a valid choice
to proceed pro se. Lower court opinions have found the following
matters important: the nature of the charges, potential penalties,
possible defenses, offenses that are included, the facts that the government is represented by counsel and that a layperson is not
equipped like an expert lawyer, and the advantages of having a
trained attorney.

A valid waiver also requires a **voluntary** choice to relinquish a right. Godinez v. Moran, 509 U.S. 389, 113 S. Ct. 2680, 125 L. Ed. 2d 321 (1993). In the contexts of coerced confessions and *Miranda* waivers, "voluntary" means "not coerced" by the government. Subjective attributes of the individual are relevant, but some amount of external pressure is required to render a confession or a *Miranda* waiver "involuntary." Purely internal forces cannot suffice. See Chapter 6, section B.3; Chapter 7, section B.4.c. An officially coerced choice to forgo trial counsel and represent oneself would clearly be invalid. Moreover, subjective attributes such as background, age, intelligence, educational level, and mental health are clearly relevant to the voluntariness of a waiver of counsel. Whether a waiver of trial counsel may be found involuntary solely because of some form of internal compulsion is unclear.

Finally, for a waiver of the right to counsel to be valid, the accused must be **mentally competent**. Id. A defendant is competent to waive counsel if he **"has sufficient present ability to consult with his lawyer with a reasonable degree of rational understanding . . . and . . . has a rational as well as factual understanding of the proceedings against him."** Id.

iii. **Uncertainty of the need for admonishment and inquiry.** In *Faretta*, the Court observed that the accused **"should be made aware** of the dangers and disadvantages of self-representation, so that **the record will establish"** a knowing choice. This passage has created a serious division of opinion in the lower courts with regard to the need to admonish every accused and to inquire about her awareness.

Some courts have held that a trial court must conduct "a 'searching inquiry' with an accused before allowing him to conduct his own defense." They have mandated hearings with specific warnings, advice, and questions. See McDowell v. United States, 484 U.S. 980, 108 S. Ct. 478, 98 L. Ed. 2d 492 (1987) (White, J., dissenting from denial of certiorari). Unless a judge follows the prescribed procedures, a waiver is invalid even if the record establishes that the accused was aware of relevant matters and made a voluntary choice to forgo counsel. See Chapter 7, section B.3 (for a discussion of an analogous approach to the *Miranda* warnings).

Other courts "have taken the position that no specific inquiries or special hearings must be conducted before an accused's exercise of his *Faretta* rights will be considered 'knowing and intelligent.'" See McDowell v. United States. So long as the record contains sufficient evidence of a knowing and voluntary choice to relinquish counsel, a waiver is valid.

This conflict between the lower courts has not been resolved by the Supreme Court.

iv. **Requirement of an ability and willingness to abide by the rules of procedure and courtroom protocol.** The *Faretta* Court observed that a trial court can "**terminate self-representation** by a defendant who **deliberately engages in serious and obstructionist misconduct.**" According to the Court, "the right of self-representation is not a license to abuse the dignity of the courtroom" or "a license not to comply with relevant rules of procedural and substantive law." To exercise the right of self-representation an accused must be "**able and willing to abide by rules of procedure and courtroom protocol.**" McKaskle v. Wiggins. Consequently, defendants who engage in deliberate misconduct, defendants who are unable to refrain from disruptive behavior, and defendants whose incapacity to follow the rules and procedures of the courtroom makes an orderly and decorous proceeding impossible all may be denied the right to proceed pro se.

 # EXAMPLES AND ANALYSIS

If a defendant tries in several different ways to introduce an item of evidence but each time runs afoul of a rule of law or procedure, a judge cannot terminate the entitlement to act pro se simply because of his lack of legal knowledge or skill. However, if the accused ignores a court's rulings and deliberately repeats efforts to introduce evidence in ways that do not comply with proper procedure, a judge may be able to terminate the accused's self-representation based on the defendant's unwillingness to abide by rules of procedure. Moreover, if the accused has a mental disorder that causes her repeatedly to engage in inappropriate courtroom conduct—including scurrilous and lewd remarks—a court apparently has the authority to terminate self-representation on the ground that the defendant is unable to abide by rules of protocol.

v. **Judge's authority to appoint "standby counsel."** "[E]ven over the objection of the accused," a trial judge may always appoint " '**standby counsel**' to aid the accused if and when the accused requests help, and to be available to represent the accused in the event that termination of the defendant's self-representation is necessary." Faretta v. California. Moreover, despite "the defendant's objection," standby counsel may assist the defendant "in overcoming **routine procedural or evidentiary obstacles** to the completion of some specific task . . . that the defendant has shown he wishes to complete" and may also help "to ensure the defendant's **compliance with the basic rules of courtroom protocol and procedure.**" These kinds of uninvited participation by standby counsel are constitutionally unobjectionable. McKaskle v. Wiggins.

c. **Substance of and deprivations of the right of self-representation.** This subsection outlines the substance of the right of self-representation—the specific entitlements it grants to criminal defendants. At the same time, it describes the different ways in which a defendant can be deprived of the pro se right.

    i. **What a pro se defendant must be allowed to do.** If a defendant validly waives counsel and there are no grounds for denying the pro se right, the Constitution commands that he be allowed to represent himself. A denial of self-representation violates the Sixth Amendment.

    In addition, the "right of self-representation plainly encompasses certain **specific rights to have [one's] voice heard.**" McKaskle v. Wiggins. The "defendant must be allowed to control the organization and content of his own defense, to make motions, to argue points of law, to participate in voir dire, to question witnesses, and to address the court and the jury at appropriate points in the trial." Id. While a judge can put the same limits on a pro se defendant that she could put on a lawyer, she must let the accused do all the things that a trained attorney would be allowed to do. A judge who prevents an accused from participating in these ways violates the Sixth Amendment.

    A court *may allow* an accused to be represented in part by counsel and in part by himself. Nonetheless, an accused is **not constitutionally entitled to such "hybrid representation."** McKaskle v. Wiggins. A defendant may be forced to choose between the right to counsel and the right of self-representation.

    ii. **What standby counsel must be prohibited from doing.** The right of self-representation includes more than the right to participate fully. It also includes **protection against "unsolicited and excessively intrusive participation by standby counsel."** McKaskle v. Wiggins. A judge may appoint standby counsel over the accused's wishes and need not "absolute[ly] bar . . . standby counsel's unsolicited participation" in the trial. Nevertheless, the Constitution "impose[s] some limits on the extent of [such] participation." Id.

    In general, the *Faretta* right guarantees to the defendant both an entitlement to have "**actual control over the case** he chooses to present" and an entitlement **to have the jury perceive him as representing himself.** Id. The nature of the specific limits on standby counsel's participation depends on whether a jury is present.

Outside the presence of the jury, the right of self-representation is not infringed on "if the pro se defendant is allowed to address the court freely on his own behalf and if disagreements between counsel and the pro se defendant are resolved in the defendant's favor" on matters "normally . . . left to the discretion of counsel." Thus, counsel should not be allowed to "substantially interfere with any significant tactical decisions, or to control the questioning of witnesses, or to speak *instead* of the defendant on any matter of importance." Id.

In the presence of the jury, there is an additional restraint on participation by standby counsel. Counsel must not be allowed to "destroy the appearance" or "the jury's perception that the defendant is representing himself." Id. If standby counsel is allowed to engage in excessive unsolicited participation, the right of self-representation is violated.

An accused "can waive his *Faretta* rights." Consequently, if a defendant **expressly approves** of or **invites** participation by counsel, he cannot claim that such participation deprived him of control and he "diminishes any general claim" that counsel interfered with the jury's perception of him. If a defendant elects to have counsel participate, his "complaints concerning **subsequent unsolicited participation** lose much of their force." Moreover, if the accused invites or agrees to "substantial participation by counsel, **subsequent appearances** by counsel must be **presumed to be with the defendant's acquiescence**" unless the accused "expressly and unambiguously" requests that "counsel be silenced."

iii.   **Unavailability of "ineffective assistance" claims.** When a defendant validly chooses self-representation instead of representation by trained counsel, she forgoes the clear advantages of legal expertise and takes the risk that her own performance will be considerably less effective. She cannot later claim that her own poor performance constituted "ineffective assistance of counsel." Faretta v. California; McKaskle v. Wiggins; see also section C.2 above (discussing the right to "effective assistance" and the elements of an "ineffective assistance of counsel" claim).

iv.   **Inapplicability of harmless error analysis.** An accused can be deprived of the right of self-representation in various ways, including outright denial of a valid request, erroneous rejection of an acceptable waiver, restrictions on the defendant's participation at trial, or excessive participation by standby counsel. **No violation**

of the pro se right can be harmless. McKaskle v. Wiggins. A conviction that is the result of a trial at which a defendant was deprived of the entitlement to represent himself *must* be reversed.

There are two reasons that violation of the *Faretta* right cannot be harmless. First, standard harmless error analysis focuses on whether a mistake at trial had a negative effect on the defendant's chances for acquittal. Because denials of self-representation would ordinarily improve the "fairness" of the defendant's trial and enhance the chances for acquittal, most, if not all, violations of the *Faretta* right would be harmless. McKaskle v. Wiggins. Incentives to honor the right of self-representation would be undermined.

Perhaps more important, the *Faretta* right is designed primarily to safeguard "the dignity and autonomy of the accused." When the right of self-representation is infringed on, there is always harm to those values. Put otherwise, violations of the pro se right are never harmless because they always deprive the defendant of the interests that underlie the right.

REVIEW QUESTIONS AND ANSWERS

Question: In 1997 Polly was charged with driving under the influence of narcotics (DUI). Driving under the influence is a misdemeanor, punishable by up to one year in jail or a fine of $2,000 or both. An individual who has two prior DUI convictions, however, may be charged with a felony, punishable by up to five years in state prison or a fine of up to $10,000 or both. Because Polly had been convicted in both 1989 and 1992 for DUI, the prosecutor charged her with a felony on this occasion. Although indigent, she was denied appointed counsel at the 1989 trial; after conviction, she was sentenced to pay a fine of $500. Polly asked to represent herself in 1992 and the judge granted her request without ascertaining whether she was aware of the risks of self-representation. She was convicted and sentenced to pay a fine of $2,000. Polly claims that the use of these convictions to support a felony conviction will violate her right to counsel. Is her claim valid?

Answer: No. The Constitution does not guarantee counsel to misdemeanants who are not punished by actual imprisonment. A conviction that is valid because it does not result in actual imprisonment is also valid for the purpose of elevating the level of a subsequent offense and enhancing the sentence that is available for that offense. Polly's first and second DUI convictions were valid because her trials resulted only in fines. Although the record of the second trial does not contain an adequate showing that she "knowingly" waived her right to counsel and chose self-representation, the conviction is valid because Polly had no right to counsel at that trial.

Question: Arlene was charged with arson in connection with a bombing at an animal research center. She retained Ben, a famous civil rights attorney, to represent her. Prior to trial, the judge ruled that the parties could not make opening arguments to the jury unless they could "show good cause to believe that opening arguments would promote a fair outcome." Because neither side made an attempt to "show good cause," there were no opening arguments. A two-hour lunch break was called while Arlene was in the midst of her direct testimony. The judge ordered Ben "not to talk to your client about her testimony" during that break. At the end of the two-week trial, the judge ruled that each side would have 15 minutes "to sum up for the jurors." The defense raised objections to each of these rulings. Arlene was convicted. Should the judge's rulings be upheld on appeal?

Answer: While each of the rulings may be the basis for a reversal of Arlene's conviction under existing precedents, none clearly violates the right to counsel.

The restrictions on opening and closing arguments: The holding of Herring v. New York is instructive, although not controlling, in this case. Therein, the Court held that a denial of any opportunity to present **closing** argument in a **bench trial** is unconstitutional. According to *Herring*, government restrictions that deprive counsel of "the opportunity to participate fully and fairly in the adversary factfinding process" or that improperly restrict counsel's ability to "defend[ ] a criminal prosecution in accord with the traditions of the adversary factfinding process" deprive the defendant of effective assistance. Partisan advocacy is an important function of counsel in the adversary system. Unreasonable restrictions on partisan advocacy may well deprive an accused of the Sixth Amendment entitlement.

Herring dealt only with closing argument in a bench trial. In part, the Court's reasoning rested on the fact that summation provides the parties with a final chance to persuade the factfinder after all the evidence is in. Arlene's initial claim pertains to opening argument. It is arguable that opening argument is also a vital part of partisan advocacy in setting the stage for the evidence to come. This may be true particularly when the trier is a body of laypersons unschooled in the law and unlikely to detect the significance of each bit of evidence. If opening argument is a vital part of partisan advocacy, the judge's ruling here probably should be deemed unconstitutional. The defendant should not have to "show good cause" why counsel should be allowed to participate in ways that *presumptively* further the objectives of our adversary system.

In addition, *Herring* specifically authorized judges to place reasonable restrictions on closing argument in a bench trial. Undoubtedly, a judge has the same power in a jury trial. The question in Arlene's case is whether the 15-minute limit on closing argument to the jury was "reasonable." A two-week trial would logically seem to require a longer period for summation, but perhaps the issues were sufficiently simple and the evidence sufficiently clear to allow adequate summation in a short time. The resolution of Arlene's claim regarding closing argument is unclear and could be bolstered by a demonstration in the record that the legal and factual issues were complex or that the evidence was extensive.

The restriction on consultation: In general, defendants have the right to consult with counsel. According to Perry v. Leeke, however, judges may bar all consultation between attorney and client during "brief" recesses between the accused's direct testimony and cross-examination in which it is "a virtual certainty that any conversation . . . would relate to ongoing testimony." It must be "appropriate to presume that nothing but testimony will be discussed."

The break here was during Arlene's direct testimony. It is arguable that Perry v. Leeke is inapplicable at that point in the trial and that the defendant's right to consult was violated. On the other hand, Perry v. Leeke held that the defendant has no right to discuss her testimony while it is in progress. Whether a break is during direct examination, between direct and cross-examination, or during cross-examination, it would seem appropriate to presume that only testimony will be discussed—so long as the break is sufficiently "brief."

It seems quite unlikely (though possible) that a two-hour lunch break is sufficiently brief to permit a ban on consultation. That time span alone gives rise to a cognizable likelihood of an interest in and need to discuss other topics. Moreover, such breaks provide the opportunity for mid-day strategy sessions. Nonetheless, the judge barred only consultation about the defendant's testimony. Because there is no right to discuss ongoing testimony, such a prohibition might be allowable during a longer break. It is arguable, however, that any restraint on consultation runs a risk of chilling attorney-client discussions about matters the defendant has a right to discuss.

Question: Vinny and Thelma were married. In the summer of 1997, they operated a day camp. By fall, they were bankrupt. In early 1998, based on the allegations of several different adolescents about events at the camp, Vinny and Thelma were charged in separate indictments with multiple counts of contributing to the delinquency of a minor and lewd and lascivious acts with a minor. Danielle was appointed to represent both codefendants. The prosecutor intended to try Thelma first in order to keep open the possibility that she would testify against Vinny at his trial. On the morning before Thelma's trial began, Danielle told the judge that she could "foresee a chance that I won't be able to maximize both defendants' chances for a fair verdict or a good bargain." The judge immediately responded that "the chance of conflict seems small considering the separate trials that are scheduled." Both Thelma and Vinny were convicted. Both now appeal. How should the appellate court rule?

Answer: Both convictions should be reversed under the opinion in Holloway v. Arkansas. When a judge is notified by counsel for codefendants that a possible conflict exists, the judge must either appoint separate counsel or ascertain that the risk of a conflict is too remote to warrant separate counsel. The judge here did neither. The mere fact that codefendants' trials are separate should not be a sufficient basis for finding that the risk of conflict is "remote." Separate trials may reduce the risk, but joint representation still entails serious risks that an attorney will be unable to pursue zealously a favorable outcome (either a verdict or a plea bargain) for both clients.

A judge's failure to fulfill the obligation to appoint separate counsel or inquire adequately into the remoteness of the risk is automatically reversible error. Neither an actual conflict nor prejudice need be shown.

Question: Ricky Joe was charged with first-degree murder. His father retained Walter to represent him. Walter was overburdened with work and failed to look into the circumstances surrounding Ricky Joe's confession. Consequently, he did not learn that Ricky Joe had made an "equivocal" request for counsel upon receiving the *Miranda* warnings. Under a controlling precedent in the jurisdiction at the time of Ricky Joe's trial, an officer's failure to clarify an equivocal request for counsel prior to continuing with custodial interrogation rendered any waiver given by a suspect invalid. If Walter had moved to suppress the confession, this precedent would have instructed the trial judge to suppress Ricky Joe's confession.

After a trial at which the confession was a significant piece of the government's evidence, Ricky Joe was convicted and sentenced to death. He has collaterally attacked his conviction on Sixth Amendment grounds. Between the conviction and the collateral attack, the Supreme Court decided Davis v. United States, 512 U.S. 452, 114 S. Ct. 2350, 129 L. Ed. 2d 362 (1994) (discussed in Chapter 7, section B.6.a). Under *Davis*, officers have no obligation to clarify ambiguous requests for counsel. How should the appellate court rule?

Answer: According to Lockhart v. Fretwell, the appellate court should affirm the conviction. An "actual ineffectiveness" claim requires a defendant to show deficient performance and prejudice. Ricky Joe can probably show that the failure to research his *Miranda* claim was outside the wide range of reasonably competent assistance. When a confession is a significant part of a case, it is particularly important for defense counsel to examine the relevant facts and research the pertinent precedents. Walter failed to do so without good reason. A heavy workload cannot justify such a dereliction.

Nonetheless, Ricky Joe will not be able to show prejudice. The "significant" role of the confession does suggest that there is a "reasonable probability" that but for Walter's error the result of the trial would have been different. The suppression claim would have succeeded, and without the confession there is quite arguably a "reasonable probability" that Walter would not have been convicted. The prejudice analysis, however, cannot focus on "outcome determination" alone. Here, the "different outcome" would have been based on "erroneous law"—the precedent that, according to the later opinion in *Davis*, misinterpreted *Miranda*'s requirements. Walter's deficient performance cannot have "undermined confidence in the outcome" of the trial because it led to a "more reliable" verdict by preventing the trial court from relying on mistaken law. A defendant can suffer prejudice within the meaning of *Strickland* only if counsel's deficient performance "renders the result unreliable or the proceeding fundamentally unfair." Lockhart v. Fretwell. A lawyer's error must "deprive the defendant of a[ ] substantive or procedural right to which the law entitles him." Id. Because Walter's error did not have such an effect on Ricky Joe's trial, an ineffective assistance claim should not succeed.

Question: Jamie was charged with criminal trespass in connection with a protest at a federal facility. A public defender was appointed to represent her. Jamie disagreed with her attorney's strategy. She filed a formal, written request with the court, seeking to "act as my own counsel." The trial judge thoroughly warned Jamie of the risks, inquired extensively into her understanding, satisfied himself that she was acting voluntarily, and agreed that Jamie could act as her own counsel. The judge then warned Jamie as follows: "I am going to appoint Ms. Winston to act as standby counsel. I will not allow you to make political statements or put U.S. government policy on trial. You will be required to stay within the bounds of the law. If you insist on exceeding them or ignoring my rulings, I will have Ms. Winston take over for you."

Early in the trial, during cross-examination of a government official, Jamie began to ask questions designed to demonstrate the immorality of U.S. government policy. The judge informed her that she could "not pursue that line of questioning." Jamie proceeded to other topics. Later, while Jamie was examining the first defense witness, the judge repeatedly upheld prosecution objections to the form of her questioning. Exasperated, Jamie cursed. The judge warned her. At that point, Ms. Winston intervened, offering a proper formulation of Jamie's question. Jamie told her to "shut up and sit down." The trial judge warned Jamie once again. Finally, during direct examination of her third witness Jamie once again began to ask questions aimed at the propriety of U.S. policy. The judge interrupted her, declaring, "I have had enough of your conduct. Your right to represent yourself is hereby terminated. Ms. Winston, please finish with this witness and with closing argument." Jamie was convicted and has appealed. Does she have a valid claim that her right of self-representation was violated?

Answer: The question is debatable. First, the judge seems to have gotten a valid waiver of counsel from a person who was competent to choose self-representation and had a right to do so. The judge had the power to appoint standby counsel and could warn Jamie that she would have to stick to proper, legal defenses during the trial. Similarly, each of the four warnings at trial seem proper.

Jamie could complain of counsel's unsolicited effort to help her formulate her question. Under McKaskle v. Wiggins, however, there is no bar to standby counsel, even over the accused's objection, assisting "the pro se defendant in overcoming routine procedural or evidentiary obstacles to the completion of some specific task, such as introducing evidence . . . , that the defendant has clearly shown [she] wishes to complete." That would seem to be what Ms. Winston did here.

The only argument that would have a cognizable chance of success is a claim that Jamie's behavior was insufficient to permit termination of her Sixth Amendment right. *Faretta* stated that termination was allowable if the defendant "deliberately engages in serious and obstructionist misconduct," and *McKaskle* indicated that the pro se right can be lost if the defendant is not "able and willing to abide by rules of procedure and courtroom protocol." Even when her conduct is added up, Jamie's two attempts at questioning U.S. policy, her cursing, and her uncivil comment toward the standby lawyer who had intervened might not meet these standards for termination. If they do not, the judge violated Jamie's constitutional right when he ordered standby counsel to finish the trial, and her conviction would have to be reversed.

19 THE RIGHT TO TRIAL BY JURY

CHAPTER OVERVIEW

The Sixth Amendment provides that "[i]n all criminal prosecutions, the accused shall enjoy the **right to a . . . trial, by an impartial jury,**" and Article III, section 2 of the U.S. Constitution provides that "[t]he Trial of all Crimes . . . shall be by Jury." The history of trial by jury "reveal[s] a long tradition attaching great importance to the concept of relying on a **body of one's peers** to determine guilt or innocence **as a safeguard against arbitrary law enforcement.**" Williams v. Florida, 399 U.S. 78, 90 S. Ct. 1893, 26 L. Ed. 2d 446 (1970). Inclusion of the right to a jury trial in the Constitution "reflect[s] a fundamental decision about the exercise of official power, . . . [an] insistence upon **community participation** in the determination of guilt or innocence . . . as a **defense against arbitrary law enforcement.**" Duncan v. Louisiana, 391 U.S. 145, 88 S. Ct. 1444, 20 L. Ed. 2d 491 (1968). Because it interposes a group of ordinary citizens between the accused and the state and thereby provides "an inestimable **safeguard against the corrupt or overzealous prosecutor and against the compliant, biased, or eccentric judge,**" the right to jury trial is **essential to fundamental fairness.** Id.

This chapter discusses the right to trial by jury. Specifically, it addresses the following topics:

- **The scope of the right to trial by jury.** Although the terms of both the Sixth Amendment and Article III, section 2 provide an entitlement to trial by jury for "**all** crimes" and "**all** criminal prosecutions," the Supreme Court has recognized the historical division between "**serious**" and "**petty**" crimes. Defendants are **only** entitled to jury trial **for serious crimes.**

- **The meaning of the "jury" entitlement.** A jury is a group of laypersons. The Constitution does not prescribe a requisite **size** for that group. Despite the fact that the common law eventually settled on juries made up of twelve persons, the Supreme Court has held that juries **do not have to have more than six persons.** It is often said that a jury is "a body of one's peers." The Constitution does not specify any requirements for the **constituency** of that body. Nevertheless, the Court has concluded that implicit in the purposes served by the right to jury trial is a demand that jurors be chosen from a **fair cross-section of the community.**

- **The process of jury selection.** The process of jury selection is regulated by at least three different constitutional provisions: the **Sixth Amendment** guarantee of an "impartial" jury, the **Due Process Clause** promise of "fundamental fairness," and the **Equal Protection Clause** protection against "discrimination." The first two extend to defendants a limited entitlement to have certain questions asked of prospective jurors during voir dire. The latter imposes limitations upon the parties' ability to use peremptory challenges to eliminate potential jurors.

- **The substance of the jury guarantee during trial.** Defendants are entitled to **impartial** and **competent** jurors who **decide** cases **based on the evidence.** When there is sufficient reason to believe that a juror may not meet these criteria, a **remedy** is needed. The appropriate remedy depends, in part, on whether the problem surfaces during or after the trial. A hearing into the potential infirmity may suffice or a mistrial or new trial may be necessary.

- **Jury deliberations and verdicts.** Jury deliberations and verdicts give rise to a number of legal issues. This subsection discusses the prerogative of **nullification,** the **unanimity** requirement for verdicts, the problem of **inconsistent verdicts,** and **post-verdict inquiry** into jury deliberations and decisionmaking.

- **Waiver of the right to trial by jury.** Like other constitutional rights, the right to trial by jury **may be knowingly and voluntarily waived.** There is, however, **no constitutional right to waive** a jury and insist upon a bench trial.

A.   SCOPE OF THE RIGHT TO TRIAL BY JURY

Article III, section 2 of the Constitution states that "the Trial of **all** Crimes . . . shall be by Jury" and the Sixth Amendment provides that "[i]n **all** criminal prosecutions, the accused shall enjoy the right to a . . . trial, by an impartial jury." Nevertheless, the Supreme Court has concluded that the Constitution does **not** guarantee a right to jury trial **for all offenses.**

1.   "Petty-Serious" Crime Dichotomy

"[D]efendants accused of **serious crimes** [must] be afforded the right to trial by jury." Baldwin v. New York, 399 U.S. 66, 90 S. Ct. 1886, 26 L. Ed. 2d 437 (1970). Those accused "of **petty crimes or offenses**" do not have a

Sixth Amendment entitlement to trial by jury. Duncan v. Louisiana. The critical distinction between "petty" and "serious" crimes defines the scope of the entitlement to trial by jury.

2. **Distinction Between "Petty" and "Serious" Crimes**

Whether a crime is "petty" or "serious" depends **solely** on the **maximum authorized penalty,** a reflection of the legislature's judgment about the seriousness of the offense. Blanton v. City of North Las Vegas, 489 U.S. 538, 109 S. Ct. 1289, 103 L. Ed. 2d 550 (1989). "[T]he **maximum authorized period of incarceration**" is the primary criterion because it is "the most powerful indication of whether an offense is 'serious.' " Id.

An offense with a maximum authorized period of incarceration of **more than six months is serious.** Baldwin v. New York. If the maximum authorized incarceration is **six months or less,** the offense is **presumptively "petty."** Blanton v. City of North Las Vegas. In "rare situation[s]," the defendant can overcome the presumption that such an offense is petty. To do so, an accused must "demonstrate that any **additional statutory penalties,** viewed in conjunction with the maximum authorized period of incarceration, are **so severe that they clearly reflect a legislative determination that the offense in question is a 'serious' one.**" Id.

The distinction between petty and serious offenses depends completely on **"statutory penalties."** The **only** "impositions" that count are **"penalties resulting from state action,** e.g., those mandated by statute or regulation." Id. The nature of an offense, the stigma it carries, and the likely community reaction to a conviction are apparently irrelevant. In addition, so long as the maximum authorized term of incarceration is six months or less, "it is immaterial" that a "minimum term of imprisonment" must be imposed. Id.

Legislatures often authorize monetary fines as punishment for offenses. The **magnitude of the authorized fine** that will cause an offense to be deemed "serious" is **uncertain.** An offense that is punishable by a maximum jail term of six months, or a maximum fine of $5,000, or both is "petty." United States v. Nachtigal, 507 U.S. 1, 113 S. Ct. 1072, 122 L. Ed. 2d 374 (1993). In addition, the magnitude of fine that renders an offense serious for an individual defendant does not necessarily render the same offense serious for an institutional defendant such as a corporation. See Muniz v. Hoffman, 422 U.S. 454, 95 S. Ct. 2178, 45 L. Ed. 2d 319 (1975) (holding that for a large corporation or labor union a $10,000 fine does not render a crime serious).

The right to trial by jury for an offense depends on the maximum authorized statutory penalty **for that offense alone.** A defendant has a Sixth Amendment right to a jury for an offense only if the statutorily authorized maximum penalty renders that offense "serious." Lewis v. United States, — U.S. —,

116 S. Ct. 2163, 135 L. Ed. 2d 590 (1996). Consequently, if a defendant is charged with multiple "petty" offenses and those offenses are tried jointly at a single trial, there is **no right to a jury.** Id. The right to trial by jury does **not** attach simply because the aggregate authorized maximum penalty is greater than six months in prison or because multiple convictions and sentences actually result in a sentence of imprisonment in excess of six months. Id.

 # EXAMPLES AND ANALYSIS

1. An individual convicted of driving under the influence of alcohol (DUI) may be punished by a minimum of two days in jail and a maximum of six months. As an alternative, a defendant may be ordered to perform 48 hours of community service in distinctive dress that identifies her as a DUI offender. In addition, a defendant may be fined from $200 to $1,000, will automatically lose her driver's license for 90 days, and must attend, at her own expense, an alcohol abuse education course. Repeat offenders are eligible for higher penalties. May an individual charged with DUI for the first time insist on trial by jury?

According to the unanimous Supreme Court opinion in Blanton v. City of North Las Vegas, the Constitution does **not** grant a right to trial by jury for this "petty" offense. First, the maximum authorized incarceration period of six months gives rise to a presumption that the offense is petty. Second, the additional statutory penalties are not sufficiently severe to reflect a legislative judgment that the offense is "serious." The authorized fine is well within the constitutional limit. The "alternative" community service is less serious than six months in prison. The license suspension is "irrelevant" if it is concurrent with incarceration and is "not . . . that significant" if it follows incarceration. The alcohol abuse course is a "de minimis" imposition. And the possibility of higher "recidivist penalties" is of "little significance" because such penalties are "commonplace" and do not apply to first-time offenders.

2. Suppose that the individual in the preceding situation was charged not only with DUI, but also with possession of marijuana and interference with official acts. All three offenses are scheduled for trial together. Is the defendant entitled to a jury trial?

The defendant has a right to a jury trial only for offenses that are serious. When multiple offenses are tried together, the right does not depend on the aggregate of maximum statutorily authorized sentences or on the actual sentence imposed on the defendant. Instead, each offense must be judged against the *Blanton* standards. In the preceding hypothetical, the defendant would have a right to a trial by jury only for an offense that qualifies as "serious."

3.   Crimes with No Authorized Maximum Penalty: The Special Case of Criminal Contempt

Whether a crime is serious or petty is ordinarily dictated by the "maximum authorized penalty." For some offenses, most notably criminal contempt, "no legislative penalty is specified and sentence is left to the discretion of the judge." Codispoti v. Pennsylvania, 418 U.S. 506, 94 S. Ct. 2687, 41 L. Ed. 2d 912 (1974). Because there is no legislative judgment regarding the seriousness of such offenses, their "pettiness or seriousness . . . [must] be judged by the **penalty actually imposed.**" Id.; see also Frank v. United States, 395 U.S. 147, 89 S. Ct. 1503, 23 L. Ed. 2d 162 (1969). An actual sentence that is longer than six months requires a trial by jury; an actual sentence of six months or less does not. Codispoti v. Pennsylvania.

The question is more complicated in situations where multiple contempt convictions and sentences are imposed. If a judge **summarily** finds an individual guilty of multiple criminal contempts **during a trial,** she may impose a sentence of up to six months in prison for each conviction and may require the sentences to be served consecutively without triggering the entitlement to a jury. While no single sentence can be longer than six months, a defendant can be sentenced to more than six months of total prison time. See id.

For **nonsummary** criminal contempt prosecutions conducted after trial, the outcome is different. If the contempt charges "ar[i]se from a single trial, [are] charged by a single judge, and [are] tried in a single proceeding," the cumulative punishment imposed **cannot exceed six months** unless the defendant is afforded a jury. Id. However, multiple post-trial contempt convictions and sentences do not require a jury if none of the sentences exceeds six months and if the sentences run concurrently. See Taylor v. Hayes, 418 U.S. 488, 94 S. Ct. 2697, 41 L. Ed. 2d 488 (1974).

 # EXAMPLES AND ANALYSIS

1.   Bart swears repeatedly at witnesses during his trial. The judge holds him in contempt 10 separate times. The first nine times, the judge sentences Bart to 90 days in jail. The last time, the judge orders Bart to serve one year in jail. The sentences are to run consecutively. Was Bart's right to trial by jury violated?

Yes. The sentence of one year in prison for the tenth contempt was impermissible absent a jury determination. Summary contempts may be punished by up to six months, and sentences for multiple summary contempts may run consecutively, but no single sentence may exceed six months. Nonetheless, the violation does not require a new trial. If the sentence for the tenth contempt is reduced to six months, the trial of that offense without a jury becomes constitutional. See Taylor v. Hayes.

2. Bart's lawyer, on three occasions, misbehaved during his trial. The judge charged him with contempt. After Bart's trial had concluded, the judge tried the contempt charges without a jury. What is the maximum sentence the judge can impose in the absence of a jury?

Because these contempts arise from a single trial, have been charged by a single judge, and are being tried in a single proceeding, the judge can impose three six-month sentences that run concurrently. The judge may not impose any single sentence or any combination of consecutive sentences that requires the attorney to spend more than six months in prison. See Codispoti v. Pennsylvania.

B. MEANING OF THE RIGHT TO TRIAL BY JURY

The Constitution guarantees a trial by "jury" but does not define that term. This section explores the meaning of the term—specifically, the questions of **jury size and constituency.**

1. Jury Size: The Number of Persons Needed To Constitute a Jury

A jury is a group of peers or laypersons drawn from the community. Although a jury clearly must include more than one or two persons, the Constitution does not specify the minimum number of persons necessary to constitute a "jury."

At the time that our Constitution was drafted, a "requirement of 12" persons had been part of the common law for at least 400 years. Williams v. Florida, 399 U.S. 78, 90 S. Ct. 1893, 26 L. Ed. 2d 446 (1970). Nevertheless, the Supreme Court has concluded that the Framers did not intend to constitutionalize the 12-person requirement. According to the Court, juries composed of **six persons are constitutional,** id., while juries of **fewer than six are not,** Ballew v. Georgia, 435 U.S. 223, 98 S. Ct. 1029, 55 L. Ed. 2d 234 (1978) (declaring five-person jury unconstitutional). Even serious charges that carry severe sentences may be tried by six-person juries. See Williams v. Florida (approving six-person jury trial for robbery charge that led to sentence of life imprisonment).

The right to trial by jury safeguards against arbitrary and oppressive law enforcement. A group of laypersons drawn from the community provides protection against judges and prosecutors, promotes the accurate resolution of factual disputes, and ensures verdicts that reflect the common sense of the community. According to the Supreme Court, a body of six persons can adequately serve these functions while a smaller group cannot.

EXAMPLE AND ANALYSIS

A state wanting to save time and money passes legislation authorizing juries of six in capital trials. The juries decide both the guilt or innocence of the defendants and the sentences. Is the legislation constitutional?

No jurisdiction currently authorizes juries of fewer than 12 for capital charges. On the one hand, it is *arguable* that juries in capital cases must include more than six persons to ensure the reliability of the decisionmaking and provide an extra safeguard against arbitrariness by the judge or prosecutor or bias by the jury. Other cases have found a need for more stringent constitutional safeguards in capital cases. On the other hand, the Court's opinion in *Williams* provides support for an argument that juries of six are sufficient to serve the functions entrusted to juries—even in capital cases.

2. **"Fair Cross Section" Requirement**

The only thing that the text of the Sixth Amendment specifies about the "constituency" of a jury is that it must be "impartial." Nonetheless, the Supreme Court has concluded that the guarantee includes a **fair cross section requirement.** See Taylor v. Louisiana, 419 U.S. 522, 95 S. Ct. 692, 42 L. Ed. 2d 690 (1975); Duren v. Missouri, 439 U.S. 357, 99 S. Ct. 664, 58 L. Ed. 2d 579 (1979).

a. **Textual basis for and purposes of the fair cross section requirement.** Early opinions recognizing a fair cross section requirement seemed to find it implicit in the concept of a **"jury."** In Holland v. Illinois, 493 U.S. 474, 110 S. Ct. 803, 107 L. Ed. 2d 905 (1990), however, a bare majority of the Supreme Court concluded that the fair cross section demand is based on the requirement that juries be **"impartial."** But see id. (Marshall, J., dissenting) (maintaining that the requirement is derived from the term "jury").

The fair cross section requirement has three purposes: (1) to " 'guard[ ] against the exercise of arbitrary power' and ensure that the 'common-sense judgment of the community' will act as 'a hedge against the overzealous or mistaken prosecutor' "; (2) to "preserv[e] 'public confidence in the fairness of the criminal justice system' "; and (3) to "implement[ ] our belief that 'sharing in the administration of justice is a phase of civic responsibility.' " Lockhart v. McCree, 476 U.S. 162, 106 S. Ct. 1758, 90 L. Ed. 2d 137 (1986).

b. **Meaning and content of the fair cross section requirement.** The fair cross section requirement focuses on the **"venires"** or **"pools"** from which "petit juries" are selected, not on the petit juries themselves. The Sixth Amendment requires that "petit juries must be **drawn from**" or "**chosen from** a fair cross section of the community." Taylor v. Louisiana. The fair cross section requirement **does not demand** that either the "petit juries actually chosen" or the venires or pools from which they are chosen "mirror the community and reflect the various distinctive groups in the population." Id. There is no entitlement "to a jury of any particular composition." Id. The fair cross section requirement does demand that "jury **wheels, pools of names, panels, or venires** from which juries are drawn **must not systematically exclude distinctive groups in the community and thereby fail to be reasonably representative thereof.**" Id.

There is ongoing debate over whether the fair cross section requirement has *any* application to **petit juries.** One view is that it speaks only to exclusion from venires and does not bar even the systematic exclusion of distinctive groups from petit juries. Another view holds that while a petit jury need not "mirror the community," the Sixth Amendment would be violated by systematic exclusion of a distinctive group during the selection of a petit jury. One thing is settled: The government's **use of "peremptory challenges"** to "systematically exclude" a distinctive group from the petit jury **does not violate** the fair cross section requirement. See Holland v. Illinois (holding peremptory challenges immune from challenge on fair cross section grounds); but see section C.6 below (discussing the availability of an "equal protection" challenge to the "discriminatory" use of peremptory jury challenges).

c. **Elements necessary for a prima facie violation of the fair cross section requirement.** "[T]o establish a prima facie violation of the fair-cross-section requirement, the defendant must show (1) that the group alleged to be excluded is a **[sufficiently numerous and] 'distinctive' group** in the community; (2) that the **representation** of the group **in venires** from which juries are selected is **not fair and reasonable** in relation to the number of such persons in the community; and (3) that this underrepresentation is due to **systematic exclusion** of the group in the jury-selection process." Duren v. Missouri. A defendant has **standing** to raise a fair cross section claim whether or not he is a member of the group allegedly excluded. A man, for example, can succeed with a claim that women were unconstitutionally excluded from his venire. See Taylor v. Louisiana; Duren v. Missouri.

   i. **A group that is sufficiently numerous and distinctive.** First, the group alleged to have been excluded from the jury selection process must be **"sufficiently numerous"**—it must be of a certain size or magnitude in the community from which jurors are chosen. Some groups are too small to qualify as the basis of a fair cross section claim. It is not clear how large a group must be to qualify.

      Second, the group must be **"distinct" from other groups in the community.** It must have "a flavor, a distinct quality"; it must "bring to juries . . . perspectives and values" that are different from those of other groups in the community. Taylor v. Louisiana.

ii. **Representation in the venire that is not fair and reasonable.** Representation in the venire is not fair and reasonable if the percentage of a group's members in venires is significantly lower than the percentage of that group's members in the community. For example, if a group comprises approximately 50 percent of the community and only 15 percent of venires, its representation is not fair and reasonable. The minimum amount of disparity necessary to satisfy this element is not clear.

iii. **Underrepresentation because of systematic exclusion.** The disparity between the representation of the group in the community and its representation in venires must be the **result of** some aspect of the jurisdiction's **jury selection system.** Underrepresentation caused by random chance is not unconstitutional. A defendant need not establish, however, that a group was intentionally excluded—that is, that the system was designed to serve a "discriminatory purpose." See Duren v. Missouri. Rather, an accused need show only "systematic disproportion"— a deficiency of representation traceable to some aspect of the jury selection process. Id.

The "systematic" nature of exclusion in a given case can be inferred from the combination of (1) a particular feature of the jury selection process that makes exclusion of the relevant group possible, (2) the points in the selection process at which the group's representation diminishes, and (3) the fact that underrepresentation of the group in venires is recurrent. Thus, in Duren v. Missouri, the Court concluded that the exclusion of women was "systematic" because (1) the state's selection process allowed women to "opt out" of service at various points without having to provide a reason; (2) the numbers of women in the pools dropped dramatically at each of these points; and (3) the underrepresentation of women in jury pools occurred repeatedly.

d. **The government's opportunity to justify systematic exclusion.** Establishment of a prima facie violation of the fair cross section requirement does not end the constitutional analysis. If the government justifies the exclusion caused by its system of jury selection, there is no violation of the Sixth Amendment.

To justify the systematic exclusion of a distinctive and sufficiently numerous group from jury venires, the government must show "that **a significant state interest** [is] manifestly and primarily advanced by those aspects of the jury-selection process . . . that result in the disproportionate exclusion." Id. Mere "rational grounds" are not sufficient. Id. The exclusionary process must advance a weightier concern, "an important interest."

Moreover, the government must show that the aspect of the process that promotes a significant state interest is **"appropriately tailored to [serve the] interest."** Id. If it results in exclusion that is broader than necessary to further the important state interest and if a narrower approach would not have the same exclusionary impact on the distinctive group, the selection process is not "appropriately tailored." Put simply, if a state can achieve its objective without infringing on or with less infringement on an accused's interest in having a fair cross section, a jury selection process is unjustifiable and, therefore, unconstitutional.

 # EXAMPLE AND ANALYSIS

In Duren v. Missouri, the state allowed women to "opt out" of jury service in order to ensure that "members of the family responsible for the care of children [would be] available to do so." The Court suggested that the interest posited by the state was "significant" enough to serve as a justification for exclusion. Nonetheless, the Court struck down the state's jury selection system because it was not "appropriately tailored to this interest." The exemption for women was "overinclusive" insofar as it led to the exclusion of women who did not care for children. An exemption that allowed those who care for children to "opt out" of jury service would not have excluded those women and thus would have infringed less on the defendant's interest in having the perspectives and values of women in his jury pool.

C. JURY SELECTION

The petit jury that will decide a criminal case is selected from a much larger venire or panel summoned to the courthouse. The selection process consists of **voir dire** and **challenges** of prospective jurors. Voir dire is the process during which the judge or the parties or both question potential jurors. Challenges are the mechanism through which the parties and judge remove jurors from the pool. Both the voir dire process and juror challenges are regulated by rules adopted in each jurisdiction. See, e.g., Federal Rule of Criminal Procedure 24. The rules and processes vary considerably from jurisdiction to jurisdiction. This section does not discuss the variety of state and federal rules and procedures but, instead, focuses almost exclusively on constitutional regulations pertinent to voir dire and juror challenges.

1. A Brief Description of the Voir Dire Process

During voir dire, the parties or the judge or both ask the jurors questions about their backgrounds, their experiences, their opinions, and other matters that bear on their suitability to decide the case. A question may be addressed to a group of jurors or to one specific juror. Trial judges have broad discretion to control the voir dire of prospective jurors. See Ristaino v. Ross, 424 U.S. 589, 96 S. Ct. 1017, 47 L. Ed. 2d 258 (1976). Subject to the limited constitutional regulation discussed below, the judge decides which questions will be asked.

One object of voir dire questioning is to determine whether there is anything that renders a juror subject to a challenge for cause. A juror may be unqualified to serve, for example, because of mental incompetence, an irremediable bias of some sort, or exposure to matters that make her incapable of deciding the case solely on the evidence. If disqualifying information is revealed on voir dire, the judge should excuse the juror "for cause." See section C.4 below. Answers to voir dire questions can also help the parties decide which qualified jurors they prefer to have or not have on the jury. The parties can exercise their peremptory challenges in light of the jurors' answers.

2.   The Due Process Entitlement to Specific Voir Dire About Racial Prejudice: The Rule of Ham v. South Carolina

A trial before jurors with prejudice against the accused is fundamentally unfair. Both the **Due Process Clause** and the **Sixth Amendment** guarantee defendants a right to be tried by **impartial** jurors. To a very limited extent, the guarantee of juror impartiality restricts a judge's discretion to control the voir dire of prospective jurors. More specifically, in some cases **the judge must question prospective jurors specifically about racial prejudice** when a defendant requests such questioning. See Ham v. South Carolina, 409 U.S. 524, 93 S. Ct. 848, 35 L. Ed. 2d 46 (1973); Ristaino v. Ross.

a.   The showing necessary to establish an entitlement to voir dire about racial prejudice. To be entitled to have jurors questioned specifically about racial prejudice, a defendant must show that there is a **"constitutionally significant likelihood** that, absent questioning about racial prejudice, the **jurors would not be"** impartial. Id. A **"significant likelihood that racial prejudice might infect [the] trial"** is required. Id. To determine whether there is a "significant likelihood" of prejudice, a judge should consider "all of the circumstances"—including the race of the defendant, the race of the victim, whether "racial issues" are somehow involved in the case, and any other factors likely to "intensify any prejudice" that a juror harbors. Id.

 EXAMPLES AND ANALYSIS

In Ham v. South Carolina, the Court held that a refusal to make specific inquiries about racial prejudice on request by the defendant denied due process. There was a significant likelihood of prejudice because the accused was a prominent civil rights activist and his defense to the charge of narcotics possession was that he had been framed because of his civil rights activities. Because racial issues "were inextricably bound up with the conduct of the trial," and because both the defendant's reputation and his defense were "likely to intensify any prejudice that individual members of the jury might harbor," the Constitution required "a voir dire that included questioning specifically directed to racial prejudice." Ristaino v. Ross.

In Ristaino v. Ross, the defendant claimed that because he was a black man accused of a crime of violence against a white victim there was a sufficient likelihood of prejudice to trigger the due process entitlement to specific questioning. The Supreme Court rejected the claim, holding that the fact that the crime charged involves "interracial violence" does not by itself give rise to a "constitutionally significant likelihood" that racial prejudice "might infect [the] trial." There can be little doubt that there is *some* risk of race prejudice in such circumstances. The risk of impact on the jurors is simply *insufficient* to trigger a constitutional right to specific questioning about race.

___

b. **Entitlement to specific questioning about other kinds of prejudice.** The limited entitlement to specific questions about racial prejudice clearly extends to cases that involve a significant likelihood of ethnic prejudice. See Rosales-Lopez v. United States, 451 U.S. 182, 101 S. Ct. 1629, 68 L. Ed. 2d 22 (1981) (treating racial and ethnic prejudice alike for purposes of the "nonconstitutional" entitlement to voir dire questions in federal court). It is unclear whether a defendant is ever entitled to specific questions concerning prejudice on other bases such as religion, national origin, or sexual orientation. On the one hand, special circumstances could make it more likely that such prejudices would operate. On the other hand, these other types of prejudice could be considered insufficiently prevalent or intense to require a due process safeguard.

c. **The special case of "capital sentencing" proceedings: The rule of Turner v. Murray.** As noted above, an accusation of interracial violence is ordinarily not sufficient to trigger the due process entitlement to specific questioning. The rule is different, however, for **capital sentencing proceedings.** Because capital sentencing juries have **greater discretion** and because the **stakes are higher** for the accused, a defendant has the constitutional right to have potential capital sentencing jurors asked specifically about racial prejudice when an offense involves interracial violence. Turner v. Murray, 476 U.S. 28, 106 S.Ct. 1683, 90 L.Ed.2d 27 (1986).

Although this right to specific inquiry does not extend to the guilt-innocence determination, if the same jury is responsible for both the trial and sentencing phases the question about prejudice will surely be asked prior to trial. Nonetheless, if a court violates the defendant's due process right by refusing to make specific inquiries, a conviction is valid. A defendant is only entitled to have the unconstitutional death sentence set aside. See id.

3. "Supervisory Power" Standard for Voir Dire in Federal Courts

The supervisory power over the administration of criminal justice in the federal courts, see Chapter 3, section D, provides greater voir dire protection for those charged with federal offenses. **Federal defendants** are entitled to specific voir dire questioning of prospective jurors "where the circumstances . . . indicate that there is a **reasonable possibility that racial or ethnic prejudice might . . . influence[ ] the jury.**" Rosales-Lopez v. United States. There is no need to show a "significant likelihood" of prejudice; a "reasonable possibility" is sufficient.

 # EXAMPLE AND ANALYSIS

Jorge, an illegal alien from Mexico, is charged with possession of narcotics and assault on an officer. Before trial, his appointed counsel requests that jurors be asked whether they harbor any prejudices against Hispanic persons. The judge denies the request. After he is convicted, Jorge appeals the judge's denial. How should the appellate court rule?

The hypothetical does not discuss whether the charges were state or federal. If the charges were tried in state court, the court should affirm. There was no due process entitlement because the facts presented did not give rise to a "significant likelihood" that ethnic prejudice would infect the jurors' decisions. If the charges were tried in federal court, Jorge might have been entitled to questioning by virtue of the "supervisory power." If the victim of the alleged assault was of a different race, Jorge would have been facing a charge of "interracial violence." According to the Supreme Court's opinion in Rosales-Lopez v. United States, such offenses do create a "reasonable possibility" of prejudice that triggers the supervisory power entitlement to specific voir dire questioning.

4. Challenges for Cause

The bases for excusing a juror **for cause** may be specified in a statute or rule of court or may be left unspecified. In general, a party may challenge a prospective juror for cause if there is reason to believe the juror will not be impartial, competent, qualified, or able to decide the case based on the evidence at trial. If a party establishes an adequate basis for concluding that a juror is not fit for service, the judge should grant a challenge for cause and excuse the juror.

Trial judges typically have broad authority to determine whether jurors should be excused for cause, and their determinations are rarely overturned. For example, if a juror has been exposed to potentially prejudicial information or has expressed an opinion about guilt or innocence, a judge ordinarily may credit the juror's declaration that she will set aside the information or opinion and render an impartial decision. Appellate courts are reluctant to second-guess denials of challenges for cause. See, e.g., Patton v. Yount, 467 U.S. 1025, 104 S. Ct. 2885, 81 L. Ed. 2d 847 (1984) (refusing to set aside trial judge's determination of impartiality based on jurors' statements and emphasizing the deference due such determinations).

In rare, extreme cases in which circumstances make it highly likely that a juror will be incurably biased or unable to set aside an impression he has formed, a judge is required to excuse the juror for cause despite the juror's assertions that he is able to reach an impartial decision based on the evidence. In those instances, proof that a juror is *actually* partial is unnecessary because the circumstances justify an *inference* of partiality. Failure to remove such a juror can violate a defendant's rights to due process and an impartial jury. See Irvin v. Dowd, 366 U.S. 717, 81 S. Ct. 1639, 6 L. Ed. 2d 751 (1961) (where voir dire reflects "deep and bitter prejudice" in the community, jurors' "statement[s] of impartiality can be given little weight" and a "presumption of prejudice" is required); see also Smith v. Phillips, 455 U.S. 209, 102 S. Ct. 940, 71 L. Ed. 2d 78 (1982) (O'Connor, J., concurring) (suggesting that there are "some extreme situations that would justify a finding of implied bias").

Although it is unlikely, a court could commit constitutional error by excusing jurors for cause at the request of the government. If qualified, capable jurors are removed because of a view or attitude that could benefit the accused, a claim that the impartiality of the jury was compromised might succeed. Thus, for example, in Witherspoon v. Illinois, 391 U.S. 510, 88 S. Ct. 1770, 20 L. Ed. 2d 776 (1968), the Supreme Court upheld a claim that the trial judge had impaired the neutrality of the jury by removing all jurors with some objections to capital punishment. According to the law, the excluded jurors were not disqualified from service in capital cases. By removing them, the judge deprived the defendant of their input and created a risk that the actual jury selected would be predisposed toward the prosecution's case.

5. Nature and Source of Peremptory Challenges

A challenge for cause must be supported by some reason for concluding that the juror is not capable or qualified. In contrast, a **peremptory challenge** permits a party to remove a prospective juror without giving a reason. A party may use a peremptory challenge after a judge rejects a challenge for cause or may do so without making a challenge for cause. The party may have a tangible, objective basis for striking the juror or may be operating on the basis of a vague, subjective impression or hunch. In any case, a party ordinarily is free to strike the juror without explanation.

The right to peremptory challenges is granted **by statute.** There is **no constitutional right** to peremptories. See Swain v. Alabama, 380 U.S. 202, 85 S. Ct. 824, 13 L. Ed. 2d 759 (1965); Batson v. Kentucky, 476 U.S. 79, 106 S. Ct. 1712, 90 L. Ed. 2d 69 (1986). Nonetheless, peremptory challenges have long been a part of our criminal justice system and are an "important" right of the accused, see Swain v. Alabama, because they are a "means of assuring the selection of a qualified and unbiased jury." Batson v. Kentucky. Despite arguments that the costs of peremptory challenges outweigh their advantages, they remain an integral part of jury selection in both the federal and state courts.

Statutes or court rules grant each side a certain number of peremptory challenges. Defendants are often entitled to more peremptories than the government, and the number possessed by each side can vary based on the severity of the charge.

There are two methods of exercising peremptories. In the "challenge" system, the parties are presented with one juror at a time and are given the option of striking that juror. A decision to use or preserve a peremptory must be made with respect to a particular juror rather than the entire pool. In the "strike" system, after jurors are removed for cause a group is assembled that is equal to the total number of peremptories held by the parties plus the number of jurors to be seated. The parties then use their peremptories to remove jurors from this group. The "strike" system enables the parties to compare jurors and use challenges to eliminate those they deem least favorable.

6. **Equal Protection Clause Restrictions on the Exercise of Peremptory Challenges: The Doctrine of Batson v. Kentucky**

Ordinarily, the exercise of a peremptory challenge is uncontestable. A party can remove a juror for no reason or on an "arbitrary and capricious" basis. See Swain v. Alabama. There is, however, one significant constitutional limitation on the exercise of peremptories. The Fourteenth Amendment **Equal Protection Clause** prohibits certain kinds of **intentional discrimination** in the exercise of peremptory jury challenges. Batson v. Kentucky. The Equal Protection restriction is currently confined to **race and gender discrimination,** but could be extended to other kinds of discrimination.

a. **A brief history of Equal Protection Clause constraints on peremptory jury challenges.** In Swain v. Alabama, the Supreme Court recognized that the Equal Protection Clause does impose some restrictions upon peremptory challenges. The Court acknowledged that peremptory strikes rooted in race-based hostility toward the juror or a belief that a particular race is not capable or qualified for service would be unconstitutional. The Court held, however, that a defendant could **not** establish an equal protection violation by relying solely on a prosecutor's use of peremptories **in a particular case.** This holding was supported by two reasons. First, in an individual case such strikes might well be explained on the basis of the legitimate assumption that jurors would be favorably disposed to a defendant of the same race. Second, the institution of peremptory challenges could be destroyed by frequent inquiry into the bases for strikes. The *Swain* Court held that a defendant could establish an equal protection violation **only by proof** that the **government in case after case had struck jurors of a particular race so that no juror of that race had ever served on a jury in that jurisdiction.**

In Batson v. Kentucky, the Court overruled *Swain*, holding that an accused **can** establish an equal protection violation on the basis of the prosecutor's use of peremptory strikes **in his case alone.** Two main reasons supported the Court's decision. First, *Swain* placed a "crippling burden" on defendants seeking to show unconstitutional discrimination. Second, the removal of a juror on the **"assumption" that the juror will be partial to a person of her race is forbidden by the Equal Protection Clause.**

Batson raised a number of questions about the nature and scope of the Fourteenth Amendment restrictions on peremptories. Some of those questions have been addressed in subsequent opinions. The result is an extensive body of controlling doctrine.

b.   **Details of the *Batson* doctrine.** *Batson* prescribed a framework for evaluating claims of intentional discrimination in the exercise of peremptories. Equal protection claims concerning the use of peremptories must be analyzed within the *Batson* "three-step" framework, as modified and developed by later cases. "**First,** the defendant must make a **prima facie case** that the prosecutor has exercised peremptory challenges on the basis of race. **Second,** . . . the burden shifts to the prosecution to [**rebut** the prima facie showing by] articulating a **race-neutral explanation. Finally,** the trial court must determine **whether the defendant has carried his burden of proving purposeful discrimination.**" Hernandez v. New York, 500 U.S. 352, 111 S. Ct. 1859, 114 L. Ed. 2d 395 (1991).

> **Note:** The *Batson* doctrine was originally formulated for situations in which a **defendant** claims that the **prosecution's** use of peremptory challenges to strike **members of the defendant's race** constitutes unconstitutional **race discrimination** in violation of the **defendant's equal protection right.** The language of the doctrine (and, consequently, much of the discussion in this out-

line) is cast in terms of government peremptory use and a defense claim of race discrimination. It must be noted at the outset, however, that post-*Batson* developments have expanded the scope of the original doctrine in several important ways.

First, a defendant can succeed with a claim that members of **any race** have been excluded because the Court has held that the accused has standing to raise the **jurors' equal protection rights.** See Powers v. Ohio, 499 U.S. 400, 111 S. Ct. 1364, 113 L. Ed. 2d 411 (1991).

Second, the **prosecution** can rely on *Batson* doctrine to object to the **defense use** of peremptory challenges because the Court has held that criminal defendants may not exercise peremptories to discriminate intentionally against jurors. Georgia v. McCollum, 505 U.S. 42, 112 S. Ct. 2348, 120 L. Ed. 2d 33 (1992).

Finally, either side could succeed with a claim that the opponent has used peremptory challenges to discriminate **on account of gender.** *Batson* doctrine prohibits purposeful gender discrimination and could govern discrimination against other groups who qualify for more than "rational basis" review. See J.E.B. v. Alabama, 511 U.S. 127, 114 S. Ct. 1419, 128 L. Ed. 2d 89 (1994).

Each of these developments is discussed in greater detail below. Students should keep them in mind when reading the description of *Batson* doctrine that follows.

i. **Step one: A prima facie case of intentional race discrimination.** The defendant must establish a **prima facie case** of intentional discrimination on account of race. The "defendant **first** must show that **he is a member of a cognizable racial group** and that **the prosecutor has exercised peremptory challenges to remove from the venire members of the defendant's race. Second,** the defendant is entitled to rely on the fact . . . that **peremptory challenges . . . permit[ ] 'those to discriminate who are of a mind to discriminate.' Finally,** the defendant must show that **these facts and any other relevant circumstances raise an inference that the prosecutor used [peremptory challenges] to exclude the veniremen from the petit jury on account of their race.**" Batson v. Kentucky.

Several things about the *Batson* formulation of the prima facie case merit mention. First, the original *Batson* doctrine prescribes the showing necessary for a *defendant* to show that *his* equal protection right has been violated. A defendant also has standing to raise a juror's equal protection right not to be excluded from jury service on account of race. Powers v. Ohio. Consequently, a *Batson* claim can succeed even though the jurors stricken are **not members of the defendant's racial group.** To establish a prima facie case today, an accused must show only that members of **a racial group** have been removed on account of race.

Second, the fact that peremptory challenges allow those who are inclined to discriminate to do so is a **constant**—that is, it is always true and requires no showing.

The last element of the prima facie case requires a defendant to show that the removal of members of a particular race and *other facts* give rise to an inference of race discrimination. "Other facts" that are relevant include a " 'pattern' of strikes against" jurors of a particular race and the nature of questions asked and statements made by the prosecutor on voir dire. Any other fact suggesting a racially discriminatory motive is relevant.

At the first step, the question for the trial judge is whether the defendant has established a prima facie case of purposeful race or gender discrimination. The showing must be sufficient to carry the defendant's burden of proving an equal protection violation. If a prima facie case is established, the court must proceed to step two. If the defendant fails to establish a prima facie case, his claim must fail.

ii. **Step two: Rebuttal of the prima facie case.** "Once the defendant makes a prima facie showing, **the burden shifts to the State to come forward with a neutral explanation** for challenging [the] jurors." Batson v. Kentucky. At the second step, a judge should be concerned **only** with the **facial validity** of the reasons proffered, not with whether they are believable or persuasive. Purkett v. Elem, 514 U.S. 765, 115 S. Ct. 1769, 131 L. Ed. 2d 834 (1995).

To be "facially valid," the reasons offered for the strikes need only be **race-neutral.** They do **not** have to be **related to the particular case** to be tried. See Hernandez v. New York. An explanation is **not race-neutral** if "a discriminatory intent is inherent in the . . . explanation." Id. An explanation **is race-neutral** if it is "based on **something other than the race of the juror.**" Consequently, the explanation that a juror was challenged because he is black or because of the assumption that a black juror "would be partial to the defendant because of their shared race" is not race-neutral. See Batson v. Kentucky. More generally, any reason based on a "stereotypical assumption[ ]" about a juror on account of her race—that is, an assumption that a juror will think or behave in a certain way because of her race—is not race-neutral. See Hernandez v. New York. Finally, the mere fact that a reason has "disproportionate impact" on a particular race or gender does not render it facially invalid. See id.

The Supreme Court has refused to resolve the "difficult question of the breadth with which the concept of race should be defined for equal protection purposes." Hernandez v. New York. It remains possible that a reason that appears to be race-neutral may be so closely tied to race that it should be "treated as a surrogate for race" and deemed facially invalid. Id.

There is one ostensibly race-neutral explanation that is facially invalid as a rebuttal to a prima facie case. A prosecutor **may not "rebut** the defendant's case merely **by denying that he had a discriminatory motive or 'affirming [his] good faith** in making individual selections.' " Batson v. Kentucky. This "explanation" cannot suffice because it would render the "Equal Protection Clause '. . . but a vain and illusory requirement.' " Id. Intentional discrimination would be much too easy to conceal and much too difficult to detect.

If the reasons proffered for peremptory strikes are not facially valid, a trial judge should rule in favor of a defendant's equal protection claim. If race-neutral explanations are furnished, the judge must proceed to step three of the *Batson* inquiry.

 # EXAMPLE AND ANALYSIS

In Hernandez v. New York, the defendant alleged that peremptory strikes used against bilingual jurors who spoke English and Spanish were unconstitutional. The record established that the jurors were stricken not because they spoke Spanish but because each juror had indicated a potential unwillingness or inability to follow the official courtroom translation of Spanish testimony. The Supreme Court upheld the strikes but left open the possibility that an explanation that jurors were removed because of "proficiency in a particular language" might not be race-neutral.

Note: One thing that is made clear by the *Hernandez* opinion is that *Batson* doctrine is concerned with discrimination on account of race **or ethnicity.**

iii. **Step three: Resolution of the claim of intentional discrimination.** After a prima facie case of intentional discrimination is made and race-neutral explanations are proffered, the "trial court then [has] the duty to **determine if the defendant has established purposeful discrimination.**" Batson v. Kentucky. Taking into account **all the circumstances,** including the **credibility** of the rebuttal explanations, the judge must decide whether it is **more likely than not** that **in fact** the peremptory challenges were used to remove jurors **on account of race.** The task is to evaluate "the prosecutor's state of mind." Hernandez v. New York.

In making this "step three" evaluation, relevant factors include, inter alia, the "demeanor of the attorney who exercises the challenge," see id., whether the reason has a disproportionate impact on a particular group, see id., and whether the reason has any ostensible relationship to the case to be tried. Purkett v. Elem.

The determination of discriminatory purpose "lies 'peculiarly within a trial judge's province.' " Hernandez v. New York. It is "a finding of fact of the sort [that must be] accorded great deference on appeal." Consequently, a court's step three determination should be overturned only if an appellate court is "convinced that" it is "**clearly erroneous.**" Id.

c. **Extension of the *Batson* doctrine to defense use of peremptories.** The *Batson* doctrine was designed to deal with the prosecutor's discriminatory use of peremptories. It has been expanded, however, to bar **intentional discrimination by the defense in the exercise of peremptories.** Georgia v. McCollum. When exercising peremptory challenges to help select a jury, the defense is functioning as a **"state actor."** Id. Intentional discrimination by such a state actor violates a challenged **juror's right to equal protection.** And the prosecution, as a party in the case and as the representative of all people, has **standing** to assert the juror's rights by objecting to the defense's discriminatory use of peremptories.

The identical doctrinal analysis described in subsection b above applies when the government objects to the defense exercise of peremptory challenges. A judge is constitutionally obligated to respond to a valid government equal protection objection by preventing further discrimination by the defense and by remedying any harm that has already been done.

d. **Extension of the *Batson* doctrine to discrimination on account of gender.** The Equal Protection Clause also **forbids** purposeful discrimination **on account of gender** in the exercise of peremptories. J.E.B. v. Alabama. The doctrinal framework for evaluating claims that a party has discriminated on account of gender is identical to that governing race discrimination claims. A party may not exclude a juror because of gender. Nor may a party strike a juror based on any "stereotypical presumption" about the way that a person of a particular gender will think.

According to the *J.E.B.* majority, "[p]arties **may** . . . exercise their peremptory challenges to **remove** from the venire **any group or class of individuals normally subject to 'rational basis' review.**" A party cannot succeed with a claim that her opponent has acted unconstitutionally by intentionally striking members of a group that is entitled to neither "heightened" nor "intermediate" equal protection scrutiny. Whether *Batson* doctrine extends to **any classifications other than race or gender** is an open question. Historical considerations could support the conclusion that only race and gender discrimination are regulated. However, the special need to protect any class that merits higher than "rational basis" review could support the extension of *Batson* to those classes. Classifications currently subject to "strict" or "intermediate" equal protection scrutiny include religion, national origin, legitimacy, and, in some cases, alienage. Whether *Batson* doctrine applies to any of those categories is debatable.

EXAMPLE AND ANALYSIS

Larry is charged with statutory rape for allegedly engaging in intercourse with a 15-year-old girl. The prosecutor strikes men from the jury panel because she believes that "men will be much more sympathetic to the defendant than women." The defense strikes women because "they will more likely identify with the victim and be hostile toward the defendant." Both sides have engaged in unconstitutional gender discrimination. The prosecution's strikes are based on the mere assumption that a man would be more favorably disposed toward a male charged with statutory rape. The defense's strikes are based on the mere assumption that women would be predisposed toward a female victim and against the male accused. Judges "may not accept as a defense to [gender] discrimination the very stereotype the law condemns." Powers v. Ohio.

Of course, if a juror indicated that he or she has an actual gender bias, the juror may be stricken for cause or peremptorily. The law does not forbid, indeed it requires, the exclusion of a person who *is not impartial*. It simply forbids peremptory challenges on the basis of *assumptions* rooted in gender or race.

----

e. **Remedies for *Batson* violations.** If the prosecution violates the defendant's or a juror's equal protection rights by an intentionally discriminatory use of peremptory challenges, a conviction must be reversed. If the defense violates jurors' equal protection rights and the accused is convicted, it is unclear whether reversal is required. According to one view, a defendant may not rely on "his own" unconstitutional action to overturn a conviction. Another view holds that a *Batson* violation by either side requires the remedy of a reversal. The lower courts have split over the question of remedy.

The more difficult question is the appropriate **remedy** when a trial judge finds an unconstitutional use of peremptory challenges by either party while jury selection is in progress. The *Batson* majority made "no attempt to instruct [state and federal] courts how best to implement [the *Batson*] holding." Two options are available to the trial judge. The judge can either "discharge the venire and select a new jury from a panel not previously associated with the case, or . . . disallow the discriminatory challenges and resume selection with the improperly challenged jurors reinstated on the venire." Batson v. Kentucky. The "reinstatement" approach has the virtue of vindicating the rights of the stricken jurors, but it runs the risk that those jurors will be hostile to the party who attempted to discriminate against them. The "discharge" approach would eliminate that risk but would be more costly. In *Batson*, the Supreme Court "express[ed] no view" on whether either approach "is more appropriate." Lower courts have employed both.

D.   SUBSTANCE OF THE JURY GUARANTEE DURING TRIAL

Once a properly constituted jury is selected, the trial begins. At trial, an accused is constitutionally entitled to have the jurors function in ways that guarantee fair treatment and a fair outcome. This section discusses the trial entitlements extended by the jury guarantee and possible remedies for deprivations of those entitlements.

1.   Guarantee of Impartial and Competent Jurors Who Render a Decision Based on the Evidence Presented at Trial

An accused has a right to jurors who are **impartial** and **competent** and who **decide the case based on the evidence** presented in court. To satisfy the Constitution, each and every juror must meet these criteria. If any of them does not, a verdict is constitutionally infirm. See Parker v. Gladden, 385 U.S. 363, 87 S. Ct. 486, 17 L. Ed. 2d 420 (1966) (defendant is entitled to be tried by twelve, not nine or ten, impartial and unprejudiced jurors).

a.   Requirement of impartiality. The Sixth Amendment explicitly guarantees trial by an "**impartial** jury." Moreover, a trial by jurors who are not impartial is contrary to the guarantee of fundamental fairness extended by the Due Process Clause. See Ristaino v. Ross, 424 U.S. 589, 96 S. Ct. 1017, 47 L. Ed. 2d 258 (1976) (both the Sixth Amendment and the Due Process Clause guarantee an impartial jury). In general, this means that the jurors must evaluate evidence without bias or prejudice against the defendant. Impartiality can be threatened by prejudices that are part of a juror's makeup, by information that a juror has acquired outside the courtroom, or by extraneous influences brought to bear on a juror.

b. Requirement of competence. A defendant is also entitled to **competent** jurors—those who are capable of understanding the evidence and reaching a rational decision. See Tanner v. United States, 483 U.S. 107, 107 S. Ct. 2739, 97 L. Ed. 2d 90 (1987) (implicitly recognizing entitlement to jurors that are physically and mentally competent); Smith v. Phillips, 455 U.S. 209, 102 S. Ct. 940, 71 L. Ed. 2d 78 (1982) (recognizing an entitlement to jurors "**capable** . . . [of] decid[ing] the case solely on the evidence"). If a juror, because of physical or mental impairment, is unable to receive, comprehend, or process the evidence in a rational way, fundamental fairness is lacking. Thus, a juror could be incompetent because of an inability to hear or see, a psychosis that produces delusions or illogical thinking, or drug abuse that clouds her mental processes.

c. Requirement of a decision based on the evidence. The "requirement that a jury's verdict '**must be based upon the evidence developed at the trial**' goes to the fundamental integrity of all that is embraced in the constitutional concept of trial by jury." Turner v. Louisiana, 379 U.S. 466, 85 S. Ct. 546, 13 L. Ed. 2d 424 (1965). "Due process means a jury **capable and willing to decide the case solely on the evidence before it.**" Smith v. Phillips. Jurors must be able and willing to put aside information they have obtained about a case before trial. They must not consider "facts" learned outside the trial process and must avoid external influences on their decisionmaking.

 # EXAMPLES AND ANALYSIS

1. In Parker v. Gladden, a bailiff made prejudicial comments to the jurors about the defendant's "wicked" nature and suggested that a higher court would correct a guilty verdict if there was anything wrong with it. The bailiff's comments threatened to bias the jurors against the defendant and created a risk that they would take their responsibilities less seriously and base their decisions on matters not in evidence.

2. In Tanner v. United States, the defendant alleged that during the trial the jurors had consumed alcohol, ingested drugs, and fallen asleep. If the allegations had been proven, the defendant would have shown a deprivation of his entitlement to competent jurors.

2. Remedies for Deprivations of the Entitlement to Impartial, Competent Jurors Who Render a Decision Based on the Evidence

The jury selection process—specifically, voir dire, challenges for cause, and peremptory challenges—is designed to ensure that jurors will conform to the constitutional requisites of impartiality, competence, and decisionmaking based on the evidence. When the preventive process of selection fails in some way, a remedy is necessary. The availability of a remedy and the nature of the remedy required depend, in part, on whether the potential infirmity is discovered *during* the trial or *after* a verdict is rendered.

During the trial, if there is reason to believe that a juror is biased, incompetent, or unwilling or unable to decide based on the evidence, a judge may **remove the juror and replace her with an alternate juror.** If there is adequate proof that a juror cannot satisfy the constitutional criteria, the judge must remove her. Mere allegations that a juror is deficient in some respect will not necessarily require removal. A judge may inquire into the juror's capabilities and may determine that the juror is capable and qualified. Nonetheless, if a sufficient risk is demonstrated, a judge may opt to replace a questionable juror to safeguard against later reversal of a conviction. If it is shown that the jury has been irreparably tainted in some way or if there are insufficient alternate jurors to replace those who are compromised, the only satisfactory remedy may be a **mistrial.**

After a verdict is rendered, a sufficient showing that a juror was deficient in some way requires that a conviction be reversed and a new trial held. Nevertheless, "due process does not require a new trial every time a juror has been placed in a potentially compromising situation." Smith v. Phillips. It is not enough for a defendant to show a "contact or influence that might theoretically [have] affect[ed] the[juror's] vote." Id. Instead, when there is evidence that a trial juror's performance was constitutionally defective in some way, the proper remedy is **a post-trial "hearing in which the defendant has the opportunity to prove actual bias"** or some other flaw in the juror's decisionmaking. See id.

A new trial is required **only if** the defendant proves that the juror was **actually** biased, incompetent, or improperly influenced. In most cases in which a defendant proves something that could have prejudiced a juror or rendered him incapable, a judge can deny a new trial based on the juror's affirmation that he rendered an impartial decision based on the evidence. Assessments of juror credibility are ordinarily entrusted to the sound judgment of the court.

For example, in Smith v. Phillips, after the defendant was convicted he learned that a juror had applied for a job with the prosecutor's office while the trial was in progress. Recognizing that the juror could have developed a disqualifying bias in favor of the prosecutor, the judge held a post-trial hearing and satisfied himself that the juror had, in fact, been impartial. The Supreme Court affirmed the trial court's decision not to grant a new trial.

In some cases, however, an event or influence may be so powerful or corrupting that a judge cannot rely on a juror's affirmation that she was unaffected or uninfluenced. The likelihood of harm to the defendant's right to a fair verdict by an impartial trier may be so high that a court must presume that a juror did not satisfy the constitutional requirements. In that case, the only satisfactory remedy is a new trial. (If such an event or influence is discovered during the trial, the judge must either replace the juror or grant a mistrial.)

EXAMPLE AND ANALYSIS

In Turner v. Louisiana, sequestered jurors were placed in the care of two deputies who were also key prosecution witnesses. The Supreme Court reversed the defendant's murder conviction without considering whether the jurors and deputies actually discussed the case or whether the jurors would have been willing to declare that they were uninfluenced by the out-of-court contact with the deputies. The "close and continual association" between the two key witnesses and the jurors was deemed "prejudicial" because the relationship "could not but foster the jurors' confidence in . . . their official guardians . . . [a]nd [the defendant's] fate depended upon how much confidence the jury placed in these two witnesses." In essence, the risk that the jurors had been influenced against the accused by matters not in evidence was so high that unfairness had to be presumed and a new trial was required. See also Parker v. Gladden (when bailiff who was shepherding jurors made prejudicial comments about the accused that were heard by at least some of the jurors, "the conduct of the bailiff 'involve[d] **such a probability that prejudice** [would] result that it [was] deemed **inherently lacking in due process'** ").

> **Note:** After a verdict is rendered, the accused may be more restricted in trying to prove certain kinds of impairments of juror functioning than he would be if the problem were discovered during the trial. For further discussion of this issue, see section E.4 below.

E. JURY DELIBERATIONS AND VERDICTS

When both sides have presented their evidence, the judge instructs the jurors about the relevant law. The jurors then engage in deliberations designed to reach a verdict. Additional issues concerning the entitlement to trial by jury can arise at this stage of the trial. Those issues include jury nullification, the requirement of unanimity, inconsistent verdicts, and the impeachment of verdicts by juror testimony.

1. Desirability of and Entitlement to Instructions About "Jury Nullification"

Nullification is the process by which jurors return a verdict of acquittal even though the law and facts should lead to a conviction. A jury might "nullify" because it believes that a particular law is unjust or because it believes that the conviction of a particular defendant would be unjust. See United States v. Dougherty, 473 F.2d 1113 (D.C. Cir. 1972). A jury in a state with a populace that believes strongly in the "right to bear arms" might, for example, disagree with a law that criminalizes the possession of weapons. Or a jury might acquit a defendant charged with trespassing on federal property if it believes that the defendant was engaged in a justifiable protest against some unacceptable government policy.

There can be no doubt that juries possess the "power" or "prerogative" to engage in nullification. See United States v. Dougherty; see also United States v. Powell, 469 U.S. 57, 105 S. Ct. 471, 83 L. Ed. 2d 461 (1984). Because the Double Jeopardy Clause prohibits retrial following even an egregiously erroneous acquittal and because jurors cannot be punished for disregarding the law or evidence, a jury is free to nullify and its decision to acquit a defendant is unreviewable. United States v. Dougherty. The questions are whether the exercise of this undoubted "prerogative" is a desirable feature of our system of trial by jury and whether the accused is entitled to have the jury informed about its nullification power.

The Supreme Court has never directly addressed jury nullification. The limited law on the question is the product of lower court opinions.

a. **The lower courts' attitude toward nullification.** The majority and dissenting opinions in United States v. Dougherty thoroughly discuss nullification. The majority's approach is fairly reflective of the typical judicial attitude toward nullification.

   In *Dougherty*, a defendant who was charged with a crime that grew out of a protest asked that the jury be instructed about its nullification power. The trial court refused the instruction and barred defense counsel from arguing nullification. A majority of the court of appeals sustained the trial judge, holding that an accused has **no entitlement to a nullification instruction.** The court suggested that jury nullification is a desirable phenomenon in rare and compelling cases—those in which the law leads to unjust results. Nonetheless, there is no need to tell jurors of their prerogative because they are likely to have sufficient awareness of it and to be capable of exercising it when the occasion arises. Instructions about the nullification power would be unwise and dangerous because they could lead to excessive use of the option and, ultimately, to anarchy.

b. **The Supreme Court's attitude toward nullification.** Both its discussions of the functions of juries and its passing references to the phenomenon of nullification suggest that the Supreme Court's attitude toward nullification is consistent with that of the lower courts. In Duncan v. Louisiana, 391 U.S. 145, 88 S. Ct. 1444, 20 L. Ed. 2d 491 (1968), the

Court concluded that the main function of the jury is to "guard against the exercise of arbitrary power." Jurors provide "the commonsense judgment of the community as a hedge against the overzealous or mistaken prosecutor and in preference to the professional or perhaps overconditioned or biased response of a judge." This description of the jury's role suggests some room for proper use of the nullification prerogative. In the occasional case in which a result dictated by the law is arbitrary or unjust, the common sense of the community ought to intervene. Nonetheless, it seems highly unlikely that the Supreme Court would recognize an entitlement to nullification instructions. According to the Court, when a jury ignores the law and does justice in an individual case, it has assumed " 'a **power**' " that it has " '**no right to exercise**.' " United States v. Powell. This description of nullification indicates that its use ought to be rare or exceptional and that jurors should not be invited or encouraged to use their inherent power to nullify.

2. Requirement of Unanimous Jury Verdicts

The **Sixth Amendment** guarantee of trial by jury **includes the right to a unanimous verdict.** A conviction in federal court is invalid unless all the jurors agree that guilt has been proven beyond a reasonable doubt. Apodaca v. Oregon, 406 U.S. 404, 92 S. Ct. 1628, 32 L.Ed.2d 184 (1972).

The **Fourteenth Amendment** Due Process Clause, however, **does not include a right to a unanimous verdict** when a jury includes 12 persons. Apodaca v. Oregon; Johnson v. Louisiana, 406 U.S. 356, 92 S. Ct. 1620, 32 L. Ed. 2d 152 (1972). According to the Court, neither the requirement of proof beyond a reasonable doubt nor the entitlement to trial by jury necessitates a unanimous verdict. A conviction in state court by an 11-1, 10-2, or 9-3 vote is constitutional.

The **Due Process Clause does require unanimous verdicts by six-person juries in state courts.** A 5-1 vote in a state court cannot be the basis for a conviction. Burch v. Louisiana, 441 U.S. 130, 99 S. Ct. 1623, 60 L. Ed. 2d 96 (1979). It is **undecided** whether nonunanimous verdicts in state trials before juries of more than six but fewer than twelve jurors are valid. Thus, it is unclear whether an 8-1 vote by a nine-person jury would be a constitutionally acceptable basis for conviction of a serious offense.

3. Constitutionality of "Inconsistent" Jury Verdicts

The same jury might render two **verdicts that are logically inconsistent**. For example, a jury might convict a defendant of one offense while acquitting him of a lesser included offense. A jury might also convict an individual charged as an accomplice while acquitting the principal on whose guilt the accomplice's liability depends. The evidence presented at trial may render it impossible to reconcile the two verdicts. In sum, it may be clear that they rest on contradictory premises.

Logical inconsistency is problematic. Some jurisdictions, as a matter of policy, prohibit inconsistent verdicts by the same jury. The **Constitution, however, does not forbid inconsistent jury verdicts.** A conviction is constitutional even though it is inconsistent with another verdict returned by the same jury. See United States v. Powell.

Inconsistent verdicts rendered **by a judge following a bench trial are also constitutional.** The fact that a trial judge's conviction of one defendant is logically irreconcilable with her acquittal of another defendant does not invalidate the conviction. Harris v. Rivera, 454 U.S. 339, 102 S. Ct. 460, 70 L. Ed. 2d 530 (1981).

4. Inquiry into Deliberations and "Impeachment" of Verdicts

A common law rule restricting the use of juror testimony to impeach verdicts still has substantial influence today. That rule and the current federal rule are the subjects of this subsection.

a. **Common law prohibition on the use of juror testimony to impeach verdicts.** Our common law developed a "near-universal" rule "flatly prohibit[ing] the admission of juror testimony to impeach a jury verdict." Tanner v. United States, 483 U.S. 107, 107 S. Ct. 2739, 97 L. Ed. 2d 90 (1987). The rule did not preclude jurors from testifying about "extraneous" or "external" influences on their deliberations, but it applied only to "internal" matters bearing on those deliberations. The main reasons for the rule were to ensure frank and free deliberations and to prevent the harassment of jurors after trial. See id. The effect of this prohibition is to restrict a defendant's ability to establish matters that, if proven, "would in some instances lead to the invalidation of verdicts reached after irresponsible or improper juror behavior." Id. The rule can foreclose what may be the only available means of proving that a defendant was deprived of an impartial and competent jury that decided the case based solely on the evidence.

b. **Federal Rule of Evidence 606(b).** The general prohibition on the impeachment of verdicts by juror testimony about internal matters continues today. This outline does not discuss the variations in state rules on the subject. Instead, the discussion here focuses on the rule that controls in federal court—Federal Rule of Evidence 606(b). The rule exemplifies a typical approach and provides a vehicle for addressing issues raised by the prohibition on juror testimony.

Federal Rule of Evidence 606(b) provides, in part:

> Upon an inquiry into the validity of a verdict or indictment, a juror may not testify as to any matter or statement occurring during the course of the jury's deliberations or to the effect of anything upon that or any other juror's mind or emotions as influencing the juror to assent to or dissent from the verdict or indictment or concerning the juror's mental processes in connection therewith, except that a juror may testify on the question whether extraneous prejudicial information was improperly brought to the jury's attention or whether any outside influence was improperly brought to bear upon any juror.

Several aspects of the rule are noteworthy. **First,** it restricts testimony **only upon inquiry into a verdict.** Jurors are free to testify about anything prior to the entry of the verdict. During either the trial or the deliberations, an accused who learns of some internal impropriety is entitled to call a juror to the stand to testify about the impropriety because the prohibition of Rule 606(b) is effective only after the jurors return their verdict.

Second, the rule restricts **only** testimony about so-called **internal matters** and specifically allows jurors to testify about the effects of **"extraneous prejudicial information"** or **"outside influence[s]."** The distinction between "internal" and "external" matters is "not based on whether the juror [is] literally inside or outside the jury room when the alleged irregularity [takes] place; rather, the distinction [is] based on the nature of the allegation." Tanner v. United States. Thus, an external influence such as an attempted bribe by a crime victim could occur in the jury room. And an internal matter such as comments about the defendant evincing racist attitudes could occur outside the jury room.

Third, although the rule refers to juror testimony regarding "any matter or statement occurring **during the course of the jury's deliberations,"** its prohibition is **not** restricted to internal matters that occur after the jury is instructed and retires to discuss the case. In Tanner v. United States, the Supreme Court construed the rule to preclude post-verdict juror testimony about internal matters that occurred during the course of the trial.

Fourth, the rule prohibits **only juror testimony;** it does not prohibit nonjurors from testifying about "internal matters." Thus, a court clerk or a waiter in a restaurant could testify about internal matters affecting the jurors' deliberations. This does not mean, however, that an outsider can testify about what a juror has told her about an internal matter. There is a second sentence in Rule 606(b) that bars the introduction of a juror's "affidavit or evidence of any statement by him concerning a matter about which he would be precluded from testifying."

EXAMPLE AND ANALYSIS

In Tanner v. United States, a convicted defendant sought to use juror testimony to prove that the jurors had abused narcotics and alcohol during his trial. If the allegations of some jurors were true, members of the jury might well have been "incompetent" to serve at various points during the trial. Nonetheless, the Supreme Court held that Rule 606(b) barred juror testimony because the legislative history indicated that Congress intended to treat intoxication as an "internal matter," not an "outside influence."

---

c. **Constitutionality of restrictions on juror testimony to impeach verdicts.** Like its common law antecedent, the federal rule can impede or preclude an accused from proving a valid claim that he was deprived of his Sixth Amendment entitlement to an impartial, competent jury. The **constitutionality** of a rule that severely restricts a defendant's opportunity to prove the deprivation of a fundamental right is certainly questionable. In Tanner v. United States, however, the Supreme Court rejected the defendant's contention that Rule 606(b) unconstitutionally restricted his ability to demonstrate a Sixth Amendment violation. The Court upheld the validity of the rule, reasoning that there were other methods of guarding against juror impropriety and other avenues of proving unconstitutional juror behavior and that the infringements on Sixth Amendment interests caused by the rule were outweighed by the benefits for the jury system produced by the rule.

F. WAIVER OF THE RIGHT TO TRIAL BY JURY

The right to trial by jury can be waived. Patton v. United States, 281 U.S. 276, 50 S. Ct. 253, 74 L. Ed. 854 (1930). A judge can allow a defendant to give up the right to trial by jury and submit to a bench trial if the defendant provides a **knowing and voluntary** waiver.

Some states grant defendants a **right to waive a jury** and insist on a bench trial. However, most states and the federal system provide that an accused **may waive** his entitlement to a jury **only if** he has the consent of the prosecutor or the approval of the judge or both. In Singer v. United States, 380 U.S. 24, 85 S. Ct. 783, 13 L. Ed. 2d 630 (1965), a defendant challenged the constitutionality of the federal rule conditioning waiver on both the prosecutor's consent and the judge's approval. The Supreme Court rejected the challenge, holding that there was **no constitutional right to waive a jury trial or to have a bench trial.** Consequently, jurisdictions are free to put conditions on a defendant's ability to waive a jury.

If "compelling" circumstances rendered "an impartial trial by jury" either "impossible or unlikely," an accused might have an unconditional Sixth Amendment or due process entitlement to insist on a bench trial. See Singer v. United States. The likelihood of such circumstances, however, is remote.

REVIEW QUESTIONS AND ANSWERS

Question: Jasper was charged with 17 counts of cruelty to animals for abandoning livestock on a farm during the heat of summer. His motion for a jury trial was denied, and, after a one-day bench trial, he was convicted of all 17 counts. The judge sentenced Jasper to the maximum six-month sentence for each offense, suspended seven of the sentences, then ordered that the ten remaining sentences should run consecutively. Jasper appeals, claiming his right to trial by jury was denied. Does his claim have merit?

Answer: No. At a joint trial of multiple offenses, each offense is judged separately. Each of these offenses is petty because the maximum sentence for each is six months in jail, and the facts do not mention other authorized penalties that could make the offenses "serious." The fact that Jasper was sentenced to five years in jail is irrelevant to the question of jury entitlement.

Question: Heather is tried in state court for first-degree murder by a nine-person, all-male jury. She is convicted by a 7-2 verdict and sentenced to life in prison. She appeals, claiming that she was entitled to "twelve jurors, a unanimous verdict, and a cross section on her jury that included at least one or two women." What result on appeal?

Answer: Heather is not entitled to 12 jurors. Juries need include no more than six members even though the offense carries a life sentence. Heather may be entitled to a unanimous verdict. Nine-to-three verdicts by 12-person juries are acceptable, but six-person juries must be unanimous. It is uncertain whether juries of more than six but fewer than twelve must be unanimous or have a better "ratio" than 7 to 2. Finally, Heather's "cross section" claim is without merit. The "fair cross section requirement" does not require petit juries to mirror the community. It does not command that any group be represented on a jury, but forbids unjustified "systematic exclusion" from the jury pool. Heather has not shown systematic exclusion on these facts.

Question: Christine, a self-described "born again, fundamentalist follower of Jesus Christ," was charged with trespass, criminal mischief, resisting arrest, and assault on a police officer after a pro-life demonstration at a clinic turned violent. At trial, Christine's counsel asked the judge to inquire about whether prospective jurors have any animus against Fundamentalist Christians, asserting that Christine's defense would be that she was "compelled to do what she did by the commands of her faith and her God." The judge denied the request. Did the trial judge act correctly?

Answer: The question is arguable, but the trial judge's decision is likely to be sustained. Judges generally have broad discretion to control voir dire. In state court, that discretion is limited by the Due Process Clause. If the circumstances of a case give rise to a "constitutionally significant likelihood" of racial prejudice infecting the jurors' decisions, specific inquiry about bias is required. It is unclear whether specific inquiry about religious bias is ever required. If not, Christine has no claim. Even if religious bias is a concern of this branch of due process doctrine, it is debatable whether the nature of the offense and Christine's predicted defense give rise to a sufficient risk to justify specific inquiries of the jurors. Moreover, a judge may well rule that the proposed defense is not legally valid. In that case, the risk of bias would be even less.

Question: In the preceding case, Christine's counsel used all the defense's peremptory challenges to strike women. The prosecutor objected. Counsel explained each of the strikes, providing reasons that were gender-neutral, but none of them had any clear or logical connection to the case. The trial judge stated: "While these reasons are silly and probably will not help the defendant avoid truly unsympathetic jurors, I believe that they are the true reasons and, therefore, uphold the strikes." What result on appeal by the government?

Answer: The judge's ruling should almost certainly be upheld. The strikes of women probably give rise to a prima facie case of intentional discrimination. In any event, whether a prima facie case was established is moot in light of the fact that the defense explained the strikes. At step two of the inquiry, the only issue is gender neutrality. The reasons here qualify. The final step requires the judge to determine whether the objecting party (the government here) carried its burden of proving intentional gender discrimination. The judge here was dubious of the merits of the reasons, but specifically found that they were the true motivations for the strikes. This finding that no purposeful or intentional discrimination on account of gender was proven must be sustained on appeal unless it is clearly erroneous. The facts given do not provide evidence of "clear error."

Question: Billy Joe Wayward was charged with three counts of first-degree sexual assault in connection with an attack on his cousin. The prosecution alleges that Wayward repeatedly raped his cousin when she refused to have sexual relations with him voluntarily. After a jury convicted him of all three counts, Wayward learned that one juror had been paid a sum of money by the victim's father in order to make sure justice was done. Another juror reported that three of the jurors had referred to Billy Joe as "white hillbilly trash" and that one of them had said, "We all know how they feel about relations with relatives. If he didn't rape her, he probably slept with his sisters at least." An affidavit from the bailiff states that he heard jurors make these comments. Were Billy Joe's rights violated? To what relief is he entitled?

Answer: There is a good chance that Billy Joe's right to trial by an impartial jury that decides based on the evidence was violated. At the very least, he is entitled to a hearing to determine whether one juror was influenced by a bribe and whether bias infected the decisionmaking of other jurors. If a single juror was extraneously influenced or biased because of Billy Joe's social status or operated on the basis of matters not introduced into evidence at the trial, a new trial is in order.

The circumstances that require a court to disregard juror assurances that they decided the case properly—without bias and based on the evidence—are rare. Nonetheless, it is arguable that taint should be presumed or "imputed" to the jurors in this case. A payment by the victim's father might be so potentially corrupting that a juror's assertion that his decision was not influenced cannot be believed. Moreover, it could be argued that any juror who refers to a defendant as "white hillbilly trash" and suggests that the defendant is predisposed toward sexual relations with relatives cannot be believed when he denies bias and claims to have rendered a decision based on the evidence.

The jurisdiction might have a rule against juror testimony being used to prove an "internal" impropriety that could impeach a verdict. In this case, however, the juror's report of bias among the jurors is apparently supportable by nonjuror testimony—the report of the bailiff. Such testimony is admissible even when juror testimony is barred.

In sum, there are solid bases for a judge to find a constitutional deprivation. A hearing into actual bias or improper influence is required, and impropriety in the verdict might even have to be presumed. There would seem to be admissible evidence with regard to each impropriety.

Question: Simone was charged with manslaughter after her one-month-old baby was found dead in her crib. The infant died as a result of trauma to her brain stem. Fearing that jurors might not judge her fairly, Simone asked for a bench trial. The judge concluded that "community interest in the case renders a decision by jurors imperative" and denied Simone's request. Was the ruling correct?

Answer: If the jurisdiction allows the judge to reject an attempted waiver of the right to trial by jury, there is no constitutional impediment to denying an attempted waiver and forcing a defendant to submit to trial by jury. No facts here suggest a reason to believe that a fair verdict by a jury is not possible.

20 THE GUARANTEE AGAINST DOUBLE JEOPARDY

 CHAPTER OVERVIEW

The Fifth Amendment **Double Jeopardy Clause** provides that **"[n]o person . . . shall . . . be subject for the same offense to be twice put in jeopardy of life or limb."** This guarantee "can be traced to Greek and Roman times, and . . . became established in the common law of England long before [our] Nation's independence." Benton v. Maryland, 395 U.S. 784, 89 S. Ct. 2056, 23 L. Ed. 2d 707 (1969). Because the protection against double jeopardy "represents a fundamental ideal in our constitutional heritage," it has been made applicable to the states through the Fourteenth Amendment Due Process Clause. See id.

It is often said that the Double Jeopardy Clause affords three specific protections. "It protects against **a second prosecution for the same offense after acquittal.** It protects against **a second prosecution for the same offense after conviction.** And it protects against **multiple punishments for the same offense.**" North Carolina v. Pearce, 395 U.S. 711, 89 S. Ct. 2072, 23 L. Ed. 2d 656 (1969). While this concise summary is accurate, it does not capture the full range of the guarantee's protection or the complexity of the protections it does describe.

The **purposes** served and **interests** protected by the Double Jeopardy Clause are summarized in an oft-repeated passage from Green v. United States, 355 U.S. 184, 78 S. Ct. 221, 2 L. Ed. 2d 199 (1957):

> The underlying idea . . . is that the State with all its resources and power should not be allowed to make **repeated attempts to convict** an individual for an alleged offense, thereby subjecting him to **embarrassment, expense and ordeal and compelling him to live in a continuing state of anxiety and insecurity, as well as enhancing the possibility that even though he may be innocent he may be found guilty.**

In addition, the double jeopardy provision safeguards a defendant's " 'valued right to have his trial completed by a particular [jury].' " Crist v. Bretz, 437 U.S. 28, 98 S. Ct. 2156, 57 L. Ed. 2d 24 (1978). These purposes and interests have guided Supreme Court interpretations of the clause.

This chapter explores the basic protections afforded by the Double Jeopardy Clause and the complex doctrines that give specific content to those basic protections. The chapter is organized around the two core double jeopardy protections—the safeguard against **successive prosecutions** and the shield against **multiple punishments.**

With regard to **"successive prosecutions,"** this chapter discusses:

- **The "attachment" and "termination" of jeopardy.** The Fifth Amendment protects against being "twice put **in jeopardy.**" The protection against "successive prosecutions" is violated when a person is put in jeopardy a first time and is then subjected to a second jeopardy. For a second jeopardy to be possible, a first jeopardy must **"attach"** and **"terminate."**

  Consequently, it is important to identify the point at which jeopardy **attaches.** That point varies depending on whether the case involves a jury trial, a bench trial, or a guilty plea. Moreover, because a violation requires two jeopardies, it is also vital to identify the point at which jeopardy **terminates.** Many different events can terminate a jeopardy and raise a bar to further prosecution.

- **The meaning of the "same offense" in the successive prosecution context.** The Fifth Amendment protects only against twice being put in jeopardy **"for the same offense."** Even if one jeopardy has attached and terminated, a second jeopardy for a "different" offense is permissible. As a result, the meaning of the phrase "same offense" is of critical importance in interpreting the guarantee.

In discussing the double jeopardy protection against **"multiple punishment,"** this chapter considers:

- **The requirement of credit.** When a person serves time for an offense, has the conviction overturned, and is convicted and resentenced, the Double Jeopardy Clause does not prohibit a "higher" sentence the second time. It **does require credit** for the time served.

- **The meaning of the "same offense" for purposes of the protection against multiple punishment.** The double jeopardy protection against "multiple punishment" prohibits **multiple sentences at one trial** if those sentences are imposed **"for the same offense."** The meaning of the phrase "same offense" in this context, however, is *different* from its meaning in the **"successive prosecutions"** context.

- **The prohibition on multiple punishments at separate trials.** In some situations, the "successive prosecutions" strand of double jeopardy protection poses no barrier to two proceedings because one of the proceedings is "civil" and, therefore, does not put an individual "in jeopardy." The individual may still be protected against "punishment" resulting from that civil proceeding if a "punishment" for the same offense resulted from a prior "criminal" proceeding.

- **The "exception" to the general rule allowing sentence increases.** Ordinarily, when a conviction is overturned, the Double Jeopardy Clause does not prohibit a judge from imposing a higher sentence upon reconviction. There is one significant "exception" to this rule. When a defendant has been once put in jeopardy of capital punishment at a trial-like sentencing proceeding and that jeopardy has terminated the protection against "successive prosecutions" prevents the government from putting him in jeopardy of the death penalty a second time.

A. THE PROTECTION AGAINST "SUCCESSIVE PROSECUTIONS" FOR THE "SAME OFFENSE"

The main safeguard provided by the Double Jeopardy Clause is the **protection against "successive prosecutions" for the "same offense."** This safeguard is not an absolute bar to multiple trials. In many situations, a person may be tried twice or more for the same crime. The safeguard against successive prosecutions applies only when **one *jeopardy* has attached and terminated** and **a second *jeopardy* for the same offense is contemplated.** This section discusses the points at which jeopardy attaches, the events that terminate jeopardy, and the meaning of "same offense" in the successive prosecution context.

1. "Attachment" of Jeopardy

Jeopardy can attach only at a proceeding in which a person is put at *risk of a criminal conviction*. As a result, jeopardy ordinarily attaches only at **criminal trials.** Truly "civil" proceedings cannot constitute jeopardy. For example, a trial instituted to seek payment of a "civil" fine or penalty or the "civil" forfeiture of an item used in a criminal enterprise does not put an individual "in jeopardy" even though the basis of the fine, penalty, or forfeiture is an act that also constitutes a crime.

Although juvenile proceedings are typically classified as civil, **jeopardy does attach** at a **juvenile adjudicatory hearing** at which the **object is to determine whether the juvenile committed** an act that would be prosecuted as **a crime** if she were an adult and at which the **potential consequences** of the adjudication **involve stigma and deprivation of liberty.** See Breed v. Jones, 421 U.S. 519, 95 S. Ct. 1779, 44 L. Ed. 2d 346 (1975).

a. Point of attachment in jury trials. In a criminal trial before a jury, **jeopardy attaches when the jury is sworn.** Crist v. Bretz. Prior to that point, a person is not in jeopardy.

b. **Point of attachment in bench trials.** In a criminal trial before a judge—a bench trial—**jeopardy attaches when the first witness is sworn,** id., or **at the beginning of the introduction of evidence,** Serfass v. United States, 420 U.S. 377, 95 S. Ct. 1055, 43 L. Ed. 2d 265 (1975). These two different descriptions of the point of attachment have given rise to a minor dispute regarding the point of attachment in a bench trial. One view holds that jeopardy **attaches when the witness takes the oath.** The other view holds that jeopardy **attaches only when the witness actually starts to testify.** Both are plausible interpretations of the Court's language. The difference between the two views would have practical impact only in the rare case where a trial ends after the first witness takes the oath and before she speaks a word of testimony.

c. **Point of attachment when an accused pleads guilty.** Although there is no controlling Supreme Court precedent, the general view is that when a defendant forgoes trial and pleads guilty, **jeopardy attaches when the trial court unconditionally accepts the guilty plea.**

 ## EXAMPLES AND ANALYSIS

1. At Max's first trial, after 11 jurors have been selected, a judge grants the prosecution's motion for a mistrial. Before a second trial begins, Max moves to dismiss the indictment against him on double jeopardy grounds. Does Max have a potentially valid claim?

No. Because the jury was not sworn, jeopardy had not attached at the first trial. Without an initial jeopardy, there can be no second jeopardy.

2. Now suppose that Max waives his right to trial by jury at his second trial. After the prosecution's first witness answers two questions—"What is your name?" and "Where do you reside?"—the trial judge declares a mistrial. Max moves to prevent a third attempt to try him, claiming a double jeopardy violation. Is his claim potentially valid?

Yes. Max was put in jeopardy once at the bench trial because the first witness was sworn and began to testify. If jeopardy terminated with the mistrial, the third attempt to try him will violate his protection against double jeopardy.

2. **"Termination" of Jeopardy**

If an initial jeopardy has attached but not terminated, there cannot be a second jeopardy. Instead, there is one "continuing" jeopardy. Consequently, it is critical to determine what events constitute **terminations of jeopardy.**

A variety of different events—acquittals, convictions, mistrials, and dismissals—can terminate a jeopardy.

a.   **"Acquittals."** The most venerable rule in all double jeopardy jurisprudence is that **an acquittal terminates jeopardy.** See United States v. Scott, 437 U.S. 82, 98 S. Ct. 2187, 57 L. Ed. 2d 65 (1978). The government cannot have an acquittal overturned on appeal and cannot seek to retry an offense following an acquittal because "such a verdict **end[s] an accused's jeopardy.**" Price v. Georgia, 398 U.S. 323, 90 S. Ct. 1757, 26 L. Ed. 2d 300 (1970).

A **verdict of "not guilty"** rendered by either a jury or a judge **is an acquittal of that offense.** Moreover, **a verdict of "guilty" for a lesser included offense is an acquittal of a greater, inclusive offense** when the trier of fact has had a full opportunity to return a verdict on the greater offense. Id. In addition, a ruling by a trial judge at either a bench or a jury trial **is an acquittal** if the ruling " 'actually represents a **resolution [in the defendant's favor], correct or not, of some or all of the factual elements of the offense charged' "** or if the ruling is based on a **"defense"** that establishes " **'the criminal defendant's lack of criminal culpability.' "** United States v. Scott. This is true no matter what "label" the trial judge gives the ruling. Id.

An acquittal terminates jeopardy **even if** it is " **'egregiously erroneous.' "** See Arizona v. Washington, 434 U.S. 497, 98 S. Ct. 824, 54 L. Ed. 2d 717 (1978). No matter how "mistaken [an] acquittal," it terminates jeopardy. Even if an acquittal results from " 'erroneous evidentiary rulings or erroneous interpretations of governing legal principles,' " it stands as a bar to a second jeopardy. United States v. Scott.

 EXAMPLE AND ANALYSIS

In Price v. Georgia, the defendant had been tried for murder and convicted of voluntary manslaughter. His conviction was reversed based on an erroneous jury instruction. He was retried for murder and again convicted of voluntary manslaughter. The Supreme Court held that his second trial for murder was an impermissible second jeopardy for an offense of which he had been "implicitly acquitted." The remedy for this violation was a **new trial** for voluntary manslaughter. However, if the defendant had been convicted of **murder** at his second trial, the remedy for the double jeopardy violation would have been a **reduction** of the murder conviction to **voluntary manslaughter unless** the defendant could demonstrate **a reasonable probability that he would not have been convicted of manslaughter if he had not been tried for murder.** Morris v. Mathews, 475 U.S. 237, 106 S. Ct. 1032, 89 L. Ed. 2d 187 (1986).

When jurors choose the lesser, nonbarred offense, there is a reasonable probability that they "compromised" on that offense because of the presence of the barred, greater offense. The defendant is entitled to a new trial without that unconstitutional risk of compromise. When a jury chooses the greater, barred offense, however, the verdict demonstrates that the jurors did not compromise. Reduction of the conviction to the nonbarred, lesser included offense that the jury necessarily found proven is a sufficient remedy *unless* the defendant can establish some other basis for finding a reasonable probability that but for the presence of the barred, greater offense the jury would not have convicted him of the nonbarred, lesser offense. Id.

---

b.　"Convictions." An **unreversed conviction terminates jeopardy** and bars further jeopardy for the same offense. Brown v. Ohio, 432 U.S. 161, 97 S. Ct. 2221, 53 L. Ed. 2d 187 (1977). If a defendant does not appeal a conviction or if it is affirmed on appeal, jeopardy for the offense has ended.

When an appellate court **reverses a conviction for trial error, jeopardy does not terminate.** Ball v. United States, 163 U.S. 662, 16 S. Ct. 1192, 41 L. Ed. 300 (1896); Burks v. United States, 437 U.S. 1, 98 S. Ct. 2141, 57 L. Ed. 2d 1 (1978). When an accused appeals a conviction and an appellate court reverses on the basis of trial error, the jeopardy that attached at the first trial **"continues"** through the second trial. Ball v. United States.

When an appellate court **reverses a conviction on grounds of insufficient evidence,** however, **jeopardy is terminated.** Burks v. United States. An appellate reversal for insufficiency is considered equivalent to an acquittal entered by the trial judge based on insufficiency. In judging the sufficiency of the evidence to sustain a conviction, an appellate court must consider **all the evidence admitted at trial,** even evidence erroneously admitted. Lockhart v. Nelson, 488 U.S. 33, 109 S. Ct. 285, 102 L. Ed. 2d 265 (1988). Consequently, if a record contains sufficient evidence to sustain a conviction but an appellate court reverses the conviction because evidence of guilt was erroneously admitted at trial, retrial is permissible. It does not matter that the record would be insufficient without the erroneously admitted evidence; sufficiency is judged on the basis of all the evidence admitted at trial. The conviction has been reversed for "trial error." Id.

If an appellate court finds the evidence in the record insufficient and also agrees with the government contention that the trial court **erroneously excluded evidence** that would have prevented insufficiency, it is *arguable* that a reversal of the conviction does not terminate jeopardy and bar retrial. See Burks v. United States. While that conclusion seems inconsistent with the principle that acquittals by trial courts based on erroneous evidentiary rulings terminate jeopardy, in *Burks* the Supreme Court specifically held open the possibility that retrial *might* be permissible in that situation.

Some appellate courts are authorized to reverse convictions based on the **"weight of the evidence."** A "weight of the evidence" reversal does not reflect a conclusion that the evidence is *insufficient* to support the conviction; rather, it reflects a determination that the evidence is sufficiently weak to raise serious questions about the justice of the conviction. Sitting as the "thirteenth juror," the appellate court reverses the conviction and grants a new trial. Because reversals based on the weight of the evidence **do not terminate jeopardy,** they do not bar retrial. Tibbs v. Florida, 457 U.S. 31, 102 S. Ct. 2211, 72 L. Ed. 2d 652 (1982).

EXAMPLE AND ANALYSIS

Zeke has been charged with aggravated assault and has raised a self-defense claim. In this jurisdiction, the prosecution has the burden of disproving the defense once the defendant produces sufficient evidence that he acted in self-defense. After the jury convicts him, Zeke appeals his conviction, claiming erroneous instructions and insufficient evidence to rebut his claim of self-defense. If the appellate court agrees with either of Zeke's claims and reverses his conviction, may he be tried again consistent with double jeopardy principles?

If the appellate court reverses the conviction for instructional error, Zeke may be tried again. Jeopardy continues when a reversal for trial error occurs. If the appellate court reverses on the ground of insufficient evidence to carry the government's burden of disproving self-defense, Zeke's jeopardy terminates. He may not be retried. It does not matter that the evidentiary insufficiency pertains to a "defense" on which the government bears the burden of proof. In *Burks*, the defendant succeeded when his conviction was reversed because of insufficient evidence to disprove his insanity.

---

c. **"Dismissals."** A "dismissal" is a **ruling in the defendant's favor "on grounds unrelated to guilt or innocence."** United States v. Scott. It is a decision by the court that the defendant cannot properly be convicted of the offense charged for some reason other than a "lack of criminal culpability." See id. If a ruling in the accused's favor does not resolve an element of the offense or rest on a "defense" that establishes the defendant's lack of culpability, it is not an acquittal but is instead a "dismissal." Typically a dismissal represents a judgment "that a defendant, although criminally culpable, may not be punished" because the

Constitution or some other law prevents punishment. See id. Whether a ruling is a dismissal or an acquittal requires a close examination of its nature and basis; the trial judge's "label" is **not determinative**.

i.   **Dismissals requested by the defense. A defense-requested dismissal is not a termination of jeopardy.** See id. Thus, if the government appeals the dismissal and it is reversed, retrial is permissible. The same is undoubtedly true if the dismissal originates with the court and the **defense expressly consents to it.** See subsection d below (discussing requests for and consents to mistrials). **Note:** If a dismissal is not reversed, retrial is not permissable because a valid ruling in the defendant's favor has been entered.

ii. **Dismissals not requested by the defense.** The prosecutor is not likely to seek a dismissal, but a trial judge may grant a dismissal sua sponte—on her own initiative. A dismissal that is **not requested by or consented to by the defendant is a termination of jeopardy.** Consequently, no matter how erroneous the ruling, it is final for double jeopardy purposes and **bars a retrial.** See United States v. Scott (holding only that dismissals sought by the defense can be reversed and retried).

EXAMPLE AND ANALYSIS

Cleo was on trial for contributing to the delinquency of a minor. At the end of the government's case, Cleo moved for a "judgment of acquittal," claiming that the prosecutor had singled her out from other women who had committed the same offense and had decided to prosecute her on the basis of her race. The trial judge granted Cleo's motion, ruling that "an acquittal is in order because of the prosecutor's patent discrimination." The government wishes to appeal the ruling and try Cleo again. May it do so without violating the Fifth Amendment?

Yes. Unless the judge's ruling is other than it appears to be, the prosecutor may appeal it and, if successful, may retry Cleo. Cleo alleged that the prosecution had "singled her out for prosecution on the basis of race." She asserted that although she may have committed the offense, the prosecutor had selectively prosecuted her on a racially discriminatory basis. Assuming that the judge's ruling was an endorsement of that claim, it rested "on grounds unrelated to guilt or innocence" and did not reflect a "lack of culpability" on Cleo's part. The "label" on the ruling is not dispositive; whether a ruling is an acquittal or a dismissal depends on its character. Consequently, the trial judge granted a "defense-requested dismissal," which does not terminate jeopardy.

If the basis of the judge's ruling was instead that Cleo had not committed the offense but had been charged with it because of her race, then it would reflect a "lack of culpability" and would be an acquittal. No matter how egregiously erroneous the acquittal, Cleo could not be retried because jeopardy had terminated.

---

d. Mistrials. A **mistrial** is a ruling by a trial court that a particular trial cannot or should not be continued. In ordering a mistrial a judge is not ruling in favor of either side but is contemplating that the trial will be started over. As with other rulings by a court, for purposes of the Double Jeopardy Clause the trial court's characterization of a ruling (the "label") does not control. Substance governs over form. Consequently, the nature of the ruling must be evaluated.

i. Mistrials requested or consented to by the defense. As a general rule, a **mistrial requested or consented to by the defense does not terminate jeopardy.** United States v. Dinitz, 424 U.S. 600, 96 S. Ct. 1075, 47 L. Ed. 2d 267 (1976). Retrial is permissible. There is, however, an **exception** to the general rule. If the defense request or consent is the result of **governmental conduct intended to goad or provoke the defendant into moving for a mistrial,** the mistrial terminates jeopardy and bars further proceedings. Oregon v. Kennedy, 456 U.S. 667, 102 S. Ct. 2083, 72 L. Ed. 2d 416 (1982). This exception does not apply whenever action by the prosecutor or court seriously damages the defendant's chances for an acquittal or a fair trial and makes a mistrial the only attractive option for the defendant. It applies **only** when governmental **intent to goad or provoke the mistrial request** is proven. Id.

The general rule that jeopardy is not terminated applies if the defendant explicitly **requests** the mistrial or if the idea originates with the court or prosecutor and the accused expressly **consents** to the mistrial. It is unclear whether **silence** by the defense in the face of a court's expressed intent to grant a mistrial can qualify as "consent."

ii. Mistrials granted on the court's initiative or at the request of the prosecutor. As a general rule, a mistrial **granted over the defendant's objection on the court's initiative or at the request of the prosecutor terminates jeopardy and bars a retrial.** Arizona v. Washington, 434 U.S. 497, 98 S. Ct. 824, 54 L. Ed. 2d 717 (1978). An **exception** to the general rule is made for mistrials granted because of **manifest necessity.** In those cases, jeopardy is not terminated and retrial is constitutional. Id.

"Manifest necessity" requires a showing that there is a " **'high degree'** " **of need** to end a trial. If "the ends of public justice would be defeated" by allowing the trial to go forward, there is manifest necessity for a mistrial. Id. The manifest necessity standard **does not require** a showing that it is **impossible** to continue **or** that there is **no alternative** to the current trial. An event that seriously prejudices the prosecution's opportunity for a fair trial will ordinarily constitute manifest necessity. Manifest necessity may also be found if the best result that the state could secure is a conviction that is reversible at the request of the defendant. See Illinois v. Somerville, 410 U.S. 458, 93 S. Ct. 1066, 35 L. Ed. 2d 425 (1973). It is possible, but unlikely, that manifest necessity could be found based on a threat to the *defendant's* interests in a fair and just outcome.

To determine whether there is manifest necessity, a trial judge should take **all the relevant circumstances** into account and should consider options other than ending the present trial. There is no manifest necessity for a mistrial if a threat to the fairness of the current trial can be avoided by an **alternative remedy** that allows the trial to continue. A cautionary instruction to jurors, the replacement of a tainted juror with an alternate, and continuance of the trial are all possible alternatives that could render a mistrial unjustified. In reviewing decisions to grant mistrials, appellate courts ordinarily should be deferential to the judgment of the trial judge. See Arizona v. Washington.

The "classic case" of manifest necessity is a "hung jury." If a jury is truly deadlocked and unable to reach a verdict, there is manifest necessity for a mistrial and retrial is permissible. Id. Nonetheless, if a court immediately declares a mistrial when a jury first reports an inability to reach a verdict, manifest necessity might not be found. To make sure that there actually is a "high degree of need" to grant a mistrial, the trial judge should give the jurors ample time to work out their differences and should explore the feasibility of instructions designed to break a deadlock. If the judge acts hastily, retrial may be barred.

 # EXAMPLE AND ANALYSIS

During opening argument, defense counsel repeatedly refers to government misconduct toward her client that is irrelevant to the charges being tried. Repeatedly, the trial court warns counsel not to mention the misconduct. Eventually, the court sua sponte declares a mistrial, stating that the "prejudicial arguments of counsel have created too great a risk of taint against the government." Can the prosecution retry the defendant?

Probably. In Arizona v. Washington, a case involving a similar scenario, the Supreme Court held that in light of the deference due to the trial court the decision to grant a mistrial could be sustained on the basis of "manifest necessity." It is arguable in such a case that the judge first should have tried alternative measures such as cautionary instructions to the jurors to ignore the argument of counsel and inquiry of the jurors to ascertain whether they have been biased. If the risk of bias created by the argument is sufficiently high, Arizona v. Washington suggests that a court can defensibly conclude that neither instructions nor inquiry will be satisfactory and that the only adequate way to ensure a fair trial for the government is to declare a mistrial.

---

3. Proceedings That Constitute a "Second" Jeopardy

The preceding subsections discussed various events that "terminate" jeopardy. **Following a termination of jeopardy, the Fifth Amendment** protection against "successive prosecutions" **bars a second "jeopardy."** The question, then, is what constitutes a "second" jeopardy?

"[A]ny further proceedings devoted to the resolution of factual issues going to the elements of the offense" will amount to an unconstitutional second jeopardy. Smalis v. Pennsylvania, 476 U.S. 140, 106 S. Ct. 1745, 90 L. Ed. 2d 116 (1986). A "retrial"—an entirely new trial—is a second jeopardy. Moreover, the "resumption" of a trial at the point at which it ended is a second jeopardy if a conviction cannot be entered without "further proceedings devoted to the resolution of factual issues going to the elements of the offense." If a proceeding involves the introduction of further evidence, additional jury deliberations, or simply further findings or conclusions by a trial judge, it constitutes a second jeopardy and is forbidden following the termination of an initial jeopardy. See id.

Appellate review and reversal of a ruling that terminates jeopardy is **not barred by double jeopardy** *if* a conviction can be entered without "further proceedings devoted to the resolution of factual issues going to the elements of the offense." Without such proceedings, there is no second jeopardy. For example, if a trial judge grants a motion for judgment of acquittal on grounds of evidence insufficiency after the jury has returned a guilty verdict, the trial judge's ruling can be reversed on appeal because the result would merely be reinstatement of the jury verdict without "further proceedings." See United States v. Scott. Moreover, if an intermediate appellate court reverses a conviction for insufficiency, the government can appeal that reversal to a higher appellate court. If the higher court disagrees with the intermediate court's conclusion, the conviction can simply be reinstated without further jeopardy.

EXAMPLE AND ANALYSIS

After Amy is convicted of child endangerment following a jury trial, she moves for a judgment of acquittal. The judge grants her motion, declaring that the government had not proven the requisite mens rea beyond a reasonable doubt. May the government seek reversal of the trial judge's ruling?

Yes. Though the ruling is an acquittal, if the court of appeals agrees with the government that there was sufficient evidence, the result will be reinstatement of the jury's guilty verdict, not "further proceedings." Because there will be no second jeopardy, reversal and reinstatement are constitutional.

4. **Meaning of "the Same Offense" in Successive Prosecution Contexts**

The language of the Fifth Amendment restricts the double jeopardy protection against "successive prosecutions" to situations in which multiple jeopardies are "for **the same offense**." This subsection explores the meaning of those critical constitutional terms.

a. **"Same sovereign" requirement.** For two offenses to be "the same," they must be against **the same sovereign.** If the two offenses are defined and prosecuted by different sovereigns, the **"dual sovereignty" doctrine** precludes double jeopardy protection. Heath v. Alabama, 474 U.S. 82, 106 S. Ct. 433, 88 L. Ed. 2d 387 (1985). Two "entities" are separate sovereigns if they "draw their authority to punish the offender from distinct sources of power." Id. Thus, the federal government is a separate sovereign from each of the 50 states, see Abbate v. United States, 359 U.S. 187, 79 S. Ct. 666, 3 L. Ed. 2d 729 (1959), and each state is a separate sovereign. Heath v. Alabama. Municipalities, however, are not separate from the states in which they are located because their sources of sovereign power are the same. Id.

 EXAMPLE AND ANALYSIS

In Heath v. Alabama, the defendant was charged with a murder that began in one state and ended in another. Georgia prosecuted him first and accepted a guilty plea to murder in exchange for a life sentence. Alabama prosecuted the defendant for the same murder, securing both a conviction and death sentence. The Supreme Court rejected the defendant's double jeopardy claim. Even though Georgia could not have tried the defendant a second time for the murder, Alabama, a separate sovereign, could do so because its prosecution was not for the *same* offense.

b.   **"Same act or transaction" requirement.** For offenses to be the same, they must be **based on the same act or transaction.** Brown v. Ohio, 432 U.S. 161, 97 S. Ct. 2221, 53 L. Ed. 2d 187 (1977). Even if the statutory elements of the two charges are identical, if the bases of these charges are two different acts—that is, if the defendant has twice committed the very same crime—there is no bar to "successive prosecutions."

c.   **"Elements" test of Blockburger v. United States.** "[S]eparate statutory crimes" can be "the same" for Fifth Amendment purposes. Even though two crimes are **"not . . . identical either in constituent elements or in actual proof,"** they may still be "the same offense." Brown v. Ohio. In sum, the fact that two offenses are contained in different provisions of a jurisdiction's code and are defined to contain different elements does not mean that the double jeopardy protection against "successive prosecutions" is inapplicable.

The **sole standard** for determining whether two offenses are the same is **the *Blockburger* test.** See United States v. Dixon, 509 U.S. 688, 113 S. Ct. 2849, 125 L. Ed. 2d 556 (1993). According to that test:

> [W]here the same act or transaction constitutes a violation of two distinct statutory provisions, the test to be applied to determine whether there are two offenses or only one, is **whether each provision requires proof of an additional fact which the other does not.**

Blockburger v. United States, 284 U.S. 299, 52 S. Ct. 180, 76 L. Ed. 306 (1932). "This test emphasizes the **elements** of the two crimes." Brown v. Ohio. If each offense, by definition, **requires** the government to prove an element that the other offense does not require the government to prove, the two offenses are **not the same.** If every element that must be proven to establish one offense also must be proven to establish the other offense, the two **are the same.** In effect, two offenses will be the same only if **all** the elements of one of them are also elements of the other.

Consequently, a "lesser included offense" and the greater offense that includes it—assault and assault with a deadly weapon, for example—are **always the same** for Fifth Amendment purposes. If jeopardy has attached and terminated for one of the offenses, an accused may not be put in jeopardy for the other. Moreover, the order of the prosecutions does not matter; a first jeopardy for either offense will preclude a second jeopardy for the other. Brown v. Ohio.

Under the *Blockburger* test, a court must sometimes look beyond the "generic" or "abstract" elements of the offense in the penal code—those contained in the statutory definition—and examine the elements that actually have been or will be proven. See Harris v. Oklahoma, 433 U.S. 682, 97 S. Ct. 2912, 53 L. Ed. 2d 1054 (1977); United States v. Dixon. This is the case when an abstract statutory element of an offense can be proven in a variety of ways that all necessitate the proof of other statutory elements.

Felony murder provides a good illustration. The offense is typically defined as "the killing of another human being in the course or further-ance of **a felony.**" The "felony" element of felony murder is established by proof of the statutory elements of any of an array of different felonies. In a particular case, the prosecution may prove a rape, an arson, a burglary, or an armed robbery. In applying the *Blockburger* test, the relevant "element" is not "a felony" in the abstract but the elements of the specific felony that has been or will be proven by the state. See Harris v. Oklahoma. Thus, if the prosecution tries an accused for arson and obtains an unreversed conviction, a subsequent trial for "felony murder" based on the same arson will violate the Double Jeopardy Clause. Because the two offenses are the "same," successive prosecut-ions are prohibited.

EXAMPLE AND ANALYSIS

In United States v. Dixon, two defendants were prosecuted for contempt and for other crimes in successive trials. For one defendant, the contempt charge was based on a court order that the defendant not commit any criminal offense. The government had to prove that he knowingly violated the court order. The criminal charge was a narcotics offense that required proof that the defendant had possessed cocaine with intent to distribute it. The defendant was first tried for and found guilty of criminal contempt based on his possession of cocaine with the intent to distribute it. The Supreme Court held that this contempt prosecution and conviction barred the prosecut-ion for the crime of possession with intent to distribute. The Court looked behind the generic "violation of a court order" element of contempt and found that in the defendant's contempt trial that element actually required proof of the elements of possession of cocaine with intent to distribute it. It then concluded that the narcotics crime that was charged did not contain any element that was not in the contempt charge. Consequently, under *Blockburger* the two offenses were the same, and the second prosecution was barred.

The other defendant in *Dixon* was first prosecuted for and convicted of contempt for violating a court order that required him not to "molest, assault, or in any manner threaten or physically abuse his wife." He was then charged with the crime of "assault *with intent to kill*" based on the same assault that was the basis for the contempt conviction. The Supreme Court found no double jeopardy bar to a trial for the crime.

At the contempt trial, the government had actually been required to prove a knowing violation of a court order and a simple assault. The criminal offense required proof of an assault and an intent to kill. Each offense required proof of an element that the other did not—the contempt required a knowing violation of a court order and the crime required an intent to kill. Consequently, under *Blockburger* the two offenses were not the same and the second prosecution was not barred.

---

5. Exceptions to the Prohibition on "Successive Prosecutions for the Same Offense"

When two separate statutory offenses qualify as the same under *Blockburger*, the "successive prosecution" protection of the Fifth Amendment ordinarily prohibits two jeopardies. There are limited exceptions to this bar—cases in which the state may prosecute for an offense despite the fact that the defendant has already been in jeopardy for another offense that is the "same" under *Blockburger*.

First, when the government has prosecuted one "less serious" offense, it may try a defendant for a second, "more serious" offense if it was "**unable to proceed** on the more serious charge at the [time of the first prosecution] because the **additional facts necessary to sustain that charge ha[d] not [yet] occurred.**" Brown v. Ohio. **Second,** following an initial prosecution for a "less serious" offense, a state may prosecute a second, "more serious" offense if it was "**unable to proceed** on the more serious charge at the [time of the first prosecution] because **the additional facts necessary to sustain that charge . . . ha[d] not [yet] been discovered despite the exercise of due diligence.**" Id. In essence, if the government pursues a lesser charge at a time when a greater charge could not be proven *either* because the offense had not yet been "completed" or because officials had not yet discovered matters essential to proving the greater offense despite diligent investigation, a subsequent prosecution for the greater charge is constitutional.

Finally, there is an exception to the successive prosecution bar in situations where **the defendant is "solely responsible" for successive prosecutions** of the two offenses that are "the same." See Ohio v. Johnson, 467 U.S. 493, 104 S. Ct. 2536, 81 L. Ed. 2d 425 (1984). This exception does not apply if the prosecution bears some or all of the responsibility for the successive prosecutions. If a judge accepts a defendant's guilty plea to a "lesser charge" and enters a judgment of conviction over the objection of a prosecutor who wishes to pursue a "greater crime" that is the same offense under *Blockburger*, the state is not barred from later trying the accused for the greater crime. Ohio v. Johnson. And if a defendant either moves to sever the trial of two offenses that are the same or opposes government efforts to have two offenses that are the same consolidated for one trial, a jeopardy for one of the offenses will not bar a jeopardy for the other offense. See Jeffers v. United States, 432 U.S. 137, 97 S. Ct. 2207, 53 L. Ed. 2d 168 (1977).

6.   The "Collateral Estoppel" Doctrine of Ashe v. Swenson

Even though two offenses are not "the same offense" under the *Blockburger* test, successive prosecutions may be barred by a **collateral estoppel doctrine** that is implicit in the Fifth Amendment safeguard. See Ashe v. Swenson, 397 U.S. 436, 90 S. Ct. 1189, 25 L. Ed. 2d 469 (1970). The collateral estoppel doctrine applies only when "**an issue of ultimate fact has once been determined [in a defendant's favor] by a valid and final judgment.**" Id. When that is the case, double jeopardy principles prohibit the **same government** from relitigating that **same issue** in a criminal proceeding against the **same defendant.** A bar arises because the accused has been put "in jeopardy" once for a particular **element** of an offense and has been **acquitted of that element.** The final resolution of the element **in the defendant's favor** precludes a contrary finding on the same element in a later prosecution.

To raise the collateral estoppel bar, a defendant has "the burden . . . to demonstrate that the issue was actually decided in the first proceeding." Dowling v. United States, 493 U.S. 342, 110 S. Ct. 668, 107 L. Ed. 2d 708 (1990). Because juries do not specify the bases of their verdicts and because there are often multiple possible explanations for an acquittal, it is not easy for a defendant to demonstrate that a particular issue was actually decided in his favor.

 EXAMPLES AND ANALYSIS

Derek is charged with 10 counts of armed robbery based on an incident in which a masked individual held 10 customers at gunpoint in a supermarket and demanded their belongings. At Derek's first trial, there is no dispute that the victim was robbed. The only issue is whether Derek was the robber. The jury acquits Derek. May Derek be tried for any of the other nine robbery charges?

No. Because the sole issue in the first trial was identity, the only rational basis on which the jury could have acquitted Derek was that the government had not proven beyond a reasonable doubt that he was the robber. He was acquitted of this "issue of ultimate fact." Each of the other nine robbery counts will require proof that Derek was the robber. Because of the acquittal, he cannot be put "in jeopardy" again for that element. Collateral estoppel bars the other nine trials. See Ashe v. Swenson.

Suppose that the trial for robbery of the first victim involved two issues—whether Derek was the robber and whether the victim was actually robbed. Both were genuinely disputed and the government's evidence regarding each had serious weaknesses. Would an acquittal raise a collateral estoppel bar to trial for any of the other nine charges?

No. The defendant would have to show that the issue of identity was actually decided in his favor at the first trial. On these facts, he could not carry his burden. If the jury acquitted Derek because they were unconvinced that the first victim was robbed, he has not been acquitted of any issue that will arise in the other nine trials that involve different victims.

If Derek had been convicted at the first trial, could he have been tried for the other nine robberies? Yes. Collateral estoppel requires resolution of the issue "in the defendant's favor." Moreover, while an unreversed conviction will bar a second trial for the "same" offense, none of the 10 offenses here is the same because each requires proof of the robbery of a different victim.

B.   THE PROTECTION AGAINST "MULTIPLE PUNISHMENT" FOR THE "SAME OFFENSE"

The Double Jeopardy Clause also provides protection against **multiple punishment for the same offense.** This protection contains three separable safeguards. First, it insures that an accused receives **credit for time served** when she is resentenced following the reversal of an initial conviction. Second, it guards against **cumulative punishment at one trial for two crimes that are the same offense.** Third, it prohibits **multiple punishments** for the same offense **that result from separate "civil" and "criminal" proceedings.**

The Double Jeopardy Clause also gives rise to one safeguard against "punishment" that is actually a part of the protection against **"successive prosecutions."** At least in **capital sentencing situations,** the Fifth Amendment **prohibits a second "jeopardy" for a death sentence after an accused has once been "acquitted" of the death penalty**—that is, sentenced to life imprisonment. Because it pertains to punishment, this "successive prosecution" protection is discussed at the end of this section.

1.   The General Rule Allowing Sentence Increases and the Requirement of "Credit" for Time Served

When an accused is convicted of an offense and sentenced to a term of imprisonment and the conviction is reversed on appeal for trial error, retrial is constitutional. See section A.2.b above. In nearly all cases, the Double Jeopardy Clause **does not preclude a higher sentence** if the accused is convicted and sentenced a second time. North Carolina v. Pearce, 395 U.S. 711, 89 S. Ct. 2072, 23 L. Ed. 2d 656 (1969). A higher sentence is not forbidden because the imposition of the initial sentence is **not** considered an **implicit acquittal of the higher sentence** that could have been imposed. Bullington v. Missouri, 451 U.S. 430, 101 S. Ct. 1852, 68 L. Ed. 2d 270

(1981). For sentencing purposes, when the first conviction is reversed, the constitutional "slate is wiped clean." North Carolina v. Pearce. The Double Jeopardy Clause **does require,** however, that upon resentencing the accused be given **credit for time served** under the initial sentence. Id. The accused may not be imprisoned for longer than the duration of the second sentence minus the amount of time initially served. The accused is also constitutionally entitled to any "credits" earned during the initial sentence for good behavior or other reasons. Id. The basis of the credit requirement is simple. If time served were not credited, the accused would clearly suffer **multiple punishment for the same offense**—that is, he would be serving two sentences for one crime.

 # Example and Analysis

Manny was convicted of mail fraud. The maximum sentence for the offense is 10 years. Manny was sentenced to seven years in prison. After serving six months, his conviction was overturned. Upon retrial, Manny was again convicted. The trial judge imposed a 10-year sentence. Does the sentence violate the double jeopardy protection against multiple punishment?

If the judge gives Manny credit for the six months he has served, the sentence does not offend double jeopardy. Manny cannot be made to serve 10 additional years because then he would be serving a total of 10 years and six months for an offense with a maximum of 10 years. The "increase" in the sentence following the retrial—that is, from seven years to 10 years—does not offend double jeopardy. It may, however, violate the Due Process Clause. See Chapter 21, section F.

---

2. Prohibition on "Cumulative Punishment" for the Same Offense at a Single Trial

When an accused is tried at a single trial for two separate statutory crimes, the Double Jeopardy Clause forbids a court from imposing **cumulative punishment** if the two crimes are the **same offense.** Albernaz v. United States, 450 U.S. 333, 101 S. Ct. 1137, 67 L. Ed. 2d 275 (1981). Both concurrent and consecutive sentences are considered "cumulative punishment" and therefore are forbidden.

Whether two statutory crimes are the **"same offense"** for purposes of this bar on cumulative punishments at a single trial is **not** determined by the same standard used for purposes of the double jeopardy bar on successive prosecutions. For successive prosecution purposes, the *Blockburger* test is controlling. See section A.4 above. For cumulative punishment purposes, the sole question is **whether the legislature intended to authorize cumulative punishment.** "With respect to cumulative sentences imposed at a single trial, the Double Jeopardy Clause **does no more than prevent . . . greater punishment than the legislature intended.**" Missouri v. Hunter, 459 U.S. 359, 103 S. Ct. 673, 74 L. Ed. 2d 535 (1983). Consequently, the two offenses are the **"same" only if the legislature did not intend them to be punished cumulatively.**

The *Blockburger* test is a *guide* to legislative intent. Albernaz v. United States; Missouri v. Hunter. If two offenses are the same under that test, there is a presumption that the legislature **did not intend** cumulative punishment. Multiple sentences would be contrary to both legislative intent and the Fifth Amendment. See Rutledge v. United States, — U.S. —, 116 S. Ct. 1241, 134 L. Ed. 2d 419 (1996). If two offenses are not the same under *Blockburger*, there is a presumption that the legislature **did intend** cumulative punishment. Multiple sentences are constitutional. Either presumption, however, can be rebutted by evidence of a contrary legislative intent. If two offenses are the same under *Blockburger* but there is evidence of a legislative intent to punish them cumulatively, it is constitutional to impose two sentences after one trial. Missouri v. Hunter. If two offenses are not the same under *Blockburger* but there is evidence that the legislature did not intend to authorize cumulative punishment, two sentences would be invalid. In sum, the scope of double jeopardy protection against cumulative punishment at one trial is wholly dictated by the intent of the legislature.

 # EXAMPLE AND ANALYSIS

Brenda was arrested near a church that had been burned to the ground. The pastor was killed in the blaze. Brenda was charged with and convicted of both arson and felony murder based on the killing in the course of the arson. Are sentences for the felony murder and the arson constitutional?

Possibly. The two offenses are the same under *Blockburger* because arson does not require proof of any element that is not also included in felony murder based on the arson. Therefore, a presumption arises that the legislature did not intend cumulative punishment. If the legislature did not intend it, then cumulative punishment is neither statutorily nor constitutionally permitted. However, if there is proof that the legislature intended cumulative punishment, the Fifth Amendment is not violated by such punishment.

3. Prohibition on Multiple Punishments Imposed After Separate Proceedings

As discussed in the previous subsection, a legislature can authorize multiple punishments for two offenses that are the same under the *Blockburger* test **if** the punishments are imposed at a **single trial.** However, a legislature cannot authorize multiple punishment for two offenses that are the same under *Blockburger* **if** the punishments are imposed after **separate trials.** See United States v. Halper, 490 U.S. 435, 109 S. Ct. 1892, 104 L. Ed. 2d 487 (1989); Department of Revenue of Montana v. Kurth Ranch, 511 U.S. 767, 114 S. Ct. 1937, 128 L. Ed. 2d 767 (1994). If both trials are criminal, this multiple punishment protection is superfluous because the bar on "successive prosecutions" will preclude the second trial and thus the second punishment. If one of the trials is "civil," however, it cannot constitute a "jeopardy." See section A.1 above (discussing the meaning of "jeopardy"). The safeguard against "multiple punishment" is the only available double jeopardy protection in that situation.

a.   Standards for determining whether a sanction is punishment for double jeopardy purposes. The protection provided by this branch of double jeopardy doctrine depends ultimately on whether a state-imposed sanction is properly characterized as "punishment." See United States v. Halper; Department of Revenue of Montana v. Kurth Ranch. The question is whether a particular sanction is ***"so punitive as to constitute punishment for the purposes of the Double Jeopardy Clause."*** United States v. Ursery, — U.S. —, 116 S. Ct. 2135, 135 L. Ed. 2d 549 (1996). On the one hand, a sanction **may not be** punishment for double jeopardy purposes even though it has some "punitive aspects" and does constitute "punishment" for purposes of a different constitutional provision. Id. On the other hand, a sanction **can be** punishment even though it results from a "civil" proceeding and even though the legislature did not intend it to be punitive. See United States v. Halper.

The precedents in this area are not easily summarized. The Supreme Court's analysis has varied depending on the kind of sanction at issue. It seems fair to say that there is no single, dispositive standard for determining whether a sanction is punishment. Pertinent criteria include the **intent of the legislature,** the **history** of the particular type of sanction, and the **character of the sanction.**

   i.   Intent of the legislature. If a legislature intends a sanction to be punitive, it will constitute punishment. The absence of a punitive intent, however, does not preclude the conclusion that a sanction is punitive in character. See United States v. Ursery (treating legislative intent as an initial, but not dispositive, inquiry).

   When legislative intent is not made explicit, it can be gleaned from a variety of criteria, including **the nature and characteristics of a proceeding, the bases for imposing a sanction,** and **the inconsistency between the legislative label and the sanction's nature.**

EXAMPLES AND ANALYSIS

In United States v. Ursery, the Court found that the legislature intended civil forfeitures to be remedial, not punitive, because they had a civil title, were "in rem" in form, and were surrounded by procedural mechanisms of a sort ordinarily associated with civil actions.

In *Kurth Ranch*, the Court suggested that a supposed "property tax" had a "penal and prohibitory intent" because it hinged on the commission of a crime, was exacted only after arrest, was imposed on an activity that was "completely forbidden," and was levied on goods not owned or possessed by the taxpayer.

---

ii. **Historical understanding of the sanction.** The **historical and traditional understanding** of a particular sanction is also relevant. The fact that a sanction has historically been viewed as **"civil and remedial"** rather than **"criminal or punitive"** can indicate that the sanction is not punishment for Fifth Amendment purposes. United States v. Ursery. Moreover, the fact that prior **precedents** have vindicated the historical understanding of a sanction as nonpunitive can also be influential. Id.

iii. **Character of the sanction.** The most important criterion is probably the **character of the sanction.** If the nature of the sanction and the purposes it serves are punitive, it should qualify as punishment. If the nature of the sanction and purposes it serves are nonpunitive—if they are remedial, for example—the sanction should not be classified as punishment.

A "civil . . . sanction constitutes punishment **when the sanction . . . serves the goals of punishment, . . . retribution and deterrence.**" United States v. Halper. When the purpose or effect of a sanction is to punish—to impose hardship in order to make an offender suffer for a wrong done to society and to deter both the offender and others from future wrongdoing—a sanction will qualify as punishment. In addition, the facts that a sanction results from an "in personam" proceeding against an individual, is based on a criminal act, and requires proof of "scienter" can all indicate a punitive character. See United States v. Ursery.

If a sanction serves **"remedial purposes,"** it is **not punishment.** United States v. Halper; United States v. Ursery. "Remedial" purposes can include **compensation** of the state for losses incurred and the expenses of investigation and detection; **the removal of illegal or regulated items from circulation** in society; **the confis-**

cation of property used in violation of the law; the prevention of profit from illegal acts; or the deterrence of certain activities or abatement of a nuisance.

For a **"compensatory"** sanction to be remedial the amount of the sanction does not have to be precisely equal to the government's losses and expenses. Because the government is entitled to "rough remedial justice," a remedial sanction can be an "approximation" of the state's losses. United States v. Halper. However, if a purportedly compensatory sanction "bears no rational relation to the goal of compensating the government for its loss" and is seriously "disproportionate" to that loss, the sanction will be considered punishment. Id. Thus, in *Halper*, a civil compensatory sanction was found to be "punishment" because it was so much larger than any potential government losses or expenses that it could not be explained as "remedial" and had to be considered "retributive" and "deterrent."

Even though **"deterrence"** is a goal of punishment, it is also an acceptable "remedial" purpose. This can be true despite the fact that the activity sought to be deterred is also criminalized conduct. United States v. Ursery.

While most nonpunitive civil sanctions are remedial in one of the ways listed above, a sanction need not be "remedial" to avoid the double jeopardy ban on multiple punishments. It must only be "nonpunitive." Thus, a sanction that does not serve remedial purposes but is not punitive in character—a true revenue-raising measure, for example—will not come within the bar on multiple punishments.

In addition, the fact that a sanction results from an "in rem" proceeding can be a further indication of a "remedial" character. Id. Finally, even though a sanction is tied to criminal acts, it is not necessarily punitive. Id.

 # EXAMPLE AND ANALYSIS

In United States v. Ursery, the Court held that civil forfeitures under three different statutes were remedial in character, not punitive. The Court found it "most significant" that the forfeitures served "important nonpunitive goals"—encouraging property owners to take care to avoid using their property for illegal purposes and insuring that persons did not profit from illegal acts. Moreover, the sanctions were the product of "in rem" proceedings that did not require proof of a guilty mind. Neither the "deterrent" aspects of the forfeitures nor the fact that imposition was tied to illegal acts precluded the conclusion that the sanctions were remedial.

---

b. **Individualized, case-by-case assessment versus categorical evaluation of sanctions.** A **civil, "compensatory" penalty** such as a fine must be **judged on an individualized, case-by-case basis.** See id. To determine whether a civil penalty is remedial or punitive, the amount of the specific penalty imposed in a case is measured against the allegedly remedial purposes served by the penalty. In the "rare" case in which the magnitude of the sanction is seriously **"disproportionate"** to its remedial objectives and the **sanction cannot be explained as "solely remedial"** but **"can only be explained as also serving retributive or deterrent purposes,"** the sanction **will be deemed punitive. To the extent that it exceeds the legitimate remedial objectives,** it is subject to the double jeopardy bar on multiple punishments after separate trials. To avoid unconstitutionality the penalty must be **reduced** to a level at least roughly proportionate to the compensatory purposes it is designed to serve. United States v. Halper.

Thus, in United States v. Halper, the Court concluded that a $130,000 civil fine was so disproportionate to any losses caused by the defendant and the expenses incurred by the federal government that it could not be considered "solely remedial" and had to be considered "punishment." Because the sanction was "not rationally related to the goal of making the government whole," it had to be reduced to a proper level.

Other kinds of sanctions are **judged categorically.** In determining whether these are punitive, courts must look to the type of sanction imposed rather than the individual sanction imposed in a specific case. Thus, in *Kurth Ranch*, a purported "tax" on the possession and storage of dangerous drugs was deemed punishment because of the general nature of the tax and without regard to its application to particular individuals. Moreover, in *Ursery*, civil forfeitures under three different statutes were found to be nonpunitive without regard to their size or their impact on particular individuals.

Note: Earlier, it was noted that there would seem to be no "general" standard for determining whether civil sanctions are punishment. In *Ursery*, the Supreme Court used a "two-part test" to determine whether civil forfeitures are "punishment" for double jeopardy purposes. The **first** inquiry is **"whether [the legislature] intended proceedings . . . to be civil or criminal."** The **second** is **"whether the proceedings are so punitive in fact"** that they **" 'may not legitimately be viewed as civil in nature,' "** despite the legislative intent. The Court may intend this test for use as a general analytical tool for determining whether sanctions that are judged *categorically* are punishment. On the other hand, the Court may intend the test for use only in "civil forfeiture" cases and not as a general standard for other categories of sanctions.

c. **Possible additional limitations on the scope of the protection against multiple punishment at separate trials.** The prohibition on multiple punishment imposed in separate criminal and civil trials can apply only when the two sanctions are imposed **"for the same offense."** The Double Jeopardy Clause is not concerned with multiple punishment for "different" offenses. For purposes of this strand of double jeopardy protection, the *Blockburger* test is almost certainly controlling. See section A.4 above. If two offenses are "the same" under *Blockburger*, multiple punishments after separate trials are forbidden despite a legislative intent to impose them.

The cases in which the Supreme Court found violations of the bar on multiple punishment after separate trials involved **criminal punishments followed by civil punishment.** See United States v. Halper; Department of Revenue of Montana v. Kurth Ranch. If the order were reversed—that is, if the civil sanction preceded a criminal punishment—logic would seem to suggest the same result. No matter what the order, multiple punishment is constitutionally forbidden. Nonetheless, in *Kurth Ranch*, a majority specifically held **open** the **question whether a reversal of the order of the trials could lead to a different constitutional conclusion.**

Finally, in *Halper* and *Kurth Ranch*, the **civil trials** that resulted in punishment were **not instituted until after criminal convictions had been obtained.** Some lower courts have held that if the government pursues criminal and civil sanctions either simultaneously or very close in time, the two proceedings can be treated as a single trial and "multiple punishment" is permissible if the legislature intends it. See section B.2 above. It is uncertain whether the Supreme Court would endorse the view that separate trials may be treated as a single trial for Fifth Amendment purposes.

4. **Exception to the General Rule Allowing Higher Sentences After Retrial: The Doctrine of Bullington v. Missouri**

Ordinarily, when a defendant is retried and resentenced after a successful appeal, double jeopardy principles do not bar a higher sentence. See section B.1 above. The only double jeopardy requirement is that the defendant be given credit for time served. There is one **"exception"** to this general rule, that is, one situation in which the double jeopardy protection against "successive prosecutions" (*not* the protection against "multiple punishment") guards against a higher sentence. When an accused is put in jeopardy of the death penalty at a **trial-like capital sentencing proceeding** and is **acquitted of the death penalty,** he may not be subjected to a second capital sentencing trial—that is, he may not once again be put in jeopardy of the death penalty. Bullington v. Missouri, 451 U.S. 430, 101 S. Ct. 1852, 68 L. Ed. 2d 270 (1981). There is **an absolute bar to a second capital sentencing trial.** Two significant questions arise about the scope of the holding in *Bullington*: (1) Does it ever apply to noncapital sentencing proceedings? and (2) What is essential to make a sentencing proceeding sufficiently trial-like?

a. **Applicability of the *Bullington* exception to noncapital sentencing proceedings.** It is unclear whether the *Bullington* holding is confined to **capital sentencing trials.** One view holds that the successive prosecution strand of double jeopardy protection applies only when the accused is placed at risk of death. The contrary view holds that if a noncapital sentencing proceeding is sufficiently trial-like the bar against being put in jeopardy of a higher sentence at a second sentencing proceeding is applicable. This issue remains open.

b. **Requirements for a trial-like sentencing proceeding.** In *Bullington*, the Supreme Court concluded that the double jeopardy protection against successive prosecutions applied because Missouri's capital sentencing scheme had distinct differences from ordinary sentencing proceedings. The Court relied on several features that gave the proceeding "the hallmarks of [a] trial on guilt or innocence."

    First, the "jury . . . was **not given unbounded discretion** to select an appropriate punishment within a wide range authorized by statute." Instead, at a "separate hearing . . . the jury was presented both a **choice between two alternatives and standards to guide the making of the choice.**" Id. Ordinarily, a sentencing authority chooses any sentence within a prescribed range according to vague, general criteria that guide the choice. In *Bullington*, the choice between the death penalty and a life sentence was analogous to the choice between not guilty and guilty. Moreover, the jury's choice had to be guided by specified aggravating and mitigating circumstances, by whether the aggravating circumstances justified the death penalty, and by whether the mitigating circumstances outweighed the aggravating circumstances. These concrete criteria were considered similar to the standards that guide guilt-innocence determinations.

    Second, "the prosecution [did not] simply recommend what it felt to be an appropriate punishment [but instead] **undertook the burden of establishing certain facts beyond a reasonable doubt** in its quest to obtain the harsher of the two alternative verdicts." Id. The jury could impose the death penalty only if it "designate[d] in writing the aggravating circumstance or circumstances it [found] **beyond a reasonable doubt**" and was "convinced **beyond a reasonable doubt** that any aggravating circumstance or circumstances that it [found were] sufficient to warrant the imposition of the death penalty." Ordinary sentencings do not involve any burdens of proof, much less "beyond a reasonable doubt," a standard uniquely associated with guilt-innocence determinations in criminal trials.

Finally, the capital sentencing proceeding was in other "relevant respects . . . like the . . . trial on the issue of guilt or innocence" and unlike a typical sentencing. It involved a "separate hearing" at which the accused had the **opportunity to present additional evidence** and had the entitlement to a **jury determination** that had to be **unanimous** in order to impose the death penalty. Id.

The *Bullington* majority did not specify which features are required to make a sentencing proceeding sufficiently trial-like to qualify for the protection against successive sentencings. The issue remains open. Because any capital sentencing is likely to qualify, the issue is likely to arise only if *Bullington* governs noncapital sentencing.

c. **Effects of the *Bullington* prohibition on successive sentencing proceedings.** If a sentencing proceeding is governed by *Bullington*, any outcome that qualifies as an **"acquittal of a sentence"** for double jeopardy purposes **will bar a second jeopardy for that sentence.** See section A.2.a above. In Arizona v. Rumsey, 467 U.S. 203, 104 S. Ct. 2305, 81 L. Ed. 2d 164 (1984), for example, a trial judge erroneously interpreted the meaning of "pecuniary gain," an aggravating circumstance under Arizona law. If the judge had correctly interpreted the law, a death sentence could have been justified. The error, however, led to imposition of a life sentence. Even though it was rooted in a serious error of law, the judge's ruling was an "implicit acquittal" of the death penalty. Because an acquittal terminates jeopardy, the Supreme Court deemed a second jeopardy for the death penalty unconstitutional.

Presumably all the other doctrines that govern the attachment and termination of jeopardy at trial also apply to sentencing proceedings within the scope of the *Bullington* doctrine. See sections A.1 and A.2 above.

 EXAMPLE AND ANALYSIS

Midway through Jenny Mae's capital sentencing trial, one of the jurors becomes ill. When the prosecutor objects to replacing the juror with the sole remaining alternate, the judge declares a mistrial over the defendant's objection. Jenny Mae is then subjected to a second sentencing proceeding and is given a death sentence. She appeals the sentence, claiming a double jeopardy violation. How should the court rule?

There is a good basis for alleging no "manifest necessity" for the mistrial. If the alternate juror was qualified, there is no good reason why she could not have replaced the sick juror. Assuming no manifest necessity, the court should probably lower the sentence to life imprisonment. Jeopardy for the death penalty attached; it then terminated when the mistrial was declared over the defendant's objection. A second jeopardy for the death sentence is impermissible under *Bullington*. When a mistrial is erroneously declared during the guilt-innocence phase, a defendant may not be prosecuted at all for the offense—that is, she is entirely free of liability. When a mistrial is erroneously declared at a capital sentencing, however, a life sentence—the best result that the accused could have gotten from the jury—is surely appropriate.

REVIEW QUESTIONS AND ANSWERS

Question: Murray was indicted for possession of an explosive device and conspiracy to bomb a government building. The first government witness was Perry, a government informant. Just after Perry took the witness stand, a marshall came into the courtroom and announced that a bomb threat had been received and had to be taken seriously. The judge angrily declared a mistrial. Can Murray be retried?

Answer: The constitutionality of retrying Murray depends on facts not provided. The first question is whether jeopardy attached. If it was a jury trial, jeopardy would have attached when the jury was sworn. If it was a bench trial, attachment required at least the taking of the oath by the witness and may have required the beginning of actual testimony. The facts suggest that there has been no testimony. It is unclear whether the oath had been administered to Perry. If jeopardy did not attach, Murray has never been in jeopardy. Retrial is constitutional. If jeopardy did attach, Murray was in jeopardy once. A retrial would be an impermissible second jeopardy *unless* there was "manifest necessity" for the mistrial. On the facts provided, it is unlikely that there was a high degree of need to declare a mistrial so quickly.

Question: Todd was charged with first-degree sexual assault, an offense that requires "sexual intercourse by force or violence and either the use or threatened use of a deadly weapon or physical injury to the victim." After a jury trial, he was convicted of second-degree sexual assault, defined as "sexual intercourse by force or violence." Todd appealed, and the conviction was reversed on the basis of "improper juror conduct." The government claimed, on appeal, that it had been prevented from having a full and fair opportunity to convict Todd of first-degree sexual assault because the trial judge had erroneously excluded evidence pertinent to establishing the victim's physical injury. The appellate court agreed. Over Todd's objection, he was retried for and convicted of first degree sexual assault. He now appeals that conviction. Is he entitled to relief?

Answer: Yes. In the first trial, Todd was implicitly acquitted of first-degree sexual assault when he was convicted of the lesser included offense. Even though the acquittal was based on erroneous evidentiary rulings, it terminates jeopardy for the greater offense (first-degree sexual assault). The retrial should have been confined to the lesser offense (second-degree sexual assault). Although the trial violated Todd's rights, the presumptive remedy is not another new trial but instead a reduction of the conviction to the lesser offense of second-degree sexual assault—which the jury necessarily found proven when it convicted Todd of first-degree sexual assault. Todd is entitled to a third trial for the lesser offense only if he can demonstrate a "reasonable probability" that he would not have been convicted of that offense if the jeopardy-barred greater offense had not been "present" at the trial. One way he might establish such a probability is by documenting the evidence that was relevant only to the greater offense and would not have been admissible at a trial solely for the lesser offense. Evidence of the victim's injury might fall into that category and could help support a claim that Todd is entitled to a new trial.

Question: Jenny participated in a "drag race" while under the influence of narcotics. She lost control of her vehicle and crashed into a van, killing two members of a family and severely injuring a third. Jenny was charged with driving under the influence of narcotics. She was convicted and sentenced to two years in prison. Shortly thereafter, she was charged with two counts of manslaughter. There are three different ways that the prosecution intends to prove that Jenny committed manslaughter: killing during the course of the misdemeanor of driving under the influence; killing during the course of the misdemeanor of participating in a drag race; and killing with gross negligence. Is the manslaughter prosecution constitutional?

Answer: Yes, but only two of the ways of proving manslaughter are permissible. Driving under the influence would be a lesser included offense of misdemeanor-manslaughter based on driving under the influence. The two offenses are the same. Because Jenny has already been convicted of the lesser offense and that conviction has not been reversed, she may not be put in jeopardy for the greater offense. Under the controlling *Blockburger* test, the other two ways of proving manslaughter are constitutionally legitimate. Each of them contains an element that is not included in driving under the influence and driving under the influence contains an element not included in each of them.

Question: Yancy was charged with possession of cocaine, possession of cocaine with intent to distribute, and furnishing cocaine to a minor. After a bench trial, the judge convicted him of all three offenses and sentenced him to two years in prison for possession, five years for possession with intent to distribute, and five years for furnishing cocaine to a minor. The two five-year sentences were to run concurrently, but the two-year sentence for possession was to run consecutively to the five-year sentences. Does Yancy have a valid claim that he has suffered unconstitutional multiple punishment?

Answer: Yancy may have a valid claim. The Double Jeopardy Clause forbids multiple punishments after a single trial—whether concurrent or consecutive—only if the legislature did not intend multiple punishment. When two offenses are the same under the *Blockburger* standard, it is presumed that the legislature did not intend multiple punishment. The crime of possession has no elements that are not included in possession with intent to distribute. Therefore, multiple punishment for those two offenses is presumptively prohibited. It is permissible only if the prosecution shows that the legislature intended multiple punishment.

The multiple punishments for possession with intent to distribute (and/or possession) and furnishing cocaine to a minor are presumptively permissible because the two offenses are not the same under *Blockburger*. Each requires proof of an element that the other does not. Multiple punishment is barred only in the unlikely case that the defendant establishes that the legislature did not intend multiple punishment for those offenses.

21 APPEALS OF CRIMINAL CONVICTIONS

CHAPTER OVERVIEW

The last two chapters address the final two phases of the adjudicatory process in criminal cases—direct appeals of and collateral challenges to convictions. The latter is by far the more complex and controversial topic. The former is the subject of this chapter.

A **direct appeal of a conviction** is "the final step in the adjudication of guilt or innocence." Evitts v. Lucey, 469 U.S. 387, 105 S. Ct. 830, 83 L. Ed. 2d 821 (1985). The creation of processes for the appeal of convictions reflects an unwillingness "to curtail drastically a defendant's liberty unless a second judicial decisionmaker, the appellate court, [is] convinced that [a] conviction [is] in accord with law." Id. An appeal is an assertion that error in the trial process renders a "conviction . . . unlawful" and requires reversal. Id. Some appeals assert errors that bar retrial; most posit errors permit new trials.

In most states and in the federal system, a defendant takes an initial appeal to an "intermediate" court of appeals. After an appeal to an intermediate appellate court, some defendants have the **right to further appellate review** by the highest appellate court in the jurisdiction. Most must petition the highest court for **discretionary appellate review** —for example, by writ of certiorari. State defendants may seek review by the state supreme court and, ultimately, by the United States Supreme Court. Federal defendants proceed directly from the courts of appeal to the United States Supreme Court.

This chapter covers the following

- **The defendant's right to appeal a conviction and the government's inability to appeal an acquittal.** Defendants **do not have a constitutional right to**

appeal a conviction. Rights to appeal are granted by state and federal statutes. Because of the defendant's guarantee against "double jeopardy," the government cannot have a verdict of acquittal overturned on appeal.

- **The defendant's rights on appeal.** While the Constitution does not grant a right to appeal, it does afford certain rights to defendants who exercise their statutory right to appeal. The **Equal Protection Clause** ensures the availability of transcripts and legal counsel for indigent appellants. The **Due Process Clause** guarantees the effective assistance of counsel for all appellants and demands fundamentally fair appellate processes.

- **General principles of appellate review.** Several general principles of appellate review merit brief discussion. These include the final judgment rule; the general bar on government appeal of criminal case rulings and the statutory allowance of government appeals in limited circumstances; the mootness restriction; and the general rule against reviewing issues not raised at trial and its exception—the plain error doctrine.

- **The retroactivity of rules of constitutional law.** When a new rule of constitutional law is announced, one question is whether that rule of law is "retroactive"—whether the rule governs cases that have commenced, but not become final, prior to the date of its announcement. The answer today is simple: New rules of constitutional law retroactively apply to all cases that are not final at the time the rules are announced. Consequently, appellate courts are required to apply those rules to cases on direct appeal.

- **The harmless error doctrine.** Even if a conviction is tainted by error, it will not be reversed by an appellate court if the error is **harmless.** There are three different categories of error for harmless error purposes—nonconstitutional error, constitutional "trial error," and constitutional "structural error." Nonconstitutional errors are judged by the most generous standard and are most likely to be deemed harmless. Constitutional trial errors are evaluated according to a considerably stricter standard and are less likely to be harmless. Constitutional structural errors cannot be harmless; they lead to "automatic reversal."

- **The guarantee against governmental vindictiveness for exercising the right to appeal.** The **Due Process Clause** bars the government—both courts and prosecutors—from retaliating against an accused for exercising the right to appeal a conviction. Courts may not respond **"vindictively"** by "increasing" sentences upon reconviction; prosecutors may not respond by elevating the charges at the retrial. In many circumstances, to establish a due process violation the accused has to prove "actual vindictiveness," but in certain instances a "rebuttable presumption of vindictiveness" arises.

A.   THE DEFENDANT'S RIGHT TO APPEAL AND THE GOVERNMENT'S INABILITY TO APPEAL

This section addresses the source of the **defendant's right to seek appellate reversal** of a flawed conviction and the source of the **government's inability to overturn an erroneous acquittal.**

1.   The Defendant's Right to Appeal a Conviction

"There is . . . **no constitutional right to appeal**" a conviction. Jones v. Barnes, 463 U.S. 745, 103 S. Ct. 3308, 77 L. Ed. 2d 987 (1983); McKane v. Durston, 153 U.S. 684, 14 S. Ct. 913, 38 L. Ed. 867 (1894). Instead, the right to appeal criminal convictions is granted by state and federal statutes. **All jurisdictions provide** defendants with **the right to at least one direct appeal** of a conviction. The availability of further appellate review depends on the statutes in each jurisdiction. At the end of the line for every defendant, both state and federal, is the remote possibility of discretionary review by the United States Supreme Court on writ of certiorari.

2.   The Government's Inability to Obtain Appellate Reversal of an Acquittal

The government has no entitlement to seek appellate reversal of a ruling in a criminal case unless a statute provides one. Legislatures have created some opportunities for the government to secure appellate review and correction of adverse rulings in criminal cases. See section C.2 below. Their power to do so, however, is severely constrained by the constitutional guarantee against double jeopardy.

An acquittal terminates a defendant's "jeopardy" for an offense and bars retrial for that offense. Even if egregious legal or factual errors thwarted the prosecution's efforts to obtain a justified conviction and led to an unjustified acquittal, **appellate reversal for the purpose of retrial** is impermissible. See Chapter 20, section A.2.a. This does not necessarily mean that **appellate consideration** of the government's claim of error is unconstitutional. It is arguable that **an appeal itself is not forbidden** because it does not put the defendant in "jeopardy." In the appellate court, the defendant is not put at risk of conviction, has no obligation to participate, and can suffer no consequences if the state's claim of error is sustained. See Smalis v. Pennsylvania, 476 U.S. 140, 106 S. Ct. 1745, 90 L. Ed. 2d 116 (1986) (observing that if "a successful postacquittal appeal by the prosecution *would lead to proceedings that violate the Double Jeopardy Clause,* the appeal has no proper purpose" and "would frustrate" the defendant's interest "in having an end to the proceedings").

If a government appeal following an acquittal is constitutional so long as neither a reversal nor further jeopardy is contemplated, a state could be afforded an opportunity for appellate court "advisory opinions" about the validity of trial court rulings. Such opinions could serve to clarify the law and prevent future errors. See, e.g., State v. Clark, 346 N.W.2d 510 (Iowa 1984) (validating government's appellate claim that trial court had erroneously instructed jury regarding "mistake of law" despite the fact that the defendants had been acquitted by a jury).

B. THE DEFENDANT'S RIGHTS ON APPEAL

Although a convicted defendant has no constitutional right to an appeal, "if a State has created appellate courts as 'an integral part of the . . . system for finally adjudicating the guilt or innocence of the defendant,' " it must conduct the appellate process in ways that comport with the Constitution. Evitts v. Lucey. Two Fourteenth Amendment guarantees—the **Due Process Clause** and the **Equal Protection Clause**—provide "a criminal appellant pursuing a first appeal as of right certain minimum safeguards necessary to make that appeal adequate and effective." Id.

1. Entitlement to Due Process on Appeal

The **Due Process Clause guarantees** "**fairness** between the state and the individual dealing with the state." Ross v. Moffitt, 417 U.S. 600, 94 S. Ct. 2437, 41 L. Ed. 2d 341 (1974). When an appeal of a conviction is the final step in adjudicating a defendant's guilt or innocence, a state **violates due process if** it decides the appeal in a way that is "**arbitrary** with respect to the issues involved" **or does not afford** the appellant "**a fair opportunity** to obtain adjudication on the merits of his appeal." Evitts v. Lucey. Due process guarantees the defendant "**meaningful access to the appellate system**" and "**an adequate opportunity to present his claims fairly** in the context of the State's appellate process." Ross v. Moffitt.

More specifically, **in a first appeal as of right, due process guarantees every defendant a right to the assistance of counsel.** Douglas v. California, 372 U.S. 353, 83 S. Ct. 814, 9 L. Ed. 2d 811 (1963). Moreover, counsel must render **effective assistance.** Evitts v. Lucey. In addition, if a transcript of trial court proceedings is necessary for meaningful or "adequate appellate review," the Due Process Clause guarantees appellants either a transcript or some "other means" that will "afford[ ] adequate and effective appellate review." Griffin v. Illinois, 351 U.S. 12, 76 S. Ct. 585, 100 L. Ed.891 (1956).

2. Guarantee of Equal Protection on Appeal

The **Equal Protection Clause** also regulates the appellate process. " '**Equal protection**' . . . **emphasizes disparity in treatment** by a State between classes of individuals whose situations are arguably indistinguishable." Ross v. Moffitt. States cannot subject criminal appellants to "**invidious discriminations**" that result in deprivations of the "equality [that is] demanded by the Fourteenth Amendment." Douglas v. California; Griffin v. Illinois. While "[a]bsolute equality is not required," Douglas v. California, states violate the guarantee of equal protection when they unjustifiably deny **one class of individuals** "**meaningful access** to the appellate system" **or** "**an adequate opportunity** to present [appellate] claims." Ross v. Moffitt.

The Court has struck down distinctions in the appellate process based on **financial status,** finding "invidious discrimination" when indigent persons are "effectively denie[d] . . . [the] adequate appellate review [that is] accorded to all who have money." Griffin v. Illinois. An indigent is entitled to more than "a meaningless ritual [if] the rich man has a meaningful appeal." Douglas v. California. Consequently, a state denies equal protection when it fails to afford counsel to an indigent on his **first appeal as of right.** Id. It also denies equal protection when it refuses to furnish a transcript (or suitable alternative) for an indigent when a transcript is needed for adequate appellate review. Griffin v. Illinois.

 # EXAMPLE AND ANALYSIS

In Ross v. Moffitt, the Supreme Court held that indigent defendants are not entitled to appointed counsel for purposes of seeking **discretionary review** in a state supreme court or the United States Supreme Court. The demands of due process do not require counsel because the absence of counsel at that stage does not deny "meaningful access" to the system or "an adequate opportunity" to present one's claims fairly. Equal protection principles do not require counsel because indigent defendants who lack legal assistance still have "meaningful access" to the system and "a fair opportunity" to present their claims. While such defendants are not perfectly equal to those who can afford to hire lawyers, the lack of legal assistance at this stage is not a sufficient "handicap" to violate the Equal Protection Clause.

C.   GENERAL PRINCIPLES OF APPELLATE REVIEW

This section sketches some general principles that govern the appellate process. Because these principles are not rooted in constitutional commands, a jurisdiction need not follow them. Nonetheless, they are quite likely to be followed because they reflect thoughtful judgments.

1.   Final Judgment Rule and Its Exceptions

Because piecemeal appellate review is inefficient and costly, statutes typically allow defendants to appeal only from **"final judgments"** or **"final decisions."** Ordinarily an appeal cannot be taken until a defendant has been both convicted and sentenced. See Cobbledick v. United States, 309 U.S. 323, 60 S. Ct. 540, 84 L. Ed. 783 (1940) (urging that the final judgment rule be honored in federal criminal cases).

Statutes may authorize **"interlocutory appeals"** from trial court rulings prior to final judgment. Usually the trial judge is given discretion to permit or deny an interlocutory appeal of a ruling. The exercise of this discretion should be guided by the importance of getting appellate review of an issue and the costs of allowing an appeal prior to final judgment. An interlocutory appeal of rulings made well before trial is more likely to be allowed because such an appeal will not delay the trial. An interlocutory appeal of a ruling during the trial may require the judge to stay the proceedings.

The Supreme Court has recognized a **"collateral order" exception to the final judgment rule.** See Cohen v. Beneficial Industrial Loan Corp., 337 U.S. 541, 69 S. Ct. 1221, 93 L. Ed. 2d 1528 (1949). Collateral orders may be appealed. To qualify as "collateral," the order must conclusively determine the disputed question, resolve an important issue that is completely separate from the merits of the case, and be effectively unreviewable if not appealed prior to final judgment. See Coopers & Lybrand v. Livesay, 437 U.S. 463, 98 S. Ct. 2454, 57 L. Ed. 2d 351 (1978). Examples of appealable collateral orders include the denial of a pretrial motion to dismiss an indictment on double jeopardy grounds, Abney v. United States, 431 U.S. 651, 97 S. Ct. 2034, 52 L. Ed. 2d 651 (1977), and the denial of a pretrial motion to reduce bail. Stack v. Boyle, 342 U.S. 1, 72 S. Ct. 1, 96 L. Ed. 3 (1951). Denials of motions to dismiss on speedy trial or vindictive prosecution grounds are not collateral orders and may not be appealed. See United States v. MacDonald, 435 U.S. 850, 98 S. Ct. 1547, 56 L. Ed. 2d 18 (1978) (speedy trial); United States v. Hollywood Motor Car Co., 458 U.S. 263, 102 S. Ct. 3081, 73 L. Ed. 2d 754 (1982) (vindictive prosecution).

2. General Bar on Prosecution Appeals and Statutory Allowances

The Double Jeopardy Clause frequently prohibits appellate relief for the government. See section A.2 above. Traditionally, our system of criminal justice has barred prosecution appeals from rulings in criminal cases even when a reversal would not violate the double jeopardy guarantee. Over time, however, both federal and state systems have moved away from that blanket prohibition. By statute, they have provided considerable opportunities for the government to obtain appellate review of both final judgments and interlocutory orders. The governing federal provision, 18 U.S.C. §3731, has been read "to remove all statutory barriers to Government appeals and to allow appeals whenever the Constitution would permit." United States v. Wilson, 420 U.S. 332, 95 S. Ct. 1013, 43 L. Ed. 2d 232 (1975).

The federal statute and many state provisions recognize trial court discretion to permit interlocutory government appeals from pretrial rulings granting defendants' motions to suppress government evidence. In addition, the federal statute and many state provisions allow the government to seek appellate reversal of final rulings granting defendants' motions to dismiss criminal charges, motions for new trials, and motions for judgments of acquittal *after a jury has returned a guilty verdict.* The latter does not offend double jeopardy principles because a reversal would not require further proceedings but would merely lead to reinstatement of the jury's verdict. See Chapter 20, section A.3.

3. Prohibition on Appeal of Moot Cases

In general, an appellate court will not review a case that has become **moot** after the end of trial and before the appeal has been decided. A case is moot when the appellate court's decision can no longer have any consequences. A criminal appeal may be rendered moot, for example, by the fact that the accused has "fully satisfied" her sentence. In that case, an appellate reversal may not benefit the defendant. Nonetheless, a court will not necessarily dismiss an appeal as moot when the accused has served her sentence if the conviction still has actual or even possible adverse "collateral consequences" for the defendant. See Sibron v. New York, 392 U.S. 40, 88 S. Ct. 1889, 20 L. Ed. 2d 917 (1968).

4. Rule Against Review of Issues Not Raised at Trial and the "Plain Error" Doctrine

In general, a party may not have an error corrected on appeal if it was not brought to the attention of the trial court. If a party fails to raise a claim, make an objection, or seek a ruling at trial, appellate consideration may be precluded even if the trial court erred.

An appellate court will probably not apply the "failure to raise" principle if the party did not have an adequate opportunity to raise the claim at trial, if the grounds for the claim were established by a post-trial opinion, or if there was other good reason not to raise the particular issue or claim at trial. An appellate court might also allow a defendant to assert a claim that the trial court "lacked jurisdiction over the case" even though the defendant failed to raise the issue in the trial court.

Most jurisdictions follow the **"plain error" doctrine.** According to the plain error doctrine, an appellate court should reverse a conviction on the basis of a "plain error" even if it was not raised in the trial court. Federal Rule of Criminal Procedure 52(b) recognizes the plain error doctrine in the federal system. To qualify as a "plain error" under that rule, the trial court's mistake must be **clear or obvious** and **must affect substantial rights of the defendant.** If the error qualifies, the appellate court has discretion to decide the appeal and correct the error. See United States v. Olano, 507 U.S. 725, 113 S. Ct. 1770, 123 L. Ed. 2d 508 (1993). The *Olano* Court observed that appellate court discretion to correct plain error should be exercised in order to protect an innocent defendant or to "correct a plain forfeited error affecting substantial rights if the error 'seriously affect[s] the fairness, integrity, or public reputation of judicial proceedings.' "

D. RETROACTIVITY OF RULES OF CONSTITUTIONAL LAW TO CASES ON APPEAL

A "new rule" of constitutional law is sometimes announced after a criminal case has entered the adjudicatory process but before it has become final on appeal. One question for an appellate court is whether such a "new rule of law" is **"retroactive"** to a case before it—that is, whether the court should apply the new rule in resolving an appellate claim raised by a defendant. At one time, the Supreme Court recognized degrees of retroactivity, and the question whether a particular rule of law should be applied on appeal was relatively complex. See Desist v. United States, 394 U.S. 244, 89 S. Ct. 1030, 22 L. Ed. 2d 248 (1969) (Harlan, J., dissenting). Today, a simple and straightforward principle provides a single answer to the question of retroactivity on direct appeal of a criminal conviction.

According to the prevailing law, **every "new rule for the conduct of criminal prosecutions is to be applied retroactively to all cases,** state or federal, **pending on direct review or not yet final."** Griffith v. Kentucky, 479 U.S. 314, 107 S. Ct. 708, 93 L. Ed. 2d 649 (1987). The rule applies retroactively even if it is novel and even if it is a dramatic and unexpected departure from the prior law. Thus, when a case is still in the channels of "direct appellate review"—whether the appeal is a matter of right or is subject to the discretion of the court—any rule of constitutional law that is announced before the appeal is decided **must be applied to the case by the appellate court and by any other court that later considers the case.**

> **Note:** The preceding discussion is concerned only with the retroactive application of new rules to cases that have not yet been finalized on direct appeal at the time the rules are announced. The law regarding the retroactivity of "new rules" of constitutional law to cases that have become final before the rules are announced is much more complicated. That law is discussed in the next chapter in connection with the subject of "collateral challenges."

EXAMPLES AND ANALYSIS

1. In Griffith v. Kentucky, a defendant was convicted of conspiracy to possess narcotics with intent to distribute them. While his petition for certiorari to the Supreme Court was still pending, the Court decided Batson v. Kentucky, 476 U.S. 79, 106 S. Ct. 1712, 90 L. Ed. 2d 69 (1986). The holding of *Batson*—that a defendant could succeed with an equal protection claim based solely on a prosecutor's racially discriminatory use of peremptory juror challenges in his case—was a surprising, indeed, a revolutionary, "new rule" of constitutional law. Nonetheless, because it was announced before the

defendant's conviction had become final, the Supreme Court held that it was retroactively applicable to his case.

2. In Shea v. Louisiana, 470 U.S. 51, 105 S. Ct. 1065, 84 L. Ed. 2d 38 (1985), the Supreme Court decided Edwards v. Arizona, 451 U.S. 477, 101 S. Ct. 1880, 68 L. Ed. 2d 378 (1981), while the defendant's conviction was on appeal to the Louisiana Supreme Court. In *Edwards*, the Supreme Court interpreted *Miranda* to preclude valid waivers of rights when the police "initiate" communications following a suspect's request for counsel. Even though *Edwards* announced a "new rule" of constitutional law, that rule governed the defendant's case because his conviction had not yet become final—it was in still in the channel of direct appellate review.

E. HARMLESS ERROR ON APPEAL

To guard against the waste of judicial resources, appellate courts will not reverse convictions based on **harmless error** in the trial court. All nonconstitutional errors and most constitutional errors are subject to harmless error analysis on appeal.

1. Nonconstitutional Errors: Federal and State Standards

Some errors do not implicate the Constitution. For example, a court might violate a rule of evidence by allowing the government to introduce inadmissible character evidence. The Supreme Court has said that a **nonconstitutional error** in federal court **is harmless** if the court "is sure that **the error did not influence the jury, or had but very slight effect.**" Kotteakos v. United States, 328 U.S. 750, 66 S. Ct. 1239, 90 L. Ed. 1557 (1946). An error **is not harmless** if it "had **substantial and injurious effect or influence in determining the jury's verdict.**" Id. State courts have formulated the applicable harmlessness standard for such errors in a variety of ways.

2. Constitutional "Trial Errors": The "Beyond a Reasonable Doubt" Standard

Many errors are of constitutional stature. For example, a judge might violate due process by allowing the government to introduce a coerced confession or might violate the Sixth Amendment by improperly restricting defense counsel's ability to consult with the accused. Some constitutional errors may be harmless while others can never be. The "common thread" among constitutional deprivations that are subject to harmlessness review is that they involve " 'trial error'—**error which occur[s] during the presentation of the case to the jury.**" Arizona v. Fulminante, 499 U.S. 279, 111 S. Ct. 1246, 113 L. Ed. 2d 302 (1991). For example, if a trial court mistakenly allows the introduction of unconstitutionally obtained evidence, it has committed a **"trial error"** that is subject to harmlessness review. Arizona v. Fulminante (the admission of a coerced confession in violation of the Due Process

Clause may be harmless error); United States v. Wade, 388 U.S. 218, 87 S. Ct. 1926, 18 L. Ed. 2d 1149 (1967) (the admission of an identification obtained at a lineup at which the accused was not accorded his Sixth Amendment entitlement to counsel may be harmless).

On appeal, **constitutional trial errors** are governed by a more demanding harmless error standard than nonconstitutional errors. The government must show that the error was **harmless beyond a reasonable doubt.** Chapman v. California, 386 U.S. 18, 87 S. Ct. 824, 17 L. Ed. 2d 705 (1967); Arizona v. Fulminante. An appellate court must reverse a conviction if, after reviewing the entire record, it has at least a reasonable doubt about whether the trier of fact would have convicted the defendant if the error had not occurred. See Chapter 22, section G (discussing the different harmless error standard governing constitutional trial errors on collateral review in federal court).

3. Constitutional "Structural Defects": Automatically Reversible Errors

A small number of constitutional errors are **not** subject to harmlessness review. When such an error is found on appeal, **reversal is automatic.** Constitutional violations that fall within this limited category are those that result in **"structural defect[s that] affect[ ] the framework within which the trial proceeds."** Arizona v. Fulminante. A "structural defect" is one that deprives an accused of a basic safeguard without which "a criminal trial **cannot reliably serve its function as a vehicle for determination of guilt or innocence."** Id.

Constitutional errors that are not subject to harmless error review include various deprivations of the right to assistance of counsel at trial, the failure to instruct a jury regarding the reasonable doubt standard, trial by a judge who is not impartial, an unlawful exclusion of members of the defendant's race from the grand jury that indicts her, denial of the right of self-representation, and denial of the right to a public trial.

F. CONSTITUTIONAL PROTECTION AGAINST GOVERNMENTAL VINDICTIVENESS BASED ON APPEAL OF A CONVICTION

Following most successful appeals, defendants are subject to retrial. The **Due Process Clause** imposes certain limitations on the prosecutor's authority to charge a more serious offense at the retrial and on the trial judge's power to impose a higher sentence upon reconviction.

1. Due Process Clause Protection Against Vindictiveness

The Due Process Clause guarantees fundamental fairness in the conduct of criminal prosecutions. Because it is unfair to punish or penalize an accused for exercising his rights, "**[d]ue process of law . . . requires that vindictiveness** against the defendant for having successfully attacked his first conviction **must play no part in the sentence he receives** after a new trial." North Carolina v. Pearce, 395 U.S. 711, 89 S. Ct. 2072, 23 L. Ed. 2d 656

(1969). A judge may impose a higher sentence after reconviction, but not *because* the defendant appealed an initial conviction. Similarly, a prosecutor may not vindictively "up the ante" by filing a more serious charge *because* a defendant exercised the right to appeal. Blackledge v. Perry, 417 U.S. 21, 94 S. Ct. 2098, 40 L. Ed. 2d 628 (1974).

A due process violation is established by proof that **"actual vindictiveness"** played a role in a sentencing or charging decision. See Wasman v. United States, 468 U.S. 559, 104 S. Ct. 3217, 82 L. Ed. 2d 424 (1984) (defendant entitled to relief upon showing of actual vindictiveness in resentencing); United States v. Goodwin, 457 U.S. 368, 102 S. Ct. 2485, 73 L. Ed. 2d 74 (1982) (proof that prosecutor was actually vindictive in filing charges could establish violation of due process). Because higher sentences and increased charges following appeal are constitutional if they are not vindictive and because it is quite difficult to prove improper motivation, "actual vindictiveness" claims are rarely successful. In some circumstances, however, a defendant can succeed by relying on a "presumption of vindictiveness."

2. Presumption of Vindictive Sentencing: The Doctrine of North Carolina v. Pearce

In North Carolina v. Pearce, the Supreme Court concluded that certain circumstances give rise to a **rebuttable presumption of unconstitutional vindictiveness** in sentencing. The Court considered the presumption necessary to combat a serious risk of actual vindictiveness and to protect defendants from a fear of vindictiveness that might "chill" their exercise of the right to appeal. Id. Both the risk of vindictive sentencing and the chill on defendants' rights threaten due process values.

The *"Pearce* presumption" **can arise only when a second sentence is "higher"** than an initial sentence. Nevertheless, it **does not always arise when a defendant receives a higher sentence** after successfully appealing an initial conviction. The presumption arises only when "there is a **'reasonable likelihood' that the increase** in [a defendant's sentence following a successful appeal] **is the product of actual vindictiveness** on the part of the sentencing authority." Alabama v. Smith, 490 U.S. 794, 109 S. Ct. 2201, 104 L. Ed. 2d 865 (1989). The circumstances must make it **"more likely than not that a judge** . . . [was] motivated by vindictiveness." Id.

At least four circumstances are required to give rise to a "reasonable likelihood" of vindictiveness: (1) the second sentence must be **"higher"**; (2) the first and second sentences must be imposed by the **same sentencing authority**; (3) **the sentencer must have had her judgment challenged** by the defendant **and overturned** by another court; and (4) the sentencing decisions must be **made under essentially the same circumstances.**

    a. **The sentence must be higher and must be imposed by the same sentencing authority.** The *Pearce* presumption applies only to cases in which

the same sentencing authority imposes both an initial sentence and a **"higher" sentence** after reconviction. Texas v. McCullough, 475 U.S. 134, 106 S. Ct. 976, 89 L. Ed. 2d 104 (1986). The presumption of vindictiveness hinges on the fact of a sentence **"increase"** following appeal, and there can be no true "increase" unless the "same sentencer" imposes a "higher" sentence. Id. Consequently, the presumption can arise if the same judge sentences the defendant after both trials. It cannot arise if different judges, different juries, or a judge and then a jury impose the two sentences. Id.

b.   **The sentencing authority must have had her judgment challenged and overturned.** The *Pearce* presumption is rooted, in part, in the likelihood that **a sentencing authority** whose judgment has been challenged and overturned by another authority **has a motive to respond vindictively.** The presumption, therefore, can arise if an appellate court finds error and overturns a trial court judgment. In that situation, the likelihood of vindictiveness is increased because the sentencer has a "personal stake" and a potential motivation for vindictive retaliation. However, if a sentencing judge overturns a verdict herself and grants a new trial, the presumption does not arise. Texas v. McCullough. In that situation, because the trial court has agreed with the defendant's assertion of error and has granted a new trial, there is an inadequate risk that vindictiveness has played a role in a later sentencing increase.

c.   **Both sentencing decisions must be made in essentially the same circumstances.** The fact that both an initial sentencing decision and a resentencing decision are **made in similar circumstances on the basis of presumptively similar information** enhances the likelihood that a higher second sentence is the product of vindictiveness. Thus, if a judge presides over jury trials on both occasions and sentences the accused at the end of both, a higher second sentence can support the *Pearce* presumption. However, if the circumstances surrounding the resentencing and the information available to the judge at the time of resentencing are materially different, there may be a logical, nonvindictive explanation for an "increase." If so, the likelihood of vindictiveness is insufficient to trigger the *Pearce* presumption.

In Alabama v. Smith, for example, the Supreme Court found the *Pearce* presumption inapplicable because an initial sentence followed a conviction entered on a **guilty plea** while a subsequent sentence followed a conviction after a **jury trial.** According to the Court, the likelihood of vindictiveness in such circumstances is reduced because the amount of relevant sentencing information available to a judge is likely to be greater following a trial and because the "factors that may have indicated leniency as consideration for the guilty plea are no longer present" at the resentencing.

d. Rebuttal of the presumption of vindictive sentencing. If the circumstances that give rise to a presumption of vindictiveness are present, **a "higher" sentence must be vacated unless the presumption is rebutted.** The *Pearce* Court recognized that effective rebuttal can defeat a due process claim and validate the "higher" sentence.

According to the *Pearce* Court, a judge could rebut the presumption and justify a sentencing increase only by relying on conduct of the accused or events that occurred subsequent to the original sentencing. A majority of the Court has since concluded, however, that a judge **need not rely on "subsequent" conduct or events. New, "objective information" that justifies the sentencing increase** can rebut the presumption and defeat a due process claim. Texas v. McCullough. The facts relied on must be **"new"**—they must not have been before the judge at the first sentencing. Moreover, a judge must point to **"objective"** facts—she cannot simply declare that her attitude or thinking toward the defendant or the offense changed in the interim. Finally, the facts must **"justify the increase."** New, objective information cannot rebut the *Pearce* presumption if it is irrelevant to the sentence that a defendant ought to receive or if it is simply inadequate to support the increase that occurred.

EXAMPLE AND ANALYSIS

In Texas v. McCullough, a jury sentenced a defendant to 20 years in prison after he was convicted of murder. The defendant's motion for a new trial was granted by the trial judge. After a second trial, the defendant was again convicted and opted to be sentenced by the trial judge who had presided over both trials. The judge imposed a 50-year sentence. In justifying the sentence, the judge said that she had relied on the testimony of two witnesses who had not appeared at the first trial. The testimony directly implicated the defendant in the murder and showed the part that he played. It also shed light on his life, conduct, and mental and moral propensities. In addition, the judge noted that she had learned for the first time at the retrial that the defendant had been released from prison just four months before the murder. The defendant appealed the 50-year sentence, relying on *Pearce*.

The Supreme Court rejected the defendant's due process claim for three independent reasons. First, the *Pearce* presumption of vindictiveness did not arise because a jury had sentenced the defendant the first time and the judge had sentenced him the second time. Second, the presumption did not arise because the judge had herself granted the defendant's motion for a new trial; her judgment was not overturned on appeal. Finally, even if the presumption had arisen, the new, objective information recited above was sufficient to rebut it and justify the higher sentence.

3. Presumption of Vindictive Charging: The Doctrine of Blackledge v. Perry

The *Pearce* presumption can also restrict a prosecutor's charging decision. Blackledge v. Perry. When a prosecutor files a more serious charge following a successful appeal of an initial conviction by the accused, the situation is sufficiently "analogous to the imposition of a stiffer sentence after reversal and reconviction" to justify "a presumption of unconstitutional vindictiveness." Thigpen v. Roberts, 468 U.S. 27, 104 S. Ct. 2916, 82 L. Ed. 2d 23 (1984).

The presumption of prosecutorial vindictiveness arises if (1) **higher charges** are filed after an appeal; (2) the higher charges cover the **same conduct** as the initial charges; and (3) the **same prosecutor** participated in both the initial and the subsequent prosecution. Blackledge v. Perry; Thigpen v. Roberts. The presumption may also arise even if **different prosecutors** are involved in the two proceedings. In Thigpen v. Roberts, the Supreme Court left that issue unresolved.

The presumption of prosecutorial vindictiveness is rebuttable. In Blackledge v. Perry, the Court indicated that the state could justify the filing of more serious charges following an appeal by showing that "it was **impossible to proceed** on the more serious charge" the first time. A homicide prosecution might be "impossible" initially because the victim of an assault is still alive at the time of initial trial. The victim's death prior to retrial could explain the "more serious" homicide charge and rebut the presumption of vindictiveness. See id. It is unclear whether circumstances other than "impossibility" can rebut the *Blackledge* presumption and, if so, what circumstances would suffice.

 ## EXAMPLE AND ANALYSIS

In Thigpen v. Roberts, a traffic accident in which a passenger in another vehicle was killed led to four misdemeanor charges against the defendant. After he was convicted in a "Justice of the Peace court," the defendant gave notice of appeal. According to the provisions of state law, the case was transferred to the circuit court for trial de novo. While the appeal was pending, the prosecution secured a felony manslaughter indictment against the defendant. At the new trial, the prosecutor decided not to press the four misdemeanor charges. The jury returned a manslaughter conviction and the judge sentenced the defendant to 20 years in prison. Ultimately, the defendant sought habeas corpus relief in federal court.

The Supreme Court affirmed the lower court's grant of relief, holding that the case was controlled by *Blackledge*. Because the prosecution had pursued a felony charge following the defendant's appeal and the felony charge was based on the same conduct as the misdemeanor convictions that were appealed, a presumption of vindictiveness arose. Because the presumption was not rebutted, the prosecution for manslaughter "was unconstitutional" and "[t]he resulting conviction [could]not stand."

REVIEW QUESTIONS AND ANSWERS

Question: Sam was convicted of aggravated arson. He appealed, and counsel was appointed to assist him. The intermediate appellate court affirmed his conviction. Sam then sought to petition the state supreme court to review his constitutional claims. Because the state had a policy of refusing to appoint counsel for indigents seeking discretionary review, Sam sold his home in order to pay for an attorney. The attorney was overburdened and failed to prepare the petition in timely fashion. Consequently, the state supreme court refused to consider the merits of any of Sam's appellate claims. Sam now claims that counsel rendered constitutionally ineffective assistance. Does his claim have merit?

Answer: No. Neither the Due Process Clause nor the Equal Protection Clause requires the assistance of counsel for purposes of seeking discretionary review. Because there is no constitutional right to counsel at all, an accused has no right to "effective" assistance. See Wainwright v. Torna, 455 U.S. 586, 102 S. Ct. 1300, 71 L. Ed. 2d 475 (1982). In sum, there is no constitutional foundation for Sam's ineffective assistance claim.

Question: Patricia was tried for one count of conspiracy to commit bank robbery and one count of kidnapping. She was acquitted of conspiracy and convicted of kidnapping. Patricia appeals her conviction, claiming that the trial judge gave an erroneous instruction regarding the elements of kidnapping. The contested instruction was suggested by the prosecutor at trial. Patricia's counsel did not raise any objection to it in the trial court. The government wishes to appeal the acquittal in order to have the appellate court rule on the propriety of the trial court's instruction regarding the need for a "bilateral" conspiracy under state law. What possible impediments are there to the two appeals?

Answer: Ordinarily, appellate courts do not consider issues not raised in the trial court. The failure to raise the claim regarding the kidnapping instructions in the trial court should preclude the appeal *unless* the instruction given by the judge was "plain error"—a clear and obvious mistake that affected substantial rights of the defendant.

Because of the safeguard against "double jeopardy," the prosecution cannot secure appellate relief for the acquittal of conspiracy no matter how legally erroneous the trial court's instruction. However, if the jurisdiction provides an avenue for the prosecutor to obtain an advisory appellate opinion on a matter of law, it is entirely possible that the Double Jeopardy Clause does not stand in the way even though the legal issue arises from a trial that resulted in an acquittal. In sum, the prosecutor's appeal might be permissible so long as the acquittal is left standing no matter what the merits of the prosecutor's claim.

Question: After Sadie was convicted of trespassing at a federal facility, she appealed. The state appellate court affirmed. Sadie then petitioned for review by the United States Supreme Court. The day after Sadie's petition was filed, the Court decided a case holding that a trial judge may not bar counsel from consulting with a defendant during a two-hour lunch break while the accused is testifying on direct examination. The judge had barred Sadie's counsel from consulting with her during such a break. Can Sadie rely on the holding handed down while her petition for review in the Supreme Court was pending? If so, should the Court agree with a government contention that any error by the trial judge was "harmless beyond a reasonable doubt" because the defendant and counsel had "nothing to consult about"?

Answer: Even if the Supreme Court holding about consultation bars during two-hour lunch breaks is a "new rule" of constitutional law, it is retroactively applicable to all cases not yet final at the time it was handed down. Sadie's case was pending on review to the Supreme Court and, therefore, was not yet final. The rule is applicable to her case. Moreover, violations of the right to counsel—including the right to consult with counsel—are constitutional "structural errors" that cannot be harmless. A reversal and new trial are required.

Question: After Stuart is convicted of possession of heroin with intent to distribute and sentenced to one year in prison, he appeals, alleging that the judge should have suppressed his coerced confession. His conviction is reversed. After a new trial, the same judge sentences Stuart to five years in prison, observing that "I have reconsidered the appropriateness of a mere one-year sentence for a trafficker in hard narcotics and now realize that I was much too lenient and unprotective of society. Besides, the defendant's insistence on pursuing an appeal and retrial when conviction was certain a second time shows a lack of remorse." Is the five-year sentence constitutional?

Answer: No. The same judge increased the sentence after a successful appeal in which the judge was challenged and the conviction was overturned. These facts provide the basis for a due process–based presumption of vindictiveness. The presumption can be rebutted by "new, objective" information justifying the increase. In this case, however, the judge did not point to such information; reconsideration of the appropriateness of the initial sentence does not suffice. Moreover, in explaining that the futile appeal and retrial showed a lack of remorse, the judge betrayed "actual vindictiveness." In essence, the judge was punishing Stuart for appealing and pursuing the remedy of a new trial. Punishment for the exercise of rights clearly violates due process.

22 COLLATERAL CHALLENGES AND REMEDIES

CHAPTER OVERVIEW

After the opportunities for direct appellate review are no longer available—either because they have been pursued or the time to pursue them has expired—a judgment of conviction becomes "final." Thereafter, the only avenues for seeking relief are **collateral challenges.** A request for collateral relief—such as a writ of habeas corpus or coram nobis or a motion to vacate a sentence—is different from an appeal. See Brecht v. Abrahamson, 507 U.S. 619, 113 S. Ct. 1710, 123 L. Ed. 2d 353 (1993). It is not a direct attack on a conviction. Instead, it is a "civil" action brought by a prisoner to secure relief from confinement. A petition for a collateral remedy is outside the channel of criminal case adjudication and is typically addressed to the authorities who presently have custody of the petitioner. See Fay v. Noia, 372 U.S. 391, 83 S. Ct. 822, 9 L. Ed. 2d 837 (1963); Townsend v. Sain, 372 U.S. 293, 83 S. Ct. 745, 9 L. Ed. 2d 770 (1963). Ordinarily, a request for collateral relief seeks release from "unconstitutional" confinement based on an assertion that a serious error tainted the process leading to conviction. If the petition is granted, the individual is ordinarily subject to retrial; but in a few cases, a valid claim will bar further proceedings against the petitioner. A collateral challenge typically commences at the trial court level and is subject to review in the appellate courts of the jurisdiction.

Collateral remedies are provided in both the federal and state systems. The law governing **federal collateral remedies** is the product of **statutes and judicial opinions** that interpret those statutes in light of our common law and principles of equity. In addition, each state has statutes prescribing the available collateral remedies and the limits on those remedies.

This chapter does not discuss the array of collateral remedies provided by the states. It concentrates exclusively on the **federal statutes** and the collateral relief they provide.

Most of the discussion centers around the federal collateral remedy available to state prisoners—the **writ of habeas corpus.** To a limited extent, the equivalent remedy for **federal prisoners**—the **motion to vacate a sentence**—is also considered. More specifically, this final chapter addresses:

- **The "Suspension Clause" of the Constitution.** The Constitution prohibits suspension of the writ of habeas corpus unless the public safety requires it. The Supreme Court has not determined whether this "Suspension Clause" grants a constitutional right to habeas corpus relief. Consequently, both the existence and scope of a federal constitutional entitlement to collateral relief are uncertain.

- **Federal collateral remedies and their underlying policies.** The federal statutes provide two collateral remedies—**writs of habeas corpus** for state prisoners and **motions to vacate sentences** for federal prisoners. The content of those statutory provisions and the conflicting policies that inform legislative and judicial decisionmaking about collateral remedies are sketched in this section.

- **The "in custody" and "exhaustion of remedies" requirements.** There are two relatively simple and uncontroversial prerequisites for habeas corpus relief. The petitioner must be **"in custody"** and must **exhaust available state remedies.** A federal prisoner must also be "in custody" and must exhaust the available federal remedies before moving to vacate a sentence.

- **The subject matter of collateral claims.** The statutes provide that a petitioner in custody "in violation of the laws, treaties, and Constitution of the United States" may seek habeas corpus relief or move to vacate a sentence. Almost every petitioner alleges that some **constitutional** infirmity in his conviction renders his current confinement illegal. There are two significant *substantive* restrictions on the constitutional claims that may be brought in a habeas proceeding. First, a prisoner cannot raise **a Fourth Amendment exclusionary rule claim** unless the state failed to afford him a full and fair hearing on that claim. Second, a federal court should not entertain a habeas petition if the relief sought is based on or would require the habeas court to announce a **"new rule of constitutional law."**

- **Procedural bars to collateral relief.** There are significant *procedural* bars to habeas corpus relief. One of the most litigated and significant restrictions is the **"state procedural default"** doctrine. A state's refusal to entertain a claim because a petitioner did not comply with a procedural requirement may be a sufficient basis for refusing federal habeas review. A defendant who files **multiple habeas corpus petitions** may find a claim barred either because it was **advanced and rejected in an earlier petition** or because of a **failure to raise the claim in a prior petition.** Finally, a **long delay** in filing a habeas corpus petition may be a basis for denying relief.

- **Evidentiary hearings and state court findings of fact and determinations of law.** The validity of a constitutional claim may well hinge on the resolution of disputed facts. In some circumstances, a federal court may be required to hold an **evidentiary hearing** in order to resolve those disputes. In others, the record of the state proceedings may suffice. Moreover, according to the controlling statute, a **state court's findings of fact** are ordinarily entitled to a **"presumption of correctness"** in a federal habeas proceeding. However, state court resolutions of legal questions or mixed questions of law and fact are not presumed to be correct.

- **The harmless error standard in collateral proceedings.** On direct appeal, constitutional "trial errors" are judged by a more stringent "harmless error" standard than nonconstitutional errors. In habeas corpus proceedings, constitutional "trial errors" are judged by the same "harmlessness" standard that is used for nonconstitutional errors on appeal.

Note: Congress passed the **1996 Antiterrorism and Effective Death Penalty Act** in April 1996, and President Clinton signed it into law. The Act includes several modifications to the federal statutes that govern writs of habeas corpus and motions to vacate sentences. Because the changes made by the Act have yet to be interpreted and are subject to challenge, they will not be incorporated into the discussions of the topics to which they pertain. Instead, the relevant provisions will be highlighted in special "Notes" following the discussions.

A. THE "SUSPENSION CLAUSE" OF THE UNITED STATES CONSTITUTION

Article I, section 9, clause 2 of the United States Constitution provides that "**the Privilege of the Writ of Habeas Corpus shall not be suspended,** unless in Cases of Rebellion or Invasion the public Safety may require it." According to one interpretation, this clause creates **a right to federal habeas corpus** that does extend to those in federal custody and may also extend to those in state custody. Another interpretation, however, holds that the "Suspension Clause" does not grant a constitutional right to habeas corpus relief in the federal courts. Instead, it merely prohibits Congress from making state writs of habeas corpus unavailable to federal prisoners.

The Supreme Court has at times intimated that there is a constitutional right to habeas corpus relief but has not definitively ruled on the issue. Because Congress has authorized federal courts to issue writs of habeas corpus since 1789, there has been no need to resolve that question. Consequently, whether federal and state prisoners have any constitutional right to a federal collateral remedy remains arguable. For further discussion of this question, see LaFave and Israel, Criminal Procedure §28.2(a) (2d ed. 1992).

B. FEDERAL COLLATERAL REMEDIES AND THEIR UNDERLYING POLICIES

The common law developed two collateral remedies—writs of habeas corpus and writs of coram nobis. In the Judiciary Act of 1789, the first grant of federal court jurisdiction, Congress acknowledged the importance of collateral relief by authorizing the federal courts to grant writs of habeas corpus for federal prisoners. Stone v. Powell, 428 U.S. 465, 96 S. Ct. 3037, 49 L. Ed. 2d 1067 (1976). In 1867, Congress authorized the federal courts to grant writs of habeas corpus on behalf of state prisoners. Since that time the federal remedies have been expanded, contracted, and modified in a variety of ways.

1. Current Statutes That Govern Federal Collateral Remedies

Today, 28 U.S.C. §2254 authorizes federal courts to grant writs of habeas corpus on behalf of state prisoners, while 28 U.S.C. §2255 provides an equivalent federal court remedy for federal prisoners—motions to vacate, set aside, or correct sentences.

Section 2254 sets out the grounds on which a prisoner in state custody may be granted habeas corpus relief. It then specifies that a state prisoner must "exhaust" the available state remedies before seeking habeas relief in federal court. Finally, it announces a "presumption of correctness" for findings of fact by state courts with regard to questions involved in habeas corpus petitions. It specifies the conditions under which this presumption of correctness does not arise and prescribes the showing that an applicant must make in order to rebut the presumption. Another provision, 28 U.S.C. §2244(b), provides some answers to issues raised by "successive" habeas petitions from the same state prisoner.

Section 2255 sets out the grounds on which a federal prisoner may gain release by means of a motion to vacate a sentence. This section and 28 U.S.C. §2244(a) address the subject of "successive" motions by a federal prisoner.

2. Competing Policies That Underlie Requests for Collateral Relief

On many occasions, the Supreme Court has been required to interpret and to fill in the gaps in the federal statutes. The Court's decisions have attempted to strike a balance between the competing policies that underlie requests for collateral relief.

On the one hand, there is a need to insure that fundamental constitutional rights are observed and to guarantee that every individual has a means of obtaining relief from a fundamentally unjust imprisonment. Habeas corpus is "one of the precious heritages of Anglo-American civilization" because it sets free individuals who have been "grievously wronged" by society. Fay v. Noia. It serves as a "bulwark against convictions that violate fundamental fairness," Engle v. Isaac, 456 U.S. 107, 102 S. Ct. 1558, 71 L. Ed. 2d 783

(1982), and guards against the injustice of incarcerating the innocent. See Stone v. Powell.

On the other hand, the costs of reviewing requests for collateral remedies and of granting those requests—particularly when the relief is sought by a state prisoner—are substantial. The availability of collateral relief **undermines the finality** of criminal convictions, see Wainwright v. Sykes, 433 U.S. 72, 97 S. Ct. 2497, 53 L. Ed. 2d 594 (1977), can **upset the balance between the federal and state systems,** see Coleman v. Thompson, 501 U.S. 722, 111 S. Ct. 2546, 115 L. Ed. 2d 640 (1991), can **interfere with the functioning of state criminal justice systems,** see Engle v. Isaac, and can **frustrate the efforts to punish guilty offenders,** see Engle v. Isaac; Coleman v. Thompson. Moreover, it can **drain the resources of the federal courts** and make them unavailable for other important purposes. See Stone v. Powell. Federalism, state-federal comity, and finality are perhaps the most oft-cited bases for limiting the availability of writs of habeas corpus.

The Supreme Court's interpretations of the federal statutes have not always been consistent. In large measure, the Court's vacillation has reflected shifting attitudes toward the relative importance of the competing policies. In the 1960s, a majority of the Court emphasized the importance of avoiding unjust convictions. The result was a bias in favor of more expansive habeas relief. In more recent years, the Court has been increasingly conscious of the costs of collateral challenges. The result has been a series of decisions narrowing the scope and availability of habeas corpus relief for state prisoners. These more recent opinions are the source of most of the doctrine discussed in the following sections.

C.   THE "IN CUSTODY" AND "EXHAUSTION OF REMEDIES" REQUIREMENTS

The governing statutes prescribe two threshold requirements for those seeking collateral relief from a federal court. First, the individual must be **"in custody."** Second, the individual must **"exhaust other available remedies"** before bringing a collateral challenge.

1.   In-Custody Requirement

Writs of habeas corpus and motions to vacate sentences are available only to those held **in custody** by state or federal authorities. 28 U.S.C. §§2241, 2254, 2255. Although habeas corpus relief was originally available only to those who were actually confined, other sorts of restrictions on freedom will suffice today. An individual on probation or parole can satisfy the in-custody requirement. See Jones v. Cunningham, 371 U.S. 236, 83 S. Ct. 373, 9 L. Ed. 2d 285 (1963). Similarly, an accused who is convicted and is released on his own recognizance pending appeal is sufficiently in custody for purposes of the federal statutes. See Hensley v. Municipal Court, 411 U.S. 345, 93 S. Ct. 1571, 36 L. Ed. 2d 294 (1973).

2.   Exhaustion of Remedies Requirement

Section 2254(b) provides that an "application for a writ of habeas corpus" by a person in state custody "shall not be granted unless it appears that the applicant has **exhausted the remedies available in the courts of the State,** or that there is either an absence of available State corrective process or the existence of circumstances rendering such process ineffective to protect the rights of the prisoner." This **exhaustion of remedies** requirement bars relief "if [a state prisoner] has a right under the law of the State to raise, by any available procedure, the question presented." 28 U.S.C. §2254(c). Thus, if the petitioner has the opportunity to pursue a direct appeal of her conviction or a state collateral remedy, federal habeas relief is barred.

The exhaustion of remedies requirement applies only to avenues of relief that are still open; it **does not bar habeas relief if no state remedies are still available** at the time the petitioner seeks relief in federal court. Even if the petitioner neglected to pursue state remedies when they were available, the fact that they are currently unavailable satisfies the exhaustion requirement. See Fay v. Noia; Engle v. Isaac.

> **Note: The 1996 Act and the exhaustion of remedies requirement.**
> The 1996 Act added two provisions that pertain to the exhaustion of remedies requirement. First, it permits judges to deny applications for habeas relief "on the merits, notwithstanding the failure of the applicant to exhaust the remedies available in" state courts. A court can disregard a failure to exhaust and rule against an applicant on the merits of a claim. Second, the Act provides that a state "shall not be deemed to have waived the exhaustion requirement or be estopped from reliance" on it "unless the State, through counsel, **expressly waives** the requirement." Put simply, a prisoner cannot avoid the exhaustion requirement by claiming that a waiver of the requirement should be "inferred from" the conduct of a state official.

D.   SUBJECT MATTER OF CLAIMS FOR COLLATERAL RELIEF

In general, federal collateral relief is available for those who claim that they are being unconstitutionally held in custody by state or federal authorities. There are some claims of unconstitutional confinement, however, that are not cognizable.

1.   General Predicate for Collateral Relief: "Unconstitutional" Custody

Section 2254 provides that a writ of habeas corpus is available for a state prisoner "**only** on the ground that [the petitioner] is **in custody in violation of the Constitution or laws or treaties of the United States.**" Section 2255 provides that federal prisoners may seek release "upon the ground that [a] sentence was imposed **in violation of the Constitution or laws of the United States.**" In general, federal collateral relief is available for those subject to restraints that are "contrary to our fundamental law, the Constitution." Fay v. Noia. Subject to the limitations discussed below, state or federal prisoners may seek collateral relief on the basis of any alleged constitutional defect in the process by which they were convicted and incarcerated. See McCleskey v. Zant, 499 U.S. 467, 111 S. Ct. 1454, 113 L. Ed. 2d 517 (1991) (noting that the writ extends to all dispositive constitutional claims presented in a proper procedural manner).

2. Exception for Fourth Amendment Exclusionary Rule Claims: The Doctrine of Stone v. Powell

A state prisoner's opportunity to obtain habeas corpus relief on the ground that evidence obtained in violation of the Fourth Amendment ban on unreasonable searches and seizures was used to convict him is severely restricted. If the state has afforded the prisoner a **"full and fair opportunity" to litigate the Fourth Amendment claim,** a writ of habeas corpus may not be granted. Stone v. Powell. If the accused had an adequate opportunity for consideration of the Fourth Amendment exclusionary rule claim by state courts, a federal writ of habeas corpus is unavailable even if the state court erroneously allowed the government to introduce critical evidence obtained by means of an unconstitutional search or seizure. The rationale for this restriction is simple. According to the Court, the costs of applying the Fourth Amendment exclusionary rule in habeas proceedings outweigh any deterrent gains. Id.; see Chapter 12, section A, for a discussion of the Fourth Amendment exclusionary rule.

More than once, the Supreme Court has considered government claims that there are other constitutional grounds that should not provide a basis for habeas relief if the state has afforded full and fair opportunities to litigate. The Court, however, has rejected every such effort to expand the Stone v. Powell doctrine. See, e.g., Withrow v. Williams, 507 U.S. 680, 113 S. Ct. 1745, 123 L. Ed. 2d 407 (1993) (claim that evidence should be excluded because of *Miranda* violation is cognizable on habeas); Kimmelman v. Morrison, 477 U.S. 365, 106 S. Ct. 2574, 91 L. Ed. 2d 305 (1986) (claim that defendant was denied the Sixth Amendment right to effective assistance by counsel who failed to raise a Fourth Amendment exclusionary rule claim is cognizable on habeas); Rose v. Mitchell, 443 U.S. 545, 99 S. Ct. 2993, 61 L. Ed. 2d 739 (1979) (claim of deprivation of equal protection because of discrimination in selection of grand jury foreman is cognizable on habeas); Jackson v. Virginia, 443 U.S. 307, 99 S. Ct. 2781, 61 L. Ed. 2d 560 (1979) (due process–sufficiency of evidence claim is cognizable on habeas).

 EXAMPLE AND ANALYSIS

Pete files a petition for habeas corpus relief in which he alleges that his clearly meritorious Fourth Amendment claim was erroneously rejected by the state courts and that his confinement rests on a conviction obtained in violation of his entitlement to have critical evidence of guilt excluded. The record shows a patently valid claim, a lengthy hearing in the state trial court, and full consideration of the claim in the state appellate courts. Should the federal court entertain Pete's request for collateral relief?

The answer depends on whether Pete was given a "full and fair opportunity" to litigate the claim in the state courts. That depends on the meaning of a "full and fair opportunity." A few lower courts have held that a state's failure to recognize the merits of a clearly valid claim constitutes the denial of a "full and fair opportunity" to litigate a Fourth Amendment exclusionary rule claim. There is some force to these courts' conclusion that federal courts should consider habeas petitions in those cases.

3.   Inapplicability of "New Rules" of Constitutional Law on Habeas Corpus: The "Retroactivity" Doctrine of Teague v. Lane

In Teague v. Lane, 489 U.S. 288, 109 S. Ct. 1060, 103 L. Ed. 2d 334 (1989), the Supreme Court held that "new rules" of constitutional law are ordinarily inapplicable in habeas corpus proceedings. That holding places an additional limit on the constitutional claims available to state prisoners seeking release from unconstitutional custody.

a.   *Teague* **limitation on cognizable habeas claims.** A habeas corpus applicant may properly base a claim for relief on a rule of constitutional law announced **before his conviction became final.** Such a rule is clearly applicable upon collateral review of the conviction. See Chapter 21, section D. As a general rule, however, a habeas petitioner **may not** secure collateral relief if his claim of illegal custody rests on a **"new rule"** of constitutional law announced after his conviction became **final.** Except in two rare instances, **new rules of constitutional law are not retroactively applicable to convictions upon collateral review**—that is, new rules of constitutional law do not govern cases that were finalized before the rules were announced. Teague v. Lane; Penry v. Lynaugh, 492 U.S. 302, 109 S. Ct. 2934, 106 L. Ed. 2d 256 (1989).

Not only should new rules of constitutional law not be **applied** in habeas corpus proceedings, they should not be **"announced"** in such proceedings. Consequently, a habeas applicant cannot obtain relief on the basis of a claim that *would require* the announcement of a "new rule." Teague v. Lane. To determine whether to entertain a habeas petition, a federal court must make a "threshold" determination of whether a rule advocated by a habeas petitioner would be a "new rule." See id.; Caspari v. Bohlen, 510 U.S. 383, 114 S. Ct. 948, 127 L. Ed. 2d 236 (1994). If the validation of the petitioner's claim would require announcement of a "new rule," the federal court should not entertain the application for habeas relief.

b. Meaning of "new rule." Because the *Teague* decision bars a habeas claim based on a "new rule" of constitutional law, the definition of a new rule is of critical importance. The Court has used a variety of doctrinal phrases to describe rules that qualify as new. A rule is **new** if it "breaks new ground" or "imposes a new obligation on the States or the Federal Government" or if it leads to a result "not dictated by precedent existing at the time the defendant's conviction became final." Teague v. Lane; Penry v. Lynaugh. In addition, a rule is new if there have been "reasonable contrary conclusions reached by other courts" or if a rule "was susceptible to debate among reasonable minds." Butler v. McKellar, 494 U.S. 407, 110 S. Ct. 1212, 108 L. Ed. 2d 347 (1990). Furthermore, a rule may be new even though a court states that its decision is "within the 'logical compass' of" or is " 'controlled' by a prior decision." Id.

c. Two "exceptions" to the bar on habeas claims resting on "new rules." There are **two exceptions** to the principle that "new rules" are not retroactive to cases on collateral review—that is, two instances in which new rules **do** apply to convictions already final at the time the rule is announced. If a new rule comes within one of these extremely narrow exceptions, a habeas corpus petitioner may rely on it as a basis for relief from unconstitutional custody.

   i. "Beyond the power of the criminal lawmaking authority" exception. The first exception is for new rules that place **"certain kinds of primary, private individual conduct beyond the power of the criminal law-making power to proscribe,"** Teague v. Lane, or that **"prohibit imposition of a certain type of punishment for a class of defendants because of their status or offense."** Sawyer v. Smith, 497 U.S. 227, 110 S. Ct. 2822, 111 L. Ed. 2d 193 (1990). This exception has been the subject of minimal discussion, but seems designed for rules holding that a provision of the Constitution precludes criminalizing a particular person or act. One example of such a rule is provided by Robinson v. California, 370 U.S. 660, 82 S. Ct. 1417, 8 L. Ed. 2d 758 (1962), in which the Court held that a state law punishing "addict[ion] to the use of narcotics" is invalid because it violates the Fourteenth Amendment prohibition of "cruel and unusual punishment" to punish a person for the "status" of being an addict. Lambert v. California, 355 U.S. 225, 78 S. Ct. 240, 2 L. Ed. 2d 228 (1957), furnishes another illustration. In *Lambert*, the state had charged and convicted an individual under a statute that made it a crime for a person previously convicted of a felony to fail to register with the state. The

Supreme Court concluded that such a conviction was invalid under the Due Process Clause unless the state proved that the defendant was aware of the duty to register.

ii. **"Procedures implicit in ordered liberty" exception.** The second exception encompasses new rules that **"require[ ] the observance of 'those procedures that . . . are "implicit in the concept of ordered liberty." ' "** Teague v. Lane. To come within this exception, a rule must be **a "watershed rule[ ] of criminal procedure."** It must **"implicate the fundamental fairness of the trial."** Significantly, the exception applies only "to those **new procedures without which the likelihood of an accurate conviction is seriously diminished."** Teague v. Lane. Even if a rule "improve[s] accuracy," it does not fall within the second exception unless it **" 'alter[s] our understanding of the bedrock procedural elements' essential to the fairness of a proceeding."** Sawyer v. Smith.

In sum, to be retroactive under this exception a new rule must be a mainstay of fair process *and* must markedly decrease the likelihood that an innocent person will be erroneously convicted. The exception is designed for such fundamental safeguards as the right to appointed counsel recognized in Gideon v. Wainwright and the right to trial by jury recognized in Duncan v. Louisiana. Because it is "unlikely that many such components of basic due process have yet to emerge," Teague v. Lane, the second exception will rarely provide a basis for avoiding the *Teague* bar.

 # EXAMPLE AND ANALYSIS

In Caspari v. Bohlen, a state prisoner requested habeas corpus relief based on a contention that the double jeopardy doctrine of Bullington v. Missouri (see Chapter 20, section B.4) governs noncapital sentencing proceedings. The Eighth Circuit agreed with his contention and directed the district court to grant a writ of habeas corpus.

The Supreme Court reversed, holding that the Eighth Circuit had violated the rule of Teague v. Lane. The Court reasoned that a holding that *Bullington* applies to noncapital proceedings qualifies as a "new rule" of constitutional law because a reasonable jurist would not conclude that it was dictated by Supreme Court precedents handed down prior to the date on which the prisoner's conviction and sentence became final. Moreover, it was a new rule that did not fall into either of the narrow *Teague* exceptions. Because *Teague* bars the announcement and application of such rules in habeas proceedings, the Eighth Circuit had violated *Teague* when it decided that

Bullington governed the prisoner's noncapital sentencing proceeding and granted him relief on that basis.

E. PROCEDURAL IMPEDIMENTS TO COLLATERAL RELIEF

Even if a claim is cognizable, federal collateral relief may be denied on "procedural" grounds. Procedural grounds that can bar a collateral remedy include "state procedural defaults," the fact that a claim was raised and denied in a previous petition, the fact that a claim was not raised in a previous petition, and delay in bringing the collateral challenge.

1. "State Procedural Default" Bar to Collateral Relief

If a state court has "declined to address [the merits of] a prisoner's federal claims because the prisoner has failed to meet a state procedural requirement . . . the state's judgment [may] rest on an **independent and adequate state procedural ground**." Coleman v. Thompson. As a general rule, a failure to satisfy a state procedural requirement—a **"state procedural default"**—**bars federal habeas corpus review** because "the petitioner . . . has deprived the state courts of an opportunity to address [the federal claims] in the first instance." Id. The bar applies to every kind of constitutional claim. Id.; Engle v. Isaac. An analogous doctrine governs requests for collateral relief by federal prisoners. A **federal procedural default** bars a federal prisoner's motion to vacate his sentence under 28 U.S.C. §2255. Davis v. United States, 411 U.S. 233, 93 S. Ct. 1577, 36 L. Ed. 2d 216 (1973).

There are **two "exceptions"** to the rule that a state (or federal) procedural default bars collateral relief. First, the bar is inapplicable if the petitioner establishes **"cause"** for the default and **"prejudice"** from the alleged constitutional violation. Coleman v. Thompson. Second, the bar is inapplicable if the petitioner demonstrates that a **"fundamental miscarriage of justice"** would result if collateral review were denied. Id.

a. **Need for an independent and adequate state procedural ground.** Because the "state procedural default" doctrine is premised on the fact that the state court's judgment rests on an **"independent and adequate state ground,"** the state court's judgment must actually be based on the alleged procedural default. Harris v. Reed, 489 U.S. 255, 109 S. Ct. 1038, 103 L. Ed. 2d 308 (1989). The state procedural default bar will not apply if the state court does not in fact rely on the petitioner's default as an independent basis for its rejection of the petitioner's claims. Id.

The state procedural default must be "both **'independent'** of the merits of the federal claim **and** an **'adequate'** basis for the court's decision." Id.; see also Coleman v. Thompson (noting the need for a "truly independent basis" for decision). **To be independent,** the ground must not be linked to or interwoven with the merits of the federal claim. **To be adequate,** the ground must be legally sufficient in and of itself to sustain the court's judgment. A state procedural ground is not adequate if it has not been consistently or regularly applied by the state. Dugger v. Adams, 489 U.S. 401, 109 S. Ct. 1211, 103 L. Ed. 2d 435 (1989).

The bases of state court judgments are sometimes ambiguous. When that is the case, if "it **fairly appears** that a state court judgment **rest[s] primarily on federal law or [is] interwoven with federal law,**" there is a **conclusive presumption that the state court decision does not rest on an "independent and adequate state ground."** Coleman v. Thompson (holding that no presumption arose because the state court decision did not "fairly appear" to rest on federal grounds); see Harris v. Reed. To prevent this conclusive presumption of a federal basis for its decision, the state court must include a **"clear and express statement"** that it relied on the independent and adequate state ground. Coleman v. Thompson; Harris v. Reed. In sum, if a state court decision "fairly appears" to rest on or be interwoven with federal law and does not clearly and expressly state that it is independently based on the petitioner's "state procedural default," collateral review is not barred.

 ## EXAMPLE AND ANALYSIS

In Harris v. Reed, the defendant was convicted of murder. He appealed, claiming insufficient evidence. He then sought a state collateral remedy, alleging ineffective assistance of counsel. The state court referred to a state law principle according to which issues that could have been presented on direct appeal but were not are "waived." Although the court found that all but one of the prisoner's ineffectiveness allegations could have been presented on appeal, it nonetheless reached the merits of those allegations and rejected the petitioner's claim.

The Supreme Court held that the state court judgment fairly appeared to rest on federal law—an interpretation and application of the Sixth Amendment right to counsel. Although the state rule concerning the waiver of claims not raised on appeal was an "independent and adequate" state procedural rule that could bar habeas relief, the state court merely referred to that rule and did not "clearly and expressly" rely on it. Consequently, habeas review was not precluded.

b. **"Cause and prejudice" exception.** At one time, a state procedural default barred habeas review only if the petitioner had "deliberately bypassed" the opportunity to pursue state review of her claim. See

Fay v. Noia. Today, the opportunity for collateral review following a procedural default is much more limited. See Wainwright v. Sykes, 433 U.S. 72, 97 S. Ct. 2497, 53 L. Ed. 2d 594 (1977). Habeas relief is unavailable in many cases that do not involve a "deliberate bypass" of opportunities for state review.

A prisoner can avoid the state procedural default bar by demonstrating that her claims fall within the **"cause and prejudice" exception.** To qualify, "the prisoner [must] . . . demonstrate[both] cause for the default and actual prejudice as a result of the alleged violation of federal law." Coleman v. Thompson.

i. **Meaning of "cause" for the procedural default.** To demonstrate **"cause" for a procedural default,** a habeas applicant must ordinarily show that **"some objective factor external to the defense impeded counsel's efforts to comply with the State's procedural rule."** Coleman v. Thompson. There must be "something external to the petitioner, something that cannot fairly be attributed to him." Id.

Cause for a procedural default exists if the factual or legal basis for a claim was **not reasonably available** to counsel or if some **interference by the state** made compliance with a procedural requirement impracticable. Id. The **"futility"** of presenting an objection to state courts cannot alone constitute cause for failing to object at trial. Engle v. Isaac. Moreover, defense **counsel's ignorance or inadvertence** will not constitute cause *unless* it qualifies as constitutionally ineffective assistance under the standards prescribed by Strickland v. Washington. See Chapter 18, section C.2. Nonetheless, if a constitutional claim is "so **novel** that its legal basis [was] not reasonably available to counsel" at the time of the default—that is, if "there was no reasonable basis in existing law" for the claim—there is "cause" for counsel's failure to raise it. Reed v. Ross, 468 U.S. 1, 104 S. Ct. 2901, 82 L. Ed. 2d 1 (1984).

ii. **Meaning of "prejudice" as a result of the alleged violation.** A habeas petitioner seeking to avoid the bar raised by a state procedural default must also demonstrate **"actual prejudice" as a result of the constitutional violation** alleged in the petition. Coleman v. Thompson; Engle v. Isaac. The Supreme Court has not clearly defined the meaning of "prejudice" in this context. "Actual prejudice" requires a showing that the error alleged to render the prisoner's custody unconstitutional had **an effect on the outcome** of the prisoner's trial. In Schlup v. Delo, 513 U.S. 298, 115 S. Ct. 851, 130 L. Ed. 2d 808 (1995), the Supreme Court indicated that prejudice does **not** require a showing that "it is **more likely than not**" that the defendant would not have been convicted. Some courts and other authorities have suggested that the definition is similar, if not identical, to the definition of prejudice in the "ineffective assistance of counsel" context. If so, a defendant would have to demonstrate a "reasonable probability" that but for the constitutional error the outcome of his trial would have been different. See Chapter 18, section C.2.b.ii.

 EXAMPLE AND ANALYSIS

In Coleman v. Thompson, a prisoner who had been convicted of capital murder and sentenced to death filed a state habeas corpus action. Thirty-three days after the court entered its final judgment ruling against his claims, the petitioner filed a notice of appeal. The state moved to dismiss the appeal because the petitioner's notice of appeal was untimely under a court rule that required filing of a notice of appeal "within 30 days of final judgment." The State Supreme Court granted the state's motion to dismiss. The petitioner then sought federal habeas relief.

The Supreme Court concluded that the state court's ruling on the petitioner's claims had rested on an independent and adequate state procedural ground—the rule regarding the time within which an appeal could be filed. The Court then rejected the petitioner's contention that his attorney's error in failing to file a timely appeal constituted "cause" for his procedural default. According to the Court, attorney error can constitute cause **only** if it amounts to "constitutionally ineffective assistance." Because a prisoner has **no constitutional right to the assistance of counsel** in state postconviction proceedings, the petitioner here could not establish that the failure to file a timely notice of appeal from the state court's denial of postconviction relief amounted to constitutionally ineffective assistance.

c. **"Fundamental miscarriage of justice" or "unjust incarceration" exception.** An applicant who cannot establish cause and prejudice might still qualify for the **"fundamental miscarriage of justice" or "unjust incarceration" exception** to the state procedural default bar. The applicant must "demonstrate that failure to consider the claims will result in a fundamental miscarriage of justice." Coleman v. Thompson. Because this exception rests on the "imperative of correcting a fundamentally unjust incarceration," Engle v. Isaac, it applies only in those "rare" and "extraordinary" cases in which a "truly deserving" prisoner makes a showing that he is **"actually innocent."** Schlup v. Delo; see also Coleman v. Thompson. A showing of "legal innocence"—that is, that the prisoner could not properly have been convicted under the law—is not sufficient. See Smith v. Murray, 477 U.S. 527, 106 S. Ct. 2661, 91 L. Ed. 2d 434 (1986).

A petitioner must establish that " 'a **constitutional violation has probably resulted in the conviction of one who is actually innocent.' "** Schlup v. Delo (quoting Murray v. Carrier, 477 U.S. 478, 106 S. Ct. 2639, 91 L. Ed. 2d 397 (1986)). More specifically, he **"must show that it is more likely than not that no reasonable juror would have found [him] guilty beyond a reasonable doubt."** Schlup v. Delo. Because "actual innocence" is the focus, a judge may "consider the probative force of relevant evidence that was either excluded or unavailable at trial" and may consider evidence "alleged to have been illegally admitted." Id.

Finally, a more demanding standard applies if a petitioner does not claim that he is "actually innocent" of an offense but alleges only that he is "actually innocent of the death penalty"—that is, that the facts do not justify capital punishment. He must show **"by clear and convincing evidence"** that "but for a constitutional error, **no reasonable juror would have found [him] eligible for the death penalty."** Sawyer v. Whitley, 505 U.S. 333, 112 S. Ct. 2514, 120 L. Ed. 2d 269 (1992).

2. Procedural Bars Resulting from "Multiple" Petitions for Collateral Relief

Prisoners sometimes file multiple petitions seeking collateral relief. A second or subsequent petition may raise claims that have been raised previously or may assert grounds for relief that have not been asserted in prior petitions. The **"successive petition" doctrine** defines a procedural bar to a second or subsequent petition that raises a claim adjudicated in a prior petition. The **"abuse of writ" doctrine** defines a procedural bar based on the attempt to raise a claim not asserted in a prior petition.

a. Petitions for collateral relief raising claims previously adjudicated: The "successive petition" doctrine.

A **"successive petition"** for collateral relief is one that "raises grounds identical to those raised and rejected on the merits of a prior petition." Kuhlmann v. Wilson, 477 U.S. 436, 106 S. Ct. 2616, 91 L. Ed. 2d 364 (1986). The principle of "res judicata" does not bar successive petitions for collateral relief. Schlup v. Delo. Nonetheless, because Congress "disfavor[s] . . . claims raised in second and subsequent petitions," it has decided that a habeas corpus petition "need not be entertained . . . unless the [petition] alleges and is predicated on . . . [a] ground not adjudicated" in an earlier petition. 28 U.S.C. §2244(b); see also §2244(a) (a court "shall [not] be required to entertain" a petition by a federal prisoner that presents "no new ground not heretofore presented and determined").

In interpreting the federal statutes, the Supreme Court has concluded that a federal court **"may not ordinarily reach the merits of successive claims"** for habeas corpus relief. Schlup v. Delo. A successive petition faces a presumptive procedural bar. Nonetheless, a petitioner **may be** entitled to federal collateral review of a successive petition if he makes "a showing of **cause and prejudice.**" See id. Moreover, a petitioner **is** entitled to review if he demonstrates that the "ends of justice" require collateral review because it is necessary to prevent a **"fundamental miscarriage of justice."** Id.

    i.   **Potential "cause and prejudice" exception.** It is **not certain** that there is in fact a **"cause and prejudice" exception** to the presumptive bar on "successive petitions." Moreover, if the exception does exist, the meaning of **"cause"** in this context is far from clear. In the context of a procedural default, a petitioner must demonstrate an objective reason for *failing* to raise his claim in a prior proceeding. In the "successive petition" context, the petitioner would apparently have to provide an objective reason that he should be allowed to raise his rejected claim a second time. Such a showing might overlap completely with the showing needed to qualify for the "fundamental miscarriage of justice" exception. The showing required to establish **"prejudice"** is undoubtedly the same required to excuse a "state procedural default." See subsection 1.b.ii above.

    ii.   **"Fundamental miscarriage of justice" exception.** An exception to the bar on "successive petitions" is made if the "ends of justice" require collateral review because **"a fundamental miscarriage of justice"** would occur if review were denied. Schlup v. Delo. The showing needed to satisfy this exception is identical to the showing needed for the "fundamental miscarriage of justice" exception to the "state procedural default" doctrine. See subsection 1.c above.

 # EXAMPLE AND ANALYSIS

In Kuhlmann v. Wilson, a prisoner filed a habeas corpus petition, claiming that his Sixth Amendment right to counsel against the "deliberate elicitation" of incriminating statements recognized by Massiah v. United States had been violated. His petition was denied on the merits. After the Supreme Court decided United States v. Henry, the prisoner filed a "successive petition" raising the same claim. The district court denied relief, but the court of appeals reversed and ordered habeas relief.

The Supreme Court reversed. While a majority rested the decision on the conclusion that the prisoner's right to counsel had not been violated, a plurality would have also relied on the ground that the "successive petition" raising the identical right to counsel claim should not have been granted because the petitioner had not established that the "ends of justice" required consideration of his claims.

In light of later opinions, the plurality's opinion seems sound. The "ends of justice" exception to the bar on "successive petitions" for habeas relief requires a defendant to show that a "fundamental miscarriage of justice" will occur if the petition is not considered. To establish a fundamental miscarriage of justice, the prisoner must show that the constitutional violation alleged probably resulted in the conviction of an "actually innocent" person. In Kuhlmann v. Wilson, the evidence that the prisoner was guilty of the offense was "nearly overwhelming" and the *Massiah* claim he raised did not raise any question about his guilt. Consequently, his "successive petition" should have been barred.

---

b. Petitions for collateral relief raising claims not previously raised: The "abuse of writ" doctrine. An "abusive petition" refers to claims for collateral relief that raise " 'grounds that were available but not relied upon in a prior petition.' " Schlup v. Delo. Congress's disfavor of second or subsequent petitions is reflected in the determination that a "subsequent application" for habeas corpus relief "need not be entertained . . . unless the court . . . is satisfied that the applicant has **not** on the earlier application **deliberately withheld the newly asserted ground or otherwise abused the writ.**" 28 U.S.C. §2244(b); see also §2255 (a court "shall not be required to entertain a second or successive motion" to vacate sentence "on behalf of the same [federal] prisoner").

Under §2244(b), if a subsequent petition raises a new ground and the petitioner did not deliberately withhold it from the earlier petition or otherwise abuse the writ, a court **must** consider the subsequent petition. McCleskey v. Zant, 499 U.S. 467, 111 S. Ct. 1454, 113 L. Ed. 2d 517 (1991). Note that a court is **not required to reject an "abusive petition."** Section 2244(b) does not divest courts of their traditional equitable discretion to entertain abusive petitions. Id. In McCleskey v. Zant, the Supreme Court outlined the analysis required to determine whether a petition is abusive and whether an abusive petition should be entertained.

First, "the government bears the burden of pleading abuse of the writ." Id. To do so, it should clearly and particularly note the petitioner's prior writ history, identify the newly raised claim, and allege an abuse. Abuse occurs not only when a ground is deliberately withheld but also when the failure to raise it in a prior petition is the result of "inexcusable neglect." Id.

The petitioner then has "the burden to disprove abuse." Cause and prejudice are the standards to be used "to determine if there has been an abuse of the writ through inexcusable neglect." Id. "To excuse [a] failure to raise [a] claim earlier, **[the petitioner] must show cause for failing to raise it and prejudice therefrom.**" Id. The terms "cause" and "prejudice" have the same meaning as in the procedural default context. See subsection 1.b above. The petitioner must point to an objective, external factor that impeded efforts to raise the claim in a prior petition and must show that the constitutional violation alleged in the petition had an effect on the outcome of her trial.

If the petitioner cannot demonstrate cause, the failure to raise the claim in the earlier petition "may nonetheless be excused if he or she can show that a **fundamental miscarriage of justice** would result from a failure to entertain the claim." This phrase also has the same meaning as in the procedural default context. See subsection 1.c above. The petitioner must make a "colorable showing of factual innocence," McCleskey v. Zant. She must demonstrate "that the constitutional error 'probably' resulted in the conviction of one who was **actually innocent.**" Schlup v. Delo. The constitutional violation must call into question "the reliability of the guilt determination." McCleskey v. Zant.

 # EXAMPLE AND ANALYSIS

In McCleskey v. Zant, a prisoner filed a second habeas petition in which he raised a right to counsel claim based on the *Massiah* doctrine. Because he had not raised the claim in his first petition, the court of appeals held that his second petition was abusive and denied relief.

The Supreme Court agreed with the court of appeals. First, the government had carried its burden of pleading abuse by reciting the prior writ history and the failure to raise the *Massiah* claim in the first federal collateral attack. The petitioner had not carried his burden of showing either cause and prejudice or a fundamental miscarriage of justice.

The petitioner alleged that he had not known about or been able to discover a significant document concerning the role of a government informant prior to his first petition. The government had turned the document over to him shortly before he filed his second petition. The Court concluded that other evidence that was known or discoverable at the time of the first habeas petition would have supported the petitioner's *Massiah* claim. Consequently, there was no cause for failing to raise it at that time, and the omission to do so could "not be excused merely because evidence discovered later might also have supported or strengthened the claim."

Moreover, the petitioner's claim did not come within the fundamental miscarriage of justice exception because the constitutional violation, if there was one, "resulted in the admission at trial of truthful inculpatory evidence which did not affect the reliability of the guilt determination." He could not "demonstrate that the alleged *Massiah* violation *caused the conviction of an innocent person.*"

Note: The 1996 Act and multiple petitions. The 1996 Act makes several changes to the relevant statutes pertaining to "second or successive" requests for collateral relief:

(A) **"Successive habeas corpus petitions" by state prisoners.** According to the Act, claims presented in prior habeas corpus applications "shall be dismissed." §2244(b)(1). The statute makes no mention of exceptions for cause and prejudice or fundamental miscarriages of justice.

(B) **"Abusive habeas corpus petitions" by state prisoners.** According to the Act, claims not presented in prior habeas corpus applications "shall be dismissed unless" (1) the claim is based on a "new rule of constitutional law made retroactive to cases on collateral review by the Supreme Court, that was previously unavailable" or (2) "the factual predicate for the claim could not have been discovered previously through the exercise of due diligence" and "the facts underlying the claim, if proven and viewed in light of the evidence as a whole, would . . . establish by clear and convincing evidence that, but for the constitutional error, no reasonable factfinder would have found the applicant guilty."

(C) **"Second or successive" motions to vacate sentences by federal prisoners.** The Act provides that a second or successive motion to vacate a sentence must be based on either "(1) newly discovered evidence that, if proven and viewed in light of the evidence as a whole, would be sufficient to establish by clear and convincing evidence that no reasonable factfinder would have found the movant guilty of the offense; or (2) a new rule of constitutional law, made retroactive to cases on collateral review by the Supreme Court, that was previously unavailable." §2255.

(D) **Procedures for second or successive collateral claims by federal or state prisoners.** The Act states that state and federal prisoners seeking to file second or successive requests for collateral relief must "move in the appropriate court of appeals for an order authorizing the district court to consider the application." 28 U.S.C. §2244(b)(3)(A); §2255. The court of appeals may authorize the filing of the claims "only if it determines that the application makes a prima facie showing that the application satisfies the requirements" for review described in the preceding paragraphs of this outline. §2244(b)(3)(C). Moreover, a "district court shall dismiss any claim presented in a second or successive application . . . unless the applicant shows that the claim satisfies [those same] requirements." §2244(b)(4).

3.   Delay in Seeking Collateral Relief

Under certain circumstances, both state and federal prisoners' requests for collateral relief may be denied on the basis of **delay in bringing the claims.** According to Rule 9(a) of the Rules Governing Section 2254 Cases in the United States District Courts: "A petition may be dismissed if it appears that the state . . . has been prejudiced in its ability to respond to the petition by delay in its filing unless the petitioner shows that it is based on grounds of which he could not have had knowledge by the exercise of reasonable diligence before the circumstances prejudicial to the state occurred." See also Rule 9(a) of the Rules Governing Section 2255 Cases (analogous rule for federal prisoners). This rule is based on the equitable doctrine of "laches" according to which a party should be prevented from engaging in delay that harms an opponent.

The Section 2254 and Section 2255 Rules grant courts "discretion" to dismiss petitions when equitable considerations dictate dismissal. To exercise this discretion, the **state must be prejudiced** in its ability to respond and the **petitioner must be responsible for a lack of "reasonable diligence."** A judge may not dismiss a petition simply because a lengthy delay in filing caused harm to the state's ability to secure a conviction. See Vasquez v. Hillery, 474 U.S. 254, 106 S. Ct. 617, 88 L. Ed. 2d 598 (1986).

> **Note: The 1996 Act and delay in filing a petition.** After "many [prior] attempts . . . to create a statute of limitations for federal habeas corpus actions," in the 1996 Act Congress enacted provisions that establish fixed time periods for the filing of §§2254 and 2255 claims. According to the Act, "a 1-year period of limitation shall apply to an application for a writ of habeas corpus by a" state prisoner. The period runs "from the latest of" the date on which the state judgment became final, the date on which a state-created impediment to filing was removed, the date on which a constitutional right asserted was newly recognized by the Supreme Court and made retroactive to collateral proceedings, or the date on which the factual predicate for a claim could have been discovered by due diligence. Time during which a state prisoner is pursuing state collateral remedies does not count toward the limitations period. 28 U.S.C. §2244(d)(1), (2); see 28 U.S.C. §2255 (analogous provision governing federal prisoners' motions).

F. EVIDENTIARY HEARINGS AND STATE COURT FINDINGS OF FACT AND DETERMINATIONS OF LAW

A federal court's resolution of a constitutional claim raised in a habeas corpus petition hinges on both the **facts** and the **law** relevant to the claim. This section discusses the need for and permissibility of **"evidentiary hearings"** in federal courts, the **effect of prior state court factfinding,** and the **effect of prior state court determinations of legal questions and mixed questions of law and fact.**

1. Evidentiary Hearings in Habeas Corpus Proceedings: The Holding of Townsend v. Sain

A state prisoner's claim of unconstitutional confinement often depends in large part on disputed issues of fact. Townsend v. Sain, 372 U.S. 293, 83 S. Ct. 745, 9 L. Ed. 2d 770 (1963). When factual issues are critical, constitutional rights may be subverted if the habeas applicant lacks adequate opportunities to present evidence and to have factual questions reliably resolved. Id. To prevent such subversion, a federal court has "plenary" power to hold an **"evidentiary hearing"** that affords the parties to a habeas proceeding opportunities to present evidence relevant to the issues raised. Id. The "power" to hold such a hearing, however, needs to be exercised in a responsible manner. When a state court has already fairly and adequately resolved factual issues, "relitigation" in federal court can be wasteful, costly, and intrusive on legitimate state interests.

In Townsend v. Sain, the Supreme Court determined when a federal habeas court **must** hold an evidentiary hearing. The Court concluded that a hearing is **mandatory unless** the state court has reliably found the relevant facts after affording the prisoner a full and fair hearing. More specifically, federal courts are **required to hold evidentiary hearings if** (1) the merits of the factual dispute were not resolved by the state; (2) the state's factual determination is not fairly supported by the whole record; (3) the state factfinding process was not adequate to afford a full and fair hearing; (4) there is a substantial allegation of newly discovered evidence; (5) the material facts were not adequately developed in the state court; or (6) for any other reason, the state did not provide a full and fair hearing. In cases in which a hearing is allegedly required because the **"material facts were not adequately developed in the state court,"** a prisoner must show both **"cause"** for the failure to develop the facts in the state court and **"actual prejudice"** resulting from that failure or that a **"fundamental miscarriage of justice"** would result from the failure to hold an evidentiary hearing. Keeney v. Tamayo-Reyes, 504 U.S. 1, 112 S. Ct. 1715, 118 L. Ed. 2d 318 (1992). See sections E.1.b and E.1.c above for discussions of these standards.

In all other cases, a federal court **may** hold an evidentiary hearing—that is, a federal judge has **discretion** to decide whether an evidentiary hearing would be helpful and appropriate. In exercising this discretion, a judge should consider whether a hearing would be a waste of time and whether it would undermine the integrity of state proceedings. Keeney v. Tamayo-Reyes.

> **Note: The 1996 Act and evidentiary hearings.** In the 1996 Act, Congress amended §2254 to deal with the issue considered in Keeney v. Tamayo-Reyes—whether a federal court should hold a hearing when a petitioner "has failed to develop the factual basis for a claim in State court proceedings." According to the Act, a federal "court **shall not hold an evidentiary hearing** on the claim **unless**" (1) the claim relies on (a) "a new rule of constitutional law, made retroactive to cases on collateral review by the Supreme Court, that was previously unavailable" **or** (b) "a factual predicate that could not have been previously discovered through . . . due diligence" **and** (2) "the facts underlying the claim would . . . establish by clear and convincing evidence that but for constitutional error, no reasonable factfinder would have found the applicant guilty of the underlying offense." §2254(e)(2). These standards are clearly more demanding than the "cause and prejudice" standards adopted in Keeney v. Tamayo-Reyes.

2. State Court Resolutions of Factual and Legal Questions

In 1966, Congress amended §2254 by adding subsection (d). At least in some respects, this provision "codifies" the holding of Townsend v. Sain. See Miller v. Fenton, 474 U.S. 104, 106 S. Ct. 445, 88 L. Ed. 2d 405 (1985). Subsection (d) does not deal directly with the subject of "evidentiary hearings." Instead, it prescribes the circumstances in which findings of fact by state courts must **"be presumed to be correct"** and specifies the **showing required to overcome that presumption.** The presumption of correctness limits the power of federal habeas courts to resolve factual issues already resolved by state courts. Because there is no point in conducting an evidentiary hearing if the state's resolution of an issue must be accepted, the effect of subsection (d) is to restrict the availability of federal evidentiary hearings.

a.   **The §2254(d) "presumption of correctness" for state court findings of fact.** According to §2254(d), a state court "determination after a hearing on the merits of a factual issue," evidenced in writing, **"shall be presumed to be correct."** To **rebut** this presumption and have the factual issue redetermined by the federal court, the applicant must "establish by convincing evidence that the factual determination by the State court was erroneous." The presumption of correctness applies to factfinding by both **trial and appellate** courts. Sumner v. Mata, 449 U.S. 539, 101 S. Ct. 764, 66 L. Ed. 2d 722 (1981).

The **presumption of correctness does not apply,** however, **if** (1) the merits of the factual dispute were not resolved in the state court; (2) the factfinding procedure of the state was not adequate to afford a full and fair hearing; (3) the material facts were not adequately developed; (4) the state court lacked jurisdiction over the subject matter or petitioner; (5) in the state proceeding, an indigent petitioner was deprived of appointed counsel in violation of her constitutional right; (6) the state hearing was not full, fair and adequate; (7) the petitioner was otherwise denied due process in the state proceeding; or (8) the record of the state proceeding, as a whole, does not fairly support the factual determination of the state court. §2254(d).

b. **Federal court authority to determine questions of law.** According to Townsend v. Sain, a federal habeas court **may not defer** to state court "findings of law," but has a "duty to apply the applicable federal law to the state court fact findings independently." Section 2254(d) did not alter this conclusion. Its presumption of correctness governs only state court "findings of fact." It does not require a federal court to presume that a state court's resolution of a legal question or a "mixed question of law and fact" is correct. Consequently, both purely legal questions and mixed questions of law and fact are "subject to plenary federal review." Miller v. Fenton. A federal habeas court has an "independent obligation to decide the constitutional question." Id.

Many purely **legal questions**—questions of what the law is—are easy to categorize. For example, whether a suspect must know that a lawyer has tried to contact him in order validly to waive *Miranda* protections is a purely legal question. Some **factual questions** are also easily identified. Whether a suspect was actually informed of the fact that a lawyer tried to contact him is nothing more than a question of historical fact. It is sometimes difficult, however, to distinguish "questions of fact" from "mixed questions of law and fact." The distinction is important because questions of fact are entitled to the presumption of correctness in §2254(d) while "mixed questions of law and fact" should receive "independent review" by the federal habeas court. Miller v. Fenton; Thompson v. Keohane, — U.S. —, 116 S. Ct. 457, 133 L .Ed. 2d 383 (1995).

According to the Supreme Court, **questions of fact** are concerned with determining "basic, primary, or historical facts: facts 'in the sense of a recital of external events and the credibility of their narrators . . .'" Townsend v. Sain; Thompson v. Keohane. **"[M]ixed questions of fact and law"** are different insofar as they "require the application of a legal standard to the historical-fact determinations." Townsend v. Sain; Thompson v. Keohane. While these definitions are helpful, they do not lead to clear answers in every case. Because there is no unerring principle or methodology for distinguishing purely factual questions from "mixed" questions, Miller v. Fenton, the "proper characterization of a question" often proves to be "slippery." Thompson v. Keohane.

Questions that might appear factual—such as the voluntariness of a confession and the effectiveness of counsel's assistance—have been deemed "mixed" because of their "uniquely legal dimension." Id. Other questions that encompass more than the ascertainment of "basic, primary, or historical facts"—such as juror impartiality and defendants' competence to stand trial—have been deemed factual because they are questions that a state trial court has a "superior capacity to resolve" and because a state court's resolution is unlikely to have precedential value. Id.

In sum, in classifying a question as "factual" or "mixed," the Supreme Court has tried to determine whether the state court or the federal habeas court "is better positioned . . . to decide the issue." Miller v. Fenton. If the state court is better positioned, the question is deemed factual and is entitled to the §2254(d) presumption of correctness. If the federal habeas court is better positioned, the question is deemed "mixed" and qualifies for "independent federal review." Id.

 ## EXAMPLES AND ANALYSIS

1. In Kuhlmann v. Wilson, on review of a district court's denial of habeas relief, a federal court of appeals held that the petitioner's *Massiah* right to counsel had been violated when statements that had been deliberately elicited from him by an undercover informant were used to convict him. The Supreme Court reversed, concluding that the court of appeals had erroneously failed "to accord to the state trial court's factual findings the presumption of correctness expressly required by" §2254(d). The state court had found that the undercover agent had not "elicited" the statements that were used but instead had "only listened" to the prisoner's incriminating remarks. This was a finding of fact that was entitled to the presumption of correctness. Consequently, the court of appeals' determination that the agent had "deliberately elicited" the remarks was "clear error in light of the provisions and intent of §2254(d)."

2. In Thompson v. Keohane, a habeas petitioner had pursued a Miranda claim in the state trial court. The state court had rejected the claim based on its conclusion that the petitioner had not been "in custody" for purposes of *Miranda* doctrine. A federal district court then denied habeas relief based on its conclusion that the state court's finding that the petitioner was not "in custody" was entitled to the §2254(d) presumption of correctness.

The Supreme Court reversed, holding that the question of "custody" for *Miranda* doctrine purposes is a "mixed question of law and fact" that qualifies for independent federal review. First, the custody determination involves not merely the ascertainment of historical facts but the application of a controlling legal standard to historical facts. A state trial court is in no better position to apply such a standard than a federal habeas court. Moreover, classifying the "custody" determination as a "mixed question" serves "legitimate law enforcement interests" because "the law declaration aspect of independent review potentially may guide the police, unify precedent, and stabilize the law."

Note: The 1996 Act and state court findings of fact and determinations of law. The 1996 Act adds a new subsection (d) to §2254 and replaces old subsection (d) with a new, much shorter subsection (e). Subsection (d) now provides that writs of habeas corpus "shall not be granted with respect to any claim that was adjudicated on the merits in State court proceedings unless the adjudication of the claim—(1) resulted in a decision that was contrary to, or involved an unreasonable application of clearly established Federal law as determined by the Supreme Court . . . or (2) resulted in a decision that was based on an unreasonable determination of the facts in light of the evidence presented in the State court proceeding."

Subsection (e) now provides that "a determination of a factual issue made by a State court shall be presumed to be correct. The applicant shall have the burden of rebutting the presumption of correctness by clear and convincing evidence." §2254(e)(1). The new subsection does not list situations in which findings of fact are not entitled to the presumption.

While the meaning of these changes is not entirely clear, they seem to require deference to state resolutions of legal questions and to increase the deference that must be accorded state court factfinding.

G. HARMLESS ERROR ON COLLATERAL REVIEW

The standards for determining whether constitutional errors are "harmless" on direct appeal were discussed in Chapter 21, sections E.2 and E.3. The "harmlessness" standards applicable upon federal habeas corpus review of a state prisoner's constitutional claim are different in one respect.

On direct appeal, **constitutional "trial errors"** are evaluated under the *Chapman* standard. The question is whether the error was "harmless beyond a reasonable doubt." In habeas corpus proceedings, the harmlessness of constitutional trial errors is determined according to the less demanding *Kotteakos* standard—the standard that governs nonconstitutional errors on direct appeal. Brecht v. Abrahamson, 507 U.S. 619, 113 S. Ct. 1710, 123 L. Ed. 2d 353 (1993). The question is **whether the error had "substantial and injurious effect or influence on the jury."** Id. Habeas relief may not be granted without a showing of **"actual prejudice."** Id. The question is whether the habeas judge herself " 'think[s] that the error substantially influenced the jury's decision.' " O'Neal v. McAninch, 513 U.S. 432, 115 S. Ct. 992, 130 L. Ed. 2d 947 (1995). If the judge is uncertain but has "grave doubt" about whether an error had substantial influence—that is, if the judge is "in virtual equipoise as to the harmlessness of the error"—an error is not harmless. Id.

For harmless error purposes, **constitutional "structural errors"** are presumably treated the same on habeas review as they are treated on direct appeal. Such errors are never harmless; they lead to "automatic reversal" of a conviction. See Chapter 21, section E.3.

 # EXAMPLE AND ANALYSIS

In Brecht v. Abrahamson, on habeas corpus review, a prisoner established that at his trial the prosecution had violated due process by using his post-*Miranda* warning silence to impeach him at his trial for murder. The district court granted relief because it found that the violation of the prisoner's due process right had not been "harmless beyond a reasonable doubt."

The Supreme Court concluded that on habeas corpus review the "harmless beyond a reasonable doubt" standard did not govern the sort of constitutional trial error that had been established. Instead, such an error should be considered harmless unless it had "substantial and injurious effect or influence in determining the jury's verdict." In other words, a petitioner needs to establish "actual prejudice." Under this standard, the due process violation at the prisoner's trial was harmless because the state's references to his post-*Miranda* warning silence were "infrequent" and the other "evidence of guilt was, if not overwhelming, certainly weighty."

REVIEW QUESTIONS AND ANSWERS

Question: Jake was convicted of trafficking in child pornography based on an enterprise that entailed the distribution of made-to-order pictures over the Internet. He has been in state prison for two years. Jake is seeking habeas corpus relief based on two claims. One rests on a United States Supreme Court opinion issued since his conviction, holding that the Equal Protection Clause restriction on the discriminatory use of peremptory jury challenges applies to "religion based" strikes. The other claim is that the use of statements obtained in violation of *Miranda* to impeach a defense witness is impermissible. The government responds that these claims are not "cognizable" in habeas corpus proceedings. Should the federal court consider Jake's claims?

Answer: With regard to Jake's first claim, the date on which Jake's conviction became "final" must be ascertained. If the Supreme Court precedent on which he relies was decided before that date, it clearly is retroactive to his case, and his claim is cognizable. If the Court's decision was handed down after Jake's conviction became final, then the question is whether it announced a "new rule" of constitutional law. If so, Teague v. Lane holds that the rule is not retroactive to Jake's case and that a habeas court should not consider his claim.

On the one hand, it is arguable that the holding is merely an application of a general principle recognized in the *Batson* line of cases—that is, any classification entitled to more than rational basis review is governed by the *Batson* doctrine—and is therefore not a new rule. On the other hand, it is also arguable that the extension of *Batson* to religion was not dictated by precedent and "was susceptible to debate among reasonable minds," and therefore that it is a new rule. If the holding announced a new rule, that rule would not fall within either *Teague* exception. It did not hold that conduct was "beyond the power of the criminal law-making authority to proscribe" and did not announce a "watershed rule of criminal procedure" without which "the likelihood of an accurate conviction is seriously diminished."

With regard to Jake's second claim, the question is whether validation of his claim would require the habeas court to "announce" a new rule. *Teague* would preclude relief if a holding forbidding the impeachment of a defense witness with a statement obtained in violation of *Miranda* would be a new rule. That question is debatable. On the one hand, it might be seen as a mere logical application of James v. Illinois, in which the Court held that the products of Fourth Amendment violations may not be used to impeach defense witnesses. On the other hand, it is arguable that the extension of this holding to *Miranda* was not dictated by precedent and was susceptible to debate among reasonable minds. Again, if such a holding is a new rule, it would not fall within either *Teague* exception.

Question: Bertha was convicted of attempted murder and sentenced to 20 years in prison. At trial, she had asserted that her act had been involuntary because she was in a "somnambulistic" state at the time. The trial judge instructed the jurors that Bertha had to prove her "involuntary act" defense by a "preponderance of the evidence." On appeal, Bertha claimed that the jury instructions violated due process. Her challenge was rejected because "the defendant did not comply with the rule requiring a defendant to register objections to jury instructions at or immediately after trial in order to preserve them for appellate review **and** because her claim that the jury instruction violated due process lacks merit." While her petition for a writ of certiorari was pending in the Supreme Court, the Court decided that it violates due process to require a defendant to carry the burden of establishing that her act was involuntary because a voluntary actus reus is an essential element of an offense that the government must prove beyond a reasonable doubt. Bertha seeks habeas corpus relief based on this holding. What arguments should the state make in opposition to her petition? How should the habeas court rule?

Answer: The first question is whether state collateral relief is still available. If so, the state should contend that Bertha has not "exhausted" the available state remedies.

If state collateral relief is not available, the state should contend that Bertha's "state procedural default" was an "independent and adequate" state ground for denying her relief and that it bars habeas relief. The state appellate court plainly stated that its ruling was based on both the procedural default and the lack of merit to her federal claim. The procedural ground is "independent" of federal law. If the state has consistently applied that bar, it would seem to be adequate to support the state court's judgment.

Bertha could avoid the bar of the "state procedural default" doctrine by demonstrating "cause" and "prejudice." To establish cause, she needs to show that an "objective factor external to the defense" impeded efforts to comply with the rule, that the state interfered with her ability to comply, that the factual basis for her claim was "not reasonably available," or that the claim was "so novel that its legal basis [was] not reasonably available to counsel." If she could establish cause, she may well satisfy the prejudice requirement. The burden-shifting instruction could conceivably have had a sufficient impact on the outcome of the trial to establish prejudice from the violation of due process.

Finally, Bertha could also attempt to avoid the bar to relief by arguing that a "fundamental miscarriage of justice" would occur if relief were not granted. In this case, she might succeed with a claim that the constitutional violation led to the conviction of one who was "actually innocent." The record may be such that a properly instructed, reasonable juror probably would have acquitted her because of a reasonable doubt about whether she acted voluntarily—that is, a reasonable doubt about whether she was in fact guilty of the attempted murder.

Question: Clint was convicted of tax evasion. On appeal, his conviction was affirmed. After exhausting opportunities for state collateral review, Clint filed a habeas corpus petition, alleging that the trial judge had improperly restricted his attorney's ability to consult with him. The federal court disagreed with his claim. Two years later, Clint filed a second habeas petition alleging that his right to a speedy trial had been denied. The government responded that Clint's failure to raise the claim in his first habeas petition should bar consideration. Clint maintains that the reason he did not raise the speedy trial claim initially was that the government had concealed that fact that he had been the object of a sealed indictment for several years and that such information was essential to his claim. Should the habeas court entertain the petition?

Answer: The issue is whether the "abuse of the writ" doctrine should bar Clint's claim. The government can carry its initial burden by documenting Clint's failure to raise his speedy trial claim in his first petition for a writ of habeas corpus. The burden then shifts to Clint to show "cause" and "prejudice" or that a "fundamental miscarriage of justice" would occur.

Clint might well be able to demonstrate cause. If the state withheld information that was essential to perceiving the speedy trial claim, it is fair to say both that the state interfered with his ability to raise the claim and that the factual basis for the claim was not reasonably available at the time of the first petition. In addition, Clint probably can satisfy the prejudice element. If his speedy trial claim has merit, the outcome of his trial certainly would have been different because the failure to give him a speedy trial would have **precluded** prosecution.

Clint probably could not satisfy the "fundamental miscarriage of justice" exception. He would not be able to show that the constitutional violation he suffered led to the conviction of an "actually innocent" person. Instead, his claim seems to be one of "legal innocence"—that is, that the violation of his right to a speedy trial raises a legal barrier to conviction even if he is factually guilty of the offense.

> **Note:** It is difficult to determine whether Clint could succeed under the 1996 Act because the meaning of the provision dealing with "abusive" petitions is unclear. Consideration of a claim not presented in a prior petition is allowed if "the factual predicate for the claim could not have been discovered previously through . . . due diligence" and "the facts . . . would establish . . . that, but for the constitutional error, no reasonable factfinder would have found the applicant guilty." Clint could probably show that the factual predicate "could not have been discovered." It is uncertain whether he could show that "no reasonable factfinder would have found him guilty." On the one hand, his speedy trial claim does not change the evidence of his guilt. On the other hand, the case would not have reached a reasonable factfinder because the violation would have barred a trial.

Question: Wendy was convicted of burglary and assault with intent to rob. After exhausting all other opportunities for relief, she filed a habeas corpus petition, claiming that critical evidence admitted at her trial was obtained during an illegal search of her automobile and that she had not knowingly and voluntarily waived her right to counsel and chosen to represent herself at trial. The state courts had ruled against her illegal search claim and had specifically found a valid waiver of counsel. Should the habeas court entertain her claims? Must the habeas court presume that the state court's waiver determination is correct?

Answer: The habeas court should entertain Wendy's Fourth Amendment exclusionary rule claim only if she did not receive a "full and fair" hearing on that claim in the state courts. If she did receive a "full and fair" hearing, the doctrine of Stone v. Powell precludes habeas relief.

The court should entertain Wendy's right to counsel claim. The question whether Wendy "waived" her right to counsel rests in part on determinations of historical fact such as what pressure was put on her to waive her right, what her strength of will was, what information she was told by the judge, and what other facts she knew. Such determinations must be presumed correct under §2254(d). However, the ultimate question of whether Wendy did "waive" her right to counsel is a "mixed question of fact and law." It requires the application of the legal standard that dictates the validity of waivers to the historical facts. The presumption of correctness in §2254(d) does not govern mixed questions.

> **Note:** The 1996 Act seems to change the analysis. It provides that a writ should not be granted unless the state's adjudication "resulted in a decision . . . contrary to, or involved an unreasonable application of clearly established Federal Law." This provision suggests that the state court's determination of the mixed question of whether there was a waiver should not be overturned simply because the federal court disagrees with it. The federal court must find the state court's determination to be "contrary to" clear federal law or "an *unreasonable* application of" that law.

EXAM TIPS

This section offers suggestions for responding to examination questions. It is divided into two parts. The first provides general advice regarding essay and objective examinations. Much, if not all, of this general advice is pertinent to examinations in all subjects. The second part discusses the importance of developing analytical approaches to each specific subject in criminal procedure and provides two illustrative approaches.

The suggestions included here are based on experience. They can assist your efforts to maximize your performance on criminal procedure examinations. They are not meant to discourage you from exploring other or additional avenues to success or from asking individual professors in your courses about techniques that are likely to be helpful.

A. GENERAL ADVICE ON ANSWERING EXAM QUESTIONS

Fact-pattern essay questions and objective, multiple-choice questions test different abilities and skills. Each requires a somewhat different approach. Section 1 contains advice regarding essay exams. Section 2 provides tips for answering objective questions.

1. Essay Exam Questions

Success on essay examinations is partly a product of knowledge and analytical skills, partly a product of the ability clearly and thoroughly to express your knowledge and analyses in writing, partly the product of quickness of thought and execution, and partly the product of tactics or strategy—of playing the examination game well. Most of the advice found here can improve tactics and strategies, thereby enhancing the possibility that you will be able to demonstrate fully your knowledge, analyses, quickness of thought, and talents for written expression.

   a. Identifying and focusing on the task or tasks assigned. Fact-pattern essays typically require students to discuss the legal implications of a "story." They vary in length and nature. Some are long and raise a large number of intertwined issues. Others are brief and focus on a

479

single issue or small number of issues. The task assigned—ordinarily specified in a command or question at the end of the fact pattern—may be general and open ended (e.g., "Discuss" or "Discuss the issues and arguments"), specific and narrow (e.g., "Discuss whether a search occurred" or "Was the accused entitled to a jury trial?"), or somewhere between these extremes (e.g., "Should the defendant's motion to exclude the confession be granted?").

In responding to an essay question, it is essential to identify and focus exclusively on the task or tasks assigned. (To save time and effort, it may be wise to glance at the end of the fact pattern at the outset.) If a fact pattern raises issues outside the scope of the assigned task or tasks, do not spend precious time addressing those issues. It is very unlikely that any credit will be awarded for discussions that range beyond the bounds of the assignment. Furthermore, you will rarely have excess time to spend on essay questions. If you expend time and energy on unassigned matters, you are wasting time and energy that could be spent earning credit.

b.   **Spotting and stating issues.** Issue spotting is an essential element of success on an essay examination. Within the constraints of the task or tasks assigned, you must identify the specific legal issues that merit discussion. Both the law *and* the facts provided in the question dictate the issues that should be addressed. The requirements of the law provide the bases for *potential* issues, but the facts provided in the examination determine whether those issues are actually present in a given situation.

For example, to be able to determine whether a *Miranda* issue is present, you must know the elements of *Miranda* law. Viewed in the light of those elements, the facts at hand may preclude a *Miranda* claim and render a discussion of *Miranda* law pointless. No matter how accurately you might discuss *Miranda* law, that discussion is unlikely to earn any credit because you have demonstrated knowledge that has not been requested. At the very most, and only if there is time to do so, you might state that there is no *Miranda* claim because the doctrine requires a specific element and the given facts do not include that element.

Begin a discussion by clearly and expressly stating the issue or subissue. For example, you might begin, "The first issue is whether the officers violated the *Miranda* doctrine." Or you might preface the treatment of a subissue as follows: "The next question is whether the suspect was in custody." Introductory statements of the issues make it easier to follow a discussion and may earn credit that would not be awarded if the discussion merely "implied" that the issue had been spotted.

A warning is in order. If the facts do not give rise to a particular issue—a *Miranda* claim, for example—then do not discuss *Miranda* doctrine at all. If the facts do give rise to a particular issue, then mention briefly each of the basic elements of the applicable doctrine. For example, if the facts give rise to the issue of whether officers failed to honor a request for *Miranda* counsel, you should—as economically as possible—discuss the basic elements of *Miranda* doctrine even if there are no subissues regarding those basic elements. Thus, you should specify the custody, interrogation, and warnings requirements, and should point out as briefly as possible why the facts satisfy those elements. How much effort to devote to such basics is a judgment call, but in order to set the stage for the discussion of the disputable issue—the invocation of counsel claim—a foundational sketch of this "context" should be included. **Note:** This is an area that instructors may credit differently. Students who wish to play it safe may want to consult with their instructors in advance.

The next three subsections describe the components that should be included in discussions of the issues you have spotted and stated. To enhance organization, clarity, and thoroughness, you may wish to "outline" your answer in skeletal form before writing it. Because you will rarely have excess time on essay examinations, however, you should not spend an inordinate amount of time outlining and may not wish to spend any time doing so.

c. **Explaining the law.** After an issue has been stated, explain the pertinent law. For the sake of organization and clarity, do not list *all* the issues before you discuss any of them. Instead, provide a complete analysis of *each* issue immediately after your statement of that issue.

Make your explanations of the law as complete as possible. Doctrines, rules, and standards should be explained in the *exact* language used by the court or the legislature. Do not abbreviate or paraphrase legal standards. Synonyms or variations in controlling terminology are not advisable. The more applicable law that is provided and the more thorough and accurate the presentation of that law, the greater the credit that will be earned.

In many areas of law, there may be more than one potentially governing standard for a particular issue. (In criminal law, for example, there are several definitions of the requisite actus reus for an attempt.) In criminal procedure, if a question has been answered by the Supreme Court and if federal constitutional law is applicable, there will be only one rule of law or doctrinal standard. Make that clear and do not treat dissenting views or overruled doctrines as equally plausible.

In some instances, it is advisable to explain more than one potential controlling standard on a criminal procedure examination. First, if a question of law is unsettled, say so clearly and explicitly before presenting any plausible rule of law that might be adopted. Also discuss the arguments that support or undermine each rule of law. Second, you may be asked to respond under a state constitution in a jurisdiction that has not yet resolved an issue. Because federal doctrines guide, but do not dictate, the answers under independent state constitutional provisions, you should once again entertain and explain all plausible possibilities and the arguments pro and con. Finally, you might simply be asked to present opposing views or alternative possible rules of law. In that case, discuss all rational alternatives.

d. **Applying the law to the facts.** In a fact-pattern question, the answer being sought is not an abstract discussion of a body of law. The assignment is to confront and resolve particular issues in a concrete case. While explaining the law is essential, it is only a part of the task assigned. The law must also be applied to the facts—the specific facts provided. Facts that support one conclusion should be specified, not alluded to or intimated. If there are facts supporting the opposite conclusion, they, too, should be specified. Moreover, *all relevant facts* should be incorporated in this part of the discussion. Credit will be lost if only one or two of five relevant facts are mentioned or if only the facts that support one position are mentioned.

Suppose the question is whether an officer crossed the Fourth Amendment line between a *Terry*, investigative detention and a full arrest. In your answer, first point out facts that support the conclusion that an arrest did occur: that the officer handcuffed the suspect, moved him 100 yards, held onto his identification the entire time, and that three other officers surrounded him. Then point out the facts indicative of a mere detention: the five-minute length of the encounter, the officer's statement that the suspect was not under arrest, and the open, public setting of the encounter. A failure to mention all these facts will result in less than full credit.

If any of the facts pertinent to a particular issue are unknown, point this out and discuss the relevance of the missing fact. For example, if the *Terry* question in the previous paragraph did not specify the length of the encounter, then note that this pertinent fact is missing and explain why it is relevant.

e. **Conclusions.** Students sometimes believe that conclusions—resolutions of the issues spotted—are the most important part of their answers. In fact, a conclusion may well be the least important element. A correct conclusion may be worth a small amount of credit if it comes at the end of a sound analysis, but it is not likely to be worth anything if it follows erroneous reasoning or a weak discussion. On the other hand, an incorrect conclusion is unlikely to detract much, if at all, from a well-reasoned and explained answer.

Avoid the erroneous belief that a conclusion must be definitive—that it must reflect a clear resolution one way or the other. If the law and facts do lead to such a conclusion, then state it with confidence. However, many, if not most, issues raised in essay questions are designed so that no definitive conclusion can be reached. When this is the case, do not hesitate to write answers using phrases such as "it is unclear," "it seems probable," or "it is very likely, but not certain." For example, the bottom line of the *Terry* issue discussion might be "it is unclear whether the suspect was subjected to a full arrest" or "it seems probable that an arrest occurred."

In sum, while conclusions should be stated, do not place too much emphasis on the conclusion reached. In particular, do not "force" a definitive conclusion when uncertainty is justified. Follow the law and facts to wherever they lead and express that conclusion clearly.

f. **Additional elements and aspects of a superior essay answer.**

   i. **Allocation and wise use of time.** When an essay examination comprises a number of questions, take care to allocate ample time to each question. If the instructor provides guidance, such as time estimates or weight allocations, pay attention to it. But even if the instructor does not provide guidance, it is very important to accord each question or portion of the exam enough time for a decent discussion of the basic issues. Time spent exploring minutia, peripheral issues, or fine details of one question could be much better spent spotting and discussing the basic issues of another question. It is better to do a solid job on each part than to do a perfect job on some parts and to neglect others.

   ii. **Writing form and style.** Explain yourself clearly, in language that is unambiguous to the reader who is "ignorant" of the law and facts. Cogent expression of your thoughts will maximize the credit earned. This does not mean that you must always employ precise grammar and polished constructions. Time spent ensuring exact grammar or punctuation or devising impressive syntax is likely to be time wasted. Examinations are occasions for clear and economical expression of sound analyses, not for showing off one's writing talents. Substance is the most important aspect of an answer. Clear, time-saving abbreviations can be helpful. **Note:** This is an area in which instructors' preferences may vary. If you are in doubt, ask your professor.

   The form of writing is unimportant so long as it is sufficiently legible. Neatness may count a bit in the psyche of the grader, but it is unlikely to earn much, if any, credit. Of course, if the reader has to struggle mightily to decipher word after word, there is a strong possibility that some of the message will be lost in translation—and left uncredited. Moreover, a battle to break the code may have adverse effects in the subconscious of the grader. Students with handwriting that is truly difficult to read should take necessary steps (such as writing more slowly, printing, or typing) to eliminate the problem.

iii.   **Organization.** Organization itself is not likely to earn much, if any, credit on an essay examination. Nonetheless, a well-organized answer is likely to earn more credit for two reasons. First, the student who takes up one issue or subissue at a time, explains the applicable law, then addresses the facts and states a conclusion before moving on to the next issue or subissue will inevitably be more thorough. Pertinent points of law and facts may well be overlooked if answers do not progress in a logical order. Second, points presented in an orderly fashion and in the right context are more likely to be recognized and awarded full credit. Doctrines or facts that are presented haphazardly may not be recognized, may lack the clarity that a proper context can give, or may not be expressed in a way that deserves full (or any) credit.

iv.   **Case names and citations.** Although instructors should be consulted about the importance of case names, it is unlikely that a case name will earn much, if any, credit, unless the law associated with that case is explained. Conversely, a thorough explication of the law probably will not lose much, if any, credit because it lacks a case name. On the other hand, well-known case names (such as *Miranda*, *Terry*, *Gideon*, or *Brady-Bagley*) should be included in discussions and may serve as helpful abbreviations that promote economical use of time. Do not concern yourself with proper citation; they are not likely to earn any credit.

g.   **Conclusions regarding essay examinations.** Rarely, if ever, will you have sufficient time to write answers that clearly, cogently, and thoroughly address all relevant issues and include all pertinent law and facts. The object is to do the best job possible within the time allotted and not to allow time pressure or frustration to impede the ability to do so. By following the advice furnished above and by recognizing that the object is to produce the best product you can under the constraints imposed—not to achieve some ideal—you should be able to maximize your scores on essay examinations.

The sample essay questions and answers provided in the next part of this outline should make the advice furnished above more concrete. Review these questions and answers in light of this advice.

2. Objective Exam Questions

The sole aim in an objective examination is to reason your way to the correct answers, not to demonstrate your analytical abilities. For those who find it particularly difficult to arrive at the correct answers, practice and individual work with an instructor may be desirable and even necessary. The general advice that follows may also prove helpful.

Some of the same abilities that contribute to success on essays—knowledge of the law, logical reasoning, quickness of thought—are also important to success on objective examinations. Without a sound understanding of the legal rules and the significance of different facts under those rules, you will not be able to reason to the right answer. When time is limited, quickness will serve you well, but if you sacrifice care to quickness, the result is likely to be disastrous.

a. **Read the facts, questions, and foils carefully.** Precision and exactitude are vital—both in knowledge of the law and in reading of the facts, questions, and foils. Small factual differences are often significant and can make substantial differences in legal outcomes. An error in reading even one word may well lead you to an erroneous answer. Misreading of the question may lead you to the antithesis of the correct answer. Similarly, a small misunderstanding of a foil may lead you to conclude it is sound when it is not or that it is weak when it is correct.

b. **Eliminate incorrect foils.** For any question, except the occasional one that is designed simply to test knowledge of the law, it is inadvisable simply to read it and the foils and to choose the answer that strikes you as the best. Before settling on an answer, be sure to analyze the unchosen answers carefully and to satisfy yourself as to *why* each is "wrong." To the extent possible, you should not only have a reason why the answer you choose is "correct," you should also have a reason why each of the others is erroneous. Reasons for choosing the correct answer and rejecting the incorrect foils should be based on the law studied as applied to the facts given.

c. **Cultivate and exercise good judgment.** Some objective examination questions require you to choose between or among answers of varying strength. Contrary to some student perceptions, an instructor is not likely to require a student to make hairline distinctions or to choose based on small degrees of difference in the plausibility of the foils. It is much more likely that the distinctions and differences will be substantial enough to be discernible to the student who knows the law, reads the question carefully, reasons logically, and is able to exercise good judgment. An argument with some remote or possible chance of success is simply not as good an answer as an argument that will surely or almost surely prevail.

    d. **Do not dwell on difficult questions; double-check your answers.** If you are having difficulty with a question, do not dwell on it for an inordinate amount of time. Either leave it blank or fill it in tentatively with an eye to returning if time allows. To the extent possible within the time constraints imposed, review your answers. If time to do so is limited, reread the questions that were more difficult. Double-checking may enable you to spot a fact or distinction that you missed the first time.

B. ANALYTICAL APPROACHES TO RESOLVING CRIMINAL PROCEDURE QUESTIONS

One key to success on criminal procedure examinations is having a working knowledge and understanding of the pertinent law. To gain such knowledge and understanding, there is no substitute for intense study.

Another component of success is the development of logical analytical approaches to each distinct area of the law. The effort required to develop such approaches will pay dividends by improving your abilities to spot issues and to discuss those issues clearly and thoroughly. You should be aware that the development of analytical approaches to areas of criminal procedure is not part of the exam-taking process itself. Nonetheless, it is a very helpful part of *preparing for* examinations. Moreover, the approaches you develop can serve as useful *guides and checklists* during examinations.

In this section, two illustrative approaches to areas of criminal procedure are provided as models to assist you in developing your own approaches to other topics. These illustrations are not comprehensive recapitulations of the law pertinent to the particular areas but are sketches of the inquiries that ought to be pursued. Note, however, that the law pertaining to each area does dictate the structure and content of an appropriate analytical approach. Without a clear understanding of the legal rules that govern an area, it is impossible to devise a sound analytical method of resolving issues that may arise.

It is unlikely that there is only one way to phrase or organize an analytical approach to resolving issues in a particular area. You should not assume that there is no room for variation in the phrasing or organization of the illustrations furnished. Design your approaches in ways that enable you to produce the most thorough and clear discussions of the issues.

1. An Illustrative Approach to *Miranda* Doctrine Issues

This section sketches an approach for determining whether a set of facts raises an issue or issues under the *Miranda* doctrine and for analyzing and resolving that issue or those issues. **Note:** The approach sketched here is intended to deal only with the question of whether a violation occurred; it does not address exclusionary rule issues.

a. Is *Miranda* applicable? The threshold questions. The first major question that must be confronted under *Miranda* is whether the constraints it imposes are even applicable. That depends on two "threshold" questions: custody and interrogation.

    i. Was the suspect **in custody**? The commands of *Miranda* apply only after a suspect is taken into custody by the authorities.

    ii. Did a known government agent **interrogate** the suspect? Even if the suspect is in custody, *Miranda* applies only if a known government agent interrogates him.

b. Did the authorities comply with *Miranda*? If *Miranda* doctrine applies, it imposes an array of constraints on custodial interrogation. Several questions must be asked:

    i. Did the authorities give **adequate warnings?** Compliance with *Miranda* always requires that the substance of the information contained in the *Miranda* warnings be conveyed to the suspect. The questions that should be asked are whether warnings were given and if they were complete and accurate.

    ii. Did the suspect **invoke** the **right to silence**? If so, additional safeguards apply. The following questions should be asked:

        (a) Was the suspect's statement or conduct **sufficient to invoke the right to silence**?

        (b) If not, the analysis of this issue ends. If so, did the authorities **scrupulously honor** the invocation?

        (c) If not, *Miranda* was violated. If so, did the suspect **waive** his rights?

    iii. Did the suspect **invoke** the **right to counsel**? If so, additional safeguards apply. The following questions should be asked:

        (a) Was the suspect's statement or conduct **sufficient to invoke the right to counsel**?

        (b) If so, did the **authorities initiate communications** with the suspect or did the **suspect initiate communications** with the authorities?

        (c) If the authorities initiated communications, *Miranda* was violated. If the suspect initiated communications, did he **waive** the *Miranda* rights?

iv. Did the suspect **waive** the *Miranda* rights? If the suspect invoked either the right to silence or the right to counsel, compliance with *Miranda* will ultimately require a valid waiver. Even if no right has been invoked, a waiver is essential for compliance with *Miranda*. The question in every case is whether an adequate basis for finding a satisfactory waiver is presented by the facts.

2. **An Illustrative Approach to Sixth Amendment "Speedy Trial" Issues**

The Sixth Amendment provides a right to a "speedy" trial. Analysis of whether the government violated this right requires several inquiries.

a. **When did the speedy trial right attach?** The right to a speedy trial does not "attach," and the guarantee, therefore, is inapplicable, prior to arrest or formal charge. The initial question, therefore, is whether and when the right attached.

b. **Was the application of the right suspended for any period of time?** The right to a speedy trial does not apply to any period when charges are dismissed in good faith by the government or are dismissed by a court over the government's objection. Therefore, a pertinent question is whether the right was suspended for any period of time.

c. **Was the time during which the right was applicable sufficient to trigger "balancing" analysis?** The simple question here is whether the threshold time period for claiming a speedy trial violation was satisfied. If not, there can be no violation. If so, whether the right was violated depends on the Barker v. Wingo balancing analysis.

d. **Does the four-factor balancing analysis of Barker v. Wingo favor the defendant's claim that a speedy trial was denied or the government's claim that the trial was sufficiently speedy?** According to the controlling authority, whether a speedy trial violation has occurred depends on the balance of four pertinent factors:

   i. **How long** was the **delay**? The question is whether the time period that counts was just over the threshold, exceptionally long, or somewhere in between.

   ii. **What are the reasons for** or who is to **blame for** the **delay**? To decide how to weigh this factor in the balance—which side to put it on and how much weight to give it—the following questions must be asked: Was the delay caused by the government or the defendant? If caused by the government, was there good reason for the delay? Was it caused by culpable conduct by the government or simple neglect?

    iii. Did the defendant **assert** the right to a speedy trial? Again, determining whether this factor weighs on one side or the other and how much weight it should be accorded depends on several inquiries: Did the defendant ask for a speedy trial? If so, was the request a mere formality that was contradicted by conduct indicating that the defendant did not really desire a speedy trial? If not, did the defendant have a good reason for failing to assert the right?

    iv. Was the defendant **prejudiced** by the delay? The most important question is whether the defendant has proven any actual prejudice to his defense and, if not, whether the delay was sufficiently long to provide a basis for presuming such prejudice. Another question is whether the defendant was prejudiced during the delay by deprivation of a liberty interest. Was he incarcerated or subjected to bail constraints? A final question is whether the accused suffered other kinds of speedy trial prejudice, such as anxiety, stigma, or loss of employment as a result of the pending accusation.

    v. Which side does the **balance favor**? The ultimate, determinative inquiry is whether the balance of factors tips toward the defendant's claim of a speedy trial violation or toward the government's claim of compliance with the Constitution. If the former, dismissal of the charges is required. If the latter, no remedy is necessary.

SAMPLE EXAM QUESTIONS

Question: Arlene has been charged with manufacturing and conspiring to distribute child pornography. The evidence to be introduced at her trial was discovered by means of the following investigative activities.

Sammy, an unemployed engineer, called the police to report that he had been picking up cordless phone conversations on his radio scanner. According to Sammy, "a woman who has been a party to most of them has said suspicious and troubling things." When Vic, a vice detective, asked Sammy for permission to monitor the scanner, Sammy said that he was "reluctant to get too involved." When Vic told Sammy that he was "already involved" and that "innocent citizens usually cooperate," Sammy relented. He allowed Vic to monitor his scanner for a week. Vic identified Arlene as the woman participating in the conversations and recorded several remarks implicating her in child pornography enterprises.

Two days later, Vic went to Arlene's home. He did not have a search warrant. Beverly, Arlene's 16-year-old daughter, came to the door and reported that Arlene was not home. Without telling her why, Vic asked Beverly if he could come inside. "Well, I guess that would be okay," Beverly replied, stepping back to let Vic enter. Once he was inside the foyer, Vic asked Beverly, "Would you mind if I took a quick look all around?" "Go ahead if you want to," Beverly said. On the desk in Arlene's study, in a suitcase in a basement storage room, and in the closet in Arlene's bedroom, Vic found evidence tying Arlene to the child pornography offenses.

One week later, a woman telephoned the police. The call was referred to Vic. The caller, who refused to identify herself, told Vic that she was "feeling terribly guilty about helping Arlene with her dirty business" and reported that Arlene "always keeps a good

supply of her wares in a valise in the trunk of her Mercedes."
Without obtaining a warrant, Vic went to Arlene's home the next
day. Her Mercedes was parked on the driveway. Arlene was working
in the yard. Vic approached, placed her under arrest based on the
evidence he had found in her home during his search, and asked
for permission to search her car. Arlene asked if he had a warrant.
When Vic said he did not, Arlene ordered him to leave her property.
Instead, Vic searched Arlene, found the keys to the Mercedes,
opened the trunk, removed a black valise, and found child pornography inside.

As Vic was escorting Arlene to his car, she asked if she could "go
inside for a few minutes to freshen up." "Okay," Vic replied, "but
for no more than five minutes." After Arlene left, Vic had second
thoughts and grew suspicious. Two minutes after Arlene had entered the house, Vic followed her inside and found her in the
bedroom, destroying additional evidence. Vic seized the evidence
and took Arlene to the police station.

One week later, Barry, another vice officer, came to Arlene's home
with a valid warrant to search the Mercedes. The warrant was
based on probable cause gathered wholly legally and separately
from Vic's investigation. Because Vic had already removed the
valise a week earlier, Barry found nothing in the car.

DISCUSS THE CONSTITUTIONALITY OF THE VARIOUS
ACTIONS LEADING TO THE DISCOVERY OF EVIDENCE
AGAINST ARLENE AND THE POTENTIAL ADMISSIBIL-
ITY OF THAT EVIDENCE.

Answer: The **first issue** is the constitutionality of listening to Arlene's
conversations on Sammy's scanner. The Fourth Amendment regu-
lates only the actions of government agents. Because Sammy was
acting as a private citizen when he first listened to Arlene's conversations on his scanner, there is no constitutional basis for challenging
his conduct.

With regard to the listening by vice detective Vic, the question is
whether his actions constituted a "search." The Fourth Amendment regulates only searches and seizures. Under the controlling
Katz doctrine, a search occurs when the government invades a
reasonable, justifiable, or legitimate expectation of privacy. Whether
an invasion of a reasonable expectation of privacy occurred depends
on (1) whether the person has exhibited an actual (subjective) expectation of privacy and (2) whether society is prepared to recognize
that expectation as reasonable.

It is arguable that Arlene did not exhibit an "actual" expectation of privacy because people who use cordless telephones are aware of a significant risk of interception of their conversations by other cordless phone users and those with radio scanners. One relevant question is whether cordless phone users know of such risks. Another relevant consideration is the likelihood that a cordless phone conversation will be intercepted.

Whether Vic "searched" Arlene is likely to turn on the second inquiry—whether society is prepared to recognize the privacy expectation as reasonable. On the one hand, Arlene arguably "knowingly exposed" her conversations to the public and failed to take adequate precautions to protect her privacy. Scanners are available to the public and cordless phone conversations can be legally intercepted by any member of the public with a scanner. The authorities are entitled to assume a vantage point that is legally available to the public and to receive whatever information is publicly exposed.

On the other hand, it is arguable that the risk of interception is too small to conclude that Arlene "knowingly exposed" her conversations. Scanners are not widely used by the public. Moreover, the cordless phone calls were overheard not by means of unaided human senses but by means of a sophisticated technological device that enhanced those senses.

The **second issue** is whether Vic's search of Arlene's home was reasonable under the Fourth Amendment. A reasonable search ordinarily must be based on probable cause and a search warrant. Warrantless searches are per se unreasonable, subject to a few well-delineated exceptions. Even if Vic had probable cause to search Arlene's home, he did not secure a search warrant. The question is whether the search is justified by the "consent" exception to the search warrant requirement.

To rely on consent, the government must show that consent was given, that it was voluntary, and that the person giving the consent had authority to do so. Consent does not have to be express but can be inferred from conduct. Still, the government must show more than mere acquiescence to an officer's wishes. Moreover, the consent must be shown to be voluntary by a preponderance of the evidence. While the subjective attributes of the consenter are relevant and can make a finding of involuntariness more likely, without some minimal level of coercive conduct by an officer a consent probably should not be deemed involuntary.

Here, Vic asked if he could come inside, then asked if he could take a quick look around. Beverly's grants of permission probably constituted consents. Because Beverly was only sixteen years old, she probably was quite susceptible to official coercion by an adult, male police officer. Still, because Vic did not engage in any coercive conduct, the consents should be found voluntary.

Beverly may not have had authority to consent to the searches that occurred. While it is arguable that a young child can never give a valid consent, a 16-year-old is probably mature enough to consent. Authority to consent, however, depends on "common authority." Common authority requires mutual use by a person generally having joint access or control for most purposes. Beverly probably had "common authority" over the foyer and other areas of the home. She may well not have had such authority over Arlene's study, the suitcase in the basement storage room, and Arlene's bedroom closet. It seems unlikely that these are spaces of "mutual use" or that she has "joint access to or control over them."

The government might try to rely on the "apparent authority" doctrine. That doctrine validates warrantless searches when an individual who has consented lacks authority but an officer had an objectively reasonable belief that the person had authority to consent. In this case, there are no facts indicating that it was reasonable for Vic to believe that Beverly had authority to consent to searches of the areas he searched. There is a good chance that the search of Arlene's home was unreasonable.

The **next issue** is the validity of the warrantless search of Arlene's Mercedes. Again, the question is whether the search qualifies for one of the exceptions to the warrant rule. The "search incident to arrest" exception allows an officer to search the person of an arrestee and the area within her immediate control following a lawful custodial arrest. The search of the Mercedes does not qualify because its trunk was outside the scope of a proper search incident to arrest. Moreover, Arlene's arrest may well be tainted by earlier illegalities. If the probable cause to arrest Arlene is the product of unlawful monitoring of phone conversations or an unlawful search of her home or both, the arrest would be tainted, and anything found in a search incident to that arrest could be the tainted fruit of the earlier illegalities.

The warrantless search of the Mercedes might be justifiable under the "automobile doctrine." That doctrine requires probable cause to search a readily mobile vehicle. Moreover, it *may not* apply to a vehicle that is stationary on private property belonging to the vehicle owner.

The anonymous phone call may not be enough to furnish probable cause. Under *Gates*, the "totality of the circumstances" standard is used to determine whether a showing based on hearsay establishes probable cause. The question is whether there is a "fair probability" that child pornography was in the trunk of the Mercedes. The two-prong *Aguilar-Spinelli* test has been rejected, but the two prongs are still "highly relevant" to a conscientious assessment of the weight to be given to the hearsay. According to *Gates*, a strong showing on one prong can compensate for a deficiency in the other prong. Moreover, independent police corroboration of matters reported by an informant play an important role in the totality assessment. For all showings but those that contain mere "bare bones" conclusions, there are no rigid rules barring or requiring probable cause findings.

The caller here asserted a very strong basis of knowledge—firsthand involvement in Arlene's enterprise. That could support a conclusion that she had personal knowledge of Arlene's business and habits. However, nothing was known about the caller's veracity—that is, about whether she was telling the truth. Perhaps her "guilt" for participating in the enterprise could be a basis for inferring a motive to tell the truth. If not, perhaps the caller's strong "basis of knowledge" prong "compensates" for the deficient "veracity" prong. Although Vic did not have direct corroboration of the caller's specific assertions regarding the "wares" in Arlene's trunk, the intercepted telephone conversations did provide evidence that Arlene was involved in the child pornography business. Those conversations gave meaning to and provided some support for the anonymous caller's assertions. On these facts, either a finding of probable cause to search the car or a finding that probable cause was lacking could be sustained.

In addition, the Mercedes was on Arlene's curtilage, an area in which she had a reasonable expectation of privacy. The reasoning of *Carney* and *Kilgore* suggests that the "automobile doctrine" might well apply to any readily mobile vehicle *wherever it is located*. The Court, however, has not yet applied the automobile doctrine to a vehicle that was parked on the curtilage of the vehicle owner.

A **related issue** is the reasonableness of Vic's entry into Arlene's curtilage. It is unclear whether probable cause alone justifies the physical entry of curtilage—where the car was located. The Supreme Court has not resolved the question of the showing necessary to enter the curtilage. A search warrant may be required. Probable cause may be sufficient. Or a reasonable suspicion may be enough. If a warrant is needed, the entry here might be unreasonable. If, however, the automobile doctrine does apply to vehicles parked on private property because of the exigency created by their mobility, then it is logical to assume that a warrant is not needed to enter curtilage to search or seize a vehicle under that exception.

If the automobile doctrine justifies the search, the scope was proper. Under that warrant rule exception, an officer may search wherever there is probable cause to search. Containers in the vehicle are also subject to search. If there was probable cause here, it pertained to the valise in the trunk.

If the search of the Mercedes was unreasonable, an **additional issue** is whether the evidence found in the Mercedes is admissible under the inevitable discovery exception to the Fourth Amendment exclusionary rule. If evidence is illegally obtained but the government establishes by a preponderance of the evidence that the same evidence would have been inevitably discovered by legal means, the evidence is admissible. On the one hand, Barry had a valid warrant to search the Mercedes and arrived a week after Vic. It is arguable that the pornography found by Vic would no longer have been in the trunk and, therefore, that the exception does not apply. On the other hand, Arlene had been arrested. If she remained in custody prior to Barry's arrival, the chances that the pornography would still have been in the trunk seem relatively high. It is unclear whether the government can establish that it is "more likely than not" that the evidence would inevitably have been discovered.

The **final issue** is whether Vic's second entries of Arlene's home and bedroom were reasonable. Under *Chrisman*, an officer who has made a lawful arrest has the authority to monitor the arrestee by staying literally at her elbow. If the arrestee requests permission to enter a private place, the need and authority to monitor the arrestee make it reasonable for the officer to enter that place without a warrant. As discussed above, it is unclear whether Arlene's arrest is tainted by earlier illegalities. Arlene did request permission to go into her home and Vic allowed her to do so. The fact that he did not exercise his authority to monitor her movements until after some time had passed should not affect the validity of his entry. The evidence that Vic found Arlene destroying was properly seized if the seizure satisfied the plain view doctrine. It is likely that Vic did have lawful view of and lawful access to the evidence from a place he had a right to be and that it was immediately apparent that the evidence was incriminating. If so, a plain view seizure was permissible.

Question: Pete was traveling on Highway 40 when he aroused the suspicions of Patrol Officer Ted. Acting on a hunch, Ted pulled behind Pete and put on his red lights. Pete began to slow down and pull to the side of the road, then suddenly accelerated. After a five-mile pursuit, Ted managed to force Pete's car from the road. Ted approached with his weapon drawn. He ordered both Pete and Billy, who was sitting in the passenger seat of Pete's car, to get out, patted down both of them, then asked Pete why he had fled. Pete, who appeared very unsteady, replied, "I been drinkin' and got scared." Ted arrested Pete for driving under the influence. He searched Pete and the car and ordered Billy to empty his pockets. Billy hesitantly removed a bag of narcotics from the pocket of his jacket. Ted then placed him under arrest.

After handcuffing both men, informing them of their *Miranda* rights, and placing them in the back of his vehicle, Ted began to drive to the stationhouse. On the way, Ted asked Billy where he had gotten the narcotics. Immediately, Pete ordered Billy to "shut up and tell him you want a lawyer or else." Billy lowered his eyes and muttered, "Whatever he says goes."

Pete and Billy were booked and placed in holding cells. Detective Jay, a narcotics investigator, came to Billy's cell. Jay was aware that Billy had been arrested for possession of narcotics and wondered if he might be willing to talk. Jay introduced himself and asked if he "could do anything for" Billy. Billy began to cry, saying, "I'm real worried. I don't want to go to jail." When Jay asked if he would like to talk about what happened, Billy said, "yes." After reciting the *Miranda* warnings and securing Billy's waiver, Jay asked a series of questions. In response, Billy revealed that Pete was involved in distributing large amounts of narcotics, that Pete had talked Billy into working with him, and that Pete kept a stash of cocaine in an old barbecue sitting on his back patio. Without a warrant, Jay went to Pete's home, proceeded to the patio, opened the barbecue, and found the narcotics.

Later, Jay went to Pete's cell, handed him a summary of Billy's statement, then left. When Jay returned 10 minutes later, Pete said he wanted "to tell the truth." He then confessed to possessing and distributing narcotics and offered to cooperate fully with Jay in apprehending and prosecuting his suppliers "in exchange for a deal." Jay said he didn't know if he could offer Pete anything, then left. Twenty minutes later, Jay came back to Pete's cell, recited complete *Miranda* warnings, and obtained Pete's written waiver of his rights. Jay then asked a series of direct questions and Pete once again made a full confession.

DISCUSS THE ADMISSIBILITY OF ALL THE NARCOTICS AND STATEMENTS AGAINST PETE AND BILLY. BE SURE TO CONSIDER BOTH THE LEGALITY OF THE OFFICER'S CONDUCT AND THE EXTENT OF THE PERTINENT EXCLUSIONARY RULES.

Answer: The **first issue** is the validity of the stop of Pete's car. To stop a motorist, an officer needs at least a "reasonable suspicion" of criminal activity. Initially, Ted was operating on a "hunch." He did not have adequate grounds to stop Pete. The question, however, is when Pete was "seized" within the meaning of the Fourth Amendment.

A person is seized when an officer employs physical force—any touching of the person. Initially, Ted did not touch Pete. A person is also seized when an officer employs a sufficient show of authority—one that would make a reasonable person feel not free to leave—and the person submits to that show of authority.

Ted pulled behind Pete and put on his red lights—in effect commanding him to stop. That show of authority was sufficient to make a reasonable person feel not free to leave. Pete began to pull over, but then accelerated. He did not submit; therefore, no seizure was completed. Because no seizure occurred at this point, Pete's behavior—the acceleration—was not the product of a Fourth Amendment illegality.

The question then is whether Pete's acceleration constituted a basis for stopping him. On the one hand, if Pete exceeded the speed limit or broke another traffic law, Ted had "probable cause" to stop him for a traffic offense. In addition, if his behavior constituted "flight" from a police officer, it could be indicative of a guilty mind and might be the basis for finding a reasonable suspicion of criminal activity. On the other hand, it is far from certain that Pete was fleeing and unclear what criminal activity his behavior indicated. If Pete was merely refusing to cooperate with an unfounded request to stop or if his acceleration was too slow to be considered "flight," then Ted still lacked a basis for stopping his car.

If the stop was unlawful, then Pete's conduct and statement were the product of the illegality and the arrest would also be tainted by the stop. Likewise, the narcotics found on Billy would be the product of the illegal stop.

In a proper vehicle stop, a driver may be ordered to get out of the vehicle. No additional showing is necessary. A passenger may also automatically be forced to alight. If the stop here was lawful, it was proper to order Pete and Billy to get out of the car.

The **second issue** is the legality of Pete's arrest. A reasonable arrest requires probable cause to believe the arrestee has committed an offense. Probable cause means a "fair probability." Pete's unsteady behavior furnished some evidence that he was driving under the influence, but may not have been sufficient for probable cause. His confession that he had been drinking was probably enough when coupled with his behavior, but the question is whether that confession was obtained in violation of *Miranda*. Custodial interrogation is necessary to trigger *Miranda* protection. Ted's express question concerning the reason for Pete's flight was "interrogation." Custody requires a formal arrest—not present on these facts—or its functional equivalent. The question is whether a reasonable suspect would have believed that he had been subjected to restraints comparable to those associated with a formal arrest. The issue is arguable here. On the one hand, Ted had drawn his weapon, had ordered the men from the car, and had frisked them. On the other hand, he may have done no more than was necessary to ensure a safe "traffic stop." If Pete was in custody, his confession is inadmissible because of the failure to give *Miranda* warnings.

The **third issue** is the constitutionality of the search of Billy's pockets. By *ordering* Billy to empty his pockets, Ted searched him. He did not have probable cause to arrest or search Billy. The only possible grounds for the search would be that it was "incident to Pete's arrest" because Billy was in Pete's area of immediate control. First, it is not clear that Billy's pockets were within that area. Second, even if they were it is arguable that the authority to search the area within the immediate control of an arrestee does not typically authorize the search of other persons who have independent and powerful privacy interests in their persons. If the search of Billy was illegal, then Billy's arrest was tainted. Later discoveries derived from that arrest are also potentially tainted.

The **fourth issue** is whether Billy's statement to Jay was obtained in violation of the *Miranda* doctrine. Billy may have invoked his right to counsel. To invoke counsel, a suspect must make a clear request—one that would lead a reasonable officer to conclude that the suspect does want a lawyer. An ambiguous statement indicating that the suspect "might" want assistance is not sufficient. Billy's statement that "Whatever he says goes" made after Pete ordered him to request a lawyer seems like an expression of a desire for a lawyer. One might argue, however, that the fact that he did so only on the command of Pete indicates that he did not express his own, personal desire for a lawyer.

If Billy did not invoke his right to counsel, Jay's later custodial interrogation complied with *Miranda* because Jay recited the warnings and obtained a waiver of rights before he interrogated Billy. If Billy did invoke his right to counsel, Jay may have violated the *Miranda* doctrine. First, whether or not Jay knew of Billy's request is irrelevant. According to the *Edwards* doctrine, after an invocation of the right to counsel custodial interrogation is permissible only if a lawyer is present (not the case here) or the suspect "initiates" communications. If the authorities initiate communications, no waiver can be valid.

Remarks that are routine incidents of the custodial relationship are not initiation. Remarks indicating a desire for a generalized discussion concerning the investigation are initiation. It is undecided whether statements by an officer that are not "routine" but do not concern the investigation qualify as "initiation." Although Jay wondered if Billy was willing to talk, Jay merely introduced himself and asked if he "could do anything" for Billy. This question arguably qualifies as a "routine incident of the custodial relationship." In any case, it did not evince a desire to discuss the investigation. Jay's question could constitute initiation only if it were characterized as conversation not related to "routine" matters and if such conversation qualifies as initiation by an officer. If so, Billy's waiver is invalid and the statements made in response to Jay's custodial interrogation (express questions) are inadmissible.

If Jay did not "initiate," Billy probably did so when he cried and said that he was worried and did not want to go to jail. In Oregon v. Bradshaw, a suspect's mere question, "What's going to happen to me now?" was thought to evince a desire and willingness to discuss the investigation. Billy's remark seems comparable. If Billy did initiate communications, his waiver is valid and his statement is admissible against him.

Even if there was a *Miranda* violation, Billy's statement is admissible against Pete. Pete would not have standing to assert the violation because Billy's *Miranda* "rights," not Pete's, were violated. For the same reason, Pete could not object that the *Miranda* violation tainted the search of his barbecue.

The **next issue** is whether the search of the barbecue violated Pete's Fourth Amendment rights. Jay entered Pete's curtilage and opened his barbecue. The showing needed to enter the curtilage of a home is uncertain. Probable cause *may not* be necessary. Probable cause to search is needed, however, to open a closed container. On the one hand, it is arguable that Billy's statement provided probable cause because his intimate involvement with Pete indicated first-hand knowledge and because his statement against interest was evidence of veracity. On the other hand, Pete could contend that Billy did not say how he knew the narcotics were in the barbecue and that Billy's own admission of guilt did not provide sufficient evidence of truthfulness in light of the fact that he was trying to shift blame to Pete.

Even if there was probable cause to enter the curtilage and search the barbecue, Jay's failure to obtain a search warrant may render his conduct unreasonable. It is undecided whether a search warrant is generally needed to enter the curtilage of a home. Searches of closed containers are generally governed by the warrant rule. By opening the barbecue without a warrant, Jay violated Pete's Fourth Amendment rights. The evidence obtained is presumptively inadmissible against Pete. Billy lacks standing, however, to object to the searches. He could succeed only with a claim that the narcotics were the fruit of a violation of his *Miranda* rights.

The **last issue** is whether Pete's confessions are admissible under *Miranda*. Pete was in custody in a jail cell. Before Pete's first confession, Jay did not recite *Miranda* warnings. The government might argue that the earlier warnings by Ted conveyed the relevant information to Pete; but because they were delivered considerably earlier, in a different setting, and by a different officer, it is unlikely that those warnings satisfy *Miranda*. Moreover, it is unlikely that a waiver of rights could be established. The only evidence of a waiver is Ted's warnings and the fact of Pete's confession. If Jay's action was interrogation, Pete's first confession would be inadmissible.

The question is whether Jay interrogated Pete. Interrogation requires an express question or its functional equivalent—words or acts by the police that they should know are reasonably likely to elicit an incriminating response from the suspect. By handing Billy's statement to Pete, Jay might well have interrogated him. First, the action by Jay indicates an intent to obtain an incriminating statement. Second, Billy's statement was an accusation aimed at Pete.

Pete's second confession, however, is probably admissible even though it clearly is the product of custodial interrogation—Jay's express questioning. Jay issued the *Miranda* warnings and obtained an express waiver. Even if Pete's first statement is inadmissible because Jay failed to warn him or secure a waiver, according to the doctrine of Oregon v. Elstad, the second statement, made 20 minutes later and after compliance with *Miranda*, is "presumptively attenuated" and not subject to suppression.

Question: Based on an informant's tip and additional investigation that corroborated much of the information in the tip, Officer Salinas developed probable cause to believe that Isabel had perpetrated several armed robberies of convenience stores. Without obtaining a warrant, Salinas arrested Isabel as she was waiting at a bus stop near her home.

One of the robberies had occurred eight months prior to the arrest. A clerk at the store had been shot trying to apprehend the robber. When the clerk regained consciousness three days after the shooting, he had described the robber as a "25- to 30-year-old woman, about five-and-a-half feet tall, weighing about 150 pounds, with long blond hair." Because the injuries suffered by the clerk require long-term therapy, he has remained in a care facility.

After arresting Isabel, Officer Salinas took her to the care facility. He handcuffed her to a chair in the lobby where several other persons were present. After bringing the clerk to the lobby, Salinas asked him, "Do you see the person who robbed you anywhere in the room?" The clerk looked around the room for several minutes, then pointed at Isabel and said, "She looks very familiar. Yes, I think she definitely could be the one."

Salinas then took Isabel to the police station and placed her in a holding cell. He struck a deal with Margo, a young woman who had been arrested for prostitution, offering to have her released if she could get Isabel to talk about the robberies. Salinas handed Margo a pocket tape recorder and placed her in Isabel's cell. Margo recorded a conversation in which Isabel made several inculpatory statements.

Later that day, Isabel was formally charged with eight armed robberies and one count of assault with intent to kill. After filing the charges, the prosecutor arranged a lineup that included Isabel and seven other women who resembled her. When Isabel asked for a lawyer, the prosecutor said, "If you aren't guilty, you won't need one." He then videotaped the lineup, ordering each participant to say, "Your money or your life." Thirty minutes later, when the videotape was shown to the victims of other robberies, three of them identified Isabel.

Isabel was arraigned the next morning, and she asked to have counsel appointed to represent her. The judge informed her that if she was indigent, state-funded representation would be arranged. Isabel was then taken back to her jail cell, where Molly, an undercover detective, was posing as a fellow inmate. As Molly sat and listened, Isabel began to talk about her predicament. After she had made several incriminating remarks, Isabel stopped abruptly, saying, "I guess I should keep my mouth shut. They probably have the cell bugged." "I doubt it," Molly replied. "They've been sued for doing that in the past . . . you know, for violating our civil rights. It's cost the pigs a lot of money. I don't think they want to get caught again. I'd be glad to listen if you need to keep talking." Isabel then revealed several more incriminating details about her involvement in the robberies.

Isabel was tried for the robberies. In its case-in-chief, the prosecution introduced the identifications and statements described above and also had the injured clerk make an in-court identification of Isabel. Isabel has appealed her conviction.

DISCUSS THE CONSTITUTIONALITY OF THE LAW ENFORCEMENT CONDUCT IN ISABEL'S CASE AND THE ADMISSIBILITY OF THE EYEWITNESS IDENTIFICATIONS OF ISABEL AND THE INCRIMINATING STATEMENTS MADE BY ISABEL.

Answer: The **first issue** is the validity of Salinas's arrest of Isabel. The warrantless arrest of a person in a public place based on probable cause to believe she has committed a felony is reasonable under the Fourth Amendment. Here, Officer Salinas had probable cause to arrest Isabel for armed robberies. She was standing at a public bus stop. The arrest was valid.

The **second issue** is whether the identification in the care-facility lobby is admissible. The right to counsel attaches only at or after the initiation of formal proceedings. Because she had not been formally charged, Isabel had no right to counsel. The only claim available is under the Due Process Clause, which has been construed to require the exclusion of identifications resulting from **unnecessarily suggestive** identification methods **unless** the government establishes, by a preponderance of the evidence, that the identification was **reliable.**

Isabel was the only person handcuffed to a chair in the lobby. Although several persons were present, it is unlikely that they happened to be women who were physically similar to Isabel. The method was suggestive and conducive to misidentification, and there is no evidence of the need to use such a suggestive process. The clerk's identification was the product of unnecessary government suggestion.

The government may have a difficult time establishing reliability. It is arguable that the witness was fairly certain that Isabel was the robber ("looks very familiar," "definitely could be the one"). If the initial description by the clerk matches Isabel's appearance, that would support reliability. Evidence that the clerk had a good opportunity to see her and paid close attention would also be helpful. Absent additional evidence, the government could not carry its burden. Even with such evidence, a judge might not find the identification to be reliable because the clerk lost consciousness for three days, the robbery was eight months prior to the identification, the process was highly suggestive and corrupting, and the clerk was far from "certain," saying only that Isabel looked "very familiar" and that he *thought* that Isabel "definitely *could be* the one." The lobby identification might well be barred by due process.

The later "in-court" identification by the clerk is also subject to a due process challenge as the product of the identification process in the care-facility lobby. When a witness has been subjected to an unnecessarily suggestive identification process, both the identification made during the process and any subsequent identification by the same witness are presumptively inadmissible. The government must demonstrate reliability if it wishes to use a subsequent identification. The reliability of the in-court identification is made even more doubtful by the fact that an even longer time had passed between the crime and that identification. While the suggestion present in the lobby encounter was not present, there is no showing that the in-court identification afforded the clerk an array of choices. Unless there is further evidence to support a reliability finding, the in-court identification should also be excluded.

The **third issue** is the validity of Margo's acquisition of Isabel's inculpatory statements. First, a Fourth Amendment illegal search claim cannot succeed. A search requires the violation of a reasonable expectation of privacy. When the government plants a "false friend" with a listening device or recorder in the presence of an individual, it does not violate a reasonable expectation of privacy. By voluntarily disclosing the information to the third party who is working for the state, the individual assumes the risk that that party is cooperating with and passing the information on to the state.

Second, a Sixth Amendment right to counsel claim cannot succeed because there had not yet been an "initiation of formal, adversary, judicial proceedings" against Isabel. Because she had not yet been charged, she was not an "accused" and was not entitled to counsel.

Finally, no *Miranda* claim can succeed because that doctrine does not apply unless a **known government agent** interrogates a suspect in custody. Here, Margo was an undercover operative. Even if she questioned Isabel, *Miranda* was inapplicable.

The **fourth issue** is the propriety and admissibility of the three identifications of Isabel by the robbery victims who viewed the videotaped lineup. A Fifth Amendment–due process claim cannot succeed because there is no evidence of suggestion: The lineup included seven other women who resembled Isabel, and all were asked to speak the same words. A Sixth Amendment–right to counsel claim will also fail. A defendant is entitled to counsel if adversary, judicial proceedings have been initiated **and** if there is a **trial-like confrontation** at which the accused is **physically present.** Isabel's right had attached because she had been formally charged prior to the lineup. However, Isabel was not present when the videotape was shown to the witnesses. The situation here is no different than a photo array, which does not constitute a "critical stage" because the defendant is not present.

The **fifth issue** is the propriety of Molly's conduct in the cell and the admissibility of the statements she obtained. Once again, a *Miranda* claim will fail because even though Molly was a detective, Isabel did not realize that she was a law enforcement officer. A Sixth Amendment–*Massiah* right to counsel claim should succeed in part. The right to counsel had attached because adversary proceedings had been initiated—Isabel had been "formally charged" and "arraigned." Therefore, the government was forbidden from "deliberately eliciting" statements in the absence of counsel. For there to be a "critical stage" under the *Massiah* doctrine, an undercover agent must take some action designed deliberately to elicit an incriminating response. Passive listening is not enough. Initially, Molly just "sat and listened." Any statements she obtained at that point are admissible because they were not obtained in violation of Isabel's right to counsel.

However, when Isabel stopped because of her concern about "bugs" in the cell, Molly made several remarks that not only constituted "actions" but certainly seemed designed to elicit more information from Isabel. She reassured Isabel that there was little risk of bugging—creating a false sense of security and trust—and then invited her to tell more by saying, "I'd be glad to listen if you need to keep talking." The additional incriminating details revealed by Isabel should be inadmissible under *Massiah*.

Question: Aggie and Zeke were charged with "conspiracy to bomb a federal courthouse" and "attempted extortion." Because they were indigent, Marlene, a public defender, was appointed to represent both of them. While preparing for trial, Marlene came to the conclusion that she could not effectively represent both Aggie and

Zeke and so informed the judge. The judge said that unless Marlene could demonstrate "actual harm from the joint representation," she should continue to represent both defendants.

During jury selection, after five jurors had been chosen, the prosecutor notified the judge that he was having "great trouble locating one witness" and that "another has apparently traveled to a foreign country." Claiming that he could "not properly present the case at this time," he moved for a mistrial. The defense objected, asserting that "a continuance will sufficiently serve the government's objectives." The judge ordered a mistrial because "it would seem best to start over at this early stage." Six months later, prior to the start of jury selection, the defense moved to bar the trial on double jeopardy grounds. The judge rejected the motion, a jury was chosen, and the trial began.

At trial, before the chief prosecution witness took the stand, the government requested that "all but essential personnel be barred from the trial." When the defense objected, the prosecutor explained that the chief witness was "afraid for her life and would refuse to testify honestly and completely in open court." When examined in chambers, the witness said, "Yes, I am very, very afraid and really couldn't tell what I know in front of a crowd of strangers. Aggie and Zeke have dangerous friends who would retaliate." The judge then barred the press and public during the witness's testimony.

The witness took the stand and testified in detail about conversations she had had with Aggie and Zeke. The conversations described in her testimony were much more detailed and incriminating than those the witness had recounted to the prosecution during preparation for the trial.

After Aggie and Zeke were convicted, they learned from one juror that two other jurors made racist comments about them several times during the trial. Defense investigators found a waiter who had heard one of the jurors utter racist slurs at lunch. Aggie and Zeke moved for a new trial, offering the testimony of the juror and the waiter to establish that the jurors were tainted. The judge denied the motion, stating that the evidence that the defendants wished to present was inadmissible.

THOROUGHLY DISCUSS THE ISSUES RAISED BY THIS FACT PATTERN. PRESENT ARGUMENTS ON BOTH SIDES AND THE MOST LIKELY RESOLUTION OF THE ISSUES.

Answer: The **first issue** concerns the propriety of the judge's refusal to appoint separate counsel for Aggie and Zeke. When a judge is informed by counsel of a potential conflict of interest in a joint representation situation, the judge has the obligation to inquire into the situation. Separate representation is required unless the judge determines that the chance of a conflict because of the joint representation is "too remote" to warrant separate representation. The judge's failure to satisfy the obligation constitutes a violation of the Sixth Amendment right to counsel and requires reversal of a resulting conviction. Here, the judge committed constitutional error in failing to appoint separate lawyers or look into the likelihood of a conflict. The judge's declaration that counsel had to show "actual harm" was legally incorrect. The convictions of Aggie and Zeke must be reversed.

The **second issue** is the propriety of the judge's ruling on the defense motion to bar trial on double jeopardy grounds. For a defendant to be in "jeopardy," jeopardy must "attach." Jeopardy attaches in a jury trial only when the jury is sworn. Here, only five jurors had been selected in the first trial. Because the jury had not been sworn, jeopardy had not attached. Consequently, the second trial could not constitute a forbidden second jeopardy. The judge's ruling was correct.

The **third issue** is the propriety of the order barring the press and public from the courtroom during the testimony of the chief prosecution witness. The Sixth Amendment right to a public trial belongs to an accused. While the right to have the trial open and accessible to the public is not absolute, there is a presumption of openness that can be overcome only by an overriding interest based on a showing that closure is essential to preserve higher values and that there are no reasonable alternatives to closure. Moreover, any closure must be narrowly tailored to serve the higher values—that is, it can be no broader than is necessary. Here, the defendants were entitled to have the public present for the testimony of the prosecution's chief witness unless the facts demonstrated that an overriding interest and higher values were threatened. An actual danger to the well-being of a witness could certainly be a sufficient interest. The problem in this case is that there was no specific showing of an actual danger to the witness. She merely asserted a fear of testifying publicly and a fear of the defendants' "dangerous friends." This showing does not seem specific enough to satisfy the Sixth Amendment. A finding to the contrary—that a witness's mere assertions of fear support closure—would severely undermine the right to a public trial. Moreover, it is highly doubtful that closure actually served the alleged interest—protection against retaliation. Because the witness had to testify in the presence of the defendants and defense counsel, her identity became known. Closure would seem to provide little, if any, protection against retaliation. In sum, the closure order here, while narrowly tailored to the alleged interests of the government and the witness, was not supported by an adequate showing of overriding interests and higher values.

In addition, the witness's and government's claim that she could not give honest and complete testimony unless the public were excluded runs directly contrary to one of the premises of the public trial right—that honesty is promoted if witnesses must testify in front of members of the public. Closure based on a witness's claim that she cannot be honest in public seems patently inconsistent with the Sixth Amendment right to a public trial.

The witness's testimony gives rise to **an additional issue**—whether the prosecution had a duty to reveal perjured or false testimony. The Due Process Clause forbids the deliberate use of false evidence. In addition, when the government knows that one of its witnesses has provided false testimony and allows the testimony to go uncorrected, due process is violated. If the government deliberately presents false testimony or knowingly allows it to go uncorrected, a conviction must be reversed if there is any reasonable likelihood that the false testimony could have affected the judgment of the jury. Here, it is possible that the government violated due process. The witness's testimony regarding the conversations with the defendants was more detailed and more incriminating than her pretrial descriptions. That should have alerted the prosecutor to the possibility of perjury—or at least inaccurate embellishment. If the testimony was false and if the prosecution knew of the falsehoods, Aggie and Zeke are probably entitled to reversals. Because this was the "chief prosecution witness," there was probably a reasonable likelihood that her false testimony could have affected the judgment of the jury.

The **final issue** is the correctness of the judge's denial of the motion for a new trial. A defendant has a Sixth Amendment entitlement to an impartial jury. If any juror is biased, the right is violated. Hostility toward a defendant's race is most certainly a disqualifying bias. The only question is whether the defendants were entitled to attack the verdict by means of the testimony they sought to present. Federal Rule of Evidence 606—a reflection of the common law position—bars impeachment of a verdict concerning an "internal" matter by means of the testimony of a juror. It permits jurors to testify about "external" matters and permits nonjurors to testify about anything. Racism most certainly is an "internal" matter—not an external or extraneous influence—that may affect the impartiality of a juror's decisions. In either federal court (which is probably the forum here since the allegation is conspiracy to bomb a *federal* courthouse) or a jurisdiction following the common law tradition, the juror could not testify about other jurors' racist comments. The waiter, however, could testify about them. The court should at least have granted a hearing at which the defendants had the opportunity to make a sufficient showing that one or more of the jurors were in fact tainted by racial bias. If the evidence sustained that claim, the defendants were entitled to a new trial.

Question: In October 1994, Nellie was properly arrested in connection with several burglaries and arsons at women's health and counseling clinics throughout the northeastern United States. When Nellie was properly searched incident to her arrest, officers found an unlicensed weapon. Two days later, Nellie was charged with several felony counts of burglary and arson and with misdemeanor possession of an unlicensed weapon.

Nellie's trial was scheduled for January 1995. When a key government witness disappeared, the trial was continued for three months at the prosecution's request. In April, the prosecution sought and received a six-month continuance because the lead attorney assigned to the case was "enmeshed in another trial." In October, the judge continued the trial until January 1996 because she had the opportunity to travel with a contingent of American judges to assist with judicial reform in the former Soviet Union. Nellie's counsel objected to each continuance. In early December 1995, one of Nellie's main witnesses was involved in a serious accident and fell into a coma.

Before trial in January 1996, Nellie filed a motion to suppress an incriminating statement she allegedly made in November 1995 to a cellmate who was a government informant. The judge ordered briefing and scheduled a hearing. After the hearing in March 1996, the judge requested additional briefs. After they were filed in late March, she deliberated on the motion for one month, then ruled in the government's favor.

Before the start of trial on April 21, 1996, the judge denied Nellie's motion to dismiss the charges on speedy trial grounds. Nellie then asked to represent herself, stating, "My lawyer refuses to present the defense I want to present—that I am a victim of political and religious oppression and that all my actions were justified because I was only following my conscience. The only way I can make the people aware of what is going on and unmask this sham of a justice system is to be my own voice." The judge told Nellie that she "would have to stick to legally acceptable evidence and arguments."

When Nellie replied, "I will do what my God commands me to do," the judge denied her request to represent herself.

At the beginning of jury selection, defense counsel objected to the venire, alleging that it was "more than suspicious that only 38 percent of the prospective jurors identified themselves as Christians when the community is 74 percent Christian." When the judge overruled the objection, Nellie's counsel announced, "In that case, my client wishes to waive her right to jury trial because she does not believe that the jurors will be fair." When the prosecutor objected, the judge rejected Nellie's attempted waiver.

During the defense case, the judge declared a two-hour lunch break while Nellie was on the witness stand. Over objections, the trial judge ordered Nellie and her attorney "not to discuss anything having to do with your testimony during the break." Later that day, while a priest called on Nellie's behalf was testifying on direct examination, the trial was interrupted by a bomb threat. The judge, "to maintain the status quo," ordered Nellie's attorney "not to talk to the witness or to your client." Trial resumed 10 minutes later.

At the end of a five-day trial, Nellie was convicted of all charges. On appeal, the misdemeanor possession of an unlicensed weapon conviction was reversed because of an erroneous jury instruction. Trial for that charge was rescheduled and, over Nellie's objection, was held without a jury and without the assistance of defense counsel. The record does not demonstrate effective waivers of either right. Nellie was again convicted of the charge.

DISCUSS THE ISSUES RAISED BY THESE FACTS.

Answer: The **first issue** is whether the trial judge properly denied Nellie's motion to dismiss the charges on speedy trial grounds. The right to a speedy trial "attaches" upon arrest or formal charge. Nellie's right attached in October 1994, when she was arrested. Whether the Sixth Amendment right to a speedy trial has been violated hinges on the four-factor balancing test of Barker v. Wingo. The length of the delay, reasons for delay, defendant's assertions of the right, and prejudice to the defendant are the relevant factors.

LENGTH OF DELAY

The speedy trial clock begins to run when the right attaches and continues until the accused is tried. There is no need to engage in balancing analysis unless a delay of more than five months has occurred. Delays approaching one year are sufficient to require balancing—that is, a defendant may be able to show a speedy trial violation when the delay approaches one year. In this case, the right attached with Nellie's arrest in October 1994 and continued until the trial in April 1996. This delay of 18 months is enough to trigger balancing analysis. However, because 18 months is not exceptionally long, the length of delay is unlikely to tip the balance in the defendant's favor.

REASONS FOR DELAY

Each relevant period of delay must be evaluated to determine why it occurred. The object is to determine who is to blame for each delay (that is, on whose side of the balance it should be placed) and how much weight should be given to each delay. The three-month period from October 1994 to January 1995 is unexplained. If it is the time needed for both sides to ready themselves for trial, it should not count against the government. If any portion is the result of unnecessary delay, negligence, or court congestion, it should weigh against the government—although not heavily. If any portion constitutes deliberate or bad faith delay to harass or harm the defense, it should weigh heavily against the government.

The three-month delay from January 1995 to April 1995 is caused by a government-requested continuance based on the disappearance of a key witness. This delay is justifiable and should not tip the scales against the state. The next six-month delay—until October 1995—is also caused by a state-requested continuance based on the lead prosecutor's involvement in another trial. If the attorney's involvement in the other case at this time was not the fault of the government, if it was important that the attorney finish that trial, if it was important that the lead attorney prosecute the case against Nellie, and if six months was the time needed to complete the other trial, then this delay would also seem to be justified.

It is difficult to know how to weigh the next three-month delay until January 1996. The reason for the delay was the judge's desire to assist judicial reform in the former Soviet Union. Delays caused by a judge are attributable to the government. On the one hand, the trip might be considered unnecessary and insufficiently important to justify delaying a criminal trial. Moreover, perhaps a different judge could have handled the trial. In either case, this three-month delay should tip the scales toward the defendant. On the other hand, if the judge's participation in the project was considered sufficiently important to justify the delay and if it was impractical or inefficient to change judges at this stage, the delay should not count toward the defendant's claim.

The next delay—from January 1996 to April 1996—resulted from Nellie's motion to suppress, which apparently was not filed until shortly before trial was supposed to start. The briefing, hearing, and decisionmaking process by the court took three months. There is no reason to fault the defendant for filing the motion in January. The basis for the motion—the incriminating statements to the informant—did not arise until November 1995, and the judge apparently was away until January. Nonetheless, the defendant's action did cause the delay. If the processing of the motion by the court was expeditious—that is, if the three months were reasonably necessary to resolve the claim—the time should not count against the government. Only delays caused by negligence, overcrowded courts, or some other fault of the government that unnecessarily prolonged resolution of the motion should count against the government.

ASSERTIONS BY THE DEFENDANT

Assertions of the speedy trial right count in the defendant's favor so long as there are no indications that the defendant in fact did not want a speedy trial. Failures to assert count strongly against a defendant unless there are good reasons for the failures. Here, Nellie objected to each of the three government-caused continuances. These assertions should tip the scales in her favor. Moreover, the filing of the motion—if it had any merit—should not undermine her assertions. The occasion for the motion did not arise until after the earlier assertions, and the importance of suppressing inculpatory admissions seems clear.

PREJUDICE TO THE DEFENDANT

If Nellie was incarcerated or subject to bail restraints or if she suffered particular anxiety, humiliation, or other losses because of the pendency of the charges, these sorts of prejudice should weigh on her side of the balance. The burden to show such prejudice, however, is on the defense. The most serious (and potentially weighty) form of prejudice is "actual prejudice to the defense." The fact that one of Nellie's main witnesses fell into a coma would provide considerable weight if the witness is unavailable for trial because of the delay and if the testimony would have assisted Nellie's defense.

CONCLUSIONS

It does not seem likely based on what is known that the trial court erred in denying Nellie's motion. The delay was not "excessive." Much, if not all, of the delay was justified by adequate reasons or was caused by Nellie's motion. While Nellie's assertions and the loss of a witness do count in her favor, it seems plausible to conclude that the balance tipped toward the government here. The ruling should be upheld unless there are facts showing "culpable" delays by the government and, perhaps, additional prejudice to Nellie.

The **second issue** is whether the judge properly denied Nellie's request to represent herself. The Sixth Amendment contains an implicit right of self-representation. The accused is entitled to waive the right to counsel and represent herself if she knowingly and voluntarily chooses to do so and is able and willing to abide by the rules of courtroom protocol and procedure. A judge cannot deny self-representation because the accused will not defend herself well or lacks legal ability or knowledge. A judge can deny representation if the defendant acts disruptively and refuses to (or cannot) abide by the rules of the courtroom.

The judge's ruling here is arguable. Nellie might have provided a sufficient basis for rejecting her request when she informed the court of her feelings of victimization and then responded to the court's warning that she must stick to legally acceptable evidence and arguments by saying that she would "do what my God commands me to do." The judge's warning was proper—a defendant can be held to the rules of law and the courtroom. If Nellie's answers gave sufficient reason to believe that she would not respect the rules of the court—either the rules of procedure or the rules of substantive law—the judge could deny self-representation. It is arguable, however, that her answers were ambiguous and that the risk of improper conduct was insufficient to deny her request. The judge may have erred by failing to inquire further into the meaning of Nellie's somewhat cryptic replies.

The **third issue** is whether the judge properly overruled Nellie's objection to the makeup of the jury pool. The Sixth Amendment includes a "fair cross section" requirement. The government may not systematically exclude cognizable groups from the jury pool or venire. To establish a prima facie case of a fair cross section denial, a defendant must demonstrate that (1) the allegedly excluded group is sufficiently numerous and distinctive; (2) the representation of that group in the jury pool is not fair and reasonable in relation to the group's representation in the community; and (3) the under-representation in the pool is systematic—it is caused by some feature of the jury selection system. The state can justify the exclusion by showing that a significant state interest is advanced by the exclusionary feature of the system. The state must show more than a rational basis.

In this case, if Nellie's allegations are accurate, then Christians are sufficiently numerous—74 percent of the community—and probably are distinctive. It is arguable, at least, that Christians have attitudes, viewpoints, perspectives, or ways of looking at matters that are different from those of other religious groups.

Again, assuming that Nellie's figures are accurate, the disparity between representation in the pool (38 percent) and in the community (74 percent) is sufficient to establish that the representation of Christians in her jury pool was "not fair and reasonable." The 36 percent differential is substantial enough to satisfy the second requirement for a prima facie case.

Nellie may fail, however, on the third requirement. She needs to show that the disparity is "systematic," not the result of random chance or some variable not attributable to the selection system. While the disparity in her pool provides some evidence, it falls short of establishing "systematic exclusion." Nellie needs additional evidence that the system is to blame—evidence such as disparities in other jury pools or some facet of the system that focuses directly or indirectly on Christians and leads to their removal or allows them to avoid service on juries. Without such proof, the judge's ruling should be sustained. If such proof is provided, the government could attempt to sustain the ruling by showing that the particular aspect of the system that resulted in exclusion advances a significant interest.

The **next issue** is the propriety of rejecting Nellie's attempted waiver of her right to trial by jury. The accused has no right to waive a jury and insist on a bench trial unless perhaps there is clear and strong proof that a jury could not fairly and impartially decide the case. A state may condition waiver on the prosecutor's consent or the court's approval or both. In this case, the judge's decision to reject the waiver after the prosecutor objected is constitutional. There was an allegation but no showing that the jurors could not fairly judge the case.

Another issue is whether the two orders barring consultation violated Nellie's Sixth Amendment right to counsel. A defendant has an absolute right to consult with counsel prior to testifying and probably at all other times that she is not on the witness stand. The right to consult is subject to some restriction while an accused is testifying. During "brief" recesses between direct and cross-examination in which it is virtually certain that the only subject that will be discussed is the defendant's ongoing testimony, a judge may prohibit consultation. A recess must be so "short" that it is appropriate to presume that the only subject to be discussed is the ongoing testimony. Prohibitions of consultation during "brief" recesses at other junctures *during* the defendant's testimony are also probably allowable.

The first order may be invalid. The two-hour lunch break during Nellie's testimony would not seem to be "brief" or "short." In duration, timing, and nature, this break would seem to be one in which conversations would go beyond the ongoing testimony. The judge, however, did not bar all consultation. It is arguable that the judge's order "not to discuss anything having to do with your testimony" was so limited that it did not infringe on the defendant's right to consult. There is no right to discuss ongoing testimony, the only subject of the court's restrictive order. It is also arguable, however, that such an order is impermissible because it threatens or chills the defendant's entitlement to full and free consultation about all other matters. It is unclear whether a limited order not to discuss testimony during a "long" break is constitutional.

The second order was invalid insofar as it ordered Nellie's attorney not to talk to Nellie. Although the break of merely 10 minutes was brief, Nellie was not testifying. She had an absolute right to consultation. This violation of her Sixth Amendment right justifies reversal without a showing of prejudice. Insofar as the order barred the attorney from speaking to the priest who was testifying, it did not interfere with Nellie's right to consult. While it is arguable that the order interfered with counsel's right to present a defense, such an argument is unlikely to succeed. If the concern with undermining cross-examination and impeding the search for truth justifies a denial of consultation with the defendant herself during a brief break while she is testifying, it surely justifies a bar on talking to a defense witness during a brief break.

The **final issues** are whether the retrial violated Nellie's right to a jury or her right to counsel. Nellie objected to the trial and did not waive either right. The questions are whether she was entitled to a jury and whether she was entitled to the assistance of counsel. A defendant has the right to trial by jury for "serious" crimes but not for "petty" crimes. A crime is serious if a sentence of more than six months in prison is authorized. A crime is presumptively petty if a sentence of six months or less in prison is authorized. In rare cases in which a defendant can show additional statutory penalties that are sufficiently onerous to reflect a judgment that the crime is serious, a crime can qualify as serious even though no more than six months in jail is authorized. To determine whether misdemeanor possession of an unlicensed weapon is serious or petty and, thus, whether Nellie's right to jury trial was violated, the statutorily authorized penalties must be ascertained.

A defendant has the right to appointed counsel for a misdemeanor charge if the trial results in any actual imprisonment. A defendant may also have the right to retained counsel for a misdemeanor no matter what sentence is imposed. If a defendant is tried without a lawyer, no sentence of imprisonment is permitted. Because Nellie was tried without a lawyer, a sentence of imprisonment here would be unconstitutional. In addition, even if Nellie was not sentenced to a term of imprisonment, if she was denied the right to *retain* counsel with her own funds, it is arguable that the trial and conviction were unconstitutional.

Question: Law enforcement authorities believed that George was the head of an organized crime syndicate involved in prostitution, gambling, and illicit narcotics. After two members of a rival syndicate were murdered execution-style, George and his associate, Michael, were indicted for two counts of capital murder. The indictment charged that Michael had carried out the executions on George's orders. After George was arrested, he retained an attorney to represent himself and Michael.

Prior to trial, the defense moved to suppress significant evidence found in a search of George's home. The government claimed that George's wife had consented to the searches. Under a controlling decision that has subsequently been reversed, the consent would have been deemed invalid because George's wife had consented against his will and out of anger or vindictiveness. The motion to suppress would have been successful if defense counsel had relied on this decision, but he failed to find it or present it to the court. The court denied the motion to suppress.

George and Michael were tried together. During jury selection, defense counsel objected that the prosecutor was "striking persons of Italian descent." When asked to respond, the prosecutor asserted first that George had "no standing to raise the claim because he is not Italian." In addition, she listed reasons for striking the jurors—one had "a brother who has been convicted of narcotics trafficking," one was "a registered Libertarian Party member," one was "a professor of political science," and one was "an artist." The judge ruled that the last two jurors had to be reinstated "because your reasons have nothing to do with this case, and, besides, I do not believe that they are the real reasons for your actions."

During the trial, several occasions arose in which defense counsel was forced to choose between actions that would be advantageous to one defendant and disadvantageous to the other. On each occasion, because he was being paid by George, the lawyer chose the action that favored George.

Midway through the trial, a government jury consultant learned that the mother of one juror had been killed several years earlier when she was caught in a crossfire between members of rival organized crime families. In voir dire, the juror had not mentioned the event and had not disclosed that he had undergone extensive counseling to help him deal with his mother's death. The jury consultant did not tell the prosecutor until after the trial had ended. At that point, the prosecutor informed George's counsel.

George was convicted and Michael was acquitted of both murders. George moved for a new trial on two grounds: that his "convictions could not be valid in light of Michael's acquittals"; and that "the jury was tainted by the participation of the juror whose mother was killed and by the government's failure to disclose what it learned about that juror during the trial." The judge denied the motion because "Michael's acquittals are irrelevant" and because "there was no evidence that the juror was in fact biased."

At George's capital sentencing hearing, the jurors were unable to agree on a sentence. Eleven voted for death, but one insisted on a life sentence because her conscience would not allow her to vote for capital punishment. The governing law allowed the judge either "to declare a hung jury or impose life sentences." The judge declared the jury "hung" and scheduled another sentencing proceeding. The second jury was also unable to agree because two jurors refused to vote for the death penalty. This time, the judge imposed two life sentences. Afterward, the prosecution learned that the jurors who had held out for a life sentence had done so because their families had been threatened by George's sons. The judge granted the government's request to vacate the life sentences and hold another sentencing proceeding. The third proceeding resulted in unanimous jury decisions to impose two death sentences on George.

DISCUSS THE CORRECTNESS OF THE VARIOUS RULINGS AND DECISIONS OF THE JUDGE AND DISCUSS ANY OTHER CLAIMS THAT GEORGE MIGHT RAISE BASED ON THESE FACTS.

Answer: The **first issue** is whether counsel's failure to rely on the controlling decision regarding consent was "ineffective assistance." The Sixth Amendment guarantees that both retained and appointed counsel must render effective assistance. An actual ineffectiveness claim requires a showing of both "deficient performance" and "prejudice." Performance is deficient if it is not "reasonably effective"—if it falls outside the "wide range of professionally competent assistance." Certainly, counsel must research and raise controlling precedents. Here, counsel's failure to raise or rely on a controlling decision was deficient performance because that decision would have validated George's motion to suppress and led to the suppression of "significant evidence."

Prejudice requires a showing of a "reasonable probability that but for counsel's errors the result of the proceeding would have been different." In addition, counsel's errors must have rendered the result of the trial unreliable—factually or legally incorrect—or the proceeding fundamentally unfair. Because the evidence was "significant," there may well be a "reasonable probability" that the result of the trial would have been different if counsel had raised the precedent and the evidence had been suppressed. Nonetheless, counsel's error did not render the trial less reliable—that is, it did not render the outcome less accurate either factually or legally. A successful motion to suppress would have kept probative evidence from the trier of fact. Moreover, the decision that would have led to suppression was legally incorrect. Under what is now known to be the "correct" law, the evidence would not be suppressed. Consequently, the deficient performance did not impair the legal or factual accuracy of the result. Nor did the "error" deprive the defendant of any "procedural right" to which he was entitled. Under the "correct" law, the Fourth Amendment does not call for suppression. Because George cannot show prejudice, his ineffective assistance claim must fail.

The **second issue** is whether the trial judge's ruling on the defense objection to the prosecutor's peremptory challenges was correct. Under *Batson* doctrine, the Equal Protection Clause forbids the prosecution from exercising peremptories to strike jurors on account of race. This prohibition almost certainly applies to strikes on account of "ethnicity." Consequently, the defense should be able to raise a *Batson* challenge based on the prosecutor's strikes of persons of Italian descent. Moreover, there is no need for the defendant to be a member of the group improperly stricken. A defendant is entitled to raise jurors' equal protection rights.

According to *Batson*, the first step requires the defendant to establish a prima facie case of intentional discrimination. The facts here are sketchy. Apparently, the prosecution did use four challenges to strike jurors of Italian descent. The judge's request for explanations suggests that he found a prima facie case of discrimination. In any case, because the judge asked for explanations and the prosecutor responded, the analysis should proceed to the second step. In that step, the prosecution has the burden of providing "race-neutral explanations'' for its strikes. The sole question is whether the reasons offered are "facially valid.'' Each of the reasons offered here is facially valid because it is "race neutral''—that is, each was based on something other than race and was not "closely tied to race.''

The third step of *Batson* analysis requires the court to decide whether the defendant has sustained a claim of "intentional discrimination.'' The judge apparently found that the first two jurors—the one whose brother had a narcotics conviction and the one who was a Libertarian—had not been stricken because of their ethnicity. However, the judge rejected the reasons proffered for striking the other two jurors because these reasons did not relate to the case and because he doubted the prosecutor's sincerity. While a reason can be "facially valid'' even though it does not relate to the case, the lack of pertinence to the case can be a factor in deciding whether a reason given was the real reason for a strike. Here, the judge did not believe the prosecutor's explanations that he struck the two jurors because one was "a professor of political science'' and the other was "an artist.'' Assessment of the credibility of a party proffering explanations for peremptory challenges is a matter entrusted to the trial judge. The credibility finding in this case and the resulting conclusion that the peremptories had been used to discriminate may be overturned only if they are "clearly erroneous.'' Moreover, the judge's reinstatement of the two improperly stricken jurors was an appropriate remedy for the *Batson* violation that was established.

The **third issue** is whether a conflict of interest deprived George of effective assistance of counsel. Unless a judge is on actual or constructive notice of a conflict of interest (a claim not supported by the facts here), a defendant can establish a Sixth Amendment deprivation based on a conflict only by showing that an "actual conflict of interest adversely affected counsel's representation.'' In this case, George can show an actual conflict—several times, counsel was "forced to choose'' between the two defendants' interests. Because counsel favored George each time, however, George cannot show that the representation he received was "adversely affected.'' Consequently, his claim should fail.

The **fourth issue** is whether the trial judge improperly denied George's motion for a new trial based on the "inconsistency'' between Michael's acquittals and George's convictions. The verdicts here are logically inconsistent—George's complicity in the murders requires proof that Michael, the principal, committed the murders. Nonetheless, the Constitution is not offended by inconsistent verdicts from the same jury. Because the inconsistency may be caused by mistakes in the acquittals or lenity toward Michael and because of the policy against inquiry into juror deliberations, George cannot succeed with his claim. The judge was correct to conclude that the acquittals were "irrelevant."

The **fifth issue** is whether the trial judge improperly denied George's new trial motion based on the allegedly tainted juror and the government's failure to disclose what it knew about that juror during the trial. A defendant is entitled to impartial jurors. One biased juror can taint a verdict. When allegations of bias surface after trial, due process is generally satisfied by a hearing with an opportunity to prove actual bias. The possibility of bias here—rooted in the fact that the juror's mother had been killed by organized crime, the juror's need for "extensive counseling," and George's supposed ties to organized crime—probably entitled George to a hearing into the juror's bias. The trial judge should have afforded him that opportunity. If bias was proven at such a hearing, George would have been entitled to reversal of his convictions.

The prosecution's fault in not disclosing information about the juror during a trial, however, is not a basis for relief. The culpability of the prosecutor is not relevant to due process analysis. If the juror was biased, George is entitled to a new trial whether or not the prosecutor was at fault. But if the juror was not biased, George is not entitled to a new trial even if prosecutorial fault is established.

The **final issue** is whether the third proceeding that resulted in two death sentences violated the guarantee against double jeopardy. The bar on successive prosecutions contained in the Double Jeopardy Clause ordinarily does not pertain to sentencing processes. The imposition of one sentence is not an acquittal of other sentences. In a "trial-like" capital sentencing proceeding, however, an "acquittal of the death penalty" precludes later imposition of the death penalty. In addition, a mistrial without the request or consent of the defendant does not terminate jeopardy if there is "manifest necessity" for the mistrial.

When the first jury was unable to agree, state law allowed the judge to declare a hung jury. If the jury truly was deadlocked, the hung jury declaration was effectively a "mistrial" for manifest necessity. If the jury was not truly deadlocked (the relevant facts here are absent or ambiguous), then the "mistrial" was granted without manifest necessity, and the second capital sentencing proceeding violated double jeopardy.

In any case, when the second jury was "hung" and the judge imposed life sentences, he effectively "acquitted" George of the death penalty. An acquittal—even one that is egregiously erroneous—ordinarily terminates jeopardy and bars further proceedings. The effective acquittals here terminated George's jeopardy for the death sentence. The third sentencing proceeding and the death sentences that resulted violated George's double jeopardy rights. If the acquittal bar applies, the death sentences must be vacated.

Although the Supreme Court has never endorsed an exception to the rule that an acquittal bars further proceedings, it has never ruled out a possible exception for acquittals procured by fraud or other illegal means. There is room to argue here that the "threats" by George's sons against the jurors who did not vote for the death sentence justify an "exception" to the most venerable rule that even an erroneous acquittal terminates jeopardy. If there is an exception for acquittals procured by sufficiently culpable conduct, that exception *may* apply here because the defendant's sons threatened jurors and may well have prevented them from sentencing George to death. These threats may be the sole reason that George ultimately received the life sentences. The exception may not apply, however, unless George is shown to have been somehow involved in his sons' conduct. If this case does fall within an exception to the general rule, then the third proceeding would be valid and the two death sentences should be upheld.

GLOSSARY

abuse of the writ doctrine. A procedural bar to a prisoner's collateral challenge in federal court based on the failure to raise a claim in a prior petition seeking collateral relief.

abusive petition. A claim for collateral relief that raises grounds for relief that were available but not relied on in a prior petition.

acquittal. A determination by a judge or jury that an accused is not culpable of a criminal offense.

adequate state grounds. A basis for a state court judgment that rests on state law and is sufficient in itself to support the judgment.

administrative (or regulatory) searches. Searches conducted as a part of the enforcement of a regulatory scheme that is designed to promote societal interests other than enforcement of the criminal laws.

adversary (or adversarial) system. A system of criminal justice in which the outcome is determined by a contest between opposing parties (adversaries) before a neutral arbiter.

alibi defense. A defense to a criminal charge that consists of a claim that the accused could not have committed the crime because she was elsewhere at the time of the offense.

apparent authority doctrine. The doctrine that recognizes the constitutionality of searches based on consent by a person who does not have actual common authority to give consent but who is reasonably believed to have such authority.

appeal. The direct process by which a party that has lost in the trial court asserts error and requests relief from an appellate court.

appellate review. The process in which trial court proceedings are reviewed for error by an appellate court.

appointed counsel. An attorney who is designated by a court to represent an indigent defendant and whose services are paid for by the state.

area within an arrestee's immediate control. The area immediately surrounding an arrestee into which she might reach to grab a weapon or disposable evidence and which may be automatically searched incident to a lawful arrest.

arraignment. An initial stage of the formal process of adjudicating a criminal case in which an accused is brought before a court and may be asked to plead to the charges. An arraignment may also involve the setting of conditions for release on bail, advisement of the accused of his rights, the appointment of counsel, and the setting of a date for the next stage of the process.

arrest. An official seizure of a person that entails a substantial deprivation of personal liberty; the taking of a suspect into physical custody by an agent of the state; may be either a formal arrest or a de facto arrest.

arrestee. An individual who is arrested.

arrest warrant. A document issued by a magistrate authorizing an officer to arrest a criminal suspect. An arrest warrant is valid only if it is based on probable cause to believe that the suspect committed an offense.

at the elbow of the arrestee exception. An exception to the Fourth Amendment search warrant requirement that authorizes officers to enter private places in order to stay with an arrestee and maintain the integrity of an arrest.

attachment of jeopardy. The point in the criminal process at which a person is put at risk of conviction; the point at which the protections of the Double Jeopardy Clause become applicable.

automobile doctrine. An exception to the Fourth Amendment search warrant requirement authorizing the warrantless search of a mobile vehicle on probable cause.

bail. The financial or other conditions under which an accused individual may obtain release from confinement prior to trial or pending appeal of a conviction.

basis of knowledge. The facts and circumstances from which an informant has reached a conclusion that an individual has committed an offense or that items of interest are located in a particular place; one of the "prongs" of the two-pronged *Aguilar-Spinelli* test for assessing hearsay as the basis for probable cause showings.

Batson **doctrine.** The Equal Protection Clause–based doctrine that prescribes the showing needed to raise a successful claim of unconstitutional discrimination in the use of peremptory jury challenges.

bench trial. A trial in which the judge serves as the trier of fact rather than a jury.

beyond a reasonable doubt. The constitutionally required burden of proof on the government in a criminal case with regard to each essential element of a criminal offense.

burden of proof. A party's obligation to establish a degree of belief in the mind of the trier of fact with regard to a particular fact; the quantity of proof required before a particular fact will be found in favor of a particular party.

capital offense or crime. An offense for which the death penalty is a potential sentence.

Carroll-Chambers **doctrine.** Another name for the automobile doctrine exception to the search warrant requirement that authorizes the warrantless search of a mobile vehicle on probable cause.

case-in-chief. The prosecution's initial presentation of evidence to the trier of fact at trial in order to establish the elements required to sustain the charges against the accused.

cause. One of the showings needed to overcome certain procedural hurdles to federal collateral relief; an objective reason for a state procedural default or for failing to raise a claim for collateral relief in a prior petition for such relief.

challenge for cause. A challenge to a prospective juror alleging that there is some reason that the juror cannot provide competent, impartial jury service.

change of venue. The removal of the trial of a case from one location or district to another location or district.

clear and convincing proof. A burden of proof that is more than a preponderance of the evidence and less than beyond a reasonable doubt; proof to the level of a reasonable certainty.

clearly erroneous. A standard of appellate review of trial court findings of fact; a finding of fact that is unsupported by substantial evidence, that is contrary to the clear weight of evidence, or that leaves the reviewing court with a definite and firm conviction that a mistake has been committed.

closing argument. The lawyers' final statements to the trier of fact that summarize the evidence and posit the conclusions that should be drawn.

closure. The practice of excluding members of the public (and press) from attending a formal part of the criminal process.

codefendant. An individual who is charged with the same offense as (and may be tried jointly with) another defendant.

coerced (or involuntary) confession. An incriminating statement obtained from a suspect or an accused by means that overbear the will of the individual.

collateral attack. A process for attacking the legality of confinement that is outside the channel of direct appeal of a conviction.

collateral estoppel. A bar to relitigating an issue of fact that has already been determined in earlier proceedings between the same parties.

collateral order doctrine. The doctrine permitting the appeal of an order that is not a final judgment but is separable from the ultimate merits of the litigation.

comity. The principle that calls on courts to respect the laws or decisions of another jurisdiction.

common authority. The actual authority over premises that enables an individual to give constitutionally valid consent for the authorities to conduct a search. Common authority is based on mutual use by persons generally having joint access to or control over premises for most purposes.

competent. One of the criteria for a constitutionally acceptable juror; the mental capability to understand the evidence in a case and to reach a rational decision.

concurrent sentences. Multiple sentences for criminal offenses that are to be served at the same time.

confessions. Extrajudicial inculpatory statements obtained from a suspect or an accused.

conflict of interest. A position in which an attorney's duties or obligations to a party he or she represents run contrary to other duties or obligations of the attorney, often those owed to another party that he or she represents.

consecutive sentences. Multiple sentences for criminal offenses that are to be served separately with one commencing after the other has been completed.

consent search. An official search of a private place pursuant to permission granted by a person with authority; one of the exceptions to the Fourth Amendment search warrant requirement.

continuance. An adjournment or postponement of a proceeding or trial to a later time.

continuing jeopardy. A doctrine holding that a particular event—such as appellate reversal of a conviction or dismissal of a charge—does not terminate jeopardy for an offense.

conviction. A determination by a trier of fact that an accused is guilty of an offense.

counsel. An attorney; one of the fundamental rights guaranteed by the Sixth and Fourteenth Amendments.

critical stage of the prosecution. An informal or formal pretrial encounter between the accused and the prosecution that poses sufficient threats to the fairness of the trial to trigger the accused's entitlement to the assistance of counsel.

cross-examination. The questioning of a witness by a party opposed to the one who has called the witness to give testimony.

cumulative punishment. The imposition of more than one criminal sentence for one offense or multiple offenses. Cumulative punishment may be concurrent sentences or consecutive sentences.

curtilage. The outdoor area immediately surrounding and associated with the home to which the protections of the Fourth Amendment extend.

custodial arrest. The process of taking a suspect into actual, physical custody.

custodial interrogation. The express questioning of, or the use of other methods of interrogation on, a person who has been taken into custody or otherwise deprived of her freedom of action in a significant way; the prerequisite for *Miranda* doctrine protections.

custody. One of the prerequisites for *Miranda* doctrine protections; a formal arrest or the functional equivalent of a formal arrest.

deadly force. Force that the actor uses with the purpose of causing, or with the knowledge of a substantial risk that it will cause, death or serious bodily harm.

defendant. The accused; an individual formally charged with a criminal offense.

deliberate elicitation. One of the prerequisites for attachment of the right to counsel extended by the *Massiah* doctrine; some action, beyond mere listening, designed deliberately to evoke incriminating disclosures from an accused.

derivative evidence. Evidence that is not directly and immediately obtained from an illegality but that is derived indirectly from such an illegality.

deterrence. The discouragement of future official illegalities achieved by excluding illegally obtained evidence from court proceedings; an objective of the exclusionary rules.

direct appeal. The process by which a party asserts error in a trial court ruling or judgment and seeks reversal of that ruling or judgment by an appellate court.

direct examination. The questioning of a witness by the party who has called the witness to give testimony.

disclosure. The giving of information or evidence to one's opponent.

discovery. The formal and informal processes by which a party to a case is permitted or entitled to receive information or evidence in the possession of his or her opponent.

dismissal. A ruling in favor of an accused based on grounds other than a determination that the accused lacks criminal culpability.

dismissal with prejudice. A dismissal that does not permit the reinstitution of charges by the government.

dismissal without prejudice. A dismissal that permits the reinstitution of charges by the government.

double jeopardy. The constitutionally forbidden consequence of putting an accused in jeopardy for an offense after an initial jeopardy for the same offense has attached and terminated.

Double Jeopardy Clause. The Fifth Amendment provision that prohibits the government from twice placing a person in jeopardy for the same offense.

drug testing. Searches of the human body by means of blood, urine, or breath tests designed to determine the presence of narcotics.

Due Process Clauses. The Fifth and Fourteenth Amendment provisions that prohibit the federal and state governments from depriving persons of "life, liberty, or property, without due process of law."

due process defense. A possible defense to a criminal charge based on the claim that government officials' excessive involvement in the commission of the offense renders prosecution of the accused fundamentally unfair.

entrapment defense. A defense to a criminal charge based on the claim that government agents engaged in improper actions that induced the defendant to commit an offense.

Equal Protection Clause. The Fourteenth Amendment provision that bars states from denying any person "the equal protection of the laws."

evidence preclusion. A sanction for violating a discovery requirement that prohibits the offending party from introducing evidence at trial.

excessive bail. Conditions for release from confinement pending trial or appeal that are more onerous than those that are justified by legitimate government interests such as preventing flight and protecting against danger to the community.

Excessive Bail Clause. The Eighth Amendment provision that bars the government from requiring excessive bail.

exclusionary rules. The rules that prohibit the government from introducing illegally obtained evidence in certain situations.

exculpatory evidence. Evidence that suggests or indicates that the defendant is not guilty of the offense charged.

exigent circumstances or exigency. An exception to the Fourth Amendment search warrant requirement based on a showing of a specific need to act quickly, before there is time to secure a warrant.

fair cross section requirement. The implicit Sixth Amendment demand that bars the state from systematically excluding certain groups from the jury pool or venire.

final judgment rule. A principle of appellate review that holds that ordinarily an appeal may be taken only from a final judgment.

forfeiture. The loss of property to the state resulting from an illegal act.

formal arrest. The process of arresting a person by explicitly informing the person that he is under arrest.

formal complaint. A document alleging that an individual has committed an offense.

functional equivalent of a formal arrest. Official restraint on the physical freedom of an individual to a degree ordinarily associated with a formal arrest; official actions of such a nature that a reasonable person would believe that he has been placed under restraints on freedom comparable to those associated with a formal arrest.

good faith exception. An exception to the Fourth Amendment exclusionary rule applicable when officers have conducted an illegal search or seizure in reasonable reliance on a warrant issued by a neutral and detached magistrate.

government agent. An individual who is working for or acting at the request or instigation of the state; a person who is acting to serve government interests rather than purely private interests.

grand jury. A body of citizens charged with deciding whether there is adequate justification to issue an indictment.

guilty plea. An accused's formal, in-court admission that she is guilty of an offense.

habeas corpus. A form of collateral attack on a conviction in which a prisoner challenges the legality of his confinement outside the channel of direct appeal; the federal collateral remedy by which state prisoners seek relief from allegedly illegal confinement.

harmless error. An error in a trial proceeding that did not affect the outcome substantially enough to justify reversing a conviction and granting a new trial.

hearsay. Information in support of a probable cause determination that is not known firsthand by the affiant but has instead been provided by a third party (often an "informant") who is not present before the magistrate or judge.

hot pursuit. A variation of the exigent circumstances exception to the search warrant requirement that authorizes officers to enter dwellings and other private places when they have immediately and continuously pursued a suspect who has entered that place.

hung jury. A jury that is unable to reach the degree of consensus required to render a verdict.

immediate evidence. Evidence that is obtained directly and immediately as a result of illegal official conduct.

impartial jury. An explicit Sixth Amendment right that assures the accused of a petit jury that has no bias or prejudice against her.

impeachment. The process of casting doubt on the credibility of a witness by, for example, introducing inconsistent statements of that witness or other evidence that contradicts the witness's testimony.

inconsistent verdicts. Two or more verdicts rendered by the same petit jury that cannot logically or rationally be reconciled with each other.

independent source. An exception to the exclusionary rules that permits the introduction of evidence that is legally obtained when an official illegality has independently led to the discovery of the very same evidence.

indictment. A document returned by a grand jury that charges an individual with a criminal offense.

indigent. A person with insufficient financial ability to retain defense counsel; one who is entitled to have state-appointed legal representation.

inevitable discovery. An exception to the exclusionary rules that allows illegally obtained evidence to be introduced if the government shows that it would inevitably have discovered the evidence by legal means.

informant. An individual who provides law enforcement authorities with information regarding a criminal activity; an anonymous informant is an informant whose identity is not known to the authorities.

information. A document prepared by a prosecutor charging an individual with a criminal offense.

initial appearance. The first time that an accused appears in court; a preliminary stage of a criminal proceeding in which a defendant is informed of the charges against him and of his rights.

initiation of adversary judicial proceedings. The point at which an individual formally becomes an accused as a result of an indictment, information, arraignment, preliminary hearing, or other type of formal charge; the point of attachment of the Sixth Amendment right to counsel.

initiation of communications. An expression by a suspect of a desire or willingness for a generalized discussion with the authorities relating directly or indirectly to the investigation; *Miranda* doctrine prerequisite for the resumption of interrogation after a suspect has invoked her right to counsel.

interlocutory appeal. An appeal of a matter during the pendency of a proceeding and prior to the entry of final judgment.

interrogation. One of the prerequisites for the application of the *Miranda* doctrine; express questioning or its functional equivalent—that is, words or acts on the part of the police (other than those normally attendant to arrest and custody) that the police should know are reasonably likely to elicit an incriminating response from the suspect.

inventory search. An exception to the Fourth Amendment search warrant requirement applicable to searches of vehicles that are lawfully impounded and arrestees who are lawfully arrested and incarcerated.

involuntary (or coerced) confession. An incriminating statement obtained from a suspect or accused by means that overbear the will of the individual.

jeopardy. A risk of conviction.

joint representation. Legal representation of two or more codefendants by one attorney, often (but not necessarily) at the same trial.

jury. A group of citizens entrusted with finding the facts and rendering a verdict at a trial.

jury challenges. Mechanisms for objecting to and seeking to eliminate prospective jurors from the pool of those eligible for service in a case; may be for cause or peremptory.

jury nullification. A jury's power or prerogative to return a verdict of acquittal that is contrary to that which is dictated by the facts and law; a jury's decision to ignore the law explained in the court's instructions.

jury selection. The various processes designed to obtain an impartial and competent body of jurors to hear the trial of a case.

knock and announce principle. A doctrine holding that the reasonableness of a search under the Fourth Amendment can hinge, in part, on whether officers knocked and announced their presence and purpose prior to entry.

knowing waiver. The requirement that an individual have a sufficient awareness and comprehension of certain matters before a decision to waive or relinquish a constitutional right will be considered valid.

lawful arrest. An arrest that is based on probable cause to believe that an individual has committed an offense and, possibly, on an arrest warrant.

lawful impoundment. The taking of a vehicle or other item of property into official custody based on a showing that there are sufficiently weighty governmental interests justifying such action; the taking of a vehicle into official custody based on a need to ensure traffic flow, safety, or community convenience; an essential prerequisite to a lawful vehicle inventory.

manifest necessity. The high degree of need to declare a mistrial that is required to avoid a double jeopardy bar to retrial when a mistrial is neither requested or consented to by the defendant.

material evidence. Evidence in the possession of the authorities that is exculpatory and that, if disclosed to the defense, would engender a reasonable probability of a different trial outcome; exculpatory evidence that the prosecution is constitutionally obligated to disclose to the defense.

***Mendenhall* standard.** The doctrinal standard for determining whether a suspect has been seized for purposes of the Fourth Amendment; whether a reasonable person would not feel free to leave or walk away from an officer.

***Miranda* doctrine.** A doctrine based on the Fifth Amendment privilege against compulsory self-incrimination that requires officials to abide by certain procedural safeguards to ensure the admissibility of statements obtained by custodial interrogation.

***Miranda* warnings.** The advice that, according to the *Miranda* doctrine, must be given to suspects subjected to custodial interrogation.

mistrial. A court's termination of an ongoing trial without a resolution of the merits in favor of either party as a result of an occurrence that makes continuing the trial impractical or unfair.

mixed question of law and fact. A question that is neither purely a question of law nor a question of historical fact but requires the application of a legal standard to a set of facts.

motion to vacate a sentence. The federal collateral remedy by which federal prisoners seek relief from allegedly illegal confinement.

multiple punishment. The imposition of more than one punishment for a single criminal offense.

neutral and detached magistrate. A judicial authority who has the authority to issue search or arrest warrants, who has no biases or prejudices for or against the issuance of warrants, and who is not attached to the executive/law enforcement branch of government.

nolo contendere. A plea to a criminal charge in which an accused does not admit guilt but declares that he will not contest a criminal charge and which has similar consequences, from the standpoint of criminal liability, to a guilty plea.

nullification. A jury's power or prerogative to return a verdict of acquittal that is contrary to that which is dictated by the facts and law; a jury's decision to ignore the law explained in the court's instructions.

oath or affirmation requirement. The explicit Fourth Amendment demand that the showing of probable cause required to issue a valid warrant be "supported by Oath or affirmation" of the person providing the showing to the magistrate.

objective entrapment. The form of the entrapment defense that is concerned with the conduct of government agents and that judges eligibility according to whether that conduct would induce a reasonable person not prepared to commit an offense to do so.

objective standards. Standards that hinge on an assessment of what a reasonable person would believe or do rather than an assessment of what a particular individual would believe or do.

open fields. Privately owned, undeveloped lands outside the curtilage of the home and not within the protection of the Fourth Amendment protection against unreasonable searches.

particularity requirement. The explicit Fourth Amendment requirement that warrants "particularly describ[e] the place to be searched and the persons or things to be seized."

peremptory challenges. A device by which a party may strike or eliminate a prospective juror without providing a reason.

petit jury. The body of citizens that is selected to find facts and render a verdict at a trial.

petty crime. An offense for which an accused is not constitutionally entitled to a trial by jury because the authorized penalty is six months of imprisonment or less and any additional statutory penalties are not sufficiently onerous to classify the offense as serious.

plain error. An error whose impact on a trial is so substantial that an appellate court will take cognizance of and remedy it even though it was not raised by a party at trial.

plain view doctrine. The Fourth Amendment doctrine that permits officers to act without a warrant to seize items to which they have lawful access when it is immediately apparent that those items are incriminating.

plea bargain. An agreement between the prosecution and the defendant whereby the defendant agrees to enter a guilty or nolo contendere plea in exchange for concessions or inducements from the state.

postconviction remedies. A device provided to seek relief from illegal confinement based on a criminal conviction that is outside the direct channel of trial, conviction, and direct appeal.

pre-accusation delay. The time after the commission of an offense and prior to an arrest or the filing of a formal charge by the government.

preclusion sanction. A penalty for violating a discovery rule, requirement, or order that prohibits a party from introducing evidence.

preliminary hearing. A pretrial adversarial proceeding for the purpose of determining whether there is probable cause for requiring an accused to stand trial for an offense.

preponderance of the evidence. A burden of proof requiring a party to establish that a proposition is "more likely than not" true in order to prevail on an issue; the burden of proof for civil cases and some determinations in criminal cases (such as issues involved in suppression hearings).

pretrial motion. A request by a party for a ruling on a matter prior to a trial, including such requests as motions for dismissal, motions for a continuance, and motions to suppress evidence.

preventive detention. The practice of detaining an accused prior to trial or pending appeal to prevent flight, harm to the judicial process, or danger to the community.

private party. An individual whose actions are not regulated by the Constitution because she is not employed by the government and is not acting at the request or behest of the government.

privilege against compulsory self-incrimination. The Fifth Amendment guarantee that in any criminal case no person shall be compelled to be a witness against himself.

probable cause. The Fourth Amendment showing ordinarily required to render a full search or arrest reasonable; a fair probability or a substantial chance; more than a mere possibility and less than a preponderance of the evidence.

probable cause to arrest. A showing of a fair probability that a particular person has committed an offense.

probable cause to search. A showing of a fair probability that an object in which the government has a legitimate interest is presently in a place that is sought to be searched.

pro se representation. A defendant's legal representation of herself without the assistance of trained counsel.

protective sweep of a home. A cursory search of a dwelling for persons who pose a danger to officers that is conducted in connection with an in-home arrest.

public right of access. The First Amendment right of the public to be present at criminal trials and other phases of the criminal process.

public safety exception. The sole exception to the requirement of *Miranda* safeguards during custodial interrogation that applies when officers ask questions "reasonably prompted by a concern for the public safety."

race-neutral. Type of reason given for a peremptory jury challenge other than race or a stereotypical assumption about a person based on that person's race.

random drug testing. Drug tests that are administered to a person without an individualized, articulable suspicion that the person has used drugs.

reasonable (or legitimate or justifiable) expectation of privacy. The interest that must be violated in order for a "search" regulated by the Fourth Amendment to have occurred; the interest protected by the Fourth Amendment restrictions on government searches.

reasonable probability. A level of likelihood that is more than a mere possibility and less than a preponderance.

reasonable suspicion. The level of justification required to justify searches and seizures that are less intrusive than ordinary, full searches and seizures; a showing that is less than probable cause and more than an inarticulate hunch.

reliability of an identification. A showing that an identification of a suspect is the result of a witness's observations at the time of an offense rather than unnecessarily suggestive governmental identification techniques; the showing that the government must make under the Due Process Clause in order to introduce an identification made by a witness who has been exposed to an unnecessarily suggestive identification technique.

retained counsel. An attorney who is chosen by and whose services are paid for by an accused.

retroactivity. The application of a rule of law to a case that has already entered the criminal process at the time the rule of law is announced.

right of self-representation. The Sixth Amendment entitlement of an accused to conduct her defense personally, without the assistance of counsel.

right to consult. The Sixth Amendment entitlement of an accused to discuss matters with his attorney.

right to counsel. The Sixth Amendment right of an accused to retained or appointed legal assistance.

right to counsel of choice. The Sixth Amendment right of an accused to choose the retained lawyer that will conduct her defense.

right to effective assistance of counsel. The Sixth Amendment right of an accused to reasonably competent legal representation.

right to a public trial. The Sixth Amendment right of an accused to have the public present at trial and other significant phases of the criminal process.

school search doctrine. Fourth Amendment doctrine that permits warrantless searches of schoolchildren by school authorities without probable cause.

search. One of the governmental actions that is regulated by the Fourth Amendment; a governmental invasion of a reasonable expectation of privacy.

search incident to arrest. An exception to the Fourth Amendment search warrant requirement for searches of the persons and areas within the immediate control of persons lawfully arrested.

search warrant. A document issued by a magistrate that authorizes the search of a place for specified objects.

seizure. One of the governmental actions that is regulated by the Fourth Amendment; a seizure may be of a person or of property.

seizure of a person. An official deprivation of the liberty interest of a person effected by physical force or by submission to a show of authority that would make a reasonable person not feel free to leave.

seizure of property. Any official meaningful interference with an individual's possessory interest in an item of property.

selective incorporation. The prevailing view regarding the relationship between the Bill of Rights guarantees and the Due Process Clause of the Fourteenth Amendment; the process of determining whether rights specified in the Bill of Rights are part of the due process that states must afford.

self-representation. An accused's personal conduct of the defense of a criminal charge without the assistance of a trained lawyer.

sentencing hearing. The postconviction phase of a criminal proceeding in which a judge or jury determines the appropriate sentence.

sequestration. The isolation of jurors from exposure to other persons and to publicity during the pendency of a trial.

serious crime. An offense for which an accused is constitutionally entitled to a trial by jury because the authorized penalty is greater than six months of imprisonment or because other statutory penalties are sufficiently onerous to classify the offense as serious.

speedy trial. An explicit Sixth Amendment right of an accused designed to ensure expedition in the processing of a criminal case following an arrest or formal charge.

staleness. A description applied to information that at one time furnished probable cause to search a place but that, because of the passage of time, is no longer current enough to furnish probable cause; also applied to warrants issued on the basis of probable cause that has gone stale.

standing. A person's stake in a controversy that permits the person to raise a particular legal claim.

state actor. An individual employed by or otherwise acting on behalf of the government; one whose actions are subject to constitutional regulation.

statute of limitations. A statutory provision that prescribes the maximum time period during which a criminal charge may be brought following the commission of an offense.

stop and frisk. A limited detention of an individual for investigation and a patdown of the individual's outer clothing in order to determine whether he is armed; a less intrusive seizure and search that is justifiable on less than probable cause.

sua sponte. Description of an action taken by a judge of her own will, not in response to a request by the parties.

subjective entrapment. The form of the entrapment defense that is concerned with the culpability of the accused and that judges eligibility according to whether the accused himself was predisposed to commit the crime or was in fact induced by the government to do so.

successive petition. A request for habeas corpus relief that raises a claim identical to one raised in an earlier request for such relief.

summation. A party's closing argument to the jury in which the evidence is summarized and conclusions are drawn.

supervisory power. The inherent authority of the federal judiciary over the administration of justice in the federal courts.

suppression hearing. A proceeding to decide the merits of a defendant's request that evidence be excluded from the trial ordinarily because of a claim that officials illegally obtained the evidence.

Suspension Clause. The constitutional provision found in Article I, section 9, that prohibits suspension of the writ of habeas corpus unless required by the public safety.

temporary detention (also known as investigative detention or *Terry* detention). A seizure of a person that is less restrictive of the person's liberty than an arrest; a restriction on physical freedom that does not require probable cause but can be constitutional on the basis of a reasonable suspicion.

termination of jeopardy. The point at which jeopardy for an offense ends so that placing an accused in jeopardy for that offense again would violate the prohibition on double jeopardy.

***Terry* doctrine.** The Fourth Amendment doctrine that sustains the validity of warrantless stops and frisks on less than probable cause; the doctrine holding that searches and seizures that are less intrusive than full searches and arrests can be justified on the basis of a reasonable suspicion.

totality of the circumstances test. Any doctrinal standard that calls for an assessment of all facts that are relevant to a given determination rather than one fact or a limited number of discrete facts.

trial. The phase of the criminal process in which the trier of fact hears evidence and argument and determines guilt or innocence for an offense.

trier of fact. The person or persons who have the task of resolving factual issues in a trial; the jury in a jury trial; the judge in a bench trial.

"true bill." Another name for an indictment; a document issued by a grand jury upon finding probable cause to charge an accused with an offense.

unanimous verdict. A verdict on which all of the jurors agree.

unnecessary suggestion. A prerequisite for a claim that an eyewitness identification must be excluded under the Due Process Clause; aspects of an official identification procedure that unfairly and without good reason indicate to a witness that a particular person should be selected.

venire. The panel or pool of jurors summoned to court from which a petit jury is chosen.

verdict. The trier of fact's decision regarding guilt or innocence.

voir dire. The part of the jury selection process in which the parties or the judge or both question the prospective jurors.

voluntary. Something done by a person that is not the product of a will overborne by official coercion.

voluntary waiver. A decision to relinquish a right that is not the product of a will overborne by official coercion.

waiver. A relinquishment or surrender of a right or other protection.

warrant. A document issued by a judge that authorizes either an arrest or a search.

writ of habeas corpus. A form of collateral relief granted by a court ordering the release of an individual confined by government authorities.

TABLE OF CASES

TABLE OF STATUTES

Table of Federal Rules

INDEX

impeachment use exception, 235-237
independent source doctrine, 219, 220
inevitable discovery exception, 220-222
Krull variation of good faith exception, 233
Leon-Sheppard good faith exception, 230-232
live-witness testimony, 225
presumptive attenuation, 226, 227
rationales, 210-214
scope, 214, 215
standing, 215-218
Exigent circumstances searches, 65-69
Eyewitness identification. *See* Identification evidence

Failure to raise principle, 439
Fair cross section requirement, 375-378
Fair trial
admonishing jurors, 329
basic right, 323, 324
change of venue, 326
closure/limited closure, 325, 326
continuance, 326
instructing jurors, 328
prejudicial publicity, 324
presence/conduct of media, 324, 325, 329, 330
questioning jurors, 327
restricting disclosure of information, 325
safeguards, 325-330
sequestration of jury, 329
False/perjured testimony, 255
Faretta rights, 357-363
Federal Bail Reform Act of 1984
bail pending appeal, 272, 273
bail pending trial, 271, 272
preventive detention, 275, 276
Federal Rules of Criminal Procedure
guilty pleas, 292, 293
jury selection, 378
plea bargaining, and, 284, 285
Federal Speedy Trial Act, 308-310
Federal supervisory power, 17, 18
Fifth Amendment. *See* Double jeopardy, *Miranda* doctrine
Final judgment rule, 437, 438
Fingerprinting, 98
First Amendment, 320
First appearance, 341
Forfeiture proceedings, 238
Fourteenth Amendment, 14, 145. *See also* Due process
Fourth Amendment. *See* Search and seizure
Frisk, 102. *See also* Stop and frisk doctrine
Fruit of the poisonous tree, 218

Gates totality of the circumstances test, 42, 43
General warrants, 50
Glossary, 523-535
Good faith exception, 229-235
Government involvement in commission of crimes. *See* Excessive government involvement
Government suggestion requirement, 202
Grand jury proceedings, 9, 238
Guilty pleas

antecedent constitutional violations, 291, 292
challenges to validity, 290
claims of innocence, and, 289
competency to plead, 289
Federal Rule of Criminal Procedure II, 292, 293
ineffective assistance challenge, 290-292, 352
requirements of valid plea, 285-289

Habeas corpus. *See* Collateral challenges
Handcuffing, 98
Harmless error
appeals, 441, 442
collateral challenges, 473, 474
duty to disclose exculpatory evidence, 257
government restriction on counsel, 348
pro se right, 363
Hearsay, and informants, 40-43
Hot pursuit, 66, 67
Human bodies, searches of, 131, 132
Hung jury, 11, 412
Hybrid representation, 361, 362

Identification evidence
due process, 201-207, 214
right to counsel, 193-199, 213, 214
Impeachment use exception, 235-237
Independence of state constitutions/statutes, 15, 16
Independent origin inquiry, 196-198
Independent source doctrine, 219, 220
Indictment, 9
Indigents
appeals, 437
bail, and, 270, 271
right to appointed counsel, 337-339
Ineffective assistance of counsel, 344, 345
appellate proceedings, 343, 344
conflicts of interest, 353-356
deficient performance, 349-352
government restrictions, 345-349
guilty pleas, 290, 352
right to consult, 346, 347
Inevitable discovery exception, 220-222
Informants, 40-43
Information, 9
Innocent home-dweller's constitutional rights, 63
Interlocutory appeals, 438
Inventory searches, 74-78
Investigatory course, 4
Invidious discrimination, 436, 437
Involuntary confession doctrine. *See* Due process clause and confessions

Jury nullification, 393-395
Jury trial, 369-401
capital sentencing proceedings, 380
challenges for cause, 381, 382
criminal contempt, 373
fair cross section requirement, 375-378
federal defendants, 381